Human Resource Development

Learning, Knowing and Growing

Fourth Edition

Brian Delahaye
Sarojni Choy

Human Resource Development: Learning, Knowing and Growing
Fourth edition, first printing

Author
Brian Delahaye and Sarojni Choy

ISBN: 978-0-7346-1232-8 (print)
ISBN: 978-0-7346-2130-6 (ePDF)

Disclaimer

All reasonable efforts have been made to ensure the quality and accuracy of this publication. Tilde Publishing and Distribution assumes no responsibility for any errors or omissions and no warranties are made with regard to this publication. Neither Tilde Publishing and Distribution nor any authorised distributors shall be held responsible for any direct, incidental or consequential damages resulting from the use of this publication.

Published by:
Tilde Publishing and Distribution
PO Box 72
Prahran VIC 3181 Australia
www.tilde.com.au

TUP-HumanResourceDevelopment-Delahaye-4e1p

Dedication

For Brian:

Dedicated to the memory of my parents, Len and Evelyn –
true models of courage and caring.

For Sarojni:

To my late dad who taught me the value of education.

Contents

Acknowledgements ix
Prologue .... **xi**
    An introduction to the textbook xi
Chapter 1: Introduction to HRD **1**
    The business environment 2
    Management re-engineering 5
    The traditional management approach 9
    Knowledge capital 10
    Complexity theory and managing knowledge capital 12
    The adult learner 18
    The HR developer and the management of knowledge 20
    Within a wider theoretical context 22
    The context of HRD 23
    The design of this textbook 24
    The 4th edition – a different approach 27
    How to use this book 27
    References 28
Chapter 2: Continuing education and training **31**
    Introduction 32
    The importance of continuing education and training 34
    Implications of continuing education and training for HRD practitioners 36
    Learning experiences for continuing education and training 36
    Models of continuing education and training and their implementation 38
    The future of VET 42
    References 43
Chapter 3: Adult learning **45**
    The foundation of HRD 46
    Learning 46
    Adults as learners 47
    Basic types of learning 49
    Generation of knowledge 52
    Knowledge creation and adult learning 54
    Critical thinking 71
    Unlearning 75
    Holistic adult learning 77
    The practical application of adult learning 80
    The four stages of HRD 83
    References 83
Chapter 4: Individual differences in adult learners **87**
    Introduction 88
    Ethnocentricity 88
    Celebrating individual differences 89
    The characteristics of adult learners 90
    The impact on the HR developer 106
    Globalisation 110
    Diversity and the organisation 113

References 114
Chapter 5: HRD needs investigation - An overview **118**
The importance of HRDNI 119
HRDNI defined 120
The purpose of HRDNI 121
Organisational awareness 122
The investigation plan 132
Selecting a HRDNI method 133
Face value? 136
The HRDNI report 137
The need for HRDNI 139
References 140
Chapter 6: Performance appraisal and career development **142**
The importance of performance appraisal 143
Performance appraisal within performance management 143
A natural process 144
A unique process 145
Impact on the HR developer 146
Types of performance appraisal 147
Job analysis – constructing the predetermined standard 148
Observing the performance 153
The comparison 155
Feedback 160
Action plans 162
Input into the developmental system 163
Surveillance system 163
Legal issues 164
Career management 164
Knowledge creation and maintenance 172
References 173
Chapter 7: Interviewing and focus groups **176**
Qualitative research 177
Interviewing 181
Structured and unstructured interviews 195
The focus group 198
Analysing qualitative data 205
The beginning of learning 209
References 209
Chapter 8: Design - The two main considerations **212**
Defining the role of the HR developer 213
Constructive alignment 214
The hierarchy of learning outcomes 215
The learners 229
A designer's checklist 243
References 244
Chapter 9: Other design considerations **247**
The indirect factors 248
An overview of the design process 255
Some basics for design 257

The product 259
The HR developer as a designer 264
References 266

Chapter 10: Implementing the structured learning strategies 268
The role of the HR developer 269
Managing and coordinating the program 270
Micro skills 270
The structured learning strategies 274
The semi-structured learning strategies 276
The challenge to the HR developer 287
References 288

Chapter 11: Implementing the unstructured learning strategies 290
The role of the HR developer 291
The assumptions 294
Problem-based learning 294
Contract learning 298
Action learning 303
Change interventions 307
Mentoring 311
E-learning 314
Blended learning 321
The implementing stage 323
References 324

Chapter 12: Evaluation 329
Misconceptions about evaluation 330
Assessment of learning 332
Kirkpatrick's four levels 346
The presage factors 352
Timeout 357
The scientific models 357
Cost-benefit analysis 360
The evaluation plan 362
The evaluation report 363
Whose responsibility? 364
The need for dialectic thinking 364
References 366

Chapter 13: Workplace learning 368
Moving into the shadow system 369
The workplace as a site for learning 369
Challenges to workplace learning 371
The supervisor as the HR developer 371
Learning spaces 372
Managing workplace learning 373
Individual change 382
Individual adult learning 384
The challenge of workplace learning 390
References 391

Chapter 14: Creating and embedding new knowledge 393
From maintaining to creating 394

An overview of the shadow system 394
The guiding principles of the shadow system 398
The three roles of the shadow system 399
Extraordinary management processes 401
Summary 412
Exporting to the legitimate system 412
Control – to be or not to be? 417
The nexus of work and learning 418
References 419

Chapter 15: Organisational culture, leadership and knowledge management 422
Knowledge as an asset 423
A systems approach 425
The legitimate system 427
Workplace learning 433
The shadow system 433
Bounded instability 437
Organisational culture 439
Summary 446
Leadership 446
The role of the HR developer 448
References 451

Glossary **455**
Index **471**

Acknowledgements

For Brian:

In many ways, this book is a history of my professional life. I commenced as a trainer in the then PMG Department nearly 40 years ago and was so fortunate to be influenced by older, and much wiser, trainers who had been adult teachers during the 1930s, instructors in the Second World War in the various defence forces and then technical instructors in the 1950s and 1960s. Their words of wisdom still resound in my mind – "Teach a little, test a little", "Teach a little well", "If in doubt, go into an activity" and my favourite "If anything will stuff up your session, it will be this new-fangled technology" – the fact that they were referring to the overhead projector adding a piquant reminder to review all aspects of session preparation. Even in the present modern times, these words are not only astute but also so relevant. I was fortunate to meet and interact on a personal basis with such key adult educators as Malcolm Knowles and Reg Revans. In addition, my development was strongly enhanced by Australian movers-and-shakers in organisational development and self-directed learning such as Bob Dick, Charles Margerison and Geoff Prideaux. If I can see further, it is because I stand on the shoulders of these giants.

On a personal basis, to my children – the original four, the newer four, the 'adopted' ones and now the ones of the grandchild variety – I appreciate so much your constant love and steadfast respect. Finally and always, to my life partner, wife and soul mate, Yvonne, your love and enduring support continue to be the wind beneath my wings.

For Sarojni:

I first came across the first edition of this book as a student when the seeds of my interest in adult learning theories and their applications were just beginning to germinate. This interest was nurtured under supervision and guidance from Brian Delahaye and I commenced my contributions to the development of workplace trainers and workers. He remains an inspiration and a role model as I continue to advance my career in vocational, professional and continuing education and training. I was honoured when asked to be a co-author.

For both of us:

Undoubtedly though, the group of people who have had the most impact on our professional lives has been our students. Facilitating the learning of others is a privilege and, indeed, is often a humbling process. To be a witness as adult learners struggle with new concepts, challenge the very values of their being and overcome, at times, overwhelming personal obstacles as they doggedly continue to learn and become empowered, is one of life's more inspiring experiences. Certainly by their questions and interactions, they still enrich, enhance, enrage, engage, energise and/or entrance and, in the course of events, have added immeasurably to our personal development and learning. We thank you all.

Our thanks to our research assistant Julie-Anne Jackson – finding relevant new readings and providing insightful suggestions have certainly added to the quality of this edition. Many thanks to our publishers, Tilde University Press, who have proven to be a highly professional and most helpful group of people – all authors need the wise and sagacious oversight of a publisher such as Rick Ryan and the caring support of the editing staff. We are indebted to you all.

Brian Delahaye
Sarojni Choy
April 2016

Prologue

One of the main goals in preparing the Student's Resource Guide for *Human Resource Development: Learning, Knowing and Growing* was to provide a valuable and pragmatic support system that busy students would find efficient and useful. Accordingly, the Student Resource Guide now consists of two books.

This textbook *Human Resource Development: Learning, Knowing and Growing* (4th edition) is the companion book to the workbook *Human Resource Development: Workbook* (4th edition). The **textbook** covers the theoretical foundations for good human resource development practice, while the **workbook** allows you to test and refine your knowledge on the application of these theories. Together these two publications provide a unique Student Resource Guide to help you learn the complex processes of managing human resources.

An introduction to the textbook

Trainers, instructors, adult teachers, human resource developers, workplace educators, community educators, learning consultants and knowledge managers are just some of the titles given to the people who are given the responsibility to develop individual and organisational learning. People who undertake this role are faced with a number of conflicting yet ever present pressures. Among these pressures are:

- demands to decrease the dollar and time investment in staff development,

- the increasing complexity of technology,

- the enhanced expectations of adult learners that they be treated as adults,

- the need to ensure that learning is relevant and has a commercial value, and

- the exponential growth of theories of adult learning and the management of knowledge.

Developing people in this role - whether they are called human resource developers or workplace educators or any of the other titles - has become a distinctive challenge. Further, this challenge has occurred at a time when decision makers have realised the critical importance of the knowledge asset to the future viability of an organisation.

The text *Human Resource Development: Learning, Knowing and Growing* has been designed and written to meet the needs of undergraduate and postgraduate students who wish to fulfil such roles and meet such challenges. The text offers a comprehensive theoretical and practical coverage of human resource development. The book offers a number of features to enhance learning and to provide praxis - the conversion of theory into practice:

- **Learning objectives** at the beginning of each chapter highlight the expected learning outcomes.

- **Main headings, sub-headings and sub-sub-headings** furnish an easily recognised structure to each chapter.

- **A closer look** feature which highlights a practical example or a more in-depth discussion.

- **Glossary** of key words at the end of each chapter provide a quick reference to important concepts.

Each of the four stages of human resource development - needs investigation, design, implementation and evaluation - are discussed in turn throughout the book with important theoretical principles being described and with models, recommendations and check lists presented as professional guides for actions and decisions. These discussions and descriptions are embedded within an overall understanding of the concepts of the management of knowledge capital.

The material presented in the text consists of 15 chapters. Chapter 1 introduces the importance of human resource development and locates human resource development in the theories, concepts and practices of human resource management. The chapter introduces the concept of complexity theory – the theoretical basis of the textbook and a most useful theory when examining the management of knowledge capital and the underpinning adult learning processes. Chapter 2 then introduces continuing education and training, analysing the different models and their implementation.

The next two chapters present issues that have a direct influence, and provide a deeper understanding of human resource development. Chapter 3 examines the theories and practices of adult learning. Chapter 4 emphasises the importance of, and the critical nature of, individual differences in adult learners. Chapter 5 begins the discussion on human resource development needs investigation (HRDNI) and the next two chapters explore specific methods of HRDNI - performance appraisal and career development (Chapter 6) and interviewing and focus groups (Chapter 7). Chapter 8 examines the role of two important considerations in the design of adult learning programs - the topic content and the learner - which provide an initial indication of the type of learning strategies that are most beneficial. Other considerations of the design process, and the type of program plans required, are discussed in Chapter 9. The structured learning strategies of the skill session, theory session and lecture and the semi-structured approaches of the discussion, case study, role play and experiential learning are described in Chapter 10. Chapter 11 examines the unstructured learning strategies of problem-based learning, contract learning, action learning, change interventions and mentoring and also has a discussion on e-learning. Chapter 12 explains and examines evaluation. Chapter 13 presents a discussion on workplace learning and suggests that learning in the workplace needs a workplace learning curriculum. Accordingly a model of a workplace curriculum is presented as is a new model discussing the steps used by an individual adult learner. Chapter 14 examines the creation of knowledge by examining, in depth, the role of the shadow system and the critical importance of self organising groups. The chapter also explores the process of developing a state of bounded instability in an organisation. Chapter 15 reviews the concepts examined in the previous chapters by expanding the complexity theory model introduced in Chapter 1. This model can be used as a means of understanding the management of knowledge or as a template to audit an organisation's knowledge management processes. The chapter then shows how these concepts combine with organisational culture and leadership to manage the knowledge capital of an organisation. The chapter, and the textbook, end with a suggested career development path for HR developers.

In addition, this fourth edition again features a large case study on an organisation called Pacific Lifestyle Publishing. Pacific Lifestyle Publishing is a real organisation located on the east coast of Australia. It was exciting to find an organisation that valued its staff so highly and which managed its knowledge capital so effectively and so naturally. The case study, located in the companion workbook, is used in a number of ways throughout the text. There are nearly 50 boxed notes in the main body of the text that link the theoretical concepts being discussed to the real life experiences in Pacific Lifestyle Publishing. There are also several references to Pacific Lifestyle Publishing in the theoretical discussions in the text itself.

Chapter 1

Introduction to HRD

LEARNING OBJECTIVES

After studying this chapter you should be able to:

1. Describe the negative effects of management re-engineering on organisations.

2. Explain why knowledge is a unique resource.

3. Describe how knowledge capital can be managed by complexity theory.

4. Describe the role of the HR developer in knowledge management.

The business environment

Managers now accept that the only certainty is that change will keep occurring at a rapidly escalating rate. According to Mason (2008), accompanying this rapid change is increased complexity and turbulence. New flexible work arrangements are now becoming common – for example, telework as fast broadband technology is eroding the idea of 'office' as central to the generation of work (Goodyear 2013). What is surprising is that so many organisations appear to be unprepared because such a challenging situation was predicted several decades ago. For example, McConkey (1988) suggested that the future would become increasingly more difficult. He expected:

- a dramatic increase in the environment's complexity;

- an increasing number of variables;

- an increase in the number of both domestic and world events affecting organisations; and

- a decreasing time span for planning with any certainty.

By and large, despite such warnings, managers have not adjusted successfully to the modern environment. Indeed, as Davidson, Simon, Woods and Griffin (2009) comment, with the failure of several corporations, the confusion and demoralisation within management ranks has become widespread as faith in corporate Australia and New Zealand has deteriorated.

A common theme in these corporate disasters has been the lack of training and development of staff. The systemic inadequacy of organisational implementation of human resource development has been highlighted by a litany of disasters in recent times in both Australia and New Zealand. Prime amongst these was the Homeowners Insualtion Plan.

A closer look 1.1

The Homeowners Insulation Plan

One of the most widely reported disasters of recent times involved the Australian Federal Government's Homeowners Insulation Plan (HIP). The HIP was part of an initiative of the Australian Government, released on 03 February 2009 as part of its response to the global financial crisis. The stated aim for the HIP was to retrofit insulation into the ceilings of some 2.2 million Australian existing houses in a period of two and a half years. Given this target, the HIP thus aimed to achieve an approximately fifteen-fold increase in the number of installations per year. The substantive commencement date of the HIP was 01 July 2009 – that is, only five months from its inception.

The HIP resulted in some catastrophic consequence, not the least of which were the deaths of four young men.

A Royal Commission headed by Ian Hanger AM QC produced a report entitled

Report of the Royal Commission into the Home Insulation Program on 29 August 2014. Reading this report is a very sobering experience. The report concluded that there were seven significant failings in the design and implementation of the HIP. One of the prime failings was the decision to relax training and competency requirements, and to substitute 'supervision' for insulation-specific training. The report noted that the key driver in the design of the program was the inflexible start date of 01 July 2009.

The report is uncompromising in its criticism. It accused the Federal Government of conceiving, devising, designing and implementing a program that enabled very large numbers of inexperienced workers to undertake potentially dangerous work. The report makes the damning judgment that the government should have done more to protect them. Despite construction leaders such as the Master Builders having the unanimous view that training (preferably a three-day course costing $500 for each participant) was needed, the requirement that all installers have insulation-specific training was removed. In its place, the untrained installers were to be supervised. However, the nature of supervision required was not specified in any of the formal documentation from the HIP. Indeed, the HIP provided no assurance (and none was sought to be imposed) that the supervisors would in fact supervise as they ought, especially in cases in which the installer was particularly young or inexperienced.

There are two telling final comments from Chapter 8 (on training and competencies) of the report. The first is that the decision not to provide installer training is an important illustration of a preference being given to the rapid rollout of the HIP over its careful and safe design and implementation. The second is that this lack also brought with it an almost inevitable risk that young and inexperienced installers would be exposed to the real risk of injury.

Chapter 12 of the Royal Commission's report deals with the deaths of the four young men. The chapter is harrowing reading. That chapter should be a constant reminder to trainers and HR developers that we must not tolerate unacceptable compromises on the quality of our HR programs. The programs that we design and implement must be of the highest professional standard, and we must uphold that standard to ensure that appalling outcomes, such as occurred with the Homeowners Insulation Plan, never occur again.

While the Homeowners Insulation Plan received a lot of publicity, there are many more such sad events reported in newspapers across the country.

- On the 24th of April, 2015 the Brisbane Federal Court fined a construction firm $110,000 after an employee was struck by a falling metal bridge while working on the Brisbane Airport Link. The company admitted that it did not conduct a risk assessment of the bridge before installing and using it, nor did they give the workers any information or training on how to safely use the structure. (Source: www.9news.com.au/national/2015/04/24/16/13/com-pany-fined-110k-over-airport-injury.)

- A Queensland employer was fined $135,000 over a teenager's death – the highest fine recorded against a company in Queensland under the *Electrical Safety Act*. In 2009, the teenager was electrocuted while installing insulation under the Australian Federal Government's Home Insulation Scheme. The investigation found that the company gave only minimal training to its employees and did not produce specific procedures for the installation of insulation. The teenager was one of four people who died during the roll out of the government's multi-billion dollar home insulation program. A spokesperson for Master Electricians Australia was reported as commenting that the lack of training for installers was leading to a range of problems, from electrocution to house fires, because of insulation packed too close to down-lights. (*Sources*: *The Courier-Mail* 18/11/09; 7/5/10; 15/9/10; 18-19/9/10; *The Weekend Australian* 18-19/9/10.)

- A Cable Beach resort in Broome, Western Australia, was fined $60,000 over a workplace accident that left a young worker permanently paralysed when a cherry picker tipped over. The case exposed a serious lack of training and maintenance at the resort. (*Source*: ABC Regional News 9/2/10.)

- Inadequate training and procedures led to two police officers suffering serious injuries during a drug audit in Sydney, New South Wales. The police officers were exposed to the fumes of rotting drugs during an audit of an evidence locker in March 2009. (*Source*: AAP Australian National News wire 4/8/09.)

- The coroner called for better training for hunting guides after a tourist died on a hunting trip in the Albert Burn Valley near Makarora, New Zealand. Moments after alighting from a helicopter, the American tourist slipped on wet grass and fell 160 meters over a cliff. The coroner found that the hunting guide's actions were flawed, demonstrating a lack of training and experience. (*Source*: *The Southland Times* 1/4/09.)

- After a fatal industrial accident in north Canberra, the Transport Workers Union called for compulsory training for waste collectors. The 57-year-old man was crushed to death while using a crane to lift a rubbish hopper onto the back of a truck. (*Source*: ABC Premium News 14/1/09.)

- The death of a baby at the Mareeba Maternity Unit in Queensland was blamed on a lack of training, a culture of fear, and a breakdown in procedures by staff. (*Source*: *The Cairns Post* 27/12/07.)

- A District Court judge in Sydney, New South Wales, found that the death of a patient undergoing a dental procedure while under sedation was largely caused by a deficiency in the training and accreditation of the dentist. (*Source*: *The Sydney Morning Herald* 24/6/08.)

Organisations must take responsibility for developing their staff to the highest level of competence, or such catastrophic events will continue to occur. Organisations must recognise that their staff are their most important resource; the knowledge of their staff is the component most critical for their success. Developing the knowledge of staff is a complex process that needs high levels of investment in terms of finance, time and energy. The willingness to make such a high investment, though, will depend on organisations changing their basic values concerning efficiency and effectiveness.

Management re-engineering

The initial reaction of organisations and managers to the turbulent business environment of the 1990s has been to re-focus on the most familiar, easily observed and crucial resource – finance. This focus on finance has generated a number of solutions based on rational economics – usually discussed under terms like re-engineering, outsmarting, downsizing, business process re-engineering (BPR), creating flatter structures, and cost cutting. The goal of these options was the elimination of wastage and time delays that were rampant within many organisations in the late 1980s. Quite rightly, organisations examined and reassessed core business efforts, staffing levels, and organisational practices and procedures to ensure that resources were harnessed efficiently. Organisations had to be 'lean, mean fighting machines' to meet and surmount the challenges of the new millennium.

Unfortunately, the focus on dollar savings often became the sole justification for actions in many organisations. Simplistic interpretations of management theory led to untold damage in many organisations. The error was based on the assumption that costs can be removed. In fact, costs cannot be eliminated; they can only be transferred. Organisations are made up of a number of subsystems; they are but a subsystem within the global system. Any costs saved in one part of the system re-surface either in another internal subsystem or in the external system.

A favourite strategy of re-engineering advocates is to close down a small section (or several positions) in the central office and to move the work to the strategic business units (SBUs) or operational sections without transferring extra resources to these units or sections to carry out the work. This is a cunning artifice; each section or unit has only to do a small part of the original work. The strategy can be successful provided that not too much is transferred. Similar strategies can be used to transfer the costs to the external system – for example to customers (e.g. longer waiting periods; automated telephone messages directing customers to select a number to be put through to a desired contact point; fees for a variety of services) and to suppliers (e.g. charging for display areas).

There are two schemes that are even more insidious. The first is the 'flatter structures' option – i.e. to eliminate middle management in favour of teams. The assumption is that the energy generated by team work will offset the loss of the coordinating role of the middle managers. Unfortunately, this assumption is true only in situations where the work is dependent on the group interacting and operating as a single entity – that is, as a team.

The second scheme involves the re-emergence of 'management by objectives' – often under the new name of 'strategic management performance' (SMP). The general strategy is to give a manager full responsibility for an operational section, increase the performance objectives, and decrease the resources available to run the unit or section.

This forces the manager of the unit or section to make the necessary re-engineering decisions without sullying the face of upper management. These performance management strategies suffer from the same manipulative misuses that killed management by objectives. Management by objectives was designed originally to motivate and enrich management jobs. It was based on the assumptions that the manager would be fully involved in the setting of the objectives and would have significant power over the resources needed. Only when these two assumptions are applied will SMP survive. Both the elimination of middle management and SMP, however, suffer from the same illness – they are simplistic interpretations of management theory and can be successful only in specific situations.

For example, this cost cutting has had a severe detrimental effect in many of our higher education institutions. Nankervis (2013) sees the inevitability of cutting corners in such institutions – huge numbers of students in cramped lecture theatres, minimal or non-existant tutorials, online learning materials that render lecture attendances superfluous, and invalid lecturer evaluation processes.

Provided the cost does not rebound, cost transference can turn into cost savings. A cost saving, therefore, can be defined as a cost that is permanently transferred to another subsystem. Unfortunately, if a cost does rebound, it will do so with a multiplier effect, growing to many times the original supposed savings.

Some negative effects of the 'cost-saving syndrome' include:

1. *Loss of knowledge*. Loss of knowledge occurs when staff are retrenched. This is especially evident when the 'flatter structures' option is employed. The retrenched staff's knowledge walks out the door with them. While some of their knowledge can be documented, the problem is the loss of tacit knowledge. As we will see later, tacit knowledge is the unarticulated information that forms the base for a large variety of critical decisions.

2. *Ignoring traditional but critical processes and standards*. Re-engineering favours the new. Unfortunately, the old is often discarded without due thought. Some processes and standards have an essential, timeless quality. No matter what the changes, these critical processes and standards remain true. Machinery, for example, wears out in direct relationship to usage time. Many 'renewed' organisations, however, ignore maintenance schedules to save costs. The fact that an event may have a low probability of occurring is immaterial if the cost of that event is extremely high. Some former government-run electricity generating and distribution organisations in Australia and New Zealand, now 'corporatised', are facing multi-million dollar layouts because they ignored this fact of risk management. They have proved that a rebounding cost can have a huge multiplier effect.

3. *Forgetting that loyalty is a two-way street*. The re-engineering fad concentrates almost solely on the money resource. However, another highly valuable resource is the loyalty of staff, customers and suppliers. Staff are usually very forgiving, but only up to a point. Once the pain threshold is overstepped, motivation drops very quickly and individual staff output decreases

significantly. To make matters worse, redressing the situation takes anything from four to ten times the investment of the original 'saving'. Loss of loyalty is commonly seen with the transfer-of-tasks and flatter-structures options.

4. *The 'everything is saved' mentality.* This occurs particularly with the strategy of outsourcing. For example, when a function (such as catering in a hospital) is outsourced to an outside organisation, the justification is that the new service organisation which specialises in the function (catering) can produce the product or service much more efficiently. This is sometimes true. However, it must be remembered that it is in the outside organisation's best interest to provide service at the lowest possible cost to maximise their own profits.

Outsourcing organisations often err in three areas. First, if they do not use some of the money saved to institute an auditing process of the incoming produce or service, they risk increasing the possibility of substandard or inappropriate incoming resources. The outside service organisation, often driven by a 'cost saving' mentality, will want to produce as close to the minimum standard as possible. A basic tenet of management, however, is that responsibility can never be delegated. The host organisation, therefore, is still responsible for the quality of incoming resources. Managers of organisations which outsource functions must accept that not all the cost reduction is money saved. Some investment must be made in an auditing system. Even with an auditing system, the contractor often seeks only to meet the minimum standards of the contract, invariably leading to a drop in standards.

Second, by retrenching or re-deploying the staff of the original function outsourced, knowledge is lost. Unfortunately, it is this very knowledge that is needed to make the proposed auditing system operational and viable. Worse, as no staff are dedicated to the lost function, changes and new knowledge in that function are not imported by the host organisation.

Third, the function no longer has a champion in the organisation. This means that the attention of the organisation is not drawn to the importance of the outsourced function. Because of the political nature of decision-making, absolutely minimal resources are invested in the outsourced function.

These three losses – loss of current knowledge, no importation of new knowledge, and the lack of a champion – means that the decision-making in the organisation often ignores the impact of the lost function on the other systems in the organisation. Even when the lost function is considered in the decision-making, the decision is usually founded on a sadly inadequate knowledge base.

5. *The anorexic syndrome.* Cost cutting, taken to the extreme, leaves no fat in the system – and all living organisms need some fat. In complexity theory, this fat is called 'redundancy' or 'exploratory energy'. The system makes two uses of this exploratory resource. Most obviously, the excess energy can be used in times of deficiency or stress – when new but temporary demands are placed on the organisation (for example, new government legislation requires additional

reporting), or when resources are depleted for a short period (for example, when influenza sweeps the human resource).

The second use of the exploratory energy is more subtle, yet much more crucial. The additional resources allow the organisation to search the future for opportunities or threats, and to experiment with possible solutions. As we see later in the book, this is the important role of the shadow system. The closer to uncertainty the organisation operates, the more reliant on the shadow system (and hence on the exploratory resources) the organisation is for its strategic planning.

6. *Focus on money.* Excess emphasis on cost reduction sends an unremitting message – save money at all costs. All staff should be efficiency conscious, but when attention to this theme becomes extreme, the entire focus of the staff shifts from the core business to cost reduction. Such a shift is as disastrous as it is insidious. Long-term solutions based on the future needs of the core business are sacrificed for the short-term benefits of cost saving. Staff interest, motivation and curiosity are no longer being stimulated by the core business. Staff satisfaction wanes as a focus on the satisfaction of a job well done comes a poor second to cold dollars.

In times of external environment complexity and rapid change, this first reaction of focusing on saving costs is natural – especially in light of the recent global financial crisis. If conducted in a reasoned, systemic and strategic manner, it is a vital first step. However, the cost saving strategy is good only for trimming excess fat. To survive in an environment that is convoluted and changes rapidly, a much more complex, creative and impulsive resource must be brought to bear – the human resource.

The issue of not developing the people of the organisation was highlighted succinctly by a recent report from Drake International (2010), who found that 72 percent of organisations expect to face a skills shortage this year at the same time as staff turnover accelerates. As McNally (2003) comments, rather than the usual management processes of branding, economies of scale or even capital, talented people at all levels will ultimately become the key strength of an organisation. While clamouring for clarity beyond daily stock reports, headcount reductions and restructuring, executives and managers should not lose sight of the key essential to surviving and thriving: talented, skilled, knowledgeable and agile people (Tarrant 2009). The best organisations continue to pay attention to talent management and employee engagement, even when they are required to downsize (Schweyer 2009).

There are, however, indications that some management representatives are becoming aware of the importance of people and of the value of the asset called knowledge. The Chief Executive of the National Australia Bank, John Stewart, has emphatically commented that the employee is paramount, and he believes that the sequence of events that make things happen is happy staff, happy customers and then happy shareholders (Charles 2004). Sexton (2003) reports that the Dow Jones Sustainability Index and the Human Capital Index are showing that companies with sophisticated human capital practices are outperforming other companies by a factor of nearly three. Both Sexton (2003), Stone (2008) and Tarrant (2009) cite research which shows that a firm's human resource development investment was the single most important statistical predictor of stockholder return, and that there is a correlation between profit and productivity and increased expenditure on human resource development. While such research represents the 'carrot' for managers to move towards an approach that is more people and knowledge friendly, the 'stick' is also making itself known in the form of *compliance training*. A employer can be held vicariously liable for any actions of its staff that contravene any laws – for example, sexual harassment, health and safety – unless the employer has taken all reasonable steps, including the provision of regular training on those laws, to ensure that employees comply with the law (Donaldson 2009).

Some organisations are taking the importance of developing their staff so seriously, that they are opening their own universities. For example, Mars Incorporated established the 'virtual' Mars University in Australia and New Zealand in 2006. HR Monthly (2009) reports on the impetus to ensure that the company had comparable skills across the organisation, and that Mars are aiming at a 60 percent annual increase in management and leadership training hours. The report goes on to describe how there is no campus for the university, but that the programs cover: sales, marketing, research and development, supply, procurement, finance, HR and IT, as well as generic learning streams for leadership and management, for 'lean' efficiencies, and for Mars-unique methods of operation.

The traditional management approach

Traditional management theories can be divided into two broad classifications – conventional strategic management and operational management. Conventional strategic management recommends that the external environment should be analysed by identifying and assessing the factors that have a direct influence on the organisation – the customers, the competitors, specific government legislation, etc. From this analysis, the environment can be evaluated on a scale ranging from predictable to relatively unpredictable. Based on this judgement, traditional management theories then allow the upper management of the organisation to create an appropriate organisational structure and to follow appropriate strategies. Once the strategies have been selected, they can be operationalised using the operational management functions of plan, lead, organise and control (often called the PLOC model). These theories are based on what is called the Newtonian paradigm. Newton was a sixteenth-century mathematician and physicist who inspired significant original thought in science. The basis of his theories was the assumption that objects or matter could be broken down into their component parts, measured, and then re-built. In the early nineteenth century, these assumptions were incorporated into the then new science of management, particularly by people such as Frederick Taylor (1911).

Traditional management theories are heavily influenced by these values and, even today, there is a culture among so called 'hard-nosed' managers that, if it cannot be measured, then it does not matter. Halpin and Hanlon (2009) refer to this approach as the 'machine' metaphor with an emphasis on step-by-step processes, linearity, and a search for cause-and-effect. In this machine metaphor, the only useful knowledge is formal and systematic – hard (read: quantifiable) data, codified procedures, and universal principles (Nonaka

2007). Now it is not so much that the Newtonian paradigm is wrong for management theory, it just does not go far enough – it only tells part of the story (for an in-depth and critical analysis of the traditional management theories, see Mickelthwait and Wooldridge 1996). After all, a company is not a machine but a living organism (Nonaka 2007). Writers such as Delahaye (2003) and Morgan (2006) document several severe limitations of relying only on the traditional management theories, including:

- the great difficulty in adapting to changing circumstances;

- a mindless and unquestioning bureaucracy that is destined to always perform the same actions, no matter what;

- a concentration on the detail – if in doubt, divide the detail further and undertake even more micro-measurements; and

- a dehumanising of employees.

The significant deficiency in the traditional theories is an assumption that the two main resources available to managers are time and money – and further, that one can be exchanged for the other. So, for example, if a task is taking longer than planned, one solution is to invest money in equipment or additional staff to bring the task back onto the expected time line. The modern manager, though, has to recognise that we are in the middle of the 'information age' where a third, basic resource is critical – knowledge.

Knowledge capital

In 1990, Peter Senge, in his text *The Fifth Discipline*, popularised the concept of the learning organisation, where to survive an organisation had to continually learn and adjust to an ever-changing environment. Chief executive officers (CEOs), academics and researchers eagerly grasped this concept as a viable alternative to rational economics.

However, the concept proved to be vast in its complexity and the writings of the early 1990s, while providing important insights, had difficulty providing a sound, unifying and practical picture.

The situation was becoming very frustrating for both theoreticians and practitioners. Concentrating on costs gave the organisation only the potential to become a lean, mean fighting machine. An overemphasis on costs led to highly undesirable, and possibly terminal, negative effects. Strategic human resource management (SHRM) provided some answers, but also raised more questions. As Gee, Hull and Lankshear (1996) commented, gone were the days when workers were hired from the neck down and simply told what to do. The 'Holy Grail' of the learning organisation gave a glimpse into a powerful solution, but the view was distorted and dim. What increased the frustration was that each of these potential solutions did provide some practical insights, but an integrated resolution was still out of reach.

Then, in the mid-1990s, the focus concentrated on an intriguing concept - the management of knowledge capital. It was suggested that the knowledge of an organisation was a remarkable and critical resource:

In this society, knowledge is the primary resource for individuals and for the economy overall. Land, labour, and capital – the economist's traditional factors of production – do not disappear, but they become secondary. They can be obtained, and obtained easily, provided there is specialized knowledge. At the same time, however, specialized knowledge by itself produces nothing. It can become productive only when it is integrated into a task. And that is why the knowledge society is also a society of organizations: the purpose and function of every organization, business and non-business alike, is the integration of specialized knowledge into a common task. (Drucker 1995, p. 76)

Nonaka and von Krogh (2009) and Wang and Noe (2010) agree by stressing that knowledge is a critical organisational resource that provides a sustainable competitive advantage in a competitive and dynamic economy. Pimpimon (2009) concurs, pointing out that business strategies and financial issues are not enough – successful knowledge management is essential to sustained competitive advantage.

A unique resource

Authors such as Delahaye (2003) and Sveiby (1997, 2007) suggest that knowledge is a unique resource because of several characteristics:

1. *There is no law of diminishing returns.* The law of diminishing returns states that, as long as output increases, there will come a time when the cost per unit will begin to rise – and this principle is valid in a world of limited physical resources. However, unlike coal or wool, knowledge is not intrinsically scarce. Knowledge can be conjured up by human minds from nothing.

2. *Knowledge grows from sharing.* Unlike physical resources, knowledge does not disappear from the 'giver' when shared or sold. The 'giver' retains the exact same level of knowledge. So, when knowledge is shared with someone else, it is doubled. In addition, the very act of dredging up knowledge from the unconscious mind brings new insights to the 'giver' through a process called externalisation (to be discussed below).

3. *Knowledge cannot be hoarded for long.* The competitive edge provided by knowledge is only temporary, as competitors learn from each other and, if knowledge is created once, it can be created again.

4. Unlike information, *knowledge is not subject to copyright or to patents.* No person or organisation can copyright or patent an idea; they can copyright only physical expressions of the idea.

5. *Knowledge can be created by anyone*, and this means that one organisation's competitive edge can be annihilated overnight.

6. While it may take high levels of energy to accumulate, *knowledge is one of the most enduring of resources.*

Therefore, organisations have to be able to maintain their current knowledge, disseminate specific knowledge to specific parts of the organisation, create new knowledge, and unlearn useless knowledge. Not only do the learning needs of the organisation and the learning needs of the individual have to be considered, but the interaction between the two needs has to be fostered and nurtured. As Billett (1999) comments, never have enterprises and their workers needed each other more than they do now. This link between individuals and the organisation is emphasised by Nonaka and von Krogh (2009), who suggest that knowledge creation is the process of making available and amplifying knowledge created by individuals as well as crystallising and connecting it to an organisation's knowledge system.

So what is knowledge? Nonaka (2002) sees knowledge as a multifaceted concept with multilayered meanings. Therefore, knowledge is, firstly, justified true belief, in that individuals justify their beliefs based on their observations of the world; secondly, knowledge is the capacity to define a situation and act accordingly; and, thirdly, knowledge is explicit (can be enunciated) *and* is tacit (beliefs, intuition, complex skills) (Nonaka, von Krogh & Voelpel 2006). To add to this definition, it is also worthwhile differentiating knowledge from data and information:

- *Data* – raw ciphers that, by themselves, have no meaning. For example, a list of numbers representing the responses of a subject to items in a questionnaire.

- *Information* – raw data combined into simple messages. For example, the mean and standard deviation values of the responses to items in a questionnaire.

- *Inert knowledge* – a stored flow of information that presents a considered opinion or story. For example, the knowledge in a textbook.

- *Embodied knowledge* – knowledge held in the human brain that is accessed at various times depending on conscious and subconscious cues.

This hierarchy suggests that knowledge is more complex than data and information, but that data and information can be used to construct knowledge.

Complexity theory and managing knowledge capital

The machine metaphor of the traditional management theories provides some control and direction over the management of the knowledge resources in an organisation. Nonaka *et al.* (2006) point out that traditional management theories see the primary function of managers as maintaining efficiency. This is achieved in six steps:

1. Top managers articulate knowledge visions and communicate them throughout.

2. Middle managers translate these visions into a work context by breaking down the visions into concepts, images and activities that guide the knowledge creation process.

3. Top managers deal with the knowledge system layer, and ascertain that it is both used and fed by organisational knowledge creation (for example, through the strategic planning process).

4. Top managers redefine the organisational units so that they enhance the fit with the knowledge system layer – new organisational units are initiated and others become redundant.

5. Top and middle managers provide space for learning – physical space such as meeting rooms; virtual space such as computer networks; and mental space, such as corporate goals. They bring about the right mix of people (from the view point of upper management) and promote their interaction.

6. Middle managers keep the learning spaces – physical, virtual and mental – energised and focused.

Now, these endeavours of traditional theories to manage the knowledge resource can be successful to an extent, and the processes used are essential. Unfortunately, a unitary focus is not enough in this age of information. As far as managing knowledge goes, these theories have three major limiting flaws:

- There is a focus on reductionism – the belief that, if smaller and smaller component parts can be identified and measured, then the ultimate solution will eventually be found.

- Further, there is an assumption that some universal knowledge is available that can be drawn upon, at will, by senior managers.

- The managers are solely responsible for driving the learning of the new knowledge.

What was needed was a new management approach incorporating both the machine metaphor and the living organism metaphor of Morgan (2006) and Nonaka (2007). Senge (1990) first articulated the critical importance of learning in organisational survival. Wellman (2007) identifies three reasons for organisations to ensure that learning has primacy in all organisational endeavours:

1. The capacity to learn and to apply learning is rapidly becoming one of a few truly sustainable competitive advantages.

2. Learning is an asset not unlike intellectual property, capital investment, or a skilled workforce.

3. An effective learning organisation is a central element in a healthy organisational gestalt, as it breeds a sense of optimism about the future, the ability to deal with adversity, and a healthy willingness to take calculated risks.

The advantage of the new management theories is that they incorporate the process of both the machine and the living organisms metaphors while also emphasise learning. One of the most significant writers on the new management theories is Stacey (1993, 1996, 2000, 2003, 2007). In his earlier texts (for example, Stacey 1996), he tagged the older, rationalistic approaches as 'ordinary management', and the new approaches as 'extraordinary management'. Further, he suggests that managers needed to combine the older rational skills and with these newer ideas. As Mason (2008) comments, complexity theory shares chaos theory's concern with wholes, with larger systems or environments, and with the recognition that even very slight degrees of uncertainty can grow inexorably; this, as opposed to the reductionist concerns of mainstream science with the essential of the ultimate particle. Stacey (2000) uses complexity theory – a combination of chaos theory and quantum mechanics – as the more logical and appropriate basis for management theory.

According to complexity theory, any system is drawn to two main attractors – equilibrium and inequilibrium. When applied to organisations, these two main attractors are represented by two systems – the legitimate system and the shadow system. The relationship between these two systems is represented in Figure 1.1.

Figure 1.1 The two basic systems

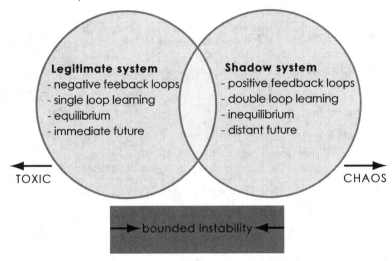

Source: Based on Delahaye 2002.

The legitimate system

The legitimate system pulls the organisation towards equilibrium, and its main aim and justification is efficiency. The legitimate system has three important roles:

- to concentrate on the near-to-certain aspects of the external environment;

- to manage the day-to-day activities of the organisation; and

- to audit any change that may affect the *status quo*.

The legitimate system is best managed by the familiar rationalist theories of ordinary management that are the basis of most management and business administration degrees, for example, the familiar circular POLC model of the plan, organise, lead and control functions (see, for example, Davidson *et al.* 2009). In large part these management theories were derived from the engineering and military fields of practice and, as discussed earlier, are all based on the Newtonian paradigm. This paradigm assumes that cause and effect can be analysed by breaking a problem down into smaller and smaller components - and these assumptions are true under conditions of close-to-certainty. Further, cohesion is achieved by basic laws. In organisations, these laws are called plans, policies and procedures. The organisation uses two processes – negative feedback loops and single-loop learning – to ensure that efficiency is achieved.

Negative feedback loops dampen any deviation from the 'norm' and bring such deviations back to the accepted or planned standard. The control function in the POLC model is a classical negative feedback loop. When some deviation (e.g. in the budget) is detected, remedial action is taken to bring the budget back into balance. Similarly, if a staff member contravenes some rule, then the disciplinary process is used to ensure that the transgression does not occur again. Single-loop learning (see Argyris 2008) passes on current knowledge without the learner challenging the veracity or usefulness of the knowledge. Efficiency is achieved as no time is 'wasted' explaining why the material being learnt is valid or why it is needed.

The legitimate system can invoke a sense of stability and can act to reassure participants that rationality and control are possible (Fitzgerald 2009); when the legitimate system concentrates on that part of the external environment that is near-to-certainty, then this sense of reassurance is justified. Further, the legitimate system is critical to the organisation, as this system produces the services or products that allow the organisation to survive. Accordingly, the legitimate system often has enormous power as it is so obviously the source of immediate survival.

The shadow system

The shadow system pulls the organisation towards inequilibrium, and its main aim and justification is creativity. The shadow system has three important roles:

- to concentrate on the far-from-certainty aspects of the external environment;

- to import and create new knowledge that will ensure the long term future of the organisation; and

- to export the new knowledge to the legitimate system.

The shadow system continually tests the internal and external environment of the organisation and, in this way, releases the self-organising potential of the natural system so that future possible opportunities, challenges and threats are explored and analysed. The shadow system allows the organisation to continually evolve in a spontaneous, self-organising manner by exploring options and generating ingenious alternatives. The shadow system relies on extraordinary management – an approach that applies chaos theory and uses the resources of redundancy, i.e. those resources that the system stores and invests in in an effort to avoid stagnation and obsolescence.

Creativity is valued above all else, and its role may be seen as 'play without apparent purpose'. The shadow system achieves creativity by tapping into the tacit and highly subjective insights, intuitions and hunches of individual employees and by making those insights available for testing and for use by the organisation as a whole (Nonaka 2007). The shadow system accomplishes creativity by using the extraordinary management processes of positive feedback loops and double-loop learning.

Positive feedback loops – feedback that enhances and amplifies – reign supreme. The ultimate aim of the shadow system is to produce a replacement for the current dominant schema, the legitimate system. Possible solutions to these future trends are promulgated and championed by the shadow system before being tested by the legitimate system for their robust potential to help the organisation survive. Double-loop learning (see Argyris 2008) occurs when the learner challenges the underlying beliefs and values of commonly-held 'truths'. Frequently, the values and beliefs that are challenged belong to the legitimate system. In challenging these beliefs and values, the shadow system ensures that the organisation will survive by pushing the legitimate system away from its comfort zone to a place where it must reconfigure itself (Dervitsiotis 2005).

While the legitimate system relies on the machine-like processes of the PLOC model, the heart of the shadow system is the self-organising groups (Stacey 2001) or as Nonaka (2007) call them, informal communities of interaction. A self-organising group (SOG) occurs when two or more people come together to discuss an issue of mutual interest. After all, the fundamental motivator of human behaviour is the urge to relate and this urge causes a self-organising effect, in the sense that people always have the potential for spontaneity and do not simply follow centrally determined rules of conduct (Stacey, 2008). Stacey (2008) then goes on to explain that, since human interaction is nonlinear, its iteration has the capacity to amplify small differences caused by spontaneity and imperfect reproduction into major qualitative changes in population-wide patterns of relating. It is in this manner that human interaction evolves in novel ways. SOGs need positive feedback loops to grow and are the most significant source of creativity, and thus for new knowledge, for the organisation.

In terms of this new management theory, it is interesting to note that traditional management champions the legitimate system, while the literature of the early 1990s on the learning organisation (see, for example, Senge 2006) advocates the shadow system. However, the current literature sees the interaction between the two systems – the legitimate and the shadow – as the hallmark of the learning organisation. The role of the modern manager is to manage both systems, and the interaction between them, simultaneously. Organisational knowledge creation is the process of making available and amplifying the knowledge created by individuals (that is, the shadow system) as well as crystallising and connecting it with an organisation's knowledge system (that is, the legitimate system) (Nonaka *et al.* 2006).

Bounded instability

It is interesting to note that the shadow system cannot operate unless there is a solid and secure legitimate system. First, the shadow system depends on the legitimate system to provide sufficient resources to operate successfully. Second, the shadow system can only explore imaginatively and with complete freedom if it knows that the legitimate system is available to ultimately curb any ideas that are too outlandish. The major problem with an overly-powerful shadow system is that, in its pursuit of creativity, it will drag the organisation into chaos and ultimate collapse.

Yet the current legitimate system has to live with the knowledge that the ultimate aim of the shadow system is to identify and design new values and structures that will make the present legitimate system obsolete. In addition, society has always assumed that inequilibrium is to be avoided, as the final outcome of that path is confusion, turmoil and anarchy. Hence, the Roman Empire, by staying firmly within the boundaries of equilibrium, remained a world force for centuries. Therefore, the assumption has always been that organisations need the stability of equilibrium – and it is in the state of equilibrium that the rationalist management theories of ordinary management operate to their fullest potential. This historical precedence has led to an innate distrust by the legitimate system of new ideas from the shadow system. In any case, considering new ideas takes up energy, and this diversion of energy decreases efficiency.

So, the natural reaction of the legitimate system to the predations of the shadow system is the use of organisational defence mechanisms. These defence mechanisms tend to keep an organisation in single-loop learning so that the underlying governing variables are not examined. Argyris (1999) describes one of these defence mechanisms as the *undiscussables*, where certain issues in organisations cannot be discussed. The reasons why are often dimmed by history – but most people in the organisation know that the issue should not be discussed. New members are soon encultured into recognising the undiscussability by nonverbals or public 'put downs'. If the new member does not take the hint, then someone with higher power will take on the responsibility to 'straighten him out'. Eerily, this enculturation into the world of undiscussables is quite overt, with the 'teacher' requiring no instruction to carry out the task. The process becomes even more bizarre, with the undiscussability of the issue becoming itself undiscussable.

Case study example

See the PLP case study on page 24 of the workbook that accompanies this text for organisational defence mechanisms.

Defensive mechanisms are designed to avoid double-loop learning and thereby maintain efficiency. However, an often lethal by-product is that such a single-minded pursuit of efficiency can draw the organisation into a toxic state. The organisation then does not re-new itself and remains static (and comfortable for those in powerful positions), and the rest of the world passes it by. The toxicity can be recognised by the high level of industrial problems, excessive sick leave among staff or high staff turnover.

Such a toxic legitimate system results in the death of the system – a slower death than being drawn into chaos by an overactive shadow system, but death just the same. In short, equilibrium does not guarantee success and longevity. An organisation in the state of equilibrium remains viable only while its external environment remains predictable and certain. The Roman Empire remained a vital force for so long because there were no dramatic changes in technology, climate or politics. When the external environment changes, the organisation that remains in a state of equilibrium will soon be by-passed.

If the separate states of equilibrium or inequilibrium are not the answer, then what is? The initial part of the answer lies in the recognition that the solution will not be a simple 'either/or' option. Rather, Stacey (1996) suggests, organisations must operate in a state of bounded instability where the organisation hovers between equilibrium and inequalibrium. Each system – the legitimate and the shadow – must be given an appropriate level of power so that exceptional efficiency is maintained, but also so that the organisation creates and incorporates sufficient new knowledge so that unforeseen and unpredictable challenges are overcome. In the foreseeable future, managers must strive for bounded instability – a state where the organisation is partly in equilibrium and partly in inequilibrium. Under bounded instability, the organisation is seen as having two complementary and dependent systems – the legitimate system and the shadow system – that are continually in tension.

The adult learner

As Nonaka (2007) points out, new knowledge always begins with the individual, and therefore an organisation cannot create knowledge without individuals. Governments, academics and managers are now recognising the unique and critical contribution that staff – and the vast majority of these staff are adults – make to the continued viability of organisations, societies, communities, and the nation.

The most recent and comprehensive investigation in adult learning in Australia – there appears to be no equivalent for New Zealand - was *Adult Learning in Australia: A Consultation Paper* (Department of Education, Science and Training 2003). This report nominates seven key action areas for adult learning:

1. Understanding the needs of adult learners

2. Building the relationships between service providers, employers, government and the community

3. Promoting the value of adult learning

4. Assisting mature age transitions

5. Supporting learning in the workplace

6. Ensuring access to opportunities

7. Engaging communities.

Source: Department of Education, Science and Training 2003.

The importance for recognising adult learning as a major theme is predicated on at least four levels (Department of Education, Science and Training 2003). First, as the workforce ages, businesses will come to rely more on the skills and knowledge of mature age workers. Second, and compounding this situation, there will be the need for all workers to continually upgrade their skills and knowledge. Third, learning enriches our culture, promotes intellectual life, and helps people achieve their potential as citizens. Fourth, adult learning enables Australia to maintain its competitive advantage in an increasingly competitive world economy.

Understanding and facilitating adult learning, then, is fundamental to the existence of HRD and the ability to manage knowledge capital. As Foley (2001) explains, learning in societal, community and organisational life is complex, contested and contextual. Therefore:

- people learn all the time, experientially and informally as well as formally;

- this learning can be positive or negative, productive or unproductive; and

- in attempting to change societies, communities and organisations, it is essential to understand the dynamics and outcomes of this formal, informal and experiential learning.

Learning at the individual and group level, then, is fundamental to the creation of knowledge and the concepts of adult learning theory will underpin all the discussions throughout this book.

A closer look 1.2

People matter at Brannigans

To Darrin Murphy, human capital is New Zealand's most valuable resource.

'It is widely recognised that, for New Zealand to grow, we must focus on building a knowledge-based economy. To do this we must continue to invest in human capital. At Brannigans, we regard people as human capital, an asset to be supported and developed to achieve full potential,' he says.

Darrin is the chief executive of Brannigans Human Capital, a newly-formed human resources consultancy company set up by a group of prominent Christchurch business and human resource consultants.

The aim of the company is to fill a niche in the Christchurch human resource market by setting up a consultancy that is both locally owned and focused on business in the Canterbury region, yet capable of operating nationally and internationally. The business will provide a complete range of human resource-related services using the broad capabilities of the people involved.

'Brannigans is staffed by a group of very talented and experienced human resource and business professionals who call Christchurch home,' says Darrin. 'Many of them have lived and worked in various other countries, developing and honing the considerable range of skills they are now making available to our South Island clients.'

Darrin Murphy brings his own unique set of skills to his position as chief executive. The former New Zealand international cricketer has a strong background of senior management experience in a number of international businesses.

His experience includes responsibility for activities in New Zealand, Australia, Asia, Europe, and North America. Recently returned from Europe, he managed the restructure of PDL Electronics' European business and its successful integration into Schneider-Electric Europe.

As well as change management, his other areas of expertise are general management, business strategy, business turnaround and financial transactions.

'While executive recruitment will be central to our operations, other services include: organisational performance, change management, employment law and employment relations, psychometric assessment, career coaching and counselling, performance management, human resources training and development, career transition, and redundancy support,' he says.

Source: The Press, Christchurch, 9 July 2003.

The HR developer and the management of knowledge

The traditional role of the HR developer has been to deliver formal programs – alternatively called courses, workshops or training – in a location away from the worksite of the workers/learners. Frequently, these formal programs were initiated by the HRD Department as the topics were generic in nature and seemed to satisfy perennial demands from the workplace. In fact, even this role is a diminished version of the full traditional responsibilities – one suspects that the craving of the legitimate system has devalued the role of HR developer to one of a face-to-face communicator.

In fact, we have been fully aware for some time of the complete traditional role of the HR developer – and, indeed, one of these roles is that of a face-to-face communicator. Dewey (1938) championed the central tenet that meaningful learning design should be founded on the learner's needs and interests. Over fifty years ago, Tyler (1949) and Knowles (1950) declared that the logical process of planned adult learning should follow the steps of: determining the learner's needs, stating objectives, choosing the content, instructors and methods, and evaluating the outcomes – steps that were given a formalised imprimatur by London in 1960. In 1974, Goldstein collated these ideas and advocated a systems approach to HRD based on the three stages of: needs assessment, training and development, and evaluation. Brookfield (1987) extended these three stages to four, commenting that there seemed to be a great deal of consensus among the various process models as to the steps involved. These steps are:

1. an *investigation stage* where needs are investigated and identified;

2. a *design stage* where aims, objectives (or goals) and content are examined;

3. an *implementation stage* where formal or informal learning activities occur; and

4. an *evaluation stage* where the worth of the learning experience is judged.

In the intervening years, a variety of techniques have been developed to achieve the aims of these four stages. These techniques have been documented in a variety of texts that usually concentrate on only one of the stages – be that on needs investigation or design or implementation or evaluation.

A number of these techniques have stood the test of time, and have proven to be exceptionally useful tools in managing the knowledge capital in organisations. The question then arises: 'Why do organisations not use these techniques consistently and in the systematic manner that is recognised as best practice?' Part of the answer lies in the penchant for managers, under pressure to produce, to look for the quick-fix solution, and in the concomitant increase in the number of fads that flooded the market in the 1980s in particular (for a fuller discussion, see Micklethwait and Wooldridge 1996). Another somewhat related answer lies in the incredibly complex efforts and long lead times needed for effective HRD. Managers under pressure for quick solutions opt for the more immediate, if illusory, results promised by management re-engineering. Finally, there is the legitimate system's unrelenting search for 'efficiency'. Accordingly, three of stages – needs analysis, design and evaluation – are often allowed to slide into oblivion. Time has shown that such ill-founded decisions increase staff frustrations while the underlying problems remain and fester.

These four stages of HRD – needs investigation, design, implementation and evaluation – are in fact a significant part of the legitimate system's contribution to the management of knowledge. They represent the 'engine room' of the traditional management of knowledge capital. The four stages produce the energy that drives the basic requirements so that the organisational knowledge is constantly identified, disseminated and reviewed. Further, a thorough understanding of the four stages is needed to successfully manage both workplace learning and learning partnerships. Accordingly, the HR developer needs to be fully proficient and competent in the four stages if the legitimate system is to have any chance of contributing to the management of the knowledge capital of the organisation.

However, the newer complexity theory shows us that the role of the HR developer must expand beyond this traditional, ordinary management role. Firstly, in today's complex business world, it is important to emphasise that the full responsibility for the development of staff rests with the *immediate* supervisor. While this has always been the case, over the past several decades, supervisors have come to concentrate more on the elements of the job that impact most directly and overtly on productivity. Therefore, being continually time poor, most supervisors were happy to see the role of developing staff relocated elsewhere – elsewhere being to an official HRD department or section. Responsibility can never be delegated, so supervisors now need to re-claim the developmental role of their staff. If, in the supervisors' considered opinion, the development can be carried out more efficiently or effectively by third party, then that third party can be given the authority to undertake specific developmental projects. The third party may be an internal consultant in the organisation's HRD department or section, or it may be an external consultant in HRD. If, however, the learning would be facilitated more effectively in the local environment (perhaps because there are preferred local ways of performing tasks, for example), then the supervisor becomes the HR developer and retains the responsibility.

The role for the modern HR developer is now much wider than the traditional role. Yes, the formal HR developer will still undertake traditional HRD tasks in the legitimate system, based on the four stages of HRD. On the other hand, the supervisor may take on the role of HR developer. Further, though, the HR developer (whether the formal or the supervisor) will be required to facilitate learning in the shadow system, and the most significant element of this facilitation is the support of the learning in the self-organising groups. The responsibilities in this facilitation of SOGs can be many and varied, but some of the most important are:

- developing the members as self-directed learners;

- developing the members in skills such as brainstorming, researching analysis and critical thinking;

- managing the group processes including the movement through the stages of group growth, problem solving, creative development, and managing internal and external networks, and, perhaps the most difficult of all

- developing managers so that they do not automatically revert to organisational defence mechanisms, but rather engage in extraordinary management.

Additionally, HR developers need to continually look for ways to keep the organisation in a state of bounded instability.

So, under complexity, the role of HRD is performed by a number of people, primarily the supervisor and the formal HR developer, and this gives the whole concept of HRD a much wider interpretation. Concomitantly, the HR developer now has a more extensive and more complex role to ensure that the organisation effectively manages its knowledge capital.

Within a wider theoretical context

To this stage, we have discussed HRD within the wider concepts of management, in particular ordinary management (for example, the PLOC model) and extraordinary management (for example, facilitating the learning of SOGs).

Undoubtedly, like most other employees, most HR developers will spend the majority of their time within the legitimate system. Accordingly, the four HRD stages of investigation, design, implementation and evaluation cannot be considered in isolation as the legitimate system has a number of overt ordinary management systems. One of the most important elements of this ordinary managerial orientation that impacts on the role of the HR developer is that of human resource management (HRM).

The functions of HRM

The functions of HRM define the roles that managers undertake as they manage the human resource of the organisation. Usually, these functions are listed as:

1. *strategic human resource planning* (SHRP), which is linked directly to the organisational strategic plan. The organisational strategic plan identifies the market niche that the organisation will occupy and the strategies that the organisation will use to service its customers. SHRP identifies the type and number of staff the organisation will need to fulfil this servicing role.

2. *recruitment,* where the community is advised that the organisation needs a certain number and type of staff. To recruit additional staff, the organisation usually advertises in newspapers, professional journals and the internet – although these days professional recruitment consultants are also used quite extensively.

3. *selection,* where the candidates who responded to the recruitment campaign are reviewed and assessed. Successful candidates are then selected for entry into the organisation.

4. *induction,* where the successful candidates are introduced to the organisation. This induction may cover procedural or even technical training, as well as socialising the selectees to the organisational culture.

5. *human resource development,* where staff are continually developed so that their knowledge, skills and abilities are updated. This function is now seen as critical to the ongoing viability of the organisation, and is often separated out from HRM. It is this function, of course, which is the subject of this book.

6. *performance appraisal*, where the performance of staff is assessed and any improvements or developmental needs are identified.

7. *career counselling*, where the long-term future of each staff member is planned for the good of the individual and of the organisation.

8. *discipline*, where aberrant behaviour is modified. The discipline function is directly affected by legal issues which proscribe both the type of behaviour that cannot be accepted by organisations and the process by which this behaviour can be encouraged to change.

9. *separations*, where staff leave the organisation – either through retirement (age or ill-health), resignation or dismissal.

While it is common for HRD to be separated organisationally from the other functions of HRM, the strong interrelationships do continue. For example, when new staff are selected, they often need specific development either to bring them up to an acceptable standard or to re-educate them to the unique skills or procedures required for that particular organisation.

Undoubtedly, the function of HRM that most strongly influences the four stages of HRD in the legitimate system is strategic human resource planning (SHRP). The development of staff must be compatible with the strategic direction of the organisation. Further, quite often a change in strategic direction of an organisation requires a significant effort to re-develop the staff. If you are not familiar with strategic planning, it is suggested you read texts such as Davidson *et al.* (2009) and Dickie and Dickie (2007).

However, the two HRM functions that feed directly into the four stages of HRD are performance appraisal and career counselling or, as it is often referred to, career development. Both of these functions are critical elements of the first stage of HRD, and are discussed in detail in Chapter 6.

The context of HRD

As indicated in Figure 1.2, HRD can be viewed as being embedded in HRM, although there is a tendency to recognise that HRD is an important entity in its own right. As far as the legitimate system is concerned, HRD is governed by the four stages of HRD. Figure 1.2 also indicates that HRD is crucially informed by four other concepts – the management of knowledge, adult learning, workplace learning, and creativity and organisational culture – all of which are receiving burgeoning interest in the academic literature. These concepts have provided a refreshing review of the role of HRD and explain why HRD has such a critical role in the management of an organisation. Further, the literature on the creation of knowledge, on adult learning, on workplace learning and on organisational culture presents cogent explanations for the application of HRD within the wider context of *both* the legitimate system and the shadow system, and also provides distinct guides for decision-making within the HRD framework.

This wider theoretical context of HRD, then, has provided the logical basis for the design of this textbook.

Figure 1.2 The wider theoretical context of HRD

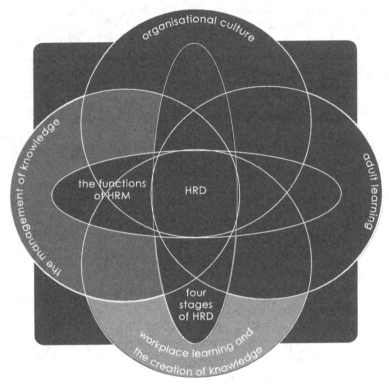

The design of this textbook

The next three chapters take a wider view – more the external environment within which HRD survives. Chapter 2 examines continuing education and training as, in these contemporary times, there is an expectation of lifelong learning. Accordingly, external learning institutions such as universities TAFE colleges and registered training organisations often provide a basis for professional development. Indeed, at times, such educational institutions can become learning partners with organisations. As adult learning provides such a fundamental underpinning of HRD and knowledge management, Chapter 3 examines the significant adult learning theories and their practical application. The theories and concepts discussed in this chapter are fundamental to understanding the topics covered in all the following chapters in the book, and it is suggested that Chapter 3 be read very carefully. Chapter 4 emphasises that individual adult learners are different. They have different cultural, social and economic backgrounds; they have lived different histories and have different personality patterns. Any design for learning and harnessing creativity must take account of the foundation adult learning theories and of the rich diversity of adult learners.

An overview of HRD needs identification – the first of the four stages of HRD – is provided in Chapter 5. A definition of, and the purposes for, the human resource needs identification (HRDNI) are discussed. The two levels of awareness – surveillance and investigation – are examined and various techniques for data gathering and data analysis are discussed. The chapter emphasises that the key outcome of the HRDNI is the *identification of the learning outcomes* (objectives or competencies). Then, the results of the investigation should be included in a report. Finally, suggestions are also made about selecting appropriate HRDNI methods and how to plan a HRDNI.

The HRDNI surveillance level methods of performance appraisal and career development are examined in Chapter 6. Performance appraisal and performance management are discussed, concluding that performance appraisal is a subset of performance management. Performance appraisal is a natural and unique process in organisations, although most managers do not realise that there are two basic types – administrative and developmental. Administrative performance appraisal is used for administrative decision-making in the organisation, for example, about promotions and salary increases. Developmental performance appraisal is used for identifying the developmental needs of individual staff members and, accordingly, is very useful for HRDNI. All performance appraisals should be based on a current job analysis before performance is observed and comparisons made with the key effectiveness areas and job specification. Feedback is then given with an appropriate interview before action plans for the development of the individual are instituted. Linked very closely to performance appraisal is the function of career development. Career development focuses on the long-term development of the individual and is discussed in Chapter 6.

Research skills are foundational to conducting a HRDNI. Generally, research skills are divided into qualitative and quantitative. The qualitative skills are, generically, the same as the skills that a HR developer uses when facilitating and managing learning. So, Chapter 7 discusses the two qualitative investigative methods of the interview and the focus group. Ways of appropriately structuring each of these interventions and the required skills needed to manage the processes of data gathering – questioning, listening, paraphrasing, probing and summarising – are examined. The differences between structured and unstructured interviews/focus groups are also explored. The reader should note that these competencies are fundamental to the HRD practitioner and need to be assimilated as elementary skills to understand the following chapters. Quantitative research requires complex knowledge in the areas of questionnaire design and statistical analysis. This knowledge is beyond the scope of this text, and the reader is asked to refer to other textbooks on the topic.

The book then comes to the second of the four stages of HRD – design. Of critical importance is the concept of *constructive alignment* – identifying learning strategies that are most likely to achieve the defined learning outcomes. Chapter 8 then goes on to suggest that there are two main considerations when designing learning experiences for adults – the content and the learner. The content consists of the topics the learner will learn. This chapter puts forward a hierarchy of learning outcomes (HLO) that prioritises the content into a hierarchy. This hierarchy is divided into five major categories – programmed knowledge, task, relationships, critical thinking and meta-abilities – that move from the least complex (programmed knowledge) to the most complex (meta-abilities). These five major categories are further divided into subgroups of outcomes, and each subgroup is broken further down into elements of outcomes. This HLO can then be associated with selecting appropriate learning strategies – with the structured learning strategies being most suited to programmed learning, and the unstructured learning strategies being more suited to the meta-abilities category. This matching of learning outcomes to learning strategies is a relatively simple indicator of appropriateness. Any such initial decision would need to be reviewed and adjusted in light of the second main indicator – the learner. Learners can differ on a variety of characteristics – including current knowledge, motivation, learning orientation and learning styles – and this variety of needs should be reflected in the final design of the learning experience.

Chapter 9 examines other considerations that can be used to refine the design of the learning experience. These variables include: the strategic orientation of the organisation, the organisational culture, the needs of the key stakeholders, and the limiting effects of the resources available. As an overview, the whole design process is reviewed by examining the common curriculum design theories of the rational model, the interaction model, and the platform model. Finally, it is emphasised that the design stage is not complete until all the HRD operational plans are documented. These operational plans include: session plans, the program, the resource plan, the marketing plan, the budget, and the evaluation plan.

The next two chapters move onto the third of the four stages of HRD, implementation. Chapter 10 examines the structured learning strategies. The structured learning strategies discussed are: the skill session, the theory session, the lecture, the discussion, the case study, the role play, and experiential learning. However, where a learning strategy transforms from structured to unstructured is a moot point, as only the first three – the skill session, the theory session and the lecture – could be considered fully structured. In these three learning strategies, the HR developer makes all the decisions on what will be learned, on how it will be learned, and on how it will be assessed. In the other four learning strategies, starting with the discussion, the learner takes over more responsibility, with this responsibility increasing as the case study, then the role play, and then the experiential learning strategies are used. So these last four strategies become more unstructured.

Chapter 11 examines the fully unstructured learning strategies of contract learning, action learning, change interventions, mentoring and e-learning. The ways and means of managing the process, rather than directing the content, are examined in full – as are the various skills required of the HR developer.

Chapter 12 explores the fourth of the HRD stages: evaluation. Again, the importance of *constructive alignment* is emphasised here – the assessment of learning must be appropriate to the defined learning outcomes and integrate with the chosen learning strategies. Ways of assessing learning are examined, including skills resting, objective tests, subjective written tests, performance tests, learning diaries and portfolio assessment. Kirkpatrick's four levels of evaluation are discussed. One disadvantage of Kirkpatrick's model is that the presage or input factors are not addressed, and so the ways of evaluating the program design, the implementation and the implementing HR developer are also examined in this chapter. Two other approaches to evaluation – the scientific model and the cost-benefit analysis – are then discussed. Finally, the need to develop an evaluation plan is emphasised.

Chapter 13 begins the move away from the processes used into the legitimate system and begins the examination of the shadow system. The chapter explores workplace learning by examining the challenges to workplace learning, and then providing a model for managing learning in the workplace and a model of individual adult learning. The chapter emphasises the primacy of the supervisor in the development of staff.

Chapter 14 examines the processes used to create and embed new knowledge into the everyday work practices of the organisation. The chapter discusses: the three roles of the shadow system, the importance of self-organising groups, communities of practice, networks, and learning partnerships. Finally, the chapter describes how the new knowledge is exported to the legitimate system to achieve a state of bounded instability.

Chapter 15 discusses the mutually dependent concepts of organisational culture, leadership and knowledge management. It begins by providing a comprehensive model for managing the knowledge capital of the organisation using an expanded version of Figure 1.1. Types of organisational culture are then discussed with the suggestion that, when managing knowledge, a multi-dimensional interpretation of organisational culture is needed, rather than a uni-dimensional approach. Finally, the chapter discusses how transactional and transformational leadership can combine with organisational culture to manage the knowledge capital of the organisation.

The 4th edition – a different approach

This 4th edition is, in effect, two books. The first is this textbook, which now concentrates solely on the theoretical and practical application of these theories. The companion book – the workbook – contains all the activities that can make your learning journey easier. Accordingly, the workbook contains the Pacific Lifestyle Publishing case study and, for each chapter, case studies, possible examination questions and multiple choice questions.

The possible examination questions are divided into three types:

- For review – These questions simply ask you to restate the facts on the theories and parts of theories discussed in the chapter.

- For analysis – these questions ask you to delve deeper into the theories and parts of theories. For example, you will be asked to compare and contrast, differentiate between, describe situations or top explain a theory or parts of theories.

- For application – these questions ask you to apply the theories or parts of theories and to justify your choices or decisions.

You might like to read Chapter 8 and examine the hierarchy of learning outcomes and identify how these three types of questions represent different levels of learning – from shallow to deep.

Also in the workbook is a large case study, the Pacific Lifestyle Publishing. This case study is cross-referenced with the various theories in this textbook so that you can see the practical use of these theories.

How to use this book

Being in the written form, this book is based on a linear logic that assumes all readers will wish to start with the wider view of continuing education and training (Chapter 2) and the underpinning adult learning theories (Chapter 3), and then go on to examine individual differences in adult learners (Chapter 4) before working through the four functions in sequence – needs investigation (Chapters 6 to 7), design (Chapters 8 and 9), implementation (Chapters 10 and 11) and evaluation (Chapter 13). The role of the supervisor as a HR developer is then explored in Chapter 13, and the role of the shadow system in Chapter 14. Chapter 15 examines the management of knowledge by discussing how appropriate leadership styles can combine with an appropriate multi-dimensional culture to manage the organisation's knowledge capital.

However, two factors may make this assumption of linear logic unsuitable. First, the needs of individual readers - perhaps those with more advanced knowledge of HRD or perhaps because of different learning styles – may indicate that a different order be followed. Second, the four stages of HRD are very closely interlinked and, indeed, overlap in some parts. Further, as already discussed, these four stages impact on, and are affected by, the functions of HRM, the theories of knowledge creation, and the new management theories. So, some readers may prefer to examine first the four stages of HRD (Chapters 6 to 12), as these four stages are the main theme of this book. Some readers may wish to start with one of the other stages – implementation, for example, rather than needs investigation. Other readers may be more intrigued by the creation of knowledge and organisational culture, and may prefer to go straight to Chapters 14 and 15 before exploring the four stages of HRD. Those of who are interested in workplace learning, however, may prefer to start with Chapter 13.

So, while a decision had to be made on the ordering of the concepts in this book, readers are free to follow a different path if they wish.

References

Argyris, C 1999, *On organizational learning*, 2nd edn, Blackwell, Cambridge, Mass.

Argyris, C 2008, 'Learning in organizations', in T G Cummings (ed.), *Handbook of Organizational Development*, Sage Publications, Los Angeles..

Billett, S 1999 'Guided learning at work.', in D Boud & J Garrick (eds.), *Understanding Learning at Work*, Routledge, London.

Brookfield, S 1987, *Developing Critical Thinkers: Challenging Adults to Explore Alternative Ways of Thinking and Acting*, Jossey-Bass, San Francisco.

Charles, M 2004, 'NAB boss prepares to wield the knife', *The Courier-Mail*, 7 February, p. 75.

Davidson, P, Simon, A Woods, P & Griffin, R W 2009, Management, 4th edn, John Wiley & Sons Australia, Brisbane.

Delahaye, B L 2003, 'Human resource development and the management of knowledge capital', in R Wiesner & B Millett (eds.), *Human Resource Management: Challenges and Future Directions*, John Wiley & Sons Australia, Brisbane.

Dervitsiotis, K N 2005, 'Creating conditions to nourish sustainable organizational excellence', *Total Quality Management & Business Excelence*, 16(8/9), pp. 925-943.

Department of Education, Science and Training 2003, *Adult Learning in Australia: A Consultation Paper*, Legislative Services, Canberra.

Dewey, J 1938, *Experience and Education*, Kappa Delta Pi, New York.

Dickie, L & Dickie, C 2007, *Cornerstones of strategic management*, Tilde University Press, Prahran, Vic.

Donaldson, C 2009, 'Falling in line with learning', *Human Resources Leader*, 181, July, pp. 24-25.

Drake International 2010 Gearing up for Growth.

Drucker, P 1995, *Managing in a Time of Great Change*, New York: Truman Talley Books/Dutton.

Fitzgerald, T 2009, 'The tyranny of bureaucracy: Continuing challenges of leading and managing from the middle' *Educational Management and Administration Leadership*, 37(1), pp. 51-65.

Foley, G 2001, *Strategic Learning: Understanding and Facilitating Organisational Change*, Centre for Popular Education, Sydney.

Gee, J P Hull, G & Lankshear, C 1996, *The New Work Order: Behind the Language of the New Capitalism*, Allen and Unwin, Sydney.

Goldstein, I L 1974, *Training: Program Development and Evaluation*, Brooks/Cole, New York.

Goodyear L 2013, 'Telework: The future of work?', *Human Resource Monthly*, November, p. 9.

Halpin, C & Hanlon, P 2009, 'Interaction of the legitimate system and the shadow system in organisations: Its impact on creativity', A paper presented to the *11th Annual Conference of the Irish Academy of Management*, September, Dublin.

HR Monthly, 2009, *Life at Mars*, May, p. 31.

Knowles, M S 1950, *Informal Adult Education: A Guide for Administrators, Leaders, and Teachers*, AAAE, New York.

London, J 1960, 'Program development in adult education', in MS Knowles (ed.), *Handbook of Adult Education in the United States*, AAAE, Chicago.

Mason, M 2008, 'What is complexity theory and what are its implications for educational change?', *Educational Philosophy and Theory*, 40(1), pp. 35-49.

McConkey, D D 1988, 'Planning in a changing environment', Business Horizons, 31(5), pp. 64-72.

McNally, B 2003 'Human Resource Management: the challenges of globalisation', in R Wiesner & B Millett (eds.), *Human Resource Management: Challenges and Future Directions*, John Wiley & Sons Australia, Brisbane.

Micklethwait, J & Wooldridge, A 1996, *The Witch Doctors*, Heinemann, London.

Morgan, G 2006 *Images of organisation*, Sage, London.

Nankervis, A 2013, 'Higher education blues', *Human Resource Monthly*, October, p. 14.

Nonaka, I 2002, 'A dynamic theory of organizational knowledge creation', in C.W. Choo & N Bontis (eds.), *The Strategic Management of Intellectual Capital and Organizational Knowledge*, Oxford University Press, New York.

Nonaka I & von Krogh G 2009, 'Tacit knowledge and knowledge cobversion: Controversy and advancement in organizational knowledge creation theory', *Organization Science*, 20(3), pp. 635-652.

Nonaka, I 2007, 'The knowledge creating company', *Harvard Business Review*, July-August, pp. 162-171.

Nonaka, K von Krogh, G & Voelpel, S 2006, 'Organizational knowledge creation theory: Evolutionary paths and future advances', *Organizational Studies*, 27, p. 1179- 1208.

Pimpimon, K 2009, 'Knowledge management for sustained competitive advantage in mergers and acquisitions', *Advances in Developing Human Resources,* 11(3), August, pp. 375-387.

Schweyer, A 2009, 'The impact of this great recession on the US workforce', *Human Resources Leader,* 181, July, pp. 14-15.

Senge, PM 1990, *The fifth discipline: The art and practice of the learning organisation.* Random House: Milson's Point, NSW.

Senge, PM 2006, *The fifth discipline: The art and practice of the learning organisation,* Doubleday, New York.

Stacey, R D 1993, 1996, 2001, 2003, 2008, 2011, *Strategic management and organisational dynamics,* 1st to 6th edn, Pitman Publishing, London and Prentice Hall/Financial Times, New York.

Stone, R J 2008, *Managing Human Resources,* 6th edn, John Wiley & Sons Australia, Brisbane.

Sveiby, K E 1997, *The new organisational wealth: Managing and measuring knowledge-based assets,* Berret Koehler, San Francisco.

Sveiby, K E 2007, 'Disabling the context for knowledge work: The role of managers' behaviours', *Management Decision,* 45(10, pp. 1636-1655.

Tarrant, D 2009, 'Trains of thought', *HR Monthly,* May, pp. 28-31.

Taylor, F W 1911, *The principles of scientific management,* Harper, New York.

Tyler, R 1949, *Basic principles of curriculum and instruction,* University of Chicago Press, Chicago.

Wellman, J 2007, 'Lessons learned about lessons learned', *Organization Development Journal,* 25(3), Fall, pp. 65-72.

Wang, S & Noe, RA 2010, 'Knowledge sharing: A review and directions for the future', *Human Resource Management Review,* 20, pp. 115-131.

Chapter 2

Continuing education and training

LEARNING OBJECTIVES

After studying this chapter you should be able to:

1. Explain the difference between education and training.

2. List the importance of continuing education and training.

3. Discuss the implications of continuing education and training of HRD practitioners.

4. Describe the learning experiences for continuing education and training.

5. Analyse the different models of continuing education and training and their implementation.

Introduction

Historically, training and education were seen as different identities. Training originated through guilds and apprenticeships when young participants worked alongside trade experts to gain competencies for particular vocations. Training concentrates on gaining knowledge, skills and attributes to build capacities for specific occupations so that individuals remain employable, and sustain on-going employment – it is in this way that individuals become economically productive citizens. Training may include both manual (e.g. trade related) as well as mental skills (e.g. mathematical calculations, computing, marketing). Other than apprenticeships, training was seen as a process that was predominantly conducted within organisations and strongly focused on the skills and knowledge required by the organisations.

Education, on the other hand, was associated with schooling and the furthering of knowledge. Its purpose was to develop intellectualism and allow individuals to form foundations that would facilitate entry into employment, as well as for lifelong learning. The focus of education in the early days was more liberal (associated with philosophical thinking, and creation of knowledge – for purposes of enlightenment) and emancipatory (to assist in overcoming educational disadvantage, social exclusion and discrimination, and forms of inequalities – to advance progressive social change), and to a lesser extent instrumental (e.g. preparation for employment).

Nowadays, the focus in education is more instrumental in that there are increasing imperatives for human and social capital. It has also become a lot more commercialised – a commodity that is valued in monetary terms. For instance, discourses about return on investment when employers and other sponsors provide funding for education (and for training), and for qualifications in return for what is paid for (purchased in a sense) by individuals, signal greater prominence for commoditisation of education. Training as an investment with anticipated immediate returns is particularly challenging for HR practitioners. For individuals it is not just a qualification that is of interest and demand; a qualification forms only one of many requirements for gaining employment. On the whole, the provision of education continues to be regulated by government systems and covers a broad range of topics that may impinge on vocational requirements and provide credentials in the form of qualifications. Its primary focus is not necessarily about preparation for employment.

So, to see education and training as separate from each other is unconstructive because both are necessary for the development of the 'whole person' and is now a necessary lifelong process to sustain lengthening and longer working lives. Essentially, vocational education and training is directly aligned to learning for work. While some see this as the holistic and integrated development underpinning knowledge and broad-based, transferable work and life skills, others perceive it as a relatively narrow band of employment-related or job-specific skills and competencies (Andersen *et al.* 2004). Many HR practitioners would relate more to the latter perspective.

However, these separate interpretations are not conducive to a life-long learning agenda and tends to guard the human capital imperatives rather than the on-going development of global citizens who can operate in a global competitive environment. Therefore, beyond the years of compulsory education, continuing education and training provisions need careful planning and facilitation to serve important purposes. Importantly, development of workers' core competences in academic education and vocational education and training (VET) systems that are not fully able to respond to labour market needs will compromise the supply and demand of industry-relevant skills.

It is important for HR practitioners to understand the difference so that they know when to focus on the educational aspect and when a training focus is more appropriate for developing the workforce for particular sites or industries. Typically, the decision around these aspects will be based on when (and at what point) workers need to be developed and how best their learning can be arranged.

As suggested earlier, authorities that support, finance or govern further learning see education and training as an investment with expected explicit returns translated as employment, productivity and economic outcomes. This is a view echoed by industry, as well as many individuals. Other benefits of good education and training, such as personal development for lifelong existence and development of the wider society, are less spoken about. Education and training are expected to serve a diverse group of individuals and agencies – young people preparing for entry into employment; those currently in employment; those temporarily unemployed; those aspiring for career change; enterprises; and governing bodies.

A demand for vocationally related learning has stretched its provisions beyond the traditional agents (i.e. public and private vocational education and training institutions) to now include schools offering vocational education and training, enterprises, universities, adult and community education providers, professional associations, and other community groups. These agents, including HR practitioners, provide accredited and/or unaccredited training and serve a diverse group of citizens. Among all of them, it is the HR practitioner group that has the ability to respond speedily to the development of workers to meet immediate industry requirements, largely because they are not constrained by the lengthy processes of curriculum reforms such as in formal education systems. It is this group of agents who cannot afford education and training in isolation from the day to day changes in nature and organisation of work and influence of technology on organisational productivity.

Fundamentally, the core of education and training is about learning. It can be described as either formal (e.g. as part of an approved curriculum) and formally supported (as in scheduled episodes of mentoring or coaching, etc.), or informal (e.g. through interactions with co-workers). All forms contribute to the development of an individual's capacities. Appropriate provisions of experiences, pedagogic practices and administrative arrange-ments can meet the needs for individual participation, and expectations and interests of employers and governments. This implies that education and training is no longer considered as the specialty of the schooling system with schools, registered training organisations and universities alone. Traditionally these educational institutions have well-structured education and training programs, but also have limitations in providing authentic vocational experiences for their participants. Hence provision of education and training has necessarily extended beyond traditional educational sites into workplaces.

This extension has in some ways blurred the divide between education and training. In an attempt to accommodate some of these arrangements, schools, universities offering accredited training, and registered training organisations tend to integrate the educational curriculum with learning in the workplace and deliver work integrated learning programs. Even so, the skills and capacities of HR practitioners play a significant part in shaping these types of arrangements because they are best placed to appropriate learning in the context of particular vocations and work sites. It is in the practice settings of each workplace that knowledge is codified and shared meanings and understandings are created to serve particular purposes in culturally appropriate ways.

In contemporary times, when there are constant changes in knowledge and work practices, both education and training have become lifelong processes with bigger focus on employment so that individuals remain employed and industries maintain a competent workforce, and continue to sustain their business in a competitive global environment. In this chapter, we consider education and training as a necessary amalgamation for appropriate development of vocational capacities and life skills. Much is written about education and training for pre-employment and, indeed, even today there is considerable focus and resourcing for the preparation of individuals to gain employment. Yet, although continuing education and training remains a priority, Billett and his colleagues (2012) argue that current purposes and processes of education and training do not adequately meet the needs of workers and industries. They went on to research and develop models for continuing education and training. We will look at these later in the chapter. Let us first briefly discuss the importance of continuing education and training.

The importance of continuing education and training

The challenges of routine, unpredictable changes and a highly competitive global marketplace are experienced by all types of organisations as well as individual workers. At an operational level, new concepts, technology, regulatory compliance, and industrial restructuring continue to drive the pace and extent of changes to the nature of work and productivity. Consequently, to remain competitive, organisations need to upskill and reskill their workforce, and workers need to continue learning through continuing education and training to remain employed and employable across their working lives. Learning forms a significant source of competitive advantage for organisations and creating environments conducive for learning and development can improve individual as well as organisational performance (Ellinger 2004). Human resource practitioners play a pivotal role in the continuing educating and training of individuals.

Individuals engage in continuing education and training to achieve three broad goals:

1. to sustain employability, that is, remaining employed until their 70th year;

2. to secure employment when changing occupations; and

3. to develop further their capacities for advancement and promotion.

Demands for learning through continuing education and training call for important functions to be performed by HRM practitioners responsible for workforce development. Realistically, much of the learning for continuing education and training can take place through everyday experiences in the workplace and, if needed, be supplemented with provisions by registered training organisations (RTOs) or other agents. This means that HRM practitioners have specific responsibilities in achieving four types of objectives associated with continuing education and training:

1. promoting and directing individuals' learning in particular ways;

2. enabling access to knowledge that might not otherwise be accessible to individuals in their workplace;

3. promoting particular kinds of learning through targeted curriculum and pedagogic practices in either educational or workplace settings; and

4. certifying individuals' learning for employment-related purposes (Billett *et al.* 2012, p. 11).

To achieve these four objectives, HR practitioners are required to assume a professional role in providing relevant experiences, pedagogic practices and administrative arrangements. These roles relate to empowering and developing workers to enhance services and productivity. The benefits of learning are optimised if these objectives closely align with the individual's purposes for participating in continuing education and training. Individual's work-related goals can be broadly purposed to sustain employability, secure new employment when occupations are transformed or no longer in demand, and seek promotion.

Some of these goals also require accreditation of continuing education and training towards a recognised award. Furthermore, there may be other personal benefits that contribute to activities outside of the workplace. These objectives suggest that learning through continuing education and training is a lifelong activity so, as strategic actors and change agents, HR practitioners need to operationalise a combination of structured, incidental as well as unstructured learning and development to meet individual and employer needs.

Employers' objectives may, on the other hand, relate to maintaining a highly competent workforce to meet current and emerging work and service requirements (Smith & Billett 2003), remain competitive, and retain staff; and for compliance in order to meet regulatory requirements and/or maintain registration or licencing. A range of incentives and support are available for continuing education and training to meet compliance. These are regulatory through government sources. Besides, different levels of government tend to support learning and continuing education and training as these sustain the supply of skilled workers who can remain employed and adequately meet the nation's economic imperatives (Rubenson 2009).

Moreover, when there is greater demand in a particular industry, governments tend to boost support for continuing education and training to develop the capacity of a workforce to meet the requirements. Indeed, supporting and investing in continuing education and training and lifelong learning to strengthen the interdependent relationships between work, workers and workplaces is now a vital economic and political priority (OECD 2010, 2013).

Implications of continuing education and training for HRD practitioners

Individual, employer and government imperatives for continuing education and training have extended the traditional role of HR practitioners of providing training and advising employees to non-traditional roles such as consulting and supporting. These non-traditional roles require a balancing of business goals against learning through the provision of support, training, and knowledge sharing (Tjepkema *et al.* 2000). In an Australian study Harris, Simons and Bone (2000) noted five functions of HRD practitioners (workplace trainers). These are:

1. foster an environment conducive to learning where communication is most prominent;

2. working and learning with co-workers;

3. arranging work process to assist learning;

4. promoting independent and self-directed learning; and

5. integrating and facilitating learning from various sources outside the workplace.

These and other roles suggested in literature give an indication of the complexity of HR practitioners' work to support continuing education and training. Furthermore, the diversity of outcomes for individuals, employers, industries, governments and society highlight the importance of continuing education and training. It is not surprising then to see a heightened interest in models of continuing education and training and its contributions to social cohesion and economic prosperity. It is necessary for workers to participate in a range of work activities and to engage in various social interactions. Kira (2010) contends there are two conditions that will facilitate their learning: 1) learning-conducive work; and 2) learning-conducive work practices.

Learning experiences for continuing education and training

While the primary focus in the workplace is on work-related outcomes, concomitantly these sites offer rich pedagogical opportunities for workers to continue developing their occupational capacities, albeit independently as well as interdependently. Because workers need knowledge that is most relevant to particular workplace, it becomes necessary for them to join workplace communities, participate and support one another (Sparrow & Heel 2006). This makes learning through work clearly relational in that knowledge is mediated by contextual and situational factors in the workplace. It is no surprise then that an Australian study by Billett *et al.* (2014) found that workers and their managers preferred learning for continuing education and training to take place in the context of work.

Interactions during daily work experiences lead to three types of competence: i) practical skills and knowledge required in specific occupations and job-tasks; ii) knowledge related to the work community and organisation; and iii) knowledge that helps assess one's work and ways of working and acting (Paloniemi 2006, pp. 443-444). Marchand (2008) argues that the most common approaches to learning are through observation, mimesis (i.e.

imitation) and practice. However, the quality of learning relies on the individuals' efforts and capacities as observers, imitators and initiators. In any case, there is a range of experiences that contribute to workers' continuing education and training. Here is a short list (Billett *et al.* 2012):

- *Everyday learning through work – individually.* This form of learning is often self-directed and could include online, books, etc., where workers try to work things out themselves or practice work tasks to improve speed or accuracy. It involves self-reflection and enables workers to build self-confidence through trial and error, and if successful, they are able to take on more complex tasks. However, their success in learning alone relies on prior knowledge, skills and understanding of expected outcomes.

- *Everyday learning through work – assisted by other workers.* That is, working and sharing with another person on the job. They may include co-workers, buddies, supervisors/managers, mentors, or industry experts, each with different perspectives to offer. For example, nurses in an aged-care facility work as buddies to complete particular work tasks and learn from each other in the process. Such arrangements are deliberate practices in aged-care facilities. However, in workplaces where such arrangements are not part of the organisational structure, workers still prefer to have access to others in proximity to seek assistance if and when required.

- *Everyday learning + group training courses at work from employer.* Some employers sponsor group training courses at the work site. Such courses may include mandatory courses on new regulations and technology and may be offered by in-house trainers, external trainers or vendors. Some of these courses may even be accredited.

- *Everyday learning + training courses away from work (offsite).* Workers may choose to attend courses off site. Some of these may include courses that are sponsored by their employers. The main issue with courses offered off site is that workers should be able to apply what they have learnt when they return to work.

- *On-site learning with individual mentoring: one-to-one.* Not all workplaces have mentoring arrangements, but workers who are afforded such opportunities tend to engage in rich learning from more experienced workers and experts in the workplace.

- *Small group training at work – external provider.* Employers also hire external providers to deliver customised training to workers in the workplace. Such provisions are offered to groups of workers and may include accredited training. However, it is important that external trainers are able to appropriately link their training to the context of the specific workplace.

- *Individual training at work – external provider.* Workers may also receive individual training at their work site from external providers. The important thing about the services of external providers is that the quality of instruction is high, and workers are able to access them if they need further clarification.

These experiences are summarised in Figure 2.1.

The list suggested by Billett *et al.* (2012) stresses the significance of learning in the workplace. You can read more about workplace as a learning site in Chapter 13. Furthermore, there is greater emphasis on learning instead of individuals being taught. This means that HRD practitioners and other education and training facilitators – be they teachers, workplace trainers, supervisors or experienced workers/experts – need to assist individuals in directing their own learning. See Chapter 13 for details on the role of the HDR practitioner and workplace supervisors. In any case, facilitators need to first conduct a needs analysis plan. Chapter 5 details how to go about completing a needs analysis task. Basically, the needs analysis is intended to inform the planning and delivery of learning for continuing education and training in appropriate ways. There are different models of continuing education and training that can facilitate delivery. We will now look at the models recently developed by Billett *et al.* (2014).

Figure 2.1 Workplace and individual practices promoting learning through work

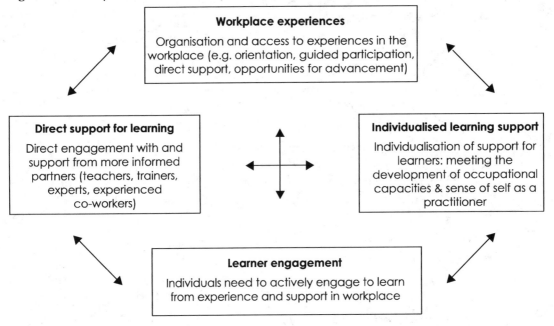

Source: Billett et al. *(2012, p. 39).*

Models of continuing education and training and their implementation

A three-year study by Billett *et al.* (2014) funded by the National Centre for Vocational Education Research (NCVER) proposed four main models of continuing education and training. These were: 1) wholly work-based experiences; 2) work-based experiences with direct guidance; 3) work-based experiences with educational interventions; and 4) wholly educational institution-based experiences. Each model is briefly described below.

Wholly work-based experiences

Workers learn in the context of their work by engaging in activities and interactions with other workers. Some of that learning would be individually done, commonly by observing and repeating what is accepted practice at their particular work site. Other forms may be supported by co-workers. Learning in this model is easily accessible, directly relevant to workers' tasks, and purposely undertaken to meet immediate performance requirements. Wholly work-based experiences extend what individuals already know. Successful implementation of this model relies on workers being self-directed. They must: have the ability to identify their own learning needs; be given agency to access opportunities; and, be able to evaluate their learning. However, we cannot assume that all workers have abilities. HRD practitioners therefore need to check the capacities of individuals to engage in learning on their own. Supervisors and managers, on the other hand, need to support workers' learning by providing access to resources and opportunities to enrich their experiences. A site-specific workplace learning curriculum is a helpful means to providing structure if workers need more direction. Furthermore, a culture where workers are rewarded for learning in the workplace would encourage a larger number of workers to actively engage in learning.

Work-based experiences with direct guidance

In this model, individuals may receive direct guidance from more experienced co-workers, supervisors or other experts to develop knowledge and skills that cannot be acquired individually. The objective here is to be able to learn and immediately put that into practice. Common forms of guidance could include mentoring, coaching and demonstration. However, those providing guidance must be considered as credible sources of learning, and are available to assist when needed. Workplace supervisors can facilitate this model of learning if they are competent as trainers, mentors and guides, and can provide constructive feedback in a timely manner. Similarly, managers in workplaces need to recognise the contributions of supervisors and also provide opportunities to both supervisors and workers to engage in purposeful learning. Registered training providers can assist by helping workplaces structure a learning curriculum that can build capacities for training on a one-to-one basis.

Work-based experiences with educational interventions

In this model, learners are supported by trainers from registered training providers (on or off site) to assist with integrating and reconciling what they learn in the workplace with theoretical and conceptual ideas common in the formal curriculum. There is often a particular interest in accreditation or certification of what the teachers/trainers offer. Workers need to have relevant literacy and numeracy skills to be able to gain from this model of learning. Furthermore, they need to see value in certification for career-long benefits. Here, workplace supervisors can take an active role in approving educational interventions and value assessment and certification. Managers' abilities to work in partnership with registered training organisations can supplement the types of support needed for this model of learning in the workplace.

Wholly educational institution-based experiences

Workers generally engage in this model to develop the types of skills set or capacities that cannot be learnt in their workplace. A decision to engage in this model may indicate intentions to change roles, seek promotion or change occupations altogether. Whatever the purpose, workers need to accommodate their learning within work, family and personal commitments. Workplace supervisors can support this model by allowing workers with time-off for learning and providing access to internal expertise if approached by workers. It is likely that workers engaging in this model may not necessarily want their supervisors or managers to know about their learning, especially if they intend to change workplaces or occupations. Workplace managers may agree to sponsor part or full time studies, depending on the expected benefits for the workplace. Registered training organisations can assist by giving recognition for current competencies and providing support to extend the development of workers' competencies.

The success of the first three models relies on supportive and enriching learning spaces and affordances in the worksite. See Chapter 13 where these concepts are elaborated. The models suggested above have implications for new roles and responsibilities for workers, supervisors, managers, and training providers. Primarily they all need to maintain a shared value for learning by cultivating and supporting learning. However, the cost associated with providing and engaging in continuing education and training is often a major barrier for many workers. Most workers rely on support from their employers, while others fund these themselves. Employer-supported vocational and continuing education and training are well established in many European countries. The systems in Germany and Finland, for instance, exemplify the strength of partnerships with industries, governments and education and training providers in developing and sustaining a highly productive workforce. Both these countries benefit economically as well as socially – the outcomes of continuing education and training also translate into the well-being of citizens.

Employer-supported learning opportunities have multiple benefits. A well-trained workforce contributes to high levels of productivity, and employees greatly value learning support and are more likely to remain loyal and continue to sustain good returns. The downside is that well performing employees are also more vulnerable to poaching by other employers, and when this happens it is a loss to those who provide support for workers' development. Employer support can be in the form of reimbursement of tuition fee (partial or full), allowing time away from work to engage in learning, offering opportunities during daily work-experiences to practice what they learnt, or rewards for improvements in performance after engagement in learning. These affordances may be distributed differently among full-time and part-time employees, the length of service to the employer, or employees of different ranks. Furthermore, affordances in small, medium and large workplaces may vary greatly. Whatever the case, workplaces need an accommodating culture of lifelong learning, promotion of excellence, and support for workers' learning for continuing education and training. However, lifelong learning is primarily an individual responsibility; therefore, workers need to play an agentic role in their capacity building. From the perspective of HRD practitioners, continuing education and training must contribute to growth and jobs, and this can be achieved if learning focuses on the needs of both employers and learners. Their expertise in content development, education and training pedagogies for adults, delivery of training and assessment, and the positioning of various learning opportunities within the overall business context of particular occupations or workplaces play a central part. Strategies for many of these roles are discussed in various chapters in this book.

Markedly, the role of HRD practitioners is made easier if workplace managers and individual learners can clearly communicate what they want and need. Workplace managers can include learning as an integral part of their enterprise's business plan so that learning for continuing education and training is afforded as a useful investment through provision of opportunities for workers to learn in the course of their daily work. Chapter 13 explains how workplace supervisors can contribute to workers' learning. A learning plan could also include engagement and collaboration with registered training organisations to customise what is needed by specific sites and at the same time maintain quality assurance. However, education and training providers need to be more flexible in their approach to curriculum development and delivery in terms of the modes (e.g. blended learning, workplace learning) and timing.

Effective provision of learning for continuing education and training also demands that staff from registered training organisations need to maintain currency of knowledge and expertise in their vocational areas and to gain a comprehensive knowledge and understanding of the work environment and contexts of workplaces. In addition, up-to-date knowledge of regulations, compliance requirements and industrial relations procedures and appropriate applications for where they assist workers with their continuing education and training are essential. Of course, they also need to learn about the diversity among workers and their specific learning needs. So, teachers from registered training organisations need to become lifelong learners themselves. In the same vein, workers also need to assume new roles. That is, unless they value learning in the workplace, it is unlikely that they will appreciate learning in the context of everyday work. This is not surprising because often workers see the workplace as the principal site for work and associate learning with schooling. They may not appreciate the pedagogical opportunities that can enrich their learning in the workplace. Learning as schooling is often interpreted in terms of learning as a product (acquisition of discrete items of knowledge or skills; Hager 2004, p. 3) instead of learning as a product *and* process which is recommended for lifelong learning.

Eraut (2007) suggests that work processes such as 'participation in group processes, working alongside others, tackling challenging tasks and roles, consultations, problem solving, working with clients' (p. 409) lead to learning as a by-product. Processes such as supervision, coaching, mentoring, shadowing, etc., are pedagogical practices that support learning processes in the workplace. Choy (2010) contends that just having a basic conceptual understanding of workplace pedagogies is not sufficient. It means that individuals use only a few cognitive processing strategies and this constrains their learning. Furthermore, it is important that workers learn ways that pedagogical opportunities in the workplace can contribute to their learning because learning skills that were used for classroom based-learning are not always helpful when it comes to learning in the workplace. Regardless of the learning skills, it is important for facilitators to appropriately design learning episodes and create spaces for on-going support and practice. See Chapter 14 for more on this. Further to learning skills, Billett (2009) advocates that learners need to take an agentic role in accessing and utilising opportunities available in the workplace. Additionally, they need to develop personal qualities such as self-direction, motivation and openness to a learning culture (by receiving learning support and also contributing to others' learning). On the whole, workers need to make a commitment to engage in learning. These accounts show that learning for continuing education and training and its provisions are not without challenge. You will learn more about the challenges and how communities of practice and learning networks play an important role in workers' learning in Chapter 13.

The future of VET

Approaches to human resource development in many organisations has resemblance to provisions through vocational education and training in that the focus is on skilling workers so that they can appropriately contribute to productivity in workplaces. The types of provisions through VET influences ways in which HR practitioners go about establishing, designing and developing training in workplaces. The VET sector continues to play a significant role in training skilled workers needed to sustain the labour market for Australia's economic development. It has evolved from a predominantly jurisdiction-based system in the 1970s to increased Commonwealth investment and support between the 1970s and 1980s. In this way, Commonwealth efforts allowed Technical and Further Education (TAFE) in Australia to become a vehicle for economic and social change. At the time, growing youth unemployment and criticisms about the apprenticeship system triggered another set of impetus leading to Commonwealth, states and territories agreeing to a shared responsibility for a nationwide-approach to VET. Reforms under a national approach included the introduction of competency-based training with occupational standards; recognition of prior learning; greater involvement of industry; and an open national training market. In the 1990s, the Australian National Training Authority coordinated and facilitated joint investments by the governments through a range of national training reforms. Between 2000 and 2012, VET focused more on the demand side with new technical colleges and increased support for apprenticeships. So VET has continued to evolve to make a significant contribution to the nation. However, it needs to remain dynamic to sustain a nation operating in a highly competitive global environment. Therefore, more reforms are obligatory.

Current thinking about further reforms concentrate on balancing local and national skills needs, consensus around eight different VET systems, meeting the needs of a future workforce, consumer information, policy coherence and interaction with other service systems (Commonwealth of Australia 2014). Government efforts around VET signify crucial contributions of the system worthy of reforms and investments because VET not only prepares workers for entry into employment, but also develops the foundations for future employment and earning capacities. These provisions for many are the start of on-going learning that workers need to maintain in order to adequately respond to influences of emerging technologies and globalisation impacting on both the nature of work and work organisation. Hence, in recent years VET has become very prominent in government policy and public debate – primarily driven by industry responding to economic goals, globalisation and free market economics (Anderson, Brown & Rushbrook 2004). With more active involvement by industry, governments have assumed a purchasing role instead of being a key provider, while still maintaining centralised controls over the objectives and outcomes of VET. Such controls are evident in the national standards, a competency-based training framework, Australian Qualification Framework, performance-based contracts and outcome-based funding, etc. Furthermore, the principles of competition, user choice, and voucher schemes, for example, drive the demand-driven training market. These have particular implications for HR practitioners who need to operate within an overarching national and international setting instead of local organisation level only. Standards, quality, portability of skills have become important considerations that encompass education as well as training, and accommodating both into HR practices will allow organisations to achieve broader goals. Importantly, HR practitioners need to appreciate that education and training cannot be seen as separate from each other.

References

Billett, S. (2009). Realising the educational worth of integrating work experiences in higher education. *Studies in Higher Education*, 34 (8).

Billett, S., Henderson, A., Choy, S., Dymock, D., Beven, F., Kelly, A., James, I., Lewis, J., & Smith, R. (2012). *Continuing education and training models and strategies: An initial appraisal.* Adelaide: National Centre for Vocational Education Research.

Billett, S., Henderson, A., Choy, S., Dymock, D., Beven, F., Kelly, A., James, I., Lewis, J., Smith, R. (2014). *Towards more effective continuing education and training for Australian workers.* Adelaide: National Centre for Vocational Education Research.

Commonwealth of Australia (2014). Reform of the Federation. White Paper. Issues Paper 4. Commonwealth of Australia: Canberra.

Choy, S. (2010). Students' conceptual knowledge about workplace pedagogies and applications to learning in the workplace. *13th Annual Conference of the Australian Vocational Education and Training Researchers Association*, 7-9 April 2010, Surfers Paradise, Australia.

Ellinger, A. (2004). The concept of self-directed learning and its implications for human resource development. *Advances in Developing Human Resources, 6*(2), 158-177.

Eraut, M. (2007). Learning from other people in the workplace. *Oxford Review of Education, 30* (4), 403 – 422.

Hager, P. (2004). Conceptions of learning and understanding learning at work. *Studies in Continuing Education,* 26:1, 3-17.

Harris, R., Simons, M. & Bone, J. (2000). *More than meets the eye? Rethinking the role of workplace trainer.* Adelaide, National Centre for Vocational Education Research (NCVER).

Kirra, M. (2010). Routine-generating and regenerative workplace learning. *Vocations and Learning,* 3, 71-90.

Marchand, T.H.J. (2008). Muscles, morals and mind: Craft apprenticeship and the formation of person. *British Journal of Education Studies*, 56 (3), 245-271.

Organisation for Economic Co-operation and Development (2010). *Reviews of Vocational education and training: Learning for jobs.* OECD: Paris.

Organisation for Economic Co-operation and Development (2013) . *Economic Policy Reforms: Going for Growth 2013.* OECD: Paris.

Paloniemi, S. (2006). Experience, competence and workplace learning. *Journal of Workplace Learning,* 18 (7/8), 439-450.

Rubenson, K. (2009). The Impact of Welfare State Regimes on Barriers to Participation in Adult Education: A Bounded Agency Model.

Smith, A. & Billett, S. (2003). *Enhancing employers' expenditure on training*. NCVER, Adelaide.

Sparrow, J., & Heel, D. (2006). Fostering team learning development. Reflective Practice, 7, 151-162.

Tjepkema, S., Horst, H.M. ter, Mulder, M. & Scheerens, J. (2000). *Future challenges for HRD professionals in Europe. Final report*. Enschede, Programme on Targeted Socio-Economic Research (TSER).

Tynjala, P. (2008). Perspectives into learning in the workplace. *Education Research Review*, 3(2), 130-154.

Chapter 3

Adult learning

LEARNING OBJECTIVES

After studying this chapter you should be able to:

1. List the assumptions underpinning pedagogical and andragogical learning.

2. Discuss the basic types of learning – classical conditioning, behaviour modification and modelling.

3. Explain and discuss the four knowledge generation processes.

4. Explain and distinguish the three levels of learning – instrumental, communicative and emancipatory.

5. Define the role of critical thinking in the process of adult learning.

6. Discuss the two models of unlearning.

7. Describe the holistic adult learning model.

8. Describe the time delay in learning.

9. Describe the effect of stress on learning.

The foundation of HRD

A constant theme underpinning any endeavour in human resource development is the body of knowledge that forms the theories, principles and approaches that describe our understanding of how adults learn. Historically, most learning efforts have been directed at children and youths. Interest in adult learning intensified in the nineteenth century, primarily because leading citizens felt a responsibility for the religious and moral salvation of uneducated adults, who formed the very large majority of the world's population at that time (Grattan 1955).

There has been considerable argument through the ages as to whether adults can learn. Until recently, it was thought that when human beings reached biological maturity, they reached a learning plateau on which they remained for a few years before beginning to deteriorate (Jarvis 2010). In these days of life-long learning, it may seem strange that such an issue could even be debated. We can thank Thorndike (1928) for concluding that adults can indeed learn – although even he had reservations! More recent research shows that this view is pessimistic as the adult brain is flexible and can learn (for a discussion, see Blakemore & Frith 2005).

Learning

Learning is defined typically as a relatively permanent change in behaviour or behaviour potential resulting from one's experiences (Sigelman & Shaffer 2009). Tovey and Lawlor (2008) see learning as a complex process that occurs throughout life – learning allows humans to adjust to the many changes that occur in everyday life, from the simplest to the highly intricate. Davis, Sumara & Luce-Kapler (2002) see learning as a process through which one becomes capable of more sophisticated, more flexible, and more creative action.

These usual definitions of learning apply to most organisms. However, humans are a distinctive species on this Earth. As Kolb comments:

> Human beings are unique among all living organisms in that their primary adaptive specialization lies not in some particular physical form or skill or fit in an ecological niche, but rather in identification with the process of adaption itself – in the process of learning. We are thus the learning species, and our survival depends on our ability to adapt not only in the reactive sense of fitting into the physical and social worlds, but in the proactive sense of creating and shaping those worlds. (Kolb 1984, p. 1)

So Kolb (1984) defines learning not as fixed and immutable ideas where change can be measured, but as a process whereby concepts are derived from, and continuously modified by, experience. Further, learning is not the specialised realm of one function, such as cognition or perception, but involves the integrated functioning of the total organism – thinking, feeling, perceiving and behaving. Brookfield (2009) goes further by pointing out that learning is not a rational, bloodless, ascetic phenomenon. He believes that learning is an activity invested with such significance by learners, and where their fragile egos face such potentially serious threats, that they must also experience it emotionally. Scott and Harker (2004) support this view by contending that real learning is only achieved by seeking challenges and by engaging in demanding and often threatening environments.

One could expect, therefore, the topic of adult learning to be complex and intriguing. While most organisms can adapt their behaviour, humans are unique in that learning is their primary adaptive mechanism. This learning is experienced emotionally as well as cognitively.

Adults as learners

The scientific or traditional school of learning dates back to the middle ages. Learning was then the prerogative of the upper class, the clergy and artisans. In the 1800s, when schooling became compulsory for children in a number of countries, the basic themes of control and imparting of a defined body of knowledge became imbedded in the educational system. Berte (1975) describes this as the Lancastrian system – the mass production of students through a totally prescribed and regimented sequential curriculum. While the methods advocated by the traditional educators have been criticised over the years, there is no doubt that such schooling provided a basic level of education across a wide section of the world's population. So the traditionalists were certainly doing something right. One of the leading lights of the traditionalist school was E. L. Thorndike. While he had a predilection for laboratory experimentation – he felt research in a classroom led to contamination – his contribution to education cannot be minimised. His *Laws of Readiness, Exercise and Effect* are still central tenets of adult education today.

The artistic stream, the members of which were sometimes referred to as the 'progressives', criticised the traditionalists on two levels – firstly for assuming that the learner was an empty vessel and the teacher the fount of all knowledge; and secondly, for a preoccupation with the notion of pre-given universal 'information' (Nonaka & von Krogh 2009). Progressives felt that learning was a totality, a gestalt. They valued the expression of individuality, learning through experience, the importance of the learner's needs and the dynamism of active learning. John Dewey, the champion of the progressives, expressed the differences as follows:

> To imposition from above is opposed to expression and cultivation of individuality; to external discipline is opposed free activity; to learning from tests and teachers, learning through experience; to acquisition of isolated skills and techniques by drill is opposed acquisition of them as a means of attaining ends which make direct vital appeal. (Dewey 1938, pp. 19-20)

The progressive school of thought was the precursor of modern self-directed learning. Carl Rogers (cited in Long 2002, pp. 47-48) suggests that adults are different in the learning context because they:

- are in a continuing process of growth, not at the start of a process;

- bring with them a package of experiences and values;

- come to the learning experience with intentions;

- bring expectations about the learning process;

- have competing interests; and

- already have their own set patterns of learning.

It is therefore reasonable to expect that adult learning and facilitating adult learning will be different from the processes used in child learning.

Table 3.1 Assumptions of the pedagogical and andragogical models

Characteristic	Pedagogy	Andragogy
1. The need to know	Learners know only what the teacher teaches if they want to pass and get promoted.	Adults need to know why they need to learn something before undertaking it.
2. The learner's self-concept	The learner's self-concept eventually becomes that of a dependent personality.	Adults have a self-concept of being responsible for their own decisions.
3. The role of experience	The learner's experience is of little worth as a resource for learning,	Adults come into an educational activity with both a greater volume and a different quality of experience from youths.
4. Readiness to learn	Learners become ready to learn what the teacher tells them, when they want to pass and get promoted.	Adults become ready to learn those things they need to know and be able to do in order to cope effectively with their real-life situations.
5. Orientation to learning	Learners have a subject-centred orientation to learning; they see learning as acquiring subject matter content.	Adults are life-centred. They must perceive that learning will help them perform tasks or deal with problems that they confront in real-life situations.
6. Motivation	Learners are motivated to learn by external motivations,	The most potent motivations are internal pressures.

Source: Based on work by Knowles, MS 1980, The Modern Practice of Education: From Pedagogy to Andragogy, *2nd edn, New York, Cambridge Books; Knowles, MS 1998,* The Adult Learner: A Neglected Species, *5th edn, Gulf Publishing.*

The proposition that adults may use learning processes different from those of children was launched in the English-speaking world by Edward C. Lindeman (1926). For the next 70 years this theme was championed by Malcolm Knowles, a writer and educator who is considered to be one of the leading thinkers and proponents of adult learning. Originally, Knowles believed that the pedagogical (from *peda*, a child) suppositions of learning were only relevant to children and that adults operated under a different set of assumptions, which he labelled 'andragogy' (from *andra*, an adult). In short, pedagogy followed the traditionalists – that there was a fixed body of knowledge and this knowledge should be delivered to the learner in a controlled manner. Andragogy, on the other hand, followed the precepts of the progressives – learning should follow the needs of the learner and allow the learner to be responsible for the learning. For a full discussion on andragogy, see Henschke (2009).

This stance was epitomised in the title of his 1970 text *The Modern Practice of Adult Education: Pedagogy versus Andragogy*. However, by 1980 this stance (and the subtitle of the book) had become *From Pedagogy to Andragogy*. Knowles recognised that, under certain situations, adults could learn best under the assumptions of pedagogy and at other times the andragogical process would be more appropriate.

Accordingly, pedagogical learning strategies used in HRD are often referred to as structured, other-directed or dependent, and andragogical approaches as unstructured, self-directed or independent. These descriptions indicate that in pedagogical learning, a person other than the learner takes the responsibility for deciding what will be learned, how it will be learned, and what will be assessed, while in andragogical learning the learner takes these responsibilities. The circumstances when pedagogical or andragogical strategies are most appropriate are discussed in Chapter 8; Chapter 10 discusses the pedagogical or structured learning strategies used in HRD, and Chapter 11 explores self-directed or andragogical learning strategies. We will return to the effects of pedagogy and andragogy on HRD throughout the book.

Knowles is correct – adults are different. Even though some of the theories, principles and approaches discussed later in this chapter are based on general considerations of teaching and learning, it should be recognised that some of the andragogical assumptions will always apply in adult learning. These include the following.

- The learning should be relevant to the real-life situations and problems. This enhances the motivation of the learner as well as embedding the new learning into a context.

- The learning should incorporate the rich experiences of the adult learners, thus utilising that abundant resource, the tacit knowledge of the adult.

- The learning should involve the adult learner, at least to some extent, so that the individual's sense of self-responsibility ensures that the learning is transferred back to the operational site.

We now go on to examine some of the general theories and principles that apply to all human learning. However, bear in mind the three andragogical assumptions.

Basic types of learning

Writers, psychologists and researchers agree that there are three fundamental types of learning – classical conditioning, behaviour modification, and modelling (or observational learning). Of the three, the last two – behaviour modification and modelling – are of significant interest in the development of the human resource in organisations.

Classical conditioning

This is the world of Ivan Pavlov and his salivating dogs. Pavlov noticed that when dogs smelt food (the unconditioned stimulus) the dogs salivated (the unconditioned response). He then rang a bell (the conditioned stimulus) whenever the food was presented to the dogs. After a while, he did not present the food but just rang the bell – and the dogs salivated (the conditioned response).

In humans, classical conditioning is strongly involved in the learning of emotional responses. Consider the individual who has just picked up his new car, with its distinctive 'new' smell of leather and paint – but who unfortunately has an accident, causing anxiety and fear. In the future, the smell of a new car may result in increased heart rate and sweating as the conditioned response of anxiety and fear returns. Such responses can be unlearned through counter-conditioning. Accordingly, the area of classical conditioning is usually associated with counselling and psychotherapy rather than human resource development.

Behaviour modification

Behaviour modification has its foundations in behaviourism (Watson 1925). Behaviourism posited that any analysis of human development should be based on observations of overt behaviour rather than on unconscious motives or unobservable cognitive processes. Behaviourists further held that learning was merely a matter of accumulating a series of stimulus–response (S–R) associations. Thorndike (1913, 1928), investigating ways that these S–R connections could be strengthened or weakened, identified the Law of Effect – i.e. when an experience is followed by a reward, the relationship is strengthened.

Behaviour modification was explored more fully by Skinner (1953). Skinner conducted a wide variety of experiments showing that a behaviour could be magnified or modified by a reward (operant conditioning). He suggested that there were two types of rewards (or reinforcements) – positive and negative.

Positive reinforcement occurs when a reward is added to the situation. A negative reinforcement occurs when something unpleasant or undesirable is *removed* from the situation – e.g. when you feel the cold and put on a jumper or pullover, thus avoiding the unpleasant sensation of feeling cold.

For a new behaviour to be developed, a new reward (either a positive or negative reinforcement) must follow. Hence the basic rule – to create a new behaviour, first implement the reward. Initially, the reinforcement should occur every time the behaviour is exhibited. However, for long-term behaviour change, it is better to switch to non-scheduled reinforcement – where rewards occur at intermittent and unpredictable intervals. The poker machines in the local club operate very effectively on this unpredictable, positive reinforcement schedule.

Managers frequently use operant conditioning to develop staff. If a staff member is new to a task, a significant part of the development plan should be to provide rewards by acknowledgement, words of praise and providing opportunities for more challenging and interesting work as the staff member exhibits appropriate behaviour and achieves expected levels of productivity. However, this example exposes one of the limitations of operant conditioning. Skinner believed that humans were passively shaped by the environment – in other words, only external or extrinsic rewards were valuable. This viewpoint follows Watson's original exhortations to acknowledge only observable behaviour. These days we also acknowledge the power of intrinsic rewards – those motivations within a person that can also reward behaviour. So, in our example, the reward inherent in the manager's kind words is the sense of pride or satisfaction generated within the staff member.

Case study example

See the PLP case study on page 13 of the workbook that accompanies this text for behaviour modification.

Modelling

Bandura *(1977)* believed people have far more sophisticated cognitive abilities – they are cognitive beings whose active processing of information from the environment plays a major role in learning and human development. Sigelman and Shaffer (2009) believed that nowhere is Bandura's cognitive emphasis more evident than in his highlighting of observational learning (modelling) as the most important mechanism through which human behaviour changes. Human beings (and other animals) attend to the behaviour of others of their kind, tending to imitate that behaviour (Gardner *et al.* 1981). This is learning to do new things by observing how particular models do them and then imitating the behaviour of those models. Indeed, people are more likely to model their behaviour on that of a significant other than to take notice of verbal counsel to behave in a certain manner.

Case study example

See the PLP case study on page 14 of the workbook that accompanies this text for an example on modelling.

Zimbardo (2007) suggests that a model's observed behaviour will be at its most influential when:

- the model is perceived positively, that is, seen to be of high status, liked, and respected;

- the model's behaviour is visible and salient – stands out as a clear figure against the background of competing models;

- it is within the observer's range of competence to enact the behaviour; and

- the model's behaviour is seen as having reinforcing consequences – that is, there are appropriate rewards and punishments.

As Zimbardo (2007) points out, the advantage of modelling is that it enables us to acquire large, integrated patterns of behaviour without going through the tedious process of gradually eliminating wrong responses and building up the right ones through trial-and-error – to say nothing of profiting from the mistakes and successes of others. It should also be noted that modelling is the basis of the knowledge generation process of socialisation (tacit to tacit) discussed later in this chapter.

So, behaviour modification and modelling provide some initial insights into how people learn. They are likely to perform a behaviour if that behaviour results in a reward.

However, given the andragogical assumptions in Table 3.1, adults are also likely to make individual assessments of the reward. Modelling is useful for acquiring large, integrated patterns of behaviour. Again, the andragogical assumptions may play a part in the adult's decision as to whether to follow the lead of the model. However, modelling does have some significant links to the knowledge creation process of socialisation. So, given the right conditions (i.e. andragogical assumptions), modelling can be a dynamic learning process for adults.

Generation of knowledge

As indicated in Chapter 1, the concept of knowledge is a critical resource for individuals and organisations. Nonaka and von Krogh (2009) believe that knowledge has assumed an increasingly justifiable and important role in organisational science. From the point of view of adult learning, the generation of knowledge is fundamental to existence within organisations. Of critical importance to adult learning and knowledge management is the indisputable fact that only humans can generate knowledge.

Nonaka and others (Nonaka 1991; Nonaka & Takeuchi 1995; Nonaka, Takeuchi & Umemoto 1996; Nonaka & Konno 1998; Nonaka & von Krogh 2009) have presented a model based on tacit and explicit knowledge that places the management of the organisation's knowledge capital firmly within the auspices of human resource development.

Tacit knowledge is a corner stone in organisational knowledge creation theory. It covers knowledge that is unarticulated, and tied to the senses, movement skills, physical experiences, intuition, unarticulated mental models or implicit rules of thumb (Nonaka & von Krogh (2009) – for example, wine tasting, crafting a violin, or interpreting a complex seismic printout of an oil reservoir. Tacit knowledge is in the mind of the individual, although the individual may be unaware of it or unable declare it. With time, tacit knowledge becomes more important for solving the problem or challenge, as the tacit knowledge is more efficient to task solutions.

Explicit knowledge is the knowledge that the individual can declare and formulate into sentences. It is captured in drawings and writings. Explicit knowledge has a universal character, supporting the capacity to act across contexts. It is accessible through conscious thought. Unfortunately, a number of learning institutions, both within and outside organisations, give a primacy to explicit knowledge – that is, they tend to equate information with knowledge. It should be recognised, though, that explicit knowledge is rooted in tacit knowledge. One advantage of explicit knowledge is that it can be shared at low cost among individuals.

Tacit and explicit knowledge are not totally separate; they are mutually complementary entities and inherently inseparable. Thus tacit and explicit knowledge interact with, and change into, each other during the creative activities of human beings. Nonaka and von Krogh (2009) suggest that tacit and explicit knowledge are the two ends of a continuum.

Using tacit and explicit knowledge as a base, Nonaka and others built a model explaining the four processes used to create or generate new knowledge. The model is based on two types of knowledge movement between the tacit and explicit domains (Nonaka & von

Krogh 2009). Firstly, by bringing together individuals with different biographies, their personal subjective knowledge can be socially justified and brought together with other's knowledge so that knowledge keeps expanding – a social process. Secondly, there is an individual process where knowledge alternates between tacit and explicit within the individual, thereby increasing the individual's capacity to act.

1. *Combination (explicit to explicit).* One of the most common and obvious paths of knowledge creation, this process uses lectures, discussions, documents, meetings, and electronic and computerised communication. Combination involves the conversion of explicit knowledge into more complex sets of explicit knowledge. Your reading of this book is a classic example of combination. The fact that the words have been expressed means that the ideas are explicit knowledge. As you read, the explicit knowledge is combined with your own explicit knowledge. Through a process of sorting, combining, or categorising your current knowledge and the explicit knowledge in this book, you reconfigure your existing knowledge.

2. *Externalisation (tacit to explicit).* This process occurs when tacit knowledge is translated and expressed into forms that are comprehensible to the conscious mind of the individual and to others. Converting knowledge from a tacit to an explicit form is an inherently creative act using metaphors, analogies, and images. Externalisation always occurs when an individual writes thoughts and ideas on paper. While certain aspects of the conscious mind are transposed easily into the written word, the writer usually finds that some other ideas embedded in the subconscious mind also surface and give the original conscious thoughts a richer meaning and context. Reflection is one of the main forms of externalisation, through writing, discussions with others or contemplative thinking. Writing takes the reflection out of the psychological domain and forces a reconciliation with reality; while in discussions, the comprehensibility, truth, appropriateness and authenticity of the assertions can be contested (Taylor 2009).

3. *Internalisation (explicit to tacit).* The process of internalisation is seen most easily when an individual is 'learning by doing'. For example, there is a big difference between your reading about the techniques in this book and you doing them. In Chapter 7, we discuss interviewing. When one reads about interviewing skills, they may seem logical and straightforward. When one tries to interview someone, however, attempting to combine questioning, paraphrasing, summarising, probing, and taking notes, the process may not seem be so easy! It is this whole body experience of 'learning by doing' that converts explicit knowledge into tacit knowledge. Internalisation also occurs when an individual reflects on an experience – which explains some academics' penchant for setting learning diaries as assignments to encourage internalisation. Although reflection can be a conscious act, it can also occur instinctively in the subconscious mind with little awareness of the learner. It is also suspected that internalisation can occur through re-experiencing another's experiences through methods such as oral stories or diagrams and models.

4. *Socialisation (tacit to tacit).* This is an osmotic process where complex information is exchanged. It is often seen where a learner watches and interacts with an expert. While often accompanied by the combination process, socialisation is also a whole body experience where various nuances and nonverbal messages are received and synthesised into a complex appreciation of an intricate archetype. Socialisation, therefore, depends on modelling.

This four-phase paradigm of knowledge creation – combination, externalisation, internalisation and socialisation – provides an interesting and detailed look at how new knowledge can be generated. Most organisations have used the combination process as the main, and often only, means of creating knowledge. One very strong message from the writings of Nonaka and others is that organisations must actively encourage the use of the other three knowledge-creating processes.

In addition, integral to the knowledge creation processes, is the need for individuals, groups, and organisations to interact with others who have different biographies and diverse constructs of the world. So the concepts discussed in Chapter 4 on the positive management of individual differences also have a significant bearing on the creation of knowledge.

Knowledge creation and adult learning

Over the last decade or so, Jack Mezirow has formulated a comprehensive, idealised and universal model of adult learning. He calls this model transformative learning (1994) or transformational learning.

Taylor (2007) believes that transformational learning offers a theory of learning that is uniquely adult, abstract, idealised, and grounded in the nature of human communication. While some of his concepts are not always easy to follow (and not without their critics), Mezirow's contribution has a lot of value. Mezirow has suggested (1990, 1991, 2000, 2009) that there are three domains of adult learning – instrumental, communicative and emancipatory. There is an approximate relationship between the four phases of knowledge generation and the three domains of adult learning. This relationship can only be approximate, as knowledge generation is based on the tacit-explicit continuum, so the learning episode frequently incorporates elements of both tacit and explicit knowledge. Table 3.2 represents a relationship in its most simplistic form.

Table 3.2 Relationship between knowledge generation model & transformational learning

Knowledge generation	Transformational learning
Combination	Instrumental
Externalisation, combination, internalisation	Communicative
Internalisation & socialisation	Emancipatory

Instrumental learning

Instrumental learning involves the process of learning to control and manipulate the environment or other people. It is often task-oriented problem solving – i.e. how to do something or how to perform. This type of learning also allows us to establish the 'truth' by empirical tests and objective measurement – we can measure changes resulting from our learning in terms of productivity, performance or behaviour. In instrumental learning, the explicit knowledge from one person is assimilated by another person – i.e. the knowledge generation process of combination.

Combination/instrumental learning assumes that there is a set of universal information which should be transmitted to the learners. In organisations, this combination/ instrumental learning is the primary form of knowledge generation in the more formal learning episodes. It is evident in two spheres of activity:

- *Procedural training,* where all organisations have set procedures for achieving outcomes. These procedures are important and are a significant part of the organisation's knowledge capital (Sveiby 1997). As discussed in Chapter 1, the more fanatical followers of re-engineering have seen the opportunity for significant cost savings by reducing procedural training – with the resultant devaluation of the organisation's internal structures. Procedural training is the main contributor to the organisation's combination process of knowledge generation (Nonaka & Takeuchi 1995). It is a prime contributor to the organisation's well-being and survival. Organisations must continue to invest in procedural training to ensure the knowledge that forms the backbone of the organisation's competitive edge is widely disseminated.

- *Empirical research,* where instrumental learning involves determining cause–effect relationships through task-oriented problem solving. Further, the outcomes of instrumental learning can be proven by empirical testing (Mezirow 2000). This may occur, for example, during human resource needs investigations (see Chapter 5) when determining the reasons for customer dissatisfaction or the skills needed to use a new piece of equipment.

Principles of learning

Our understanding of instrumental learning has been predominantly shaped by the assumptions of the traditional school of thought and the research of writers such as Thorndike (1913, 1928). From these assumptions and research come a number of principles of learning that are frequently cited in texts on human resource development (e.g. Delahaye & Smith 1998; De Simone & Harris 2009; Goldstein 2002; Stone 2010). These writers agree that these principles underpin the needs investigation, design, implementation, and evaluation of learning experiences. A number of these principles have been recognised for over 100 years; some have come from the research of the traditionalist educators of the early 1900s, and some have been the result of more recent research, particularly in the area of human perception.

Some of the more important principles for adult learning are:

- *starting with the known.* In 1853, James Hole made the statement 'to raise the working man [sic] we must take hold of him where he is, not where he is not'. Lack of political correctness and indifferent grammar aside, this is a worthy maxim that all human resource developers should have engraved on their memory. Any learning episode must start at the learner's current level of knowledge or perspective and then gradually progress.

- *readiness to learn.* Thorndike's Law of Readiness (1913) states that if the individual is ready to learn, he or she will find the experience more satisfying. While this tenet may seem obvious, it is more often honoured by its absence than its presence in most learning designs.

- *part learning.* Based on his experiments in the 1880s, Ebbinghause found that, to learn new material, it is more efficient to space practice than to mass it (see Grattan, 1955). This has led to two themes. First, any material for learning should be separated into reasonably sized pieces before being presented to the learner. Miller (1956) coined the term 'chunking' to describe the process. Typically, adult learners tend to store information that is given in smaller chunks. The usual 'rule of thumb' is seven (+ or -2) (i.e. adults will remember information when it is divided into chunks of five to nine elements). The second theme assumes spaced learning.

- *spaced learning.* The concept of chunking presumes a space between the chunks. The question then becomes how the space should be constructed. The most obvious answer is to allow time between the chunks, although too much will allow the forgetting process to kick in. A second option is to use an activity associated with the information learned.

- *active learning.* Delahaye and Smith (1998) suggest using an activity to reinforce the previous chunk of information. They called this option 'active learning'. The basic premise is that there is a difference between hearing about a concept and doing the concept. This idea has strong links with the knowledge-creation process of internalisation where the 'whole body' experience becomes important. The saying 'I hear and I forget. I see and I remember. I do and I understand' encapsulates active learning quite well.

- *overlearning.* Another insight from Ebbinghause's work was that when something is learned, it is not forgotten at an even rate. Rather, most is lost very quickly and the rest is forgotten at a slow and fairly even rate. Thorndike (1913) established his Law of Exercise to combat this phenomenon – the more connections are used, the stronger they become. Hence, repetition increases retention. However, such repetition is often in conflict with an adult's power of self-responsibility – repetition can be quite boring. The design of any learning episode needs to incorporate repetition in a subtle, but effective, manner. McGehee and Thayer (1961) call such repetition 'overlearning' – practising beyond the point in time when the material or task is mastered.

- *multiple sense learning.* Delahaye and Smith (1998) point out that humans are visual animals. It has been shown that we take in about 80 percent of our information through sight and about ten percent through hearing. The use of multiple-sense learning means combining all the senses, although in reality educators are advised to concentrate on designing appropriate and effective visual aids – the talking side seems to come naturally!

- *feedback.* Feedback is critical to learning. De Simone & Harris (2009) suggest that feedback has two dimensions. Informational feedback provides understanding on what has been done correctly and what needs improvement. Motivational feedback occurs when the recipient values the information. Both dimensions are important. The following three steps provide a good model for giving feedback:

  - advise what the learner did well;

  - advise one to three areas for improvement that the learner may concentrate on next time (any more than three tends to become overwhelming);

  - suggest ways (or have the learner suggest ways) that these improvements could be made.

- *meaningful material.* The information being presented has to be acceptable and useful to the learner. McGehee and Thayer (1961) have shown that the more meaningful the material being presented, the more likely it will be learned and remembered. Delahaye and Smith (1998) suggest that the material presented should be meaningful to the learner in two ways: it should be linked to the learner's past, and it should be relevant to the learner's future.

- *transfer of learning.* De Simone & Harris (2009) discuss a concept of Thorndike and Woodworth (1901) called 'identical elements'. The more similar the learning and the performance situations, the more likely it is that the learning will be transferred to the working situation. The human resource developer should always endeavour to 'bring the workplace into the training room' by using, as far as possible, the exact working materials and equipment during the learning episode.

Case study example

See the PLP case study on page 14 of the workbook that accompanies this text for a manager using feedback.

While the traditional school has given us some important insights into adult learning, there is no doubt that some of the values of the school are at odds with the needs of adults. In particular, the assumptions that knowledge is a fairly fixed body of information (see Berte 1975), the impersonal and structured curriculum, and the controlling nature of the expert (see Howe 1977) are the very opposites of the values of andragogy enunciated by Knowles.

On the other hand, a significant amount of learning within organisations is instrumental learning – showing staff how to manipulate their workplace environment, whether it is using a machine, completing a form or entering information into a computer. Such procedural knowledge is the lifeblood of most organisations. The potential for conflict with the andragogical values, however, underlines the need for thoughtful and careful design of learning experiences for adults when using instrumental learning (see Chapters 8 and 10).

While the pathway of learners combining transmitted explicit knowledge with their own existing explicit knowledge is an obvious process, there is no doubt that, under certain conditions, learners could use new explicit knowledge to develop tacit knowledge. Driven by a high level of motivation (see Chapter 8), a learner could conceivably reflect deeply on new explicit knowledge and create new tacit knowledge or even engage in Mezirow's emancipatory learning domain (see Nonaka & von Krogh 2009).

Techniques and strategies for facilitating combination/instrumental learning are discussed in depth in Chapter 10.

A closer look 3.1

Combination and emancipatory learning

As part of a mentoring program, the protégé raised serious concerns about the levels of stress caused by a heavy workload. After some discussion, it became apparent that there were two prime causes of the heavy workload – poor time management and a reticence to make decisions on priorities. A possible drive underpinning these actions was a personal value of the protégé to be of service and assistance to others.

The mentor provided information (explicit knowledge) on setting priorities and also on ways to manage time. The information included using such practices as keeping a planning diary, allocating sufficient future time for each task that would be undertaken, allowing some time for unexpected tasks, and keeping in mind that the statement 'I did not have time' is not a matter of fact but a matter of opinion. The protégé was advised only to accept tasks that were essential to major responsibilities of the protégés role and for career development.

The protégé obviously reflected on this explicit knowledge and engaged in the knowledge generation process of combination. The following week the protégé showed the mentor a planning diary that incorporated time allocations for all tasks that were to be carried out over the next nine months. The details of this time allocation were more detailed and complete in the near term but, as could be expected, less so in the long term, because of limited data on the future tasks.

Over the following weeks, there was evidence that the protégé, reflecting on and internalising some of the explicit knowledge provided during the combination process, had created tacit knowledge. The mentor also observed evidence that the protégé had engaged in emancipatory learning, with changes to some basic frames of reference being noticeable. The evidence observed by the mentor included reports from the protégé of turning down requests from others and a noticeable focus on key tasks that were needed to complete important responsibilities. The protégé appeared to have changed the personal value of being always of service to others to a more balanced view of also considering the protégé's self.

Communicative learning

Communicative learning is most commonly associated with externalisation, combination and internalisation, which is why communicative learning is such a powerful knowledge-generation domain.

Communicative learning differs from instrumental learning on two counts. First, communicative learning involves the dynamics of understanding others rather than how to control or manipulate the external environment. In communicative learning, the approach is one in which the learner attempts to understand what is meant by another through speech, writing, drama, art or dance. You are involved in communicative learning as you are reading this text. However, such learning goes deeper than mere words. Communicative learning – trying to understand what someone means – often involves values, intentions, feelings, moral decisions, ideals, and normative concepts which may be defined only by their contexts – like freedom, love, beauty, and justice (Mezirow 1994, 2000).

Second, Mezirow (1994, 2000) contends that, instead of attempting to determine 'truth' (as occurs in instrumental learning), communicative learning seeks to establish the validity, or justification, for personal beliefs. In other words, we validate or justify contested beliefs through discourse (Mezirow 2009). It should also be noted that communicative learning is seldom amenable to empirical testing.

Debate

When considering a verbal interaction with another, the paradigm that most readily comes to mind is a debate. In a debate, one party attempts to convert the other to the 'true' or 'correct' point of view. Argyris (2008) refers to this type of interaction as 'model I theory-in-use' and believes that there are four governing processes. The debater:

- strives to remain in unilateral control;
- minimises losing and maximises winning;
- suppresses negative feelings; and
- gives the appearance of being rational throughout the interaction by defining clear objectives and evaluating their behaviour in terms of whether or not they have achieved them.

In carrying out these processes, there are two underlying strategies. First, the communicator debates without encouraging enquiry. This strategy is designed to maintain control and eventually win. Second, to maximise the chance of winning, the communicator avoids upsetting others and remains rational, trying to save face for both parties. A debate, then, has more to do with instrumental learning as the search is for 'truth'. However, when knowledge leaves the most basic level where 'truth' is an identifiable entity (e.g. water is made up of two atoms of hydrogen and one atom of oxygen), then a debate becomes much less useful.

For communicative learning, an interaction called discourse is much more productive.

Rational and reflective discourse

As espoused by Knowles (1998), one major defining feature of adult learners is the need to understand the meaning of what others communicate. This need to understand values, ideals, feelings and moral decisions can only be achieved through discourse. Mezirow (2000) sees discourse as the specialised use of dialogue devoted to:

- the search for common understanding; and

- the justification of an interpretation or belief.

> *Discourse is used here to refer to that special kind of dialogue in which we focus on content and try to justify beliefs by giving and defending reasons and by examining the evidence for and against competing viewpoints. We search out those who we believe to be most informed, objective and rational to seek a consensus in the form of a best collective judgement. We settle for a best judgement, given careful assessment of reasons, arguments and evidence. [When new evidence is encountered], then the process of discourse continues, often in a series of one-to-one encounters, including authors of published texts. (Mezirow 1994, p. 225)*

There are two sequential elements to discourse – rational and reflective.

Rational discourse can be defined as a discussion that allows each party to understand the position of the other party and, in turn, to have his or her own position understood. Brookfield (1995) describes this process as 'democratic discourse' and defines it as the ability to talk and listen respectfully to those who hold views different from our own. Rational discourse, then, uses externalisation and combination for one party and combination and internalisation for the other party in each interaction.

Case study example

See the PLP case study on page 3 of the workbook that accompanies this text for rational discourse.

Reflective discourse involves a critical assessment of beliefs, points of view, or ideas and follows rational discourse. Reflective discourse requires a provisional suspension of judgement about the truth or falsity of ideas, or the belief or disbelief in them, until a better determination can be made (Mezirow 2000). The listener can then proceed to change or not change, accept or not accept the beliefs, points of view, or ideas – that is, to learn. Reflective discourse uses the internalisation process of knowledge generation.

Discourse, and therefore communicative learning, is more likely to be successful (Mezirow 2009) when, in addition to minimum levels of personal security, health and education, the learners:

- have more accurate and complete information;

- have equal opportunity to participate;

- are free from coercion and distorting self-deception;

- are open to alternative points of view and care about how others think and feel;

- have the ability to weigh evidence and assess arguments objectively;

- have awareness of the context of ideas and taken-for-granted assumptions, including one's own;

- have a willingness to seek understanding, agreement, and a tentative best judgement as a test of validity until new evidence, perspectives, or arguments are encountered and validated.

It is interesting to compare this list with model II theory-in-use (Argyris 1999). Model II is essentially a description of his double-loop learning, (a key requirement for the organisation's shadow system – see Chapter 1) where an individual or organisation examines or changes the underlying governing variables or the master programs:

- the interaction is based on valid information;

- the participants have free and informed choice; and

- the participants keep testing the validity of the choices, especially as the choices are being implemented.

Discourse and knowledge generation

Rational discourse can be seen in the knowledge-generating processes of Nonaka and Takeuchi (1995). When considered at the individual level, there are two major pathways for knowledge to be generated. Using the first pathway, person A selects some knowledge from his tacit level, perhaps using an analogy, and converts this to explicit knowledge (externalisation) which is then declared to person B. Person B adds this declared knowledge to her explicit knowledge (combination) and some elements of this new explicit knowledge may then progress into her tacit knowledge (internalisation). This may then trigger a previously unrelated thought in person B that is then converted into her explicit knowledge (externalisation) and is declared to person A. Person A adds this to his explicit knowledge (combination) and, in turn, some of this explicit knowledge may progress to his tacit knowledge (internalisation) – and so rational discourse would continue.

Two points need to be acknowledged in this externalisation–combination–internalisation interaction (the first pathway). First, it is difficult to be precise on the amount or type of knowledge that is internalised; as this knowledge is moving from the explicit (declarable) to the tacit (non-declarable) level, the individual concerned is most probably unaware of what has been transferred. Second, this externalisation–combination–internalisation path can be used in the debating method as well as in rational discourse. In the debating method, however, internalisation is unlikely to occur as the listener is more concerned with defending a point of view rather than understanding the other's world of values and beliefs.

The second pathway connects the tacit levels of knowledge in the two individuals via socialisation. Again, this will occur with both debate and rational discourse. In debate, the tacit knowledge exchanged is more likely to be about power – attempting to sway the other to the 'true' point of view. In rational discourse, the two communicators pick up messages about feelings and emotions – they read nonverbals, for example – and this additional information enhances the level of knowledge of each of the communicators.

Usually, in communicative learning, both pathways are used providing what Nonaka and Takeuchi (1995) describe as 'total body communication' – shared experiences, not just cognitive experiences but at the bodily level as well – so that the emotions and senses are also involved. They also add that such learning is not only a forum for creative dialogue but a medium for sharing experience and enhancing trust.

A closer look 3.2

Pathway 1: Communicative learning using knowledge-generation processes

In a class on adult learning, I was discussing Mezirow's three levels of learning – instrumental, communicative and emancipatory. Some of my input had come directly from my explicit knowledge – by this time in my career, I knew the basics of Mezirow by heart! However, some had come from my tacit knowledge – for example, when I shared a long-forgotten story about my abhorrence of some personal use of power. This explicit and tacit knowledge was declared to the class and was hopefully to be combined with their explicit knowledge to widen their explicit knowledge.

One of the class members, a principal of a primary school, commented that the three levels" most probably occurred in children as well. From my explicit knowledge I replied that there was certainly research in the area, and that it usually indicated that their emancipatory level was being developed, but that with adults the expectation was that the belief systems had already been developed and the emancipatory level was to do with change or transformation.

As I was declaring this explicit knowledge, I had a sudden memory of a TV documentary I had seen the previous week on siblings in the human race. The presenter had said that siblings were hardwired to compete and fight with each other, but fortunately hardwired not to kill each other. I could easily picture this segment of the documentary. I then related this picture to the class and went on to suggest that perhaps children were hardwired to learn at different levels depending on their age – instrumental learning between 1 and 5, communicative learning between 6 and 12 and emancipatory learning in their teens. Thus, with the interaction with the class member, my externalisation–combination–internalisation process created new knowledge.

I have since learned that this 'hardwiring' concept is not new in childhood education and is much more complicated than the interaction in my class suggested. As viewed from my own development, this is immaterial for two reasons. First, the interaction had generated new information for me and the class members. Second, without this new insight, I would not have continued my queries with other professional colleagues at a later date, consequently increasing my (albeit limited) explicit and tacit knowledge of childhood learning.

The importance of communicative learning

Because of the difficulty in measuring objective outcomes of communicative learning, it is often underestimated or dismissed. A number of initiatives of the 1980s – such as industrial democracy, empowerment and total quality management – failed, or did not have the expected impact, because the techniques of instrumental learning were used instead of the principles of communicative learning (see the discussion on *Management re-engineering* in Chapter 1). Communicative learning, a deeper and more complex process than instrumental learning, tends to have a more profound and long-term impact on the organisation's ability to survive. In addition, communicative learning, particularly through rational discourse and rational reflection, has a developmental effect on critical thinking and, as we shall see later, on critical reflection.

Communicative learning is involved in all the four steps of HRD. At the needs investigation stage, the researcher is attempting to uncover the deep, underlying values, beliefs, and 'views of the world' of the information provider; during the design stage, the developer will need to make judgements on how knowledge that is more complex than facts (i.e. beliefs and values) can be presented; during implementation, the facilitator will be constantly looking for opportunities to use communicative learning; and at the evaluation stage, the evaluator will need to look beyond the simple facts and figures to gauge the level of complex learning that has occurred and its effect on the organisation.

Emancipatory learning

Mezirow (2009) believes that emancipatory learning requires individuals to transform their basic frames of reference – hence the term 'transformational learning'. Originally, Mezirow called these frames of reference 'meaning structures' and Argyris (2008) refers to them as 'master programs in the individual's head' that dictate the kind of meanings and behavioural strategies the individuals will or will not produce.

Frames of reference, then, are those deep-seated underlying values and belief systems that guide, shape and dictate our everyday attitudes and behaviours. As Scott and Harker (2004) explain, we see the world through the paradigm filters that have been painstakingly built on the platform of our earlier experiences of the world. We need these frames of reference. Every day we are bombarded with a variety of signals, cues and stimuli. If we tried to assess and judge each one of these inputs, we would become quickly overwhelmed. So, frames of reference provide us with a predisposition to act. Mezirow (1990) suggests that what we do and do not perceive, comprehend, and remember is profoundly influenced by our frames of reference.

A hierarchy of assumptions

Along with our tacit knowledge, we all have frames of reference. Frames of reference include personality traits and dispositions, genealogy, power allocations, world views, religious doctrine, aesthetic values, social movements, psychological schema or scripts, and learning styles and preferences (Mezirow 2009). In his earlier writings, Mezirow (1990, 1991) suggested that there are two types of frames of reference: meaning perspectives, and meaning schemes. While he has provided some fairly good descriptions of meaning perspectives over the years, the definition of meaning schemes is still somewhat unclear. However, Brookfield (1995) uses the term 'assumptions' and suggests that there is a hierarchy of three – paradigmatic, prescriptive and causal.

Paradigmatic assumptions

Paradigmatic assumptions are the same as Mezirow's meaning perspectives (Mezirow 1990, 1991, 1994), now referred to as 'habits of the mind' (Mezirow 2000). These assumptions are the basic axioms we use to order the world into fundamental categories. Paradigmatic assumptions are the broad sets of predispositions that are the foundation for the prescriptive and causal assumptions. They provide us with criteria for judging right and wrong, bad and good, true and false, appropriate and inappropriate.

Paradigmatic assumptions are acquired uncritically in childhood through the knowledge-generation process of socialisation, often within a context of emotionally charged relationships with parents, teachers, or other important adults. We may not recognise them as assumptions, even after they have been pointed out as such. Instead, we insist that they are objectively valid renderings of reality. When paradigmatic assumptions are challenged and changed, the consequences for our lives are often explosive.

Mezirow (1990, 1994, 1996) sees that there are three major sources of paradigmatic assumptions (or meaning perspectives or habits of the mind):

- *sociolinguistic* – such as ideologies, social norms, language codes. The first two – ideologies and social norms – imprint us with power perceptions and social relationships, especially those currently prevailing, that are legitimised and enforced by institutions in our society. The ways we address people, both verbally and nonverbally, as well as the accompanying emotions, come from this sociolinguistic foundation. Mezirow gives an illuminating example of language codes:

   > *A good example is the English language. The English language is a real problem in one specific way. We don't have any words between the polarities. Everything is big or little, fat or thin, rich or poor, beautiful or ugly. We don't have any intermediate words. A number of [other] languages have them. Certainly that's a severe limitation that forces us to think, and feel and see in certain ways (Mezirow 1996, p. 9);*

- *psychological* – the way that neuroses and psychoses and personality tend to limit the individual's responses to the external environment. So, some people are extroverted, gaining their energy from the external environment and interacting with others; other people are introverted, happily working with the images and thoughts within their own mind (see Myers 1995);

- *epistemic* – the individual preferences for taking in information. For example, people have different learning styles, e.g. pragmatist, activist, theorist or reflector (see the discussion in Chapter 8) and different sensory preferences for taking in information, e.g. print, visual, aural, interactive, tactile or manipulative, kinaesthetic or manipulative, olfactory.

Prescriptive assumptions

These assumptions provide us with guidance on what ought to be happening in a particular situation, given that we all yearn to live in an ordered world. The prescriptive assumptions can be identified by the words 'ought' or 'should' or 'must' in conversations.

Mezirow (2000) refers to this level of assumptions as 'points of view' – sets of immediate specific expectations, beliefs, feelings, attitudes and judgements. These points of view tacitly direct and shape a specific interpretation and determine how we judge, typify objects, and attribute causality (Mezirow 2000).

Causal assumptions

Causal assumptions help us understand how different parts of the world work and the conditions under which processes can be changed. These assumptions are usually stated in predictive terms 'If I smile when I look at a stranger, I will be accepted'.

In summary, then, how one views and categorises experiences, beliefs, people, events and the self involves structures of assumptions and expectations through which our thoughts, feelings and habits are filtered, formulated and enacted into behaviour (Mezirow 2009).

A closer look 3.3

Some paradigmatic assumptions

Rational Emotive Therapy (RET) is an approach to counselling developed by Albert Ellis (see Ellis & Whiteley 1979). An underpinning foundation of RET is that adults take simple preferences, such as a desire for approval or success, and make the mistake of re-interpreting these simple desires as dire necessities. Ellis believed that it is our unthinking acceptance of early-indoctrinated irrational thoughts that keeps dysfunctional attitudes and behaviours active and functioning within us. A number of authors (e.g. Corey 1991, George & Christiana 1995, Hansen, Rossberg & Cramer 1994) suggest that there are at least eleven irrational thoughts that operate as hegemonic paradigmatic assumptions:

- it is absolutely essential that I be loved and/or approved of by every significant person I meet;

- I have to be completely competent and perfect if I am to be considered worthwhile;

- some people are wicked, bad, and awful, and it is essential that these people are blamed and punished to the fullest extent of their transgressions;

- it is terrible and catastrophic when things in my life are not the way I want them to be;

- all my unhappiness is caused by outside events and these events are beyond my control;

- there are many things that are dangerous and harmful and I should constantly worry and be concerned about them;

- it is easier to run away from difficulties and responsibilities than it is to face them;

- I need to be dependent on others and have someone else stronger than me to lean on;

- past events in my life determine my present behaviour and I cannot change the events or my behaviour;

- I should be very concerned and upset by other people's problems; and

- there is always a correct and precise answer to every problem, and it is catastrophic if I cannot find it.

These eleven paradigmatic assumptions are hegemonic assumptions as they work against our long-term best interests. It is much better that we accept and love ourselves because of our imperfections. Further, by accepting responsibility for ourselves, we are more likely to find long-term and satisfying solutions to the many challenges that life presents to us.

The role of frames of reference

These assumptions of frames of reference – paradigmatic, prescriptive and causal – selectively order and delimit learning by defining our horizons of expectation which significantly affect the activities of perceiving, comprehending and remembering. In addition to dictating how an individual acts, our frames of reference have three important qualities:

- They filter information, accepting information that supports them and rejecting information that does not. This means they are rarely changed without some effort on the part of the individual. Argyris (1999) points out that just because individuals experience inconsistency between their actions and their beliefs does not necessarily mean that they will change either the action or belief.

- They are very well defended by the psyche of the individual so only particular change processes are likely to have any effect on them. As Scott and Harker (2004) point out, when a person has invested time and emotional energy in making sense of their personal reality, logic is not particularly persuasive! The defence mechanism is quite sophisticated and complex. Our understanding of it is incomplete. Argyris (1999) has suggested that one such defence mechanism is the use of espoused values – values which an individual claims are his or her underlying master programs. However, there is a difference between an individual's espoused values and his or her theories-in-action. Theories-in-action can only be identified by observing behaviours. We have all heard of the boss who says, 'My door is always open' but, when an employee tests this invitation, he or she receives significant negative nonverbal indicators that the boss is not really interested. In fact, this separation of espoused versus theory-in-action is so strong that individuals often use a paradigmatic assumption (or, if you like, theory-in-action or master program) while simultaneously advising others not to do so (e.g. 'Your big problem is that you always criticise other people' or 'I have told you a million times not to exaggerate.').

▪ Any change to a frame of reference is usually accompanied by a highly emotional reaction. The emotions may be negative, such as anger or fear, or positive, such as wonder or excitement or satisfaction. More frequently, the emotions are a mixture of positive and negative. An individual challenging a personal hegemonic assumption will experience fear of the unknown in letting go of a faithful servant (the paradigmatic assumption or theory-in-action) but will experience also the sense of freedom and excited anticipation of a future unconstrained by the stultifying theory-in-action.

Changing frames of reference

For most people, the majority of their frames of reference operate as they should – guiding the individual, with relative safety, through the paths, traps and quagmires of everyday life. However, some of our frames of reference are what Brookfield (1995) calls 'hegemonic assumptions' – assumptions and practices that seem to make our lives easier but actually work against our own best long-term interests. Mezirow (1996a, p. 11) refers to these hegemonic assumptions as 'all libidinal, linguistic, epistemic, institutional or environmental forces that can limit an individual's options and rational control over one's life, but have been taken for granted or seen as beyond human control'.

Meyer and Land (2005) refer to this opportunity to challenge hegemonic assumptions as 'conceptual gateways' or 'portals' that lead to a previously inaccessible (and initially perhaps troublesome) way of thinking, thereby leading the learner on through a transformational landscape in a kind of epistemological steeplechase. So, for example, when an adult learner believes he is hopeless at using a computer, this would be classified as a causal assumption. This causal assumption may be based on a paradigmatic assumption that 'book learning is a waste of time'. However, if this adult learner wishes to succeed at further learning, he will have to challenge these hegemonic assumptions (both causal and paradigmatic). Emancipatory learning is the liberation from these hegemonic assumptions.

There are two ways to change a frame of reference. One, the *incremental approach* (Mezirow 2000), is to gradually change an associated cluster of causal and prescriptive assumptions. This is often achieved through communicative learning and modelling (the knowledge-generation process of socialisation). By exposure to others' values and belief systems, an individual can gradually change a series of causal and prescriptive assumptions and, eventually, an entire paradigmatic assumption.

For example, many new Doctor of Philosophy candidates become overawed by the various journal articles and texts they must read. The written word takes on the veracity of the Holy Grail, simply because it has been published in a journal or by a publishing company. Such candidates copy automatically what is written without due thought – an action called 'reporting the literature'.

However, after watching their doctoral supervisor challenge several writings – commenting on both the worthy and inappropriate contributions to a particular theoretical stance (note the knowledge-generation process of socialisation here) – the candidate starts to recognise that published material is not necessarily the pure truth (a causal assumption). After several demonstrations, the candidate reads a journal article and identifies components that are supported by other literature and parts that are contrary to other literature. After doing this with several journal articles, the candidate then summons the courage to put these reasonings onto paper – a process called 'analysing the literature'. After several episodes of analysing the literature, the candidate suddenly realises that, when reading a journal article and not understanding it, her first response is not to castigate herself and assume that she is dim witted. Rather, she first questions the writing ability of the author, then the quality of the content, and finally cross-checks to see whether, indeed, she has been mistaken. Thus the paradigmatic assumption that someone who has had a journal article published must be superior to a mere doctoral candidate is broken.

The second way that frames of reference can be changed is the *epochal approach* (Mezirow 2000) – the result of a disorienting dilemma such as a divorce, death of a loved one, or change in job status (Mezirow 1990). The individual is faced with an undeniable and significant fact or event that is at odds with the paradigmatic assumption – a state of mental conflict called 'cognitive dissonance'. Under cognitive dissonance, given that the fact or event is indisputable, the individual experiences distress and is then motivated to reduce this distress by changing the paradigmatic assumption. Mezirow (2009) suggests that the individual passes through the following phases:

- a disorienting dilemma;

- self-examination with feelings of guilt or shame, sometimes turning to religion for support;

- a critical assessment of assumptions;

- recognition that one's discontent and the process of transformation are shared and that others have negotiated a similar change;

- exploration of options for new roles, relationships and actions;

- planning a course of action;

- acquiring knowledge and skills for implementing one's plans;

- provisionally trying out new plans;

- renegotiating relationships;

- building competence and self-confidence in new roles and relationships; and

- a reintegration into one's life on the basis of conditions dictated by one's new perspective.

Critical reflection

Whether the paradigmatic assumptions are transformed by the sudden, and usually traumatic, occurrence of a disorienting dilemma or by the slower conversion of a cluster of causal and prescriptive assumptions, there is one common process that must transpire

– that is, critical reflection. Taylor (2007) reports that research has confirmed the essential position of critical reflection in transformational learning.

Critical reflection refers to questioning the integrity of deeply held assumptions and beliefs which occurs when an individual discerningly examines the very foundations and justifications for his or her beliefs (Taylor 2009). Critical reflection is more than reflection (Brookfield, 2000). It is certainly deeper than the reflective discourse used in communicative learning. Critical reflection makes explicit and analyses that which was previously implicit and uncritically accepted. The individual may ask such questions as:

- What are these habits of thinking that I have fallen in to?
- What are the frames of reference that support these habits? and
- Where did these frames of reference come from?

Brookfield (1995) sees two elements that allow reflection to become critical. First, when reflection is used to understand how considerations of power undergird, frame and distort processes and interactions. Second, when assumptions and practices that seem to make our lives easier but actually work against our own best long-term interests are questioned.

Mezirow (1990) and Taylor (2009) emphasise the differences of reflecting on the content, process and premises of problem solving. These can be linked to the three levels of assumptions:

- *content reflection* – where we focus on what we perceive, feel, think and act (this level concentrates on causal assumptions by examining the content of the problem);

- *process reflection* – where we focus on how we perform the functions of perceiving (this level concentrates on prescriptive assumptions by examining the processes); and

- *premise reflection* – which raises the awareness of why we perceive (this level concentrates on paradigmatic assumptions by examining the basic presuppositions or fundamental beliefs underpinning the problem).

Premise reflection is the least common of the three but is the basis for critical reflection (Taylor 2009).

A closer look 3.4

An example of critical reflection

Managers sometimes experience difficulty in conducting a performance appraisal on particular members of their staff. If a manager wished to become critically reflective on the problem, he or she could examine each of the three levels:

- *content reflection.* The manager would consider the various indicators he or she used – observations of behaviour, the quality of reports written, and the number of errors. By looking closely at those indicators, the manager would be critically reflecting at the content level,

- *process reflection.* If the manager asks such questions as 'Have I seen enough of this staff member to make such judgements?' or 'Were all the errors directly attributable to that particular staff member?', then the manager is examining the process of problem solving and will analyse the prescriptive assumptions underlying these questions.

- *premise reflection.* When the manager examines the very foundations of the decision for any personal biases that may have occurred, then he or she may ask a questions such as 'Why do I expect such precision in all that the staff do?' This question strikes at the very heart of the decision. 'Are my expectations too high?', 'Do I always produce such perfect work?', and 'Am I always error free?' These are confirmatory questions that could easily follow to check on the veracity of the paradigmatic assumption.

Comment

Whether the manager then progresses through transformational learning and changes the paradigmatic assumption depends on whether the disorienting dilemma was strong enough to challenge the paradigmatic assumption or whether the content and process reflections changed a cluster of related causal and prescriptive assumptions. For example, suppose the manager's judgement on the performance appraisal had been overturned by a higher authority – the CEO or an appeals board (as exist in some public service organisations). Such a decision, contrary to the one that the manager made, may strike at the heart of the manger's paradigmatic assumption and be so disorienting that the manager proceeds directly to the premise reflection stage.

Or the contrary decision may be one of a series, and the manager may reflect on the content and process stage over several cycles and gradually realise that the content and process reflections are identifying a common theme like – 'Why do I not like a staff member to dress so casually?', 'Why should a report use headings and subheadings?', or 'Can a staff member really be error free?'. Then the manager could conclude that this common theme is really concerned with a deeply held belief about precision, and that such an extreme belief no longer has a place in his or her work as a manager.

The importance of emancipatory learning

Emancipatory learning looks at changing frames of reference – paradigmatic, prescriptive and causal – and is a very complex, value-laden, and emotional process. Transformational learning is learning that transforms problematic frames of reference to make them more inclusive, discriminating, reflective, open, and emotionally able to change (Mezirow 2009).

At the heart of transformational learning is the process of critical reflection where the individual actively examines those assumptions or frames of reference to see if they still have a place in the individual's current life. The challenge to the frame of reference may have come from:

- reflecting on new explicit knowledge (an unusual event only occurring when there is high motivation to change);

- an episode of rational discourse where, by deeply appreciating another's inner world, a personal value is challenged and changed; or

- a disorienting dilemma in one's personal life.

The critical reflection by the learner on this additional data results in transformational learning.

Hegemonic assumptions (those assumptions that seem to make our life easier but in fact work against our long-term best interests) are usually recognised as worthy of change. However, in the modern management of organisations, managers often need to become aware of the 'mind maps' of staff for comparison with the strategic or legal imperatives faced by the organisation. Debilitating inconsistencies between the assumptions of the individual and the obligations of the organisation may demand the alteration of the individual's assumptions. For example, many public service departments have undergone significant change in recent years. Under the old bureaucratic model, a public service department made decisions based on the policies of the department, whether or not those policies made sense. Now the public service organisations are expected to operate a service to clients. Some public servants had great difficulty changing to this new way of making decisions and needed to go through transformational learning to make the adjustment.

If organisations are to succeed in surviving the dynamic environments in which they now operate, staff will need to examine continually their own basic assumptions. Further, managers will be expected to become experts in the various strategies that facilitate the emancipatory learning process. Ironically, becoming adept at facilitating such change will mean that managers will need to work through transformational learning themselves.

Table 3.3 The relationship between types of knowledge, knowledge generation and transformational learning

Types of knowledge	Knowledge generation	Transformational learning
Explicit	Combination	Instrumental
Tacit	Combination Externalisation Internalisation	Communicative
Frames of reference	Internalisation Socialisation	Emancipatory

Critical thinking

When discussing transformational learning, Mezirow (1990) concentrates on changing frames of reference. However, there is certainly more to individual higher level learning than this. One area of importance that is also discussed in the literature is critical thinking.

Critical thinking is different from critical reflection. Critical reflection involves the deep examination of the very foundations and justifications of one's beliefs and values. Critical thinking, however, impinges on our knowledge of a topic or the logic we use to change our knowledge of a topic. So, for example, during rational discourse, an individual may identify gaps in his or her knowledge or some dissonance between one concept and another. In closing the gap in the knowledge, the individual may simply add new knowledge. In challenging the dissonance between concepts, the individual may work through a decision-making process that clarifies the situation.

The knowledge-generation processes of externalisation and internalisation play a large part in critical thinking during rational discourse and rational reflection. As the two learners empathically disclose and listen, they are attempting to articulate tacit knowledge into explicit knowledge. The interaction helps the disclosing party to formulate and make concrete the formerly undefined tacit knowledge. As this tacit knowledge becomes explicit, the listener tries to digest the new explicit knowledge and create new tacit knowledge or change current knowledge. This process forms part of the individual's critical thinking ability.

Revans (1982) has suggested that 'Learning = Programmed Knowledge + Questioning Insight' (L = P + Q). He sees programmed information being available in the textbooks and journals in the library and being 'the stuff of traditional education'. He goes on to say that traditional instruction prepares one for the treatment of puzzles or difficulties from which escapes are thought to be known, even though the escapes or solutions might be hard to discover and call for the skill of experts (Revans 1998). The parallels of programmed knowledge with instrumental learning and explicit knowledge are obvious. The process of formulating questions and working logically through the various options, comparisons and alternatives is to Revans, however, the real hallmark of learning. This questioning insight, therefore, deals with the resolution of problems and the acceptance of the concomitant opportunities about which no single course of action is to be justified by any code of programmed knowledge. This process of questioning is the basic foundation of critical thinking.

The literature gives surprisingly diverse views on the definitions of and approaches to critical thinking. Typically, textbooks on the topic rely heavily on the technicalities of logic. They provide detailed discussion of the anatomy of argument, inductive and deductive reasoning, the role of premise, and fallacies of argument. These concepts, however, throw little light on the processes of critical thinking. There is some agreement on what can be termed the components of critical thinking – i.e. problem solving, creativity, evaluation, dialectic thinking and logical reflection.

Problem solving

Problem solving tends to be seen as a major focus of critical thinking. In the learning literature, two processes – one by Dewey and one by Revans – provide some insight into the problem-solving component of critical thinking.

Scientific problem solving

As far back as 1910, Dewey suggested a robust problem-solving model that has stood the test of time. The model has been used extensively in textbooks over the years, and generally follows seven steps:

- defining the problem;
- identifying possible solutions;
- evaluating each solution;
- selecting a solution;
- planning the implementation;
- implementing; and
- evaluating to see whether the original problem has been solved.

It is surprising to see the number of people who define a problem in the words of a possible solution – e.g. 'We need team building'. In fact, team building is often just one possible solution – the problem is usually low productivity. There could in fact be a number of possible solutions to low productivity – improved communications, better control systems, lower staff turnover and so on.

The scientific problem-solving model helps the critical thinker first to identify the real goal. Another mistake that is often made is to analyse possible solutions as they are raised. Identifying possible solutions is a creative activity requiring positive feedback loops whereas evaluation is a logical, auditing exercise using negative feedback loops. As we know, negative feedback loops destroy creativity. To gain clarity of thinking, the two elements should not be mixed – that is, possible solutions should be identified first, and then each of the solutions be evaluated. Finally, the model ensures that the problem-solving activity results in an action, and that the outcome of the action is compared against the original problem that needed solving.

System beta

In describing the way managers should solve problems, Revans (1982, 1998) believed that a five-step process (which he called 'System Beta') should be used. The five steps of System Beta are:

- *survey* – a stage of observation where the critical thinker collects data and finally admits that some dissonance or contradiction is occurring;
- *hypothesis* – a stage of theory, conjecture, and testing (the critical thinker may make suppositions, or even guesses, at new relationships between the observed variables);
- *experiment* – practical tests are carried out to compare the new speculated relationships or guesses with some standard (the standard may come from a reliable authority – a textbook or person – or even be some activity such as a rehearsal or a pilot study);

- *audit* – actual and desired results are compared (this may be highly objective – with the comparison of measurements; or highly subjective – such as personal assessment of the outcomes or a debate or discussion with another party);

- *review* – the speculated relationships between variables are retained or rejected.

This five-step process provides a simple yet vigorous paradigm that can be used to enhance critical thinking. While it has similarities to the scientific problem-solving model, System Beta emphasises the role of observation and experimentation in critical thinking.

These two models – one by Dewey and the other by Revans – provide some insights into the critical thinking process. However, both are in the realms of explicit knowledge and there is a suspicion that professionals rely more on tacit knowledge for problem solving. Such tacit problem-solving knowledge can be built only by experience, often using the socialisation process with the novice professional working alongside the master.

Creativity

Creativity is associated with novel responses. To act creatively, one brings previously unconnected elements together in new, unusual or adaptive ways. Creativity involves formulating possible solutions to a problem (note the link with problem solving here) or explanations for a phenomenon (Rudinow & Barry 2007). Boden (2004) believes that the goal of creativity is exploration – where the terrain explored is the mind itself. The individual draws on a wide reservoir of knowledge, a deep well of experience, and combines this with a vivid imagination and courageous intuition. Creativity is therefore a product of processing information in unique and imaginative ways.

Evaluation

Evaluation in critical thinking is largely about testing for what is both relevant and significant – as Rudinow & Barry (2007) remark, distinguishing the relevant from the irrelevant, the significant from the trivial. They go on to suggest that evaluation involves determining and assessing the reasons for a position, trying to find out whether a position is worth holding, thereby serving as a basis for further discussion and inquiry.

Evaluation relies on a standard to provide a basis for comparison. When this standard comes from an individual's explicit knowledge, the link between the standard and the issue being reviewed can be readily articulated. However, the standard can also come from the individual's tacit knowledge or even from his or her frames of reference; in these cases the logicality of the link is more difficult to assert. This difficulty, however, is not a reasonable justification for assuming that the evaluation is not valuable.

Dialectic thinking

Sometimes referred to as relativistic thinking, dialectic thought allows the mind to accept that an entity has opposing attributes. For example, electricity can have both positive and negative qualities: on the one hand it provides warmth, and on the other it may cause fatalities. It is believed that dialectic thought is a characteristic of adults and is a trait that differentiates adults from youths (Labouvie-Vief 1985). Adults understand that all knowledge is relative and non-absolute, and that thoughts, emotions, experiences, people and objects embody contradictory aspects (Perlmutter & Hall 1992). Recognising that an object or phenomenon may have ephemeral qualities beyond the obvious and formal attributes allows an individual to imagine a wider variety of possibilities and options.

Logical reflection

Schon (1983, 1991) has commented on the importance of reflection in adult learning. Logical reflection is an important aspect of critical thinking as the adult learner reviews the problem solving, the results of being creative, and evaluates the issue under examination. So, where reflective discourse and critical reflection focus on the inner world of the individual (that is the individual's frame of reference), logical reflection concentrates on the outer world of a particular problem or challenge. It is through the logical reflection process that the adult adds to the store of explicit and tacit knowledge. Further, adult learners may conclude, through logical reflection in the critical thinking process, that critical reflection is needed to examine certain aspects of their frames of reference – thus creating a link between critical thinking and critical reflection.

The amalgam of critical thinking

Critical thinking, then, is a higher order thought process that is complex and multifaceted. Questioning is a key activity in the process; the interaction between explicit and tacit knowledge often generates insights that appear magical. Critical thinking appears to be comprised of the components of problem solving, creativity, evaluation, dialectic thinking and logical reflection. Further, it is apparent that these components mix and merge as the creative activity progresses. Finally, it is also suggested that critical thinking interacts vigorously with the frames of reference and the explicit and tacit knowledge of the individual.

Unlearning

Recently, there has been growing interest in the concept of 'unlearning'. Starbuck (1996) suggests that people seem to have difficulty in discarding ineffective or obsolete methods and theories, but that learning often cannot occur until after there has been unlearning.

It is interesting to reflect that the concept of unlearning has only recently become a phenomenon worthy of consideration in adult and organisational learning. Centuries ago, an individual's knowledge would last a lifetime; indeed knowledge would be passed down generations and still be highly useful. This has changed over the last several decades until, as we pass into the new millennium, knowledge becomes rapidly obsolete – hence the need to consider the unlearning process. Surprisingly, there has been very little written on the topic.

When discussing unlearning, a differentiation should be made between individual and organisational unlearning. Unfortunately, as pointed out by Becker (2008a), most definitions of unlearning refer to both individual and organisational levels as if they are the same entity. In this text, we will discuss individual unlearning in this chapter and organisational unlearning in Chapter 13.

For individuals, Hedberg (1981) considers that obsolete knowledge is simply 'overwritten' – a process that is different to forgetting. With forgetting, the individual unconsciously loses knowledge, whether the knowledge is useful or not. Hedberg, however, suggests that the individual consciously erases obsolete knowledge in favour of knowledge that is more serviceable. Consider the situation where an individual is changing from a word processing package that uses keys for sending control instructions to the computer, to one that uses a mouse and a menu display. Hedberg's model assumes that the learner will overwrite the old knowledge on the key control with the new knowledge for the mouse control.

Klein (1989), however, believes that the new knowledge sits beside the old knowledge – hence the name 'parenthetic model'. He further suggests that the old knowledge can be dredged up if the individual returns to the original context. So, in our example, if the individual has to use an old word processing package depending on keys for control of the computer, then the individual can happily revert to the old knowledge. Klein's model certainly seems closer to reality, although it does ignore the effect of Thorndike's Law of Exercise. If the old knowledge is not used for some time, certain elements of the old knowledge will be lost (i.e. forgotten). If you have ever tried to go back to a word processing package that uses keys for control rather than a computer mouse, you will know what this is like. There is usually a frantic hunt for an old instruction manual!

The underlying assumption of both models – overwriting (Hedeberg 1981) and parenthesis (Klein, 1989) – is that the knowledge being changed is what could be called 'professional tacit' knowledge. *Professional tacit knowledge* is that which professionals use to make decisions and which becomes a basis for their explicit knowledge. As we know from Mezirow (1994), there is more to learning, and therefore unlearning, than that. Adults also operate on their frames of reference. So, when we consider individual unlearning, we must examine both professional knowledge and frames of reference.

We have already discussed the reluctance people have in changing their frames of reference. Such change may be achieved after a concerted effort of changing a number of prescriptive and causal assumptions or may occur relatively after experiencing a disorienting dilemma. Several authors also discuss the reluctance that individuals may have in releasing hard-earned professional knowledge. Indeed, Becker (2008b) has shown that those who have been longer in a single organisational position have the most difficulty in unlearning past practices, whereas those who had a breadth of experience across a number of roles tended to find it easier in relinquishing past practice. In addition, Becker (2008b) found that some individuals were simply more comfortable with change, something many of them put down to individual personality. So, we can say that unlearning deep and personally meaningful knowledge is likely to be difficult.

Managing unlearning

When managing unlearning, organisations need to consider a number of issues. Becker (2007) found that organisations need to overcome a number of barriers, including:

- *feelings and expectations.* Prior to a change, staff often believe that the new way sounds more difficult than the old way, and expect the change to be difficult to make. During the change, a higher level of experience in the job made it more difficult for the individual to make the change.

- *individual inertia.* Individuals were less likely to change if they were comfortable with the old way of doing things and felt the old way was acceptable.

- *history of organisational change.* The willingness to unlearn will be affected by how well the organisation has handled change in the past. Any negative experiences with change in the past will increase the suspicions of the staff and create a barrier that will need addressing.

However, if staff were well prepared prior to the change, had a positive outlook, and understood why the new change was needed, then unlearning was more likely to occur.

There are a number of factors that organisations can use to encourage unlearning. Becker (2007), Becker (2008a & b) and Becker and Hyland (2008) discuss the following:

- *explaining the need for change.* The organisation needs to explain, fully and openly, why the old way needs to be changed and why the organisation decided to use the new way. This information helps staff to understand why the new way is better so that they become less worried about whether the organisation has made the right decision.

- *organisational support and training.* The support mechanisms utilised by the organisation should allow the individual to the chance to unlearn both formally and informally. The support should include:

  - written information that is useful and relevant, able to be readily applied to their jobs, and distributed in time to help the individual to learn the new ways;

  - training sessions that are useful and relevant, give real-life examples, a chance to practice the new ways, and give information that can readily be applied when an individual returns to work.

  - implementing the new ways as soon as possible after the planning stage makes it easier to change to the new ways.

- *continuing support after implementation.* After the new way has been officially implemented, the staff will continue to make judgements on the new way. Initially, they will continue to compare the new and old ways; they may find the new way more difficult for some time. Some staff will take time after the implementation to become used to the new way, so the organisation will need to provide continuing reassurance and support.

- *positive experience and informal support.* Staff with experience in their jobs and with the organisation generally appear to accept changes more readily. This is only true, however, when they have the positive support of their supervisors and colleagues, and providing that their colleagues do not oppose the new way. This element makes the need for organisations to provide organisational support and training critical.

Holistic adult learning

In the past, organisations erred by viewing human resource development merely as instrumental learning. If an organisation's only competitive edge is the speed at which it can learn, then the individual staff member will need to be viewed as a learning entity – a holistic view of the human resource learning process is needed. Figure 3.1 provides an overview of the total entity of a learning adult.

Figure 3.1 Holistic adult learning

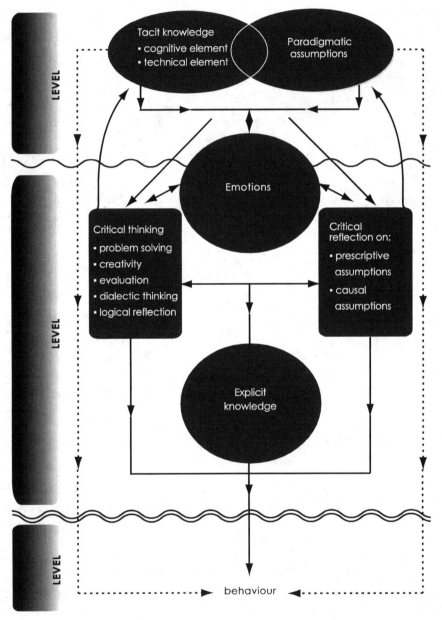

Tacit knowledge and paradigmatic assumptions are held in the subconscious mind of the individual. Further, Nonaka (2002) sees tacit knowledge as involving both cognitive and technical elements. The cognitive elements centre on 'mental models', in which human beings form working models of the world. These mental models include schemata, paradigms and viewpoints that help the individual perceive, define and interact with the world.

The technical element covers concrete knowhow, crafts and skills that apply to specific contexts. These two elements of tacit knowledge – cognitive and technical – combine with paradigmatic assumptions to create a powerful subconscious control. Meyer and Land (2005) call this combination the inter-relatedness of the learner's identity with thinking and language. Both tacit knowledge and paradigmatic assumptions are unarticulated and therefore difficult to define and virtually impossible to measure. The two elements most probably overlap and interact but, with our present knowledge of adult learning, the exact nature of their relationship is not understood. What is now recognised is the power of both these elements of the subconscious mind in the life of the individual. As organisations come to rely more and more on the judgement, knowledge and commitment of people, the ability to provide opportunities for individuals to change, develop and adjust the tacit knowledge and paradigmatic assumptions becomes critically important. The emphasis here is on 'provide opportunities'. While there are definite moral dilemmas for organisations in attempting to manipulate tacit knowledge or paradigmatic assumptions, the change processes are so subtle and difficult it is doubtful that organisations could overtly force any change across a mass of staff.

Case study example

See the PLP case study on page 8 of the workbook that accompanies this text for an example of using tacit knowledge.

Partly in the subconscious level and partly in the conscious, emotions are an element of learning that White Anglo-Saxon Protestant values would prefer to ignore. Yet emotions are a strong intervening variable in all but the most instrumental of learning events. Writers such as Brookfield (2009) recognise that it would be quite unnatural for learners not to experience learning emotionally. He goes on to compare teaching to the educational equivalent of white-water rafting (1990, p. 2) and learning as a gloriously messy pursuit in which surprise, shock and risk are endemic (1990, p. 1). The emotional energy of all stakeholders in a learning event is a powerfully pervasive force which, if ignored, will invariably lead to antipathy at the best or outright rebellion at the worst.

At the higher levels of the conscious mind are the processes of critical thinking and critical reflection. Critical thinking involves the problem-solving processes, creativity, evaluation, dialectic thinking and logical reflection. Critical reflection at the conscious level occurs on the prescriptive and causal assumptions. Critical reflection and critical thinking interact, most probably constantly and vigorously. For example, critical reflection on a prescriptive assumption would almost certainly require problem solving and creativity, and most probably would also involve evaluation and dialectic thinking as well. There could also be occasions, as an individual logically reflects on the critical thinking process, when the individual realises that a causal, prescriptive or even paradigmatic assumption is the real barrier to progress. The individual would then have a choice of critically reflecting on these assumptions. Further, both of these critical thinking and critical reflection processes are influenced by the functions of tacit knowledge, paradigmatic assumptions and the emotions. Critical thinking and critical reflection, in turn, affect explicit knowledge.

These functions and processes in the subconscious and conscious levels, of course, operate within the individual. To a second party, the only evidence of action is in the behaviour of the individual. This behaviour can be influenced by explicit knowledge, the prescriptive or causal assumptions, or by the critical thinking processes – or even a combination of all three. Further, the behaviour of the individual can be directly influenced by his or her paradigmatic assumptions and tacit knowledge.

Holistic adult learning, then, recognises the incredible complexities involved in the learning of adults. Appropriate learning experiences will depend on the nature of the change required and the emotional and motivational forces affecting the individual at the time. This totality of the human learning experience becomes a prime underlying meta-process crucial to the four stages of change: needs investigation, design, implementation and evaluation.

The practical application of adult learning

Adult learning is indeed a complex and intriguing process. Historically, most organisations have viewed human resource development as merely instrumental learning – as procedural training and task-oriented problem solving. This view is based on the belief that learning in organisations is merely the transmission of explicit knowledge from one person to another, the knowledge-generation process of combination. Such a stance presumes that the knowledge being transmitted has an indefinite life and will be suitable for any occasion.

This is partly true for some of the knowledge that is essential to the organisation's continual survival. Equipment that has an expected lengthy production life in a manufacturing company will be operated in a specific manner and needs to be serviced in a certain way at specific periods of time. As new staff are hired to work the equipment they will need to be trained in its safe operation. Instrumental learning is therefore an important component both in organisational learning and in ensuring that the organisation's knowledge capital is passed on to those who can use it to produce income.

However, in today's complex business world, instrumental learning by itself is rarely enough – organisations operate on more than just explicit knowledge. Much of what happens in organisations – decisions judgements, predicting – relies on the tacit knowledge of all the knowledge workers in the organisation. Teaching someone the safe operation of a piece of equipment is often only the start. The belief system of the individual – e.g. that safety is their responsibility – may also need to be changed and this can be achieved only through communicative and emancipatory learning. And such a change is only the start. Most organisations are trying to survive in very competitive and turbulent environments; they are becoming more dependent on staff who accept a wider responsibility – to identify new knowledge that will help the organisation survive. This challenges an even wider paradigmatic assumption than 'safety is my business'. 'The future success of the organisation is also my business' is a paradigmatic assumption that a majority of workers will look at askance. Yet, if organisations are to survive the future, this is the very belief system that is needed.

As a conclusion to this chapter, we will examine two issues that a facilitator of adult learning will need to keep in mind. The first is the time delay that often occurs before full competence occurs. The second is the effect of stress on problem solving and therefore learning.

A time delay

For adults, learning rarely occurs at only one of the instrumental, communicative, or emancipatory levels. More frequently, adult learning occurs at two or even all three levels. Learning for adults is a complex affair. Not surprisingly, learning for adults is not instantaneous – a fact frequently overlooked by managers and supervisors. For adults, this time delay in learning can be depicted as the four steps shown in Figure 3.2.

Figure 3.2 The time delay in learning

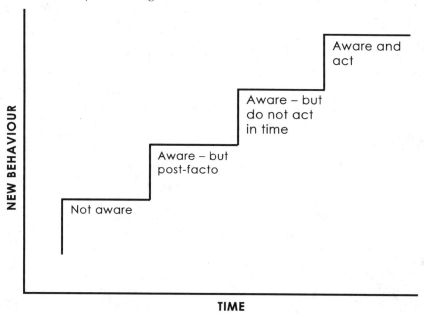

At first, the adult is unaware that learning is needed until some feedback awakens the realisation for a need. Once the realisation that learning is needed is stimulated, the learner rarely acts on this new learning on cue. Often, the feedback occurs again, and after this feedback is received, the learner remembers that a new behaviour was required. Still the learner tends not to implement the new learning. The event occurs again and, simultaneous with the error occurring, the learner remembers the new behaviour that was needed – just too late! Finally, at the fourth step, the learner does undertake the new activity in time to avert the error.

Accepting that this time delay occurs is an important element of being a good facilitator of adult learning. Of course, the time delay experienced will depend on a number of circumstances – the motivation and learning maturity of the learner being the most important. The acceptance of the time delay does require the development of patience on the part of the facilitator and the active use of the learning principles, especially over learning, spaced learning and active learning. The facilitator will also need to use the successive approximations process – using the three-step feedback process:

- identifying what the learner has done correctly;

- identifying one or two changes for the future; and

- suggesting how the changes can be made;

and continuing this three-step process to gradually guide the learner to full and complete accomplishment.

Stress and learning

There appears to be a natural assumption that, when adults are faced with a problem or opportunity, they will automatically engage in problem solving and learning. This situation is true when the stress is at acceptable levels (optimal arousal conditions). However, there is an inverted-U shaped relationship between stress and learning – if the stress is too low then there is little motivation to learn. On the other hand, if the stress is too high, then a different set of circumstances arises.

When under high levels of stress, humans secrete hormones (such as cortisol and noradrenalin) which act on the brain. One effect of this flooding of hormones on the brain is to shut down the working memory part of the brain, such as logical or problem-solving, as well as memory retrieval (see, for example, Arnsten 2009; Tranel *et al.*, 2006). The effect of this is shown in Figure 3.3.

Figure 3.3 The effect of stress on problem solving and learning

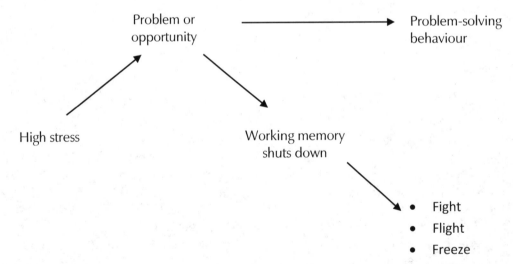

With high levels of stress, logical thinking and memory retrieval shuts down. The adult will then go into one of the three avoidance techniques – fight, flight or freeze.

These avoidance techniques have served humans well over the centuries – there is nothing like a flood of hormones to persuade an individual stay very still in the near presence of a sabre-toothed tiger, or to motivate him to fight or flee.

These avoidance behaviours are less useful in the modern business world but are still incredibly strong. Just being in a training room can be very stressful for some adults –

perhaps because of negative memories from childhood. The message for facilitators of adult learning is to ensure that the learners will only experience reasonable levels of stress, so that the adult is fully engaged in the learning. Some suggestions include:

- ensuring that the learner is moving from the known to the unknown, in reasonably sized steps;

- ensuring that the learning environment is supportive and positive;

- ensuring that the feedback is informational and motivational, using the three-step process;

- looking for behaviours that indicate that a frame of reference is being challenged and then handling the learning process as transformational learning; and

- always being conscious of the time delay in learning.

The four stages of HRD

The concepts of adult learning covered in this chapter should become a consistent theme in the four stages of HRD:

- *the investigation stage,* where the investigatory strategies and tools need to be selected and devised with the level of learning in mind. Survey questionnaires are ideal for instrumental learning, but the interview and focus group are more likely to mine the rich context of communicative and emancipatory learning.

- *the design stage,* where all aspects of adult learning (the basic learning types of behaviour modification and modelling; the principles of learning; rational discourse; and the considerations of challenging a paradigmatic assumption) come together. Undergirding these decisions are the contributions of the knowledge-generation processes of externalisation, combination, internalisation and socialisation.

- *the implementation stage,* where human resource developers must have the skills to use the appropriate learning strategies. Instrumental, communicative and emancipatory learning all demand competence in specific skills and a thorough understanding of the values underpinning each approach.

- *the evaluation stage,* where the circle is completed. The evaluation method used relies heavily on the level of learning. While instrumental learning is more susceptible to cost–benefit analysis and facts and figures, such objective data merely provides gross indicators for communicative and emancipatory learning. For these two deeper levels a more active research strategy is required.

References

Argyris, C. 1999, *On Organizational Learning,* 2nd edn, Blackwell, Cambridge, Mass.

Argyris, C 2008, *Teaching smart people how to learn,* Harvard Business Press, Boston, Mass.

Arnsten, A F 2009, 'Stress signalling pathways that impair prefrontal cortex structure and function', *Nature Reviews Neuroscience,* 10, pp.410-422.

Bandura, A 1977, *Social Learning Theory,* Prentice Hall, New Jersey.

Becker, K L 2007, *Unlearning in the workplace: A mixed methods study*, unpublished doctoral thesis, Queensland University of Technology.

Becker, K L 2008a, 'Unlearning as a driver of sustainable change and innovation: Three Australian case studies', *International Journal of International Management*, 42(1/2), pp. 89-106.

Becker, K L 2008b, 'Fostering unlearning to facilitate change and innovation', in *Academy of Management 2008 Annual Meeting Proceedings – The Questions We Ask*, Anaheim, California.

Becker, K L & Hyland, P 2008, 'Overcoming barriers to innovation by facilitating unlearning', in *Inside the Innovation Matrix*, Australia Business Foundation, North Sydney, NSW.

Berte, N R (ed.) 1975, *New Directions for Higher Education*, Jossey-Bass, San Francisco.

Blakemore, S J & Frith, U 2005, *The Learning Brain*, Blackwell, Oxford

Boden, M A 2004, *The Creative Mind: Myths and Mechanisms*, 2nd edn, Cardinal, London.

Brookfield, S D 1995, *Becoming a Critically Reflective Teacher* Jossey-Bass, San Francisco.

Brookfield, S D 2000, 'Transformative learning as ideology critique' in J Mezirow, (ed.), *Learning as Transformation: Critical Perspectives on a Theory in Progress*, Jossey-Bass, San Francisco.

Brookfield, S D 2009, *The Skilful Teacher: Technique, Trust and Responsiveness in the Classroom*, 2nd edn, John Wiley & Sons, Hoboken..

Corey, G 1991, *Theory and Practice of Counselling and Psychotherapy*, 4th edn, Brooks/Cole, Pacific Grove: California.

Davis, B, Sumara, D J & Luce – Kapler, R 2002, *Engaging minds: Learning and teaching in a complex world*, Erlbaum, Mahwah, New Jersey.

Delahaye, B L & Smith, B J 1998, *How to be an Effective Trainer*, Wiley, New York.

De Simone, R L & Harris, D M 2009, *Human Resource Development*, 5th edn, Harcourt Brace, Fort Worth.

Dewey, J 1910, *How We Think*, D C Heath, New York.

Dewey, J 1938, *Experience and Education*, Capricorn Books, New York.

Ellis, A & Whiteley, J (eds.), 1979, *Theoretical and Empirical Foundations of Rational Emotive Therapy*, Brooks/Cole, Pacific Grove, California.

George, R L & Christiani, T S 1995, *Counselling: Theory and Practice*, 4th edn, Allyn and Bacon, Boston.

Gardner, G, Innes, J M, Forgas, J P, O'Driscoll, M, Pearce, P L & Newton, J W 1981, *Social Psychology*, Prentice Hall, Sydney.

Goldstein, I 2002, *Training in Organisations*, 4th edn, Brooks/Cole, Pacific Grove, California.

Grattan, C H 1955, *In Quest of Knowledge: A Historical Perspective on Adult Education*, Association Press, New York.

Hansen, J C, Rossberg, R H & Cramer, S H 1994, *Counselling: Theory and Process*, 5th edn, Allyn and Bacon, Boston.

Hedberg, B 1981, 'How organisations learn and unlearn', in W H Starbuck & P C Nystrom (eds.), *Handbook of Organisational Design Volume 1*, Oxford University Press, Oxford.

Henschke, J A 2009, *Strengthening a global perspective of andragogy: An update for 2009,* a paper presentation session for the Commission of Professors of Adult Education (CPAE) conference, Cleveland OH, November.

Howe, MJA 1977, *Adult Learning: Psychological Research and Application,* Wiley, Chichester.

Jarvis, P 2010, *Adult Education and Lifelong Learning: Theory and Practice,* Routledge, Milton Park, Oxen.

Klein, J I 1989, 'Parenthetic learning in organizations: Toward the unlearning of the unlearning model', *Journal of Management Studies,* 26(3), pp. 29 1-308.

Knowles, M S 1980, *The Modern Practice of Adult Education: From Pedagogy to Andragogy,* 2nd edn, Cambridge Books, New York:.

Knowles, M S 1998, *The Adult Learner: A Neglected Species,* 5th edn, Gulf, Houston, Texas.

Kolb, D A 1984, *Experiential Learning: Experience as the Source of Learning and Development.* Prentice Hall, Englewood Cliffs, New Jersey.

Labouvie-Vief, G 1985, 'Intelligence and cognition', in J E Birren, & K W Schaie, (eds.), *Handbook of the Psychology of Aging,* 2nd edn, Reinhold, New York.

Lindeman, E C 1926, *The Meaning of Adult Education,* New Republic, New York.

Long, H B 2002, *Teaching for Learning,* Krieger, Malabar, Florida.

Meyer JHF & Land R 2005, 'Threshold concepts and troublesome knowledge: Epistemological considerations and a conceptual framework for teaching and learning', *Higher Education,* 49, pp. 373-388.

McGehee, W & Thayer, P W 1961, *Training in Business and Industry,* Wiley, New York.

Mezirow, J 1990, *Fostering Critical Reflection in Adulthood: A Guide to Transformative and Emancipatory Learning*: Jossey-Bass, San Francisco.

Mezirow, J 1991, *Transformative Dimensions of Adult Learning* Jossey-Bass, San Francisco

Mezirow, J 1994, 'Understanding transformational theory', *Adult Education Quarterly,* Summer, 44(4), pp. 222-32.

Mezirow, J 1996, 'Transformational learning', *Training and Development in Australia,* March, 23(1), pp. 9-12.

Mezirow, J 2000, 'Learning to think like an adult: Core concepts of adult learning theory', in Mezirow, J, (ed.). *Learning as Transformation: Critical Perspectives on a Theory in Progress.* Jossey-Bass, San Francisco.

Mezirow, J 2009, 'Transformative learning theory', in Mezirow, J & Taylor E W (eds.) *Transformational learning in practice: Insights from community, workplace and higher education.* Jossey-Bass, San Francisco.

Miller, G A 1956, 'The magical number seven plus or minus two: Some limits on our capacity for processing information', *Psychological Review,* 63, pp. 81-97.

Myers, I B with Myers, PB 1995, *Gifts Differing,* 3rd edn, Consulting Psychologists Press, Palo Alto, California.

Nonaka, I 1991, 'The knowledge creating company', *Harvard Business Review,* November – December, pp. 96-104.

Nonaka, I 2002, 'A dynamic theory of organizational knowledge creation' in CW Choo, & N Bontis (eds.), *The Strategic Management of Intellectual Capital and Organizational Knowledge* Oxford University Press, New York..

Nonaka, I Takeuchi, H & Umemoto, K 1996, 'A theory of organisational knowledge creation', *International Journal of Technology Management*, 11(7/8), pp. 833-845.

Nonaka, I & Takeuchi, H 1995, *The Knowledge Creating Company: How Japanese Companies Create the Dynamics of innovation*, Oxford University Press, New York..

Nonaka, I & Konno, N 1998, 'The concept of "Ba": Building a foundation for knowledge creation', *California Management Review*, 40(3), Spring, pp. 1-15.

Nonaka, I & von Krogh, G 2009, 'Tacit knowledge and knowledge conversion: Controversy and advancement in organizational knowledge creation', *Organization Science*, 20(3) pp. 635-652.

Perlmutter, M & Hall, E 1992, *Adult Development and Aging*, 2nd edn, Wiley, New York.

Revans, R W 1982, *The Origins and Growth of Action Learning*, Studentlitteratur, Sweden.

Revans, R W 1998, *ABC of Action Learning*, 3rd edn, Lemos & Crane, London.

Rudinow, J & Barry, V E 2007, *Invitation to Critical Thinking*, 6th edn, Cengage Learning, London.

Schon, D A 1983, *The Reflective Practitioner: How Professionals Think in Action*, Basic Books, New York.

Schon, D A 1991, *Educating the Reflective Practitioner: Toward a New Design for Teaching and Learning in the Professions*, 6th edn, Josse-Bass, San Francisco.

Scott, T & Harker, P 2004, *The Myth of Nine to Five: Work, Workplaces and Workplace Relationships*, Thorogood, London.

Sigelman, C K & Shaffer, D R 2009, *Life'-span Human Development*, 6th edn, Brooks/Cole, Pacific Grove, California.

Skinner, B F 1953, *Science and Human Behavior*, MacMillan, New York.

Starbuck, W H 1996, 'Unlearning ineffective or obsolete technologies', *International Journal of Technology Management*, 11(7/8), pp. 725-37.

Stone, R J 2010, *Managing Human Resources*, 3rd edn, Milton, John Wiley & Sons Australia.

Sveiby, K E 1997, *The New Organizational Wealth: Managing and Measuring Knowledge-Based Assets*, Berret Koehier, San Francisco.

Taylor E W 2007, 'An update of transformative learning theory: A critical review of empirical research', *International Journal of Lifelong Learning*, 26(2), pp. 173-191.

Taylor, E W 2009, 'Fostering transformational learning', in J Mezirow, & EW Taylor (eds.), *Transformational learning in practice: Insights from community, workplace and higher education*. Jossey-Bass, San Francisco, CA.

Thorndike, E L 1913, *The Psychology of Learning*, Teacher's College, New York.

Thorndike, E L 1928, *Adult Learning*. MacMillan, New York.

Tovey M D, & Lawlor DR 2008, *Training in Australia*, 3rd edn, Pearson Education Australia, Frenchs Forrest, NSW.

Tranel, D Adolphs, R & Buchanan, TW 2006, Impaired memory retrieval correlates with individual differences in cortisol response but not autonomic response, *Learning & Memory*, (13(3), pp. 382-387.

Watson, J B 1925, *Behaviorism*, Norton, New York..

Zimbardo, P G 2007, *Psychology and Life*, 18th edn, Pearson/Allyn & Bacon, Boston, Mass.

Chapter 4

Individual differences in adult learners

LEARNING OBJECTIVES

After studying this chapter you should be able to:

1. List the disadvantages of ethnocentricity.

2. Explain the benefits of harnessing the power of individual differences.

3. Describe and explain the different individual characteristics of adult learners including age, impairment, gender and cultural backgrounds.

4. Describe the developmental needs of an organisation operating in a global environment.

5. Explain the benefits to the organisation of diversity.

Introduction

The adult population in Australia and New Zealand outnumbers the children. Further, people are living longer; this has two results. First, the adult population will continue to grow in numbers. Second, with differing experiences, each individual adult will refine and develop their personal frame of reference, thus expanding individual differences. In addition, Australia and New Zealand are multicultural societies, and this multiculturalism is reflected in all organisations. Multiculturalism can be defined as an acceptance, without prejudice or discrimination, of cultural differences within an organisation (or even a nation) with full equity for all. Davidson, Simon, Woods and Griffin (2009) suggest that the changing demographics of the contemporary labour market are affected by the broadening of gender roles, the strengthening profile of indigenous people, the higher profile of ethnicity issues, and the growing population of people with disabilities.

These influences of sheer numbers, individual differences, and multiculturalism lead to diversity. For a discussion on diversity and multiculturalism in the workplace see Schermerhorn *et al.* (2011, pp. 47-52).

Ethnocentricity

Ethnocentricity is one of the biggest restraints on constructively mobilising the asset of diversity and individualism in organisations. Ethnocentricity is the belief in the intrinsic superiority of one's own cultural norms. Unfortunately, this belief is often accompanied by feelings of paternalism, or even dislike and contempt, for other groups.

A process that often accompanies ethnocentricism is stereotyping. *Stereotypes* are developed through generalisations which are often based on prejudice, and which often result in discrimination (Davidson *et al.* 2009). Stereotyping can be negative (for example, all males lack feelings) or positive (for example, all Africans are good at sports). All stereotypes lack accuracy and can impede learning.

Both ethnocentricity and stereotyping may have been useful in ancient times when insecurity and local warfare were the norm, but neither has any place in multicultural societies such as Australia and New Zealand. In the organisational sphere, ethnocentricity and stereotyping are typified by discrimination and harassment. Discrimination is the unfair treatment of an individual or a minority group based on some prejudice. Harassment is a particular form of discrimination designed to humiliate, offend, intimidate or otherwise make a person feel unwelcome or inadequate. Sexual harassment may be direct (e.g. the expectation of performing a sexual behaviour to gain a benefit) or indirect (e.g. using sexually explicit material or nudity on an overhead transparency). Harassment is a particularly insidious and nasty type of discrimination; it is illegal in Australia, New Zealand, and many other countries.

It should also be noted that, in New Zealand and Australia, an employer will be held legally responsible if an employee harasses or discriminates against another. Harassment and discrimination have their basis in fear – fear of not understanding the other person's beliefs, fear of looking a fool, or fear that the other person is better is some way and will pose a threat. Such reactions are not acceptable in today's society – rather diversity and individual differences should be celebrated. For a deeper discussion on the legal issues surrounding discrimination and harassment see Chapter 18 'Managing Diversity' in Stone (2010).

Celebrating individual differences

Adult learners differ on a number of characteristics; these very differences being a rich source of creativity, breadth of knowledge, and problem-solving potential. Accordingly, organisations need an organisational culture that celebrates differences among its people. Individual differences offer organisations an unprecedented opportunity to ensure creativity and viability. This very diversity of backgrounds, cultures, ways of knowing, and views of the world provides an almost limitless supply of options and perceptions.

Organisations must be careful that the potential of this energy is harnessed so that every challenge and threat faced by the organisation will be fully examined and objectively analysed to make certain that the most feasible alternative actions are taken to ensure the organisation's future. As Stone (2010) comments, such organisations can gain a competitive advantage whereby employee differences present opportunities to:

- improve staff management practices;

- alter the workplace and work practices in ways which increase efficiency and safety;

- make products and facilities more accessible to and appropriate for clients and customers; and

- identify new products, services, and markets.

Davidson *et al.* (2009) present six arguments to demonstrate how diversity contributes to competitiveness. Organisations that manage diversity well have higher levels of productivity and lower levels of turnover and absenteeism, leading to:

- cost advantages;

- a reputation among women and minority groups as good places to work;

- advantages in acquiring qualified staff from these groups;

- a marketing advantage resulting from being better able to understand different market segments;

- greater creativity and innovation;

- an increased pool of information, giving a higher probability of realistic problem solving; and

- greater systems flexibility resulting from the need to manage a diverse workforce. This systems flexibility allows organisations to respond more appropriately and quickly to environmental changes.

As Theophanous (1994) argues, social justice and economic growth can be complementary if both are pursued in such a way that the capacity to do both is maximised.

For the HR developer, then, the first step in helping the organisation to manage its diversity, achieve social justice and economic growth, is to acknowledge the differences between adult learners. Further, in a dynamic organisation, creative leadership positively values differences (Scott & Harker 2004).

The characteristics of adult learners

Adult learners differ on a number of characteristics. Problems in learning and knowledge generation occur when social constructions of what is right and wrong are projected into learning episodes by those with power. This, of course, comes back to the personal frames of reference of those powerbrokers. Powerbrokers may be within the organisation (e.g. managers) or outside the organisation (e.g. union officials). So what is seen as 'true' learning by certain powerbrokers in an organisation may be contaminated by the very personal characteristics that those powerbrokers hold dear.

The HR developer as the *designer* of the learning programs is one of the internal powerbrokers. In Chapter 9, it is suggested that the designer of adult learning experiences becomes very familiar with his or her personal frame of reference and how this frame of reference may contaminate the design process. The HR developer as the *implementer* is another role where power can be used with undue influence (e.g. ignoring certain learners during the learning episode).

For the HR developer, the diversity in individual differences is both a dynamic opportunity and professional challenge. There is the opportunity for HR developers to harness the energy and the challenge of using their professional skills and knowledge to explore and meld the variety of values, knowledge and historical wisdoms – wisdom that has been honed over the millennia as the various national cultures absorbed and learned their lessons from history.

For HRD, the literature identifies age, impairment, gender, and cultural backgrounds as characteristics within adult and organisational learning that are vulnerable to social constructions and personal values. Basic hegemonic assumptions (see Chapter 3) by powerbrokers about any of these characteristics – for example, younger people learn more quickly than older people or that people from certain racial backgrounds learn differently – can inhibit, interfere with, or contaminate learning to an extraordinary degree.

Age

Adult educators interact with learners of the widest age range. Generally, the literature assumes that adulthood commences at approximately 18 years and continues into the eighties and nineties. This wide age range brings with it a variety of issues to be considered by the HR developer. There are two issues that are particularly worthy of understanding:

- the stages in an adult life cycle; and
- the impact of historical events on an adult learner's expectations.

The stage models

Authors such as Levinson and Levinson (1996) and Sheehy (1995) suggest that adults move through a series of age-related stages in their life cycle. Each of these stages relates to particular needs and represents a transition in the adult's outlook and behaviours. In general, these stages start with the late teens and early twenties where young adults search for meaning in their lives. The mid-twenties to the mid-thirties are focused on raising a family and security. The mid-thirties to mid-forties are often seen as a time of crisis when the adult questions his or her life achievements thus far, and perhaps opts for a different career direction. In the fifties, the adult is coming to terms with personal mortality; and the late sixties are seen as the years of contentment, or sorrow for lost opportunities.

While each of these *stage models* appears to have some face validity, the research on which the concepts are based has been criticised for concentrating on white, male, middle-class subjects. Certainly, not every adult conforms to these sequences. Many adults meet life-changing circumstances – perhaps ill health or losing a life partner – that necessitate attention to other needs and wants. Further, the recent literature on the X-generation and the Y-generation indicates that age groups may have different agendas than those suggested by the stage models (see, for example, Gozzi 1995; Howe & Strauss 1993; Lankard 1997; Martin & Tulgan 2001).

However, a sufficient proportion of the adult population conforms to the suggested stages for the HR developer to make some initial (albeit gross) assumptions. Those who are in long-term relationships and who have children are often searching for security, and some find this security in accumulating career-related knowledge and skills. By their mid-thirties, a number of adults are looking at career changes and may need assistance in identifying possibilities and knowledge-based resources. Staff in their late fifties are often a wealth of knowledge, and this knowledge should be accessed as an important knowledge silo (see Chapter 15) for the management of knowledge capital.

Historical embeddedness

Baltes (1987) has suggested that the critical historical moments experienced by an individual may affect the perception of that individual. Historical moments are those events that were important to large societies at a particular time; they are differentiated from those events that were more individual. An historical moment may have been the war in Vietnam, the death of Princess Diana, the 11 September 2001 terrorist attacks in the US, or the Bali nightclub bombings. As such, these momentous occasions have often affected significant proportions of the population of a particular age and influenced their outlook on certain organisationally initiated learning episodes. For example, the suspect actions of lending institutions that led to the recent global financial crisis may generalise into distrust of the concepts of financial management by some staff over the age of twenty.

The HR developer needs to consider these historical moments when interacting with adult learners. First, the historical moment may have had an indelible effect on the frame of reference of the adult learner; this indelible effect may have been positive or negative. For example, a question relating to federal government decisions asked during a needs investigation may bring what appears to be an irrational, negative response from a Vietnam War veteran. This information needs to be treated with care and confidentiality. Second, those who have experienced an historical moment may have a wealth of knowledge that can be shared with other learners. When relevant, the HR developer should look for opportunities to tap into such a rich tapestry of information.

Older learners

Most developed countries (including Australia and New Zealand), are facing structured aging. Structured aging results from the combined effects of increased longevity and reduced fertility (Chappell *et al.* 2004). In Australia over the next 40 years, for example, growth of the workforce is expected to slow almost to zero, while the population of those over 65 will almost double (Foster, 2008).

As the workforce increasingly matures, retaining employees with critical skills, creating career paths to help senior employees break out of career plateaus, and retraining senior employees whose skills have become outdated and require further development, will pose special challenges for organisations (Beaver & Hutchings 2005). Yet few organisations have recognised this critical threat, and fewer still have moved beyond mere lip service to meeting the challenge. As Armstrong-Stassen & Templer (2005) found, most organisations have a long way to go towards the full utilisation and development of their older employees.

Some of the key barriers to adult participation in learning and development, though, are the negative stereotypes about their abilities to learn and their worth in the workplace. Additionally, older employees may lack confidence, have low self-esteem, and be less likely to see that they will gain sufficient return from an investment in training and education (Foster 2008).

Bennington and Tharenou (1998) have refuted a number of stereotypes about the older learner by finding that they do not have memory loss, declining intelligence, lower performance, or less creativity. The older learner can keep abreast of change and new knowledge. Patrickson (2003) points out that those now aged over 50 tend to have a high level of computer literacy, are more accustomed to re-skilling and multi-skilling, and have had to come to terms with flexible usage of labour. Further, they have matured in a climate of multiculturalism and are therefore very aware of workforce diversity issues. Because of their rich experience and extensive backgrounds in the technical aspects of the tasks, they are valuable reservoirs of knowledge. The ageing workforce, then, presents organisations with numerous challenges that will become more pronounced over the next several decades (Hedge 2010).

One key challenge is in adjusting learning designs and strategies and creating supportive environments to meet the needs, preferences, and learning styles of the older learners. When designing learning experiences for older adults, Delahaye and Ehrich (2008) suggest that three factors should be considered:

- The *presage factors* present prior to the learning experience. Some hurdles that are frequently reported as facing older learners include increased anxiety, perhaps caused by fear of rejection; fear or dislike of learning because of negative experiences while at school; strong frames of reference; and a preference for planning and controlling their own lives, rather than entrusting them to a stranger.

- Several elements should be present in the *learning environment* for older learners, including having a similar aged cohort; a supportive climate that is safe, nonthreatening and less formal; and a preference for peer support, mentoring and tutoring.

- They will engage in *complex learning processes*, using their own judgement in selecting appropriate learning options. They will switch from being *dependent learners* (with one-on-one mentoring and structured formal and informal learning) to being *independent learners* by 'having a go by themselves', actively reflecting on experiences, using failure as feedback process, and practicing in private. This rapid switching of learning processes is often supported by *passively seeking knowledge* by standing back and watching, on the one hand, and *actively seeking knowledge* by assertively controlling their learning and using social interactions purposively on the other.

A closer look 4.1

Older but wiser: by Brent Jones

Organisations both public and private have been busy looking into the social and economic impacts of the ageing workforce. With nothing less than the future prosperity of the nation at stake, the aim has been to identify the trends and predict their long-term implications.

Now the time has come to get specific. Progressive organisations must go beyond broad discussions and look closely at their own operations. They need to form strategies for securing continuing supplies of skilled labour in the medium to long term in an increasingly competitive market. Those that act now will stand a better chance of being well placed to take advantage of business opportunities that open up as populations around the world age in a globalising marketplace.

The number of young people entering the Australian workforce annually has fallen significantly, and this will escalate. Retention of older workers has become a primary strategy for averting labour and skills shortages, and for limiting ballooning health and welfare costs. Understanding exactly what the ageing population will mean for a particular organisation is a complex, demanding task, and its relevance may not be immediately clear. Each organisation will need to look at its own circumstances, conduct research, analyse data, hold discussions with stakeholders, and plot the course best suiting its needs.

A lot of questions will have to be asked, including:

- How will we be affected by the projected labour supply and market conditions?

- What is the business case for age diversity and the continuing employment of older workers, and what benefits can they bring to the organisation?

- What messages need communicating to ensure that all employees understand the necessity for recruiting, developing and retaining workers as they age?

- Does our organisation's age profile reflect that of the broader working population?

- How well are we managing age balance and do we stereotype older workers?

- Do the older workers we already have feel positive about their work and status?

- Are our management practices adapting to the demands of an ageing workforce, and what areas need improvement?

- How do we implement required changes across the organisation?

- How do we compare with other organisations?

- How do we develop a global age-management plan?

Human resource management professionals will play a major role in helping organisations to answer these questions and find ways to manage workforces as they age. It will be a challenge, but it is a unique opportunity to demonstrate the contribution they can make to both the financial and social wellbeing of their organisations and the nation as a whole.

HR professionals are well equipped to meet the challenge. Research shows that HRM areas such as recruitment, learning and development, and health and safety have a major impact on older workers and their attitude to work. There is a strong case for the immediate creation of a special professional development program to give HR practitioners leading-edge knowledge and skills in managing an ageing workforce.

Source: *HR Monthly*, February 2004, pp. 34–5.

Youth learners

Recent research has focused on the differences between adult and youth learning. Choy and Delahaye (2003) found that youth learners had a tendency to have a:

- preference for the 'feel good' elements of self-directed learning, such as having a friendly and adult relationship with their educators, but did not want the responsibility of deciding what should be learned or how it should be learned;

- respect for the credibility of their teachers or facilitators, especially the depth of their knowledge of a topic;

- belief that gaining credentials is one of the most important outcomes of learning; and

- perception of themselves as complex wholes and that formal learning is only one of the roles in their lives. The other two important roles were their social life and part-time work.

Adult educators, involved in facilitating the learning experiences of youth, would need to take these perceptions into account when designing learning experiences. This topic will be discussed further in Chapter 10.

With governments in both New Zealand and Australia stressing the importance of vocational education, there is an emphasis on apprenticeship training and most apprentices are in their teens. This very fact will bring HR developers and organisations into direct contact with learners between the ages of 15 and 25 years, and mean that they will be more involved in vocational education and training (VET) initiatives.

However, there is some debate over the definition of adulthood. Some people would suggest that the age of 21 years defines the beginning of adulthood and others, referring to the right to vote in Australia, would argue for the age of 18 years. Some researchers in adult learning suggest that the age separation should begin at 24 years. Hall and Brier (2007) report that, during the last decade, research on adolescent brain development has produced insights into adolescent behaviours. Neural transformation takes place during the teen years – particularly in the prefrontal cortex, the cerebellum and the limbic cortex – and this means that young adults are still maturing in the areas alertness, attention, planning, working memory and regulating emotional and impulse control. Hall and Brier (2007) suggest that youth learners should be defined as those between the ages of 17 and 25.

Accordingly, several writers (e.g. Brady & Kennedy 2003, Kasworm 1989, Lankard 1997 and Martin & Tulgan 2001) have suggested that youth may benefit by being considered as learners who demonstrate some different needs to children or adults. The debate often focuses on the different values of the so called Generation X, Generation Y and the millennial generation.

Choy (2000) and Choy and Delahaye (2001, 2003), as a general view, argue that youth learners present the following characteristics:

- They tend to be surface learners with a low readiness for self-directed learning. Surface learners tend to use simple learning strategies such as rote learning and do not search for a deep understanding of the topic. Surface learners are usually driven by utility motivation, for example, learning just to pass the subject or competency.

- They will tend to enjoy the 'feel good' aspects of informal learning in the workplace, but prefer not to have the responsibility for making decisions on what should be learned and how such learning should be assessed.

- Generally they respect the professional knowledge of the instructor (for example, the trainer or the college lecturer) and therefore prefer that their instructor be responsible for, and in charge of, the learning.

- They perceive that learning (especially in an educational institution) is only one part of their life world. Two other significant roles in their lives are their social life and work. They perceive themselves as being complex wholes, not defined by one role or another. This perception clashes with the typical stance of learning institutions that often assume being a student is the only role for youth.

- There is a pragmatic recognition of credentialism among youth. They recognise that they must gain qualifications to gain employment. Concurrently, they also recognise the importance of gaining work experience to complement their qualifications. This provides further justification for the role of being a part-time worker.

- They are quite critical of formal learning institutions that claim to operate under self-directed learning assumptions, yet structure learning experiences based on traditional teaching practices and use assessment that rewards easily measured explicit knowledge.

To increase self responsibility, educators can address the adolescent cognitive issues of planning and organising by providing some scaffolding to assist in learning – for example, maintain firm due dates, allow them to experience negative consequences so that the importance of planning sinks in, keep a handy record of assignments and class activities, provide specific note taking, and provide process management techniques (see Chapter 11) to encourage development rather than providing content answers (Hall & Brier 2007). For addressing adolescent emotional issues, these authors go on to recommend that the learning facilitator:

- models calm, stabilising behaviour;

- develops curiosity by encouraging students to create hypotheses and choose their own project topics; and

- focuses on the positive and on what can be done to improve difficult situations.

Youth learners will present a special challenge to HR developers – whether the HR developer is a trainer, a community educator, a supervisor in the workplace or a lecturer in a university. Recognise, however, that the characteristics discussed above are a generalisation. Some youth learners, for example, will be attracted towards self-directed learning. Alternatively, some adult learners will conform exactly to the profile of the youth learner. As usual, individual differences will have to be taken into account when designing learning experiences.

A closer look 4.2

School-to-work transition

In both New Zealand and Australia, educational authorities and employers are focusing on the advantages of undertaking school-to-work development programs. Such programs encourage a seamless transition for youth to move from the familiar environment of school to the unknown environment of the workplace. These programs provide the youth with 'whole body learning' (see Chapter 3) about the values and expectations of the working world. The school students can make worthwhile comparisons with their present life style and gradually prepare for the changes that may be required. From the employers' point of view, the school leavers assimilate more readily into work life, are often already trained in the generic attributes such as communication and team work and need less direct supervision.

In Australia and New Zealand, this school-to-work transition has been introduced and supported by the new apprenticeship schemes where, in the last two years of their school life, students commence apprenticeships and traineeships, and spend one or two days each week at work.

Impairment

In Australia and New Zealand, with their well-developed health systems, good health is usually taken for granted. Indeed, good health is often assumed to be a prerequisite for attendance at voluntary or paid employment. Such a utopian view is not, however, entirely correct. In both Australia and New Zealand, nearly one in five people have some form of disability. 'Impairment' is the term used in legislation to cover the variety of disabilities – either mental or physical – that can present a challenge to an individual in the working or learning environment.

As people age, certain biological changes occur. These changes can have an impact on health. Senses, particularly sight and hearing, often deteriorate in middle age. Reaction times on physical or motor skills may not be as fast as they once were. The incidence of other debilitating conditions, such as arthritis and cardiovascular disease, may increase with age. Of course, health impairments may become manifest at an earlier age. Loss of sight, hearing, mobility, or other abilities may occur at birth or can be caused at any age by disease or accidents. Some refugees who have taken up residence may have endured torture and abuse before coming to Australia or New Zealand, and now experience debilitating anxiety and stress. Yet many people with these impairments or disabilities are still very active and productive members of the workforce.

While medical and technological advances have provided some corrective measures for these impairments, learning can still be a challenge because of health-related limitations. The HR developer must help the learner meet these challenges so that the important role of learning – important to the individuals and the organisation – can continue.

Gender

It is hard to imagine that a little over 50 years ago, married women were not allowed to work in the federal public service. In addition, women were paid less than their male counterparts for performing exactly the same jobs. A number of other large organisations of that time had similar policies. Such policies had negative emotional and financial effects on many individuals and families.

One puzzling feature was that organisations with such discriminating policies did not recognise the extraordinary opportunities lost because they were essentially only tapping one half of the possible employment pool. These days, while there is still some distance to travel for complete equity, notable advances have been made. Women now have a significant presence in the professions and in higher educational institutions.

However, there are still serious concerns over the limited representation of women in the upper levels of management in all industries. In New Zealand, despite a 50 percent participation rate, 60 of the top 100 NZX companies have no women on their boards (New Zealand Management, 2009). In Australia, women comprise only eight percent of board directorships and only one in ten of executive management positions (Ham 2010) and the average gender pay gap was 12 percent (Hartevelt 2008). In New Zealand, the 2001 census showed that 40 percent of the 'administrative, managers and legislative' were women. However, the pattern of vertical sex integration remains resistant to change with only three percent of CEOs in the top 200 private sector being women (Olsson & Pringle 2004). Further, as Bern (1993) comments, males and male experiences are seen as the norm or standard, and female and *other sexual orientations* are viewed as a sex-specific deviation from that norm – and this stance is still relatively common in organisations today.

Interest in feminist pedagogy has focused attention on the concerns of women in the teaching–learning interaction. Merriam, Caffarella and Baumgartner (2007) initially categorised the perspectives on oppression and empowerment of women in adult learning into two groups – liberatory models and gender models. The *liberatory models* highlight the structures and systems in society and organisations that oppress through power and control. Of particular concern is how these structures and systems are reflected in the learning episodes of the organisation; they may consist of reproduction (e.g. males dominating classroom discussions) or resistance (e.g. females shunning developmental opportunities because of the psychological discomfort of operating in a male-dominant learning environment).

The *gender models* emphasise the emancipatory process as the individual becomes free from hegemonic assumptions (see Chapter 3) about the role of being a female learner. In this model, a connected approach to learning is advocated, where life experiences are valued, where a woman can have a voice and, hence, an identity. Merriam *et al.* (2007) now recommend a synthesis of both the liberatory and gender models may be the best approach. For an in-depth discussion of feminist pedagogy see Belenky, Clinchy, Goldberger and Tarule (1997), Hart (1992), Merriam *et al.* (2007) and Tisdell (1995).

Knights (1995) proposes at least three points that should be of concern to HR developers when considering female learners in an organisation.

- HR developers need to look beyond learning processes that accentuate competitive debate and 'objective' truth. Learning that features authentic understanding and relations and connectedness (see communicative learning in Chapter 3) with others should also be emphasised. These learning processes that emphasise relations and connectedness are often referred to as the relational models (see Brown & Gilligan 1992).

- HR developers need to recognise that women who have been away from the workforce for a period of time (for example, being engaged in child rearing) may not have the technical qualifications or the confidence to engage in organisational development activities. Specific action is needed to support and develop women in these situations.

- With women still bearing the brunt of home management duties, difficulties can arise with attendance at organisational development activities, particularly at residential workshops or during after-school periods. Again, the HR developer needs to ensure that other developmental alternatives are available.

'Gender' was deliberately chosen as the heading for this section so that the debate on individual differences and diversity might include homosexuality, bisexuality and trans-sexuality. That people with a different sexual orientation may view knowledge and learning from a different perspective than that advanced by the dominant male narrative has rarely been considered in human resource development or in adult education. As Hill (1995) has pointed out, the disenfranchisement of other sexual orientations that starts in preparatory schooling continues through all levels of adult education; Ellis (2008) contends that, while homophobia is not an overwhelming problem on campuses, it is still a significant one. There is very limited reported research on other sexual orientation learning preferences, although D'Augelli (1994) provides a solid starting point for such research. The liberatory and gender models also provide a reasonable starting point for understanding the learning challenges and processes of adult learners with other sexual orientations.

However, as Burnett (2003) points out, homophobia is the dominant factor inhibiting the learning of gays and lesbians. Unfortunately, homophobia is often seen as the last acceptable form of bigotry within our society. Burnett (2003) further points out that people with other sexual orientations often feel disconnected from those around them, often experiencing a 'splitting of self'. They are attempting to deal not only with issues of peer pressure, sexuality and personal identity, but also with a society that fears and rejects them. While lesbian, gay, bisexual, and transgender individuals may not be identified easily, the adult educator still has a demonstrable responsibility to ensure that such learners are not victimised nor stigmatised. As Burnett (2003) emphasises, educators have a duty of care to all learners in their care.

The HR developer must analyse the gender roles within the learning environment, first to ensure that power either from individuals or from organisational structures and systems does not interfere in any way with the individual and organisational learning processes; and second, to question the nature and the construction of the knowledge being covered in both the formal and informal learning episodes that occur within the organisation. For further reading on gender issues see Hunter (1992), Kim (2009), Smith and Hutchinson (1995) and Pierce and Delahaye (1998).

Cultural backgrounds

Any discussion of culture is vexed by differing definitions and by confusions with race, religion and ethnicity. In New Zealand and Australia, there has also been an increasing interest in cultural identity and a resurgence of cultural politics. While this resurgence has created a healthy awareness of multiculturalism, discussion of culture can also be confused by political agendas where varying groups push particular viewpoints to gain a political or economic advantage. In addition, culture should not be considered as only a national affair. In South-East Asia, for example, religion is taken very seriously, religious creeds being a way of life with beliefs transcending national boundaries. Culture, then, is a multifaceted construct; uni-dimensional interpretations should be avoided, particularly as culture is a changing and dynamic phenomenon (compare, for example, the Australia and New Zealand of the 1950s with their current states).

However, despite these enigmas, the literature does provide some guidance through the maze. Noe (2009) sees culture as the set of assumptions group members share about the world and how it works and establishes the ideals worth striving for; Triandis (2004) suggests that culture imposes a set of lenses for seeing the world so that individuals select, interpret and process information to act in an established manner. This is a similar interpretation to that of Mezirow (1990) who includes culture as a construct of the individual's frame of reference (see Chapter 3). As Hall (1989) points out, culture is not innate, but is learned by the individual and, by being shared within a group, defines the boundaries of values and thus behaviours. To provide a more specific understanding, this text will concentrate on what Gudykunst and Kim (2005) refer to as an 'intercultural' interpretation – where a person from one culture is experiencing life in a different culture.

Gudykunst (2004) contends that the most useful frameworks of culture are those which examine the low-context/high-context styles of communication and the individualist–collectivist constructs. In *low-context cultures,* primacy is given to the content of the message in any communication (Hall 1989). Being direct and linear is valued so that 'what' is said is more important than 'how' it is said (i.e. being 'up-front' and clear). The mass of information is explicit and purposeful.

In *high-context cultures,* the content of the message is downgraded and the situational context – how the message is said, the nonverbals, what is not said, the overall theme of the communication episode and even the relationship between the participants – is most consequential (Hall 1989). In high-context communications, the relational interaction surmounts the actual wording, so literal interpretations of wording are of diminished importance. In high-context cultures, there is a greater distinction between insiders and outsiders. Further, low-context cultures tend to change faster than high-context cultures.

Hofstede (2005) has suggested that cultures differ on an individualist–collectivist continuum. *Individualist cultures* prize self-reliance, creativity, independence, solitude, and equality (Triandis 2004). The individual is encouraged to self-actualise and use her or his own judgement, even when it is in contention with societal norms. In *collectivist cultures* individual goals defer to group goals. Characteristics of reciprocity (what one does for another, the other reciprocates), humility, harmony, dependence, and proper action are honoured (Triandis 2004). Behaviour for pleasure is subordinated to social norms and duty defined by the group, and readiness to cooperate with the group is fundamental.

The western-influenced societies of Australia and New Zealand have low-context, individualist cultures. This is not to say that there is a homogeneous entity in Australia or New Zealand, but there is a tendency for self-reliance, competitiveness, the attainment of individual goals, creativity and action to be valued highly. These values tend to be reflected in our educational systems and in the learning processes used within organisations. The challenge for the HR developer is to recognise the deep bearing that a culture may have on a specific learner or group of learners. For example, indigenous Australians have a profound respect for their elders, and learners from many South-East Asian countries have a high regard for authority. Also, in South-East Asia 'face communication' equates with the Western concept of self-esteem, so that 'losing face' is the same as losing self-esteem, which can impede learning. Expectations that such learners will indulge in active debate with the trainer or teacher in front of class will ultimately cause confusion and disappointment for both parties.

As a starting point, HR developers should not automatically assume that learners will conform to the low-context–individualist behaviours and cues. First, even within the individualist orientations of the Australian and New Zealand cultures, there exist elements of collectivism. For example, individuals from certain rural locations, or from within industry groups, often have similar views on life. Second, if the learning episode to be designed or conducted will include learners from differing cultures, then the HR developer will need to investigate and understand the mores and ethics of those cultures before designing or implementing the learning experience. For further information see Bempechat and Ellicott (2002), Brislin and Yoshida (1994), Hofstede (2005), Holton and Hedrick (1990) and Thorpe, Edwards and Hanson (1986). For learning issues of adults with non-English-speaking backgrounds (NESB) see Federation of Ethnic Communities Councils of Australia (FECCA) (1996).

We will now discuss the cultural backgrounds of two groups of people important to Australia and New Zealand – the indigenous Australians and the Maoris. The reader should note that the following two sections were written by a non-indigenous person attempting to understand and value the complexities involved.

Indigenous Australian learners

Non-indigenous HR developers should seek the advice of indigenous communities and elders when planning, designing and implementing learning programs for indigenous adults. A very good article to read is Boyd (2010). This article describes the experiences of a number of companies, including Rio Tinto, the Mantra Group and Theiss, with the recruitment, selection and career development of indigenous Australian adults.

Indigenous Australians are the Aboriginal and Torres Strait Islander people. While sometimes erroneously regarded as a homogenous group, there is a great diversity between these people – socially, culturally, and linguistically – at both macro and local levels. One of the key messages of the following paragraphs is the need to gain a clear understanding of the importance of the local communities and the links with the land, spiritual beliefs, and class.

Garvey, Rolfe, Pearson & Treloar (2009) believe that issues for adult indigenous learners are likely to be similar to those experienced by non-indigenous learners. It is important to note, however, that these issues may be exacerbated by the learners' educational background, race, and experience of discrimination, cultural background and language barriers. The issues provide a salient basis for the design and implementation of learning experiences for adult indigenous Australians.

As Jorgensen, Grootenboer, Niesche & Lerman (2010) point out, for too long there has been a reliance on two customary approaches of pedagogical design. The first, the deficit model of learning, is based on the assumption that indigenous learners bring very limited knowledge to the learning experience. The second, the ethno-educational approach, occurs when the curriculum takes an indigenous activity and searches for the 'western' knowledge within that activity. Both of these approaches have been found to be ineffective and inappropriate, as such approaches reinforce the high status of western knowledge while subjugating the indigenous activity. The learning curriculum must be developed by respecting and recognising Aboriginal culture and customs (Byrne, 1993).

A third strategy is therefore needed. This strategy is called variously the *bicultural approach*, the *two-way learning method* and the *indigenous standpoint theory*. In the bicultural approach, both the western and indigenous ways of knowing are recognised as legitimate, coming together to the benefit of both cultures. As Miller (2005) asserts, indigenous and western bodies of knowledge and ways of learning are equally relevant.

When some suggestions by Byrnes (1993), Clapham (1999), and Miller (2005) to improve indigenous adult learning are examined, we can see a variety of underlying commonalities between the indigenous ways of learning and the western ways of learning (see Chapter 3). It is interesting to note that, while some of these learning approaches have only been used by western cultures in the last 50 years, they have been part of Australian indigenous culture for centuries.

Table 4.1 Commonality between indigenous Australian and western ways of learning

Indigenous	Western
Students should be given time and space to take in and process information	The principles of learning of *part learning* and *spaced learning*
Information should be presented in a variety of ways, including audio-visual resources	The principle of learning of *multiple sense learning*
The past experience of Aboriginal learners must be the basis for further development	The principle of learning of *starting with the unknown*
The resources provided must enable students to assess their own learning needs	The principle of learning of *feedback*
Flexible training programs that are able to evolve and change with community development goals, and are evaluated according to their relevance and effectiveness for communities	The *andragogical* approach
Using demonstrations	See *the skill session* in Chapter 10

Clapham (1999) goes on to emphasise that the building up of self-esteem is important, and Byrne (1993) discusses the importance of the teacher being a learner as well as a teacher – continually evaluating the learning processes, planning and responding as the lesson progresses rather than sticking to a pre-arranged plan, and encouraging group work and self-directed learning. Again, the western concepts of andragogical assumptions discussed in Chapter 3 are evident here; they are worth repeating:

- the learning should be relevant to the real-life situations and problems of the learner;

- the learning should incorporate the rich experience of the adult learners, thus utilising that abundant resource, the tacit knowledge of the adult; and

- the learning should involve the adult learner, at least to some extent, so that the individual's sense of self-responsibility ensures that the learning is transferred back to the operational site.

The unstructured learning strategies discussed in Chapter 11 move a long way towards satisfying the requirements of Byrne (1993) and Clapham (1999). So, in some ways, some western philosophies of adult learning are relevant to indigenous learning. Perhaps the divide is not as daunting as first envisaged.

The western contribution to indigenous learning, however, only scratches the surface when designing and implementing learning episodes for adult indigenous Australians. The Aboriginal terms of reference, values, and beliefs provide the critical and foundational platform of learning for indigenous adults. Clapham (1999) believes that the indigenous way of knowing is more holistic and more esoteric, and will use social, historical and cultural (including the recognition of supernatural forces) as the key basis for learning.

Garvey *et al.* (2009) point out that the individualised emphasis of western learning may be significantly different from the indigenous experiences of learning which occurs in a community-oriented setting of family, extended family, and community. Further, the knowledge required to operate in Aboriginal society is spiritual knowledge together with an interlinked understanding of the social position of the indigenous learner and their complex obligations. Finally, the centrality of the elders in indigenous knowledge is fundamental to the success of any learning experience. Elders are seen as the as the only true repositories of knowledge; and they give status to knowledge by imparting it to others (Byrne 1993).

The research by Jorgensen *et al.* (2010) highlights the importance of conducting a needs investigation before designing a learning experience for indigenous adult learners. However, as Lloyd and Norrie (2004) comment, such a process is only effective when the various parties share common world views (the communicative learning discussed in Chapter 3). So, while Chapter 5 discusses the skills and processes of HRD needs investigation, more will be needed when designing learning experiences for indigenous learners. Miller (2005) suggests that this should start with an understanding of individuals' backgrounds, their needs and aspirations, and then negotiate course content and delivery around these foundations.

Nearly three decades ago, Trudgen (1983) suggested that non-indigenous facilitators of learning (that would include most HR developers) need to become learners from Aboriginal people before they will be able to impart non-Aboriginal concepts effectively to Aboriginal people. So the HR developer will need to:

- become immersed in the culture and achieve a deep understanding of the beliefs of the indigenous people who will be trainees – for example, not looking someone in the eye may be considered shifty by a 'mainstream' Australian but for many indigenous Australians it is the height of politeness (Boyd 2010);

- engage genuinely with the elders to examine ways in which the non-indigenous knowledge can be incorporated into the indigenous culture, and also to identify the active part that the elders can play in the learning experience;

- identify ways to ensure that the new knowledge will not threaten the local indigenous culture;

- when the new learning is incorporated into the local indigenous culture, identify ways that the new skills and knowledge can be migrated back into the western world (for the example, a mine site) where the skills and knowledge will be used; and

- identify ways to overcome the negative experiences adult indigenous learners may have had in their previous education (for a discussion on the history of Aboriginal education, see Reynolds 2009).

For further discussion on indigenous Australians learners, please see the following:

Closing the gap on indigenous disadvantage: The challenge for Australia, 2009 (viewed 30/04/2009), Department of Families, Housing, Community Services and Indigenous Affairs Canberra, Commonwealth of Australia at:

> www.fahcsia.gov.au/sa/indigenous/pubs/general/Documents/closing_the_gap/ default.htm

Partners in a Learning Culture at:

> www.dest.gov.au/NR/rdonlyres/E879AF00-53E7-4087-812A-5064A50E0BFB/ 6398/THEWAYFORWARDfinalJune05.pdf

and

Partners in Learning a Learning Culture – the Way Forward by the Australian national Training authority (2005) at:

> www.dest.gov.au/sectors/training_skills/policy_issues_reviews/key_issues/nts/ vet/aitac.htm

Maori learners

Non-Maori HR developers should seek the advice of Maori communities and elders when planning, designing and implementing learning programs for Maori adults.

Some of the suggestions made for adult indigenous Australian learners are also applicable for adult Maori learners. Both cultures have deep spiritual connections to the land and their ancestors, and strong links to their communities and families. As Papuni and Bartlett (2006) comment, two of the most striking Maori values are respect for place, especially for home topography, and honouring of family and ancestors. So, in the traditional *mihimihi* (introduction of self), the individual first refers to the voyaging histories that have made the individual (such as the mountains that sheltered ancestors, the rivers that provided water, and the place the family calls home) and, then in the last sentence, lets the listener know the individual's name.

While Zepke & Leach (2002) suggest there is some question whether western constructs from adult learning have any place at all in Maori contexts, a number of their suggestions for Maori preferences for learning show underlying commonalities with western approaches, as shown in Table 4.2.

Table 4.2 Commonality between Maori and western approaches to learning

Maori	Western
Consideration of learners' contexts	The principle of learning of *meaningful material* (Chapter 3)
Emphasise the practical	The principle of *learning by doing* (Chapter 3)
Orient towards the group as well as the individual	The learning strategies of *discussion, case study and role play* (Chapter 10)
Have the learning related to real life tasks	The *andragogical approach* (Chapter 3)

A Maori worldview, with its strong oral traditions, places a high value on knowledge (Smith 1999). Durie and Hermansson (1990) believe that, for Maoris, knowledge is obtained from the relationships they have with their families, their ancestors, the land and the sky. This leads to some significant issues for the HR developer to consider. These issues include:

- the fact that Maori learning has always been lifelong and life-wide, long before these concepts became fashionable in adult education circles (Merriam *et al.* 2007);

- the tendency (e.g. Hemara 2000, Smith 1999, Zepke & Leach 2002) for Maori learning to be holistic, incorporating the four dimensions of the person – *wairua* (spiritual), *hinengaro* (intellectual), *tinana* (physical) and *whatumanawa* (emotional);

- reciprocal learning (Merriam *et al.* 2007) – *ako*, the Maori word for learning, entails historical and cultural dimensions and does not differentiate between those who dispense knowledge and those who acquire it;

- traditional methods of teaching which include *waiata* (song/poetry), *whakatauaki* (proverbs), *korero tawhito* (history) and *whakapapa* (genealogy) (Hemara 2000); and

- the centrality of people to any activity of living, and the strong connection to extended family (see Merriam *et al.* 2007 and Papuni & Bartlett 2006).

The importance of conducting a needs investigation before designing a learning experience for Maori adult learners cannot be stressed strongly enough. The HR developer must recognise that the learning commences with this initial interaction. So, while Chapter 5 discusses the skills and processes of HRD needs investigation, more will be needed when designing learning experiences for Maori learners. Always involve Maori communities and elders in any planning and implementation of learning programs for Maori adult learners.

Some concluding comments on cultural backgrounds

Both New Zealand and Australia now have rich multicultural societies; this very richness is the source of valuable knowledge that can be harnessed to energise and strengthen the viability of any organisation. To add to the enduring and fertile culture of the original indigenous and Maori cultures, we have seen an influx of western European values and practices and, more recently, the integration of Asian and African cultures and the beliefs and values of other major religions, such as Islam, Buddhism and Hinduism.

These national cultures and religions have been practised for many centuries. They emphasise knowledge and learning. For example, in Islam, learning is lifelong; it is an individual's responsibility to seek knowledge from the cradle to the grave – seeking, reflecting and sharing knowledge is the noblest of all (Merriam *et al.* 2007). Interestingly, Merriam *et al.* (2007) go on to report that Islam recognises the equal importance of both learning and teaching, with those who have knowledge having a responsibility to develop others. The teacher–student relationship is sacred; *adab* (discipline of body, mind and spirit) must be observed when one interacts with one's teacher.

The impact on the HR developer

The HR developer is closely and deeply affected by diversity in two ways. First, HRD is at the forefront in maximising the use of this most valuable asset. Whether this be in exploring options among learners when facilitating a learning episode, or when encouraging actors in the shadow system to investigate new knowledge, the HR developer has to ensure that the advantages of a diverse workforce are allowed to exert a positive influence on the outcome.

The second way diversity affects the HR developer is during the learning process itself. As Jarvis (2010) points out, learning rarely occurs in 'splendid isolation', but is intimately related to the world in which the learner lives. The HR developer must 'start where the learner is' (see Chapter 3) as the history, culture and values of the learner are important components of the learner's world.

A closer look 4.3

Conflict in the classroom

During a discussion on United States foreign policy, Ahmed, an Arab student, shouts, 'You Americans are imperialists. You have never helped any country unless it was in your own interests! The only reason you went to Somalia was to establish military control in the Arab world.'

John, an American student, becomes defensive, seeing his classmate as 'out of control'. In an effort to calm things down, he employs objectivity and inductive logic. He lowers his voice and says in an unemotional, deliberate manner, 'I don't support imperialism. And if you look at the facts, you'll find that we often help others for purely altruistic reasons. There's no strategic interest in our being in Somalia.'

The affective–intuitive or deductive style of rhetoric is common in the Middle East. Ahmed emotionally begins with his conclusion, supported only by limited evidence. John calmly suggests he consider 'the facts', causing the disagreement to become a conflict. From Ahmed's point of view, John rejected both his position and his sincerity.

Acknowledging Ahmed's feelings and suggesting other interpretations, John then says something like, 'Ahmed, I know you believe that the U.S. government is imperialistic, but there are many Americans who think the intention of the U.S. involvement in Somalia is altruistic, designed to prevent Somalis from starving.'

To get across the affect and content of his position, Ahmed becomes even more emotional. 'You Americans only put your arm around others to hold them still as you stab them in the back!'

Mr Smith, Ahmed's teacher, pleased with the exchange of opinion, smiles and says, 'I'm sure you two can continue this lively discussion on U.S. foreign policy in the cafeteria.' After all, these are adults interacting in the classroom. He does not want to interfere, but he needs to stop things getting out of hand.

Ahmed, however, concludes that his teacher is irresponsible. Americans view conflict and its resolution as the responsibility of the disputants. The teacher wants to stay out of it. Ahmed expects a third-party intermediary to step in to prevent anyone from losing face. The teacher is the only person who can play this role. He is indirectly responsible for whatever happens between students in the classroom. And, if he does not assume his responsibility to intervene, he may be held accountable for perpetuating the conflict.

Source: Weaver, C R 1995, 'Communication and conflict in the multicultural classroom', *Adult Learning*, 6(5), pp. 23–4.

Hofstede (2005) has suggested that cultures differ on 'power distance' as well as on the individualist–collectivist continuum, and that this concept can be very useful for the HR developer during interactions with learners. Power distance concerns the degree of deference that one individual (e.g. a learner) gives to another (e.g. a HR developer). Williams and Green (1994) believe that a learner from a high power distance culture would be more likely to see the HR developer as an expert and authority figure, and prefer the more structured learning strategies (see Chapter 10) while a learner from a low power distance culture (such as Australia) would prefer the more facilitative, unstructured learning strategies described in Chapter 11. A brief comparison of the cultural variables is provided in Table 4.3. However, the HR developer is cautioned against making any simple judgements based on this comparison. For example, a number of Australian learners are more comfortable with a high power distance relationship.

Other than these considerations of low–high context, individualist–collectivist, and low–high power distance, and the specific comments made in the sections for indigenous Australians and Maoris, research has provided the HR developer with little specific advice on designing learning programs. Some thoughts providing a starting point include:

- the need to conduct a comprehensive HRDNI;

- the need to chart common ground;

- recognising misconceptions about cultural approaches to learning;

- facilitating the likelihood of creative outcomes;

- respecting different communication preferences; and

- sensitivity to the food requirements of people from different cultures.

Table 4.3 A brief comparison of low-context and high-context cultures

Low-context cultures	High-context cultures
■ Primacy given to the content of the message ■ Information is explicit and purposeful ■ Literal interpretation of the wording is important	■ Primacy given to the context of the message ■ The relational activity between the parties surmounts the actual wording ■ Literal interpretation of the wording is not important
Individualist cultures	**Collectivist cultures**
■ Prize self-reliance, creativity, independence, solitude and equity ■ Individual encouraged to self-actualise ■ Expected to use own judgement	■ Honour obedience to authority, duty, harmony, dependence and 'proper' action ■ Deference of individual goals to group goals ■ Readiness to cooperate with group is fundamental
Low power distance cultures	**High power distance cultures**
■ The HR developer is more of a colleague and friend ■ Preference for the more unstructured learning strategies	■ The HR developer is an expert, authority figure ■ Preference for the structured learning strategies

Source: Based on work by Knowles (1980b, 1990).

Conducting a comprehensive HRD needs investigation is paramount in the successful design and implementation of any learning program for adult learners. HR developers must recognise that the HRD needs investigation not only provides the complete and detailed data, but is also the very beginning of any learning program. The initial involvement of the individual and the immediate community sets the scene for the learning, initiates the analytic and creative cognitive processes of the individual, provides motivation, and establishes commitment and a sense of responsibility and ownership. The HR developer should reflect on his or her own frames of reference (see Chapter 3) about the characteristics discussed – e.g. age, impairments, gender and cultural backgrounds. This reflection is likely to be more productive the more specific the behaviours that are considered – for example, how comfortable one is about accents or religious beliefs.

When considering these so-called differences, it is often productive to chart the common ground. For example, the characteristics of reciprocity, harmony, dependence and proper action are valued in the trade union movement as well as in collectivist cultures.

The HR developer must recognise the universal misconceptions about how certain nationalities or cultures learn. In Australia, for example, it is sometimes believed that learners from Asia rely on rote learning rather than on a deep learning approach. Researchers such as Kember, Wong and Leung (1999) and Purdie and Hattie (2002), however, report that learners from Asia do not necessarily rely on rote learning, often differentiating between different stages of memorisation – memorising with little understanding, memorisation to understand, and understand and memorise.

Working with intercultural groups can result in very creative outcomes. Some basic work at the beginning of the learning episode by the HR developer can increase the probability of such a creative result. This initial work can be as simple as a 'getting to know you exercise' (such as finding out one fact about another learner) or a carefully facilitated (see Chapter 11) value-sharing interaction.

The developer should acknowledge and respect different communicative preferences. The western world has an espoused belief (see Chapter 3) in the benefits of quiet, logical discussion. As Weaver (1995) points out, however, in some Latino, Arab and African cultures, sincerity is demonstrated by stating a position with great emotion, hyperbole, and overstatement; the use of metaphors and poetic phrases is considered an indication of sophisticated rhetoric, whereas a calm, unemotional response is a sign of insincerity and lack of personal commitment (see 'A closer look 4.3').

If the learning program is a residential workshop, or if food is to be provided, the developer should ensure that suitable food (e.g. kosher, halal or vegetarian) is available.

To help the organisation manage its diversity positively, Davidson *et al.* (2009) suggest specific strategies on which the HR developer should concentrate. These include:

- *diversity training* as a specific developmental activity designed to enable members of an organisation to function better in a diverse workplace. Cross-cultural training helps employees learn how they are both like and unlike others. Awareness training, as well as the organisational mission statement and policy, can identify legal obligations and ramifications. Both these types of training will depend on communicative learning rather than instrumental learning (see Chapter 3). Wilson (1996) warns that standalone programs are unlikely to be successful, that the development should have top management support, be open to all staff, and include organisation-wide interventions.

- *developing managers and supervisors* in team building, conflict resolution and decision-making to ensure that equity and diversity measures are addressed and biases are overcome at the workface. As Wilson (1996) points out, such communication and negotiation skills are really part of good management anyway, but managers need to be pro-active in using these skills in diversity management.

- *developing and fostering members of minority or disadvantaged groups* in leadership, conflict resolution, and dispute resolution as well as providing literacy programs for speakers of English as a second language (see FECCA 1996). There is also a significant proportion of persons whose first language is English but who have literacy and numeracy problems needing special consideration.

- *recognising prior learning and qualifications* gained elsewhere, as this offers flexibility in assessing organisational and individual needs, and broadens opportunities for both individuals and the organisation.

For the HR developer, the equal opportunity approach tended to emphasise the development of staff in the areas of recruitment and selection (Wilson 1996). Thomas (1994) believes that the HR developer needs first to gain top management commitment, undertake a cultural audit as part of the HRDNI, and ensure that any intervention has very clear objectives to provide a focused approach so that not too many issues are covered at once. With positive management of diversity, the HR developer anticipates ways in which differences between learners can be used as an empowering and emancipatory force, also looking at the different ways that knowledge is constructed and interpreted. Ewert, Rice and Lauderdale (1995) emphasise that, by promoting intercultural skills and studying non-western world views, the organisation's ability to generate new knowledge is enhanced remarkably (see Chapter 15).

Globalisation

For many Australian organisations, the world has become a global village; and globalisation has become an important strategic issue. As Stone (2010) comments, an organisation with its headquarters in Australia and major operations overseas is no longer unique.

Globalisation is not simply the involvement in the economic and industrial activities of another country (e.g. in erecting and managing a factory in another part of the world). It also includes interacting on a global scale with people from a variety of cultures in the normal course of one's job in Australia (e.g. buying imported parts, exporting, being part of a foreign subsidiary, or just competing with foreign imports). The advent of modern communications technology (e.g. the internet and email) has broken the historic geographical isolation of Australia. Whether staff are operating from an Australian base or are expatriate staff in another country, simply selling the best product or the best service is not enough. Australian organisations must fully understand their clients, suppliers, and peers, whatever culture they come from.

In helping the organisation deal with globalisation, the HR developer will have at least two major areas of interest. First, staff – whether they are expatriates, repatriates (those re-entering Australia or New Zealand), inpatriates (overseas staff entering Australia or New Zealand for the first time) or interacting with other countries from an Australian base – need to be developed in the skills and attitudes appropriate to other countries. Second, the HR developer may be required to arrange, design, or implement learning experiences in another country.

Developing staff

An increasingly important part of the HR developer's role is in developing staff so that they can operate in differing cultural contexts. Many expatriates experience culture shock induced by the removal of familiar cues; even basic actions, such as making a telephone call, can become nightmarish experiences (Stone, 2010). Whether they be expatriates, repatriates, or inpatriates, Furuya, Stevens, Bird, Oddou and Mendenhall (2009),

Hutchings (2003), Mamman (1994) and Tadmore (2006) suggest that, in order to improve intercultural effectiveness, several areas have to be addressed. These include:

- Enhancing self-adjustment through cross-cultural and language training.

- Being aware of the *different communicative processes* that are used to acquire and use knowledge. Many countries operate on the high-context model of interactions; staff need to become adept at reading the context within which the message is delivered rather than concentrating on the content of the message.

- Acquiring knowledge of the host culture and specifically being able to demonstrate culturally appropriate behaviours. For example, in many collectivist cultures, high importance is attached to developing and fostering relationships before becoming involved in business transactions. For inpatriates, the 'laid back' lifestyle in New Zealand and Australia is often mistaken for a casual attitude to work.

- Recognising that sex role equality is often higher in an individualistic culture than in a collectivist society. This calls for careful consideration of male–female interactions, for both expatriate males and females. For expatriate females, dress codes may need to be accommodated to enhance intercultural effectiveness. For expatriate males, initial communication with females may need to be initiated through a male relative.

- Raising the awareness of the expatriates and inpatriates of their own core frameworks and developing skills in being able to establish psychological or physical buffers between oneself and the new local culture.

- Full articulation in the host country's language may not be necessary; in many countries, being able to speak English is seen as a socially desirable quality. However, some knowledge of the language can be of considerable assistance in developing business relationships. Being able to offer a greeting in the appropriate language is often looked upon with favour. Overall, though, the importance of linguistic ability will vary from country to country; the expatriate (or those living in Australia but interacting with people from another country) will need to understand both the social implications of being able or not able to speak the language and the implications of their accent when speaking the host language. For inpatriates, the idioms of Australian and New Zealand speech may require some period of adjustment.

- Repatriates will need the support of the organisation for successful re-integration into New Zealand or Australia when they return; the move should not be seen as a demotion, expatriates' knowledge should be strategically used, and organisational recognition of the cadre of global managers should be provided.

Developing staff to the levels of competency required to interact within the global village requires more than instrumental learning. Learning experiences based on communicative and, at times, emancipatory learning are needed. These deeper levels of learning use more energy, both for the organisation and the individual learner. For the organisation, the more unstructured learning strategies (see Chapter 13) will have to be utilised; these strategies take more time and require the facilitative skills of an experienced HR developer. For the individual learner, achieving the desired level of learning outcomes demands commitment and a willingness to examine one's beliefs and values – activities that can be personally exhausting.

Overseas learning interventions

Marquardt and Engle (1993) contend that, for the HR developer, managing and conducting learning interventions outside one's home country differ on several factors:

- the presence of learners from a *variety of nations* – from the local or host country, from the parent organisational country, and from third countries (i.e. from countries other than the local or parent countries);

- the overriding *dynamic of culture* will affect all aspects of the learning experience, with intercultural interactions (between two or more cultures within a nation), cross-cultural interactions (crossing cultures and national borders) and multicultural interactions (involving many cultures);

- *administrative issues* including transport, host government relations, language translation, and housing;

- the *political environment* of the host country may need to be considered – whether the government is democratic or totalitarian; the skills and ability levels of the local labour and the wages paid to them; the likelihood of terrorism and kidnapping; the existence and quality of health facilities; and the weather.

- the *role of the HR developer* may differ in various cultures, with some preferring a more laid-back and friendly approach, and others expecting an authoritative, disciplined and even remote expert figure; and

- the *distance* from the parent country, which can present challenges for communication with supervisors and for supply lines for equipment and materials.

The HR developer also needs to consider the impact of culture on the four stages on HRD. Marquardt and Engle (1993) provide an excellent discussion of specific issues the HR developer needs to consider. For example, during HRDNI, it is difficult for respondents in some cultures to admit that there are problems or even become involved in such an investigation.

In Australian Aboriginal society, for example, asking questions is often seen as bad manners (see Byrnes 1993). In collectivist cultures, even acknowledging that problems exist may cause the respondent's manager to 'lose face'. Establishing learning objectives may be regarded as presumptuous or threatening, or even be against religious beliefs if the future is seen to be preordained and beyond the manipulation of humans.

When designing programs, the HR developer needs to bear in mind that some cultures prefer a didactic, deductive and rote style of teaching; the Australian preference for independence, involvement (e.g. using experiential learning), and generalising from specifics may not be acceptable.

It is in the implementation stage that significant differences between cultures become most obvious. In some cultures, the teacher/HR developer/facilitator is viewed as an omniscient fountain of knowledge, and is expected to live up to this high ideal. The Australian casual and friendly attitude may run counter to this expectation. Simple actions like leaning on a desk (undignified) and asking questions (the teacher is the content expert and the learner should not have to help him or her) can lead to loss of credibility.

Further, during implementation, the expatriate HR developer often works with a local HR developer. This has advantages in overcoming language barriers and helps the expatriate HR developer to understand the local culture. In some cultures, however, the teacher–learner dichotomy between the expatriate HR developer and the local HR developer may be exacerbated. Finally, there can be significant differences as to who evaluates, what is evaluated, and how and when evaluation is carried out – particularly in cultures that value hiding feelings, not prying into the feelings and thoughts of others, and where protecting the 'face' of an honoured person or guest is paramount.

The challenges for the HR developer managing and conducting a learning program in another country can be immense. Indeed, it can be argued that being an expatriate HR developer is a special and unique career move. The most important factor that emerges is that the HR developer concerned must become very knowledgeable about the culture where the learning program is to be mounted. There are very few texts available for the global HR developer. Marquardt and Engle (1993) have provided a practical and detailed text with a number of sensible suggestions and specific tips for operating in various world cultures, and this text is highly recommended. Iles (1996) provides an organisational view of HRD's role in an international or global organisation.

Diversity and the organisation

Most organisations will have to confront existence in a changing and complex environment. One of the most valuable assets that will help the organisation to survive and prosper from such change and complexity is a sophisticated and diverse workforce. As Ewert, Rice and Lauderdale (1995) comment, organisations that view diversity as a problem, focus their developmental efforts on avoiding legal difficulties whereas those that hold the 'value-in-diversity' perspective define differences as opportunities to mobilise all of the organisation's human resources on behalf of the common good. Diversity provides a rich accumulation of perceptions and knowledge. By fostering and managing this diversity positively, the organisation handles uncertainty and challenge in a sophisticated manner that ensures success.

Adults differ on many qualities. This chapter has examined four:

- age;
- health;
- gender; and
- culture

that are considered to be particularly pertinent to adult learning. Such differences have to be acknowledged, celebrated and mobilised. In addition, though, the HR developer must recognise that individual learners are a combination of many of these differences. For example, a learner may be young, female, adult, and paraplegic – or a male Maori elder with an abundance of wisdom but limited formal education. Acknowledging these differences, and the variety of accumulated experiences and perceptions, provides an inexhaustible source of knowledge and truth.

References

Belenky, M F, Clinchy, B M, Goldberger, N R & Tarule, J M 1997, *Women's Ways of Knowing: The Development of Self Voice and Mind, 10th anniversary edition*, Basic Books, New York.

Bern, S L 1993, *The Lenses of Gender: Transforming the Debate on Sexual Inequality*, Yale University Press, New Haven, Con.

Bempechat, J & Elliott, J G (eds.) 2002, *Learning in Culture and Contexts: Approaching the complexities of achievement motivation in student learning*, Jossey-Bass, San Francisco.

Bennington, L & Tharenou, P 1998, 'Older workers: Myths, evidence and implications for Australian managers', in R J Stone (ed.), *Readings in Human Resource Management, Volume 3*, John Wiley & SonsAustralia, Brisbane.

Brislin, R & Yoshida, T 1994, *Improving Intercultural Interactions: Modules for Cross Cultural Training Programs*, Sage, Thousand Oakes, Cal.

Brown, L M & Gilligan, C 1992, *Meeting at the Crossroads: Women's Psychology and Girl's Development*, Harvard University Press, Cambridge, Mass.

Boyd, C 2010, 'Untapped resource', *HR Monthly*, August, pp. 12-19.

Burnett, L 2003, 'We don't have any of *them* at our school! Lesbian, gay, bisexual and transgender student, teacher and parent invisibility issues', *Australian Journal of Middle Schooling*, 3(1), pp. 39-45.

Byrnes, J 1993, 'Aboriginal learning styles and adult education: Is a synthesis possible?', *Australian Journal of Adult and Community Education*, 33(3), pp.157-71.

Clapham, K 1999, 'Andragogy and Aboriginal Australian learning styles', *Indigenous Education around the World: Workshop papers from the World Indigenous People's Conference*, New Mexico.

D'Augelli, A R 1994, 'Identity development and sexual orientation: Toward a model of lesbian, gay and bisexual development.', in E J Trickett, R J Watts and D Birman (eds.), *Human Diversity: Perspectives on People in Context*, Jossey-Bass, San Francisco.

Davidson, P, Simon, A Woods, P & Griffin, R W 2009 Management, 4th edn, John Wiley & Sons Australia, Brisbane.

Durie, M & Hermansson, G 1990, 'Counselling Maori people in New Zealand', *International Journal for the Advancement of Counselling*, 13, pp. 107-118.

Ellis, S J 2008, *Diversity and inclusivity at university: A survey of the experiences of lesbian, gay, bisexual and trans students in the UK*, Sheffield UK, Sheffield Hallam University Research Archive.

Ewert, M Rice, J K & Lauderdale, E 1995, 'Training for diversity: How organisations become more inclusive', *Adult Learning*, May/June, pp. 27-2 8.

Federation of Ethnic Communities' Councils of Australia (FECCA) 1996, Life *Long Learning for All: Adult and Community Education and People of Non-English Speaking Backgrounds*, Australian Association of Adult and Community Education, Jamison Centre, ACT.

Furuya, N, Stevens, M J, Bird, A, Oddou, G & Mendenhall, M 2009, 'Managing the learning and transfer of global management competence: Antecedents and outcomes of Japanese repatriation effectiveness', *Journal of International Business Studies*, 40, pp. 200-215.

Garvey, G, Rolfe, I E, Pearson, S & Treloar, C 2009, 'Indigenous Australian medical students' perceptions of their medical school training', *Medical Education*, 43, pp. 1047-1055.

Gozzi, R 1995, 'The Generation X and Boomers metaphors', *Et Cetera*, 52(3), pp. 331-335.

Gudykunst, W B 2004, *Bridging Differences: Effective Intergroup Communication*, 4th edn, Sage, Thousand Oaks, Cal.

Gudykunst, W B & Kim, Y Y 2005, *Communicating with Strangers: An Approach to Intercultural Communication*, 4th edn, McGraw-Hill, New York.

Hall, E T 1989, *Beyond Culture*, Anchor Books edition, New York.

Hall, M & Brier, G 2007, 'From frustrating forgetfulness to fabulous forethought', *The Science Teacher*, 74(1), pp. 24-27.

Ham, M 2010, 'Inequality in the corporate world has deepened in the past two years', *Sydney Morning Herald*, 15 May, p. 11.

Hart, M 1992, *Working and Educating for Life: Feminist and International Perspectives on Adult Education*, Routledge, London.

Hartevelt, J 2008, 'It doesn't pay to be female', *The Press*, 27 December, p. A4.

Hemara, W 2002, *Maori pedagogies: A view from the literature*, New Zealand Council for Educational Research, Wellington.

Hill, R J 1995, 'Gay discourse in adult education: A critical review', *Adult Education Quarterly*, 45(3), pp. 142-58.

Hofstede, G 2005, *Cultures and Organisations: Intercultural Cooperation and Its Importance for Survival*, 2nd edn, McGraw-Hill, New York.

Holton, R & Hedrick, C (eds.) 1990, *Cross Cultural Communication and Professional Education*, Centre for Multicultural Studies, Flinders University, Adelaide.

Howe, N & Strauss, B 1993, *13th Generation*, Vintage Books New York.

Hunter, R 1992, *Indirect Discrimination in the Workplace*, Federation Press, Sydney.

Hutchings, K 2003, 'Cross-cultural preparation of Australian expatriates in organisations in China: The need for greater attention to training', *Asia Pacific Journal of Management*, 20, pp. 375-396.

Jarvis, P 2010, *Adult education and lifelong learning: Theory and practice*, London, Routledge.

Jorgensen, R Grootenboer, P Niesche, R & Lerman, S 2010, 'Challenges for teacher education: The mismatch between beliefs and practice in remote indigenous contexts', *Asia-Pacific Journal of Teacher Education*, 38(2), pp. 161-175.

Kim, R 2009, *A report on the status of gay, lesbian, bisexual and transgender people in education: Stepping out of the closet into the light*, Washington DC, National Education Association.

Kember, D, Wong, A & Leung, D Y P 1999, 'Reconsidering the dimensions of approaches to learning', *British Journal of Educational Psychology*, 69, pp. 323-43.

Knights, S 2000, 'Women and learning', in G. Foley (ed.), *Understanding Adult Education and Training*, 2nd edn, Allen & Unwin, St. Leonards, NSW.

Lankard, B A 1997, 'New learning strategies for Generation X'. *ERIC clearinghouse on Adult, Career and Vocational Education,ERIC Digest No. 184*, Columbus, Ohio.

Levinson, D & Levinson, J D 1996, *The Seasons of a Woman'sLife*, Knopf, New York.

Lloyd, D & Norrie, F 2004, 'Identifying training needs to improve indigenous community representatives' input into environmental resource management consultative processes: A case study of the Bundjalung Nation', *Australian Journal of Environmental Education*, 20(1).

Mamman, A 1994, 'Intercultural effectiveness: Implications for Australian expatriates and business people', in R J Stone (ed.), *Readings in Human Resource Management, Volume 2*, John Wiley & Sons Australia, Brisbane.

Marquardt, M J & Engie, D W 1993, *Global Human Resource Development*, Prentice Hall, Upper Saddle River, NJ.

Martin, C A & Tulgan, B 2001, *Managing Generation Y*, HRD Press, Amherst, Mass.

Merriam, S B, Caffarella, R S & Baumgartner, L M 2007, *Learning in adulthood: A comprehensive guide*, 3rd edn, San Francisco, John Wiley & Sons.

Mezirow, J 1990, Fostering Critical *Reflection in Adulthood: A Guide to Transformative and Emanciatory Learning*, Jossey-Bass, San Francisco.

Miller, C 2005, *Aspects of training that meet Indigenous Australians' aspirations: A systematic view of research*, Adelaide, NCVER.

New Zealand Management, 2009, 'Where are the women leaders?', 56(10), pp. 5-6.

Noe, R A 2009, *Employee Training and Development*, 5th edn, McGraw Hill, Boston.

Olsson, S & Pringle, J K 2004, 'Women executives: Public and private sectors as sites of advancement?' *Women in Management Review*, 19(1).

Papuni, H T & Bartlett, K R 2006, 'Maori and pakeha perspectives of adult learning in Aotearoa/New Zealand workplaces', *Advances in Developing Human Resources*, 8(3), pp. 400-407.

Patrickson, M 2003, 'Human resource management and the ageing workforce', in R Wiesner & B Millett (eds.), *Human Resource Management: Challenges and Future Directions*, John Wiley & Sons Australia, Brisbane.

Pierce, J & Delahaye, B L 1998, 'Human resource management implications of dual-career couples', IinR J Stone (ed.), *Readings in Humanz Resource Management, Volume 3*, John Wiley & Sons Australia, Brisbane.

Purdie, N Hattie, J 2002, 'Assessing students conceptions of learning', *Australian Journal of Development and Education Psychology*, 2, pp. 17-31

Reynolds, R J 2009, '"Clean, clad and courteoue" revisited: A review history of 200 years of Aboriginal education in New South Wales', *The Journal of Negro Education*, 78(1), pp. 83-94.

Schermerhorn, J R, Davidson, P, Poole, D, Simon, A, Woods, P & Chau, S L 2011, *Management*, John Wiley & Sons, Brisbane.

Scott, T & Harker, P 2004, *The Myth of Nint Five: Work, Workplaces and Workplace Relationships*, Thorogood, London.

Smith, C & Hutchinson, J 1995, *Gender: A Strategic Management Issue,* Business and Professional Publishing, Sydney.

Smith, L T 1999, *Decolonizing methodologies: Research and indigenous peoples,* Zed Boks, New York.

Stone, R J 2010, *Human resource management,* 7th edn, John Wiley & Sons Australia, Brisbane.

Tadmore, CT 2006, 'Acculturation strategies and integrative complexity as predictors of overseas success', *Academy of Management Best Conference Paper.*

Theophanous, A C 1994, *Understanding Social Justice: An Australian Perspective,* 2nd edn, Elikia Books, Carlton South, Vic.

Thomas, V 1994, 'The downside of diversity', *Training and Development,* January, 60-62.

Thorpe, M, Edwards, R & Hanson, A (eds.) 1986, *Culture and Processes of Adult Education,* Open University, London.

Tisdell, E J 1995, *Creating Inclusive Adult Learning Environments: Insights from Multicultural Education and Feminist Pedagogy: Information Series No. 361,* ERIC Clearing House on Adult, Career and Vocational Education, Columbus, Ohio.

Triandis, H 2004, *Culture and Social Behavior,* McGraw Hill, Boston, Mass.

Trudgen, RI 1983, *Aboriginal traditional economic system in Central and East Arnhemland,* Northern Regional Council of Congress, Darwin.

Weaver, G R 1995, 'Communication and conflict in the multicultural classroom', *Adult Learning,* 6(5), pp. 23-24.

Williams, T & Green, A 1994, *Dealing with Difference: How Trainers Can Take Account of Cultural Diversity,* Gower, Aldershot, England.

Zepke, N & Leach, L 2002, 'Appropriate pedagogy and technology in a cross-cultural distance education context', *Teaching in Higher Education,* 7(3), pp. 309-321.

Chapter 5

HRD needs investigation

An overview

LEARNING OBJECTIVES

After studying this chapter you should be able to:

1. Describe the four categories of a human resource development needs investigation (HRDNI).

2. Discuss the purpose of a HRDNI.

3. Explain how the surveillance stage of a HRDNI can give early indicators of HRD requirements.

4. Describe the influence of the strategic plan has on the HRDNI.

5. Describe the two parts of the investigation stage of the HRDNI.

6. Discuss the issues to be considered when creating a realistic action plan for a HRDNI.

7. Explain how to select appropriate HRDNI methods.

8. Identify the three forces that may impede a HRDNI.

9. List the elements of a HRDNI report.

The importance of HRDNI

Human resource development needs investigation (HRDNI) often goes by other names: HRD needs assessment or even the older training needs analysis (TNA) are quite common. Yet HRDNI is much more than these alternative names suggest. Certainly, analysis and assessment are involved, but other processes such as data gathering, description, verification, classification, and interrelationships are also present.

In the HRDNI, the HR developer becomes an investigator who carries out all these activities. Most organisations will conduct a variety of needs analyses or investigations into a variety of issues. However, the HRDNI is the only systematic way of collecting data that will assist in making a decision on

- whether a HRD solution is required, and

- on the most appropriate solution (Tovey & Lawlor 2008).

In these days of change and pressure, it is easy to dismiss HRDNI as an unnecessary and time-consuming impost. Such a stance is fraught with danger. Stone (2010) reports that one Australian survey showed that 70 percent of training was a waste. As Goldstein (2002) comments, while there is a temptation to begin human resource development without a thorough HRDNI, learning programs are designed to achieve goals that meet certain learning outcomes. As is common in today's turbulent climate, yes–no decisions are rarely suitable and are usually an indication of lazy management. Rather, as writers such as Swart *et al.* (2005) and Tovey and Lawlor (2008) emphasise, a HRDNI should be conducted in as organised and systematic manner as possible in order to maximise the potential benefits of any learning intervention.

HRDNI spans both the legitimate system and the shadow system, and accordingly becomes dependent on a close relationship between the supervisor and upper management (Browning & Delahaye 2010). Upper management has the responsibility to

- monitor the strategic needs of the organisation;

- communicate these needs through the strategic plan;

- ensure that the organisation has sufficient resources to implement the strategic plans; and

- audit the success of the implementation through strategic control systems.

The supervisor then has two responsibilities:

- firstly, to ensure that staff have sufficient skills and knowledge to implement the strategic plan; and

- secondly, to appraise the daily performance of staff.

When a staff developmental need arises, the supervisor then arranges for the staff member to be developed.

A closer look 5.1

Six key areas of organisational change

There are six key areas of organisational change that have an impact on human resource development.

1. Pressures for workforce productivity have intensified with organisations looking for more systematic and 'breakthrough' ways of being low cost yet high quality producers of goods and services.

2. The pace of change continues to accelerate with the bottom line being that organisations that complete the work in less time have a competitive edge.

3. Organisations continue to shift their focus to the customer and quality, as well as trying to complete work in less time.

4. The arena for an organisation's planning and action is now very global; relationships are more complex, with some competitors being suppliers, customers or partners, blurring the boundaries between the organisation and its external environment.

5. Business strategies now depend even more on the quality and versatility of the human resource. This is especially the case in organisations in which people's knowledge, attitudes, skills and willingness to change are critical to the organisation's competitive advantage.

6. Work structure and design are changing dramatically with the boundaries between individual jobs blurring, with more team accountability and flexible, multi-skilled job designs.

Source: Based on Stone 2010 and PA McLagen, 'Models for BIRD practice', *Training and Development Journal*, vol. 43, no. 9, September 1989, p. 50.

HRDNI defined

At its most basic, a HRDNI is a process that identifies the gap between what is currently happening and what should be occurring. Rothwell and Kazanas (1989, p. 81) suggest that, traditionally, 'what is' and 'what should be' are considered. Tovey and Lawlor (2008) concur, believing that a HRDNI detects the difference between expected performance and actual performance of an individual or group, thus leading to the identification of any performance gap.

However, this traditional stance on HRDNI – sometimes called 'gap analysis' – focuses too much on performance deficiencies. A HRDNI process should also be future-oriented, pro-active and positive, rather than being reactive and negative. Accordingly, writers such a Brinkerhoff (1986) suggest that there are four categories of HRDNI:

1. *a performance deficiency*, which concentrates on the measurable difference between what the organisation expects and what is actually occurring – the gap analysis. So, for example, a construction supervisor may expect that a gang of carpenters will

take three days to erect a house frame, but sees that one gang is averaging four and a half days.

2. *a diagnostic audit*, which focuses on the future rather than on existing problems or issues by searching for ways that will lead to more effective performance or prevent performance problems. For example, an organisation should always be searching for new technological advancements that will maintain the organisation's competitive edge. This category of HRDNI would emphasise the impact of the strategic planning process of the organisation (discussed in Chapter 5).

3. *a democratic preference,* in which staff and managers may become aware of programs that they perceive will meet their unique needs. Such options have the advantage of having high acceptability when staff are involved fully in the decisions. The democratic preference category empowers staff to consider their own developmental needs. Opportunities for democratic preference often surface in the developmental performance appraisal (discussed in Chapter 7).

4. *a pro-active analysis,* where the emphasis of the search is on future problems and challenges, before such issues are evident. As such, this category is firmly in the arena of the shadow system as the organisation operates close to the edge of uncertainty and pro-actively searches for new knowledge.

So, the concept of HRDNI can have multiple meanings. It may refer to:

- a one-off investigation (as in the performance deficiency category);

- an ongoing surveillance of the knowledge levels within the organisation; or

- a scanning of future problems and challenges that may confront the organisation.

However, a strong warning must be raised. Too often there is an automatic assumption that organisational problems are caused, and can be subsequently fixed, by the training and development of staff. Organisational problems have many possible causes. It is therefore more accurate to depict HRDNI as part of a general needs analysis. Further, the general needs analysis must be conducted first. If the general needs analysis indicates that lack of staff development may be the cause, or if the solution will eventually involve staff development (e.g. if new equipment is to be installed), *then* a HRDNI can be carried out.

The purpose of HRDNI

The importance of conducting a HRDNI was underlined by the findings of van Eerde, Tang and Talbot (2008) who, when investigating 398 organisations in New Zealand, found that a systematic and comprehensive investigation of development needs before making decisions about HRD was strongly associated with better organisational effectiveness. HRDNI, then, is based on the powerful premise that diagnosis should come before action. This prior emphasis on diagnosis is common to all professions – engineers, for example, survey the building site and then draw construction plans, and doctors ask questions, conduct a physical examination and take tests before making a decision.

Diagnosis is a two-part process – the gathering of accurate and relevant data and the impartial analysis of that data. Such a careful diagnosis ensures that the aim of the development is well defined and understood and that the subsequent developmental effort will be both effective and efficient.

A HRDNI, then, is a process that identifies and defines an organisation's HRD needs. Overall, the HRDNI should focus on three levels – the needs of the organisation, the task, and the person (Rudman 2010; van Eerde *et al.* 2008). De Simone and Harris (2009) suggest that a HRDNI is a study that can be used to identify:

- an organisation's goals and its effectiveness in reaching these goals;

- discrepancies between employees' skills and the skills required for effective job performance;

- discrepancies between current skills and the skills needed to perform the job successfully in the future; and

- the conditions under which the HRD activity will occur.

The HRDNI seeks answers to such underlying topics as:

- *the content and learning objectives* – What is going well? What needs improvement? What content needs to be covered? What examples are there of good practice? What examples are there of bad practice? How can this content be categorised – is it explicit or tacit knowledge; is it to do with the frames of reference of the learners? Are we seeing cause-and-effect or do the variables under investigation merely have a correlational relationship?

- *the population* – Who needs to be developed? What are their levels of knowledge, skills and abilities? Are there groups of potential learners or is the issue more individually based? How motivated are they? How do they prefer to learn?

- *the resources needed* – What resources are needed to conduct the learning experience? What resources are available? What is the overall time frame within which the development should be achieved? What has to occur first, what second and so on?

- *the context and organisational politics* – What are the organisational political ramifications of the issue under investigation? Who is likely to support it? Who besides the learner will benefit? Who is likely to feel threatened by the outcomes of the learning? What are the opinions of the key stakeholders? What are the levels of outcome likely to be accepted by the key stakeholders – do they want the learners to be highly proficient or will a coping level be accepted? What level and type of resources are the key decision makers willing to invest in the learning outcomes?

Organisational awareness

Organisations are continually being exhorted to be pro-active, and in the arena of HRD, the imperative is no less. Delahaye and Smith (1998) suggest that organisations need to operate at two levels of awareness – surveillance and investigation.

The surveillance stage

The manager of the HRD department or section, as well as individual HR developers, need to ensure that the external and internal environments of the organisation are constantly surveyed.

Organisational strategic plan

Usually, the *external environment* is initially monitored via the strategic plan of the organisation's legitimate system. The organisational strategic planning process commences with a SWOT analysis (strengths, weaknesses, opportunities and threats), and once this data is analysed, the organisation's mission statement (which defines the organisation's competitive edge), strategies and strategic objectives are defined. Mintzberg (2003) calls the result of this formal strategic planning process the *intended strategic plan.* For an in-depth discussion on strategic planning see Dickie and Dickie (2007). It is critical that the HR developer is guided by the themes in the organisation's strategy. Stone (2010) strongly emphasises the point that HRD must be aligned with corporate strategic objectives.

To achieve this end, the HR developer must be engaged in the organisational strategic process in three ways.

- Firstly, the HR developer must have a strong voice in the strategic planning process itself.

- Secondly, the HR developer must understand clearly the strategic direction of their organisation, because designing learning and developmental programs that do not fit into the organisation's strategic objectives would not make sense. In essence, a learning program must enhance the competitive edge of the organisation and/or help the organisation overcome any weaknesses.

- Thirdly, when the organisation changes its strategic orientation, staff usually has to be developed in new skills and knowledge.

The HR developer will be expected to design, implement and evaluate these new learning programs. The involvement of the HR developer in the strategic planning process cannot be stressed strongly enough. Unfortunately, as Stone (2010) goes on to point out, strategic HRD is virtually non-existent in many organisations.

As well as in the legitimate system's strategic plan, the external environment is monitored through the shadow system. Mintzberg (2003) calls the result of this informal strategic planning process the *emergent strategic plan.* Supervisors have a very important role to play here. (This role is described in more fully in Chapter 13 and Chapter 15). The HR developer may or may not be involved in this emergent strategic planning process.

HRD strategic plan

In addition to providing inputs for, and being guided by, the organisational strategic plan, the HR developer should also scrutinise the local external environment so that any minor adjustments can be made. For example, the local supply of a particular type of employee may be limited, and this can mean that specific training workshops have to be planned and conducted. Finally, the HR developer needs to monitor the political and legal arenas to evaluate recent changes to laws and regulations. In this way, the HR developer can construct a HRD strategic plan, guided by the organisational strategic plan and the additional information gathered on local conditions. Again, any changes identified can often become the topic of courses and workshops.

The internal environment

The *internal environment* of an organisation is monitored by tapping into the various organisational information systems. Some of the more important information systems are:

- the *quality control system*, which is an important indicator of the effectiveness of the organisation. If the quality standards are not being maintained, then customer needs are not being met and resources are being wasted. Now the cause may or may not be a human resource problem, but monitoring of the quality control system will give the HRD needs analyst an early warning of possible issues.

- the *financial system*, which provides a measure of the basic health of the organisation. If cost budgets are being exceeded, or if cash flows are too low, then the organisation is in serious trouble. Again, early warnings of such basic troubles give the HRD needs investigator some lead time in which to carry out further investigations.

- *staff turnover and sick leave* figures, which frequently reflect the state of staff morale. Again, there may be other causes of high staff turnover (e.g. not paying high enough wages) but high staff turnover and high levels of sick leave may be indicators of serious staffing problems such as bad management practices, low conflict resolution abilities, and lack of skills leading to feelings of ineptitude. Some of these problems may be resolved through appropriate human resource development strategies.

- *safety reports*, which can signify the extent of a safety problem (by the number of reports) and the type of safety problem (by the content of the reports). Safety is a serious issue, not simply because of the grave legal consequences, but also because of the potential cost in human suffering.

- the *performance appraisal system*, which, these days, comes under a number of different headings – performance review, performance management, performance counselling, and staff development system. Whatever the name, they all have one thing in common – they compare the performance of the individual or the team to requirements of the job. The performance appraisal system is one of the most critical surveillance processes available to the organisation. It provides an early warning system of problems and opportunities in human resources and also furnishes complex details of individual staff development needs. Yet performance appraisal systems frequently become one of the worst designed, badly managed and de-motivating practices in the organisation. (Because of its critical nature, the performance appraisal system will be discussed in detail in Chapter 6.)

- *managerial observation*, which provides a 'real time' assessment of the operations of an organisation. Managers and supervisors should always be alert to the ongoing activities in their area and be especially vigilant for any unusual occurrences.

Keeping a constant surveillance of such organisational information systems (sometimes referred to as the control function or control systems) can give the HR developer early indicators of human resource development requirements. Once warned, the HR developer can then proceed to the specific investigation – the stage on which most writers concentrate when addressing HRDNI.

The investigation stage

Once an early warning of an opportunity (e.g. from the strategic plan or from the shadow system) or a problem (e.g. from safety reports) is received, the HR developer then commences a specific investigation. The investigation stage is in two parts – the gathering and the data analysis.

Data gathering

There are a number of data gathering methods. Two of the most common are qualitative approaches – the interview and the focus group. These methods will be discussed fully in Chapter 7. Other data collection methods include those discussed below.

Organisational records

This is usually an automatic extension of the surveillance stage. The organisational system that has alerted the analyst in the first place is examined in deeper detail. So if customer complaints indicate that the incidence of grievances has risen above the acceptable standard, the investigator will examine all the complaints recorded over an extended period of time. The analyst may also be alerted to other organisational records. For example, in a hotel, where the original complaints are about room service, the investigator may need to look at the rosters at the reception office because guests' telephone calls are re-routed through the reception desk when the room service area is busy or unattended.

A closer look 5.2

Whose responsibility?

So far in this book we have discussed the four stages of HRD in the context of the role of the HR developer. However, the question must be asked, 'Whose responsibility is the development of staff in an organisation?'

The answer is that the responsibility is that of the line managers and supervisors. The line managers and supervisors are the ones who have the direct responsibility to manage the resources that will result in the satisfaction of customer needs. As part of managing these resources, the line manager and supervisor are responsible for managing the knowledge assets under their control.

So, what is the HR developer's responsibility? First, the HR developer should be responsible for identifying and promulgating policies on HRD. Second, the HR developer undertakes those parts of the four stages of HRD that are delegated to the HR developer by the managers and supervisors. So, a manager may ask that a HRDNI be undertaken or that a training course be designed and implemented by a HR developer. The HR developer is then accountable for that HRDNI or that training course. Note, though, that the manager still holds overall responsibility for the end result – the completed HRDNI results or trained staff.

Also recognise that there are some HRD activities that only the manager or supervisor can do. As a general rule of thumb, the managers and supervisors are fully responsible for some of the specific information systems in the surveillance stage. For example, the manager or supervisor must undertake the performance appraisal of staff. This cannot be delegated to another person such as a HR developer. The manager or supervisor is also responsible for implementing and using the various information systems or control systems that indicate the success of that part of the organisation for which they are responsible. In addition, as will be discussed in Chapter 13, the supervisor/manager is fully responsible for workplace learning, including the day-to-day HRDNI in the workplace, as well as supporting the creativity in the shadow system. The investigation stage, though, can be delegated to another person such as a HR developer.

The wise HR developer keeps an eye on the systems in the surveillance stage, though, so that a warning of an impending need is identified early. In addition, the HR developer and the supervisors and managers need to be fully cognizant of the strategic plan of the legitimate system.

Observation

The investigator may observe a staff member completing some task to gain a deeper insight into the complexity of the skills needed. This observation may involve a listing of the sequence of the steps taken to complete the task or even a time measurement of particular parts of the job. A particular problem with this technique is ensuring that the act of observing does not contaminate the outcome. It is sometimes difficult for the person observed to act naturally when being observed. This can be particularly so, for example, when a safety issue is being examined and the person being observed is afraid of making a mistake.

A closer look 5.3

The observation method

Unstructured observations

Observations can be divided into two types – structured and unstructured – and the observer can undertake one of two roles – nonparticipant observer and participant observer.

Structured observations

In a structured observational study, the investigator develops a set of characteristics of activities or behaviours to be observed before doing the observation. The observer then indicates how many times the predetermined activities or behaviours occur.

Non-participant role

The investigator does not become involved in any of the activities or behaviours but remains 'at a distance'. The investigator observes the activities, records the activities in a systematic way and then analyses the data at a later time. However, by being a passive bystander, the nonparticipant observer may only gain a superficial understanding of the phenomenon being studied.

Participant role

The observer also becomes an 'actor' in the episode by becoming part of the team or work group that is being observed. It is felt that the participant role allows the observer to feel all emotive and social detail of any activities. However, the participant observer role contaminates the data that comes from the investigation.

For further information on the observational method see Cavana, Delahaye & Sekaran 2001.

Case study illustration

See the PLP case study on page 13 of the workbook that accompanies this text for a manager using observation.

Assessment centres

Assessment centres are used by other HRM functions – such as selection and performance appraisal – as well as for HRDNI. Assessment centres are special locations where specially trained people observe employees carrying out tasks. Often, senior line managers of the organisation are trained as assessors and are teamed with psychologists as observers. The assessments can be made on individuals or on groups. Rothwell and Kazanas (1989) describe the process as one where individuals are interviewed, tested, and asked to participate in various individual and group exercises. The exercises are based on the activities of a job, as identified through a job analysis, and the performance of the individuals is assessed by trained evaluators.

The expense of the procedures usually confines their use to highly paid employees so that the return on investment is higher. However, several writers believe that, for the management level, assessment centres are superior to any other technique in identifying management potential and, at the same time, taking part in a centre is a powerful management training experience for both the participants and their higher management assessors (see, for example, Bernthal *et al.* 2001; Byham 1983; Starkey 2006).

Critical incident technique

The critical incident technique (CIT) was first described by Flanagan (1954). The essence of CIT is to discover the tasks and skills that are critical to good performance. As such, the CIT often compares good operators and mediocre operators. One of the challenges is that the critical skills are often based on tacit knowledge and so the analyst is often involved in the externalisation process of knowledge creation by trying to surface the tacit knowledge. CIT usually relies on interviewing, and during this interaction, the analyst is often involved in concretisation – helping the interviewee to make more concrete definitions of generalised responses.

Data analysis

Once the data has been gathered it must be analysed. The analytic techniques depend on the type of data collected – either qualitative or quantitative. The analysis of qualitative data is discussed further in Chapter 7. The key outcome of the HRDNI is to define what the learners should be able to achieve after completing the designed learning experiences. These key outcomes have been called, variously, the learning objectives, competencies and learning outcomes.

Learning objectives

The term 'learning objectives' (sometimes called 'training objectives') has been used commonly in training and development since the early 1950s. Delahaye and Smith (1998) suggest that a learning objective should have three components:

1. a *terminal behaviour statement,* which defines the observable behaviour that the learner should demonstrate at the end of the learning experience (e.g. repair a Barthon-Lewis drill press);

2. *standards,* which define how well the learner should perform the behaviour (e.g. in 20 minutes); and

3. *conditions,* which describe the physical environment under which the learner *is* expected to perform the terminal behaviour (e.g. using only hand tools).

Each of these components of a learning objective has some influence on the design and implementation of the learning program. The terminal behaviour statement indicates the content or topics to be learned. The standards dictate the length of time that the learning program may take. For example, the learners would need more time to practise the skills if the standard was 10 minutes rather than 20 minutes. The conditions can affect both the length of the learning program and the content covered. In the example above, if the conditions allowed the use of power tools, the practice may be shortened (as the learners could complete the task quicker) but there would need to be additional content input about using the power tools. To add to the decision-making required of the HR developer (both for conducting the HRDNI and also for designing the program), sometimes the need for conditions in the learning objectives becomes superfluous. For example, if the terminal statement is 'to list all the moving components of a steam railway engine, without error', the conditions would be 'using a pen and paper'. However, most tests in a classroom assume that a pen and paper would be available, so quite often that phrase is omitted.

Learning objectives came under severe criticism during the 1970s, mainly in the school education system rather than in workplace education, for being too reductionist – the reduction of the results of learning to trivialities. In some cases, this was certainly the case when basic motor skills (e.g. pick up the screw driver) were included in the list of objectives. Generally, however, learning objectives as defined by Delahaye and Smith (1998) continue to serve very well in the delivery of adult and workplace learning.

Competencies

The concept of competencies has become more popular in workplace education over the last decade. Rudman (2010) believes that the use of competency frameworks was intended to provide employees with clearly defined objectives and managers with a consistent assessment tool that could be used across organisational and other boundaries. Competencies were introduced in conjunction with the Australian Quality Training Framework and the New Zealand National Qualifications Framework.

Table 5.1 provides an example of two elements from one of the competencies in Certificate IV in Training and Assessment. This sample of elements covers just two of four elements for the competency, 'Contribute to assessment'. A competency statement was originally intended to cover a combination of skills, knowledge, abilities and attitudes. Further, competencies were intended to be observed in the workplace and the person being observed was expected to demonstrate the competencies several times in this workplace situation.

Writers (see, for example, Hager & Gonczi 1991; Lovat & Smith 2003; Stone 2010) have listed a number of concerns about competencies, among them being:

- Competence does not necessarily equate with performance.

- While the approach claims to be objective, in reality, it is no more objective than any other approach.

- The utility of the process can be outweighed by the time investment needed to establish it. Further, on-the-job tasks often change (e.g. because of new technology) and the time-consuming process of developing competencies cannot always mirror this speed of change.

- Competencies deny the pluralism in society and are overly instrumentalist and highly bureaucratised.

- Competencies focus on the individual and ignore the training process.

- In addition to these concerns is the practical reality of how competencies are now presented. Competencies are invariably broken down into 'elements', and broken further into 'performance criteria'. In a high number of instances, these performance criteria now invoke the same criticism as was aimed at learning objectives, in that they are often too reductionist – or, as Wolf (1993) comments, are a never-ending spiral of specification.

Table 5.1 Example of elements and performance criteria of a competency – from the Certificate IV in Training and Assessment (TAAA04)

Unit Number & Name	Element	Performance criteria
TAAASS301B Contribute to assessment	1. Clarify role and responsibilities in the assessment process	1.1 Purpose of assessment is discussed and confirmed with relevant people using appropriate communications and interpersonal skills. 1.2 Benchmark/s for assessment are discussed and confirmed with qualified assessor. 1.3 The assessment plan is accessed, read and clarified with qualified assessor.
	2. Confirm organisational arrangements for evidence gathering	2.1 Nominated assessment methods and assessment tools to be used in collecting evidence are clarified with the qualified assessor to ensure the instruments to collect evidence and the procedures to be followed are clear. 2.2 The assessment context including candidate's characteristics and any need for reasonable adjustments are discussed and confirmed with relevant people. 2.3 Resource requirements are confirmed and arranged in consultation with relevant people. 2.4 Documentation setting out relevant assessment system policies and procedures, legal/organisational/ethical requirements and any other relevant advice on assessment is accessed and confirmed with relevant people.

Source: National Training Information Service, downloaded from www.ntis.gov.au/Default.aspx?/ trainingpackage/TAA04/unit/TAAASS301B#.

However, the competency movement has been quite useful to HRD. First, as Delahaye and Smith (1998) comment, competencies have raised the awareness of HR developers that the outcome of a learning experience must be exported to the workplace. What is important here is the idea that competency is concerned with what people do and not simply with their knowledge or skills, or the rigidly defined task requirements of the job (Rudman 2010). Second, various jobs and positions within industry that were previously accorded only informal acknowledgement (e.g. administrative positions and workplace trainer positions) now have official recognition through qualifications. Third, the official recognition of competencies in the Australian Quality Training Framework and the New Zealand National Qualification Framework has meant that qualifications can be transported from organisation to organisation and from state to state. In addition, qualifications based on competencies can be used for recognition of prior learning (RPL) and for articulation to higher level qualifications.

HR developers tend to prefer to use learning objectives rather than competencies when designing and implementing learning experiences. First, the competency–elements–performance criteria hierarchy is sometimes too reductionist to be useful. Second, standards and conditions are invariably not present in competencies, thereby providing only a limited picture of the desired learning achievements. Thirdly, there is the requirement that competencies be tested in the workplace several times. Such a requirement usually places too great a demand on the limited time of the HR developer. Of course, when a qualification is based on competencies, then the HR developer has no choice but to ensure that the competencies are assessed appropriately.

For an in-depth discussion of competencies see Harris *et al.* (1995) and Rudman (2010).

Learning outcomes

The overall problem with both learning objectives and competencies is that they are suitable mainly for instrumental learning. Both learning objectives and competencies describe ways that the learner can manipulate or cope with their working environment. As Lovat and Smith (2003) comment, some of the most important knowledge, skills, and materials – for example, any creative and problem-solving activity – cannot be reduced to such specific terms. Therefore, it is very difficult to compose learning objectives or competencies for communicative or emancipatory learning.

Accordingly, when communicative and emancipatory learning are involved, it becomes customary to describe the intended results of the learning experience as learning outcomes. Learning outcomes (e.g. positively handle conflict situations in the workplace) subsume a number of highly interactive and complex skills, knowledge and abilities. Gonczi (1999) calls learning outcomes 'integrated competencies'. He suggests that integrated competencies are first, combinations of attributes linked with tasks. Second, any competency is invariably linked with other competencies. For example, while the HRDNI investigator is gathering facts from a staff member, she or he is also building a relationship with that staff member. Third, integrative competencies (or learning outcomes) are normative and evolving as professional practitioners constantly ask the question, 'How ought I to act in this situation?'

The problem, of course, is that learning outcomes (or integrative competencies) are a relatively generalised statement compared to learning objectives. So HR developers, when they are involved in designing or implementing learning experiences based on learning outcomes, often also formulate tentative learning objectives to represent the skills, knowledge and abilities subsumed under the learning outcome. Such learning objectives are recognised as being only representative of the rich mix that makes up a learning outcome. However, these tentative learning objectives do provide the HR developer, whether in the designing, implementing or assessment role, with a more explicit goal on which to focus.

Prioritising the outputs

Recognising the various constraints on using learning objectives and learning outcomes, the HR developer conducting the HRDNI usually prioritises the expected learning achievements. If the expected learning achievements involve communicative or emancipatory learning, then learning outcomes are used. If instrumental learning is involved, then learning objectives are used. Further, to assist the designer, the HRDNI investigator will often include a hierarchy of tentative learning objectives under any learning outcomes listed.

A pivotal role

Learning objectives and learning outcomes play a pivotal role in the other three stages of HRD. As discussed in Chapter 8, they are one of the two main considerations when the HR developer is designing a learning experience. Learning objectives and outcomes also provide the HR developer with a focus during the implementation. When conducting learning sessions, the HR developer is always assessing the learners to judge the extent to which they are progressing towards the designated terminal behaviour. Finally, the learning objectives and outcomes provide the evaluation plan with its basic comparison – were the intended learning objectives and outcomes achieved?

Other components

As well as analysing the data for learning objectives and learning outcomes, the investigator will examine the data for answers on other components – indicators of the appropriate curriculum to be used, the target population of learners, the type of HR developers who should be involved in the implementation of the learning experience, the possible locations where the learning episodes could take place and the possible resources that will be needed to design and implement the learning episodes. These other components are discussed more fully later in the chapter under the HRDNI report.

The investigation plan

The investigation stage of the HRDNI, as with any activity, should be based on a realistic action plan. The following need to be considered for such a plan:

1. *An operational base.* The HR developer who is the investigator will require a physical location from which to conduct the investigation. A desk, filing space and a telephone are the usual basic requirements. However, these days, a personal computer with appropriate word processing, statistical and qualitative analytic packages is also high on the list of essentials.

2. *An authority base.* The investigator is usually an 'interloper', even when an internal consultant. Therefore, some official authority is needed to allow the investigator access to records and to use the time of the staff. Often this

authority base comes in the form of an official letter from someone with appropriate power in the organisation.

The support needed to undertake a HRDNI should not be underestimated and, at this planning stage, the investigator should carefully consider the ramifications. As Goldstein (2002) comments, an intervention, such as a HRDNI, is a procedure that interrupts organisational members' daily routines and patterns of work behaviour and therefore the success of a HRDNI largely depends on the extent of support offered by the organisation and its members towards the investigatory process.

3. *Identification of the key role players in the investigation.* The more obvious role players will be the staff who do the actual work and other people who may have specific information germane to the investigation. However, you may need to consider:

    -   *the initiator.* This is the person or group who first called attention to the HRD need. While this person (or group) can give valuable indicators of the problem, it is also essential not to be biased by this person's perceptions or opinions.

    -   *the decider.* This is the person who has the power to decide whether the investigation, and even the eventual developmental episode, will go ahead. It is essential to anticipate the rationale of this person's involvement.

    -   *the loose connections.* These are the people who, initially, may seem to have nothing to offer the investigation but who can provide valuable and unusual insights, for example, non-customers.

4. *Identification of other sources of information.* Sources worth investigating include company records, business plans, minutes of meetings and control systems.

5. *Review of the appropriate investigation methods.* There are a variety of investigation methods available, each of which has strengths and weaknesses (see Table 5.2). The investigator usually selects a multi-method combination, bearing in mind the objectives of the HRDNI and ensuring that the advantages and disadvantages of those methods selected offset each other.

6. *Establishment of appropriate time frames for the investigation.* Often, it is better to start at the end (the date when the investigation should be finished) and work backwards, listing all the key actions that have to be taken and allowing for the amount of time investment that each action needs.

7. Allowing time for the analysis of the data and writing up the report.

Selecting a HRDNI method

Selecting a suitable investigatory method is a complex decision often owing more to art than science. However, there are two parameters that can impose some logic onto the decision.

The strategic orientation

Organisations have a specific strategic orientation which defines the market niche that they will capitalise on. This strategic orientation can provide a crude initial indicator of the type of HRDNI method that may be most useful. For example, an organisation facing a predictable environment will tend to be more interested in trends rather than cause-and-solution. Such an organisation also has a preference for less costly interventions – lower cost is how they usually differentiate their product. Therefore, low cost, fact-providing methods such as the survey questionnaire and organisational records analysis tend to more appropriate. An organisation facing an unpredictable environment will need methods that provide rich and complex material – the interview and focus group.

Advantages and disadvantages of HRDNI methods

Several writers (e.g. Steadman 1980; Smith, Delahaye & Gates 1986; Goldstein 2002) describe the advantages and disadvantages of the various HRDNI methods. These writers recommend that the investigator tries to maximise the advantages and minimise the disadvantages of the various HRDNI methods according to the situation being faced by the investigator. Table 5.2 provides a list of advantages and disadvantages.

Table 5.2 Advantages and disadvantages of HRDNI investigatory methods

Method	Advantage	Disadvantage
Interviewing	<ul><li>Involves and hooks the individual giving information</li><li>Provides complex information including feelings and opinions</li><li>Encourages the knowledge-generation process of externalisation</li><li>Allows deeper probing of issues because of the face-to-face nature</li><li>People more willing to disclose controversial information</li><li>Can flexibly investigate a variety of issues</li><li>Good for identifying relationships, causes and problems</li></ul>	<ul><li>Can be quite time consuming</li><li>Some people find the personal approach intrusive</li><li>Relies on a skilled interviewer.</li><li>Subjective analysis of data</li></ul>
Focus groups	<ul><li>More time efficient than an interview</li><li>Individuals can creatively bounce off the ideas of others</li><li>Encourages the knowledge-generating process of externalisation</li><li>Permits on-the-spot synthesis of different viewpoints</li><li>Can flexibly investigate a variety of</li></ul>	<ul><li>Arranging logistics can be difficult – facilitator, information givers, equipment, room</li><li>The views of one person can predominate</li><li>People less willing to disclose controversial information</li><li>Subjective analysis of data</li></ul>

Method	Advantage	Disadvantage
	issues	
Survey questionnaires	▪ Can gather information from large groups of people ▪ The data can be analysed objectively ▪ Issues to be investigated can be targeted very specifically ▪ Data can be easily summarised and reported ▪ Some decision makers feel more at home with hard data ▪ Relatively inexpensive	▪ Does not allow flexibility of investigation into other issues ▪ Has a built-in bias because the issues are decided upon by the investigator ▪ Low involvement of staff ▪ Needs return rates high enough to allow confident predictions ▪ Analysis depends on special skills, data recording, use of computers and analytic tools ▪ Are of limited utility in identifying cause and solutions
Organisational records	▪ Can provide an excellent, guiding overview ▪ Identify the historical context of the issue ▪ Can provide measurable evidence of problems ▪ Can indicate possible trouble spots ▪ Information can usually be gathered quite easily	▪ Do not indicate cause and effect ▪ Tend to reflect only the past history ▪ No indications of the complexity of the issue
Observation	▪ Direct gathering of data by the investigator – no interpretation of others' perceptions ▪ Highly relevant data on the issue ▪ Good for cross-checking data gathered by other methods	▪ The very presence of the observer can contaminate the outcome (e.g. the observee acting unnaturally) ▪ Requires a highly skilled investigator with both process and content knowledge ▪ Can depend on 'serendipity' – sometimes something occurs and sometimes it doesn't
Assessment centres	▪ Very appropriate for upper level and management positions ▪ Gathers very complex data	▪ Very expensive ▪ Can result in 'psychological' casualties when some individuals are confronted with unacceptable weaknesses
Critical incident technique	▪ Gathers very useful, rich and appropriate data ▪ Individuals tend to relate to the information because of its relevance	▪ Questions over the validity and relevance of the data are often raised ▪ The data has to be representative over time

Face value?

When investigating problems in, or future challenges for, organisations, the investigator must always bear in mind that initial impressions may not always be accurate. There are three forces to be aware of:

1. organisational politics;
2. espoused theory; and
3. organisational defence mechanisms.

Organisational politics

Politics are a normal part of business life. Emphasising certain points while obfuscating other points to bring about a preferred outcome is, in many ways, human nature. It may be an unconscious process driven, for example, by individual frames of reference, or may be quite overt because an individual sees particular personal or group benefits if facts are interpreted in a particular way.

Espoused theory vs. theory-in-action

These are discussed in more detail in Chapter 14. Argyris (1999) has suggested that the way people say they will behave and the way they actually behave often differ in reality. He calls the way that people say they will behave 'espoused theory' and the manner in which they actually behave as 'theory-in-action'.

Case study illustration

See the PLP case study on page 518 of the workbook that accompanies this text for an example of espoused theory and theory-in-action.

Organisational defence mechanisms

Again, these will be discussed more fully in Chapter 14, but need to be kept in mind while investigating issues for a needs identification. Argyris (1999) has identified a hegemonic process he calls organisational defence mechanisms. These mechanisms are designed to protect powerful members of the organisation. In practical terms, certain events surrounding, or behaviours of, powerful people (or even those under the protection of powerful people) become 'undiscussable' – no one is allowed to talk about the events or behaviours. Any attempt to investigate these protected issues will result, initially, in all types of avoidance actions. If the investigator attempts to pry further, then some organisational proscription will ensue. The ultimate in organisational defence behaviours is where the undiscussable becomes undiscussable – i.e. the very act of talking about the undiscussability of an event or behaviour cannot be discussed. Any proscription or punishment from contravening the 'undiscussability of the undiscussable' is amplified accordingly.

Between a rock and a hard place

These three forces – organisational politics, espoused theory and organisational defence mechanisms – cannot be dismissed lightly as they place the investigator 'between a rock and a hard place'. On the one hand, they cannot be ignored but on the other, 'bravely treading where angels fear to tread' can lead to disastrous results – no information, incorrect information, forfeited credibility and even a lost career. In these situations, the analyst needs good judgement – a quality that can be gained only by experience and excellent investigative skills. These investigative skills are discussed under interviewing and focus groups.

The life of a needs investigator is not always easy, and perhaps we can borrow from the experienced air pilots' adage – there are old investigators and there are bold investigators but there are no old, bold investigators!

The HRDNI report

The end result of all this investigative effort – gathering data and analysing it – is the HRDNI report. The HRDNI report should cover at least the following issues:

- *Explain the reason for conducting the HRDNI.* This section describes how the need came to the attention of the investigator, perhaps through the strategic plan or because of an indicator from one of the information systems being monitored in the surveillance stage. If someone higher in the management hierarchy ordered the investigation, then this is usually noted as well.

- *Describe the investigator's position in the organisation, qualifications and experience.* This gives the reader some background on how the information and analysis is likely to be interpreted and should also bring credibility to the report.

- *Describe the investigative processes used.* This would cover the methods used to gather and analyse the data, the people contacted, and the organisational records accessed. This section allows the reader to make judgements on the accuracy of the conclusions drawn and also allows the investigation to be replicated. As we see in Chapter 7, accuracy and replicability are two important and basic foundations of scientific research. Further, this description provides valuable information for the planning of the evaluation stage (see Chapter 12).

- *Define the learner population.* The target population of learners needs to be described accurately – what sections or departments they come from, what levels in the organisation they belong to, what professional/technical positions they occupy, the salary levels, and the total number of learners in the target population.

- *Define the learning outcomes and learning objectives.* As discussed earlier, these are the key goal of the HRDNI and need to be documented carefully and fully. Preferably, they should also be presented in a hierarchy of outcomes and associated objectives to provide the HR developer, who will later design the learning experience, with as much assistance as possible. If qualifications based on competencies are needed, they should be fully described and linked to the

Australian Quality Training Framework or the New Zealand National Qualifications Framework.

- *Justify the design of a learning experience to achieve the learning outcomes and objectives.* The HRDNI report is not just a device to communicate information; it is also a persuasive document. The need for the learning has to be sold to key stakeholders. These key stakeholders may be the chief executive officer (CEO), upper management, or the managers whose staff are to be developed. Sometimes key stakeholders outside the organisation, such as union officials, also have to be convinced of the need for the development. Arguments based on needs identified in the strategic planning process, on logic, or on decision support mechanisms such as cost benefit analysis (see Chapter 12) are often used.

- *Note information to assist with the later design of the learning experiences.* Such information would cover:

    - the curriculum, which describes the content to be taught and the methods to be used. During the needs investigation, information is gathered on the content that needs to be covered. Further, practical examples of best practice can be gathered, as well as examples of not-so good-practice that can then be used as examples during the course (see the principle of learning, 'transfer of learning', in Chapter 3.

    - appropriate learning strategies. These are also canvassed during the needs investigation. The design of learning experiences is discussed in Chapters 10 and 11 and, as we shall see, the appropriate learning strategy depends on a number of variables (see Chapter 8 and 9). However, at this stage of the HRDNI, the needs investigator will be interested in the preferences of the potential learners, perhaps gathering information on learning styles, for example. There may also be indicators of the type of strategies that are not acceptable by individuals or by the organisational culture. Certainly the investigator will be trying to assess whether the learning should be instrumental, communicative or emancipatory.

    - The HR developers and facilitators need not only the content knowledge but also the ability to conduct the appropriate developmental activity. Developers and facilitators provide a focal point for the learning experience and must be selected carefully.

    - The learning can occur in a variety of locations from on-the-job, to in-house classroom, to live-away courses, to 'virtual' reality. Recommendations on the preferred choices of location should be given.

    - A variety of resources are required to conduct a developmental activity – for example, HR developers, classrooms or workshops, visual aids, and guest speakers, to name a few. In addition, a financial budget will be needed.

- *Plan the evaluation* prior to the implementation of the developmental activities to ensure that the expected outcomes are achieved. Quite often the later evaluation of the learning experience uses the same methods as that used for the HRDNI. It is often helpful when planning the evaluation, therefore, to know the methods and processes used in the HRDNI so that they can be duplicated.

So the HRDNI report is an important document that has multiple goals. It needs to communicate information that will provide significant assistance to the later design stage. In addition, it needs to persuade key stakeholders to support the later stages of design, implementation, and evaluation.

The need for HRDNI

The HR developer needs to be aware of a pragmatic reality – not everyone embraces HRDNI with a passion. De Simone and Harris (2009) comment that, despite its importance, many organisations do not perform a needs analysis as frequently or as thoroughly as they might. They go on to suggest a number of reasons:

1. A HRDNI can be a difficult, time-consuming process.

2. Action is valued over research.

3. Fads, demands from senior management and the temptation to copy the HRD programs of widely admired organisations or competitors appear to be a more attractive option.

4. There is a lack of support for needs assessment, as decision makers often think in terms of bottom-line, or monetary, justification. The problems with this viewpoint were canvassed in Chapter 1 under management re-engineering.

HR developers need to sell the importance of HRDNI to key decision makers in the organisation. As Stone (2010) comments, organisations cannot hide from the strategic imperatives of inadequate and inferior human resource development, particularly with the increasing pressures of international competition. There are several important precepts that underlie HRDNI:

- HRDNI is a dynamic and continuous process. It is not a one-off event, nor does it occur just at the lower levels of the organisation. In reality, it is incorrect to refer to 'a' HRDNI as the process should be ever present and ongoing, covering the whole organisation and its environment.

- The investigation stage is a means to an end. It is established to satisfy a demand, whether that demand is to surmount a challenge, take advantage of an opportunity or to overcome a weakness in the organisation.

- The whole HRDNI process is an investment of resources – usually time and money – to ensure that the subsequent action is more efficient and effective. In other words, the cost of the learning experience will be outweighed by the savings in costs of solving the problem, or the increased earnings of taking advantage of the opportunity.

- The overall aim of the HRDNI is to ensure that not only is there an increase in efficiency and effectiveness, but there is a decrease in the risk that inappropriate action will be taken.

The key to organisational survival is the knowledge capital of the organisation. One of the most basic processes that ensures this knowledge capital is utilised efficiently and effectively is the HRDNI. Successful organisations recognise this and regard HRDNI as an important investment in the future survival of the organisation.

References

Argvris, C 1999, *On Organizational Learning,* 2nd edn, Cambridge, Mass: Blackwell.

Bernthal, P, Cook, K & Smith, A 2001, 'Needs and outcomes in an executive development program', *Journal of Applied Behavioural Science*, 37(4), 99, 488-512.

Brinkerhoff, R 0 1986, 'Expanding needs analysis.' *Training and Development Journal,* 40, pp. 64-65.

Browning, V & Delahaye, B L 2010, 'Enhancing workplace learning through collaborative HRD', in M Clarke (ed.), *Cases and readings in HRM and sustainability*, Tilde University Press, Melbourne, Vic.

Byham, W C 1983, 'The use of assessment centres in management development', in B Taylor and G Lippitt (eds.), *Management Development and Training Handbook,* London: McGraw-Hill.

Cavana, R Y, Delahaye, B L & Sekaran, U 2001, *Applied Business Research: Qualitative and Quantitative Methods,* Brisbane: John Wiley & Sons Australia.

Delahaye, B L & Smith, B J 1998, *How to be an Effective Trainer,* 3rd edn, New York: Wiley.

DeSimone, R L & Harris, D M 2009, *Human Resource Development*, 5th edn, Fort Worth: Harcourt Brace

Dickie, L & Dickie, C 2007, *Cornerstones of strategic management*, Tilde University Press, Melbourne, VIC.

Finagan, J C 1954, 'The Critical Incident Technique', *The Psychological Bulletin,* 51(4).

Goldstein, I L 2002, *Training in Organizations,* 4th edn, Belmont, California: Brooks/Cole.

Gonczi, A 1999, 'Competency-based learning: a dubious past an assured future?', in D Boud & J Garrick (eds.), *Understanding Learning at Work,* London: Routledge.

Hager, P & Gonczi, A 1991, 'Competency-based standards: A boon for continuing professional education?', *Studies in Continuing Education,* 13(1), pp. 24-29.

Harris, R, Guthrie, H, Hobart, B & Lundberg, D 1995, *Competency-based Education and Training: Between a Rock and A Whirlpool,* South Melbourne, Vic: MacMillan.

Lovat, T J & Smith, D L 2003, *Curriculum: Action on Reflection Revisited,* 4th edn, Wentworth Falls, NSW: Social Science Press.

Mintzberg, H, 2003, *The strategy process: Concepts, contexts and cases*, Pearson Education, New York.

Rothwell, W J & Kazanas, H C 1989, *Strategic Human Resource Development*, 4th edn, Englewood Cliffs, New Jersey: Prentice Hall.

Rudman, R 2010, *Human Resource Management in New Zealand*, 5th edn, Auckland, Pearson Education.

Smith, B J, Delahaye, B L & Gates, P 1986, 'Some observations on TNA', *Training and Developmental Journal,* August, pp. 63-68.

Steadman, G T 1980, *The Basics of Organisations.* Sydney, NSW: Butterworths.

Starkey, A 2006, 'How assessment data can inform coaching', *People Management*, 12(17), pp. 50.

Stone, R J 2010, *Managing human resource*, 3rd edn, John Wiley & Sons, Australia, Brisbane.

Swart, J, Mann, C, Brown, S & Proce, A 2005, *Human resource development: Strategy and tactics*, Elsevier, Amsterdam.

Tovey, M D & Lawlor, D R 2008, *Training in Australia*, 3rd edn, Pearson Education, Frenchs Forest, NSW.

Van Eerde, , W, Tang, KCS & Talbot, G 2008, ' The mediating role of training utility in the relationship between training needs assessment and organizational effectiveness', The *International Journal of Human Resource Development*, 19(1), pp. 63-73.

Wolf, A 1993, *Assessment Issues and Problems in a Criterion-based System*, London: Further Education Unit.

Chapter 6

Performance appraisal and career development

LEARNING OBJECTIVES

After studying this chapter you should be able to:

1. Explain performance management and describe the relationship of performance appraisal to performance management.

2. Identify the ways that HR developers are involved in performance appraisal.

3. Differentiate between the two types of performance appraisal.

4. Describe the job analysis process.

5. Describe the observation and comparison process.

6. Describe the types of feedback and the role of action plans.

7. Define career development and explain the roles of career counselling and career management.

The importance of performance appraisal

Performance appraisal systems should achieve outcomes in the following areas (Jafari, Bourouni & Amiri 2009):

- Be a basis for HRDNI;
- be a basis for evaluation;
- encourage the development of staff;
- make comparisons between individuals;
- be cost effective; and
- be free from error.

Performance appraisal, then, provides the most direct and dynamic link between on-the-job performance and human resource development, a fact underlined by the research of Brown and Heywood (2005). Performance appraisal is not only the prime organisational system for HRDNI – a good performance appraisal system provides an automatic and highly valid basis for the evaluation of all learning and developmental endeavours.

Yet performance appraisal is one of the most misunderstood functions of human resource management. It is frequently (and inappropriately) used as a replacement for psychological counselling, and as a discipline process. Such improper application of this critical human resource management function has led to an almost inherent swirl of persisting mistrust as a constant companion to performance appraisal. As Glendinning (2002) comments, this has often led to a process that everyone loves to hate. In attempts to make performance appraisal more palatable, it has been given a variety of new names – performance evaluation, performance assessment, staff development, and performance counselling – to name a few. It is as if managers believe that, by anointing the process with a new name, they will be allowed to avoid the effort and energy that are essential to make a performance appraisal system a success.

While certain performance appraisal activities must take place for an organisation to flourish – for example, staff need to be assessed for salary increments – these activities are often forced underground, or given only cursory attention, because of its undeserved threatening reputation. Worse, the most positive and helpful features of performance appraisal are lost.

Partly as a result of this negative reaction, and also because of the perceived need that a results orientation is essential to survival, a new term has entered the lexicon of management theory – *performance management*.

Performance appraisal within performance management

Performance management concentrates on the overall achievements of the organisation and ensures that all actions are linked strongly and directly to the strategic direction of the organisation. Stone (2010) sees the key elements of performance management as:

- being the creation of a shared vision of the organisation's strategic objectives;

- having performance objectives for each strategic business unit, function, team and individual;

- using a formal review process of progress towards these objectives; and

- linking performance evaluation with employee development and rewards to motivate and reinforce desired behaviour.

Armstrong (2006) and sees performance management as bringing new, integrating features:

- it is regarded as a normal interactive process between managers, individuals and teams, not an administrative chore imposed from above;

- it is based on agreements, accountables, expectations and development plans – it measures and reviews performance by reference both to input/process factors and output/outcome factors;

- it is a continuous process, not relying on a once-a-year formal review.

- it treats the performance review as a joint process which is concerned primarily with looking constructively towards the future;

- it can provide the basis for performance-related pay decisions; and

- it attaches much more importance to the 'processes' of forming agreements, managing performance throughout the year and monitoring and reviewing results.

When texts such as Cummings and Schwab (1973) and Aguinis (2009) are examined, we see that a number of these 'new' features have always been viewed as part of an ideal performance appraisal system, and especially the connection between performance appraisal and strategic planning.

Indeed, some writers, such as Glendinning (2002), use the terms 'performance management' and 'performance appraisal' interchangeably. However, there is no doubt that performance management takes a wider organisational view in its appraisal process. Performance appraisal, therefore, is usually seen as a subsystem of performance management.

Performance management unites performance appraisal with the other organisational subsystems and strategies. Performance appraisal concentrates on the individual and provides a unique set of information for HRDNI. Accordingly, this text will use the familiar term 'performance appraisal' to differentiate the challenging, frustrating and exciting process that concentrates on the human resources, from the performance management of the other systems in the organisation.

A natural process

A dictionary definition of appraisal usually includes the words 'measure' and 'value', so when appraising something, we are measuring the extent of its value to us. In fact, appraisal is a natural process. We make hundreds of judgements on a variety of events each day. Deciding what to eat, for example, is an appraisal process, albeit one made largely unconsciously.

Any appraisal has four stages, namely:

- having some predetermined standard;
- observing some event or object;
- comparing this observation against the predetermined standard; and
- taking some action.

With the food example, we usually have some predetermined standard in our unconscious mind about what will satisfy our hunger. If, for example, we are in a cafeteria, we observe the options that are on offer; we then compare them with our predetermined unconscious standard, and make a purchase decision.

So, making appraisals is quite normal a process in our everyday lives.

A unique process

Human interactions are complex events and, in organisations, these interactions need to be ongoing and constant. One important component that helps to ensure that these interactions continue in a positive manner is trust – but trust is a delicate organism. Performance appraisal can play a unique role in engendering or destroying trust.

Figure 6.1 shows that communication is the key.

Figure 6.1 The trust relationship

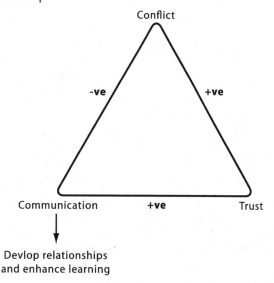

Source: Based on Dick, R 1979, 'Communication skills: non-defensive communication for improved relationships and problem solving', Paper No. 2, Brisbane: Organisational Studies Unit, University of Queensland.

The greater the communication between the manager and the staff member, the more trust there is. The more there is trust the higher are the levels of communication. Conversely, the less trust, the more conflict will ensue; the less communication, the more conflict; the more conflict, the less trust and communication. So, an intensively negative relationship develops. The only way that trust can be increased is by increased communication – and performance appraisal can provide an excellent vehicle for meaningful communication between manager and staff member.

Performance appraisal is also unique because of its pivotal role in HRD. It is not just a dynamic tool for HRDNI. By its very nature, it can also be a powerful and continuing developmental event.

The communicative engagement between manager and staff member can be escalated to true communicative learning for both parties. By interacting with the appraiser, the staff member is involved in the knowledge creation process of externalisation (as the staff member uncovers ideas and thoughts), and of internalisation (as the staff member integrates the suggestions made by the appraiser).

Finally, the performance appraisal system becomes an essential part of the evaluation of the investment of developmental activities. After the implementation stage, the appraiser and the learner should be involved in another performance appraisal to see whether the developmental needs identified in the original performance appraisal have been achieved. Where to position the topic of performance appraisal in a textbook is therefore a moot point – whether to place it in the needs investigation, the implementation stage, or the evaluation. In this text we have chosen to discuss performance appraisal at the HRDNI stage because of the rich and complex material that a performance appraisal can uncover for the HRDNI. However, reference will be made to the various aspects of performance appraisal throughout the book.

It could also be said that these two unique elements – trust, and its pivotal nature in HRD – provide some insight into the reasons some managers shy away from performance appraisal. Trust is delicate, and the thought that a mistake in the communication episode may damage it can become overwhelming. The very complexity that its pivotal nature in HRD denotes only adds to the stress. Conversely, the two elements also explain why so many managers continually hope that a new name for performance appraisal will make life easier!

Impact on the HR developer

Despite the fact that appraisal is a normal process, the difficulties managers and organisations seem to encounter demand that the HR developer be totally familiar with the performance appraisal as a unique and high-impact system. HR developers will find themselves involved in performance appraisal in a variety of ways:

- In both the surveillance and investigatory stages of HRDNI, performance appraisal is a very important input.

- HR developers are often asked to design, develop and instigate performance-appraisal systems into the organisation because of their distinctive position and knowledge.

- HR developers are usually asked to develop both the managers and the appraisees in the reciprocal skills necessary to conduct performance appraisals.

- As stewards of the creation and maintenance of knowledge, HR developers need to ensure that the special interaction between managers and staff fulfils the fruitful opportunities offered. The appraisal interaction between manager and staff member is a dynamic developmental episode when handled correctly – but an absolute disaster when handled incorrectly.

- The results of performance appraisals provide specific and indispensable information for the evaluation stage.

The keys to successful performance appraisal are sound and caring values, open communication and the involvement of the appraisee. There are eight principles for a successful performance appraisal system – namely:

1. the recognition that there are two types of performance appraisal systems – administrative and developmental;

2. the use of a cascade process – upper managers are appraised first, then those managers appraise the operational managers who then appraise their supervisors who then appraise their operational staff;

3. establishing a standard for performance based on a current job analysis;

4. observing the events using appropriate observation methods;

5. using realistic comparisons between the observed data and the predetermined standard;

6. taking action through the use of appropriate feedback methods;

7. creating action plans;

8. recognising that the action plans must become the inputs for a developmental program.

Types of performance appraisal

For some time, writers have suggested that there are two basic purposes for performance appraisal – administrative and developmental (see, for example, Cummings & Schwab 1973; Fisher, Schoenfeldt & Shaw 2006). Some of the reasons for administrative performance appraisal include making decisions for salary increments, promotions, retrenchments and succession plans. The administrative performance appraisal is therefore a critical part of the control function in an organisation. While the focus up to the 1990s was more on administrative performance appraisals, the current emphasis is on staff reactions to appraisal and the social context in which these appraisals occur (Brown & Heywood, 2005). So the contemporary approach accentuates individual development. Developmental performance appraisals concentrate on identifying, honestly and accurately, the developmental needs of an individual for successful present and future performance in an organisation.

Case study illustration

See the PLP case study on page 11 of the workbook that accompanies this text for types of performance appraisal.

These two needs – administrative and developmental – are conflicting in nature. In administrative performance appraisal, the appraiser has the final responsibility for all the decisions on salary increments, promotions or retrenchments. In other words, the appraiser is judge and jury. Under developmental performance appraisal, however, the appraiser undertakes the role of helper and ally – a role that becomes very difficult with administrative performance appraisal. One of the most common mistakes occurs when organisations try to make one performance appraisal system cover both administrative and developmental processes. Two performance appraisal systems are required if an organisation is to perform successfully in today's competitive environment.

This is not to say that no developmental outcomes can emanate from an administrative performance appraisal. If someone is assessed for promotion and found to be limited in some area, then a manager would be negligent not to organise some developmental experience for that individual. Whether an administrative outcome can originate from a developmental performance appraisal, however, is a matter of debate. The main variable is trust. If a trusting relationship exists between the appraiser and appraisee then the information volunteered by the appraisee during the developmental performance appraisal may be used, without negative effect, for some administrative purpose. If the trust factor is not high, and the appraisee believes that the information may be used for future administrative decisions, then the appraisee is more likely to filter the information to ensure that the best picture is painted of him or her.

Many managers have difficulty accepting that there are two types of performance appraisal. They are often confused at the expectation that they conduct both but, at the same time, keep them separate. However, many of our life roles expect this duality. As a parent, we have both nurturing and disciplinary sides. Teachers and university lecturers are expected to be both adviser and assessor. In Chapter 3, we discussed dialectic thinking – the ability to recognise that an entity has opposing attributes. These opposing attributes apply to performance appraisal, which can be both evaluative and developmental. One way to split the two types of appraisal, of course, is to conduct them at different times, and this works quite well for most managers. However, keeping the basic schism between them is not always easy as both processes have commonalities. The first of these commonalities is the job analysis.

Job analysis – constructing the predetermined standard

Stone (2010) believes that job analysis is a basic HR activity because it focuses attention on what employees are expected to do. Figure 6.2 shows the wide variety of purposes for a job analysis and this list serves to underline the importance of the activity. Three of the purposes for the job analysis relate to those for performance appraisal – identifying the developmental needs (1), the administrative prerogatives of decisions on pay and pay equity (2), and promotional processes (5).

Figure 6.2 Purposes of job analysis

1. To identify the developmental need.

2. To maintain external and internal pay equity.

3. To identify the working conditions (such as levels of temperature or noise).

4. To identify the machinery or equipment to be used.

5. For selection and promotion processes.

6. To ensure that health and safety legislation is not violated.

7. To ensure that discrimination laws are adhered to.

8. To ensure that award provisions are adhered to.

9. As a basic input to the human resource planning process, and to determine recruiting needs.

10. To ensure all jobs contribute to the strategic direction of the organisation.

There are two stages in the conduct of a job analysis:

- gathering and recording information on a job; and

- creating the two basic documents – the job description and the job specification.

Gathering data for a job analysis is carried out using many of the same methods as used for a HRDNI analysis – for example, interviewing, focus groups and questionnaires. Additionally, the engineering approaches of time and motion studies, ergonomic analysis and micro-motion studies are sometimes carried out. There are even questionnaires designed to analyse a wide variety of jobs (e.g. the Position Analysis Questionnaire by EJ McCormick and the Management Position Description Questionnaire by WW Tornow and PR Pinto).

Whatever the procedures used, the data gathering process of job analysis is designed to answer two particular questions:

- 'What are the tasks and duties of the occupant of this particular position?' and

- 'What are the expected outputs/outcomes of these tasks and duties?

Additionally, the context of the job – for example, the relationship to other positions, the conditions under which work is performed – will also be of interest to the job analyst.

The two basic job documents

Once the data has been gathered it is analysed to create the two basic job documents – the job description and the job specification (sometimes called 'position description' and 'position specification'). These two documents then become the predetermined standard for the performance appraisal as a comparison point for the occupant's behaviours and abilities.

The job description

A typical job description contains a lot of information about the position (see the example in Figure 6.3). The initial information in the job description identifies the position by title, department and position number. The second segment of information defines the relationship of the position to other positions – who the person reports to, and the subordinate staff and other internal and external contacts. These two segments provide the contextual or background information of the position.

The third segment, and usually the largest, delineates the job duties (Fisher *et al.* 2006) or domains (Schuler *et al.* 1992). As can be seen by the example in Figure 6.3, the job duties list the activities that are carried out by the position occupant. The list defines the role of the position.

Figure 6.3 A job description

Position title:	**Department:**
Administrative Selection Officer	Human Resources Directorate
Salary scale: Level 6 Administrative	**Position no.:** HROO4l1
Supervisor: Manager, Staff Selection	**Subordinate staff:** Nil
Internal contacts:	**External contacts:**
Manager, Strategic Planning	Recruitment consultants
Manager, Payroll	Advertising agencies
Line managers	

Position summary

Select staff for administrative positions throughout the company.

Duties

1. Conduct job analyses using quantitative and qualitative methods.
2. Arrange selection of applicants for administrative positions.
3. As chair of the Selection Panel, conduct selection processes of administrative applicants.
4. Write legally defensible reports on the selection decisions.
5. Arrange the commencement of the selected applicant.
6. Advise unsuccessful applicants.

Performance indicators

1. 90% of selected staff remain with the company for at least 6 months.
2. 98% of selected staff are assessed as satisfactory by their line manager at the 3-month probation performance appraisal.

Finally, the outputs/outcomes expected of the position are listed. Stone (2010) refers to these outputs/outcomes as *performance indicators*. The importance of performance indicators was originally recognised in the early 1960s, when they were called 'key effectiveness areas' and were the total focus of an approach called 'management by objectives' (MBO) (see 'A closer look 6.1').

The performance indicators for the position of Administrative Selection Officer (Figure 6.3) have been defined quite explicitly. They pass the two basic tests of performance indicators – i.e. they are observable and measurable. This is not always possible in all jobs, as some have outputs that are difficult to measure. For example, the performance indicators for a HR developer are usually more generally described because the successful outcomes are about the extent to which people have been developed. The results of such development are often not evident until some time after the learning episode that the HR developer facilitated. This is particularly so when the learning episode was based on communicative or emancipatory learning. In these cases, the manager and the HR developer would need to meet and agree to more specific indicators.

For performance appraisal, then, two of the main outcomes of the job analysis are the job duties and the performance indicators. These two elements make up the job description. It is interesting to note that, in New Zealand under the *Employment Relations Act 2000*, it is mandatory for the employee to be given a copy of the job description and to have the employee sign the document before commencing work.

A closer look 6.1

Management by objectives

First used in the 1960s, management by objectives (MBO) was seen as an exciting management tool that freed staff from the strictures of bureaucratic control, bequeathed self-control, unleashed their creativity and allowed their dynamic energy to be focused on the task at hand. This management nirvana was to be accomplished quite simply. In a consultative process between the manager and staff member, goals or objectives were defined – in an observable and measurable form – and the staff member then proceeded to meet the objectives. These observable, measurable objectives were called 'key effectiveness areas' (see Reddin 1971).

The basic tenet of MBO made some simple assumptions. Firstly, that the staff member would be highly motivated by being involved in the mutual objective-setting process. Secondly, that the staff member's goals and the organisational goals would be unilaterally common. Thirdly, that the resources needed by the staff member to achieve the set objectives would be unfettered and easily available. Fourthly, that the staff member had all the skills required, for the present and in the future, to meet the objectives.

MBO programs gradually fell into disfavour during the 1970s because the results were very limited. Programs floundered for a number of reasons, but largely because they did not adhere to the basic assumptions. Some of the assumptions were quite naïve – who could expect every staff member's personal objectives to coincide with those of the organisation? Others were impossible to achieve – no staff member has total control over the resources needed. Yet others felt manipulated – what staff members would disagree with a manager's stated expectation of the objectives? In addition, Armstrong (2006) saw MBO schemes failing because:

- they became a largely top-down process with insufficient dialogue between

- managers and the staff member;

- they became bureaucratic and centralised;

- quantifiable factors were emphasised at the expense of qualitative factors and behavioural aspects of performance.

While the pure concept of MBO has left us, the legacy of key effectiveness areas is still an essential and powerful ingredient in managing the performance of staff. These days we see that the key effectiveness areas (or performance indicators as they are called in this book) to be part of the story for performance appraisal. The other part is supplied by the characteristics of the job specification. Together, these two parts give the appraiser a more holistic view of the individual's performance and what can be done to improve performance. Secondly, as Drucker (2007) recognised some time ago, performance indicators not only provide a focus for an individual's job, but also define the contribution of that job to the immediate work unit, the contribution the immediate work unit makes in assisting other work units achieve their objectives (and, reciprocally, how those units contribute to the immediate work unit's objectives), and how all these contributions help the organisation achieve its strategic objectives. 'Right from the start, in other words, emphasis should be on teamwork and team results' (Drucker 2007).

The job specification

The job specification lists the characteristics (sometimes referred to as knowledge, skills and abilities) that the position occupant needs to carry out the duties and successfully achieve the performance indicators. The job analyst interprets and extrapolates the job specifications directly from the list of duties. Figure 6.4 shows a possible job specification for the position of Administrative Selection Officer described in Figure 6.3. As you can see, characteristic numbers 1, 2, 3 and 4 come from the duty listed number 1 in the job description. If you go down each of the characteristics, you will be able to relate each to one of the duties in the job description. The job specification is the third major outcome of the job analysis.

If you think of the job specification and the list of duties and the performance indicators in the job description, they represent three of the characteristics of an open system (von Bertalanffy 1956):

- an input stage (the job specification);

- a throughput stage (the duties); and

- an output stage (the performance indicators).

This is a very handy way to view the three major components of a job analysis.

The job specification defines the characteristic that the individual puts into the job; the job description describes how the individual's inputs combine with the other energy inputs (for example, materials, machinery, plans) to produce the observable and measurable outputs of that endeavour.

Figure 6.4 A job specification

Position title:	**Position no.:**
Administrative Selection Officer	HROO4l1

Characteristics of position holder:

1. Knowledge and ability to design and administer survey questionnaires.
2. Knowledge and ability to analyse quantitative data using parametric and non-parametric statistics.
3. Knowledge and ability to design and conduct interviews and focus groups.
4. Knowledge and ability to analyse qualitative data.
5. Ability to write reports that are clear, concise and legally defensible.
6. Ability to organise selection panels and schedule selection interviews.
7. Knowledge and ability to administer personality inventories.
8. Knowledge and ability to conduct selection interviews.
9. Experience in chairing committees.
10. Knowledge of, and experience in administering, discrimination and EEC laws and regulations.
11. Knowledge of company forms and procedures for the commencement of staff.
12. Ability to counsel and handle mild conflict situations

The predetermined standard

It was suggested earlier that appraisal was a natural process, and an example of selecting food in a cafeteria was given. However, most of us do not give the process of making a decision over food much conscious thought, and the identity of the predetermined standard on what food we like is usually implanted deeply in our subconscious. The problem with performance appraisal of individuals in organisations is that the process is often just as unconscious. Unfortunately, and similar to our food example, the predetermined standard is often hidden in the appraiser's unconscious mind and may have no validity. The role of the job analysis is to ensure that the predetermined standard for performance appraisal is valid, open, and indisputable. This is achieved through the job analysis and, from this process, the performance indicators and the job specification become the predetermined standards.

Case study example

See the PLP case study on page 10 of the workbook that accompanies this text for uses of the job description for selection and orientation.

Observing the performance

If performance is to be assessed it must be observed, which raises two questions: 'What is observed?' and 'Who does the observing?'

The what

What is observed is defined by the performance indicators and the job specification of the position. Information on the performance indicators is usually quantitative, because performance indicators are observable and measurable. This means that whoever is conducting the appraisal needs to gather the measurements physically over the period of time that is being used as the appraisal period. In our example in Figure 6.3, the appraiser would need to ensure that the information on the staff selected by the Administrative Selection Officer (who has stayed and who has left; the opinions of the managers on the selected staff) is readily available or can be gathered before the appraisal is conducted.

Judgements regarding the characteristics within the job specification are often largely subjective. For example, with the characteristic 'Ability to write reports that are clear, concise and legally defensible' there is the opportunity to count the number of spelling and grammar mistakes, but this quantitative data does not give a full representation of the quality of the report writing. Someone needs to make a judgement on the descriptors 'clear', 'concise' and 'legally defensible'. This judgement, even when professional and tenable, is still subjective. To make this judgement, however, the appraiser still needs to gather information over the period in question. So the manager may read samples of the Administrative Selection Officer's reports – say, two each week for 6 months – and make notes on the strengths and weaknesses of the report writing style and content. Based on this information, the appraiser can then make a more informed judgement.

The critical incident technique is an additional option used in the gathering of data to ensure that the comparison stage is fully representative. For performance appraisal, the critical incident technique is a means of eliciting data about effective or less effective behaviour that is related to examples about actual events – critical incidents (Armstrong 2006).

By keeping a record of these highs and lows over the entire appraisal period, the appraiser can track trends and make realistic conclusions. In summary, then, the information gathered for the performance indicators is usually quantitative, while that for the job specification is generally qualitative. This differing emphasis – quantitative for the performance indicators and qualitative for the job specification – is an important dichotomy, particularly for the administrative performance appraisal. In making the critical, but potentially contestable, decision in administrative performance appraisal on another's career, the appraiser will need more than the subjective opinion of the judgement on the job specifications. The support of quantitative evidence on the performance indicators is a safety net that cannot be ignored. The performance indicators are also useful for developmental performance appraisal, but they tend to play a more informing, rather than confirming, role.

The who

The most obvious person to do the observing is the supervisor of the appraisee and indeed, this is the case in most organisations. Certainly, for the administrative performance appraisal, the supervisor has the legal and professional responsibility.

For the developmental appraisal, the net is sometimes thrown wider, and the opinions of other people are sought. This wider net most frequently occurs with managers, and the term '360-degree appraisal' has become popular over the last few years (see Bannister 2003 and Maylett 2009).

The principle behind 360-degree appraisal is based on the concept of 'role theory' (for a full discussion see Katz & Khan 1978). Role theory assumes that the tasks a person carries out as part of their job (or role) do not happen capriciously. Nor is the role defined solely by the supervisor. Each role occupant receives messages from role senders. These messages are called 'expectations'. Based on a number of decision processes:

- possible rewards;

- the power of the role sender to cause problems;

- the charismatic power of the role sender; and

- personal preferences and values

the role occupant accepts or rejects specific expectations in the stream of messages and thus constructs the most preferred role. Of course, various role senders are always attempting to sway the judgement of the role occupant, and so the dynamics of organisational life continue. However, out of the tensions, a relatively stable role is created and maintained. The 360-degree appraisal selects representatives from the various role senders and formalises the process of message sending. The appraisee may therefore receive information, not only from the supervisor, but also subordinates, peers, clients, and suppliers.

The full period

The final point to be emphasised is that the information must be representative of the full period over which the appraisee is being assessed. For a 6- or 12-monthly appraisal, there is not much point in using data from only the previous month. There could be all types of reasons why this single month of data is biased – from personal traumas to problems that are organisationally wide. This means that the appraisers and role senders – whether for administrative or developmental appraisal – need to keep records of the observed behaviours for the entire period of the appraisal. As suggested earlier, the critical incident technique is a useful approach.

The comparison

Once the data and information has been gathered, attention then turns to the comparison of the occupant's performance with that expected when looking at the performance indicators and the job specifications. This comparison is best achieved by using some permanent or semipermanent visual record. One of the more practical approaches is to create a 'form' with two basic sections – one for the performance indicators and one for the job specifications.

The visual record

For the performance indicators, a simple list with space for the quantitative figures usually suffices. For the position of Administrative Selection Officer (Figure 6.3) this would simply mean having the two indicators –

- 'selected staff remaining' and

- 'assessed as satisfactory'

together with the appropriate figures. Some organisations include a history of the figures so that the performance indicators can be compared across a number of assessments (see Figure 6.5).

Figure 6.5 Performance indicators

Position title: Administrative Selection Officer		Position no: HR00411			
Performance indicator		**March**	**June**	**September**	**December**
Selected staff remaining	Total selected	22	15	28	30
	Total remaining	20	10	25	27
	% Remaining	91%	67%	89%	90%
Performance indicator		**March**	**June**	**September**	**December**
Assessed as satisfactory	Total assessed	20	10	25	27
	% satisfactory	100%	100%	98%	93%

Making decisions at this comparison stage on the characteristic of the job specification is often a complex and difficult task. In response to this perceived threat, a plethora of processes have been recommended over the years:

- forced choice;

- forced distribution;

- ranking;

- paired comparisons; and

- behavioural observation scales

to name a few. However, these particular processes have limited practical use in modern performance appraisal, so they will not be discussed further in this book. If you are interested in them, Rudman (2003) provides an in-depth discussion, and Blume, Baldwin and Rubin (2009) provide some recent research on forced-distribution scales.

Two approaches that provide some reasonable levels of objectivity are

- the graphic rating scale and

- the behaviourally anchored rating scale.

The comparison for the job specification segment is usually handled differently for the administrative appraisal and the developmental appraisal. For the administrative process, each characteristic in the job specification is assessed on a 'satisfactory or not satisfactory' basis. However, organisations may have to consider the use of BARS for administrative performance appraisal in the near future.

A closer look 6.2

Graphic rating scales and BARS

Graphic rating scales are very similar to Likert scales, except the requirements that the scale have an uneven number of points and that the mid-point be either neutral or passing are waived. In reality, most graphic rating scales conform to the Likert scale requirements. For a performance appraisal episode, the graphic rating scale is simply placed after each characteristic of the job specification. The appraiser then reads each characteristic and circles the rating that he or she believes best represents the appraisee's level of competence.

Behaviourally anchored rating scales (BARS) are a more complex form of graphic rating scale. Rather than having a generic word such as 'Good' or 'Fair' to describe each point, a description of the behaviour that is represented by that point is provided. The same is done for each point on the scale. If there are five points on the scale, then five behavioural descriptors are given. This process is followed for each characteristic in the job specification. For a full description of the development of BARS see Schneier and Beatty (1979a, 1979b).

For the first characteristic of the job description for the Administrative Selection Officer (*Knowledge and ability to design and administer survey questionnaires*), the behavioural descriptors for a BARS may be:

1. **(Poor)** Can write understandable question items but has no concept of reliability and does not understand the basics of statistical analysis.

2. **(Fair)** Can write understandable question items that have content validity and can calculate descriptive statistics.

3. **(Satisfactory)** Designs question items that are valid; understands the concepts of validity and reliability, and can give basic instructions on the requirements for statistical analysis of results.

4. **(Good)** Designs valid and reliable questionnaires and has a good knowledge of multivariate statistics.

5. **(Excellent)** Proves validity and reliability of questionnaires, chooses samples appropriately, and analyses results using appropriate computer packages.

The process for designing BARS is time consuming, expensive and complex. Swan (1991) suggests that there are usually several groups involved. One group of job-knowledgeable individuals identifies specific sets of effective and ineffective behaviours (or incidents) for the job; a second job-knowledgeable group assigns these incidents to the job specification characteristic that best describes it; a third job-knowledgeable group rates the collection of incidents, within each characteristic, on a scale (1 to 5 or 1 to 8, whichever is chosen). A fourth group may then be charged with validating the BARS for each characteristic. The BARS is then often pilot-tested. Because of the cost and complexity, BARS is not often used. However, with the legal climate surrounding human resource management, organisations may be forced to consider the process in the near future as a viable option for administrative performance appraisal schemes.

For the developmental process, a more detailed comparison than the 'satisfactory' or 'not satisfactory' is needed to provide data that is rich enough for a HRDNI. Unfortunately the use of BARS is usually too expensive. Basically, the appraiser needs answers to questions such as:

- to what extent does the job occupant have the skill, knowledge or ability? and

- what does the job occupant need to do to become better at the job specification?

To answer these questions each characteristic in the job specification can be assessed using two different decision mechanisms:

1. A judgement on each characteristic in the job specification can be made using a graphic rating scale. A graphic rating scale forces the assessor to make a clear decision on the extent to which the appraisee is satisfactory or not satisfactory on that characteristic. For developmental performance appraisals, a graphic rating scale has the advantage of being easily and inexpensively created, gives the appraiser a reasonably objective measure and, most importantly, provides a sound starting point for meaningful discussions.

2. The appraiser provides some qualitative information by answering the question, 'Why is the appraisee not a 5?' (if using a five-point Likert scale). If the '5' has been circled (the staff member is rated as excellent on that characteristic), then the appraiser should justify that decision by writing reasons in the space provided.

One of the advantages of these justifying statements is that they can be translated into learning objectives very easily.

Figure 6.6 shows an example of a form for this dual judgement for three of the characteristics of the job specification for the Administrative Selection Officer. This visual record or 'form' should not be confused with a bureaucratic form. First, it is there merely to assist making the comparison between the staff member's actual performance and the expected performance. Second, it provides a focal point and catalyst for the discussion between the appraiser and appraisee. Third, the 'form' is not a permanent entity, as a new 'form' should be constructed for each performance appraisal and be based on the results of a recent job analysis.

Figure 6.6 Making a decision on the job specifications

Position title:	**Position no:**
Administrative Selection Officer	HR00411

Characteristics of position holder:

1. Knowledge and ability to design and administer survey questionnaires

   a) _____

1	2	3	4	5
Poor	Fair	Satisfactory	Good	Excellent

   b) Why not a 5? _____

   _____

   _____

2. Knowledge and ability to analyse quantitative data using parametric and non-parametric statistics

   a) _____

1	2	3	4	5
Poor	Fair	Satisfactory	Good	Excellent

   b) Why not a 5? _____

   _____

   _____

3. Knowledge and ability to design and conduct interviews and focus groups

   a) _____

1	2	3	4	5
Poor	Fair	Satisfactory	Good	Excellent

   b) Why not a 5? _____

   _____

   _____

[and so on for each specification]

Case study example

See the PLP case study on 12 of the workbook that accompanies this text for visual record.

Two additional points

Two points should be noted. First, the performance indicators and the job specification are linked in this judgement mechanism. If the job occupant is achieving satisfactory results for the performance indicators then it would be difficult to judge any of the job specification characteristics as 'unsatisfactory'. However, if a performance indicator is below standard then the cause may be traced to some problem in one or more of the job specification characteristics.

Second, while it has been suggested that the judgement relating to the job specification for the administrative appraisal should be on a 'satisfactory' or 'not satisfactory' basis, the appraiser can use graphic rating scales. However, this is riskier in the administrative process as the appraiser will need to justify the decision (e.g. 'Why a 3 and not a 4?'). For an in-depth discussion of rating and appraisal see DeNisi (1996).

The who again

The final issue to be decided is who should do the comparisons. In the administrative appraisal the manager or supervisor really has the final responsibility. While the appraisee sometimes is given the opportunity for some input, the manager or supervisor is the one who has to make the final decisions. However, with the developmental process, the appraisee is commonly involved to a marked degree. This involvement has two benefits. First, the appraisee is more likely to own the outcome. Second, the appraisee can provide some unique insights into the various judgements to be made. Further, as discussed previously, the 360-degree appraisal can also be used to great benefit in the developmental appraisal as the additional information provided allows more informed decisions.

Feedback

Recent research has found that the amount and quantity of feedback is a critical aspect in the acceptance of performance appraisal systems (Blume *et al.* 2009). There is consequently no doubt that the feedback step is an important part of the performance appraisal.

Over the years, the feedback process has been referred to under a variety of names, with 'performance appraisal interview' being most common, although 'performance review discussion' is becoming more popular. Whatever the name, a number of managers find the interpersonal, face-to-face nature of the performance appraisal interview a difficult and distressing task. However, there is little point in conducting the comparisons unless the appraisee is going to be advised of the outcome.

There are several reasons for this apparent reluctance. First, many managers believe that they do not have the interpersonal skills needed for such a complex and possibly emotionally charged interaction as a performance appraisal review. The interviewing skills discussed in Chapter 7 are of critical relevance in this regard. Another reason for the reluctance of managers is that they do not perceive that there are appropriate feedback models for particular situations.

Maier (1976) has proposed three different performance appraisal interviews – namely:

- tell-and-sell;
- tell-and-listen; and
- problem solving.

These three approaches are still seen as the basic options today (see, for example, Fisher *et al.* 2006, Schuler *et al.* 1992). In the tell-and-sell interview the appraiser has already pre-judged the situation and simply tells the appraisee of the decision. This type of interview assumes that there is a power differential between the appraiser and the appraisee – that is, the appraiser has a great deal more power than the appraisee. This power differential comes from either having a higher position in the organisation or because the appraiser has a broader and more relevant knowledge base.

The tell-and-listen interview allows some appraisee involvement in the interaction. The appraiser advises the appraisee of the decision and the reasons for the decision, and then invites comments from the appraisee. At the very least, it is assumed that this involvement will encourage the appraisee to accept the decision and, at best, that the appraisee will provide new and unique information that will enhance the decision. In the problem-solving interview, the appraiser and the appraisee have equal power, with the assumption that each comes to the interaction with valuable and unique information. The aim is to combine this information for the most beneficial result.

Generally, the tell-and-sell and the tell-and-listen are most suitable for the administrative appraisal. The base line is that, in the administrative process, the appraiser (who is usually the manager or supervisor) has the responsibility to make the final decision. The responsibility cannot be fobbed off onto the appraisee. Indeed, the appraiser will often lose credibility if he or she attempts to transfer this obligation.

The problem-solving interview is most appropriate for the developmental appraisal. It is crucial for the appraisee to have ownership of the final recommendations if meaningful development is to occur. In addition, the complexities of designing appropriate learning experiences means that the appraisee's personal preferences and insights are just as important as the expert judgement of the appraiser.

Case study example

See the PLP case study on page 11 of the workbook that accompanies this text for problem-solving performance appraisals.

As with any general rule, there are exceptions to having the tell-and-sell and the tell-and-listen for the administrative appraisal and the problem-solving for the developmental appraisal. The decision pivots on the job maturity of the appraisee. If the appraisee has a good knowledge of the job, and a deep interest in it, then it is more likely that the administrative process will be based predominantly on the common problem-solving approach. An appraisee with very high job maturity will already know how he or she compares with the job specification.

Commonly, with a job-mature staff member, the common problem-solving interaction is based on force field analysis (see Chapter 10) where the facilitating and inhibiting factors in the occupant's role are identified and ways of overcoming the inhibiting factors are planned. The appraiser still has the responsibility for the final decision, but with a high job maturity, the appraisee's and the appraiser's assessments are very likely to agree. On the other hand, an appraisee of low job maturity (perhaps he or she has recently commenced in the position) is unlikely to have sufficient knowledge to make worthwhile comments on his or her performance even in the developmental performance appraisal. In this situation, the tell-and-listen interview would be more efficient and effective.

Action plans

An interview is ephemeral in nature – the spoken words disappear into thin air and the only history is in the memories of the participants. Unfortunately, memories are not as infallible as we would like to believe. A more permanent and reliable record is needed.

For the administrative appraisal, the usual record is a report either especially written for the occasion (as in a promotion), or as a pre-printed form (as is common with a salary increment). The report, in whatever form, is then forwarded to the appropriate department – the human resource department in the case of the promotion report, or the salary and wages department in the case of the salary increment.

The more informal nature of the developmental appraisal does not negate the need for a permanent record of the decisions. In fact, a permanent record is vital if future development is to eventuate, and should be in the form of an action plan. An action plan covers the what, who and how of the decision. What are the learning objectives? Who will be responsible for carrying out the activities? By when should the activities be completed? An example of an action plan is included in Figure 6.7.

Figure 6.7 Action plan

Position title: Administrative Selection Officer		Position no: HR00411	
Learning objectives	**How to be achieved**	**Who is responsible?**	**By when?**
1. Analyse a questionnaire using descriptive statistics	Attend the Basic Statistics Course	Manager, HRM Department	20 December
2. Improve ability in chairing committees	Sit on five committees over the next month and write a reflective journal on the experiences	Administrative Selection Officer	15 November
3. List the major components of the EEO laws	Read the state EEO laws and regulations and compile a list of the major components	Administrative Selection Officer	30 October
4. Effectively counsel applicants who are not selected	Attend the Interviewing and Counselling Workshop	Manager, HRM Department	10 October
	Have developmental discussions with Manager, HRM after each counselling session	Administrative Selection Officer	Commencing on 15 October

It is common for upper management to review these action plans and to send either the action plans or a synopsis of a section's or branch's or department's action plans forward to the HRD manager.

Input into the developmental system

One of the characteristics of an open system (von Bertalanffy 1956) is that to avoid the entopic process (i.e. dying), the outputs of the system must become the inputs of another system. The results of the deliberations in the administrative performance appraisal system are always forwarded to another system – the payroll section in the case of salary increments or the selection section in the case of promotion appraisals.

However, the action plan from the developmental appraisal is still in danger of becoming a non-event. It is quite easy for the plan to be filed away and forgotten. A procedure needs to be instituted to ensure that all action plans from developmental performance appraisals become the inputs to the organisational human resource development plan. There are a variety of ways that this can occur, but usually the process becomes one of accumulation – the action plans from a section are collated, these are then coalesced into departmental requirements and this information then becomes the basis of the organisational human resource developmental plan.

Surveillance system

The developmental performance appraisal process is the key surveillance system for any HRDNI. While each action plan classifies the needs of each individual, the collation of section and departmental action plans can disclose trends which can foreshadow possible problems or challenges for the organisation. Therefore, the information on the action plans is used for two purposes:

- to design learning programs for individuals;
- to investigate trends identified from the collation of several individual action plans for further hidden needs.

The means of investigation are discussed in the following three chapters.

The information from the administrative performance appraisal can be of use for HRDNI but the degree of this usefulness is hampered by the fact that the outputs of the administrative process (i.e. the reports) are usually confidential. In practical terms, the analyst is usually dependent on the appraisers to forward 'censored' information – material on identified needs that is not tied to individual identities.

While this chapter has concentrated on the performance appraisal system as a surveillance mechanism, other systems should also be monitored. Any of the control systems – quality control, bench marks, production figures, absentee figures – must be scrutinised for trends, and these trends contrasted and compared with the trends of the performance appraisal system. A HRDNI is a pro-active role, with the qualities of curiosity and detection high among the desirable characteristics.

Legal issues

As Glendinning (2002) and Stone (2010) point out, a performance appraisal holds weight in the legal environment, and so the performance appraisal system can be either a shield against legal proceedings or a distinct legal and financial risk to the organisation. The legal ramifications need to be considered by the organisation on several fronts. First, not having a performance appraisal system poses an enormous risk. Second, the job analysis needs to produce job descriptions that are accurate, key performance indicators that are reasonable and achievable, and job specifications that are logical. Third, the performance appraisal process needs to use measures of key performance indicators and job specifications that can be proven to be reliable and valid. Finally, the performance process should be used in HRDNI (see Chapter 5) and also in the evaluation of developmental experiences (see Chapter 12).

Career management

While writers such as Inkson (2003) report that individuals seldom attribute their career decisions or outcomes to activities by their organisations, the organisation must be involved in the future of its staff to support the continuation of the strategic plan. This comparison between the needs of the individual and the needs of the organisation is called career management. Interestingly, Smith and Sheridan (2006) found that some employees were highly dissatisfied with organisations that did not take an active part in career management. Consequently, facilitating career management has benefits for the organisation on several levels.

The capabilities of staff are central to the present and future viability of the organisation. Overall then, the present abilities and future aspirations of the individual will have to be matched to the strategic objectives of the organisation, using performance management and performance appraisal (see Chapter 6). As Rudman (2010) points out, careful assessment of future appointments and career moves is critical because of the long lead times often needed for the development of people for new roles and responsibilities. Such development usually needs the implementation of the more unstructured, time consuming, and costly learning strategies of action learning and mentoring (see Chapter 11). Overall, for a balanced workforce, organisations need to ensure four types of flexibility (Atkinson 1984) to have a viable human resource plan:

- functional flexibility to ensure the availability of required skills;

- numerical flexibility to ensure the required number of people;

- temporal flexibility to ensure services for customers are available when required and projects can be completed on time;

- wage flexibility to align pay with labour demand while controlling salary and wage costs.

To meet these requirements for flexibility, staff within organisations can be categorised as primary, secondary, or peripheral (Hartmann 2003).

- A primary labour force is made up of the full-time, permanent workers. The primary labour force provides functional and temporal flexibility to the organisation. The core worker accumulates valuable knowledge about the specialisations and procedures of the organisation through workplace learning and training courses; she or he is often more committed to the ideals and culture of the organisation and can usually perform a wider range of skills.

- The secondary labour market provides numerical, temporal and wage flexibility through part-time, casual and temporary employees.

- Peripheral workers are short-term outsiders (usually self-employed) and contractual workers.

The organisation matches the needs of the staff with the organisation's requirements for flexibility, attempting to achieve a balanced mix of primary, secondary and peripheral staff. This matching process is called career management.

A closer look 6.3

The dual-career couple

With so many people gaining university or other qualifications and starting professional careers, a recent phenomenon on the employment scene has been the dual-career couple. A dual-career couple is defined as two people in a married or other significant relationship, where both partners display a high degree of commitment to their respective work roles. Dual-career couples present organisations with specific challenges, particularly in career management. There are at least four significant issues that affect dual-career couples:

1. *Relocation and job mobility.* For a dual-career couple, relocation is further complicated by the need to satisfy the career requirements of both partners simultaneously and this complication often leads to employee immobility. If the relocation option is taken, then the dilemma of coordinating two careers surfaces with the only solution being that one party subordinates his or her career for their partner.

2. *Spousal anti-nepotism.* Organisations are often ambivalent (at best) about spouses working together. Concerns about preferential treatment (real or otherwise) and inappropriate sharing of information (e.g. one partner knowing about the promotion of a friend in the organisation) are often cited as reasons for this ambivalence. A number of organisations overcome this issue by not employing dual-career couples.

3. *Flexibility in work arrangements.* Expectation of long working hours are exacerbated when partners work in the one organisation. It is often difficult for both partners to be absent from the workplace together as, if they are both in critical positions, the organisation often needs both present for critical decisions.

4. *Childcare.* The 'arrive early leave late' requirement of high-pressure careers

> creates special challenges with regard to child-care arrangements for dual-career couples. Sickness in the family, and special occasions (e.g. a school function) often require dual-career couples to make highly stressful personal decisions.
>
> With dual-career couples becoming an increasing proportion of the workforce, organisations will need to make specific strategic decisions in their career development programs if they are to attract high quality employees.
>
> *Source:* Based on information in *The International Journal of Human Resource Management*, vol. 7, no. 4, 1996, pp. 905-23, Published by ITP.

Careers

Historically, a career was seen as being successful within one organisation – a model now referred to as the 'traditional organisational career' or the 'bounded career' or 'traditional vertical career'. The *traditional vertical career* occurs within a single organisation and implies an orderly, predictable progression of upward movement accompanied by appropriate increases in salary, status, and power – and a sense of security. At the heart of the vertical career is the concept of the psychological contract. The psychological contract is characterised by a mutual understanding between the employee and the organisation that:

- the employee will work hard, cause few problems, be loyal and obey their manager's instructions; while

- the organisation will provide a good job, pay an acceptable wage, offer opportunities for advancement and generally guarantee lifetime employment (Smith & Sheridan 2006).

However, careers occur within a social context. As discussed in Chapter 1, this context has been subject to a variety of forces, from globalisation to the global financial meltdown, resulting in an environment of rapid and continuous change. Various writers, such as Briscoe and Finklestein (2009), Dries, Pepermans and De Kerpel (2008), and De Vos and Soens (2008), suggest that there has been a shift from the traditional organisational-based careers to more non-linear career forms, in particular protean careers and boundaryless careers.

The *protean career* has a self-directed orientation that implies independence from external career influences (Hall 1976). In this approach, the individual generates and evaluates career goals based on internal values rather than others' standards and drives their own career through independent self-managed strategies (Briscoe, Hall & DeMuth 2006). The protean career involves greater mobility and a more whole-of-life perspective (Hall, 2004). The name is derived from the Greek god Proteus who could change shape at will (Smith & Shreidan 2006) – reflecting the aim of the protean career to continually re-invent itself.

The *boundaryless career*, first suggested by Arthur (1994), suggests that multiple potential boundaries can be and are transcended, with the individual crossing organisational and professional boundaries (Briscoe & Finklestein 2009). This brings a seductive connotation of escaping limits and exploring uncharted territory (Feldman & Ng 2007). The boundaries that may be crossed include mental as well as physical boundaries (Sullivan & Arthur 2006). Under the boundaryless career, the psychological contract is altered – job security is replaced by employability, and the employee would need to develop new skills in self-management and self-knowledge with a focus on continuous learning. Accordingly, there is an emphasis on continually changing career paths and exploring other possibilities.

Recent research shows that a majority of employees still follow the traditional vertical career path (Dries *et al.* 2008; Smith & Sheridan 2006) with a high attachment to organisational security, no matter what their generation (Baby Boomer, Generation X, Generation Y). McDonald, Brown & Bradley (2005) report similar research results, although they also found that the trend towards protean careers is more pronounced for women than men. There is also the suggestion that upper career workers may be best placed to take advantage of the boundaryless and protean career approaches, as they have many key resources required for mobile careers, such as formal education, quality work experience, rich social networks, and a strong proactive orientation (Zeitz, Blau & Fertig 2009).

Briscoe & Finkelstein (2009) suggest that most people are neither independent and boundaryless nor captive of the organisation. Consequently, as suggested by Sullivan and Arthur (2006), it would appear that the decision on career direction is not an 'either/or' proposition, but one that may encompass a variety of options. They go on to suggest that the decision may be based on two criteria – the *degree of physical mobility* and the *degree of psychological mobility*. High physical mobility would include having skills and knowledge that are relevant to a wide variety of work situations and no personal responsibilities (such as family) necessitating remaining in one geographical location. Psychological mobility would include confidence in one's own ability and a lack of need for security.

Career development

Career development can be described as:

- on-going;

- involving a reciprocal interaction between employee and employer;

- attaining and enhancing capabilities so that the individual is not restricted to a particular job, career path or organisation;

- ensuring that the process contributes to organisational success;

- being inclusive rather than exclusive to a few;

- being formal and informal;

- ensuring that individual and work priorities influence choice about careers and developmental opportunities. (McDonald & Hite 2005)

McDonald & Hite (2005) believe that career development and HRD must be integrated, as career development is based on learning activities. Indeed, Briscoe and Finkelstein (2009) found that developmental opportunities, no matter which career concept is followed, are directly related to commitment to the organisation. Such developmental activities would include organisational-centric learning (such as training, job rotation and mentoring) and boundary-spanning learning such as that occurring through external networks, informal learning and community-based learning (McDonald & Hitte 2005). This view of HRD including organisational-centric and boundary-spanning learning will be explored further in Chapters 13 and 15.

The actual interaction between the staff member and the supervisor to discuss career development is often called career counselling.

Career counselling

As Rudman (2010) points out, career counselling is now more concerned with helping people to develop the means of reaching their career goals, however broadly defined, rather than with determining a particular set of goals. The extent to which an individual will become involved in career counselling will depend on that individual's level of motivation. Noe (2009) suggests that career motivation has three aspects – career identity, career insight, and career resilience.

1. *Career identity* is the extent to which an individual defines her or his personal values according to their work.

2. *Career insight* refers to an individual's ability to evaluate their own strengths and weaknesses and how this perception relates to their own career goals.

3. *Career resilience* reflects the extent to which the individual can cope with the problems that arise at work.

Individuals who have a high career motivation are more likely to become involved in career counselling. Career counselling can be seen as comprising five steps:

-   identifying career anchors;

-   analysing an individual's personal environment;

-   providing information on future careers;

-   constructing operational plans; and

-   making the change.

Career anchors

Career anchors are an important concept in career development. A career anchor is made up of a combination of technical skills, knowledge, and experiences. They are described by Schein (1978) as a pattern of talents, motives and values that serve to guide, constrain, stabilise and integrate individual careers. A career anchor can be used to pull one's self up a specific career but, conversely, also limits the vocational choices of an individual. For example, studying and working for many years as a civil engineer will help an individual find a job as a civil engineer or even a promotion in that profession. However, such an individual will find attempting to gain entry into electronic engineering a challenge. Such a challenge involves some 'backtracking' to gain other qualifications and work experiences. If the individual wished to make a more significant change, say to become a chef, then even more investments of time, energy and money would be required. Most people would not make such an investment and would therefore find that their present career limited their choices. As we will see, the type of career anchor discussed in this paragraph is termed 'technical competence'.

Schein (1993) describes eight types of career anchors:

1. *Technical competence.* The content – the skills and knowledge of work carried out (physical mobility).

2. *Managerial competence.* The ability to lead other people, solve problems, handle interpersonal relationships, and remain emotionally stable combined with general managerial skills and knowledge (physical mobility).

3. *Security.* Wanting the surety of a predictable future. Often people with this career anchor place a priority on families and non-work interests and are willing to sacrifice advancement to ensure certainty of time allocation to these other interests (psychological mobility).

4. *Creativity.* Finding excitement in the new, and deep enjoyment in creating new ideas or entities. People with this career anchor like to be central to the main event or task and often feel constrained in a large organisational environment (psychological mobility).

5. *Autonomy.* A need to be free to pursue one's own talents. People with this career anchor seek freedom and autonomy in decision-making (psychological mobility).

6. *Service.* Dedication to an organisation, industry or profession (psychological mobility).

7. *Pure challenge.* The need to be challenged, push personal boundaries, and explore new concepts (psychological mobility).

8. *Lifestyle.* Enjoying a certain level or form of living. This may include the physical surroundings (e.g. living in the city or by the sea), strong social support networks and available services to satisfy personal needs (e.g. health facilities or entertainment centres) (psychological mobility).

Usually, an individual has a combination of several of these career anchors. Making future choices therefore needs at least some knowledge of an individual's profile. Some career anchors are identified easily, particularly technical competence. Identifying technical competence involves an examination of qualifications and work and life experience. Other career anchors, for example security and creativity, may need expert assistance to uncover and to separate personal delusions from reality. In addition to providing insights for individuals, career orientations of individuals provide organisations with a way to understand what influences individuals to select a particular occupation or work setting (Igbaria, Greenhaus & Parsurman 1991). This is an important issue, as Trevor-Roberts and McAlpine (2003) report that research indicates that an individual's feeling of ownership of a job is stronger than the binding force that keeps an employee with an organisation.

A closer look 6.4

Happenstance theory

Life seldom progresses as one expects. Events, challenges and opportunities often transpire without any apparent reason or cause. In career counselling, happenstance theory is based on the premise that, in developing a career, unplanned events are not only inevitable, they are desirable. Accordingly, counsellors should assist clients to develop five skills to recognise, create and use chance as a career development opportunity. These five skills are:

1.   *Curiosity* – exploring new learning opportunities
2.   *Persistence* – exerting effort despite setbacks
3.   *Flexibility* – changing attitudes and circumstances
4.   *Optimism* – viewing new opportunities as possible and attainable
5.   *Risk taking* – taking action in the face of uncertain outcomes.

With today's boundaryless careers, these skills are paramount. Everyone should look at continually developing and honing each of them. Everyone has down days. The trick is to pick oneself up and regain a sense of optimism.

Always be curious. Do not accept the status quo as far as your career is concerned. Look at each new experience as an opportunity that should at least be explored. Above all, let that curiosity turn perceived set-backs into opportunities – and continually inflate your optimism to make sure that perceived set-backs are turned into opportunities.

Persistence is a key quality. Certainly, do not give up at the first obstacle. When you hear yourself say, 'I should do that' or 'I should not do this' or even worse, 'I cannot do this', examine your frames of reference (see Chapter 3). Your hegemonic assumptions may be keeping you in an inflexible, habitual mode that stifles other alternatives.

Look at changing attitudes and use problem-solving to change circumstances (see the scientific problem-solving model in Chapter 3). Any action, even non-action, has risks. The final skill, risk taking, is not about taking risks unthinkingly, but about analysing the costs and benefits of any action, and making a conscious decision about which action is most beneficial.

Source: Based on Mitchell, K, Levin, AS & Krumboltz, J 1999, 'Planned happenstance: constructing unexpected career opportunities', *Journal of Counselling and Development: JCD*, 77, p. 118.

It is interesting to note that Shein (1996) believes that those anchored with stability technical competence and, to some extent, managerial competence, will find it difficult to survive in the current environment. He argues that those with autonomy, entrepreneurship, and pure challenge are better suited to survive in the twenty-first century. The importance of the five skills discussed in 'A closer look 6.4' – curiosity, persistence, flexibility, optimism and risk taking – are critical to these last-mentioned career anchors.

An individual's personal environment

The individual needs to make a realistic analysis of her or his personal operating environment. Most people have at least three parts to their lives – their work life, their family life, and their leisure life. A person's leisure life would include hobbies and sports. Some people have more roles – for example, studying for further qualifications. Given that time is finite, people often find a role conflict occurs – time invested in one part of one's life precludes time put into another part of one's life. An initial and important stage of analysing one's personal environment is to examine the extent of role conflicts and a careful prioritising of the roles.

An allied concept to personal environment roles is the life-cycle model. This model suggests that an individual moves through identifiable life stages. Noe (2009) classifies these stages as:

- *Exploration stage* (mid-teens to early 20s) – where the individual identifies potential careers by examining personal interests and values, discussing alternatives with friends, family, and significant people in their lives. Additional information such as education and training is also needed. This exploration stage continues into the initial employment assignments where expectations are tested against reality.

- *Establishment stage* (late 20s to early 40s) – where individuals find their place in a career or an organisation, achieve financial and career success, and establish a desirable lifestyle. They tend to be self-directed learners and contribute to the benefit of the organisation, colleagues, staff, and their society.

- *Maintenance stage* (mid-40s to late 50s) – where the individual has many years of experience and deep levels of knowledge about his or her career and organisation. People in this stage have concerns about keeping up to date and being seen as a positive contributor. A major issue for organisations is ensuring that such employees do not plateau.

- *Disengagement stage* (60s) – where the individual prepares for a life role outside an organisation or career. In Australia and New Zealand, it has been assumed that this stage would finish at 65. However, there are political and economic concerns about retirement commencing at 65 and signs that society and government will be encouraging people to continue working until their mid-70s. A major issue for organisations who have staff in this stage is ensuring that their knowledge does not walk out the door with them. Staff at this disengagement stage will often find motivation by becoming mentors and instructors.

Information on future careers

Staff need to be encouraged to find out information on options within careers or changes in careers. Specifically, information should be gathered on:

- what qualifications are needed;

- how much supervised experience is required;

- employment opportunities;

- locations of employment;

- expected working hours (e.g. a number of hospitality positions have quite anti-social hours of work); and

- costs of gaining qualifications and experience, and effects of such a change on present lifestyle.

Constructing action plans

Career advancement or changes do not just happen. The individual should construct action plans to make the change. Such plans usually include a time line (e.g. when to start studying, when to start work experience, when to sell the house, when to move to a new location). As with any such, a budget should also be compiled.

In addition, it is a good idea to incorporate a reality check into the process. The reality check may include visiting a work site, undertaking a 'work shadow' role for a few days (following a person who is already in the career position around their work place), or even applying for a position in the chosen career direction and experiencing the selection process, including the interview.

Making the change

The final step is making the change. This, above all, needs courage. Stone (2010) suggests some specific questions:

- How will the specific change affect each member of your family?

- Is the new employer financially stable?

- Is the culture 'fit' of the new organisation appropriate?

- Is the physical environment of where you will be working suitable to you?

The dual nature

Career development has a dual nature and aim. The process must start with the individual, especially in these times of the boundaryless career. The individual will always be concerned with future earnings and security, and career counselling must be based on this premise. However, the future of the organisation must also be addressed. The process of career management places the contributions of the individual within the strategic imperatives of the organisation.

Knowledge creation and maintenance

A well-designed developmental performance appraisal system and a dynamic career development program form the basic building block for the creation and maintenance of knowledge. The critical feature of a learning organisation is a culture that sets high values on learning. The fundamental expectation is that learning will occur. The developmental performance appraisal and the career development program establish this expectation.

- First, it brings together key people to focus on the development of one person.

- Second, this close interaction increases the trust between the players. The more communication that occurs, the less conflict ensues and higher levels of trust result. Conflict has a great deal of difficulty existing where there are high levels of trust and communication.

- Third, the constant interaction regularly emphasises the importance of an individual's development. This regular emphasis eventually becomes a permanent custom.

- Fourth, the performance appraisal system encourages the knowledge generation process of converting tacit knowledge to explicit knowledge. The frequent scrutiny of an individual's development, and the open discussion with another forces the thought mechanism to constantly cover the circle of tacit to explicit to explicit to tacit.

The subsequent learning experiences that come out of the resultant action plans only reinforce this knowledge creation process ten-fold.

In this chapter, we have consistently referred to the performance appraisal *system* and career development *program*. The emphasis on the words 'system' and 'program' convey the wider perspective and recognition that the performance appraisal system and the career development program are part of performance management. This means that the two processes are in constant and direct interaction with the other systems in performance management. In addition, both processes must contribute, significantly and overtly, to the strategic objectives of the organisation.

Above all, though, performance appraisal systems and career development are about people. As Cousens and Cousens (2000) comment, performance appraisal and career development schemes that work are geared for continuous improvement. They seek to empower people and are necessarily based on respect for people.

References

Aguinis, H 2009, *Performance management*, 2nd edn, Pearson Prentice Hall, Upper Saddle River, NJ.

Armstrong, M 2006, *Performance Management* 3rd edn, Kogan Page, London.

Arthur, M 1994, "The boundaryless career: A new perspective for organizational inquiry', *Journal of Organizational Behaviour*, 15, pp. 295-306.

Atkinson, J 1984, `Manpower strategies for flexible organisations', *Personnel Management*, August, pp. 28-31.

Bannister, L 2003, `360 degrees of development', *Human Resources*, 48, January, pp. 12-13.

Blume, B D, Baldwin, T T & Rubin, R S 2009, 'Reaction to different types of forced distribution performance evaluation systems', *Journal of Business Psychology*, 24, pp. 77-91.

Briscoe, J P & Finklestein, L M 2009, 'The "new career" and organizational commitment: Do boundaryless careers and protean attitudes make a difference?', *Career Development International,* 14(3), pp. 242-260.

Briscoe, J P, Hall, D T & DeMuth, R L 2006, 'Protean and boundaryless careers: An empirical exploration', *Journal of Vocational Behaviour,* 69, pp. 30-47.

Brown, M & Heywood, J S 2005, 'Performance appraisal systems: Determinants and change', *British Journal of Industrial Relations,* 43(4), pp. 659-679.

Cousens, L & Cousens, T 2000, *Performance Appraisal: Making It Work,* 2nd edn, Springwood, NSW: Australian Education Network.

Cummings, L L & Schwab, D P 1973, *Performance in Organizations: Determinants and Appraisal.* Glenview, Illinois: Scott, Foresman and Co.

DeNisi, A S 1996, *Cognitive Approach to Performance Appraisal.* London: Routledge.

De Vos, A & Soens, N 2008, 'Protean attitude and career success: The mediating role of self-management', *Journal of Vocational Behaviour,* 73, pp. 449-456.

Dick, R 1979, `Communication skills: nondefensive communication for improved relationships and problem solving', Paper No. 2, Brisbane: Organisational Studies Unit, University of Queensland.

Dries, N, Pepermans, R & De Kerpel, E 2008, 'Exploring four generations' beliefs about career: Is "satisfied" the new "successful"', *Journal of Managerial Psychology,* 23(8), pp. 907-928.

Drucker, P E 2007, *Management: Tasks, Responsibilities, Practices,* European Group, UK.

Feldman, D C & Ng, T W 2007, 'Careers: Mobility, embeddedness and success', *Journal of Management,* 33(3), pp. 350-375.

Fisher, C D, Schoenfeldt, L F and Shaw, J B 2006, *Human Resource Management,* 6th edn, Houghton Mifflin, Dallas.

Glendinning, P M 2002, `Performance Management: Pariah or Messiah', *Public Personnel Management,* 31(2), pp. 161-78.

Hall, D T 1976, *Careers in organizations,* Scott Foresman, Glenview, IL.

Hall, D T 2004, 'The protean career: A quarter-century journey', *Journal of Vocational Behaviour,* 65, pp. 1-13.

Hartmann, I 2003, `Managing the new workforce: The challenge of mixed employment relationships', in R Wiesner & B Millett (eds.), *Human Resource Management-Challenges and Future Directions,* Brisbane: John Wiley & Sons Australia.

Igbaria, M, Greenhaus, J H & Parsurman, S 1991, `Career orientations of MIS employees: An empirical analysis', *MIS Quarterly,* 10(4), pp. 151-69.

Inkson, K. 2003, `Human resource management and the new careers', in R Wiesner & B Millett (eds.), *Human Resource Management: Challenges and Future Directions,* Brisbane: John Wiley & Sons Australia.

Jafari, M, Bourouni & Amiri, R H 2009, 'A new framework for selection of the best performance appraisal method', *European Journal of Social Sciences,* 7(3), pp 92-100.

Katz, D & Kahn, R L 1978, *The Social Psychology of Organizations,* 2nd edn, New York: Wiley. Maier, NRE 1976, *The Appraisal Interview.* California: University Associates.

Maylett, T 2009, '360-degree feedback revisited: The transition from development to appraisal', *Research Note,* Sage Publications

McDonald, P, Brown, K & Bradley, L 2005, 'Have traditional career paths given way to protean ones? Evidence from senior managers in the Australian public service', *Career Development International*, 10(2), pp. 109-129.

McDonald, K S & Hitte, L M 2005, 'Reviving the relevance of career development in human resource development', *Human Resourceds Development Review*, 4(4), pp. 418-439.

Mitchell, K E, Levin, A S & Krumboltz, J D 1999, `Planned happenstance: Constructing unexpected career opportunities', Journal of Counselling and Development, 77(2), pp. 1.

Noe, A 2009, Employee Training and Development, 5th edn, McGraw-Hill, Boston.

Reddin, W T 1971, *Effective MBO*, New York: McGraw-Hill.

Rudman, R 2003, *Performance Planning and Review: Making Employee Appraisals Work*, 2nd edn, Melbourne, Vic: Pitman.

Rudman, R 2010, *Human Resource Management in New Zealand*, 5th edn, Pearson, Auckland.

Schein, E H 1978, *Career Dynamics: Matching Individual and Organisational Needs*, Reading: Addison-Wesley.

Schein, E H 1993, *Career anchors: Discovering your real values*, Pfleffer, San Diego, Cal.

Schein, E H 1996, 'Career anchors revisited: Implications for career development in the 21st century', *Academy of Management Executive*, 10 (4)

Schneier, C E & Beatty, R W 1979a, 'Performance appraisal revisited, part I', *Personnel Administrator*, July.

Schneier, C E & Beatty, R W 1979b, 'Performance appraisal revisited, part II', *Personnel Administrator*, August.

Schuler, R S, Dowling, P J, Smart, J P & Huber, V L 1992, *Human Resource Management in Australia*, Artamon, NSW, Harper Collins.

Smith, T & Sheridan, A 2006, 'Organisational careers versus boundaryless careers: Insights from the accounting profession', *Journal of Management & Organization*, 12, pp. 223-234.

Stone, R 1 2010, *Managing human resources*, 3rd edn, John Wiley & Sons Australia, Brisbane.

Sullivan, S & Arthur, M B 2006, 'The evolution of the boundaryless career concept; Examining physical and psychological mobility', *Journal of Vocational Behaviour*, 69, pp. 19-29.

Swan, W S 1991, *How to do a Superior Performance Appraisal*, New York, Wiley.

Trevor-Roberts, F & McAlpine, A 2003, 'Psychological ownership', *Management Today*, October, p. 33.

von Bertalanffy, L 1956, 'General systems theory: General Systems', *Yearbook of the Society of General Systems Theory*, 1, pp. 1-10.

Zeitz, G, Blau, G & Fertig, J 2009, 'Boundaryless careers and institutional resources', *The International Journal of Human Resource Management*, 20(2), pp. 372-398.

Chapter 7

Interviewing and focus groups

LEARNING OBJECTIVES

After studying this chapter you should be able to:

1.   Define qualitative research

2.   Discuss the types of sampling designs

3.   Explain the pattern of a good interview

4.   Describe the listening, questioning, paraphrasing, probing and summarising processes

5.   Differentiate between structured and unstructured interviews

6.   Identify the six factors that a focus group process has in common with an interview

7.   Describe the process of conducting a focus group

8.   Explain how qualitative data can be analysed.

Qualitative research

Interviews and focus groups are qualitative research methods. As such, both approaches come under the heading of scientific research. Scientific research is based on the twin pillars of accuracy and replicability. The data gathered have to be an accurate representation of the phenomenon being investigated (if you are investigating the type of skills needed to operate a new machine, there is little point in conducting interviews on customer complaints); the cues or instruments used to gather the data have to be appropriate and accurate tools; the data have to be accurately recorded; the data have to be accurately interpreted; and the results have to be accurately reported.

In addition, if someone else conducts the same investigation then that second investigation should come up with the same results, that is, the research should be able to be replicated. It must be acknowledged, however, that these twin pillars of accuracy and replicability are ideals, as no research method entirely achieves the high standards thus envisioned. The good investigator, though, always tries to achieve these utopian ideals.

Achieving the utopian ideals

Qualitative research is open to criticism for being subjective and prone to bias. Its advantage however, is the ability to amass rich and highly useful data. Qualitative researchers, therefore, respond to the demands of accuracy and replicability in a number of ways. Writers such as Burns (2000) and Neuman (2006) list a number of options:

Trustworthiness

To a qualitative researcher integrity is everything. A qualitative researcher always endeavours to observe, report and interpret the complex field experience as accurately and as faithfully as possible.

Verification

A basic tenet of qualitative research is not to accept anything at face value. Qualitative researchers try to ensure that their research accurately reflects the evidence and have checks on their evidence and interpretations.

Triangulation is a common theme in qualitative research as an aid to verification. Cohen and Manion (2000) suggest three types.

- First, researcher–subject corroboration involves cross-checking the meaning of data between the researcher and the respondents. For confirmation of accurate reporting, this cross-checking may occur during data gathering or after interpretations of the raw data have been made.

- Second, confirmation from other sources, about specific issues or events identified, is always paramount.

- Third, two or more methods of data collection should be used and the resultant interpretations should be compared.

A final triangulation option is called researcher convergence (Huberman & Miles 1998). It involves using another researcher to analyse the raw data and then comparing the two analyses.

Acknowledging subjectivity and bias

Qualitative researchers assume that it is impossible to eliminate the effects of the bias and subjectivity of the researcher. They suggest that quantitative researchers sometimes hide behind supposed 'objective' techniques. A qualitative researcher takes advantage of personal insights, feelings and values, but uses two techniques to limit the contamination.

First, the researcher overtly takes measures to guard against inappropriate personal influences by being aware of his or her frames of reference (see Chapter 3) that may contaminate any analysis of the topic under investigation.

Second, it is common for a brief description of the researcher to be incorporated in the final report. This brief description includes any relevant personal history of the researcher that may affect the interpretations – either by providing a unique insight, or by causing subjectivity and bias. Frequently, research assumptions and biases are also shared with the reader.

Process and sequence

The passage of time is an integral part of qualitative research. The sequence of events and what happened first, second, third and so on, provides confirming evidence for the qualitative researcher.

Interpretation

Interpreting the complex behaviours, messages, forces and conditions of an event is the central theme of qualitative research. As a safeguard to accuracy, the qualitative researcher uses two techniques. The first is to report 'in the voice of the source' by using the actual words of the respondent either in the phrasing of a sentence or verbatim as an example of an opinion or fact. As Burns (2000) comments, to understand events from the viewpoints of the participants the task of the qualitative methodologist is to capture what people say and do as a product of how they interpret the complexity of their world. The second technique is to report the logic of interpretation used to come to a particular conclusion.

Referential adequacy

The comments and descriptions in the report should be of sufficient detail and richness that the reader has no difficulty in imagining the context, situations and thematics discussed (Eisner 1997). Citations of the raw data collected in qualitative research should be frequent enough to give the reader confidence that the raw data has been reported accurately and that the themes extracted are valid.

Paint the path

It is impossible to replicate a qualitative study exactly – there are too many complex variables involved. For example, just having a different researcher introduces an immediate variant to qualitative research, as the researcher is such a central part of it.

However, to help the reader of the report understand the source and theme of the interpretations, the qualitative researcher provides a detailed description of the research process in the final report. Huberman and Miles (1998) call this 'transparency' and suggest that description be provided of:

- the sampling decisions;
- data collection operations;
- database summary (size, how produced);
- software used (if any);
- an overview of the analytic strategies used; and
- the inclusion of key data displays supporting the main conclusions.

To this list could be added:

- the timing and timeliness of observations;
- spatial arrangements of interviews;
- relationships with subjects;
- categories developed for analysis; and
- protocols of analysis.

Summary

When involved in qualitative research, the HR developer as an investigator in a HRDNI needs to ensure that triangulation is built into the research design. At the very least, two methods of data gathering should be used, and preferably more. Frequently, this means the use of either interviews or focus groups and survey questionnaires, but need not be limited to this qualitative and quantitative combination. During the report-writing stage, referential adequacy and the provision of support for interpretations are prime requirements. Describing the data gathering and analysis choices – that is, *painting the path* – need to be sufficiently detailed.

Sampling

Gathering data from entire populations of respondents is usually too costly and time consuming. The usual solution to this dilemma is to gather data from a sample of the population. The problem then arises of ensuring that the sample is representative of the entire population at which the research objective is aimed. There are various types of sampling designs, but writers such as Cavana, Delahaye and Sekaran (2001), Dick (1990) and VanderStoep and Johnson (2008) discuss several useful types.

Simple random sampling

Similar to being in a lottery, every population member has an equal chance of being selected. Some random sampling processes (names in a hat; a table of random numbers) are used to identify the chosen research subjects. The simple random sampling process is totally unbiased but can become cumbersome and expensive.

Systematic sampling

Every *nth* person in the population is chosen. While this is a cheaper option, systematic bias can creep in. For example, every *nth* member of the organisation may share some common characteristic. It is unlikely, but it can occur.

Stratified random sampling

Some subgroups of people in the organisation may be expected to have different opinions or experiences (e.g. upper managers, supervisors, frontline operators). Each stratification or subgroup is identified and then a random sampling process is used for selection. This is one of the most efficient designs, but care has to be taken to ensure that the stratifications are meaningful and are appropriate to the research objective. One method used in HRDNI is called the 'slice group'. In this method the organisation is sliced from top to bottom and representatives are chosen from each level.

Convenience sampling

The first of the non-probability designs, this sampling design collects data from those in the target population who happen to be most conveniently accessible. The opportunity for systematic bias is high, but it is a very cheap option.

Purposive sampling

Purposive sampling involves specifying the types of people (based on predetermined parameters) who should be targeted. For example, the investigation may target organisational members within certain salary brackets. Specific and rich information can be gained from this method, but it is wide open to researcher bias.

Convergence sampling

Another option is to use the convergence technique. In this technique, the investigator starts by finding two people from the target population who are significantly different on some important parameter – for example, an engineer and a social worker (i.e. different professions). The selection process continues until the variations on the parameter converge to a point where there is no expected effect on the data to be provided.

Snowball sampling

This type of sampling involves using an initial group of informants and asking them to recommend further informants. In turn, these informants are asked for further recommendations and so on. Usually, the first tier of initial informants is not used as respondents and the data-gathering process commences with the second tier.

An important task

The above listing of sampling techniques ranges from probability sampling – where the participants are selected by chance – to non-probability sampling – where some bias could occur. However, the non-probability methods have the distinct advantage of quickly accessing participants who are most likely to provide rich information. For this reason, non-probability methods of sampling are more commonly used in qualitative research (Minichiello *et al.* 1995).

An important task of a HRDNI investigator is to ensure that no systematic bias occurs in the data gathered in the selection of a representative sample of respondents. At the same time, the investigator should take care not to suffer from 'paralysis by analysis'. As Kruger & Casey (2000) comment, the investigator needs to recognise that compromises are sometimes needed between the cost of finding the perfect participants and the likely increased quality of the data gathered. As a specific warning, Kruger and Casey go on to advise caution about participants who

- have expressed concern about the topic;

- are 'clones' of the supervisor;

- can be best spared by the supervisor because they are the least productive; or

- are picked from memory by the supervisor or other 'expert'.

The cautious investigator always reviews the sampling options for the most efficient and potentially worthwhile participants in the HRDNI.

Overall, then, the HRDNI investigator has to recognise that, when using the interview or focus group, he or she is involved in qualitative research and that certain protocols – achieving the high ideals and sampling in particular – should provide guiding principles to manage the process.

Interviewing

One wit has suggested that everyone claims that they are good drivers, good lovers and good interviewers. The last claim, at least, is not true! Successful interviewing is the result of the complex interaction of high-level skills, empathy and understanding of others, and an abundant curiosity. Interviews may be conducted face to face, over the telephone or via a video link. While there are some minor variations, the same general principles apply whatever the medium.

The interview provides a unique opportunity to uncover rich and complex information from an individual. The face-to-face interactive process can, under the guidance of an experienced interviewer, encourage the interviewee to share intrinsic opinions and dredge previously unthought-of memories from the unconscious mind. This rich material invariably includes tacit knowledge from the interviewee, knowledge that is often critical to the design of the developmental learning experiences needed for individuals and organisations to overcome the challenges and take advantage of the opportunities that are the hallmark of the business environment today.

The key to uncovering this rich information is a well-designed and professionally conducted interview. Socialisation and natural resistance means that people tend not to disclose information, particularly to a stranger. Further, we often 'grade' the information that we are willing to disclose. There is a difference in the responses to such questions as:

- 'How did you travel to work this morning?'

- 'What tasks did you carry out at work yesterday?'

compared to questions such as:

- 'Have you ever been convicted of taking prohibited drugs?'

- 'Would you describe your feelings when you experience your worst nightmare?'

Whether interviewees would respond to any of these questions and how much they would disclose depends a lot on the context of the interview. However, certain interview skills will increase the likelihood that the interviewee will provide the desired information. Such a well-designed interview is based on six factors:

- the pattern of the interview;

- listening;

- questioning;

- paraphrasing;

- probing; and

- nonverbal behaviour.

The pattern of an interview

A well-patterned interview has a number of benefits. The basic aim of the interview is achieved in less time by removing communication barriers and encouraging the flow of information. The interviewee feels at ease and tends to provide more complete answers. Finally, a well-patterned interview looks professional. Figure 7.1 is an overview of the pattern of an interview. This model provides a general guideline for an interviewer involved in a one-on-one interaction.

The first challenge of an interviewer is to bring the interviewee into the *rapport zone*. This is the area of minimum stress, where the interviewee will disclose all information. We all retain natural barriers so that we do not disclose personal information inappropriately. The first task of the skilled interviewer is to encourage the interviewee to lower these barriers so that information will flow more easily. This easy flow of information occurs in the rapport zone. The interview proper cannot start until the interviewee enters this zone. The interviewer will need to invest some time and energy in encouraging the interviewee to lower his or her natural barriers.

The interview pattern consists of four stages:

1. the entrance investment time;

2. activity no. 2;

3.   intimacy; and

4.   the exit investment time.

Figure 7.1 The pattern of an interview

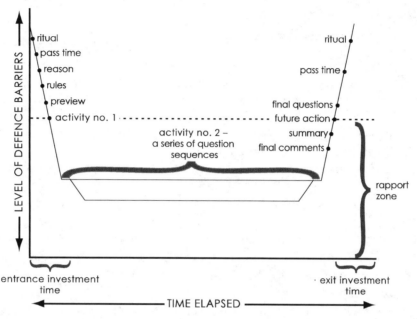

Stage 1. Entrance investment time

This is the time invested at the beginning of the interview to ensure that the interviewee enters the rapport zone. It comprises six steps:

- the ritual;

- the pass time;

- the reason;

- the rules;

- preview; and

- activity number 1.

The first two steps may seem to be superficial. However, far from being a waste of time, these exchanges provide information, as well as a time space, for the interviewee to start to become accustomed to the interviewer and the interview situation. Any attempt to 'short cut' the proceedings will often result in barriers reforming as a protection against insecurity.

Rituals

Rituals are the simple, stereotyped greetings that we use every day – e.g. 'Good Morning'. They can be regarded as common good manners. A frequent addition to the ritual is an introduction, for example, 'My name is Yvonne'.

A pass time

A pass time carries on from the ritual and extends the time space available to the interviewee to adjust to the interview situation. Common pass times include the weather ('It's a windy day today, isn't it?') and health ('How are you today?'). The point of the pass time is that it does not require a reply – in fact, a reply to a pass time is usually considered quite odd. However, a pass time should be reasonably relevant to the situation. A comment on the immediate environment may be more acceptable than the 'health' pass time for example, 'It's quite cool in here, isn't it?' Or if the interviewee has travelled to the interview location a comment such as 'Ah, good, you found the room then,' would suffice.

The reason

By this time the interviewee's mind should be coming off any events that occurred before the interview with his or her curiosity becoming piqued about *the reason* for the interviewer's presence. Needless to say, this curiosity should be satisfied immediately by sharing with the interviewee the objectives of the HRDNI. However, a decision needs to be made about the degree of specificity to be shared about the objectives of the HRDNI. If the interview is to be unstructured, then the interviewer may prefer to give a more generalised description, as anything specific may bias the direction of the interview.

The rules

Interviews are a somewhat artificial situation. In an interview, two strangers are coming together to share information in an open relationship that would normally take some time to establish. Therefore, there is a need to establish *basic ground rules* early. One frequent concern of interviewees is the confidentiality of the information and how the information will be used. Assurances need to be given at this stage. Permission on the type of recording – whether note taking or audio recording – needs to be obtained from the interviewee.

Preview

Very briefly, *preview* the interview by telling the interviewee how it will proceed. This may simply be: 'I have six questions to ask, and expect that this will take about 45 minutes'. Depending on the context, more detail can be given, but be careful not to talk for too long. The sign of a good interview is a very high proportion of interviewee activity.

The ritual, the pass time and the reason would have occupied a time space of about 60 seconds, and the rules and the preview perhaps another 30 seconds. While the interviewee may now be willing to disclose some information, it would be naive to assume that no filtering would take place. It is now time for activity number 1.

Activity number 1

The role of activity number 1 is to bring the interviewee fully into the rapport zone. When people start on a perceived relevant activity, information flows more easily, the natural barriers are forgotten, and trust increases. However, activity number 1 needs to be designed to meet two conflicting goals. On the one hand, activity number 1 has to be related the objective of the HRDNI, as any hint of artificiality will increase the interviewee's natural barriers rather than lower them.

On the other hand, it has to be recognised that the interviewee is not yet into the rapport zone, so the initial information, at least, of activity number 1 will be filtered by the interviewee. In addition, activity number 1 needs to be a based on a question that the interviewee can answer easily and is willing to answer – lack of early success on the part of the interviewee is likely to increase the barriers to the free information flow. Activity number 1, therefore, needs to be carefully planned.

One good strategy is to ask a question about the interviewee's most recent job – for example, 'I see from your application that you have worked as a technical instructor on the coal fields in Central Queensland. Would you tell us about some of the experiences you enjoyed the most?' When involved in a HRDNI, most people expect to discuss their most recent job, so they have usually prepared possible answers. In addition, what they have done recently in their job is usually fresh in their minds, so they can usually answer quite readily. Further, most of the important information about their current job is often available elsewhere (e.g. in organisational records), so if they forget some aspect through stress, there are minimal problems for the investigator.

As indicated in Figure 7.1, activity number 1 sits on the boundary between stage 1 (entrance investment time) and the rapport zone. This positioning indicates that activity number 1 helps the interviewee enter the rapport zone and, at the same time, provides some useful information. However, this information would need checking through triangulation as there is a possibility that stress or lack of trust may have filtered the data.

The entrance investment time is needed to help the interviewee reduce the natural barriers to sharing information. The entrance investment time has two conflicting roles. It needs to be detailed and take sufficient time to allow the interviewee to lower his or her natural barriers but should not take so much time that the interviewee becomes exasperated.

Stage 2. Activity number 2

As the interviewee enters the rapport zone (and this can be seen by the nonverbal clues) the interview proper can start. Activity number 2 is where the interviewer uses the skills of questioning, paraphrasing and probing. These skills will be discussed later in this chapter.

HRDNIs that are investigating explicit knowledge will remain at this step. As discussed later in this chapter, interviews that stay at the activity number 2 level are usually more structured and rely on questions that are pre-planned and content based.

Stage 3. Intimacy

HRDNIs that are researching knowledge deeper than that which is explicit will usually encounter complexity, uncertainty and emotions. This suggests that such an interview will need to progress deeper into the rapport zone. Such a step involves genuine caring and authenticity, and requires expert interviewing skills and sensitivity. Interviews at the intimacy level are usually more unstructured, relying heavily on the investigator's interview skills.

It should be noted that interviews moving this deep into the rapport zone will need to go through the steps of ritual, pass time, activity number 1 and activity number 2 before the interviewee will be deep enough into the rapport zone to risk full disclosure of emotions and inner feelings.

Stage 4. Exit investment time

Just as an investment of time was required to lower the defences of the interviewee at the beginning of the interview, so another time investment is needed to allow the interviewee to rebuild his or her natural defences. It is quite unethical for an interviewer not to provide this time space as no interviewee should be pushed defenceless into the cold outside world. There are six steps to this exit time investment:

- *Make final comments.* When the interviewer considers that all the information has been gathered, a comment can be made such as: 'Well, that is all the questions that I have. Do you have any *final comments?'* This achieves three aims. First, the interviewee can add any further information that he or she considers important. This often leaves the interviewee with a feeling of satisfaction that he or she has completed a good job. Second, it sometimes uncovers unexpected information which the interviewer may or may not choose to follow up. Third, the word 'final' gives the interviewee a cue that the interview is coming to a close.

- *Give a summary.* Some interviewers prefer to give a *summary* at this point, highlighting the main issues discussed. Again, this may encourage the interviewee to add some finer points. By explicitly stating all the issues covered, the summary emphasises that the interview was worthwhile. On the other hand, particularly if the interviewee is concerned about the amount of time the interview has taken, this step may take up too much valuable time and therefore may be omitted.

- *State future actions.* The interviewee may be curious or concerned about what will happen to the information that he or she has supplied. It is good practice to advise the interviewee of the *future actions* that you will take. This is also a good time to re-emphasise the confidentiality of these actions.

- *Give an opportunity for final questions.* To check if there are any other issues or concerns held by the interviewee, a comment can be made such as: 'Do you have any *final questions?'* This gives the interviewee the opportunity to satisfy any curiosity and also indicates that the interview is almost finished.

- *Conclude with a pass time.* A *pass time* gives the interviewee the chance to prepare to leave. Some interviewers like to use the same pass time that was used at the beginning of the interview, but such a perfectly rounded ending is most probably not needed. This pass time can also be accompanied by nonverbal behaviours such as standing up and moving towards the door of the interview room.

- *Close with an exit ritual.* In a similar fashion to the entry *ritual,* this is common good manners and a 'good-bye and a thank-you for the time' is usually all that is necessary.

Each of these steps in the exit investment time signals to the interviewee that the interview is coming to a close. They allow the interviewee to rebuild his or her defences in an orderly and dignified fashion.

Listening

Listening is the most important skill of an interviewer. Seidman (2006) suggests there are two levels of listening. First, the interviewer listens to what the interviewee is saying – the content of the reply as construed by the words used. The interviewer must concentrate on the substance to:

- make sure that the message is understood;

- assess whether the answer is on the right track; and

- make sure the answer is as detailed and complete as required.

Second, the interviewer listens for the 'unstated message' – what is not being said or what is being said verbally but is being contradicted by nonverbal messages. Does the interviewee continually avoid answering questions on a specific topic? Does the tone of voice match the verbalised message? Is he saying, 'Yes, it's OK' while looking despondent or even shaking his head?

As Kolb (2008) points out, it is the interviewee who provides the information in the form of answers. The answers are the raw data for the investigation so the interviewer must listen very carefully. This means that the interviewer must be comfortable with silence – allowing the interviewee to think – rather than rushing in and contaminating the outcome.

Questioning

While the pattern of the interview defines the overall strategy of the interview, questioning is the real heart of the process. Well-designed questions allow the interviewer to control the direction of the interview and investigate areas of relevance and interest – to say nothing of ensuring that the objectives of the HRDNI are achieved. There are two types of questions – open questions and closed questions.

Open questions

There are two aspects to the open question (Delahaye & Smith 1998). First, open questions allow the interviewee a wide choice of possible answers. While the interviewee may have only one opinion or remember only one point, as far as the interviewer is concerned the *possible opinions* or points are many. Secondly the open question should be arranged in what is called the *stem-plus-query design*. So, an open question may look like this:

> 'I am interested in the concerns you may have about the new financial system. Would you tell me about any concerns you have, please?'

Compare this to the style of questioning that is often used in ordinary conversations:

> 'What are your concerns about the new financial system?'

Compared to the ordinary style, the stem-plus-query structure of open questions gives the interviewee the subject to be investigated early in the question. This allows the interviewee to start focusing his or her attention on the topic. It also 'softens' the question as the ordinary style can become inquisitory when used in a succession of questions. In addition, as we will see later in this chapter, the stem-plus-query design fits in well with the skill of probing.

Closed questions

Closed questions are used for identifying explicit facts or for confirmation, for example:

> 'How many times have customers complained?'

> 'So, in your opinion, blue would be a better colour for the background?'

Because of the very short interviewee response the stem-plus-query structure is usually inappropriate for the closed question.

In combination

During the interview, the first question is usually referred to as the *primary question*. All other questions are called *secondary questions*. The type of questions used as primary and secondary questions lead to different questioning sequences that have different uses.

A *funnel sequence* consists of:

- an open question;
- a less open secondary question;
- a relatively closed question; and
- a closed question.

The funnel sequence is the most commonly used for investigations such as a HRDNI.

An *inverted funnel sequence* starts with a closed question and the questions then become broader until the sequence finishes with an open question. An interviewer uses the inverted funnel sequence when the interviewee is reluctant to be interviewed or if there is some uncertainty that the interviewee has any knowledge of the topic area. Theoretically, the inverted funnel sequence allows the interviewer to stop the interview early so that time is not wasted. However, as discussed later under *probing*, there are more sophisticated ways of gathering data under these difficult situations that have a higher probability of success.

The *tunnel sequence* is made up of either a series of closed questions or a series of open questions. A series of closed questions becomes an interrogation and this type of tunnel sequence is rarely used in a HRDNI (although it is a favourite of the police force!). A tunnel sequence of open questions requires high levels of interviewing skills as the interviewee can easily become bored or frustrated with the inability to cover any particular area in depth.

Paraphrasing

From the point of view of the interviewer, questions are the key to the interview as they provide the cues to which the interviewee responds. However, from the interviewee's point of view, the answers are the most important component – and who can argue? The answers provide the required material that will become the raw data of the HRDNI.

From the interviewee's perspective, the interviewee hears the questions and provides a detailed answer. The interviewer then asks another (possibly unrelated) question. The interviewee is left wondering. Has the interviewer heard my detailed answer? More importantly, has the interviewer understood the real meaning of my reply? These unspoken queries divert the interviewee's attention and, worse, de-motivate the interviewee so that less detail is given to the next question. This is not the ideal interviewing environment.

Of course, what the interviewee needs is confirmation that the interviewer has heard and does understand. This confirmation is achieved by *paraphrasing*. With paraphrasing, the interviewer repeats to the interviewee, in a concise form, the essential message of the interviewee's reply. If there has been a misunderstanding, the interviewee can then correct the interviewer's perception. As well as reassuring the interviewee that the message has been understood, paraphrasing has three additional benefits:

- as the interviewer is paraphrasing, the interviewee is often reminded of some additional information and will then provide this when the interviewer finishes paraphrasing;

- paraphrasing establishes a caring atmosphere within the interview that increases the trust between the participants; and

- paraphrasing allows the interviewee a little time to think, giving the interview a slightly slower but methodical, measured and professional quality.

A special type of paraphrasing is called reflection or *reflection of feeling*. Whereas ordinary paraphrasing concentrates on the content of the message, reflection of feeling acknowledges the emotions of the interviewee. Reflection of feelings often becomes more important during the intimacy stage of the interview. Being able to reflect feelings is a much more complex skill than ordinary paraphrasing as it demands of the interviewer the ability to empathise with the interviewee's emotions. In turn, empathising with another's feelings requires an ability to be in touch with one's own feelings. In most Western societies, feelings and emotions are second-class citizens to more factual pursuits, so developing the skill to reflect feelings often requires considerable effort. (See Cormier & Cormier 2002 and Howe 2005, for excellent discussions on reflection of feeling.)

Probing

Probing combines the funnel sequence of questions with paraphrasing and allows the interviewer to delve into the memories of the interviewee. The steps in probing are as follows:

1. The interviewer asks the primary (usually open) question, using the stem-plus-query structure.

2. The interviewee responds.

3. The interviewer makes note of the salient points of the interviewee's answer to the first primary question.

4. The interviewer paraphrases the salient points.

5. Selecting one of the salient points, the interviewer asks the first secondary question, using the salient point as the stem of the question.

6. The process continues on the first salient point, with each issue paraphrased and with the questions becoming more closed, until the interviewer is satisfied that the point has been explored fully.

7. The interviewer then briefly summarises the main issues that have come out of the first salient point. This overall summary is a special type of paraphrasing that briefly brings together what has been covered to this stage.

8. The interviewer then goes to the second salient point, using it as the stem for the next secondary question. The interviewer then continues to explore this second salient point, using the funnel sequence so that the questions become more closed and more factual information is uncovered.

9. The interviewer then progresses to the third salient point of the first primary question or goes on to the next primary question. Thus the interview becomes a series of funnel sequences.

Several points should be made about the probing process. Paraphrasing in the early stages of each funnel sequence is a must, but as the interview progresses down each funnel, paraphrasing may become annoying for the interviewee. Therefore, as the questions become more closed, paraphrasing usually becomes redundant.

The interviewer decides which salient points of the interviewee's response to explore. Some points may be explained fully as part of the response to the primary question; other points may not be worth following up. Only those points which help with objectives of the HRDNI are the ones the interviewer chooses to invest the time of the interview. The interviewer can decide how far down the funnel the questions should commence. For an interviewee who has limited knowledge of the topic, it may be easier to start with a less open question – that is, start lower down the funnel.

With interviewees who have a better knowledge of the topic the interviewer can afford to start with a broader, more open question – that is, start higher up the funnel. Finally, the interviewer decides how far down the funnel the interview should progress. Remember, closed questions are used to confirm an issue or to gather a specific fact. If confirmation or a specific fact is not needed, then the interviewer finishes that funnel sequence (usually with a summary) before the closed questions and then goes on to the next area to be explored. For a fuller discussion on the concept of probing in interviews, see Kolb (2008).

A closer look 7.1

Probing

The following is an example of an interview in which probing has been used to discover more information.

Er: As you know, there are a number of problems with the human resource information system we use in the company What type of problems have you come across when using the system?

Ee: Well, trying to access information is always a problem You know you need to find out various bits and pieces. I guess it is to do with the system not linking the various parts. When someone takes leave without pay, the system deducts the right amount from their pay but it doesn't deduct the day from their leave records. You would think that the system would do the lot, wouldn't you? And another thing, when someone goes to a training course, the system notes their training record but nothing is transferred to their department's skills matrix. We have to enter that information by hand a second time.

Er: So the main problem with the current human resource information system is that the various parts are not linked. There are two specific problems; let's concentrate on the first. Tell me more about the problems between the pay record and the leave record.

Ee: Well, when someone goes on leave without pay they fill out a form. This leave form goes to the leave clerk who enters the information into the computer under the Individual Leave Record. But then the leave clerk has to complete another form which he sends to the pay office. The computer system should automatically deduct the amount from both the leave record and the person's salary.

Er: So the leave clerk has to complete two actions – enter the leave into the computer and also complete another form. This other form that the leave clerk completes, what is it called?

Ee: Oh, that's the Salary Deduction form. It has to be signed by the manager as well.

Er: Ok, the leave clerk enters the information and also completes the Salary Deduction form when someone has leave without pay. You also spoke about the problem when someone goes on a training course. Would you tell me more about that?

Ee: Yes, when someone gets trained we have to update their personal record on the HRIS. But the personnel records of each department are separate. It's the same problem, really. We then have to open another field in the HRIS and enter the same information. It's a waste of time. And, of course, sometimes it is not always done, so it makes problems when we have to look up information – and it can cause quite a bit of confusion.

Er: So, it is the same general problem – you have to do two actions when only one entry should be all that is needed. I would just like to go back to the Salary Deduction form. You said that the manager had to sign it. If the computer did both jobs – note the leave record and also deduct the salary – how would the manager approve the salary deduction?

[and so the interview would continue]

Some points to note

- The interviewer started with an open question in the stem-plus-query format.

- The interviewee has provided information. The reply is fairly typical in that the first few sentences are not very clear. The interviewee is trying to make some sense of his or her thoughts and in the initial stages, this is often not very logical. However, as the answer progresses, the interviewee becomes more articulate.

- The interviewer paraphrased the information back to the interviewee.

- The interviewer chose to follow the first point about the leave and salary record.

- The interviewer used a closed question to identity a fact – the name of the Salary Deduction form.

- The interviewer summarised the main information from this first point, then followed up on the second point with another open question in the stem-plus-query format.

- This information was again paraphrased. There was no need for a summary on the second as the paraphrasing accomplished this objective.

The interviewer then investigated a new point disclosed by the interviewee from the earlier closed question. The interviewer could have followed up this point when it was raised but this would have interfered with the flow of the interview. Instead, the interviewer chose to make it a major third point, as the interviewer considered it to be a very important issue.

Summarising provides a break in the relentless search for information – a break for both the interviewer and the interviewee. Vanderstoep and Johnson (2008) define a summary as a restatement of the major ideas, facts, themes, or feelings that the interviewee has expressed. They suggest that summaries are like internal summaries in a good speech. From our knowledge of adult learning, a summary can be seen as a good example of at least two principles of learning (see Chapter 3):

- the recency element refreshes the interviewee's memory; and

- the feedback provided is both informational and motivational.

The advantages of recency and feedback alone emphasise the importance of the skill of summarising.

Interviewers should summarise at the end of each questioning sequence (that is, at the bottom of the funnel). This allows the interviewer to highlight the important points covered and to refresh the memories of each party of the salient points. The interviewee also has the opportunity to correct any misinterpretations that have occurred.

A closer look 7.2

Summarising

An example of inadequate summarising

Er: Yes, well, that was very interesting. You have made some very good points. They should be very useful for my enquiry. Thank you very much. Now I have some more questions.

An example of good summarising

Er: Good, thank you. Looking at my notes here, you have made four very good points about helping customers at the library. First, on the return of books. Customers have no record of the return of their books, and if there is a later enquiry, customers cannot prove that they have returned their books. Second, the returned books are not put back on the shelves quickly enough. You have found that, even though the library records indicate that a book is available, it is not on the shelves, and sometimes you have found it on the return trolleys. Third, when checking out books, you have noticed that some staff seem to be confused by the 'hold system' and have to find and then ask the supervisor what to do. However, as a fourth point, you do like the friendly and helpful atmosphere in the library. You always feel that you can go to staff members and ask questions.

Ok, is there anything you would like to add to those points? No? Right, I would like to go onto the next point which is about the computer services.

[and so the interview would continue]

Some points to note

- In the inadequate summary, the interviewer has given motivational feedback and has indicated that the interview will move on to further questions but little else has been achieved.

- In the good summary, the interviewer has provided positive motivational feedback and then gone on to list and paraphrase the four points the interviewee made. The interviewer has also referred to the notes, thereby sharing the notes with the interviewee, indicating that the notes are not a secret record but can be shared.

- In the good summary, the interviewer has given the interviewee an opportunity to add more information.

In the good summary, the interviewer has previewed the next area of questioning.

Nonverbal behaviour

The interviewer needs to be aware of nonverbal behaviour on two fronts. First, the nonverbal behaviour exhibited by the interviewer can have a dynamic effect on the interview. Second, reading the interviewee's nonverbal behaviour can provide useful insights into the progress of the interview and also useful cues on when to press for more information or when to proceed more carefully on a particular topic.

Egan (2002) has provided a robust model that can be used successfully either for appropriate interviewer behaviour or for interpreting the interviewee's orientation. This model is called the SOLER system:

- **(S)**quare on. The interviewer needs to stand or sit so that he or she is fully facing the interviewee. This gives the message that the interviewer is paying full attention to the interviewee's responses.

- **(O)**pen posture. The interviewer should not be hunched down or 'close off' the interviewee (e.g. by having arms or legs crossed so that they form a barrier). Sit up straight with an open profile. This gives the indication that the interviewer is willing to accept all the information that the interviewee will give and is usually interpreted as being non-defensive.

- **(L)**ean forward. Gently leaning forward slightly indicates involvement and interest. This posture says, 'I'm with you, I want to understand your message'. However, it should be noted that leaning too far forward has implications of aggressiveness and should be avoided.

- **(E)**yes. In our society, the eyes play an important part in communication. There are two issues to consider here. First, the distance from the eye of the interviewer to the eye of the interviewee should be at least a metre. This distance varies from culture to culture, but a metre seems to be a comfortable distance for most people. Any less and the interviewee may become unconsciously defensive with a resultant suppression of information. Any more, and the interviewee may feel that the interviewer is uninterested. Second, the amount of eye contact is important, although again this also varies between cultures. However, in most cultures there is an accepted level of contact, with too little being just as inhibiting as too much.

- **(R)**elax. A relaxed interview atmosphere is usually more conducive to easy information flow. If the interviewer models relaxed nonverbal behaviour – slower rather than jerky movements, a calm facial expression, slower speech patterns – then the interviewee is more likely to follow suit.

The SOLER system provides a useful 'checklist' at the start of the interview. If the interviewer consciously concentrates on these nonverbal behaviours at the beginning, they tend to become more automatic as the interview progresses and the interviewer becomes more interested in the topic of the interview itself.

The SOLER system also provides a very useful guide to assess the involvement of the interviewee. The more defensive the interviewee is, the more the interviewee's behaviour will appear to be anti-SOLER – the interviewee tending to stand or sit side-on, trying to make their overall profile smaller by hunching down; not keeping eye contact; and seeming to be anything but relaxed.

Such anti-SOLER behaviour is a sure sign that the interviewee is not in the rapport zone. This usually means that the interviewee has not reacted positively to the ritual and the pass time, so the interviewer will need to spend more time on activity number 1. Another option is for the interviewer to mimic, very subtly, the anti-SOLER nonverbal behaviours of the interviewee and then gradually move to the SOLER posture. Frequently, if the changes in nonverbal behaviour are carefully gauged, then the interviewee will gradually model the SOLER posture of the interviewer and, concomitantly, become more open psychologically to allowing information to flow.

A closer look 7.3

An anti-SOLER exercise

The nonverbal behaviours of the SOLER system are surprisingly strong. To test this strength, conduct the following exercise.

Ask a friend to do anti-SOLER behaviours while you talk to that friend for about three minutes on any topic. To do the anti-SOLER behaviours, your friend should sit sideways to you, cross their arms over his or her chest, lean back and look anywhere but at you. As you try to keep talking, also monitor your reactions. It is common for the speaker to try to catch the listener's attention by touching them or raising their voice. You may find that you lose your train of thought and it is common to have feelings of anger.

Structured and unstructured interviews

Interviews can be categorised as highly structured or highly unstructured, with these two points being considered as the poles of a continuum. Being on a continuum means that an interview can be described as being less structured or more unstructured. In other words there are degrees of being structured or unstructured.

The unstructured interview

An *unstructured interview* is one in which the interviewer starts with a broad, open primary question and then relies entirely on the interview skill of probing, paraphrasing, and summarising to manage the process and the direction of the interview An unstructured interview has the advantage of being unbiased by the preconceptions of the interviewer, and theoretically, more truly reflecting the world of the interviewee. The disadvantage of the unstructured interview is that it can be very time consuming and can wander from the objectives of the HRDNI. This means that no two interviews are the same, allowing the breadth of the investigation to become very wide.

The structured interview

In a *structured interview* standardised questions are carefully ordered and worded in a detailed interview schedule. Each research subject is asked exactly the same question, in exactly the same order, as all other subjects (Minichiello *et al.* 1995). Each question is pre-planned and explores a specific topic – that is, it uses the content of the questions to manage the direction of the interview. Structured interviews are used in situations where differences in interviewees' responses can be compared and interpreted as indicating real differences in what is being measured. The structured interview ensures that each interviewee answers the same questions and that opinions are canvassed for specific areas of enquiry only. However, the interview direction is biased heavily by the predetermined questions and there is usually limited opportunity for the interviewee to provide further information.

Structured or unstructured?

The decision to use a structured or unstructured interview revolves around two variables. The main variable is whether there is a reasonable amount of information on the issues already known. If there is, then specific primary questions can be formulated for each of the issues. If there is only limited information available on the issues, the interviewer will have no recourse but to use a more unstructured format and rely on interviewing skills to manage the process to ensure that the objectives of the HRDNI are accomplished.

The second variable is the interview skills of the interviewer. The unstructured interview demands that the interviewer be highly experienced. The strict scheduling of the structured interview, on the other hand, can often be used successfully by an unskilled interviewer.

The semi-structured interview

Another option, of course, is to conduct *a semi-structured interview*. There are two basic strategies for this. The first strategy is to commence the interaction as an unstructured interview – present the primary, overall question and then concentrate on managing the process by using interview skills to elicit information. When the information sought appears not to be forthcoming, the interviewer switches to planned questions based on defined, pre-identified topics – that is, questions based on content. So, for example, the investigator may start the interview with a very open question such as:

'The records indicate that customer complaints for whole company have increased in the last three months by 32 percent. In your experience, what do you see as some of the possible reasons for these complaints?'

When the interviewer has used all their probing skills to explore the respondent's ideas, they may then choose to switch to some prepared questions on topics such as:

- customer delivery systems;

- the location of the complaints office; and

- the training of staff to handle difficult customers.

These are questions based on content. Where did the investigator find the content for these questions? Most probably from the beginnings of the investigation using other needs identification methods. For example, before conducting the interviews, the investigator may have examined organisational records and gained some insights into possible causes of customer complaints.

Another strategy for semi-structured interviews is to use a pre-planned, logical approach to manage the interview process. Writers such as Tregoe (1983), Zima (1991) and Egan (2002) have each provided some insights that could be combined into a five-step model that can be used to manage the process of a semi-structured interview:

- *Exploring the current situation* – where the interviewer probes for a description of the current situation by identifying, clarifying and exploring problem situations and unused opportunities. The interviewer will tend to concentrate on:

  - what is actually happening and the identity of the issue;

  - where it is happening or the location;

  - when the event occurred; and

  - the extent of the event – how often, how serious, or how important.

- *Possible causes/options* – where a HRDNI assumes that the people at the workfront have a wealth of knowledge and the interview should provide an opportunity for this knowledge to come to the fore. If the HRDNI is examining a problem, this step will concentrate on causes; if exploring an opportunity, the options will be the emphasis. Some techniques for assisting the process include:

  - listing the historical sequence of events, which will often highlight the link that was most at risk or had the highest impact on creating the problem or the link that is easiest to repair;

  - brainstorming – asking people to come up with a long list of ideas, the more far-out the better, without assessing them;

  - asking people to compare and contrast – e.g. how it used to be with now; this product with that one; utopia with reality;

  - concentrating on what has changed.

- *Identifying untrue causes or adverse consequences* – where the investigator finds out whether the suggested cause would eliminate the problem or if the suggested option would have other effects in another system.

- *Preferred scenario* – where the investigator has people describe the preferred future scenario – defining activities that would occur, goals that would be achieved and people who would be affected. This is a good time to gather ideal examples, either in descriptive form or as actual artefacts. These ideal examples can often be used in formulating learning objectives or as part of the learning experience.

- *Planning the future* – where the investigator gathers suggestions on how the proposed scenario should be planned – identifying the resources that will be needed, the timing of key events, the people who should be involved and any dangers that should be avoided.

The three levels of interviewing

The interview is a dynamic vehicle for exploring rich and complex information in an individual. As an interaction, it is complex and dynamic, operating on three levels:

- the *content level* where the interviewer listens to and records the data information that the interviewee provides;

- the *process level* where the interviewer uses the skills of questioning, paraphrasing, probing and attending to control the direction of the interview and encourage the interviewee to provide information; and

- the *executive level.* As Seidman (2006) points out, the interviewer must be conscious of time during the interview and must be aware of how much has been covered and how much there is to go. An interviewer must be sensitive to the interviewee's energy levels and continually make judgements on how to move the interview forward.

The interview is ideally suited for investigating information from an individual. Where qualitative information from two or more people is required, the focus group is used.

The focus group

The focus group method is a research technique that collects data through group interaction on a topic determined by the researcher – the researcher's interest provides the focus while the data comes from the group interaction (Morgan 1997).

As a data-gathering device for the HRDNI, the focus group has a number of similarities with the interview. Firstly, the facilitator of a focus group must operate at the three levels – content, process and executive. As is the case with the interview, the management of the process is the most complex of these levels. Secondly, the conduct of the focus group is based on the same six factors as the interview:

- The overall pattern is based on an entry investment time, with the steps of ritual, pass time, reason, rules, preview and activity number 1, activity number 2, intimacy (if needed) and exit investment time, including final comments, summary, future, final questions, pass time and ritual.

- The ability to listen is still paramount.

- Questioning by the facilitator still guides and controls the interaction.

- The participants still need to hear paraphrasing to be reassured that their message has been received and understood.

- The facilitator probes to uncover all the information required.

- Nonverbal behaviour of the facilitator is used to encourage responses, and the facilitator observes the nonverbal behaviour of the participants to check for levels of involvement and understanding.

Differences between the interview and the focus group, however, highlight the roles that the facilitator will need to play in managing the process of a focus group. Morgan (1997) points out that the focus group method provides direct and immediate evidence about similarities and differences in participants' opinions and experiences as opposed to reaching such conclusions from *post hoc* analysis of separate statements from each interviewee. He goes on to acknowledge that the individual interviews have the distinct advantage with regard to (a) the amount of control the interviewer has and (b) the greater amount of time that each informant has to provide data. However, it is interesting to note that an investigation by Fern (1982) showed that focus groups did not produce significantly more or better quality information than an equivalent number of individual interviews.

In conducting a focus group, a facilitator has to be aware of a number of specific issues – among them being whether the focus group should be structured or unstructured, the logistics, group composition, and the processes of conducting the focus group.

Structured and unstructured focus groups

In a similar fashion to the interview, a decision needs to be made on whether the focus group should be structured or unstructured. A structured focus group is governed by predetermined, content questions while the unstructured approach uses an initial, open primary question and then relies on the skills of the facilitator to manage the process. A semi-structured focus group starts off being unstructured and then the facilitator brings in the predetermined, content-based questions.

Logistics

A focus group brings together a number of people, at a common time, in a relatively large space that is comfortable, quiet and free from interruptions. Associated equipment such as chairs, tables, audio- or videotaping facilities, visual aids and writing material is usually needed. While the steps in planning a focus group are the same as those discussed for the interview, planning the *logistics*, so that a focus group runs smoothly, can take some considerable time.

Accessing financial resources is usually more involved. Kolb (2008) suggests that resources such as the interview room, equipment, salaries, payment to the participants, refreshments, and transcription of the raw data will all add to the budget.

Group composition

The investigator has to give careful thought to the membership of the groups. One of the assumed benefits of focus groups is that the individuals in the group can 'piggy-back' and 'leap-frog' off each others' ideas, thus generating a richer accumulation of data. Unfortunately, if not carefully managed, this interaction can also contaminate the outcome, particularly when stronger participants take over the group.

Another problem that can occur with inappropriate group composition is having a group where members have backgrounds that are too diverse. The diversity of interests often results in too many, and even inappropriate, issues being raised, with the resultant time investment increasing significantly. Accordingly, there are several variables that need to be considered when assembling a group.

Homogeneity

The degree of homogeneity or sameness within the group will depend on the objectives of the HRDNI. If in-depth discussion is needed on a particular issue, then the members of the group will need to be similar on a number of elements. For example, if the perceptions of upper management on a particular situation are to be compared to those of operating staff, then there may be a need for at least two focus groups – one consisting of upper managers and another of operating staff. On the other hand, if the objective is to gather information from a wide variety of staff, then a mixture of participants may produce more relevant and richer data. Perhaps the final word can rest with Kruger & Casey (2000) who suggest that the focus group is characterised by homogeneity but with sufficient variation among participants to allow for contrasting opinion.

Representation

Quite often the entire target population cannot be canvassed, so only a sample of representatives comes together in the focus group. It is important to ensure that these representatives are likely to mirror the opinion of the target population. Previous comments on sampling should be considered here.

Strangers versus acquaintances

Whether it is preferable to select individuals who do or do not know each other is debatable. Morgan (1997) suggests that the rule of thumb favours strangers, although he acknowledges that this is not a necessity. Indeed, avoiding acquaintanceships within organisations is virtually impossible.

Size of group

There are conflicting issues to consider when deciding the optimum size of a group. The smaller the group, the more time each participant has to contribute views. However, the smaller the group, the less chance there is of representation of the target population and the more chance that one strong individual can hijack the agenda. Morgan (1997) considers that small groups can be disrupted easily by friendship pairs, 'experts' or uncooperative participants. Small groups, therefore, are likely to work best when the participants are interested in the topic and respectful of each other. Large groups, on the other hand, require considerable skill to manage, simply because of the tyranny of numbers. In addition, as groups increase in size, they tend to become more complex and formally structured (Forsyth 2006).

Krueger and Casey (2000) suggest that a rule of thumb specifies a range of six to nine, although one should not feel confined by these upper and lower boundaries. For more discussion on these issues, especially group composition, structure, and conflict, see Levine and Moreland (2006).

Conducting the focus group

Figure 7.1 also provides a very good outline for the conduct of a focus group. Focus groups rarely descend to the intimacy level as the public domain usually inhibits such disclosures. Fontana and Frey (1998) believe that the skills required by a group facilitator are not significantly different from those needed by an interviewer of individuals. The facilitator will also use the same process skills of questioning, probing and identifying nonverbal behaviour.

Fontana and Frey (1998) and Kolb (2008) go on to report that a facilitator of focus groups has three specific goals:

- first, the facilitator must keep one person or a small coalition of persons from dominating the group;

- second, he or she must encourage recalcitrant respondents to participate; and

- third, he or she must obtain responses from the entire group to ensure the fullest possible coverage.

Finally, the facilitator must keep the focus group focused on the desired outcomes. To achieve these goals there are five specific considerations that need attention while conducting focus groups.

Facilitator team

Kruger and Casey (2000) recommend considering using a *facilitator team* – perhaps with a facilitator and assistant facilitator. The facilitator concentrates on directing the discussion and recording the group's views on a white board, while the assistant takes more comprehensive notes.

Recording

Consider whether technology is needed to assist with data gathering. Audio- or videorecording devices can record a variety of detail and be a significant memory aid during the analytic stage. However, recognise that such recording can cause participants to suppress information.

Use of visual aids

When talking to a group, it is difficult to be sure that you have the attention of everyone. It is also more difficult to recognise feedback from many people. Using visual aids (i.e. multiple-sense learning) can help overcome these problems, particularly when used on the three occasions below.

- During the introduction, the *objectives* of the HRDNI can be shown on the overhead projector or PowerPoint show.

- Each *new question* can also be displayed on the overhead projector or PowerPoint show. If the question is just presented orally, misinterpretations can occur. In addition, the question can remain on the overhead projector for some time, so the participants can refer to it and keep the discussion on track.

- The *ideas* offered by the group should be recorded on a white board or similar device. This has at least three advantages. First, the person making the offer is rewarded by seeing her or his idea accepted visually. The reward is doubled if the facilitator paraphrases at the same time. Second, other participants can use an idea displayed on the white board to generate new ideas. Third, the list can be easily used to summarise at strategic points during the focus group interaction.

An alternative to questions, or in conjunction with them, is to use cues or examples that are more activity oriented or physical. Colucci (2007) suggests activity-oriented questions such as ranking options, label generation, storytelling, and role playing. Examples of work, and models or replicas can be used as physical examples. The purpose of questions, activity-oriented questions, and physical examples is to provide cues that will prod the memories and the creative thoughts of the focus group members.

Thinking time

It is often advisable to allow group members to write down ideas individually when each question or cue is presented (this is borrowed from the nominal group technique). This gives everyone a chance to collect their thoughts and tends to mitigate the overbearing predilections of opinionated individuals who like to take over the focus group agenda. If someone has written down an idea, he or she usually shares it with limited encouragement, thus assuring contribution from all members.

As an extension of this thinking time, Colucci (2007) suggests that the participants can be asked to do some preparation before the focus group meeting, such as reading references, checking the internet for a topic, or visiting a specific location.

Group dynamics

There are a variety of forces that operate within a group. Collectively, these forces are known as 'group dynamics'. Early work by such researchers as Benne and Sheats (1948) and Bales (1950) suggested that groups carry out two important functions – task and maintenance – and within these functions group members undertake a variety of roles. The *task roles* encompass all behaviours that help the group achieve the goal or objective. In a focus group this task activity is the answering of questions. They contribute to the good working relationships of the group by encouraging a collaborative attitude. Recently a number of authors have expanded on this earlier work on group roles (e.g. Dunphy with Dick 1987; Forsyth 2006; Napier & Gershenfeld 2003). Roles within each of the functions that are important to focus groups are described in Tables 7.1 and 7.2.

The facilitator must be able to differentiate between the task and maintenance functions and recognise the roles within each. Schein (1969) recommends that group facilitators stay at the process level and not stray into the content. Using this recommendation as a basic theme, the facilitator of focus groups should not become involved in any of the task roles. Rather, the facilitator should recognise and encourage the contributions of each role within the task function. So, if the group is not making any progress, the facilitator may ask the person who has been filling the initiator role for a contribution. However, it is important to recognise that any group member may fill any of the roles at various points – for example, as the discussion moves from topic to topic, different members may fill the information-giver role.

If the facilitator attends to the maintenance roles, then he or she will fulfil Schein's recommendation to concentrate on managing the process. However, group members will also often perform some of the maintenance roles. The facilitator, therefore, needs to decide when to adopt one of the roles or when to allow or encourage one of the participants to fill the role.

Table 7.1 Task roles in focus groups

Role	Function
Initiator	Provides new ideas or solutions about the problem at hand or suggests different ways to approach the problem. Is often deferred to by the group.
Information giver	Being a topic expert, provides facts and data. Acts in an advisory capacity to the group.
Information seeker	Calls for background, factual information from other members.
Elaborator	Gives additional information in the form of examples or rephrases others' contributions.
Opinion giver	Provides opinions, values and feelings.
Opinion seeker	Seeks more qualitative data, such as attitudes, values and feelings.
Coordinator	Points out the relevance of each idea and its relationship to the focus group objective.
Evaluator	Appraises the quality of the group's offerings, logic and results. Questions the validity or relevance of the facts raised by the group. Seeks clarification of vague ideas or issues.
Representative	Acts as a spokesperson for the others outside the group and speaks for the group as a whole.

Typically, the facilitator tends to assume the roles of recorder, encourager, gatekeeper, orienter and energiser. While the facilitator also assumes other roles, it is sometimes better to allow one of the group members to take on the responsibility. For example, 'tension reliever' is sometimes best occupied by a participant, particularly if the tension reliever is also the expresser. Of course, the facilitator may find the need to become the tension reliever but must be careful that this is not viewed as being flippant or as demonstrating a lack of concentration on the goal of the focus group. For further discussion on feelings and emotions within groups, see Manix, Neale and Anderson (2007).

Benne and Sheats (1948) and Bales (1950) also suggested that some idiosyncratic behaviours of individuals can militate against the achievement of the group goals. The facilitator needs to be on the lookout for these behaviours and plan ways of overcoming them. Napier and Gershenfeld (2003) suggest the need to be aware of five of these behavioural types:

- the aggressor;
- the blocker;
- the self-confessor;
- the recognition-seeker
- the dominator.

With thinly veiled sarcasm, the *aggressor* questions the very use and purpose of the focus group, making personal attacks on the facilitator and on individual group members. The *blocker* criticises every suggestion and idea. The *self-confessor* uses the audience to express personal problems, seeking sympathy and atonement. The *recognition-seeker* boasts of personal conquests and past successes. The *dominator* likes to be 'top dog' and uses strategies such as interrupting, flattery and asserting superior status.

Table 7.2 Maintenance roles in focus groups

Role	Function
Encourager	Rewards others through agreement, warmth and praise. Asks for additional examples or enquiries if others have a similar opinion.
Harmoniser	Mediates conflict between group members or between different points of view.
Gatekeeper	Ensures equal participation from members. Establishes procedures and ground rules that encourages smooth communications.
Orienter	Refocuses discussion on topic when necessary.
Energiser	Stimulates the group to continue working when discussion flags.
Expresser	Expresses the emotions the group is feeling and sometimes 'triggers' emotional responses from other members.
Confronter	Tends to take the 'hardnose' approach and exposes interpersonal conflicts. Is impatient with delays and confusion.
Tension reliever	Introduces humour when group tension is high; encourages a relaxed atmosphere.
Recorder	Provides a record of the information provided by the participants. This record is of two types – a visual record to help the group in processing the data and a permanent record for later analysis.

The thing to remember about these dysfunctional behaviours is that they are personal agenda that run contrary to the needs and goals of the group. The behaviours are games that satisfy the needs of the aberrant individual. The facilitator has a number of strategies to cope with the situations, among them the following:

- Allow the group the chance to retain control. Often the confronter is good at this role.

- Use nonverbal behaviour to discourage the individual – for example, go against the SOLER method: do not look the aberrant individual in the eyes and stand sideways to him or her.

- Do not paraphrase their aberrant offerings but reward them for positive contributions.

- Remind the group of the question by pointing to the overhead projector and restating the question.

- Summarise the progress so far and go back to the question.

- As a last resort, confess that you cannot see how the aberrant contribution helps the focus group achieve its goals. Be careful of this option as it can have negative repercussions.

Three of these considerations, in particular:

- use of visual aids;

- thinking time; and

- group dynamics

and the associated skills separate the focus group from the interview. They are also what make the facilitation of focus groups both exciting and challenging. For an excellent discussion on the techniques of focus groups with a variety of different groups and purposes, see Langford and McDonagh (2003).

Analysing qualitative data

The overall purpose of analysing qualitative data is to identify the themes and sub-themes in the raw data that will provide an understanding of the issue, opportunity, or problem that is being investigated. For a HRDNI it is well to keep firmly in mind that the most basic outcomes sought are learning objectives. Themes can be identified in two basic ways – based either on the pre-planned questions or by content analysis.

Pre-planned questions

In structured and semi-structured interviews and focus groups, pre-planned questions are used to explore certain specific topics. These cue questions, then, automatically provide themes for investigation. For example, if a question used was:

'Staff expect their supervisors to take on several roles. What do you think some of these roles are?'

then the researcher would gather a list and a description of a variety of roles based on the expectations of the respondents. One theme in the HRDNI report would therefore be a list and description of the expected roles. This theme might then be converted into a learning objective, such as:

'Describe the five main roles expected of a supervisor.'

Of course, using the pre-planned questions as the blueprint for analysis places an *a priori* structure on the outcome of the analysis. However, if the pre-planned questions have been devised carefully and are accurate cues representing the concept or issue being investigated, then any resultant contamination will be minimal.

Content analysis

The unstructured interview or focus group does not have the advantage of predetermined themes. Of course, even with the structured interview or focus group, additional data that does not conform to the predetermined questions is often gathered as well.

Content analysis is the process of identifying, coding and categorising the primary patterns in the data (Patton 2002). This type of analysis allows the themes to emerge from the raw data. There are nine steps in conducting a content analysis. Recognise, however, that these steps are not necessarily followed in a strict linear order as interaction and overlapping do occur.

- *Read* through your notes, transcripts and other evidence.

- *Code* the themes that emerge as you read through the notes and other evidence. A coding system is a means of reorganising the data according to conceptual themes recognised by the researcher (Minichiello *et al.* 1995). Coding can be achieved in a number of ways – putting an abbreviation or number representing the theme next to the sentence or paragraph containing the theme or using a highlighter pen to accent a theme. This coding process is the central activity of content analysis. As Patton (2002) comments, coming up with topics or themes is like constructing an index for a book or labels for a filing system; look at what is there and give it a label.

- *Compare* each emerging theme with the themes that emerged before it. For example, when you find what you think is a second theme, compare it to the first theme. When you find a third theme, compare it to the first and second themes, and so on. This process is called 'constant comparative analysis' (Cavana, Delahaye & Sekaran 2001).

- *Build* a data index. Maintain a list of the abbreviations with brief descriptions of the themes on a separate sheet of paper. Keep adding to this list as you discover new themes. This provides a data index and is the first stage of classification.

- *Transfer* the indicated passages to a computer file – one file for each theme – at reasonable intervals during the process (say, every couple of hours or so) or at the end of the process. These days, this is usually achieved by using a computer and word processing package. Another option is the 'cut and paste' technique – simply cut the coded segments from your notes or transcripts and paste them onto other sheets of paper under the appropriate categories. As this destroys the original documents, the cut and paste process needs to be undertaken with copies.

This transfer process classifies the data into specific categories. It provides fuller descriptions and examples of the themes. Usually, one category consists of one theme. Guba (1978) suggests two criteria for judging a theme or category:

- *internal homogeneity* – the extent to which the data in the theme 'dovetails' or holds together in a meaningful way; and

- *external heterogeneity* – the extent to which differences between themes are bold and clear.

Do not be concerned if a sentence or paragraph contributes to more than one theme. Just incorporate the sentence or paragraph in all the themes to which it contributes. However, re-examine these themes to see whether this commonality indicates a relationship.

From open coding to the written report

Stage 1 Open coding. The five steps in content analysis listed above constitute what Neuman (2006) calls 'open coding' – the first pass through the raw data where the researcher locates themes and assigns initial codes or labels in an attempt to condense the mass of data.

Stage 2 Axial coding. A second reading of the raw data is for axial coding (Neuman 2006). While additional or new ideas may emerge during this pass, the researcher's primary task is to review and examine the initial codes assigned during the open-coding step. During this second pass, the researcher asks about causes and consequences, conditions and interactions, strategies and processes, and looks for clusters of categories or concepts.

During this reading, the researcher reads through each of the theme files looking for sub-themes, relationships between sub-themes and other primary themes. One theme may split into two or more new themes, or two themes may combine to make one. Judgement is the critical element as it is the researcher who is trying to make sense of the wealth of raw data.

Stage 3 Selective coding (Neuman 2006). This occurs during a third reading of the raw data. The researcher first looks for evidence illustrating or justifying themes, and second, makes comparisons and contrasts between sub-themes and themes.

During this stage, Morgan (1997) suggests that the number of participants who mentioned a particular code be noted and whether each group's discussion contained a particular code. In other words, numerical scores can indicate the strength of opinion on a particular theme – although this should not be confused with importance, which is more a judgement of the analyst. Neuman (2006) suggests that negative evidence should also be identified, in that the non-appearance of something can also provide valuable insights. For example, an event not occurring, or the target population not being aware of certain issues, can have significant meaning.

Stage 4 The report. Surprisingly, this step is also an important last step in the analytic process – simply because of the knowledge-generation effect of externalisation. The researcher is forced to convert tacit knowledge to explicit knowledge; and logic deficiencies often come to the surface during this period. Once again, this can be an iterative process, with the researcher often revisiting the theme files and the raw data to check, question, or support various arguments enunciated in the report.

A rich, messy and complex process

Seven important comments should be made about the analysis of qualitative data:

- Analysis of qualitative data is a messy process. Even the nine steps of content analysis discussed above are relatively clean representations of reality.

- Analysis tends to start during the data gathering phase. It is difficult for the analyst not to see trends and categories as the data unfolds. Some authors argue that the analyst should ignore the urge to start analysing at the data-gathering stage. This is unrealistic. The best strategy is to acknowledge that this early analysing is natural, and record any ideas on trends or categories. However, acknowledge that these early ideas are tentative, use them as possible sources for probing questions, but do not fall into the error of assuming that reality has been found. Maintain a healthy scepticism. The analyst will work back and forward between the themes and sub-themes, and even between the themes and the raw data, again and again, until a level of satisfaction is felt that the reconstituted data is a true and accurate reflection of the phenomena being studied.

- Further, Minichiello *et al.* (1995) suggest that there can be at least two levels of data – the *manifest content* and the *latent content*. The manifest content is the data that is physically present and accountable in the evidence (e.g. the words in a quote from an interviewee). The latent content is the symbolism underlying the physically present data – or, if you like, reading between the lines. The analyst may choose to interpret the manifest or the latent content, or both. However, Minichiello *et al.* emphasise that, when reading between the lines, it is essential to continually ask whether our reading is consistent with the informant's perspective.

- Krueger (2006) suggests that the more complex the study, the more time analysis will take. He goes on to suggest that the analysis of three or four focus groups, or an equivalent amount of data from interviews, will take around 60 to 100 hours.

- The decisions are yours. Do not be overwhelmed by this. Look for the evidence that supports your choices of themes and go with it. Most people severely underestimate their ability to identify trends or themes in data – yet the human brain is superbly designed for just this purpose.

- Computer programs, such as NVIVO, can be used as an aid in content analysis. Decisions on themes (and the resultant codes), relationships between themes, between a theme and its sub-themes and between sub-themes, have to be decided on before such packages can be used. For an excellent discussion of the use of computers in qualitative data analysis see Richards and Richards (1998).

- Gathering data, analysing the data, and writing the report are not mutually exclusive activities. As Morgan (1997) comments, decisions about how to collect the data will depend on decisions about how to analyse and report the data. So, when planning the data-gathering techniques for a HRDNI, the investigator needs to project, keeping in mind the implications of the data analysis and the make-up of the final report.

- For a detailed examination of qualitative data analysis see Cavana, Delahaye and Sekaran (2001) and Neuman (2006).

It is a fact of life that the best instrument to analyse qualitative data is the human brain. This is the only instrument that possesses the required breadth of perception, complex appreciation and ability to reduce data. There is a danger of contamination. However, the principles of qualitative research are the means of mitigating this danger. Always striving for the utopian ideals of accuracy and replicability, and following the conventions of content analysis, are the hallmarks of good qualitative research.

The beginning of learning

The HRDNI is, in fact, the beginning of the learning experience for the individual and the organisation. This is particularly so with qualitative research methods like interviewing and focus groups. The interactions between the investigator and the participants are the epitome of communicative learning. Each of the parties involved is striving to understand the other's values, beliefs, and points of view while trying to ensure that their own beliefs, values, and points of view are understood.

In addition, both parties are involved in the knowledge-generation processes of externalisation and internalisation. The facilitator listens to the overt knowledge of the participant and internalises the ideas and beliefs. The participant dredges information from deep within the tacit knowledge level and, in converting this knowledge to explicit knowledge, often gains new insights into the problem, opportunity or issue.

The qualitative approaches to HRDNI also uncover a variety of variables and concepts, a number of which may need further investigation. In particular, confirmation is needed as to whether certain ideas validly coalesce to form a theme or if one variable has a relationship with another variable. This confirmation and validation process is the realm of quantitative research.

References

Bales, R 1950, *Interaction Process Analysis*. Reading Mass: Addison-Wesley.

Benne, K D & Sheats, P 1948, 'Functional roles of group members', *Journal of Social Issues*, 4(2), pp. 41-49.

Burns, R B 2000, *Introduction to Research Methods*, 4th edn, Longman Cheshire, Frenches Forrest, NSW.

Cavana, R Y, Delahaye, B & Sekaran, U 2001, *Applied Business Research: Qualitative and Quantitative Approaches*. Brisbane: John Wiley & Sons Australia.

Cohen, L & Manion, L 2000, *Research Methods in Education*, 5th edn, London: Routledge

Colucci, E 2007, '"Focus groups can be fun": The use of activity-orientated questions in focus group discussions', *Qualitative Health Research*, 17(10), pp. 1422-1433..

Cormier, W H & Cormier, L S 2002, *Interviewing Strategies for Helpers,* 5th edn, Pacific Grove, California: Brooks/Cole.

Delahaye, B L 1982, 'The structure of an interview', *Update,* Issue 29, March. Brisbane: Australian Institute of Management.

Delahaye, B L & Smith, B J 1998, *How to be an Effective Trainer,* 3rd edn, New York: Wiley.

Dick, R 1990, *Convergence Interviewing,* Chapel Hill, Qld: Interchange.

Dunphy, D C with Dick, R 1987, *Organizational Change by Choice,* McGraw-Hill, Sydney.

Egan, G 2002, *The Skilled Helper: A Problem- Management Approach to Helping,* 7th edn, Pacific Grove, California: Brooks/Cole.

Eisner, E 1997, *The Enlightened Eye: Qualitative Inquiry and the Enhancement of Educational Practice,* 2nd edn, New York: MacMillan.

Fern, E E 1982, 'The use of focus groups for idea generation: The effects of group size, acquaintanceship and moderator on response quantity and quality', *Journal of Marketing Research,* 19, pp. 1-13.

Fontana, A & Frey, J H 1998, 'Interviewing: The art and science', in N K Denzin & Y S Lincoln (eds.), *Collecting and Interpreting Qualitative materials.* Thousand Oaks: Sage.

Forsyth, D R 2006, *Group dynamics,* 4th edn,Thompson Wadsworth, Belmont, Ca.

Guba, E G 1978, *Toward a Methodology of Naturalistic Inquiry in Educational Evaluation.* CSE monograph series in evaluation, no. 8. Los Angeles: Centre for the Study of Evaluation, University of California.

Howe, M 2005, *Developing helping skills,* ACER Press, Camberwell, Vic.

Huberman, A M & Miles, M B 1998, 'Data management and analysis methods', in N K Denzin and Y S Lincoln (eds.), *Collecting and Interpreting Qualitative Materials,* Thousand Oaks: Sage.

Kolb, B M 2008, *Marketing research: A practical approach,* Sage, Los Angeles.

Krueger, R A 2006, 'Analyzing focus group interviews', *The Journal of Wound, Ostomy and Continence Nurses,* 33(5), pp. 478-481.

Krueger, R A & Casey, M A 2000, *Focus Groups: A Practical Guide for Applied Research,* 3rd edn, Sage, Thousand Oaks.

Langford, J & McDonagh, D 2003, *Focus Groups: Supporting Effective Product Development.* London: Taylor and Francis.

Levine, J M & Moreland, R L 2006, *Small Groups,* Psychology Press, New York.

Mannix, E A, Neale, M A & Anderson, C P 2007, Research on managing groups and teams: Volume 10 Affect and groups, Emerald (http://www.emeraldinsight.com.ezp01.library.qut.edu.au/books.htm?issn=1534-0856&volume=10).

Minichiello, V, Aroni, R, Timewell, E & Alexander, L 1995, *In-Depth Interviewing: Researching People,* 2nd edn, Melbourne: Longman Cheshire.

Morgan, D L 1997, *Focus Groups as Qualitative Research,* 2nd edn, Thousand Oaks: Sage.

Napier, R W & Gershenfeld, M K 2003, *Groups: Theory and Experience,* 7th edn, Bostor Houghton Mifflin.

Neuman, W L 2006, *Social research methods: Qualitative and quantitative approaches,* 6th edn, Pearson/Allyn and Bacon Boston.

Patton, M Q 2002, *Qualitative Evaluation and Research Methods*, 3rd edn, Newbury Park: Sage.

Richards, T J & Richards, L 1998, 'Using computers in qualitative research', in N. K. Denzin and Y S Lincoln (eds.), *Collecting and Interpreting Qualitative Materials*, Thousand Oaks: Sage.

Schein, E H 1969, *Process Management*, Reading Mass: Addison-Wesley.

Seidman, I E 2006, *Interviewing as qualitative research*, 3rd edn, Teacher's College Press, New York.

Tregoe, B J 1983, 'Questioning: The key to effective problem solving and decision making', in B Taylor and G Lippitt (eds.), *Management Development and Training Handbook*, 2nd edn, London: McGraw-Hill.

VanderStoep, S W & Johnson, D D 2008, *Research methods for everyday life: Blendingqualitative and quantitative approaches*, Jossey-Bass, San Francisco.

Zima, J P 1991, *Interviewing: Key to Effective Management*. New York: MacMillan.

Chapter 8

Design
The two main considerations

LEARNING OBJECTIVES

After studying this chapter you should be able to:

1. Explain what is meant by the term 'constructive alignment'.

2. Describe the five major categories of programmed knowledge, task, relationship, critical thinking and meta-abilities in the hierarchy of learning outcomes (HLO).

3. Explain how the HLO can indicate the preferred learning strategy.

4. Explain the effect of the learner's current level of knowledge on the design process.

5. Describe how learning experiences can be designed to encourage higher levels of learner motivation.

6. Explain the effect a learner's learning orientation can have on the design process.

7. Describe how learning styles can be incorporated into the design process.

Defining the role of the HR developer

Having finished the first of the HRD stages, the HRDNI, we now move onto the second stage: the design of learning experiences – sometimes called curriculum design or curriculum development. Before we begin, however, an early word of advice: in this text, for the sake of logical understanding, we are examining each of the four stages in turn. However, there are strong links and significant overlaps between the four stages. Accordingly, we will frequently make reference to the material discussed in the previous chapters on HRDNI and also to Chapter 3, 'Adult learning'.

Henson (2006) defines curriculum as both the plan and the experiences spelled out in that plan. Smith and Lovat (2003) believe that curriculum is the reality that is created for the learner. This is an important issue and all designers need to be constantly aware that, by selecting and rejecting, the design process defines a reality for the learner. Whether that reality is useful or meaningful for the learner depends on the professional decisions made by the designer.

Henson (2006) and Marsh (2004) believe that curriculum design should consider three issues

- the knowledge that is of most worth to the learners;

- the activities that are most effective in enabling the learners to acquire this knowledge; and

- the most appropriate way to organise these activities.

A fourth feature could be added – the knowledge should be of worth to the organisation. Therefore, it could be said that the task of the designer is to create a learning experience consisting of a series of linked and appropriate learning strategies that will provide the maximum opportunities for the learners to achieve the desired learning outcomes effectively and in the most efficient manner.

There are four important variables in this definition:

- the learning strategies, which will provide the learners with the opportunities to learn;

- the learning outcomes, which define the levels of knowledge, skills and abilities that the HRDNI has deemed the learners should achieve;

- the learners, whom the HRDNI has identified as needing the development; and

- contextual variables (such as the number of learners and the time allowed for the learning), that impact on the design of learning experiences.

The learning strategies are discussed in Chapters 10 and 11 as these strategies describe the third stage of HRD: implementation. These learning strategies include: the skill session; theory session; discussion; case study; role play; experiential learning; contract learning; and action learning to name a few. If you are unfamiliar with these strategies, you may prefer to have a quick look at Chapters 10 and 12 before reading further. The contextual variables will be discussed in Chapter 9. The other two variables identified in the definition – the learning outcomes and the learners – are the topics of this chapter.

In this second stage of the HRD process, then, the HR developer takes on the role of the designer. In this role, the HR developer will find that designing a learning experience for adults is part science and part art. The 'art' input comes from the tacit knowledge of the designer, and this complex understanding can be gained only by experience. However, scientific research has given us insights into the way adults learn, and these insights provide an integrating paradigm on which to make informed decisions.

Constructive alignment

The learning outcomes are derived from the HRDNI report. As discussed in Chapter 5, these learning outcomes may also be framed in terms of learning objectives or learning competencies. The learning outcomes are derived from the knowledge, skills, and abilities that the HRDNI has identified as being essential for the development of the targeted learners. The learning outcomes therefore represent the knowledge, skills, and abilities that are to be covered by the learners. The HRDNI has also identified and defined the targeted learners.

Designing a learning experience, then, is linking the learning outcomes and the learners via the appropriate strategies. That seems simple enough, but unfortunately, the life of the designer is not that easy. The link between the learning outcomes and the learner and the learning strategies is surprisingly intricate. Further, there is another intervening consideration – the assessment. While we will be discussing assessment in Chapter 12, assessment is a dynamic part of the learning process and experience. There must therefore, be a relationship between the learning outcomes, the learning strategies and the assessment of the learning.

Figure 8.1 Constructive alignment (based on the work of Biggs & Tang 2007)

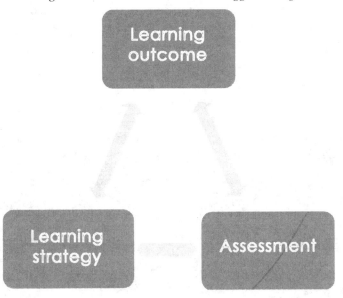

In 1999, John Biggs coined the term 'constructive alignment' (Biggs 1999). Constructive alignment occurs where the behaviours described in the intended outcomes are mirrored in both the teaching/learning activities the learners undertake and the assessment tasks

(Biggs & Tang 2007). Constructive alignment is a very important concept in the design of learning, as it integrates the three elements that impact on the experiences of the learner and emphasises that one element cannot be considered without the other.

While the next section of this chapter will concentrate on the relationship between the learning outcome and the learning strategies, the designer must always bear in mind the relationship between the learning strategy and the assessment tasks. From the learners' point of view, assessment always defines the actual, as compared to the intended, curriculum – an effect called *backwash*. Now, as Biggs & Tang (2007) point out, when the assessment is aligned to what the learners should be learning, backwash can work positively, encouraging appropriate learning. Alternatively, of course, backwash can have a negative impact, where the learner quickly sees through any rhetoric and recognises that, for example, while the facilitator may be emphasising the value of deep learning, the assessment only requires or encourages shallow learning.

We discuss the relationship between the learning outcomes and assessment, and the impact of assessment on learning, in Chapter 12.

The hierarchy of learning outcomes

The first important variable to be considered in the design stage is the learning outcomes. The content to be covered in a learning experience is defined in the HRDNI report by the list of learning outcomes and by the descriptions of the types of information, skills and abilities within the report itself. It has already been suggested in Chapter 5 that the HRDNI investigator can help the designer by prioritising the learning outcomes between those relevant to instrumental, communicative or emancipatory learning. This provides a very basic start to prioritising the learning outcomes.

One of the most well used approaches to categorising learning outcomes was provided by Gagne (see Gagne, Briggs & Wager 2004). Gagne suggested that learning outcomes could be grouped under the headings of: intellectual skills; cognitive strategies; verbal information; motor skills; and attitudes.

This categorisation provides some indications of appropriate learning strategies (e.g. the use of the skill session for motor skills) but does not cope well with the wide variety and complexity of potential learning outcomes.

After reviewing a number of studies into managerial and professional competencies, Delahaye (1990) compiled a hierarchy of learning outcomes (HLO) that can be linked to learning strategies. Recently, the writings of Ge and Hardre (2010) and O'Carroll, (2009) have added further insights. The HLO, while originally based on managerial and professional competencies, can be generalised to form a useful hierarchy for any learning outcomes (see Figure 8.2). As an overall view, it can be seen that the HLO moves from explicit knowledge to tacit knowledge or, in another perspective, from instrumental learning at the top, to communicative learning in the middle and emancipatory learning at the bottom.

This HLO indicates that there are five major categories – programmed knowledge, task, relationships, critical thinking and meta-abilities. These categories occupy four levels with programmed knowledge being the least complex, moving to meta-abilities at the most complex. The task and relationship groupings are at the same levels of complexity.

The five categories are presented as a hierarchy for four reasons:

- First, in moving from the top to the bottom, the categories become more complex.

- Second, the top category, 'programmed knowledge', has more to do with explicit knowledge, whereas the further they are towards the bottom, the more the categories enter the realm of tacit knowledge.

- Third, the categories at the top respond best to structured learning strategies whereas those at the bottom respond better to unstructured learning strategies.

- Finally, each category is dependent on an individual achieving competence in the categories above it.

However, while the five categories are presented as discrete entities, overlaps and interactions between the sub-groups, and between elements within the categories, do and must occur. Each of the categories will now be discussed, with comments in a 'closer look' indicating the most appropriate learning strategy that can be used to develop the various elements. Bear in mind, however, that the HLO provides an initial indicator of possible learning strategies only. The learner, the second main consideration discussed later in this chapter, must be given prime consideration in the design decision.

The programmed knowledge category

Programmed knowledge can reside either in the textbooks and journals in any library or be the knowledge declared by experts (Revans 1982). Nonaka and Takeuchi (1995) refer to this type of knowledge as explicit knowledge. As shown in Figure 8.2, programmed knowledge can consist of basic facts and skills, professional/technical information and procedural skills. Examples of basic facts include the number of staff in an organisation or the exchange rate of the dollar. Basic skills are the psychomotor skills – those that are completed automatically, like writing or using a screwdriver. Of more complexity is professional/technical information, which may be factual (e.g. water is made up of hydrogen and oxygen) or more complicated, having detailed complexity. Senge (1990) defines detailed complexity as occurring when many variables are involved. These variables are usually interactive but can be assessed and calculated to predict a cause-and-effect sequence (e.g. an engineer designing a bridge to meet certain load and wind force conditions). The idea of a cause–effect sequence suggests that certain detailed complex information is basic to the whole sequence, providing 'building blocks' for more advanced information later in the sequence.

Procedural skills have been nominated as the final element in this category. Delahaye and Smith (1998) define procedural skills as those involving procedures or psychomotor skills linked in a series, and where the order of psychomotor activities is crucial. Defusing a bomb, for example, would come under this element of procedural skills. It should also be noted that procedural skills often rely on professional/technical information as well as on psychomotor skills. So the successful bomb disposal expert would need to know the engineering, electronic and chemical composition of the bomb as well as having the procedural skills to carry out the defusing safely. Indeed, selecting certain procedural skills may depend on some detailed complexity information – one could well imagine that different chemicals would need different approaches to be rendered safe.

Figure 8.2 Hierarchy of learning outcomes

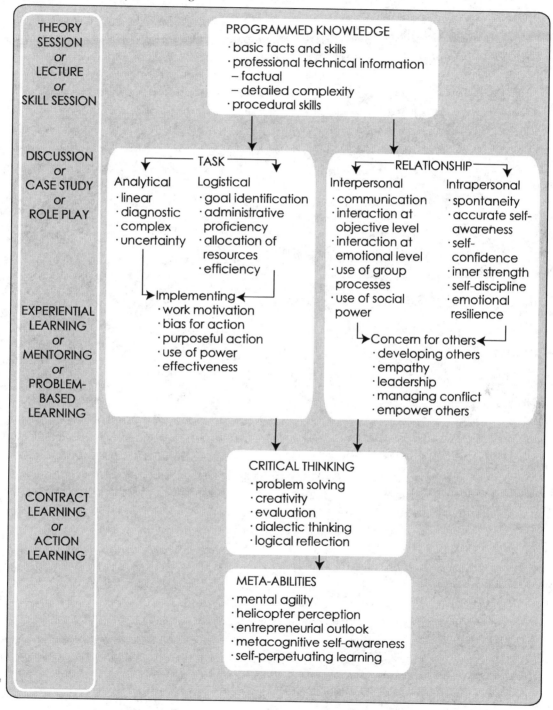

A closer look 8.1

Application of the programmed knowledge category

The programmed knowledge category is at the level of instrumental learning – the knowledge is meant to give the learner facts, information and skills that are needed to manipulate the workplace environment (see Mezirow 2009). However, the designer needs to differentiate between skills and information. The skill session is used for skills acquisition while the theory session or the lecture is usually the most appropriate for information. The skill session, theory session, and lecture are seen as the most structured of the learning strategies.

A further differentiation is information that can become basic 'building blocks' for more advanced information. The designer needs to ensure that these basic building blocks are learned before the more advanced information is presented to the learners.

When this differentiation has been made, the designer then completes session plans (see Delahaye & Smith 1998, pp. 97–111) for each of the skill sessions, theory sessions and/or lectures, along with associated support material, such as overhead projector transparencies, board plans, and specifications of required material and equipment. These session plans describe and cover the details of information and skills that the presenter (trainer, lecturer, teacher or HR developer) has to impart to the learners.

As with any instrumental learning, the designer should ensure that the basic principles of learning discussed in Chapter 3 – start with the unknown, readiness to learn, part learning, spaced learning, active learning, overlearning, multiple-sense learning, feedback, meaningful material and transfer of learning – are fully utilised throughout the design of the sessions.

The task category

The task category has three subgroups – analytical, logistical and implementing. Each of these subgroups has a number of elements which also form hierarchies. The analytical and logistical subgroups are of equal complexity.

The analytical subgroup

The analytical subgroup consists of four elements:

- linear analysis;
- diagnostic analysis;
- complex analysis; and
- analysis under uncertainty.

Linear analysis consists of simple information-processing skills (e.g. collating and identifying trends) and the ability to understand cause-and-effect relationships.

Diagnostic analysis is the ability to use existing programmed knowledge to explain or interpret an assortment of data. For example, a TV repair technician may use an algorithm (sometimes called a 'yes–no' chart) to explore the cause of a breakdown, with the algorithm providing assistance with the diagnostic analysis.

In complex analysis an individual uses a store of problem-solving and decision-making procedures or programs from which relevant selections can be made to solve a problem. For example, a HRDNI investigator may use Dewey's seven-step scientific problem-solving model (define the problem, identify possible solutions, evaluate each solution, select a solution, plan, implement, evaluate).

Analysis under uncertainty, the most complex of the analytical subgroups, is the ability to identify, analyse and solve problems under conditions of incomplete information. Senge (1990) refers to this as 'dynamic uncertainty', where cause and effect are distant in time and space and where the consequences are subtle and not obvious.

A closer look 8.2

Application of the analytical and logistical subgroups

The HRDNI report will often concentrate on the programmed knowledge that the learners need to acquire. The designer may then be left with the need to deduce whether the learners also need to assimilate analytical and logistical abilities. If the learners will be required to put the information and skills to practical use, then they will usually have to be developed in the appropriate analytical and logistical abilities. Of course, a good HRDNI report would already have covered this eventuality, but the designer should not take for granted such extrapolation.

The initial elements, particularly linear- and goal-identification, are usually most appropriately developed by the theory session, the lecture, and the skill session. Diagnostic analysis and administrative proficiency may best be imparted by one of these structured learning strategies. However, if the HRDNI report indicates that these two elements are reasonably complex, then a discussion or case study may be the method of choice. Certainly, however, the more complex elements of the task subgroup – complex analysis, analysis under uncertainty, allocating resources and efficiency – tend to need communicative learning (see Mezirow 2009) as offered, for example, by a discussion session or case study strategy. The designer may also bear in mind the knowledge-generation processes of internalisation and externalisation as the discussion session is aimed at encouraging these processes.

When considering the design of a full learning experience (e.g. a workshop or course extending over a number of days), the usual sequence of learning starts with the imparting of the information through the theory session or lecture, and then the deeper exploration of this information through reading case studies or practising in a controlled environment using a 'complex task' skill session, and then conducting discussion session to identify successful options, approaches and sequences as well as distinguishing paths that will lead to failure.

The analytical subgroup often interacts with the programmed-knowledge category. Once the programmed knowledge has been learned, the individual is usually required to put the information into practice. This practical use relies heavily on the analytical elements. However, while this interaction exists, there is no doubt that acquiring analytical competence is more difficult and more complex than learning programmed knowledge. Learning programmed knowledge is more about memorisation and repetition, while the analytical elements usually require an acquisition of protocols and decisions on options. Hence, the task category is placed a more complex level than the programmed knowledge category.

The logistical subgroup

At approximately the same level of complexity as analytical, the logistical subgroup consists of four elements:

- goal identification;
- administrative proficiency;
- resource allocation; and
- efficiency.

Goal identification is about concisely and accurately defining the goal or target that must be achieved.

Administrative proficiency covers the interactive skills of planning and organising. Planning includes the ability to foresee what activities need to be completed to achieve a goal and also the ability to make logical decisions. When organising, an individual brings together the various resources that are needed to achieve a specified goal, in a logical sequence.

While administrative proficiency is a more cerebral activity, *resource allocation* needs the courage to actually place the resources in the planned location. Allocating resources is a watershed element, as the logistics go beyond thinking and into observable and committed action.

Efficiency is the concern with doing something better, using efficient methods, and setting realistic goals and standards of excellence. While an individual can carry out the elements of goal identification, administrative proficiency and allocating resources, carrying out these actions efficiently requires a deeper level of commitment and ability.

While the analytical subgroup and the programmed knowledge category often interact directly, the logistical subgroup usually plays a supporting role. To analyse a technical or professional problem, the individual needs to identify preferred goals, plan and organise resources, and carry out the analysis in an efficient manner. For the TV repair technician, knowledge of the electrical circuitry and an understanding of appropriate diagnosis protocols will be insufficient if the technician does not plan, organise and allocate resources (time, spare parts, and equipment). If efficiency is not present, then one would have to wonder at the future employment prospects of the technician.

The implementing subgroup

The implementing subgroup of the task category is a deeper and more complex set of five elements:

- work motivation;
- bias for action;
- purposeful action;
- unilateral power; and
- effectiveness.

This is very much a results-oriented subgroup, having a high concern for ensuring that a positive outcome is achieved.

Work motivation is an attitude that emphasises self-motivation and enthusiasm with a strong belief in the primacy of work.

A bias for action concentrates this work motivation towards a desire to accomplish something, such as solving problems and overcoming obstacles.

Purposeful action channels the individual's energy towards a specific goal to ensure a positive outcome. However, this drive is tempered with common sense and an appreciation for the larger picture.

A significant but more sophisticated competence is the appropriate use of unilateral power – the ability to give directives and gain compliance. Unilateral power derives its energy from a variety of sources – the most common being knowledge expertise, position in the organisation and logical ability.

Finally, ensuring effectiveness – that the goal is achieved fully and successfully with the least expenditure of resources – is the overall aim of any task-oriented process.

A closer look 8.3

Application of the implementing subgroup

With the implementing subgroup, the HR developer as a designer is entering the challenges of emancipatory learning (see Mezirow 2009). All the elements of the implementing subgroup deal with frames of reference, although more with causal and procedural assumptions than with paradigmatic assumptions.

Accordingly, the learning strategies of choice tend to be experiential learning and mentoring, or perhaps problem-based learning. These strategies confront the learner with irrefutable evidence of inconsistencies in personal causal and procedural assumptions and encourage the reflection needed for deep internalisation and externalisation. In addition, particularly with mentoring, there is the opportunity for socialisation.

The relationships category

The relationships category consists of three subgroups:

- interpersonal;
- intrapersonal; and
- concern for others.

Like those in the task category, these three subgroups are on two levels, with the interpersonal and intrapersonal seen as equivalent in complexity. As with the analytic and logistical subgroups, there is a strong interaction between the interpersonal and intrapersonal subgroups. Further, there is often a strong relationship between analytic/logistic and interpersonal/intrapersonal.

The interpersonal subgroup

The interpersonal subgroup consists of five elements:

- communication;
- interaction at the objective level;
- interaction at the emotional level;
- use of group processes; and
- use of social power.

Very few people in the workplace operate in isolation. This means that some form of communication must occur. Communication can take three forms – written, oral and nonverbal. Oral and nonverbal communication frequently operate in tandem. Competence in communication is the most basic requirement for interpersonal abilities.

To communicate logically and meaningfully, an individual must be able to interact at the objective level. Objectivity means being relatively impartial and unbiased about others' views, and not being limited by subjectivity.

A more complex ability is being able to interact at the emotional level, recognising that there is a fundamental difference between working with 'things' and working with 'people'.

Using group processes needs high competence at the three preceding elements – communication and interacting at the objective and emotional level as well as knowledge of group processes.

The appropriate use of social power is often not acknowledged in polite circles, but is a necessary, strong, and subtle tool in interpersonal relations. Social power comes from other people's acceptance that an individual can influence them. This acceptance may be based on charisma, 'likeability' and trust. Together with unilateral power, its partner in the task subgroup, social power used inappropriately can be very destructive, so it is an energy that must be handled with care.

A closer look 8.4

Application of the interpersonal subgroup

The basics of the first two elements – communication and interacting at an objective level – can often be learned through the structured strategies of the theory session and, to a lesser extent, the lecture. The theory session has the advantage of incorporating active learning which provides opportunities of converting cognitive understanding into practical application. The more complex levels of these two elements usually require more complex learning strategies such as discussion and case study.

The other three elements – interacting at the emotional level, use of group pressure and use of social power – usually need the development or change of causal and procedural assumptions. Because these three elements assume that there will be interactions with other people, the learning strategy of the role play is particularly effectual. Mentoring and experiential learning are also viable options. When using role play, mentoring, and experiential learning, full use should be made of modelling, as this is ideal for learning large, integrated patterns of behaviour (see discussion in Chapter 3).

The intrapersonal subgroup

The intrapersonal subgroup deals with the ability of the individual to manage his or her self; 'intra' meaning within or inside. This subgroup is on a similar level of complexity to the interpersonal subgroup, and a number of the elements within each subgroup often develop in tandem. The intrapersonal subgroup has six elements:

- spontaneity;
- accurate self-awareness;
- self-confidence;
- inner strength;
- self-discipline; and
- emotional resilience.

Spontaneity is the ability to express oneself freely and easily; it has strong links with the communication element of the interpersonal subgroup.

Accurate self-awareness is the ability to assess one's strengths and weaknesses honestly and realistically.

Self-confidence, the ability to express confidence and be decisive, is a closely allied element. Both self-awareness and self-confidence are needed for interacting at the objective and emotional level.

Inner strength means having a tolerance for uncertainty, being resistant to stress, and being willing to handle ambiguity.

Closely aligned to inner strength, but at a slightly deeper level, is self-discipline – the ability to subordinate one's personal needs or desires for a greater good (the needs of another or for the organisation or for a principle or for a higher order goal).

Both of these elements – inner strength and self-discipline – are linked to the use of group processes and social power (elements of the interpersonal subgroup), and analysis under uncertainty and efficiency (elements of the analytical category).

The final element, emotional resilience, is at a deeper level and might almost be regarded as a separate subgroup. Emotional resilience is the capacity to be stimulated by emotional and interpersonal crises rather than exhausted or debilitated by them, and the capacity to bear high levels of responsibility without becoming paralysed.

Competence at the level of emotional resilience is situational. To a large extent, the situation depends on the nature of the programmed information category. So, for example, an engineer may have high emotional resilience with engineering conundrums, but much less in an unfamiliar territory like psychological counselling. The deeper level outcomes of the subgroup concern for others and the categories critical thinking and meta-abilities are also highly reliant on the same situational context.

A closer look 8.5

Application of the intrapersonal subgroup

Similar to the interpersonal subgroup, the basics of the first two elements of the intrapersonal subgroup – spontaneity and accurate self-assessment – can often be learned through the structured strategies of the theory session and the lecture. The more complex levels of these two elements usually require more complex learning strategies such as the discussion and the case study.

For the next three elements – self-confidence, inner strength, and self-discipline – the role play is particularly useful because the learner has to examine current causal and prescriptive assumptions. However, extreme care has to be taken during the 'de-roling' and debriefing stages of the role play. Frequently, mentoring and experiential learning as follow-up strategies are also needed. Again, the use of modelling is highly recommended.

Emotional resilience is reliant on paradigmatic assumptions and more intensive and lengthy learning strategies are needed. Problem-based learning is often quite effective in raising awareness of possible hegemonic assumptions but supportive mentoring and caring feedback from another party are usually needed to develop this intricate and subtle element.

The concern for others subgroup

The subgroup 'concern for others' is dependent on the other two subgroups in the relationships category – the interpersonal subgroup and the intrapersonal subgroup. Unless these two subgroups are developed to a reasonable level, the individual will not have the skills to show concern for others. In addition, the less-developed individual usually does not have the inclination to be concerned as he or she is more interested in perceived inner deficiencies: 'How can I interact with these people?' or 'This problem is just stressing me out too much!' So, before an individual can be genuinely concerned for others, she or he has to have high levels of interpersonal competence and a well-developed sense and acceptance of self.

Concern for others is made up of five elements:

- developing others;
- empathy;
- leadership;
- managing conflict; and
- empowering others.

Developing others involves not just training staff, but having a genuine interest in helping and watching others change and become more competent; having a belief in others' ability to perform and improve; being able to provide others with accurate and honest feedback; and knowing the optimal time to give this feedback.

Empathy is the ability to get along with people, to become close to them, and 'feel what others are feeling' while maintaining a strong recognition of right and wrong, what is needed, and what is not needed.

There are many definitions and theories of leadership, but of particular relevance is being a good judge of people; being able to delegate, and mould a team; and being able to supervise autonomous and independent individuals.

A closer look 8.6

Application of the concern for others subgroups

Similar to the implementing subgroup, when considering the concern for others subgroup, the designer is engaging with the challenges of emancipatory learning. All the elements of the concern-for-others subgroup deal with frames of reference, although more with causal and procedural assumptions than with paradigmatic assumptions.

Accordingly, the learning strategies associated with choice tend to be experiential learning, mentoring and perhaps problem-based learning. These strategies confront the learner with irrefutable evidence of inconsistencies in personal, causal, and procedural assumptions; they encourage the reflection needed for deep internalisation and externalisation. In addition, particularly with mentoring, there is the opportunity for socialisation.

Linked closely to leadership is the ability to manage conflict to ensure positive outcomes. Good leaders assume that conflict is a source of energy; a good leader uses this energy to the benefit of all concerned.

Finally, there is the ability to empower others – being happy to push decision-making downwards, promoting other peoples' ownership while providing guidance and support (O'Carroll 2009).

Rather than having links between elements, the subgroups of 'concern for others' and 'implementing' (from the task category) are a two-some that ensures a project will be carried to completion. Combining work motivation, a bias for purposeful action and effectiveness with the ability to develop and lead others empathically and overcoming obstacles with the appropriate use of power and managing conflict positively, are the hallmarks of good project management. Much workplace effort these days is based on projects with teams and groups sharing a variety of professional/technical information. Project work has now become the ultimate application of professional/technical information.

The critical thinking category

The second-to-last category is critical thinking; this was discussed at some length in Chapter 3 in its application to adult learning. To review, critical thinking is based on a combination of:

- *problem solving*, which is a process of logically and accurately overcoming challenges (There are several protocols available; one of the most common in use is Dewey's seven-step scientific model. This was a component of the complex analysis element in the analytical subgroup. However, in critical analysis, problem solving interacts strongly and frequently with the other components of critical thinking.);

- *creativity*, which involves novel responses and identifying new concepts by bringing together previously unconnected factors in new or unusual or adaptive ways (it includes the ability to think laterally);

- *evaluation*, by testing for what is both relevant and significant (it relies on some predetermined standard, which comes from the individual's explicit knowledge or tacit knowledge, or even from his or her frames of reference); and

- *dialectic thinking*, which allows the mind to accept that an entity may have opposing attributes, e.g. electricity can provide light and keep us warm but it can also kill us (having dialectic thought allows the individual to imagine a wider variety of possibilities and options).

A closer look 8.7

Application of the critical thinking category

The learning strategy of problem-based learning was specifically designed to develop critical thinking, and is the strategy of choice. However, mentoring and experiential learning (with honest and accurate feedback) can also play a part.

Contract learning is another option, as it gives the learner the responsibility for making all the choices during the learning experience. Making these choices about learning alternatives, and having the responsibility for accepting the consequences, tends to exercise the individual's critical thinking ability.

The advantage of problem-based learning and contract learning is that they involve emotions and critical reflection (see Figure 3.2 in Chapter 3). Thus, the complex interplay of these three components – critical thinking, critical reflection and emotions – is brought into operation, providing a full and rich learning experience.

However, highly experienced facilitators and mentors are needed to manage this sensitive and sophisticated learning process, and designers will need to specify this requirement in any design.

The meta-abilities category

The category of meta-abilities is the deepest and most complex level in the hierarchy and conforms to the abilities of an expert – defined by Ge and Hardre (2010) as having a strategically-organised content knowledge, noticing more features and meaningful patterns of information, readily recognising related sub-sets of information relevant to problems, and having systematic approaches to problem presentation and solution.

The meta-abilities category comprises five elements:

- mental agility;
- helicopter perception;
- an entrepreneurial outlook;
- metacognitive self-awareness; and
- self-perpetuating learning.

Mental agility refers both to the mental capacity for understanding complex situations and the speed at which this is done. It means being able to grasp problems quickly and think about them, to think of several things at once, to switch rapidly from one situation and problem to another, and 'to think on one's feet'.

Helicopter perception is the ability to draw back, to see the larger picture and how the specific problem or project that is the current focus of attention fits into the overall scheme of things. This broader focus also includes the ability to read the political climate and to have a feel for what the community is looking for.

Having an entrepreneurial outlook means looking outside to see what is going on in the external environment, seeking out innovative solutions, challenging set paradigms, and rejecting the status quo (O'Carroll 2009).

Metacognitive self-awareness results in a more pragmatic self-perception (usually downward) of one's ability, with a more realistic view of the complexity of issues (Ge & Hadre 2010).

Self-perpetuating learning engenders a thirst for new knowledge and holds an attitude that one's learning never ends. It allows one to be capable of using all the various learning processes and to be able to select the most appropriate learning process for the particular situation. A self-perpetuating learner can move from the abstract to the practical and back again; and can generalise learning by applying new knowledge from one situation to another.

The category is called 'meta-abilities' to indicate that the five elements form a deep-seated, nearly invisible network that operates at a subconscious level. The five elements are well within the tacit level of knowledge and are connected to the individual's basic frames of reference – the paradigmatic assumptions. The meta-abilities allow the individual to focus simultaneously on his or her personal internal operations while monitoring the overall external situation so that the categories of programmed knowledge, task, relationships, and critical thinking will be combined to ensure the most efficient and effective outcome.

A closer look 8.8

Application of the meta-abilities category

The adult learning strategies of contract learning and action learning place the learner in a situation where all the categories of programmed knowledge, task, relationships, and critical thinking are needed. In fact, these categories are usually needed in combination to deal with these strategies. For example, the learner engaging in contract learning needs the analytical abilities to conduct the research of the relevant programmed knowledge and the logistical abilities to plan, organise, and operate efficiently. The learner:

- must ensure that the learning plans are implemented;

- must operate well on an interpersonal level (as contract learning depends to a large extent on group work and contacting experts);

- needs strong intrapersonal abilities to keep operating in the face of adversity;

- often has to manage conflict; and

- must be skilled in critical thinking.

The categories needed for managing and monitoring the external situation to ensure the learning contract keeps on track depend on the meta-abilities. Action learning exercises all the categories in a similar fashion.

The practical use of the hierarchy

Any model is a rudimentary representation of reality. For this reason, no model should be followed slavishly to the exclusion of judgement, and the HLO is no exception. The overall design of categories and subgroups in the HLO seems to be relatively robust. That there is a gradient of elements within each of the subgroups is also plausible. However, there could be argument over the placing of some of the elements. For example, the placement of 'self-discipline' as marginally deeper and more complex than 'inner strength' could be challenged. Fortunately, as the design of adult learning experiences is not a precise science, such minor quibbles are of no great importance.

The HLO brings an initial logic and predictability to the selection of suitable learning strategies by focusing the designer's attention on a reasonably specific domain of potentially appropriate learning strategies. For example, it was suggested that role play would be the strategy of choice to develop the element of 'interaction at the emotional level'. However, the designer may see that a case study may be a better way to introduce the concept, and then follow this with a period of interactions with a mentor in the workplace.

In general terms, the HLO provides a clear insight into three basic themes of curriculum design. It:

- flags the learning strategy that is most likely to achieve the desired learning outcome;

- indicates clearly which learning strategies are inappropriate and which might be inappropriate (the hierarchy indicates, for example, that the lecture is inappropriate for developing 'emotional resilience', an error that is committed by organisations attempting quick fixes in the name of cost savings);

- provides a basis for the design criterion of *simple-to-complex*. A learning episode can commence with the more programmed knowledge before moving onto the more complex outcomes of, say the task category before then moving onto the critical thinking category. In this way, as expertise develops, learners are able to cope with higher-element interactivity (van Merrienboer & Sluijsmans 2009).

For these reasons, the HLO is presented as a guide for both the novice designer and the experienced designer. For the novice designer, the hierarchy will prove useful in two ways:

- it helps the designer avoid costly errors in choosing inappropriate learning strategies;

- it provides a useful model within which the designer can safely gain experience.

The experienced designer will find the hierarchy useful as a reality check to counterbalance the creative enthusiasm which sometimes leads us astray.

The learners

We now come to the second important variable: the learner. That people are complex and multifaceted is axiomatic. To ensure the strongest possibility of the success of the learning experience, however, some order has to be imposed on the myriad competing demands of the learners. Further, most learning experiences in an organisation assume that a group of people will be involved in the learning experience. This means that some individual differences will have to be subordinated to the greater good of the group.

Within this constraint, a number of characteristics about the learner have been shown to impinge on the selection of appropriate learning strategies. The issues of age, health, gender, and culture were discussed in Chapter 4; the HR developer as a designer must continually review these issues to ensure that the diversity in the organisation is harnessed as a positive and creative force. For example, adult learners from a high context, high power distance culture will expect that the HR developer as a presenter will be an authority figure who will share her or his expertise. This expectation is appropriate for the initial levels of the HLO (e.g. professional knowledge) but runs counter to the logic of the HLO approach for the deeper levels of outcomes (e.g. developing the 'concern for others' or the 'implementation' subgroups). The designer will need to consider how learners from such cultures can be developed to accept the more unstructured learning strategies.

Adult learners also exhibit a number of specific variables that need to be considered. These include:

- the level of current knowledge of the topic content;
- motivation;
- learning orientation;
- learning cycles; and
- learning styles.

Having already made some decisions about possible learning strategies from the HLO, these characteristics of the learner should be considered as an 'overlay'. This overlay allows the designer to fine-tune the selection process, perhaps by omitting some options or perhaps by indicating that a particular learning strategy option is now highly preferred.

Current knowledge

Several authors (Biggs 1989; Candy 1991; Harris 1989; Knowles 1998) have suggested that the ability to undertake unstructured (often referred to as self-directed) learning strategies, such as contract learning and action learning, may depend on the level of knowledge that the learner has about the particular programmed knowledge that is the focus of the learning endeavour. Delahaye (1990) found there were significant differences between those with high and low prior knowledge, with resultant implications for selecting a learning strategy.

A closer look 8.9

The effect of the learner's current knowledge

As learners with limited programmed knowledge are likely to have difficulty in operating within unstructured strategies, they need to be guided through programmed knowledge. The most effective and efficient options are the skill session, theory session or lecture, and the structured discussion methods, until the learners reach a level where they can seriously examine the more advanced features and interrelationships of the programmed knowledge. Then unstructured discussions and perhaps case studies can be used.

Motivation

Several motivational theories have been discussed through the years, most of them emanating from the fields of psychology and management. Two that are relevant to our discussion of the motivation of learners are:

- the two-factor theory (Herzberg 1968); and

- the expectancy–valence theory (Vroom 1964).

The two-factor theory suggests that there are two major but different considerations to take on board when examining motivation: hygiene factors and motivator factors. The absence of hygiene factors causes dissatisfaction. Of interest to designers are:

- supervision;

- the physical conditions under which the learning takes place; and

- relationships with peer learners.

If any of these is too low, the learners are likely to become dissatisfied – with resultant negative effects on learning. Interestingly, increasing the value or quality of these hygiene factors does not motivate learners; it just takes away the dissatisfaction. So, while the learning environment should be comfortable, do not expect plush and expensive surroundings to increase motivation to learn.

The motivator factors include:

- achievement;

- recognition;

- the relevance of the topic content being learned;

- responsibility; and

- growth.

The designer should look to enhance these motivators wherever possible.

The *expectancy–valence theory* gives us a much more complicated impression of motivation. This theory suggests that motivation is a process of four sequential steps. If, when taking this decision path, the learner believes that any step is below an acceptable threshold, then the subsequent motivation of the learner decreases. The four steps, in order, are:

1. *expectancy one*, where the learner decides whether the learning task is challenging but achievable, or whether it is too easy or too hard (if the task is considered too easy or too hard the learner will become demotivated);

2. *expectancy two*, where the learner makes an educated guess whether, once the task is achieved, the expected rewards will follow (if there is a belief that the expected reward will not eventuate, then the motivation of the learner to become involved in the learning task will decrease);

3. *outcome one,* where the observable (to the learner) reward eventuates (Skinner's operant conditioning suggests that a behaviour only exists because of the reward following);

4. *outcome two,* where the observable reward does have some internal value (or valence) to the learner. If the reward does not have any valence, then the learner is unlikely to perform the learning task again.

A closer look 8.10

Design and the two-factor theory of motivation

The HR developer as a designer needs to ensure that the learning experience:

- includes opportunities for the learners to meet each other and interact so that good relationships are developed between the peer learners;

- provides opportunities for the learners to see what they have achieved (e.g. through tests of ability of knowledge learned);

- allows the learners to take some responsibility for deciding what should be learned and how it should be learned;

- provides opportunities for the learners to reflect on what they have achieved during the learning experience so that they are aware of just how much personal growth and development has occurred;

- covers the knowledge that is relevant to the learners. This issue of relevance was discussed in Chapter 3 when examining the work of Knowles. It has also been emphasised as an important issue to be analysed in the HRDNI. That relevance is again raised under motivation underlines what an important issue it is.

In addition to these design components, the designer needs to consider the physical location where the learning will take place. For example, if the learning experience is a course or workshop such physical necessities as comfortable seating, sufficient light, air conditioning/heating and suitable space need to be provided.

The relationship between facilitator or trainer and the learner, and the way the facilitator or trainer provides recognition to the learners, is beyond the control of the HR developer who is the designer. However, the designer should designate the type and quality of the facilitator or trainer needed to manage the learning experience.

One important motivational theory, developed by John Biggs (1992), has come out of the educational literature. Biggs suggested that there are three levels of motivation. While Biggs did not consider the three levels to be a hierarchy, it can be useful to consider them as such. The three levels are:

- utility motivation;

- achievement motivation; and

- interest motivation.

A closer look 8.11

Design and the expectancy-valence theory

The designer needs to ensure that:

- any learning tasks are achievable but challenging for the learners;

- observable rewards will be forthcoming (e.g. that the results of any performance tests will be given to the learners);

- based on outcome two, any rewards are of value to the learner. While rewards are an individual issue, there are a number of recognised rewards that are valued by most people. These recognised rewards were identified in the two-factor theory – achievement, responsibility and growth. The designer needs to provide opportunities for these rewards to be incorporated into the learning experience.

Utility motivation occurs when the learner consents to be involved in the learning experience because the exercise will result in some utilitarian benefit other than the content learned. This happens when a learner attends a training course and tries only hard enough to achieve a basic pass, knowing that a basic pass is sufficient to receive a raise. The content covered by the training course does not hold any interest for the learner.

Achievement motivation occurs when the learner receives intense satisfaction in achieving some measurable goal. This goal may be based on competing against a personally set standard (e.g. achieving a high distinction or answering every question correctly) or on an external standard (e.g. receiving a higher score than a peer or being in the top 10 percent of the class).

Interest motivation occurs when the learner is intensely interested in the topic content itself. The details and interrelations are all fascinating to the learner with this level of motivation.

A closer look 8.12

Design and the three levels of motivation

The learner with utility motivation will prefer an efficient transmission of information, such as the theory session or lecture. A discussion will be tolerated, especially if it is a structured discussion, but it must not deviate into areas that are not essential. However, care must be taken by the designer that any summative tests (see Chapter 12) are of a standard high enough to ensure quality performance on the job. The learner with utility motivation will not voluntarily achieve a level of performance higher than that designated.

The learner with achievement motivation needs tests that provide quantitative feedback. It is only with figures that comparisons can be made by the learner – comparisons that are the foundation of achievement motivation. So the designer should incorporate some processes that provide quantitative feedback for learners with this level of motivation.

The learner with interest motivation needs freedom in time, sources of information, and opportunities for reflection – to plumb the full depths of the knowledge being covered. The self-directing approaches of problem-based learning, contract learning, and action learning are the strategies of choice for learners with the interest level of motivation.

It is tempting to believe that interest motivation is more valuable than utility motivation. However, this decision is really that of the learner. If utility motivation achieves the goals of the learner, then utility motivation is the best level for that learner. Designers and HR developers sometimes believe that others should share their interest motivation in a particular topic when, in reality, learners have other agenda that hold precedence for them. A fairer view would be that most learners come with a mix of utility, achievement, and interest motivation, with at least one of these predominating.

Learning orientation

Knowles (see Chapter 3) suggested that learning strategies can be categorised under two basic approaches – pedagogical or andragogical. Other words are often used to describe these two basic approaches – e.g. trainer/teacher or learner-controlled, traditional or self-directed, structured or unstructured. Delahaye (1987) and Delahaye, Limerick and Ream (1994) showed that pedagogy and andragogy have an orthogonal relationship, that is they are at right angles to each other. These authors also suggested that the resulting two-dimensional space can be divided into four orientations to learning – see Figure 8.3. Extending this work, Delahaye (1995) found that the learners in each orientation stage showed different characteristics and, from these characteristics, preferred learning strategies can be inferred.

Figure 8.3 The four stages of learning orientation

Stage 3 (Low pedagogy/high andragogy)	**Stage 2** (High pedagogy/high andragogy)
Stage 4 (Low pedagogy/low andragogy)	**Stage 1** (High pedagogy/low andragogy)

PEDAGOGY

Stage 1 (High pedagogy/low andragogy)

Learners in this stage tend not to be interested in 'intellectual' analytical thought. They are certain in what they have been taught to believe and accept the 'tried and true', even when something else might be better. They respect established ideas and are more tolerant of traditional difficulties (e.g. the inadequacies of the lecture when used inappropriately). These learners tend to oppose and postpone change and spend a longer time in the 'cusp of change' – they leave the old and approach the new; find the new too imposing and try to go back to the old; find the old is no longer there and approach the new again, only to repeat the process (Cattell 1989). Some learners who have difficulty with close interpersonal relationships sometimes choose stage 1, simply because such structured learning strategies preclude interactions among learners.

A closer look 8.13

The learner in stage 1 of the learning orientation

The first challenge for the designer is to decide to which stage of orientation the learners belong. While there is a questionnaire designed for the purpose (Christian 1982), it is not readily available. However, the designer can refer to the characteristics of the typical learner described and make a judgement.

For those learners at the stage 1 orientation, two of the characteristics are distinctive. The first is a disinterest in 'intellectual' analytical thought – i.e. these learners often want only the minimal amount of information to be able to do the job reasonably competently, or just to pass the test or examination. This minimalist approach seems to be caused either by a utility level of motivation or because the learner knows very little of the programmed knowledge and his or her priority is ensuring the basics of the knowledge are understood. The second distinctive characteristic is a fairly strong negative reaction to change. Indicators are stated preferences by the learner (during the HRDNI or at the beginning of the course) for lectures and 'not these airy fairy talk fests', when discussions are proposed as learning strategies.

Learners at the stage 1 learning orientation prefer structured (or pedagogical) learning strategies such as the theory session, lecture, and skill session. Use of structured discussions is tolerated, provided there is not too much interaction between learners. If the topic to be learned is appropriate (i.e. at the introductory level of programmed knowledge), then there is no conflict with using these strategies.

However, if the topic is more in the realms of the deeper elements of the analytical, logistical, interpersonal or intrapersonal subgroups of the HLO, then the designer has a difficult decision to make. One option is that the learners are not ready to be developed to these deeper elements. This is a tough decision because of most HR developers' belief in equity for all, and also because of the organisational political pressure for everyone to be developed.

The other option is to develop the stage 1 learners to become stage 2 learners. The designer will need to provide support and encouragement for the learner to progress into stage 2. Providing this support and encouragement is not easy because considerable time and effort is needed – resources that the organisation may be unwilling to invest. Providing a course program (or a weekly subject outline it in the educational sector), albeit one that has less topic content detail, can help. The designer and the educator/trainer/facilitator will find strong dependence needs ('it is your job to decide what I need to learn, not mine') and even the transition to less dependence (as compared to full independence) needs to be handled in a caring manner. Providing opportunities to develop supporting relationships with peer learners and the educator/trainer/facilitator can also help with those learners who do not have difficulties with close interpersonal contact.

Fortunately, with most learners, the human strengths of flexibility and adaptability allow a transition to stage 2, as long as some supporting mechanisms are provided.

Stage 2 (High pedagogy/high andragogy)

The learners in this group are very complex. They are quite perceptive and would prefer to understand a point rather than make hasty judgements. They are also curious and adaptable. They have a preference for the practical and are driven by their immediate learning needs. However, they tend to be suspicious and will avoid anything far-fetched. They can also have a relatively lower self-regard and lower self-acceptance, but such feelings of inferiority may be masked by aggressiveness and stubbornness – attack being considered the best form of defence.

A key characteristic is competitiveness. Learners at this stage crave competition, a function of their high achievement motivation. They display a need to achieve an internally established personal target (e.g. a certain level of correct responses – usually 80 percent to 100 percent – or a certain grade point average – again usually set at a high level) or some external comparison (e.g. achieving a higher score than a friend or enemy). As discussed under achievement motivation, such comparisons usually need a quantitative marking process. A give-away indicator for learners in stage 2 is that, when given some qualitative feedback on a test or examination, they will ask for a quantitative score (e.g. 'If this was marked out of 20, what would you give me?').

Finally, one overriding but confusing feature of learners in stage 2 is their often stated desire to be viewed as self-directed learners. This stated desire, though, is more a preference for the 'feel good' aspects of andragogy (Choy 2000). They prefer the HR developer to be friendly, to respect and value their contributions, and to be concerned about them as a whole individual, not just as a student. They are not keen to accept the hard decisions involved in being a self-directed learner, such as making decisions on what should be learned, how it should be learned, and how such learning should be assessed.

A closer look 8.14

The learner in stage 2 of the learning orientation

The heightened perception of learners in stage 2 have often made them question the appropriateness of the structured strategies in certain situations. This is an advantage if unstructured strategies are going to be used, and unstructured discussions, case studies, role plays and research projects are usually well tolerated. However, if any of these strategies is new to the learners, then their suspicion and aggression can be triggered. If the learners are likely to question the learning strategies chosen, whether they be structured or unstructured, the designer needs to consider how the selected learning strategies will be presented.

The big advantage for the designer is that the learners in this stage are curious and adaptive. Using their willingness to understand a point of view, the designer should explain fully the objectives and processes of the proposed learning strategies. Time to allow for conflict management and discussions when aggressiveness and stubbornness come to the fore also needs to be built into any design.

Of concern to the designer is their need for competition. If there is no need to develop these learners to become self-directed learners, then the designer can build in processes so that quantitative feedback is given. However, if the intent is to develop these learners so that they can progress to stage 3, then this dependence on extrinsic feedback will need to be changed.

The facilitator should certainly start with the 'feel good' aspects of being a self-directed learner. The hard decisions, what should be learned and how, can be introduced gradually, followed by the learners taking some responsibility for assessment. These levels of responsibility can then be increased gradually.

Stage 3 (Low pedagogy/high andragogy)

These learners are the quintessential self-directed learners – or, as Knowles would call them, andragoges. They are experimenting, analytical, creative and free-thinking, and can be described as 'rebels with a cause'. The cause is usually an alternative to what they see as obstructive, unfair and oppressive traditional, structured strategies.

They usually have the ability to develop meaningful, contactful relationships, and prefer to operate within groups. Being in a group allows them to hear new ideas as well as to compare their ideas and values with others.

While being imaginative and unconventional they can also be somewhat absentminded.

They usually rate high on self-regard and self-acceptance. Recent research has shown that learners with a high academic self-concept (that is, high self-evaluation and recognition of academic ability) are more likely to engage in learning strategies that are self-directed where there are opportunities for complex cognitive abilities and self reflection (Rodriguez 2009). Such a high academic self-concept is likely to go hand-in-hand with a high level of current knowledge.

A closer look 8.15

The learner in stage 3 of the learning orientation

The learners in stage 3 readily take to the unstructured learning strategies of problem-based learning, contract learning and action learning because of the freedom from obstruction and oppression, and the opportunities for analytical thought. Their high self-regard and self-acceptance see them through any challenges and constraints imposed by the organisation and powerful others. They are willing to accept responsibility for their own decisions and actions.

The challenge for the designer comes from two fronts. The first is when structured strategies are required (for example, the HLO indicates that the theory session or lecture would be the most efficient option). In this case the designer should use the structured approaches for the bare minimum of time to cover just the absolute basics of programmed knowledge. This should then be followed with discussions to give the stage 3 learners some freedom to think and interact in groups. The designer should then move into problem-based learning, contract learning, or action learning as soon as possible.

The second challenge for the designer is that stage 3 learners may become 'rebels *without a* cause'. Their experimental nature and self-confidence can engender a belief in their own learning immortality. This results in time spent on inappropriate or even unacceptable learning objectives. For example, a group might insist on watching pornographic videos for two hours after a lunch break because they are suddenly overwhelmed by feelings of freedom of choice, and choose to exert this freedom – albeit in a somewhat feisty teenage manner. The designer needs to establish firm parameters (e.g. through the non-negotiable objectives in contract learning) of what will be acceptable and what will not. Remember, these learners are experimenting, imaginative and unconventional. The designer will have to be in a highly creative and critical thinking mode to cover all bases. If there is a loophole, these learners will find it.

Stage 4 (Low pedagogy/low andragogy)

These learners are highly mature and experienced learners. They are what Candy (1991) describes as 'personally autonomous', having an ability to conceive of goals and plans independently; having a high capacity for rational thought; exercising freedom in thought and action; fearlessly and resolutely carrying plans of action into practice; and rating high on self-mastery in the face of reversals and challenges. They have a systematic way of doing things and are decisive, although they tend to have settled opinions. While they can be easily upset by authority, they usually make few demands and are guided by an overwhelming desire to avoid conflict. This profile explains their low scores on andragogy and pedagogy as they will respond to inner demands.

This work on learning orientations has three interesting implications for curriculum design:

- the concept links learning strategies with learner characteristics, so learners who are judged to be at a certain learning orientation are more likely to be more comfortable with the learning strategies discussed in the closer look sections 8.13 to 8.16 above;

- the concept suggests that the learners can be gradually developed as independent learners by following the sequence of stage1 through to stage 4, in accordance with the recommendations of Rodriguez (2009) (Note that this idea of gradual development closely parallels the design concept of *simple-to-complex*, discussed in the section 'The practical use of the hierarchy');

- the concept of moving through each stage from stage 1 to stage 4 also parallels the findings of Ge and Hardre (2010) of developing novices to become experts. Experts differ from novices in that their thinking is far more complex, allowing them to work on the full breadth of their tasks, have more systematic approaches to problem solving, and be more reflective in their selection of solutions.

The next concept we examine – learning styles – starts with learner characteristics and from these characteristics makes extrapolations to suggested learning strategies. While learning orientation indicates a preference for particular learning strategies, learning styles refers to a preference for particular information-processing styles (Curry 1987).

A closer look 8.16

The learner in stage 4 of the learning orientation

The key to this group is their high-level of learner maturity. They will select the most advantageous learning option available. For example, they are usually quite happy to sit through a lecture on a topic when their programmed knowledge is low, as they see that this is the most efficient way to gain mastery over the initial concepts of the topic.

The designer should be aware of their reaction to authority and ensure that the reasons for selecting a particular learning strategy are explored. Providing other options allows this type of learner to choose the most personally effective approach. Fortunately, there is no problem in allowing these learners to operate individually once an agreed set of learning outcomes has been negotiated.

Learning styles

Kolb (1984) believed that learning comprised two dimensions:

- prehension; and
- transformation.

The first dimension, prehension, represents two different and opposing processes. One is 'concrete experience' (i.e. apprehension) where the learner relies on the tangible, felt qualities of the immediate experience of interacting with his or her world (e.g. interacting with others or using a tool). The other is 'abstract conceptualisation' (i.e. comprehension) where the learner relies on conceptual interpretation and symbolic representation (e.g. reading the concepts in this book).

The second dimension, transformation, deals with the way the learner transforms the 'grasped or taken-in' information. Again, this occurs in two different and opposing processes. 'Reflective observation' occurs through internal reflection (e.g. reading how to make a paper plane and making a scaled drawing after abstract conceptualisation). 'Active experimentation' is the active external manipulation of the information (e.g. reading how to make a paper plane and then making one and seeing whether it flies).

These two dimensions – prehension (concrete experience v. abstract conceptualisation) and transformation (reflective observation versus active experimentation) – are seen to have an orthogonal relationship (at right angles) intersecting at the centre of each continuum. Further, Kolb believed (1984, p. 42) that learning required both prehension (grasping information) and transformation (transforming the grasped information).

This, then, forms four styles of learners:

1. *divergers*, who assimilate information through concrete experience and transform that information by reflective observation;

2. *assimilators*, who assimilate information by abstract conceptualisation and transform it by reflective observation;

3. *convergers*, who assimilate information by abstract conceptualisation and transform it by active experimentation; and

4. *accommodators*, who take in information by concrete experience and transform it by active experimentation.

Kolb also produced a questionnaire, 'The Learning Style Inventory', that allowed an individual to identify his or her predominant approach. Another popular learning style questionnaire is Honey and Mumford's 'Learning Style Questionnaire' (1992). A comparison of these two learning styles is shown in Table 8.1.

Table 8.1 Comparing learning styles: Learning Style Inventory & Learning Style Questionnaire

The Learning Style Inventory	The Learning Style Questionnaire
Divergers generate alternative ideas and implications. They will view a situation from many perspectives and organise many relationships into a meaningful 'gestalt'. They are imaginative, feeling-oriented, aware of meaning and values, and are interested in people.	*Reflectors* are thoughtful people who like to consider all angles and implications before making a move. Then they act as part of a wider picture to include others' observations as well. They tend to adopt a low profile and have a slightly distant, tolerant, unruffled air about them. They are cautious and tend to postpone reaching conclusions.
Assimilators use inductive reasoning and create theoretical models by bringing together diverse ideas into an integrated explanation. It is important that the theories or models be logically sound and precise, rather than of practical value. They are more concerned with ideas and concepts than with people.	*Theorists* assimilate disparate facts into coherent theories and like to analyse and synthesise. They are keen on basic assumptions, principles, theories, models and systems thinking, and prize rationality and logic. They prefer to maximise certainty and feel uncomfortable with subjective judgments, lateral thinking, and anything flippant.
Convergers emphasise the practical application of ideas and operate best in situations where	*Pragmatists* are practical, down-to-earth people who like making practical decisions and solving

The Learning Style Inventory	The Learning Style Questionnaire
there is a single correct answer or solution. They tend to be controlled in their expressions of emotion and prefer technical tasks and problems rather than social and interpersonal issues.	problems. They like to get on with things, and act quickly and confidently on ideas that attract them. They tend to be impatient with ruminating and open-ended discussion.
Accommodators like to be involved in new experiences and doing things. They are action oriented, take risks and seek opportunities. They happily change themselves along with changing immediate circumstances. Where plans or theories do not fit the facts, they will solve the problem in an intuitive trial-and-error manner. They will rely on other people for information (rather than use their own analytic ability) but are sometimes seen as pushy and impatient.	*Activists* involve themselves fully in new experiences. Their days are filled with activity but they are bored with implementation and longer term consolidation. They are open-minded, not sceptical, and this tends to make them enthusiastic about anything new. They tend to act first and consider the consequences later. They are gregarious, constantly involving themselves with others, but in doing so they seek to centre all activities on themselves.

Sources: Kolb 1984, and Honey & Mumford 1992.

As seen in Table 8.1, there are similarities between diverger and reflector, assimilator and theorist, converger and pragmatist, and accommodator and activist. Learning styles are very complex, and the combined descriptions give a clearer picture of each of the styles.

The concept of learning styles has an intuitive appeal. We all know people who are more action oriented and others who prefer to sit down and think an issue through before deciding what action to take. Further, Mezirow (2009) has suggested that one of the major sources of paradigmatic assumptions is epistemic influences and that these include learning styles. It is reasonable, therefore, to believe that a particular learning style will have an impact on the way an individual learns. However, the decision is not quite as straightforward as such a belief might indicate. There are three additional issues that must be considered:

- the learning style questionnaires identify a preferred style but most people have back-up or support styles (humans, being the flexible creatures that they are, tend to be able to move from one style to another);

- in any group, it is likely that there will be a variety of preferences and this variety could easily cover all four styles;

- both Kolb (1984) and Honey and Mumford (1992) believe that successful learners use all four styles. Indeed, recent research by Armstrong and Mahmud (2008) indicates that tacit knowledge is best developed by the learner experiencing all four types of learning styles.

These three issues indicate that a designer should endeavour to incorporate all four learning styles in any learning experience. Indeed, Honey and Mumford (1992) suggest that a robust learning cycle should pass through four steps:

1. having an experience (activist);

2. reviewing the experience (reflector);

3. concluding from the experience (theorist); and

4. planning the next steps (pragmatist).

A closer look 8.17

The effect of the learner's learning style

In general, designers should look to include all four types of learning styles in the learning experience. There are two ways to do this. First, the various needs incorporated in the styles can be met by the content imparted and by the strategies used. For example, pragmatists and those with a preference for concrete experience would enjoy a film or demonstration of how a piece of equipment works (the content) and would see the skill session as a good opportunity for hands-on practice; reflectors and those with a preference for reflective observation would see the case study as providing opportunities to analyse a situation logically and would appreciate the time given to reflect on the meaning of the concepts raised in the case study.

The second way of incorporating learning styles is to have group activities where each group has at least one representative from each of the four styles. It is often beneficial to ensure that each group member knows the benefits of each learning style so that the group members can see the contributions of each style. An interesting extension is to have two activities – one where the groups are homogeneous (i.e. comprising only of members of each style) and a second activity where the groups are heterogeneous (i.e. have a representative from each style in each group). A comparison of the two activities often highlights the differences in the learning process and how valuable each of the learning styles can be.

Learner maturity

In summarising these learner attributes, we can propose an overarching characteristic that could be termed 'learner maturity'. Learners could be high on the learning maturity scale when they:

1. Have high levels of tacit knowledge of the content.

2. Are predominantly driven by interest motivation.

3. Are at the fourth stage (low andragogy/low pedagogy).

4. Are adept at using all four learning styles.

5. Consistently engage in critical reflection by emphasising premise reflection (see Chapter 3).

6. Consistently engage in emancipatory learning (see Chapter 3).

7. Achieve the meta-abilities category of the *Hierarchy of Learning Outcomes* (see Chapter 8).

8. Value self-assessment above other assessment (see Chapter 12). Of course, such ability is dependent of accurate self-awareness (see the *Hierarchy of Learning Outcomes* in Chapter 8).

A very limited level of knowledge of the topic to be learned would automatically be a low maturity learner, as would those who only have utility motivation. Having a preference for the first stage of the learning orientation would also tend to indicate low maturity while the third stage is more likely to indicate a higher level of maturity. Similar judgements could be made on learning styles (one versus two or three styles), engaging in reflection, emancipator learning and evidence of achieving the meta-abilities.

Accordingly, we could say that the unstructured learning strategies would suit high learner maturity while those with a low level of learner maturity would learn more effectively with the more structured learning strategies.

A designer's checklist

As Caffarella (2002) comments, planning a learning experience for adults is like trying to negotiate a maze. Despite this complexity, the designer must make decisions that are logical, credible and defensible. This chapter has suggested that there are two basic considerations when designing learning experiences for adults. The first is the content to be learned (which is usually defined by the learning outcomes that the HRDNI indicates are most desirable). The second important consideration is the learners.

The easiest place for the designer to start is with the learning outcomes. The HLO provides a basis for the logical selection of appropriate learning strategies. While there may be debate over some of the elements within the subgroups of the hierarchy, there appears to be reasonable logic in the link between the subgroups of outcomes and preferred learning strategies.

Figure 8.4 A checklist for designers

1. Examine each of the learning outcomes listed in the HRDNI and decide which level of the HLO describes it best.

2. Identify the 'building blocks' – the basic programmed knowledge that needs to covered first before advanced programmed knowledge is presented; the programmed knowledge needed before the learners can take on the task category elements; the relationship category elements needed and where they are needed in the learning experience; the critical thinking and meta-abilities categories that are needed so that these are placed near the end of the learning experience.

3. Identify the critical characteristics of the learners – level of knowledge, motivation, learning orientations and learning styles – and decide the effect that these characteristics may have on the overall design.

4. Explore how the learning cycle of step 1 (having an experience), step 2 (reviewing the experience), step 3 (concluding from the experience) and

step 4 (planning the next steps) could be included in the overall design.

5. Make adjustments for learner maturity.

6. Ensure that opportunities for appropriate feedback are built into the design. This feedback should be:

    -   a combination of qualitative and quantitative;

    -   from an external source, such as a HR developer; and

    -   from an internal source (i.e. the learners should be given the opportunity to compare their own performances against standards and draw their own conclusions).

Once an overall selection of preferred learning strategies has been made, the designer can then turn to the needs of the learners. A judgement on the learners' current programmed knowledge is a base indicator as to whether unstructured (andragogical, self-directed, or learner controlled) strategies can be tolerated. If the learners have a low level of knowledge, then the more structured (pedagogical, traditional, trainer/teacher controlled) learning strategies would be the preferred option, at least until the levels of knowledge have improved. After that, the designer can take into consideration other learner characteristics such as motivation, learning orientation and learning styles.

Finally, reviewing the overall design to ensure that there is frequent use of the four stages of the learning cycle will provide a unifying theme throughout the whole design. A broad checklist is provided in Figure 8.4.

References

Armstrong, S J & Mahmud, A 2008, 'Experiential learning and the acquisition of managerial tacit knowledge', *Academy of Management Learning & Education*, 7(2), pp. 189-208.

Biggs, J B 1989, 'Approaches to the enhancement of tertiary teaching', *Higher Education Research and Development*, 8(1), pp. 7-25.

Biggs, J B (ed.) 1992, *Teaching for Learning: The View from Cognitive Psychology*, Hawthorn, Vic: ACER.

Biggs, J B 1999, *Teaching for quality learning at university: What the student does*, Open University Press, Buckinghamshire.

Biggs, J B & Tang, C 2007, *Teaching for quality learning at university: What the student does*, 3rd edn, Open University Press, Maidenhead.

Caffarella, R S 2002, *Planning Programs for Adult Learners*, 2nd edn, San Francisco: Jossey-Bass.

Candy, P C 1991, *Self-direction for Lifelong Learning*, San Francisco: Jossey-Bass.

Cattell, H B 1989, *The I6PF: Personality in Depth*, Illinois: IPAT.

Choy, S 2000, 'Factors that contribute to youth learning in TAFE', Keynote address at the *Moreton Institute of TAFE Staff Annual Conference*, pp. 15-16 August, Brisbane, Australia.

Christian, A C 1982, *A Comparative Study of the Andragogical – Pedagogical Orientation of Military and Civilian Personnel*, unpublished doctoral dissertation, Oklahoma State University, Stilwater.

Curry, L 1987, *Cognitive and Learning Styles in Medical Education*, Ottawa: Canadian Medical Education.

Delahaye, B L 1987 'The orthogonal relationship between pedagogy and andragogy some initial findings', *Australian Journal of Adult Learning*, 27(3), pp. 4-7.

Delahaye, B L 1990, *Selecting Strategies for Quality Management Education*, A paper presented to the ANZAME conference, Launceston, Tas.

Delahaye, B L 1995, *The Effect of Personality on Orientation to Self-directed Learning*. A paper presented to the AARE conference, Hobart, Tas.

Delahaye, B L, Limerick, D C & Hearn, G 1994, 'The relationship between andragogical and pedagogical orientations and the implications for adult learning', *Adult Education Quarterly*, 44(4), Summer, pp. 187-200.

Delahaye, B L & Smith, B J 1998, *How to be an Effective Trainer*, New York: Wiley.

Gagne, R M, Briggs, L J & Wager, W W 2004, *Principles of Instructional Design*, rev 5th edn, Thompson/Wadsworth, Belmont, CA.

Ge, X & Hardre, P L 2010, 'Self-processes and learning environments as influences in the development of expertise in instructional design', *Learning Environment Research*, 13, pp. 23-41.

Harris, R 1989, 'Reflections on self-directed adult learning: Some implications for educators of adults', *Studies in Continuing Education*, 11(2), pp. 102-116.

Henson, K T 2006, *Curriculum planning: Integrating multiculturalism, constructivism and education reform*, Waveland press Inc, Long Grove, Ill.

Herzberg, F 1968, 'One more time: How do you motivate employees?', *Harvard Business Review*, January – February; pp. 53-63.

Honey, P & Mumford, A 1992, *The Manual of Learning Styles*, Peter Honey, Maidenhead, UK.

Knowles, M S 1998, *The Adult Learner: A Neglected Species*, 5th edn, Houston: Gulf.

Kolb, D A 1984, *Experiential Learning: Experience as the Source of Learning and Development*. Englewood Cliffs, NJ: Prentice Hall.

Marsh, C J 2004, *Key concepts for understanding curriculum*, 3rd edn, RoutldgeFalmer, London.

Martin, C A & Tulgan, B 2001, *Managing Generation* V Amherst, Mass: HRD Press.

Mezirow, J 2009, 'Transformative learning theory', in Mezirow, J & Taylor E W (eds.), *Transformational learning in practice: Insights from community, workplace and higher education*. Jossey-Bass, San Francisco.

Nonaka, I & Takeuchi, H 1995, *The Knowledge Creating Company: How Japanese Companies Create the Dynamics of Innovation*, New York: Oxford University Press.

O'Carroll, S 2009, 'Subprime leadership: Lessons to be learned', *Human Resources Leader*, 185, pp. 16-20.

Revans, R W 1982, *The Origins and Growth of Action Learning*, Sweden: Studentlitteratur.

Rodriguez, C M 2009, 'The impact of academic self-concept, expectations and the choice of learning strategy on academic achievement: The case of business students', *Higher Education Research & Development*, 28(5), pp. 523-539.

Senge, P M 1990, 'The leader's new work: Building learning organisations', *MIT Sloan Management Review*, Fall, pp. 112-128.

Smith, D L & Lovat, T J 2003, *Curriculum: Action on Reflection,* 4th edn, Tuggerah, NSW: Social Science Press.

van Merrienboer, J J G & Sluijsmans, D M A 2009, 'Toward a synthesis of cognitive load theory, four component instructional design and self-directed learning', *Educational Psychological Review*, 21, pp. 55-66.

Vroom, V H 1964, *Work and Motivation,* New York: Wiley.

Chapter 9

Other design considerations

LEARNING OBJECTIVES

After studying this chapter you should be able to:

1. Describe the effect that the indirect factors of strategic orientation, organisational culture, key stakeholders, resources, and the designer's personal frame of reference have on the design decision.

2. Describe the rational model, the interaction model, the cyclical models, and the platform model of curriculum design.

3. Describe the program plan, the session plans, the resources plan, the product marketing plan, the budget, and the evaluation plan and define the role of each.

The indirect factors

The indirect factors are the second set of considerations that the HR developer as the designer has to contemplate when designing the learning experience. These factors include:

- the strategic orientation of the organisation;
- the organisational culture;
- the key stakeholders in the organisation; and
- the amount and type of resources available.

One other indirect factor is so obvious it is often overlooked – that is, the personal frame of reference of the designer.

While these factors are indirect, they do not lack importance. Indeed, many a workshop or intervention has failed because one or more of these factors has not been taken into consideration. Further, the designer often finds that balancing and negotiating these factors takes up considerable amount of time – time which the designer would prefer to invest in considering the two direct factors discussed in Chapter 8. However, in the real world, the design role for the HR developer is one of negotiating competing demands of interested stakeholders while holding true to the exigencies of the adult learning theories.

Strategic orientation

In Chapter 1 we discussed the idea that an organisation is made up of two basic systems – the legitimate system and the shadow system. The legitimate system is responsible for the day-to-day activities and for ensuring the organisation is efficient and is successfully servicing the market niche where it holds the most competitive edge.

The legitimate system, however, is effective in operating only under conditions close to certainty. The shadow system is that part of the organisation which continually prepares the organisation to survive in the future. What happens in the future, when viewed from the present time, is far from certain. Therefore, the shadow system is a highly fluid and creative part of the organisation which identifies, examines, and provides possible solutions for the challenges and opportunities that may occur at some future time.

Together, the legitimate and shadow systems specify the current strategic orientation of the organisation. The legitimate system achieves this by defining the present market niche that is being serviced; the shadow system by exploring the future and by challenging the current philosophy, culture and strategic mission of the organisation. This fundamental conflict between the two systems creates a dynamic orientation called *bounded instability* – a healthy state of tension within the organisation where learning is continual, change is expected, thinking is pro-active, but the bottom line of productivity is never forgotten. The state of bounded instability directly influences the strategic orientation of the organisation through the strategic planning process.

Strategic planning

Several decades ago, Mintzberg (1987) pointed out that an organisation has two types of strategic plans:

- intended; and

- emergent.

The intended strategic plan is the domain of the legitimate system. It incorporates the deliberate, almost mechanistic process (including the SWOT analysis that leads to the formation of the mission statement and the selection of appropriate strategies for a specified time period) that leads to the publication of the organisation's official strategic plan. The intended strategic process usually operates on assumptions of close-to-certainty. In addition, the intended strategic planning process tends to occur once every year – but changes continue in the external environment throughout that year.

Emergent strategic plans are in response to events that were not predicted in the intended strategies. These emergent strategies come from a stream of activities, usually instigated by supervisors and managers as they deal with the day-to-day challenges that they face. In other words, they are a response by the supervisors and managers who have to work in an environment that is far-from-certain. Accordingly, the emergent strategic planning process comes within the domain of the shadow system.

The activities of the shadow system – both strategic and operational – will be discussed in detail in Chapters 13 and 14. Suffice to say, at this stage, that any strategic changes emanating from the shadow system that are accepted by the legitimate system will be embedded into the legitimate system. An essential part of this embedding process is the development of staff, and changes that need the development of staff will become part of the legitimate system's HRD process.

The legitimate system

The intended strategic plan will have a strong influence on the design of the curriculum. In essence, the type of strategy selected by the intended strategic plan should be supported by learning strategies that are appropriate to that strategy. If you are unfamiliar with the concept of strategic planning, then it is strongly recommended that you read such texts as Schermerhorn *et al.* (2011) or Dickie and Dickie (2007).

The legitimate system's strategic plan, then, will influence the design of the learning episode in two ways:

1. Operational plans are directly influenced by the strategic plan and the content that will be covered in the learning episode will be found in the operational standing plans (the policies, procedures and rules). As discussed in Chapter 8, for the purposes of curriculum design, the content is represented by the learning outcomes, which were the first of the two main design considerations.

2. The strategy that the organisation has elected to follow will influence the type of learning strategies that are considered appropriate. Strategies that organisations select can be many and varied, but one taxonomy that is discussed by both

Schermerhorn *et al.* (2011) and Dickie and Dickie (2007) is the Miles and Snow framework.

A closer look 9.1

The effect of the legitimate system's strategic plan

If we use the Miles and Snow (2003) framework as an example, we can see how the various strategies will influence the type of learning strategies that can be used by the HR developer. Dickie and Dickie (2007) provide definitions of each of the Miles and Snow strategies:

- The *defender* – seeks and finds a secure niche in a stable product area.

- The *analyser* – stresses stability and flexibility but only changes after information has been carefully gathered and analysed skilfully.

- The *prospector* – perceives a dynamic, uncertain environment and maintains flexibility to take advantage of the environmental changes. It competes by anticipating change.

- The *reactor* – lacks consistency in strategic choice and tends to perform poorly.

The *defender strategy* will constrain the designer to the structured learning strategies (theory session, lecture and skill session) as they are less costly.

The *analyser strategy* will depend on staff learning the appropriate programmed knowledge but will also expect staff to have the more basic elements of the analytical, logistical, interpersonal and intrapersonal subgroups of the HLO. Usually, these basic elements can be developed quite effectively by the structured learning strategies, although the discussion will also be used frequently. However, cost will also be an issue.

The *prospector strategy* means that the legitimate system is operating very close to the shadow system. The entrepreneurial strategy depends on staff having the 'critical thinking' and 'meta-abilities' categories of learning outcomes (to maintain flexibility and ability to predict) , so the unstructured strategies of problem-based learning, contract learning and action learning will often be used by the designer.

Organisational culture

In every organisation, there are patterns of beliefs, values, rituals, myths, and practices which combine to make shared meanings. These shared meanings form the organisational culture. Organisational culture reflects the underlying assumptions about the way work is performed in an organisation – what is acceptable and what is not; what behaviours and actions are encouraged and which are not (Mullins 2007).

Having such pervasive power, organisational culture can be expected to have some influence on what types of learning strategies are acceptable and what are not. Organisational culture will be examined in more depth in Chapter 14.

Case study example

See the PLP case study on pages 15 to 18, and on page 24 of the workbook that accompanies this text for organisational culture.

A closer look 9.2

The effect of organisational culture

The organisational culture impacts on the designer in two ways. First, the designer must be aware of what the culture will accept and what it will not accept in both the content to be learned and in the learning strategies used. The designer will often find various taboos within various organisations. For example, organisational defence mechanisms (see Chapter 3) may dictate that certain issues will not be discussed, even within the confines of a learning experience. In some organisations, the name of the major competitor cannot be spoken and even good practices used by that competitor cannot be imported into the organisation. Taboos on types of learning strategies are less common, although the use of role play is sometimes banned.

The second impact on the designer occurs when the organisational culture is seen as inappropriate. The 'inappropriateness' may have been recognised by the shadow system. More commonly, because most organisations do not manage their shadow systems well, the organisation is faced with undeniable proof that the organisational culture is no longer appropriate. Either way, the designer is faced with the need to design a change intervention (as discussed in Chapter 11).

Key stakeholders

Sveiby (1997) suggests that there are two categories of knowledge within an organisation:

- professional knowledge; and
- political knowledge.

Professional knowledge is the knowledge on which the organisation depends so that it can produce its product or service. So, an accounting firm uses accounting knowledge to provide a service to its customers.

Political knowledge comprises the political power and knowledge of the organisational procedures and processes. When referring to political power, we are not discussing government politics, but the political struggles and decision-making that goes on within organisations. Political power comes from having some control over certain assets (e.g. knowledge of certain production processes, or having the keys to the storeroom) or by having connections to people with legitimate power (e.g. the personal assistant to the chief executive officer). Knowledge of the organisational procedures and processes, together with political power, gives a person within the organisation an ability to influence and manipulate what is done and how it is done. People with organisational political knowledge are called key stakeholders.

Key stakeholders who also have legitimate power tend to be the 'movers and shakers' within the organisation. Legitimate power comes from having some official capacity in the organisation. Usually, the higher up the organisational hierarchy an individual is, the more power she or he has; a manager will tend to have more power than a first-line supervisor. HR developers, whether in the role of investigator, designer, implementer or evaluator, should be aware of key stakeholders and especially key stakeholders with legitimate power.

A closer look 9.3

The effect of key stakeholders

To be a successful designer, the HR developer has to be politically astute, as key stakeholders can make or break a learning experience. A key stakeholder may decide that a particular program will not proceed or that a particular issue will not be discussed in a learning program. For example, you may have a chief manager who refuses to allow accident targets to be discussed in a safety training program. He may believe that there is only one accident target – zero accidents. The fact that decreasing the number of accidents from over 1000 to zero is unachievable, and therefore no one can be rewarded for achieving lower levels, does not come into consideration. One might empathise with the chief manager's thought process, but the decision does not help establish a safety program.

The designer needs to be aware of the peccadilloes of the various key stakeholders in the organisation. A decision then has to be made about whether these peccadilloes will be respected or ignored. It is a brave designer who goes down the path of transgression, so if this path is chosen, the designer should be quite sure that the path is correct and that there are no other options. If, as a designer, you are faced with such an awkward decision, you may wish to review the discussion of changing frames of reference, in particular paradigmatic assumptions, in Chapter 3.

On the other hand, of course, the wise designer will also seek the support of key stakeholders when designing important or controversial learning programs. Such support will go a long way towards smoothing the passage of such plans.

Resources

The resources available to the designer often seem to be a constraint on design, but this is a pessimistic view. The designer must be realistic and make decisions within the resources available. Some of the more significant resources a designer needs to monitor are:

- time;
- number of learners;
- physical resources; and
- qualified HR developers.

The tyranny of time

Time is the constant enemy of the designer. There always seems to be so much to be learned and so little time for the learning to occur. Unfortunately, to exacerbate the situation, too many managers have little idea how time consuming learning can be (see 'a time delay' in Chapter 3). This is understandable, as managers are invariably operating in highly uncertain situations but are expected to achieve targets that are, at times, set ambitiously high by the organisation. It is no wonder that managers are usually more swayed by the short-term needs of productivity rather than by the long-term benefits of developed staff.

This creates an internal conflict for the designer. On the one hand, there is the recognition that managers need their staff to maintain production schedules. On the other hand, the designer is aware that it is professionally negligent to give learners a less-than-optimal length of time to learn a skill or to challenge a frame of reference. The hallmark of a high-quality designer is the ability to come to terms with this conflict by making decisions that are fair and of equal benefit to all, and by negotiating time frames that optimise all needs.

Sometimes, the abilities of the learners (as discussed in Chapter 8) can help the designer overcome some of the challenges of time. Learners with mature learning abilities, or with high motivation, do not always need the time investment of the average learner.

The tyranny of numbers

Sometimes, a decision will be forced on the designer to accept more than the optimal number of learners on a learning program. This decision could easily come from a key stakeholder. If the decision cannot be reversed, then the designer has to make the best of a very challenging situation. The quality of learning will undoubtedly be harmed if the numbers of learners is too high. However, the designer has to be creative and attempt to minimise the problem. For example, case studies can still be used in very large groups (even up to 100 learners). The problem is that the HR developer, who is the implementer of the program, cannot both listen and provide feedback to every group. However, some of the learners can be designated 'observers' who report back to the total group at the end of the case study. The implementer can then overview the main points raised by the observers. This is not ideal, but under the circumstances is much better than nothing.

Physical resources

A variety of physical resources are needed to mount a learning program. The first consideration is the location where the learning will take place. This may vary from a meeting room, when action learning is used, to a training room for most of the other learning strategies. Skill sessions sometimes need different types of accommodation, depending on the equipment needed to demonstrate the skill. I have seen an entire front end of an aeroplane in a training room on an air force facility. These days it is not unusual to see whole training rooms devoted to computers.

These physical resources all need funding, so money is a basic resource for any learning experience. The organisation may own or hire the rooms and equipment, but this still means that some financial backing is needed. The designer has to work within the constraints of the physical resources and the finances of the organisation, although providing an early warning of future expenditure is often appreciated by higher level decision makers. At the same time, however, the designer should not be shy of pushing the boundaries of possibility.

Qualified HR developers

No matter what the learning experience, a design is merely a plan until operationalised by a HR developer. HR developers need to be qualified in two areas – the content to be taught and the learning strategies to be used. Particularly when programmed knowledge is the focus of the learning experience, HR developers need the content knowledge both to explain the concepts and to be seen as credible, a necessity underlined by the recent research by Misko and Priest (2009). However, the best knowledge expert is worse than useless if he or she does not have the techniques and abilities to impart the knowledge. These techniques and abilities – sometimes referred to as the process of teaching or facilitating – become even more important when the learning strategies become unstructured. With fully unstructured approaches such as contract learning and action learning, the HR developer cannot even operate unless he or she has exceptional facilitation abilities.

Overall, though, it is best if the facilitator has both content expertise and the skills and knowledge of a proficient facilitator. This combination allows the facilitator to engage in both modelling and the knowledge generation process of socialisation (see Chapter 3).

A closer look 9.4

The effect of available resources

A designer needs to pay very close attention to the availability of time, physical resources and qualified HR developers. The best design can easily become a learner's nightmare if any of these resources falls below a critical level.

In addition, designers have to recognise that they are often in competition for scarce resources, and will have to be prepared to fight for acceptable levels. Indeed, this is often where the backing of key stakeholders becomes important. Even designers cannot be above the need to become involved in the political machinations of the organisation.

Designer's personal frame of reference

Because it resides within, the designer often overlooks her or his personal frame of reference. Yet, as discussed in Chapter 3, one's frame of reference has a significant impact on decisions and actions. Therefore, designers should critically reflect on their personal values and beliefs, considering the impact these values and beliefs may have on design decisions. For example, a designer may have experienced intense personal satisfaction using self-directed learning. This highly positive experience will have affected the designer's frame of reference. A problem occurs if the designer allows this positive frame of reference to sway design decisions unduly in favour of self-directed learning.

An overview of the design process

In an attempt to provide a logical conception of the design process, a number of models have been proposed over the years. The order of presentation of the decisions to be made in curriculum design discussed in Chapters 8 and 9 have, to a large part, followed a number of these models.

The *objectives* or *rational model* (Tyler 1949) is the oldest and one of the most commonly used. This model suggests that there are four steps:

1. establishment of the objectives;

2. determination of the instructional strategies;

3. organisation of the learning experiences; and

4. assessment and evaluation.

There have been variations on the theme – for example, Hansen (2006) recommends analysis; design; development; implementation; and evaluation, but Tyler's four steps remain the core of the curriculum design process. The first decision of the designer is based on the first two steps of this rational model. In Chapter 8, these two steps have been described under the HLO. The learning outcomes equate to the first step (establishment of the objectives) and the link to the appropriate learning strategies matches the second step (determination of the instructional strategies). The third step of the rational model, organising the learning experience, will be discussed in the next section of this chapter, 'The product'.

So far, no mention has been made of 'assessment and evaluation'. Planning the evaluation of the learning experience is the final duty of the designer (this is the topic of Chapter 12). As indicated earlier, the four stages of the HRD process – the HRDNI, design, implementation and evaluation – not only overlap but are also highly interactive; it is therefore overly simplistic to discuss them in a linear fashion. A textbook, however, constrains an explanation to a linear presentation, so we will continue to indicate where the major overlaps occur.

Tyler's model has received some criticism over the years but, as Print (1993) points out, a lot of these negative comments are ill-informed. By making objectives the essential first step, the model provides a clear direction for the remainder of the process (Brady & Kennedy 2007). However, while this rational model is quite sound and robust, it is a mechanical view of the design process – one more suited to learning experiences for programmed knowledge than the more complex categories of the HLO.

The *interaction model* (Taba 1962) and the *cyclical model* (Wheeler 1967; Nichols & Nichols 1978) attempt to overcome this mechanistic inflexibility by suggesting that curriculum development is a more dynamic process. The interaction and cyclical models still use the same four steps of objectives, instructional strategies, organising the learning experiences and evaluation. However, the models emphasise that the design process can start with any of the steps and follow any sequence. So, with the addition of new content, decisions are then needed on objectives, methods and assessment strategies (Brady & Kennedy 2007). Further, Taba (1962) argues strongly for the diagnosis of the needs of the learners, a recommendation strongly supported by the research of Misko and Priest (2009) which emphasised the need to customise the learning program to take account of learners' needs. Chapter 8 has followed this recommendation, with the learner being considered as one of the two direct factors influencing the design decision. In addition, this text suggests that the design process is iterative – the initial decisions are based on the HLO, but these decisions are continually reviewed by the needs of the learners and the impact of the indirect factors.

The platform or naturalistic model (Walker 1971) is based on what is perceived as a more natural process of devising a curriculum and is based on three quite separate and distinct phases:

- the platform phase;
- the deliberation phase; and
- the design phase.

The *platform phase* incorporates a hotchpotch of the shared values, beliefs, theories and perceptions of all stakeholders (including learners and the designer) about what should be changed, how it should be changed and the levels of commitment to that change. These values, beliefs, theories and perceptions may not be defined clearly or even logically. They may be based on facts or may even be politically motivated. Even so they form the basis, or platform, of future curriculum decisions.

A closer look 9.5

The design models

The rational, interactive and cyclical models tend to describe the design process for learning experiences in the legitimate system. Some aspects of the platform model are also present, of course, but the contentious issues tend to be about specific matters or about preserving and/or gaining 'territory'. For example, it is quite common in educational institutions for arguments to be based on the need for a particular curriculum design to include subject matter from a particular department – the aim being to have more students exposed to that department's subjects and hence that department receiving more money.

The platform model is particularly relevant to the shadow system when new ideas are to be incorporated into the organisation. In fact, the platform model becomes a robust foundation for the design of the change intervention that the designer has to devise and, sometimes, even facilitate. Change interventions will be discussed more fully in Chapter 11.

The *design phase* begins when the key stakeholders have achieved consensus over the conflicting viewpoints and issues. In this phase, the designer can make final decisions about the components of the learning experience (the learning outcomes to be achieved, the content to be covered, and the learning strategies to be used) and the sequence of these components.

In the *deliberation phase* the stakeholders defend their ideas and push for their own political advantage. Sometimes a decision may be achieved logically and quickly but, more often than not, the process may be drawn out, chaotic, confused and full of emotion (indicating frames of reference are involved). Further, this is the time when organisational defence mechanisms unfold. However, this phase is also a time of illumination and creativity and the designer should use this time to ensure that all possible avenues are explored. While the stages of platform and deliberation are not discrete, the latter involves a movement towards practical concerns (Brady & Kennedy 2007).

As Brady and Kennedy (2007) point out, Walker's naturalistic model provides an accurate reflection of reality, emphasises the need for meaningful debate, and allows for the healthy confrontation of conflict. However, it should be recognised that the model is more applicable for large-scale curriculum changes or those at the deeper level of the HLO.

Some basics for design

For the designer, creating a curriculum is predicated on two basic tasks – firstly selecting appropriate learning strategies (as discussed in Chapter 8) and, secondly, *sequencing* sessions which provide meaningful and effective developmental opportunities that involve using both personal tacit and explicit knowledge. The tacit knowledge is developed over time and with experience. Explicit knowledge is available from the memory of the designer or in textbooks or other writings – for example, see Chapter 3. A well-designed program is based on the theories discussed in that chapter.

In particular, the designer should consider the following basics of design.

- *Logically analyse the learning objectives to be achieved.* Refer to the HRDNI and categorise the learning objectives into three levels.

    - *Program learning objectives.* These are the behaviours that the learner must exhibit at the end of the learning program or episode. So, a program learning objective may be 'describe the use of the Hierarchy of Learning Outcomes'.

    - *Enabling learning objectives.* These divide the program learning objectives into more manageable chunks. The previous example may be divided into 'describe the learning strategies' and 'describe the learning outcome categories'.

    - *Session learning objectives.* These divide the enabling learning objectives into the sessions that will be presented. Continuing with the example, there would be a session on 'explain the programmed information category and list all the elements' and 'explain the task category and list all the elements' and so on.

- *Start where the learner is at.* This is one of the principles of learning – see Chapter 3.

- *Use building blocks.* Ensure that the learners cover the basic knowledge and skills early in the learning program and that this basic information becomes the basis for the later learning. In particular, the design would generally move from the basic learning outcomes of Programmed Knowledge to the deeper categories in the Hierarchy of Learning Outcomes (see Figure 8.2), and through the stages of the learning orientation model (see Figure 8.3) from Stage 1 through to Stage 4.

- *Move from the simple to the complex.* Provide a simple model initially and then make this model more complex as the learning program progresses. As discussed in Chapter 8, this gradual developmental design may follow the structure of the hierarchy of learning outcomes and/or the progressive movement through stages 1 to 4 of the learning orientation model.

- *Ensure that part learning, spaced learning and active learning are used sequentially.* Present one small part of the knowledge or skill and follow this with a reinforcing activity to provide a space before the next small part of knowledge or skill.

- Make sure that the *activities are based on realistic, practical tasks* from the workplace (Misko & Priest 2009). This ensures that the principles of learning of meaningful material and transfer of learning are maximised.

- As a basic model, *use the learning cycle* of:

    - having an experience;

    - reviewing the experience;

    - concluding from the experience; and

    - planning and mentally rehearsing the next step.

- While the combination process of knowledge generation is often the focus of curriculum design, make sure that there are opportunities for the learners to engage in *externalisation and internalisation* as well (see Chapter 3). Emphasising externalisation and internalisation reinforces and supports the use of the learning cycle.

- Allow for the *time delay* in learning and provide opportunities for the *successive approximations* process of encouraging learning (see Chapter 3).

- *Assure transfer of learning* by ensuring that all learning is contextually based and is highly relevant to the workplace (for an excellent discussion of transfer of learning see Tennant 1999). In the design phase, the HR developer must ensure that:

    - the learners are continually reminded of the need to transfer the learning back to the workplace;

    - the learners are provided with a variety of examples of the application of the concept, task or skill in the workplace;

    - the learning aids are a close replication of the workplace situation (e.g. if the session is to teach the learners how to complete a form, then a copy of the form has to be made available to the learners); and

- the learners are provided with opportunities to reflect on how they will transfer the learning back to the workplace – practice time is provided in situations as close to possible to the real workplace environment.

- *Incorporate opportunities for both informational and motivational feedback* (see Chapter 3). These feedback processes should present the learner with 'task feedback clues' (Evans & Butler 1992) where the learner is given opportunities to observe their own performance and draw conclusions. This feedback process should be combined with 'successive approximations of targeted expertise' (Gott 1995) where the learner is encouraged to complete the learning cycle iteratively, coming closer to the required standard on each iteration.

- Ensure that sufficient time is scheduled (Misko & Priest 2099) so that the appropriate learning strategy can be used, sufficient practice time is scheduled (active learning), an allowance is made for successive approximations and quality feedback can be given (see Chapter 3).

Case study example

See the PLP case study on page 10 of the workbook that accompanies this text for experienced co-workers helping with the transfer of learning.

The product

The result of the designer's efforts and deliberations towards the development of a final product will be a series of learning episodes. The type of learning episode will depend on who has the role of HR developer (Browning & Delahaye 2010). If the HR developer is the immediate supervisor of the learner/s, the learning episodes will take place in the workplace using a workplace curriculum. This type of learning often concentrates on what Billett (1999) describes as 'non-routine problem solving'. Such learning episodes develop problem solving and other workplace-specific behaviours that are uncommon and/or complex. Accordingly, they tend to cover the more complex aspects of the HLO, from the deeper levels of the analytical, logistical, interpersonal and intrapersonal subgroups down to the meta-abilities category. This type of learning is discussed in Chapter 13.

If the learning episodes are to take place in the legitimate system, the HR developer will be a member of a learning section that is separate to the workplace. In this case, the responsibility for the learning would have been delegated to the HR developers in the learning section and would be conducted as a formal, organisation-wide program.

The legitimate system tends to be more interested in learning episodes that concentrate on what Billett (1999) describes as 'routine problem solving'. Such learning episodes focus on the everyday workplace knowledge and skills that ensure the organisation's survival in the near future. These learning episodes tend towards single-loop learning and are largely instrumental learning, although communicative learning (e.g. in management development) is involved more frequently these days (see Chapter 3). As the formal programs tend to be offered organisation wide, the content covered – whether the facts or the analytic processes to be used – presents a fairly uniform approach to problem solving or work behaviours. These learning episodes for the legitimate system tend to be presented in formal training courses and developmental workshops within classroom situations, although e-learning (see Chapter 11), is becoming more common.

The legitimate system

For the legitimate system, the designer provides a series of plans. The exact type of plans expected by the organisation varies, but tends to include:

- an overall program and session plans;
- a resource plan;
- a marketing plan;
- a budget; and
- the evaluation plan.

The program and session plans

The program and session plans explain the content to be covered in the learning experience, the learning strategies to be used, and the expected assessment. In other words, the program and session plans become the written form of the curriculum designed by the HR developer. A program is made up of a series of sessions that are presented in a specific order.

Programs that cover only explicit knowledge and use only instrumental learning (see Chapter 3) – that is, they are aimed at programmed knowledge – tend to be quite exact about the amount of time to be invested (usually from a few hours to a few days) and about the content to be covered. These programs are usually called 'training courses' and may include information only, or skills only, or a combination of information and skills. The learning strategies are usually confined to the theory session or lecture and the skill session. Figure 9.1 shows a typical program for a training course.

'Workshops' tend to cover programmed knowledge and the less complex elements of the task and relationship categories, although workshops that cover the deeper levels of the task and relationships categories are becoming more common. Typically, workshops have a defined time frame and content, and the program itself is usually presented in a similar fashion to the training course, although discussions are used more frequently as learning strategies of choice, while case studies and role plays may also be used.

Discussions and case studies, of course, are based on communicative learning (see Chapter 3) and encourage the use of externalisation and internalisation, while role plays may move into emancipatory learning (see Chapter 3). Both training courses and workshops are made up of a series of sessions – predominantly the theory, the lecture, the skill, discussions, and sometimes case studies and role plays. The designer will also need to create the session plans and other associated material (e.g. overhead transparencies, handouts, and board plans) for these sessions. The requirements for session plans will be discussed later in this chapter.

Figure 9.1 A program for a training course

Case study example

Course objectives: To conduct a ten minute research interview using an appropriate pattern of interview, questioning techniques and responding skills.

8.00 am	Administration and introductions	Doug Hansford, Senior Consultant
8:30 am	The pattern of an interview: • Explain the four sages of an interview (a theory session).	John Stewart, Senior Instructor
9:30 am	Questioning techniques: • Discuss the difference between open and closed questions. • Explain the funnel sequence of questioning (a theory session).	Jan Carroll, Senior Instructor
10.00 am	Morning tea	
10.15 am	Practise questioning techniques	Trainees
10.30 am	Responding skills: • Explain the responding skills of paraphrasing, probing and summarising (a theory session).	John Stewart, Senior Instructor
11.00 am	Practise responding skills	Trainees
11.30 am	Nonverbal behaviour • Discuss personal reactions to the use and abuse of the SOLER system (experiential learning and discussion).	John Stewart, Senior Instructor
12.00 noon	The finer points of interviewing • Discuss ways of using interview skills (a discussion).	Doug Hansford, Senior Consultant
12.30 pm	Lunch	
1.15 pm	Plan a 10 minute interview	Trainees
1.45 pm	Conduct a 10 minute interview (with a 5 minute feedback session from fellow trainees and facilitator).	Trainees and Jan Carroll
4.00 pm	Review of personal experience: • What went well? • What can be improved? • Personal goals for improvement (a discussion).	Trainees and Jan Carroll
5.00 pm	Closure	Doug Hansford

Note: The session type in brackets is placed after each session for the information of the HR Developers who will implement the program, but is deleted on the programs given to the trainees.

For the learning outcomes, from the deeper levels of the task and relationship categories and also those in the critical thinking and meta-abilities categories, the unstructured learning strategies of problem-based learning, contract learning and action learning are used. Each of these learning strategies has its own approach to managing the learning process (see Chapter 11) and emphasises communicative and emancipatory learning.

Therefore, it is difficult to prescribe a time frame. Accordingly, a tightly defined program is usually not possible, and the designer follows the learning management process recommended for each of these unstructured learning strategies.

The resource plan

The resource plan covers all those physical and human resources (other than the learners) needed to mount the program. Typically, the resource plan will include:

- the internal and external HR developers and guest speakers;

- the training rooms, store rooms, meeting rooms, and even personal accommodation during residential or 'live away' courses;

- equipment and training aids needed – it is also a good idea to indicate whether these are to be purchased or hired;

- stationery and other materials.

In addition to listing the quantities, the plan should indicate the time the resources are needed (e.g. the exact time the guest speakers are required and their travel arrangements; when a particular video or DVD should be picked up, and the supplier of the video or DVD).

The product marketing plan

The sole business of some organisations, such as private colleges, registered training organisations, private training establishments, and consulting groups is to provide training, HR development and educational services. For these organisations, marketing their programs (or product) is a basic necessity. However, it is becoming quite common for internal HR departments to see a need to market their services. As Cafferalla (2002) points out, marketing is important for educational and HE development programs where participation is often voluntary, and potential participants may not be affiliated with the sponsoring organisations. Accordingly, most designers these days have to have some input to marketing plans.

Kotler and Keller (2006) have identified five possible roles in a purchase decision:

- the *initiator* – the person who believes that there is some need for the product;

- the *influencer* – who persuades others that the product will satisfy a critical need;

- the *decider* – who has the power to make the 'yes-we-will or no-we-won't' decision;

- the *purchaser* – who has the delegation, budget or money to make the purchase; and

- the *user* – the person who uses the product.

Five different people may occupy each role or one person may be involved in two or more of the roles. A product marketing plan identifies the people who occupy these roles, where they are located, and what benefit the product (e.g. training course) will bring to each of them. Any number of people, from inside or outside the organisation, may fill these roles. The initiators and influencers are often union delegates, potential learners, or managers. The decider is usually an upper-level manager, this person often filling the role of purchaser as well. The most obvious users of a learning program are the learners themselves, although one could argue that the manager or supervisor of the learners benefits as well (trained staff make the job of a manager that much easier).

Of course, for an internal HR developer, a lot of this information will be available from the HRDNI. Outside HR developers and consultants rely on feasibility studies for the information. The second part of a marketing plan covers the promotional tactics for the learning program. There are two major parts to promotional tactics:

- the advertising content; and
- the media.

The advertising content includes descriptions of the needs to be satisfied by the program. These descriptions should be targeted to the particular buyer role.

The choice of media tactics identifies the communication methods to be used – e.g. internal memorandum, advertising poster, advertisements in newspapers and journals (and, specifically, which newspapers and journals), radio or television. Again, the choice of media should be dictated by the particular buyer role that is being targeted.

The budget

For a single product such as a learning program, a budget consists of three main areas:

- the expected income;
- the cash expenditures; and
- the opportunity cost expenditures.

The expected income is an estimate of the income that the program is expected to generate. Calculating expected income is usually the prerequisite of organisations whose sole business is providing educational and HR development programs. Most internal HR departments of an organisation do not bother with estimating expected income.

The cash expenditures include all items on which the organisation will spend cash. Such items would include the payment of external consultants and guest speakers, the hire of equipment and training aids, the rental of floor space (e.g. training rooms), consumable materials, travel expenses, and the costs of marketing the program. Most organisations expect that cash expenditures will be included in the budget, at the very least.

Opportunity cost expenditures involve all those disbursements that would have been used on work other than the learning program. These expenditures include the wages of the learners (who would have been doing their normal work) and of the HR developers, and the depreciation on buildings and equipment. Some organisations do not require the inclusion of opportunity cost expenditures.

The evaluation plan

The final, but not the least important task of the designer is to plan how the learning program is to be evaluated. Evaluation is discussed in Chapter 12.

The HR developer as a designer

For the HR developer, the role of the designer is wide and complex. For the legitimate system, the HR developer bases the design of the learning program on the information from the HRDNI. The designer makes initial decisions based on the HLO and then moves, in an iterative process, through the learning needs of the learners and the indirect factors of strategic orientation, the organisational culture, the key stakeholders and the resources available. This iterative decision-making process results in the production of a number of plans – the program and the session plans, the resources plan, the product marketing plan, the budget and the evaluation plan. The checklist for designers presented in the previous chapter has been extended to incorporate the indirect factors in this chapter and also the various plans that need to be produced – see Figure 9.2.

For the learning that occurs in the shadow system, the HR developer's role tends to blur between that of a designer and that of an implementer. This is discussed further in Chapter 13. The craft of the designer is based on a solid foundation of scientific research. The decisions are so complex, however, and the political influences of the organisation so potentially hazardous, that science alone is not always enough. The designer needs experience – but experience comes only from practice. The novice designer will find the issues discussed in Chapters 8 and 9 to be substantial, tangible bases for gaining that experience. However, finding a knowledgeable and competent mentor will certainly assist with personal development and will also help to avoid some of the more serious dangers.

Figure 9.2 A checklist for designers

1. Examine each of the learning outcomes listed in the HRDNI and decide which level of the HLO best equates with each learning outcome.

2. Identify the 'building blocks'. Ask questions such as:

   - What basic programmed knowledge is needed to be covered first before advanced programmed knowledge is presented?

   - What programmed knowledge is needed before the learners can take on the task category elements?

   - Are relationship category elements needed and, if so, where are they needed in the learning experience?

   - What critical thinking and meta-abilities categories are needed, and where should these be developed in the learning experience?

3. Identify the critical characteristics of the learners:

    -   level of knowledge;

    -   motivation;

    -   learning orientations and learning style

    and decide the effect that these characteristics may have on the overall design.

4. Explore how the learning cycle of:

    -   step 1 – having an experience;

    -   step 2 – reviewing the experience;

    -   step 3 – concluding from the experience; and

    -   step 4 – planning the next steps

    could be included in the overall design.

5. Make adjustments for learner maturity.

6. Ensure that opportunities for appropriate feedback are built into the design. This feedback should be:

    -   a combination of qualitative and quantitative;

    -   from an external source, such as a HR developer; and

    -   from an internal source (the learners should be given the opportunity to compare their own performances against standards and draw their own conclusions).

7. Check that the proposed learning strategies are compatible with the organisational strategic plan. If there is a discrepancy, verify the logic of the choice of learning strategy. If a more expensive learning strategy is proposed, seek support from key stakeholders.

8. Analyse the organisational culture for activities or issues that are or are not acceptable. Check the impact of these on the proposed learning experiences. If fundamental changes are needed to the organisational culture, examine the alternatives of change interventions. Discuss such expected fundamental changes with key stakeholders.

9. Negotiate sufficient time for the learning experience with affected managers.

10. Design the learning program. For training courses and workshops, devise a program plan similar to that in Figure 9.1. If unstructured learning strategies are to be used, devise program plans that will manage the learning processes (see Chapter 11). Decide appropriate lengths of time for each session. Juggle these times so that all sessions fit into the time available for the program.

11. Design the session plans, including all the support material. Recognise that

this step will take some considerable time. Delahaye and Smith (1998) suggest allowing a ratio of 1:4 – for every hour that a session lasts, four hours of session planning will be needed.

12. Define the qualifications needed by the HR developers. Identify the sources (internal or external) of potential HR developers.

13. Draw up the resources plan.

14. Create the product marketing plan.

15. Calculate a budget for the resources needed. Ensure that all expected cash expenditures are included (for example, hire of rooms, rental of films, and payment to external HR developers). Seek support from key stakeholders.

16. Design the evaluation plan.

References

Billett, S 1996, 'Towards a model of workplace learning: the learning curriculum', *Studies in Continuing Education*, 18(1), pp. 43-58.

Billett, S 1999, 'Guided learning at work', in D Boud & J Garrick (eds.), *Understanding Learning at Work*, London: Routledge.

Brady, L & Kennedy, K 2007, *Curriculum Construction*, 3rd edn, Sydney, NSW: Prentice Hall.

Browning, V & Delahaye, B L 2010, 'Enhancing workplace learning through collaborative HRD, in M Clarke (ed.), *Cases and readings in HRM and sustainability*, Tilde University Press, Melbourne, Vic.

Cafferalla, R S 2002, *Planning Programs for Adult Learners*, 2nd edn, San Francisco: Jossey-Bass.

Delahaye, B L & Smith, B J 1998, *How to be an Effective Trainer*, New York: Wiley.

Dickie, L & Dickie, C 2007, *Cornerstones of Strategic Management*, Tilde University Press, Prahran, Vic.

Evans, G & Butler, J 1992, 'Thinking and Enhanced Performance in the Workplace', A paper presented to the Fifth International Conference on Thinking, Townsville, Qid.

Gott, S 1995). 'Rediscovering learning: Acquiring expertise in real world problem solving tasks', *Australian and New Zealand Journal of Vocational Education Research*, 3(1), pp. 30-69.

Hansen, J W 2006, 'Training design: Scenarios of the future', *Advances in Developing Human Resources*, 8(4), pp. 492-499.

Kotler, P & Keller, K L 2006, *Marketing management*, 12th edn, Pearson Education, Upper Saddle River, NJ.

Miles, R E & Snow, C L 2003, *Organizational strategy, structure and process*, Stanford University Press, New York.

Mintzberg, H 1987, 'Five Ps for strategy', *California Management Review*, Fall.

Misko, J & Priest, S 2009, *Students' suggestions for improving their vocational education and training experience*, NCVER, Adelaide, SA.

Mullins, L J 2007, *Management and organisational behaviour*, 8th edn, Pearson Education, Harlow.

Nichols, A & Nichols, A H 1978, *Developing a Curriculum: A Practical Guide*, 2nd edn, London: Allen & Unwin.

Print, M 1993, *Curriculum Development and Design*, St Leonards, NSW: Allen & Unwin.

Schermerhorn, J R, Davidson, P, Poole, D, Simon, A, Woods, P & Chau, S L 2011, *Management*, John Wiley & Sons Australia, Brisbane.

Sveiby, K E 1997, *The New Organizational Wealth: Managing and Measuring Knowledge-based Assets*, San Francisco, Cal.: Berrett-Koehler.

Taba, H 1962, *Curriculum Development: Theory and Practice*. New York: Harcourt Brace.

Tennant, M 1999, 'Is learning transferable?', in D Boud & J Garrick (eds.), *Understanding Learning at Work*. London: Routledge.

Tyler, R W 1949, *Basic Principles of Curriculum and Instruction*. Chicago: University of Chicago Press.

Walker, D F 1971, 'A naturalistic model for curriculum development', *School Review* 80(1), pp. 51-65.

Wheeler, D K 1967, *Curriculum Process*, London: University of London Press.

Chapter 10

Implementing the structured learning strategies

LEARNING OBJECTIVES

After studying this chapter you should be able to:

1. Identify and describe the important actions a HR developer must make to manage and coordinate a learning program.

2. Describe the micro skills of questioning, responding, using visual aids and constructing learning objectives.

3. Differentiate between structured and unstructured learning strategies.

4. Describe the structured learning strategies of the skill session, the theory session and the lecture.

5. Describe the semi-structured learning strategies of the discussion, case study, role play and experiential learning.

The role of the HR developer

After the design of the learning experience has been accepted and the appropriate approvals have been given, the implementation stage begins. To use a colloquial saying, the implementation stage is where 'the rubber hits the road'. In this third stage of the HRD process, the HR developer takes on the role of implementer and is often referred to as the facilitator, instructor, trainer, or teacher. In this role, the HR developer is responsible for implementing the design. In assuming this responsibility, the HR developer is accepting certain obligations:

- to be fully conversant with the programmed knowledge to be covered;

- to have the capability to conduct the learning strategies nominated;

- to be willing to help the learners meet the various challenges;

- to deal with the learners honestly; and

- never to place personal idiosyncratic needs above the best interests of the learners.

There is also an expectation that the HR developer will stay within the planned design. However, as Tovey and Lawlor (2008) point out, a skilled facilitator is very flexible, sometimes changing the delivery of the session on the spot if the learners are having difficulty or the prepared session is inappropriate.

The implementer needs to have the authority to make fine adjustments to the overall design. Most of these adjustments are based on the implementer's first-hand experience of the learners. While the design may have made certain assumptions, the implementer has first-hand knowledge of the learners' needs. So the implementer may make some modifications because of the learners' knowledge base or learning styles (see Chapter 8) or because of their cultural backgrounds, gender, or ages (see Chapter 4). For example, recognising that in the indigenous Australian culture, asking questions is considered bad manners (see Chapter 4) but that adult learners from this culture are comfortable with communicative learning, the HR developer may increase the amount of time scheduled for discussions. Having said this, it must be stressed that major changes would be unexpected and could be justified only by significant and transparent reasons that were not acknowledged in the original design. (NB. The question of why such a variation was not accounted for in the original design would be addressed at the evaluation stage.) Three major interacting operations occur during the implementation stage:

- management and coordination of the program, where the various support resources are brought together to ensure that the learning program runs smoothly;

- utilisation of the micro skills of the HR developer, that support the learning strategies and increase the learning opportunities of the learners; and

- application of the learning strategies, where the HR developer uses accepted practices specific to the particular learning strategy.

A less than optimal performance in any of these operations can have a deleterious effect on the learning experience. An acceptable level of performance in each leads to a reasonable learning experience for the learners. However, for a highly successful learning experience, these three operations interact to create a multiplier effect.

Managing and coordinating the program

Managing and coordinating a program is a rather invisible operation – until something goes wrong. Some problems invariably arise during a program and most of these can be dealt with quickly and quietly. However, what can seem to be a minor irritant to the HR developer can be a discordant interruption to a learner. The possibilities for problems are many and varied – e.g. a learner's name misspelt, the incorrect designation of a guest speaker, a DVD not arriving or, perhaps worst of all, morning tea not on time. The HR developer in charge of a program should check the following precautions:

- ensure all learners have been notified of their attendance at the program and have received all preparatory material;

- arrange the layout of the training room to maximise the effectiveness of the learning strategies to be used and for the comfort of the learners;

- make sure the learners' name tags, programs and stationery are distributed or are readily available;

- make sure all electrical equipment and training aids are present and in working order each morning before the sessions start (remember the HR developer's adage: 'If anything will spoil your presentation it will be equipment breaking down');

- check all safety aspects of the room and equipment;

- each morning check that the guest speakers are still available;

- check on the readiness of other HR developers and on their session requirements.

A lot of these tasks can be delegated by the implementing HR developer to a designated coordinator. However, the responsibility for ensuring that the tasks are completed is never delegated. The final responsibility always remains with the implementing HR developer, as he or she is the person who suffers the immediate consequences – and these consequences are invariably felt by the learners.

For a more detailed discussion of managing and coordinating a program see Caffarella (2002) and Delahaye and Smith (1998).

Micro skills

Micro skills are those taken-for-granted techniques used most successfully by experienced HR developers:

- questioning;

- responding;

- using the visual aids; and

- creating learning objectives.

Inconveniently, these micro skills take quite some time to develop to a competent standard. The word 'inconveniently' is used because these skills can enhance the learning process to a surprising extent. Conversely, when they are absent or used ineptly, the learning process is usually diminished markedly.

Enthusiasm

Enthusiasm, a surprisingly intangible attribute, has been shown to have significant effect on the quality of learning. Feldman (2007), after conducting a meta-analysis of research, reported that high enthusiasm and expressiveness in the topic and in facilitating the learning of the topic is strongly associated with learner achievement.

Questioning

Questioning skills were discussed thoroughly in Chapter 7. The HR developer relies heavily on open questions with a 'stem-plus-query' structure and, particularly in the discussion, frequently uses the funnel sequence of questions.

Responding

Responding skills include the processes of paraphrasing, probing and summarising. Again, these were discussed extensively in Chapter 7. From the HR developer's point of view, questioning and responding skills are tightly interwoven during any learning episode; this questioning–responding sequence is sometimes referred to as the 'trainer–trainee dynamic'. The word 'dynamic' is very appropriate as the interaction is usually fast and spontaneous, so for the HR developer, these skills need to be habitual as there is little chance to pre-plan the sequence of questioning and responding.

Visual aids

As discussed in Chapter 3, the principle of learning called 'multiple sense learning' emphasises that humans perceive the major portions of their information through the sense of sight. HR developers must be adept at the appropriate use of visual aids.

Even in our high technology world, the most commonly used visual aids are the white board and the overhead projector. The white board is not a notebook for random scribbling. Information should be presented in a clear and logical sequence that enhances the assimilation of the information by the learners. The overhead projector can provide interest and impact to a presentation but is probably most effective when used in conjunction with the white board. This combination allows the HR developer to display the main points of the presentation on the white board and provide extended detail of each point via the overhead projector (Delahaye & Smith 1998).

A more modern and popular visual aid is the computer-assisted visual package – e.g. PowerPoint. These packages confer a colourful, vibrant and dramatic edge to a presentation. The presentations based on these packages are relatively flexible and the learners can be provided with a copy of the presentation, which helps considerably with their note taking. However, they do require some specialised equipment. Another problem with such presentations is that the material on one slide vanishes when the next slide appears, making it difficult for the learner to remember the logic and the progression of the session. Again, the main points are best written on the white board and the detail explained via the PowerPoint slide. The overhead visualiser is another recent technological advance. It is very similar in construction to the overhead projector but incorporates a small video camera rather than a reflective prism in the head. This camera allows the display of a variety of photographs and graphs. It also provides a zoom capability so that particular points on the photograph can be highlighted and studied in greater detail.

Other visual aids include the chart, DVD video, films, slides, IPads and audiotapes.

A closer look 10.1

The do's and don'ts of using slide shows

1. Always plan the presentation thoroughly. For a detailed discussion on planning presentations and visual aids, see Delahaye and Smith 1998.

2. Do not crowd each slide with information. Have one idea for each slide, four words per line, and no more than six lines per slide.

3. Use reasonably large-sized fonts.

4. Use light-coloured lettering on a dark background (*note*, this is the opposite of overhead projector transparencies).

5. Do not use too many colours or different sized fonts.

6. Use pictures and cartoons sparingly, and only if they make a specific and relevant point.

7. Have a master slide at the beginning to preview the session and the same master at the end to review.

8. Include summarising slides at strategic points during the session.

9. Use the fade-in/fade-out and highlighting facilities of software like PowerPoint to focus attention on the point you are explaining.

10. Practise using your software with your presentation so that you know both its facilities and all points in your session.

11. Make sure that the light in the front of the room is dimmed a little to provide a contrast for the screen.

12. Make sure you know how to contact a technician quickly, in case something goes wrong with the equipment.

13. Make overhead transparencies of your slide show. If all else fails, you can revert to the overhead projector.

14. Make hard copies of your slides to use as handouts.

Recognise, however, that all these modern visual aids are only that – aids to learning. Spending a disproportionate amount of time on fancy visual aids will not improve learning significantly. It is the skills and abilities of a competent HR developer as an implementer that provide the most dynamic assistance to learning.

For a more detailed discussion of visual aids, the texts by Agnew, Kellerman and Meyer (1996), Delahaye and Smith (1998), Kemp and Smellie (1993), Reynolds and Anderson (1991) and Tarquin and Walker (1996) are recommended.

Learning objectives

The construction of learning objectives was discussed in Chapter 6. Based on the work of Mager (1991) and Tyler (1949), Delahaye and Smith (1998) recommend that learning objectives should describe:

- the *terminal behaviour* to be achieved by the learner at the end of the learning session (e.g. theory, discussion) or learning experience (e.g. training course) – action verbs should be used to describe this terminal behaviour;

- the *standard* to which this behaviour has to be performed – this standard describes the criteria for acceptable performance;

- the *conditions* under which the learner will be expected to perform. A statement of conditions is sometimes superfluous (e.g. if the learner is taking a paper-and-pencil test in a training room) but can become very important if the learner is expected to use a calculator half-way up a mast of a sailing ship on a windy day.

Well-stated learning objectives are critical to a HR developer for at least two reasons. They provide a clear goal which, in turn, gives a conspicuous direction for the HR developer to follow. This conspicuous direction allows decisions (on such matters as content to be learned and appropriate learning strategies) to be made quickly and precisely. Secondly, clear learning objectives describe the behaviour which, when displayed by the learner, indicates to the HR developer that the learning session or experience can conclude – as the aim of the learning session or experience has been achieved.

In the structured learning strategies, the HR developer has the advantage of planning the learning objectives beforehand. However, during the unstructured learning strategies, the HR developer is often required to formulate or adjust learning objectives at a moment's notice. Having the ability to be this flexible is a trademark characteristic of the experienced HR developer.

For a more detailed and recent discussion of learning objectives see Knowles, Holton and Swanson (2005).

The importance of micro skills

The micro skills of questioning, responding, using visual aids correctly and effectively, and creating learning objectives are often unrecognised and undervalued. Yet, these skills are the catalysts which the HR developer uses to bring together the disparate concepts being covered. Further, it is with these micro skills that the HR developer helps the learner to generate knowledge through the processes of externalisation and internalisation. The absence of these skills invariably results in the learner being left floundering in direction-less frustration. These skills are indeed a very powerful device in the toolkit of the HR developer as an implementer.

The structured learning strategies

To this point, the terms 'structured learning strategies' and 'unstructured learning strategies' have been used; these terms represent the poles of a continuum. Other terminology is sometimes used to describe these poles – scientific/artistic; teacher-controlled/learner-controlled; traditional/self-directed learning; pedagogy/andragogy. Each of these terms provides some insight into the difference between the concepts.

Structured learning strategies are based on findings gleaned from quantitative research as far back as Thorndike (1931). Teacher-controlled learning indicates that the teacher makes all the decisions on the learning process; self-directed learning signifies that the learner takes responsibility for all stages of the learning experience; pedagogy (*ped* = a boy; *agogos* = leading) means the teaching of children while andragogy (*andra* = a man; *agogos* = leading) denotes the teaching of an adult.

Where a learning strategy transforms from structured to semi-structured is a moot point, as the change is a gradual transformation. This chapter defines the following learning strategies as structured:

- skill session;
- theory session; and
- lecture.

These three learning strategies are considered structured because the HR developer takes full responsibility for what will be learned, how it will be learned, and what evidence will be produced to prove that the learning did occur.

The skill session

All communication models have a similar overall structure – an introduction, a body and a conclusion. All the structured learning strategies have this structure, and the skill session is no different.

As the name implies, a skill session is used for teaching a procedural skill. A procedural skill is one involving procedures (based on some programmed knowledge) and a sequence of psychomotor skills, where the order of the activities is crucial. A skill session is based on a set series of steps that are controlled by the HR developer. Delahaye and Smith (1998) suggest that the body of the skill session should be divided into four steps:

1. *Show,* where the HR developer demonstrates the skill in an efficient and practised manner.

2. *Show and tell,* where the HR developer again proceeds through the skill but explains each step carefully to the learners. The HR developer re-explains any step where the learners are having difficulty, and may demonstrate the skill several times.

3. *Check of understanding,* where the learners verbally describe each step, in the correct sequence, to the HR developer. This step ensures that the learners understand the skill before they are allowed to use the tools and materials and is an important component of safety training.

4. *Practice,* where the learners do the skill several times while being supervised by the HR developer. The practice step should occupy at least 50 percent of the time allotted to the body of the session.

At the end of the practice step, the HR developer should test the learners to ensure that they have achieved the learning objectives.

The HR developer needs to be highly competent at performing the skill; the logistics of organising sufficient materials and tools requires careful planning. Safety should be high on the HR developer's agenda, particularly when dangerous tools or hazardous materials are being used.

The theory session

The theory session is used to impart programmed knowledge. The structure of the theory session is shown in Figure 10.1.

Figure 10.1 The theory session

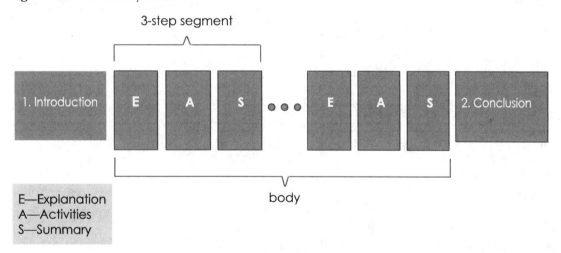

Source: Delahaye & Smith 1998, p. 30.

When planning a theory session, the HR developer must decide how many segments will comprise the body. Each segment will cover a major component of the programmed knowledge to be learned. It is quite surprising how small each of these 'major' components can be, and the learning principle of part-learning (see Chapter 3) should be used. As a general rule of thumb, five or six very minor points should make up a 'major' component.

Each 'major' component is then presented to the learners using a three-part sequence:

1. The *explanation step,* where the programmed knowledge is explained to the learners using visual aids, questioning and verbal descriptions.

2. The *activity step,* where the learners are given an activity to test whether they have understood the programmed knowledge described in the explanation step. This step can also test the learning objectives.

3. The *summary step,* where the information is briefly reviewed and any minor misunderstandings are cleared up.

Like the skill session, the theory session is a powerful learning strategy for programmed knowledge, largely because all the principles of learning discussed in Chapter 3 are in operation. You might like to review these principles of learning and note exactly where each of them is used in the recommended steps of the skill and theory sessions.

The lecture

Lectures are one of the most commonly used delivery methods; they are useful for transmitting large quantities of information, cost little to prepare, are easy to organise (Exely & Dennick 2009), and can be delivered to a large audience. However, most of the advantages of a lecture are to do with the transmission rather the learning of programmed knowledge.

The lecture is really a modified theory session. It has all the components of a theory session except the activity step. Of course, the omission of the activity step lessens the impact of the lecture as a learning strategy because several of the principles of learning are lost. However, a well-planned and well-delivered lecture can result in significant learning for a well-motivated audience. Mi (1998) believes that a lecture is effective for:

- conveying organised information, when there is an accepted body of organised knowledge;

- outlining and explaining concepts, to a knowledgeable audience to deepen the understanding of ideas and values; and

- stimulating people to think in new ways (although this is highly dependent on the motivation of the audience).

Accordingly, the lecture tends to be used most in the transmission of procedural knowledge.

The semi-structured learning strategies

Moving along the structured–unstructured continuum, we now come to the semi-structured learning strategies. These include:

- discussion;

- case study;

- role play; and

- experiential learning.

As discussed previously in the structured learning strategies, the HR developer takes full responsibility for what will be learned, how it will be learned and what evidence will be produced to prove that the learning did occur. In these semi-structured learning strategies, however, some of these responsibilities are transferred to the learner, so there are elements of unstructured learning about them.

The discussion

In a discussion, the HR developer encourages the learners to provide the knowledge that will achieve the desired learning objectives. The assumption is that, while each individual learner in the group does not have all the information, together the whole group does. It is up to the HR developer to unearth this information. So the role of the HR developer is to encourage the learners to share their explicit knowledge, thereby using the knowledge generation process of combination. There is some opportunity in the discussion to stimulate the learners' tacit knowledge (externalisation), but this knowledge-generation technique does not always occur frequently in the discussion learning strategy.

A discussion is similar to an interview in that the HR developer:

- uses questions to elicit information;

- records the information in a logical format, although with a discussion this is done on a white board rather than a notebook;

- uses responding skills to encourage the learners to contribute information;

- uses summaries at strategic points in the discussion to review the material covered and to help the learners think of new information.

In another similarity to the interview, discussions can be viewed as being on a continuum, being structured at one pole and unstructured at the other. In a structured discussion, the HR developer uses questions based on programmed knowledge to lead the learners down the path of discovery. With the unstructured discussion, the HR developer relies solely on the skills of questioning, responding, summarising, and board work (placing the information in logical classifications on the white board) to manage the learning process so that the learners achieve the desired learning objectives.

Nesbit, Leach and Foley (2004) cite Brookfield (1990) by arguing that meaningful and productive discussions are more likely to occur if the following four conditions prevail: 1) the discussion topic is stimulating; 2) the group leader is well versed in both group dynamics and the topic under discussion; 3) group members possess reasonably developed reasoning and communication skills; and 4) group members have devised and agreed on 'an appropriate moral culture' for group discussion.

Discussions are most appropriate for learning advanced programmed knowledge and the less complex elements of the task and relationship categories of the hierarchy of learning outcomes:

- linear analysis;

- some diagnostic analysis;

- goal identification;

- administrative proficiency;

- communication;

- interacting at the objective level;

- spontaneity; and

- accurate self-awareness.

The case study

The case study encourages learners to go beyond their explicit knowledge by using the knowledge-generation processes of externalisation and internalisation. These deeper learning processes are aroused and stimulated by a cue known as a case study. A particular strength of the case study is that it can reflect issues and situations within a specific context or organisation (Tovey & Lawlor 2008) which enhances transfer of training (see Chapter 3).

A case study consists of two parts:

- a narration; and

- questions.

A narration combines a description of a real-world event together with sufficient background information to orient the reader. The length of the narration varies from half a page to ten or more pages; it is designed to bring the real world into the classroom. The second part of the case study consists of the questions that the learners need to answer.

The secret to selecting or writing case studies is the learning objectives to be achieved by the session. First, the questions should be derived directly from the learning objectives. For example, the learning objective 'List three common unsafe acts that can lead to serious injury on a building site' would become 'What are the three unsafe acts that led to serious injury to Shane on the building site?' Second, the case study is written to include clues about the learning objectives (e.g. the three unsafe acts) that are described in the narrative.

Case studies should be long enough to provide sufficient information to give the learners a challenge, but not include so much useless information that reading the case study becomes boring. Reynolds (1998) suggests that the narrative should:

- be a short, written description of an actual situation;

- include enough detail for the learners to gain the experience of relating facts to one another effectively in problem solving;

- include enough detail for the learners to judge between important and unimportant information; and

- stop short of describing the final key actions and decisions, thus leaving open to the learners the choice of actions to be recommended.

When conducting the session, the HR developer can ask the learners to read the case study either beforehand or at the start of the session. Either way, individual learners should be given time to write notes which will provide a considered base for contributions to the later group discussion. To maximise the use of this time, the following five steps can be recommended to the individual learners:

1. *Read the whole case study* for a general feel of the incident or incidents being presented.

2. *Re-read* the case study to identify facts and issues.

3. *Organise* these facts and issues into a logical sequence by asking the famous four Ws – what, where, when and why.

4. *Focus on the case study questions* to see how the facts and issues provide answers.

5. *Make notes,* to be used in the later discussion, under each of the case study questions.

At the end of this preparation time, the HR developer first brings the learners together in small groups. Goldstein (2001) believes that interacting in small groups increases feedback to individual learners, allowing individuals to learn by observing others developing their respective solutions.

The HR developer then brings the whole group together and facilitates a discussion. This discussion can take a wide variety of paths. One of the most common options is a structured discussion based specifically on the case study questions. Alternatively, the small groups may be asked to present their solutions before the HR developer facilitates a review of the most preferred resolutions.

Waddell, Cummings and Worley (2004) recommend having the learners think of the discussion as a real-life meeting of business colleagues, as this can provide alternative opinions and constructive criticisms. An enhancing option is to assign the various roles in the case study to various students. This enhanced option then borders on a role play, so the comments on conducting role plays should be examined before using this option. However, when conducting the discussion, the HR developer needs to ensure that:

- the learning objectives of the session are achieved;

- the learners can identify connections between issues and also any cause-effect relationships;

- the learning that occurs is not just single-loop learning – i.e. the detection and correction of error – but that double-loop learning is also addressed so that underlying organisational values, assumptions and goals are examined and challenged (see Chapter 3); and

- the learners can generalise the learning outcomes from the specific case study to their real-life work context.

The case study is ideal for developing the diagnostic analysis, complex analysis, administrative proficiency, and allocation of resources elements of the task category of the HLO.

There can also be the added benefits of developing the elements of accurate self-awareness and self-confidence of the relationship category, as the learners test their ideas against the results of the case study discussion and find their conclusions to be valid.

For an in-depth discussion of the case study learning strategy see Killen (2007), Pigors (1976) and Reynolds (1998), and for a detailed examination of writing and conducting a case study see Delahaye and Smith (1998). For a thoughtful critique of the case study method see Argyris (1980).

The role play

The role play is similar to a case study in that the role play itself provides the cue for the generation of information that can be combined into new learning during the later discussion. As different from a narrative, however, some or all of the learners become actively engaged by acting out roles.

Delahaye and Smith (1998) suggest that there are two types of role plays. In the first, the pre-planned role play, the role players are given clear, detailed role descriptions depicting scripted behaviours that are usually quite different from the learners' usual deportment. These roles take the place of the narrative of the case study. The remaining learners in the group are given detailed observation guides that indicate what they should look for during the role play. These observation guides take the place of the case study questions. Both the roles and the observation guides are based firmly on the learning objectives for the session.

In the second type, the spontaneous role play, the selected learners are given roles in which they basically plays themselves, but try out new behaviours to expand their range of options. This second type of role play is very close to experiential learning; further comments will be made on the approach under that heading.

Whatever type of role play is used, it is the direct involvement of the learners that creates the most significant difference; the role play engenders an emotional component in the learning experience. This emotional component is both the strength and the weakness of the role play as a learning strategy.

It is the strength in that the emotional component triggers the deeper levels of learning (see Figure 3.1 in Chapter 3), encouraging critical reflection and critical thinking. It is the weakness in that, when not properly channelled by the facilitator, the energy created by the emotions can become self-destructive. As Stone (2010) points out, a successful role play does rely on the willingness of the learners to participate properly. Accordingly, the facilitator must ensure that the following steps are covered:

- The roles are written so that they are realistic and not heavily biased to release negative feelings. Negative feelings are easily initiated so the role play descriptions should he written so they are well balanced.

- The selection of the learners for the roles is taken with care and considered thought. On the one hand, the role players need some confidence that they can handle the role, but on the other the role should not create such stress to the individual that learning is blocked out.

- The learners are thoroughly briefed in the roles they are to enact.

- The observation guides are very clear so that the observers are in no doubt about what they should heed.

- The actors are debriefed carefully and thoroughly at the end of the play.

- The main themes are identified and examined fully during the discussion stage.

- The role players are observed closely during the discussion stage to ensure there is no regression to the emotions of the role.

- The learners can generalise the learning outcomes from the specific to their real-life work contexts.

The discussion needs to be closely supervised by the HR developer and combined with a very sensitive analysis of the performance and actions of the role players. To ensure that the comments and actions made during the role play are divorced from the personalities of the learners, the HR developer should be careful to refer to the roles by the role names rather than the names of the learners playing the roles. The HR developer should emphasise that the choices made by the role players were made to enrich the roles and are not regarded as being the usual performance of the persons playing the roles. Without such a sensitive review, the role play can easily become a damaging experience with learning outcomes directly opposite to those intended.

Conducted correctly, the role play is ideally suited for developing the deeper elements of the relationship category of the learning outcomes hierarchy – i.e. interaction at the emotional level; use of group processes; use of social power; self-confidence; inner strength; and self-discipline.

Indeed, recent research shows that the role play can contribute strongly to the transfer of training (see, for example, Frash *et al.* 2010; Hicks & Upton 2010; and Roscoe & Fisher 2008).

For a detailed examination of role plays see Killen (2007) and Van Ments (1994); for a discussion of writing and conducting role plays see Delahaye and Smith (1998).

Experiential learning

The term 'experiential learning' covers a number of possible approaches, with various writers providing a variety of definitions. This text will include those learning approaches which allow the learner to experiment with or experience a specific situation and to reflect on that experience or experiment.

Two conditions set experiential learning aside from other structured strategies. First, the whole learner – his or her explicit knowledge, tacit knowledge, emotions and frames of reference – is involved. Second, the learning is generated by the first-hand experience of the learner, rather than a vicarious or artificial event (such as in case studies and role plays). The situation-specific nature of experiential learning and the fact that the majority of the learning occurs within the classroom differentiates it from more unstructured learning strategies like action learning.

There are four techniques that are usually discussed under the term 'experiential learning' – namely:

- learning instruments;

- simulations;

- projects; and

- sensitivity groups.

A common theme of the four techniques is the use of the learning cycle (see Chapter 10). Each technique starts with the learner being given an experience (step 1). The learner is then expected to review that experience (step 2) and, usually with the help of a HR developer and a learning group, to draw conclusions from that reflection (step 3). Finally, the learner is encouraged to plan changes in his or her future life (step 4).

Learning instruments

A learning instrument is a device (often a questionnaire) that provides an individual with insights about his or her frames of reference (see Chapter 3). The learning instruments often measure the epistemic-based paradigmatic assumptions such as learning styles, management styles, team roles, and decision techniques. A good learning instrument provides thorough, reliable and systematic data-gathering, and a valid analysis of that data. The analysis of the data should provide the learner with personal enlightenment or a new perception of self.

Smith (1992a) suggests seven steps that the HR developer should follow in using learning instruments:

1. *Set the scene*, where the HR developer sets goals, explains terms, and clarifies the process. Establishing this base provides the motivation which encourages truthfulness in responses, discourages defensiveness, and establishes the supportive atmosphere essential to the sharing of results.

2. *Administration*, where the instrument is distributed, clear instructions are given, and questions clarified. The learners then complete the instrument.

3. *Theory input*, where an explanation is given of the theory or key concepts underpinning the instrument.

4. *Scoring*, where the learners calculate their results on a scoring sheet.

5. *Interpretation*, where the theory and concepts explained earlier are related to the scores.

6. *Posting*, where the learners' scores are made public. Usually, scores are not related to individuals but the ranges and means of the group scores are disclosed to provide information for the later discussion.

7. *Processing*, when the discussion takes place. This discussion period is really the make or break of the learning instrument technique. A shallow discussion adds little more than a lecture, while vigorous and open deliberations encourage critical thinking and critical reflection. A surprising level of emotional energy can also be generated as individuals become involved in introspection about personal values and future self development.

Learning instruments are useful for raising awareness about the relationship category of emotional resilience and for developing the initial elements of the subgroups including implementing and concern for others – particularly work motivation, bias for action, developing others, and empathy. Whether these elements will be changed or developed depends on the extent to which the individual is willing to become involved in critical thinking and critical reflection.

Simulations

A simulation allows the learner to act as if he or she were in the real-work situation. To give the learner an opportunity to act out this real behaviour, the HR developer uses a model of reality. A simulation model may take a number forms – e.g.

- a physical representation such as a flight simulator used for training pilots;

- a computer-managed game as is often used in management development; and

- the 'in basket exercise' where novice managers are asked to make a number of decisions about pieces of paper (letters, telephone messages, handwritten instructions) that are representative of a manager's normal workday.

In general, a simulation model should include a close representation of the usual work environment (at least the basic technology that is the norm for the role), sufficient information inputs to ensure that the learner has to make choices, and a mechanism to provide immediate feedback which, in turn, provides further information forcing the learner to make further choices. Hernes (1998) believes that successful simulations:

- provide a challenge to the learners so that they apply themselves, become motivated to seek new and innovative solutions, and create a desire to use the new solutions;

- have relevance to the learners' real needs (see comments by Knowles in Chapter 3); and

- are realistic so that the learners can recognise their work situation being reflected in the simulation.

Conducting simulations tends to be a much more interactive and dynamic exercise than those using case studies, role plays, and learning instruments. The HR developer is usually constantly involved, providing feedback and advice to the participants. The debriefings are usually first made on an individual basis (or at least the small group if a small group was the unit involved in the decision-making) before bringing the whole group together to discuss common trends or ideas. The HR developer should ensure that the whole group discussion raises the learning outcomes from the specific solutions to general principles that can be used in the workplace.

Simulations are designed to develop all the elements in the implementing and concern for others subgroups, as well as those in the critical thinking category of the HLO. For some examples of the use of simulations in human resource development see PNI Training Centre (2010) and Larson (2010).

Projects

A project is a defined activity that has limiting boundaries. These boundaries ensure that the project is not so large that the learner will be overwhelmed by the challenge. On the other hand, the project should be substantial enough to engender high levels of interest. The project should be workplace oriented but be of sufficient complexity to provide the learner with opportunities to see theory in practice. The experiential side of the activity often takes place outside the class room, but time should be planned so that discussion with a facilitator and a learning group can occur.

Unfortunately, learning projects can degenerate into just another task to be completed, as the urgencies of the workplace become paramount. So, for a project to be a successful learning technique, emphasis has to be given to reflection and feedback. The following seven steps are recommended for a successful learning project:

1. The project is explicitly defined with the limits described clearly and concisely.

2. The learner visits the work situation where the project is located to review the context, identify any significant features, and locate key stakeholders in the project.

3. The theories and concepts that may impact on the project are reviewed.

4. The learner uses critical thinking and critical reflection to review and contemplate new information, and to integrate theory and practice.

5. The learner discusses new insights with a HR developer and/or the learning group.

6. The previous five steps are repeated, in any order, throughout the project.

7. The learner produces a report on the recommendations for the project.

A learning diary is often included to provide further opportunities for reflection and development. Smith (1992b) suggests that a learning diary should include:

- a brief description of the experience;

- detailed observations of important events or issues;

- an analysis of these events or issues using relevant theories or concepts; and

- a description of the proposed future behaviour of the learner.

A learning diary encourages a learner to reflect deeply on the experience and to challenge any hegemonic assumptions (see Chapter 3). It is discussed further in Chapter 12.

Projects, properly managed, can be useful in developing the critical thinking category and the mental agility element of the meta-ability category.

Sensitivity groups

Sensitivity groups (sometimes called laboratory groups or T-groups) emerged from research and studies into the use of group processes for psychotherapeutic and interpersonal developmental purposes (Bion 1961 and Lewin 1951). Bion developed his ideas while helping shell-shocked soldiers from the Second World War come to terms with their terrors, while Lewin was interested in developing individual and group skills to create a harmonious and productive modern society.

Sensitivity groups are based on the belief that disclosure of deep personal issues and emotions within a highly supportive and caring group can lead to a more profound understanding of self and of one's personal relations with others. Accordingly, open and honest communication between group members and a willingness to disclose innermost feelings are the keys to productive sensitivity groups. In a symbiotic relationship, the well-known schools of therapeutic counselling of client-centred therapy (Rogers 1983) and gestalt therapy (Perls 1973) added to the rich values and processes of the sensitivity groups. The guiding beliefs of self-analysis (encouraged by unconditional acceptance by the facilitator) and staying in the 'here and now' were imported from these two schools of counselling into the sensitivity group technique.

The key to successful sensitivity groups is the HR developer (usually referred to as a facilitator) managing the process but staying out of the content. It is a reflection of Rogers's client-centred therapy in which the therapist eschews advice, reflecting only the client's meanings and feelings so that the client explores the issues and comes to personally relevant conclusions.

'Managing the process' has become the catch cry of facilitators in sensitivity groups. We came across the concept when examining interviewing (Chapter 7) and the discussion earlier in this chapter. In this, the HR developer uses processes (e.g. questioning and responding) to help learners externalise feelings and tacit knowledge. In sensitivity groups the processes became more complex than merely questioning and responding, with paradigms such as force field analysis and transactional analysis being used.

Case study example

See the PLP case study on page 8 of the workbook that accompanies this text for an example of using force field analysis.

A closer look 10.2

Force field analysis and transactional analysis

Force field analysis (FFA) is a process suggested by Lewin (1951) as a method for analysing problems that involve people. An FFA has four steps:

1. State the *objectives* to be achieved in behavioural terms (e.g. improve customer relations).

2. Identify the *driving forces* – the forces that are already present and encourage good customer relations (e.g. staff greet customers with a smile).

3. Identify the *restraining forces* – those forces that inhibit the achievement of the objective (e.g. staff lack product knowledge).

4. Plan *means of overcoming* the restraining forces (e.g. staff to attend product training courses).

The basic premise of FFA is that, once the restraining forces have been identified and overcome, the driving forces will automatically encourage the achievement of the objectives. In managing the process, the HR developer simply has the group cover each of the four steps in FFA – the group then concentrates on the actual content (e.g. 'staff lack product knowledge').

Transactional analysis (TA) is known as 'the poor person's psychology' and is a means of understanding what drives the inner self, and of analysing interpersonal relations. The heart of TA was the belief that an individual was comprised of three 'ego states':

- the parent ego state;
- the adult ego state; and
- the child ego state.

The *parent ego state* is made up of two parts – the nurturing parent and the critical parent. The nurturing parent is made up of caring messages to the self, such as 'Look left and right before crossing the road' and 'Don't worry, everything will come out all right in the end'. The critical parent gives fault-finding messages like 'You are so stupid' and 'You will never be a success'. Interestingly, parent ego messages are a simplistic understanding of frames of reference (see Chapter 3).

The *adult ego state* is based on logic and takes in factual information which is then analysed in a cause-and-effect manner.

The *child ego state* is made up of two parts. The natural child has all those childlike qualities of curiosity, excitement and living-for-the-moment. The adapted child assumes all those less-liked qualities of the manipulating child where tantrums and elements of cruelty can gain the rewards that the child-within-the-person seeks.

The HR developer would use examples from the real lives of the learners, utilising TA on these examples – first to show what is going on, and second, to 'raise the interaction'. For example, TA could be used to examine two aspects of an individual: first, to identify the basic motivations of the individual (e.g. a parent 'tape' from the parent ego saying, 'Don't even bother trying, you are hopeless'); second, to analyse the interactions between two people. This second type of analysis depends on identifying which ego state in one person is 'hooking' which ego state in the other person. So, the parent 'tape' of 'Don't even bother trying, you are hopeless' could be aimed at another person who could respond from the adapted child ego state by starting to cry.

Alternatively, rather than responding by crying (i.e. from the adapted child) the second individual may respond from the adult ego state ('What evidence do you have that I will not succeed?').

In this way, the HR developer uses TA to manage the process, while the learners contribute the content.

TA can be complicated, with other concepts such as 'games people play' being used to analyse interpersonal interactions. For further information see texts such as Harris (1967) and Jongeward and James (1973). TA dropped out of favour over the years as it can be used in a shallow and trite manner. However, there is a simplistic robustness about the concept of TA; when used correctly, it provides an easily assimilated foundation for interpersonal relations. You may have also noticed the connection of the ego states with the frames of reference discussed in Chapter 3.

Sensitivity groups were very popular in the late 1960s and early 1970s but have decreased in use over the years. Misuse of power by unskilled facilitators and the difficulty in demonstrating the relevance of the approach to workplace issues contributed to the lower interest. However, the values and techniques of sensitivity groups have been transferred to the wider field of organisational change – a learning strategy that will be discussed in the next chapter. Indeed, it is often difficult to see where sensitivity groups finish and organisational change strategies start, so close is the link between them.

Well-managed sensitivity groups develop and contribute to:

- the relationship category of the HLO;
- critical thinking; and
- the mental agility and helicopter perception elements of the meta-abilities category.

The energy for experiential learning

Experiential learning has the potential to develop the deeper levels of the task and relationship and some aspects of the critical thinking and meta-abilities categories of the HLO. However, whether this potential is fulfilled depends largely on the motivation of the learners. This motivational force is the catalyst that decides whether the learner will honestly and energetically follow the opportunities for development, or whether the learner will take the easier course and just 'play along'. The experiential learning options require a great deal of commitment and energy from the learner. A comprehensive discussion of experiential learning can be found in Higgs (1988).

The challenge to the HR developer

The discussion of learning strategies in this chapter commenced with the most structured approaches – the skill session, the theory session and the lecture – before progressing to the less structured approaches of the discussion and the case study.

The role play represents something of a watershed in this continuum of learning strategies in that it focuses strongly on the emotions of the learner as well as on the more objective or cognitive information to be learned. This means that the HR developer has not only to be adept with the programmed knowledge and the analytic procedures based on that programmed knowledge but also has to be comfortable with other peoples' emotions. Indeed, more than this, the HR developer has to regard these emotions as a form of energy and use them in a caring but productive manner when facilitating role plays and the more unstructured learning strategies.

Experiential learning involves the whole learner; the implementation of each of the techniques is based on the learning cycle of experience, review, conclude and plan. In conducting experiential learning, the HR developer becomes more a facilitator of the learning process than a teacher didactically imparting content information.

To successfully implement these learning strategies, a HR developer needs to have highly competent micro skills. These skills – questioning, responding, using visual aids, and constructing learning objectives – allow the HR developer to present information, elicit information, challenge and encourage the learners. Having the ability to use each of the learning strategies appropriately and effectively, and the micro skills to implement them, gives the HR developer the competence to present individual sessions. However, a learning experience usually consists of a number of these structured learning strategies linked together into a training program or workshop. A HR developer must be able to manage and coordinate this assembly of sessions to ensure that the desired learning experience outcomes are achieved.

While the learning strategies described in this chapter often combine to form a course or workshop, the strategies discussed in the next chapter are usually total learning experiences in themselves.

References

Agnew, P W, Kellerman, A S & Meyer, J M 1996, *Multimedia in the Classroom*, London: Allyn and Bacon.

Argyris, C 1980, 'Some limitations of the case method: Experiences in a management development program', *Academy of Management Review*, 5, pp. 291-298.

Bion, W R 1961, *Experiences in Groups*, New York: Ballantine Books.

Caffarella, R S 2002, *Planning Programs for Adult Learners*, 2nd edn, San Francisco: Jossey-Bass.

Delahaye, B L & Smith, B J 1998, *How to be an Effective Trainer*, New York: Wiley.

Exely, K & Dennick, R 2009, *Giving a lecture: From presenting to teaching*, Routledge, New York.

Feldman, K A 2007, 'Indentifying exemplary teachers and teaching: evidence from students' ratings', R P Perry & J C Smart (eds.), *The scholarship of teaching and learning in higher education: An evidence-based perspective*, Springer, AA Dordrecht, The Netherlands.

Frash, R, Antun, J, Kline, S & Almanza, B 2010, 'Like it! Learn it! Use it?', *Cornell Hospitality Quarterly*, 51(3), 3, pp. 398-414,

Goldstein, I L 2001, *Training in Organizations: Needs Assessment, Development and Evaluation*, 4th edn, Pacific Grove, California: Brooks/Cole.

Harris, T 1967, *I'm OK – You're OK*, New York: Avon.

Hernes, T 1998, 'Simulation methods', in J. Propopenko (ed.), *Management Development: A Guide to the Profession*, Geneva: ILO, pp. 251-271.

Hicks, J & Upton, S 2010, 'Jaguar Land Rover "Transition to higher performance" training program', *Industrial & Commercial Training*, 42 (5,) pp. 247-250.

Higgs, J (ed.) 1988, *Experienced-based Learning*, Sydney: ACEE.

Jongeward, D &James, M 1973, *Winning with People*, Reading, Mass: Addison-Wesley.

Kemp, J E & Smellie, D G 1993, *Planning, Producing and Using Instructional Technologies.* New York: Harper-Collins.

Killen, R 2007, *Effective Teaching Strategies: Lessons from Research and Practice*, 4th edn, Thompson, South Melbourne, Vic.

Knowles, M S, Holton III, E F & Swanson, R A 2005, *The adult learner: The definitive classic in adult education and human resource development*, Elsevier, London.

Larson, G C 2010, ' Avionics Simulation', *Business & Commercial Aviation*, 106(4), pp. 37.

Lewin, K 1951, *Field Theory in Social Sciences*, New York: Harper and Row.

Mager, R E 1991, *Preparing Instructional Objectives*, 4th edn, Belmont, California: Davis S. Lake.

Nesbit, T, Leach, L & Foley, G 2004, 'Teaching adults', in G Foley (ed.), *Dimensions of Adult Learning: Adult Education and Training in a Global Context*, Crows Nest, NSW: Allen & Unwin.

Perls, F 1973, *The Gestalt Approach and Eye Witness Therapy*, New York: Bantam.

Pigors, P 1976, 'Case method', in R L Craig (ed.), *Training and Development Handbook. A Guide to Human Resource Development*, New York: McGraw-Hill.

PNI Training Centre 2010, '*Offshore*. 70(7), p. 82.

Reynolds, A & Anderson, R H 1991, *Selecting and Developing Media for Instruction*, 3rd edn, New York: Van Nostrand Reinhold.

Reynolds, J I 1998, 'Case method', in J Prokopenko (ed.), *Management Development: A Guide to the Profession*, Geneva: ILO, pp. 272-90.

Rogers, C R 1983, *Freedom to Learn in the 80s*, Ohio: Charles E Merrill.

Roscoe, E M & Fisher, W W 2008, 'Evaluation of an efficient method for training staff to implement stimulus preference assessments', *Journal of Applied Behavior Analysis*,. 41(2), pp. 249-254.

Smith, B (1992a). 'Learning instruments', in B Smith (ed.), *Management Development in Australia*, Sydney: Harcourt Brace Jovanovich, pp. 129-139.

Smith, B 1992b 'Learning diaries', in B Smith (ed.), *Management Development in Australia*. Sydney: Harcourt Brace Jovanovich, pp. 149-154.

Stone, R J 2010, *Managing human resources*, 3rd edn, John Wiley & Sons, Brisbane.

Tarquin, P & Walker, S 1996, *Creating Success in the Classroom: Visual Organisers and How to Use Them*. Englewood, Colorado; Libraries Unlimited.

Thorndike, E L 1931, *Human Learning*, New York: Appleton-Century-Crofts.

Tovey, M D & Lawlor, D R 2008, *Training in Australia*, 3rd edn, Pearson Education Australia, Frenchs Forrest, NSW.

Tyler, R W 1949, *Basic Principles of Curriculum and Instruction*, Chicago: University of Chicago Press.

Van Ments, M 1994, *The Effective Use of Role Plays: Handbook for Teachers and Trainers*, London: Koan.

Waddell, D M, Cummings, T G & Worley C G 2004, *Organisation Development and Change*. Southbank, Vic: Nelson Australia.

Chapter 11

Implementing the unstructured learning strategies

LEARNING OBJECTIVES

After studying this chapter you should be able to:

1. Explain why knowledge is a unique asset.

2. Describe the role of the HR developer as a facilitator.

3. Describe the unstructured learning strategies of problem-based learning, contract learning, action learning, change interventions and mentoring.

4. Explain the role of e-learning in developing staff.

The role of the HR developer

The learning strategies in the previous chapter were termed 'structured' although, strictly speaking, this description only applies to the skill session, theory session and lecture. The other learning strategies – the discussion, case study, role play, and experiential learning – were discussed in a sequence that went from less structured to more unstructured. In the previous chapter, the connection between the learning strategies and the hierarchy of learning outcomes (HLO) was also emphasised – the highly structured being suitable to the programmed knowledge category while the less structured the learning strategies became, the more suitable they were to the deeper complex categories.

Another way to look at this progression is that the highly structured learning strategies rely more on the knowledge-generation process of combination and instrumental learning while the discussion, case study, role play, and experiential learning also bring in aspects of the knowledge processes of internalisation and externalisation, and communicative learning. In addition, all the learning strategies examined in the previous chapter place the responsibility on the HR developer to trigger these knowledge-generating processes.

The learning strategies discussed in this chapter place this responsibility for generating knowledge directly on the learner. There is less emphasis on combination and much more on internalisation and externalisation, and communicative and emancipatory learning. Further, the learning strategies in this chapter encourage socialisation as a significant learning channel. The first four of the unstructured learning strategies – problem-based learning, contract learning, action learning, and change interventions – use defined protocols that allow the HR developer to manage the learning process while allowing the learner to retain control over the learning itself. The final strategy – mentoring – has been designated as the most unstructured of all. Because mentoring is usually a one-on-one relationship between the mentor and the learner, the appropriate use of learning strategies can be very fluid. Learning strategies involving an emerging educational strategy, e-learning, are addressed at the end of the chapter.

In dealing with these unstructured learning strategies, the HR developer takes on a very subtle role that concentrates on managing the process but rarely becomes involved in the specific content. This 'process management' or *facilitator* role is common to all the unstructured learning strategies, so we will examine this role first. In performing this role, the facilitator undertakes a number of activities.

Support

Structured learning strategies, particularly the theory session and the lecture, are familiar to most learners. This familiarity, together with the material evidence of what the future will hold (e.g. the course program or the semester subject outline), provides the learner with a solid sense of security. The unstructured learning strategies, however, are often unfamiliar; neither is there much observable material to tell the learner what will happen in the future. The facilitator, therefore, has to provide supportive mechanisms that will ensure that learner insecurities will not impede the learning process.

There are two *supportive mechanisms* recommended by the pioneering writers (Knowles 1998; Revans 1982; Rogers 1983) in the field. The first is investing the time and encouraging supportive relationships between the learners so that they become what Revans calls 'comrades in adversity'. The second is to develop a positive relationship between the facilitator and individual learners. This relationship is not one of dependence, but one where the learner has sufficient trust to approach the facilitator as a 'sounding board' and counsellor.

Micro-skills

The *micro-skills* of questioning and responding are critical to the ability of the facilitator to stay at the process management level. When learners ask questions, they often expect answers based on content but, by and large, the facilitator should avoid 'descending into the content'. Self-directed learners are independent learners and should be encouraged to investigate options for themselves, with the facilitator questioning, reflecting, probing, and summarising. If you return to Chapter 8 and examine the concept of learning orientation displayed in Figure 8.2, you will see that the HR developer is essentially moving the learner away from stage 1, through stage 2 and into stage 3 – that is, low pedagogy/high andragogy of their learning orientation.

Malcolm Knowles (Knowles *et al.* 2005) believed that facilitators must acquire a different set of rewards – experiencing the joy of releasing learners rather than controlling them. This theme of 'releasing the learners' is one of the predominant constants in all the unstructured learning strategies. Knowles (Knowles *et al.* 2005) went on to suggest that the function of the HR developer in facilitating the unstructured learning strategies was one of process designer and manager, which required the skills of:

- relationship building;

- needs assessment;

- involvement of the learners in planning;

- linking learners to learning resources; and

- encouraging learner initiative.

Of course, this means that the facilitator must have the maturity to be able to accept and help learners with this new-found power.

Patience

For facilitators, patience is more than a virtue. It is an essential quality. The internal craving of the facilitator to intervene, give a specific example, or provide detailed advice can, at times, be overwhelming. This craving must be resisted – and to resist needs patience. Being novices to the concepts being investigated, learners will usually muddle around, procrastinate, explore dry gullies, and take the line of least resistance even when such a line will eventually take twice the time. Resisting the craving to jump in and say, 'Look, this is the best way,' requires patience.

To manipulate an old adage, the role of the facilitator is to help the learners to learn how to catch fish, not to catch the fish for them.

Active listening

Linked very closely to micro-skills and patience is the skill of listening. Listening actively is not simply using responding skills in the technical sense but really understanding and feeling what the learner is explaining. *Active listening* requires effort and concentration (see Chapter 7).

Encourage self-evaluation

Valuing *self-evaluation* above evaluation-by-others is the final bastion on the journey to becoming a self-directed learner. Most educational systems place a very high priority on evaluation-by-others. Breaking this nexus is one of the most difficult tasks of the facilitator, yet learners cannot become really independent until this transition occurs. Needless to say, we are attempting to change a very deep frame of reference here (see Chapter 3) and the transition is not easy for the learner. However, by keeping this ultimate goal of the importance of self-evaluation always to the forefront of the learning experience, the facilitator provides a constant guiding theme for the learner.

Acceptance

Rogers (1983) first commented that good facilitators can accept the troublesome, innovative, creative ideas that emerge in learners. Providing caring support, being patient, and encouraging self-evaluation releases powerful needs and forces within learners. They will experiment, they will examine issues in new ways, and they will have what they believe to be omnipotent insights. Combined with recognition that they do have a power to think, these insights will often be communicated forcefully and dramatically. The wise facilitator accepts and celebrates these new-found abilities with the learner, while also encouraging a judicious and healthy restraint.

Release the energy

Knowles (Knowles *et al.* 2005) rejoiced in the feeling of releasing the energy of others during their self-directed learning experience. The HR developer should ask the following questions:

- What is the total amount of energy available within the group of learners?
- What proportion of this energy is currently being used?
- Where is the unused energy located?
- Why is it not being tapped?
- What might be done to release this energy for accomplishing the learning objectives?

Prepared to learn

The successful facilitator is always prepared to learn – about the content being investigated by the learner and about the very process of being a facilitator. Rogers (1983) believes that facilitators have to be:

- less protective of their own beliefs;

- able to accept feedback (both positive and negative); and

- use this feedback as constructive insight into themselves and their behaviour.

It is only by being non-defensive that facilitators can deal successfully with those 'troublesome, innovative, creative ideas that emerge in learners'. Indeed, successful facilitators are always looking for opportunities to learn from the learners.

Brookfield (1995) in his text, *Becoming a Critically Reflective Teacher*, provides an excellent discussion of the developmental process needed to become a successful facilitator.

A different value system

Being a facilitator of the unstructured learning strategies requires a different value system. A facilitator uses open communication and encourages an honest relationship with the learners and between the learners. The learners are constantly challenged to examine hegemonic assumptions and to become truly independent learners by valuing self-evaluation above all else. This is not a frictionless journey for facilitators, either, and they must be secure enough in their own identity to evaluate feedback about their behaviours and beliefs honestly and forever enjoy each and every opportunity to learn.

The assumptions

All the unstructured learning strategies are based on rational or democratic discourse. As discussed in Chapter 3, Argyris (1999) and Mezirow (2009) believe that rational discourse is predicated on the critical assumption that the interaction is based on valid information. Further, they suggest that rational discourse is likely to be more successful when the participants:

- have equal opportunity to participate;

- are free from coercion and distorting self-deception;

- are open to alternative points of view;

- care about the way others think and feel;

- have free and informed choice; and

- keep testing the validity of the choices, especially as the choices are being implemented.

These assumptions, then, form the basic critical doctrine for the implementation of the unstructured learning strategies, each of which will now be discussed in turn.

Problem-based learning

As the name suggests, problem-based learning is founded on a real-life problem from the workplace. Problem-based learning reverses the traditional view of presenting information, then asking the learners to apply this information in the workplace. The proponents of problem-based learning believe that learning should revolve around professional problems that the learner would face in real life, not around academic subjects that underpin the field (Boud 1985). So the essence of problem-based learning is that the problem is presented to the learners who are then expected to find the appropriate knowledge. Stephenson and Galloway (2004) identify the objectives of problem-based learning as developing problem-solving and self-directed learning abilities, integrating learning with professional practice and motivating learners.

The problem

The problem provides the trigger needed to make the learners think. In addition, it has to be relevant and of interest to the learner (Yeo 2010). Selecting the appropriate problem is critical to the success of the learning episode. Unfortunately, however, there are no hard-and-fast rules to govern this selection process. Indeed, this dilemma reflects the strength and weakness of the problem-based approach. On the one hand, the problem should lead the learners towards the successful achievement of the learning objectives. However, the problems should not be so complex that the learners will believe that they are incapable of solving them (Killen 2003). On the other hand, the problem has to be broad enough to provide a realistic representation of a complex issue in the real world.

The problem should be multidimensional and cover a complexity of issues (Chambers 2007). There is a difference between an exercise and a problem. An exercise applies knowledge that a learner already possesses. A problem asks the learner to go out and search for appropriate knowledge. As Woods (1985) comments, in an exercise the learner already has some idea of solving the puzzle and it will just take time to work carefully through the details. With a problem, however, the learner initially has no idea of how to proceed.

Usually, the facilitator locates and presents the problem, although some writers (for example, Vilkinas & Cartan 1992) suggest the learners can bring 'problems' with them. These writers recommend a careful preparatory process where the learners first analyse their own work life by seeking feedback from peers and colleagues. The issues identified are then brought to the workshop where further analysis converts them into manageable problems.

The process

The presentation of the problem to the learners can take many forms – a written description, videotape, computer simulation, audiotape or even a combination of these media. However, once again, the guideline for the presentation is that it should reflect the same presentation sequence and quality that is encountered in real life.

If the learning experience is with a group of learners, they should be split into small groups. These small groups may be based on self-selection, although there is a danger of cliques evolving and of losing exposure to contravening ideas – self-selected small groups are often formed on the basis of common values. Another option is for the facilitator to 'force' a selection, but this has the disadvantage of the facilitator being seen to make decisions early in the process and a resultant increase in dependency. A unique option is to present both options: forming small groups, and asking learners to decide on the process of forming them.

Once the small groups have been formed, or if the learning episode will involve only one learner, the following steps should be covered by the facilitator.

1.   Have the learners read, view or listen to the problem.

2.   Encourage the students to think by asking such questions as, 'In what way is this problem similar to other problems I have solved?' and 'What is the most important piece of information I have?' (Killen 2003).

3.   Have the learners, first as individuals and then in their small groups, identify as many of the possible issues and implications of the problem as they can. Yeo (2010) believes that, at this stage, the learner is concentrating on causal reasoning. In other words, the emphasis is on content reflection where the learners focus on what they perceive, feel, think and act (see Chapter 3).

4.   Encourage curiosity by modelling inquisitive behaviour or by asking the learners to investigate how problems in the subject they are studying are solved in real life (Killen 2003).

5.   The facilitator may then ask each small group to present their findings. The idea here is to encourage each learner to identify all possible options that may need to be investigated. However, some facilitators prefer to omit this step and keep the learners operating within their own small groups.

6.   The small groups then identify possible sources of programmed knowledge that will need to be identified. Each individual learner can then investigate these sources, or the task can be divided among members of each small group.

7.   The learners report back to their small group (and full group if the facilitator prefers) on what programmed knowledge they have gathered and its application to the issues and implications of the problem.

8.   The small groups re-examine the problem to evaluate whether all the issues and implications have been resolved. At this stage, the learners are operating at the process-reflection level; they focus on how they perform the functions of perceiving. This level concentrates on prescriptive assumptions by examining the processes (see Chapter 3). The facilitator needs to be very active at this stage, asking questions and encouraging analysis by the learners, so that any omissions in logical analysis or programmed knowledge are highlighted. If omissions are identified, then the small groups return to step 4 and repeat the process.

9.   Near the end of the learning episode, the learners are encouraged to review the problem-solving processes used (Chambers 2007). The discussions should be designed to identify general principles of decision-making that can be used in the workplace or in their professional lives. At this stage, the learners are using double-loop learning (Yeo 2010) and are operating at the premise-reflection stage. Therefore, they concentrate on paradigmatic assumptions by examining the basic presuppositions or fundamental beliefs underpinning the problem (see Chapter 3).

Problem-based learning in practice

Problem-based learning focuses on providing answers to real-life situations. The proponents of problem-based learning believe that the learning is more closely linked to the learner's needs (thereby increasing motivation), providing a much broader learning experience (Hallinger & Bridges 2007). This breadth of learning is reflected in the amount of programmed knowledge covered – the learners tend to cover a broad range of interlinking topics – and the strong transference of learning to the workplace situation.

However, perhaps because of its very definition, problem-based learning tends to be more successful in situations where physical evidence of problems is evident. There are numerous reports of its use in the health professions, by medical doctors, nurses, and opticians. Problems in these professions can be readily defined, measured, and observed. In other areas, for example with the more subjective areas of management, problem-based learning has not been popular, with educators and HR developers leaning more towards the strategies of contract learning and action learning. Stephenson and Galloway (2004) find that the culturally marginalised and the socially disadvantaged and disenfranchised may find problem-based learning of limited value.

Problem-based learning is ideal for the more detailed, complex areas of professional, technical information and the task analytical and logistical subgroups of the HLO. Problem-based learning can be useful in developing outcomes in the relationship category and, depending on the problem used as the catalyst, the problem-solving element of the critical thinking category.

A closer look 11.1

An example of problem-based learning

In 1997 the University of Western Sydney became the first Australian university to offer indigenous Australians the opportunity to gain professional qualifications in the field of environmental health. For nearly 20 years before this, UWS delivered a mainstream-accredited environmental health degree through on-campus and distance education modes. PBL was used at each stage of the program alongside conventional teaching. The arrival of indigenous learners provoked a critical analysis of the suitability of both the conventional learning approach and the PBL approach. This review resulted in pedagogical changes in the PBL subjects. The changes aimed to prepare learners for work in complex, cross-cultural professional settings. In the final-year PBL subject, for example, the educational purpose shifted from being primarily concerned with the development of the individual towards learning expressed as a collaborative, strategic and action-oriented venture. In its new critical and strategic form, the PBL subject concentrates on developing the ability of learners to act on situations and to reflect on their actions in a systematic, self conscious, and reflexive way. Students engage with their peers in a variety of challenging, yet open and respectful forums. The forums are both face-to-face and internet based, involving indigenous and non-indigenous student practitioners.

Learners are asked to consider what it might take for indigenous practitioners to meet the environmental health needs of their own communities while working with the cultural differences between mainstream bureaucratic agencies and local indigenous community groups. Problems and solutions are explored in their sociopolitical, historical and cultural contexts. This contextual and critical form of PBL aims to raise students' consciousness through a continuing reflexive dialogue about their learning processes and discoveries, their questions and problems, and their management of individual and group learning. It is a framework as relevant to the learning context of mainstream professionals as it is to the learning circumstances and objectives of socially committed indigenous practitioners. And it is a framework that is driven by and grounded in the messy, real-life experiences of learning in work-based and community-based project settings (Stephenson 2002).

Source: Stephenson & Galloway 2004.

Contract learning

In championing adult learning, Knowles (1998) realised that his concept of andragogy would have to be operationalised. He achieved this practical interpretation of andragogy by promulgating an approach called 'contract learning'.

The learning contract

The heart of this strategy is a learning contract. This may seem to be an obvious statement, but many HR developers do not fully appreciate the care needed to create the learning contract or the central role it plays in managing the learning event. A learning contract has six main sections:

1. the *learning objectives,* which define the final outcome that the learner wishes to achieve. The learning objectives should be stated as terminal behaviours.

2. the *subject content* the learner proposes to cover to achieve these learning objectives.

3. the *learning methods* that will be used to learn the subject content.

4. the *evidence* that will be produced to show that the learning objectives have been achieved.

5. the *criteria* that will be used to ensure that the evidence achieves the appropriate quality standard – this criteria description will take the place of the 'standard statement' in the learning objectives; it is here the learner specifies how the evidence will be judged or validated.

6. the *date* that the evidence is expected to be submitted.

An example of a learning contract is shown in Figure 11.1. The design and layout of learning contracts are many and varied. The example given has a vertical layout. Learning contracts can also vary in the amount of information that is provided under each of the six sections. The example in Figure 11.1 gives only minimal information. Some learners prefer more-detailed descriptions, especially of the subject content.

Figure 11.1 An example of a learning contract

Learner's name: Merv Cranston

Facilitator's name: Ian Wilkinson

Learning objective: To list and discuss the skills of good interviewing

Content: 1. Questioning

           2. Paraphrasing

           3. Probing

           4. Summarising

           5. Nonverbals

Evidence: A report to be read by the facilitator and the manager, Marketing and Sales.

Criteria: 1. The report will be at least 2000 words long.

           2. All the major components of each of the interview skills will be discussed.

Date: The report will be submitted by 30 March.

Signed: _____   _____

             (Learner)   (Facilitator)

Knowles (1998) provides a form setting out the same information, but in a horizontal or landscape layout (see Figure 11.2). The advantage of Knowles's form is that several objectives can be listed with the details of the content, learning methods, evidence, criteria, and date being given for each objective across the page.

Figure 11.2 Knowles's learning contract

Learning contract for:

Name   _____

Activity   _____

Learning objectives	Learning resources and strategies	Evidence of accomplishment of objectives	Criteria and means for validating evidence

Source: Knowles 1998, p. 214.

Knowles emphasises that the learning contract is infinitely re-negotiable up until the end of the learning episode. This exhortation acknowledges that often the learners initially complete the learning contract with limited information. However, as they progress through the learning episode, the learners' knowledge improves and certain aspects may become clearer. Under these circumstances the learner could easily identify new objectives, or even realise that the original intentions were much too ambitious, and that a change in plans is prudent. So, the learners can re-negotiate up or down the learning spectrum.

The process

While the learning contract is the heart of contract learning, Knowles gives quite detailed advice on the process that should be used by the HR developer in managing the process (Knowles 1980a, 1980b, 1983a, 1983b, 1984, 1998; Knowles *et al.* 2005). He is quite adamant that the learner should not be 'thrown into the strange waters of self-directed learning and hope they can swim' (see, for example, Knowles 1980a, p. 98). Rather, the learner should be caringly and carefully prepared for the journey into andragogy (helping people to learn).

This preparation may vary on some specific points depending on the situation – for example, there are differing requirements for learning in a university compared with learning in the workplace. Further, the learner may be operating alone or as part of a learning group. However, most contract learning episodes cover the following steps:

1. The learners are introduced to the concepts of contract learning – a brief history of andragogy, the contract form, the idea of self-directed learning and self-responsibility, and a preview of the steps now being described.

2. The concept of learning objectives is discussed, both in the general sense (that learning objectives need to be stated in terms of terminal behaviour) and the specific sense (the actual learning objectives that the learner will achieve during the learning episode). Knowles readily acknowledges that some organisations, both educational and workplace, will not be in the position to allow the learner total control over what is to be achieved. Universities and colleges need to have some say over what will be learned, and some workplace organisations will need to specify what outcomes are expected of the learners. To cover this angle, Knowles suggests the use of non-negotiable and negotiable objectives. Non-negotiable objectives are the lowest level of achievement that the learners must achieve. If the learners wish to delve deeper than this minimal requirement then they can formulate negotiable objectives. For example, in university and college courses, the non-negotiable objectives are set at the pass level. If the students wish to achieve a level higher than a pass – honours or distinction – then the students suggest additional objectives that interest them but are worthy of this higher award. In a situation where the learner is going to be fully responsible for the learning and where the educational institution or workplace organisation does not wish to set specified outcomes, then only negotiable objectives are used.

3. When non-negotiable objectives are being used, the facilitator provides what Knowles calls the 'broad brush' view of the content to be learned. A broad brush view covers the main points of the content that the learners will need so that they can achieve the non-negotiable objectives. This information can be covered using a lecture or handouts or readings (specific pages or perhaps a chapter) from textbooks.

4. For the negotiable objectives, Knowles suggests that the facilitator acts as a 'traffic cop'. The facilitator may recommend to the learner certain texts to be read, or may refer the learner to a noted expert. One very useful source is the tables of contents of relevant textbooks. A list of contents provides a good broad-brush view of a particular topic, where key words and concepts can be identified very efficiently. If they are facing self-directed learning for the first time, learners often feel somewhat insecure. The idea of doing something useful and tangible, such as examining relevant content, is very reassuring for learners, so asking them to examine content is satisfying both intellectually and emotionally.

5. At this stage, some time for reflection can be very beneficial, allowing the learner to accumulate and internalise the appropriate content.

6. As well as internalising the content, most learners review the whole concept of contract learning during the reflective time. Issues, questions, concerns and doubts start to bubble and become disconcerting. This distraction can interfere with learning, so the facilitator needs to deal with the distractions by encouraging the learners to discuss them.

7. If the contract learning is taking place with a group of learners, they can be divided into small groups and asked to list all the issues, questions, concerns, and doubts. If these are disclosed within a small group, no negative queries can be attributed to an individual. The small groups, therefore, are more likely to be forthcoming and produce more information. Once the small groups have completed their list, the facilitator can combine the contributions (usually on a white board so that all can see). It is then a matter of confronting each point.

8. Some of the points can be addressed simply by providing information – for example, the query 'I'm not sure what you mean by terminal behaviour in the learning objectives' can be addressed by defining terminal behaviour more precisely. However, other points can be answered only by the learners experiencing the situation. For example, the concern of trust in the facilitator is always an issue, sometimes overt but usually covert. The learners will not be influenced by facilitator exhortations of 'Sure, you can trust me'. Trust will only be built over time and after a close examination of the facilitator's behaviour by the learners.

9. A similar process can be used for individuals using contract learning, although, of course, the safety of anonymity afforded within small groups is not available.

10. With at least some of the anxieties abating, the learners can again turn to the learning objectives they wish to attain. At this stage, learning can be enhanced when the learners discuss their insights and findings with each other. As well as

interchanging content (i.e. combination), the learners discover that the other learners are experiencing similar concerns and impediments, and feelings of loneliness tend to dissipate. Further, there is an opportunity for the knowledge-generating process of socialisation to occur.

11. At the end of this interaction, the full group of learners is encouraged to publicly generate a long list of possible competencies or issues or concepts that could be covered during the learning episode. This list is then used by individual learners to identify personally relevant matters that they can investigate.

12. The learners can then be encouraged to turn their attention to their learning contracts. They should be given a definite target date to submit their contracts, as procrastination can suffocate the best of intentions. When the contracts are submitted, the facilitator examines them and decides whether they do reflect the required intentions. If the contract is acceptable, the facilitator signs to signal an agreement. If the contract is not acceptable, then the facilitator and learner will enter a negotiation stage until the needs of the learner and the facilitator (who represents the educational institution or workplace organisation) are met.

13. With agreement on the learning contract reached, the learner follows the plan described under the learning methods section of the learning contract, always moving towards producing the evidence promised. When a group of learners is involved, it is common for the facilitator to help them identify areas of common interest, and assist the learners to identify efficient and effective learning events.

By following these thirteen steps, the facilitator manages the learning process while allowing the learner to concentrate on the content to be learned. Good support and encouragement is provided to the learner and the various decisions required for learning to continue are raised at the appropriate time.

Contract learning in practice

During the discussion of contract learning, care has been taken to differentiate between process and content. Theoretically, the content can include any of the elements in the hierarchy of learning outcomes, from the programmed knowledge to the meta-abilities categories. However, in learning contracts, the learners tend to concentrate on the programmed knowledge category, the analytical and logistical subgroups of the task category, and the interpersonal and intrapersonal subgroups of the relationship category. But, by being involved in contract learning, the learners are likely to develop competence in the implementing subgroup of the task category, the concern for others subgroup of the relationship category, and the critical thinking category.

There is also the possibility of developing the outcomes in the meta-abilities category, although this will depend largely on the motivation and perceptiveness of the learners. It is this wide range of possible outcomes that often attracts HR developers to contract learning as a robust learning strategy.

Action learning

Action learning was defined and created by Reg Revans (1980) as a self-directed process for developing managers. The key to action learning is to *take action*. If the learning contract is the heart of contract learning, then the driving force of action learning is the formula: Learning = Programmed Information + Questions (L=PI+Q). Programmed information is available from books, journals and experts. For Revans, and this is the second key to action learning, true learning comes only from the ability to *ask important questions*. Recently, however (see, for example, Marquardt, Skipton, Freedman & Hill, 2009), the formulae has been extended to L=PI+Q+R where 'R' stands for reflection. The third key to action learning, then, is *reflection*. In simplistic terms, action learning becomes a cycle of:

- reflection on the problem or challenge;

- formulating questions based on this reflection;

- searching for possible answers, firstly through programmed information (for example, textbooks or in the mind of an expert);

- reflection on these answers and formulating a possible experience;

- engaging in the experience (that is, taking action); and

- reflection on the experience and formulating questions.

So, when facilitating action learning, the HR developer will continually encourage the learners to take action, ask questions, reflect deeply on experiences, and then ask more questions and so on.

In reading the various texts by Revans (e.g. 1980, 1982), one finally realises that Revans avoids supplying explicit definitions. Indeed, he is more noted for providing insights into what action learning is not. However, two of his writings (1997, 1998) offer characteristics of action learning that can be combined to create a workable paradigm. The characteristics of action learning are:

1. Learning by doing, rather than simply acquiring information.

2. Learning to take effective action rather than just analysing a situation – conclusions should not simply be reported but be implemented, and this implementation has to be evaluated for effective learning to occur.

3. Working on a specific and defined project that is rooted in the real workplace and is of significance to the learner. The project should be about attacking a problem or opportunity rather than a puzzle. A puzzle is an embarrassment to which a solution already exists, whereas a problem or challenge has no currently existing solution.

4. Learning to identify the important questions to ask when attacking a problem or challenge.

5. Changing learners' perceptions of what they are doing and how they interpret their past experiences. (This is similar to what was discussed in Chapter 3 on changing frames of reference.)

As well as being defined by these five characteristics, action learning has three other essential elements:

- the real-life project;

- the learning set; and

- the set adviser.

The real-life project

The first important element is selection of a real-life project that will be suitable for action learning. Figure 11.3 shows the process for the identification of a suitable project.

Figure 11.3 Defining the real-life project for action learning

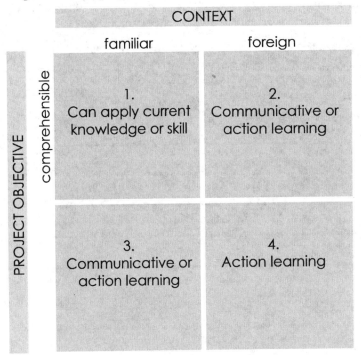

The selection of the specific and defined project can be based on two parameters – the context where the project occurs and the objective of the project. The context in which the project can occur can vary from familiar to the learner to foreign, while the project objective can vary from comprehensible to the learner to meaningless. However, it is important to recognise that the two parameters must be interpreted from the learner's point of view – that is, how the learner views the context and how the learner views the project objective.

These two parameters establish four possible situations from which the project can be selected:

- *Situation 1:* A comprehensible objective (i.e. it is understandable to the learner) occurring in a familiar context. This would occur, for example, if the learner is a sales representative facing a marketing project in the organisation in which the learner works. In this case, the learner would solve the problem that is the basis of the project by applying her or his current knowledge – and most probably learn very little. This situation is not suitable for action learning.

- *Situation 2:* A comprehensible objective in a foreign context (i.e. the project is occurring in a context the learner would find alien). This would occur if the learner is a sales representative in a manufacturing organisation but is facing a sales project in a service industry. The learner may solve the problem that is the basis of the project by talking to others who have the required context knowledge – that is, by using communicative learning. But if the problem is somewhat more complex, even for the people in the service industry (perhaps it has sales connotations), the project would be suitable for action learning.

- *Situation 3:* An objective that is meaningless (i.e. the learner does not understand what the objective means). This would occur if the learner is a sales representative facing an accounting problem in the sales department. The learner may solve the problem by talking to others who have the required accounting knowledge – that is, by using communicative learning – but if the problem is somewhat more complex even for an accountant (perhaps it has sales connotations), the project would be suitable for action learning.

- *Situation 4:* The objective of the project is meaningless to the learner and the context is also foreign to the learner. This would occur if the learner is a sales representative in a manufacturing organisation facing an accounting problem in a service industry. The learner is more likely to experience more meaning and deeper learning from situation 4. This situation is the quintessential action learning project.

Situations 3 and 4 indicate that the objective is meaningless to the learner. The obvious first step for the learner, then, is to make meaning of the objective. Only then can the learner examine the options to explore as part of the action learning process.

The learning set

Revans firmly believed that learning is a social process because people learn best from each other. In action learning, this social interaction is provided through a 'learning set', where a group of learners meets regularly to discuss their individual projects. The learning set becomes the support system, the sounding board, and the devil's advocate where individual learners can raise issues, confess to a lack of understanding, and have ideas tested and challenged – hence Revans' sobriquet *comrades in adversity*.

The set adviser

The role of the set adviser is not to teach but to help the learners learn from exposure to problems and to each other. The set adviser encourages the learning set to become a learning community. Writers such as Casey (1991) and McGill and Brockbank (2004) suggest that the set adviser has two basic tasks – to develop the abilities to:

- give; and
- receive.

The ability to *give* involves:

- formulating questions that provide maximum help rather than satisfying the curiosity of the questioner;
- giving opinions, both positive and negative in an open, honest and effective manner; and
- giving support, especially emotional.

The ability to *receive* involves encouraging each learner to search diligently for help from their peers and other sources. This may seem paradoxical to some learners where, on the one hand, they are asked to be independent but, on the other, to seek help. The difference is that dependent learners depend solely on a significant person, but in developing the ability to receive, the learners are seeking to find clues to solutions from a variety of sources.

The set adviser holds regular meetings for the learners – the comrades in adversity – who discuss individual projects with an emphasis on identifying the types of important questions that provided the most productive results. Challenges and barriers encountered are noted and the strategies used to overcome these barriers are analysed for general principles that can be used in a variety of situations.

As with any learning endeavour, the set adviser will first have the learners clearly define the learning objectives they are to achieve. This step is particularly important with Situations 3 and 4 (see Figure 11.3). Then, as an overall guide to keeping individual learners focused on their project, the set adviser uses System Beta, a process that Revans believes is needed to plan and implement a decision. System Beta comprises five steps:

1. a *survey stage*, where the learner identifies all possible options;

2. a *trial decision stage*, where the learner examines each possible option as if it is the most likely to help with the decision, imagines the possible outcomes of each option and then selects the option that is most likely to succeed;

3. an *action stage*, where the selected option is implemented, either in whole or in part, either in reality or in some simulated form;

4. an *audit stage*, where the observed results of the action stage are compared to the planned outcome; and

5. a *control stage*, where appropriate action is taken on the comparison. This action may encompass accepting success and moving to the next stage of the plan, modifying the plan or rejecting it and starting again. Whichever action is decided upon, the learner then returns to the survey stage to repeat the process.

System Beta has some striking similarities to Dewey's scientific decision-making process (see Chapter 3) and also to Honey and Mumford's learning cycle (see Chapter 8). You may wish to review these two concepts and identify the commonalities.

Action learning in practice

In action learning, the emphasis is on questioning, implementing, and reviewing. Mumford (2004) believes that action learning is different from other reality-based programs on several counts:

- the learners solve problems that entail taking risks and resolving uncertainties;

- the projects are open-ended in that there is rarely one 'correct' solution – thus the learners learn to cope better in situations of complexity and uncertainty;

- the learners are encouraged to develop their own abilities to solve problems;

- it is not just a method (e.g. a case study or a simulation), but a set of methods whereby the learner learns through action in the real world; and

- it is not used to perpetuate or diffuse existing practice but to creatively modify and replace it.

When an action learning project is selected at the situation 4 level (unfamiliar task in an unfamiliar context), the learner is likely to develop the critical thinking and meta-abilities level of the HLO (see Chapter 8). The less complex categories are also developed, especially the implementing subgroup of the task category and the concern for others subgroup of the relationship category. However, the programmed knowledge category is relegated to a certain extent in that programmed information is used as a means to an end – i.e. to allow the learner to detect new relationships between thoughts, ideas, and values.

Change interventions

Managing change appropriately to enhance the development of individuals, groups, and organisations has its origins in sensitivity groups (see Chapter 10). As early as the 1970s it was recognised that more mechanistic and structured training methods did not always allow individuals or organisations to cope with the speed or the complexity of change that was becoming evident in society. Gradually, more interest was taken in the power of people analysing and developing their own solutions to their own problems. This interest was based on a belief that people involved in the change would know all the issues and that their inability to solve the problems was caused by a block in the decision-making processes used. This belief led to the identification of the key value in managing change interventions – i.e. the facilitator managing the process and staying out of the content. For a detailed discussion of managing process see Schein (1998).

One of the fundamentals of managing the process is the use of group dynamics; this was discussed in Chapter 7. Another fundamental model used in managing the process is action research.

Action research

In managing the process of a change intervention, the facilitator uses a basic model called action research (see Figure 11.4). The action research model starts with the objective to be achieved. As usual, this objective should include a terminal behaviour statement but may or may not include standards. For example, an objective may be 'To increase customer spending by ten percent' and this includes both a terminal behaviour statement 'increase customer spending' and a measurable standard – 'ten percent'. However, the objective 'To decrease conflict within the group' does not have a standard as it is difficult to measure 'conflict'. Of course, some pseudo-measurements could be created – for example, 'There are ten percent fewer arguments each day' – but such measurements are easily faked. Change interventions are based on open communication, and pseudo-measurements are often felt to be counterproductive.

Figure 11.4 The action research model

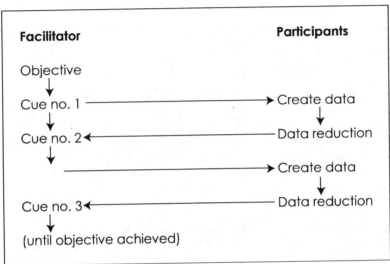

From this objective, the facilitator creates 'cue no. 1'. A cue is a catalyst that guides the participants in the appropriate direction. How does the facilitator create this cue? The decision may be based on logic. For the objective 'To increase customer spending by ten percent', the facilitator may decide that the participants already have a number of ideas so the cue may be: 'In what ways could the customers be encouraged to spend more while they are in the store?' Another way that a cue could be created from this objective is to use theory. A common theoretical base for cues is force field analysis (FFA) (see Chapter 10). From FFA, cue number 1 could become: 'What currently encourages customers to spend money?'

This cue is given to the participants – on a piece of paper, or displayed on a whiteboard or an overhead projector – and they are asked to generate data by listing a series of ideas. During this stage, the facilitator has to be aware of group dynamics (see Chapter 7) and ready to manage the task and maintenance roles as well as any idiosyncratic needs that arise.

Another technique that encourages deeper thought and deeper analysis is the individual→small-group→large-group sequence. In this technique, the individual participants are given time to think and jot down ideas by themselves before being invited to join small groups (three or four people) to share their ideas. When finished, each small group reports to the main group on their accumulated ideas. To help promulgate the information efficiently across the large group, it has become traditional for the small groups to use 'butcher's paper' (sometimes called 'flip chart paper') – large pieces of white paper, approximately one metre by three-quarters of a metre – on which each group writes ideas, hangs it from a wall, and refers to it while debriefing their ideas.

With all this information displayed and understood, the problem now likely to be faced by the whole group is an embarrassment of data – too much to handle effectively. Accordingly, the data needs to be reduced. This data reduction can be carried out by the facilitator, although this option is usually taken only if time is of the essence. Preferably, the group should make the decision on what data is less important or what pieces can be collated or combined to make a significant issue. Because a number of people are involved and issues can engender in-depth discussion, this option is time consuming. Depending on the time available and the motivation of the participants, the facilitator will have to decide which option is most feasible.

Once the data has been reduced to a workable level, and if the objective has not been achieved by the first cue, the facilitator then creates cue number 2. Again, this cue can be based on logic or theory. For example, the second cue may be based on FFA by concentrating on the hindering forces. This cue is again presented to the participants and so the action research process continues with cue number 3 being 'How can the hindering forces be overcome?'

More recently, the process of action research has broadened conceptually from the basic model presented in Figure 11.4. Based on the work of such writers as Kemmis (2007) and Somekh (2006), action research (while still emphasising the power of the participants) is often seen as a series of flexible cycles involving, holistically:

1. the collection of data about the topic;

2. the analysis and interpretation of the data;

3. the planning and implementation of strategies to bring about positive change;

4. the evaluation of those changes; and

5. a continuing cycle of data collection, analysis, evaluation, and so forth.

The key to action research is that the facilitator encourages the participants to make as many of the decisions as possible. Indeed, Somekh (2006) emphasises that action research is based on a genuine collaboration between the participants and researchers with a vision of social transformation and social justice for all.

As a final comment, there appears to be some similarities between this conceptually broader view of action research and the system beta of action learning. This is not surprising, as both are dealing with the development of human systems. The main difference is that action learning concentrates on the development of the individual, while action research focuses on the development of the social system and the target group of individuals.

Change in a social system

Change interventions are used to transform any social system. A social system is one that includes people. As a learning strategy, a change intervention can be used in a classroom or as part of workplace learning or across an organisation.

A change intervention in an organisation, or as part of workplace learning, is usually referred to as organisational development. While all change interventions are based on action research, organisational development interventions also use a variety of other, specifically designed models. The choice of model selected to help manage the change process depends on the objective that is to be achieved. These models vary from conflict management to team building to strategic planning. For detailed descriptions of these models see French, Bell and Zawicki (2005), Jeston and Nelis (2008) and Patton and McCalman (2008).

A change intervention in a classroom is often referred to as 'classroom democracy'. While action research is still the base model used, there are no other specific, recognised models designed for classroom democracy. There is high reliance on managing group processes (see Chapter 7) with a theme of devolving responsibility for learning to the learners. For a good description of classroom democracy see Dick (1992).

Change interventions in practice

Change interventions are designed to manage the learning process in any social system. While all change interventions are based on action research, organisational change interventions also use specifically designed models that suit particular situations, such as conflict resolution or team building. Change interventions in the classroom – called classroom democracy – are also based on the action research model but rely heavily on managing the group dynamics.

Most participants involved in a change intervention usually develop abilities in the implementing subgroup of the task category, the concern for others subgroup of the relationship category, and the critical thinking and meta-abilities categories of the HLO (see Chapter 8).

A closer look 11.2

A work team or a work group?

One popular demand for a change facilitator is the request for 'team building'. Managers are often seduced into believing that if their staff becomes a team, the majority of supervision problems will disappear. Sadly and frequently, such a faith in the power of team building does not survive the harsh realities of the organisational world. This is not to say that team building is a waste of time.

Team building interventions are successful with work groups who have the potential to become a team. A group has the potential to become a team when the group members are interdependent. In other words, the outputs of each team member are the inputs of another team member and/or the outputs of each team member have to be combined with the outputs of every other team member. If such interdependence is present, the dynamics of the team – the dependence on each other, the trust each has in the other members of the team, the desire not to let down other members of the team – become the glue that holds the team together and the coordinating force that ensure that the high quality goods and/or services are delivered on time and at the right place. Such special work groups will benefit enormously from a team building intervention. To see the successful use of teams, see the PLP case study on pages 2 to 4.

However, if the interdependence of work members is not present – and this is the case with most work groups – calling the work group a team will not ensure coordination, even with a team-building intervention. The only coordination processes that will be successful in work groups are the usual processes of single-use planning and control systems.

Change facilitators should be wary of falling into the team building trap. Only undertake team building intervention if you are sure that the work group members are fully interdependent.

Mentoring

As Mumford (2004) comments, the idea of an older person acting as a coach, counsellor or sponsor is one that has long existed informally and even accidently. Indeed, the very word 'mentor' comes from ancient Greek mythology when King Odysseus selected Mentor as the tutor and friend of his only son. Today, mentoring is part of the modern workplace, a tool as ubiquitous as the desktop and water cooler (Gettler 2002).

The words 'mentoring', 'coaching' and 'counselling' appear in the literature with a variety of meanings, describing a variety of relationships. Some authors (for example, Gonczi 1992 and Zey 1988) believe that mentoring is the dominant role – with coaching being a subset – while others (for example, Landsberg 2003 and McLennan 1995) see mentoring as being a subset of coaching. The argument eventually comes down to semantics and, for practical purposes, it is more important that the HR developer has consistent definitions. This text will assume that mentoring is the dominant concept.

Successful mentoring programs

Mentoring is not simply a set of techniques; it is also a philosophy. A successful mentoring program is based on an organisational belief system that values learning, where senior staff enjoy assisting talented staff to develop, and where senior staff actively accept that responsibility.

Organisations, thinking of implementing a mentoring program, need to consider the following:

- Mentors-to-be need to be developed in the role of a mentor. Mentors do not just have appropriate programmed knowledge; they are also adept at using structured and unstructured learning strategies.

- Organisations need to allocate resources to the mentor, especially the resource of time. The assumption that highly productive staff (usually the ones to become mentors) will somehow find sufficient time in their busy schedules is antiquated and short-sighted.

- The mentor must gain both extrinsic and intrinsic benefits from the program. This means that organisations need to consider meaningful rewards for those staff willing to take on the role of mentor. Just as important, each mentor should feel personal satisfaction in the improvement of the protégé. In addition, successful mentors expect to learn just as much as the protégé – in different ways, of course, but just as much in a quantitative sense.

The mentor–protégé synergy

Selecting a productive mentor–protégé team is a delicate task. The desired outcome is a complex combination of career and psychosocial functions. The protégé is not being developed in just the programmed knowledge required but in all categories of the HLO. In addition, these outcomes are being developed in the workplace for demonstrable improvement in the workplace context. Choosing a mentor is not a matter of choosing the 'closest' or the most 'accessible' person. The selection should be based on a number of considerations and after serious thought (Ho Law & Hussain 2007).

What should a protégé look for in a mentor? Odiorne (1985) believes that good mentors have the following qualities:

- they are superior performers and thus represent a model to which the protégé may aspire;

- they realise that they set an example, and behave accordingly;

- while being very supportive, they avoid usurping or interfering too much;

- they are good delegators, defining the required outcomes specifically, providing appropriate resources and support – and then leaving the person alone to work towards the desired outcome; and

- they encourage self-feedback so that the person becomes a self-directed learner.

Further, there has to be compatibility between the mentor and the protégé but this compatibility has to be about balance. It could be argued, for example, that both parties should have similar learning styles so that they can communicate and avoid misunderstandings. But similarity of learning style will not 'stretch' the protégé. There will be few new insights, less challenging of thought processes, and more limited exploration of alternative perceptions. On the other hand, too great a distance between the mentor and the protégé can lead to a less than harmonious relationship. There are two keys to a successful mentor–protégé alliance. First, the two parties have to be able to communicate – that is engage in reflective discourse (see Chapter 3). This means each recognises and accepts individual differences and each goes out of his or her way to discuss issues using words and nonverbals understood by the other. Second, the protégé should be encouraged to interact with other 'experts' and 'superior performers'. Such encouragement requires a high level of maturity on the part of the mentor.

The role of the mentor

Smith (1992) suggests that there is no universal role description for a mentor, as requirements vary according to the organisational factors, the stage of the mentor–protégé relationship, and the needs of the protégé. The role of the mentor, though, goes beyond being a HR developer. The mentor is involved in the psychosocial development based on the organisation's culture. The mentor is also closely involved with career planning, preparing the protégé's advancement for several promotions. So the mentor–protégé relationship is usually of a fairly long term. The mentor can expect to do the following:

- Use the various learning strategies appropriately. Frequently, the mentor will commence with contract learning or action learning to manage the process.

- Coach the protégé in specific skills, and task and relationship competencies. Coaching tends to be relatively performance oriented, is a very active role, and concentrates on short-term, immediate requirements (Smith 1992).

- Concentrate on the relationship category of the HLO, using counselling skills from recognised counselling approaches such as client-centred counselling, rational-emotive therapy, and gestalt therapy.

- Ensure that the protégé is involved in career-building projects by bringing the protégé to the attention of the key stakeholders in the organisation and opening the door to opportunities for advancement.

Mentoring in practice

The role of the mentor is to set up an environment wherein protégés feel good about themselves, believe in themselves, care about others and feel empowered to make a meaningful contribution (Oncken 1997). Mentors are very special people. They delight in watching others fulfil their potential, see mentoring as a challenge which will provide opportunities for learning for both parties, and are themselves highly developed in the competencies of the meta-abilities category of the HLO. The mentoring role itself is a complex set of interacting skills, knowledge, and values. The mentor has to have high levels of appropriate programmed knowledge, be competent in managing the adult learning, and have the compassion to accept the unique combination of strengths and weaknesses that make up an individual.

Hansford, Tennent and Ehrich (2002) and Ramaswami and Dreher (2007) see a number of benefits accruing from mentoring. For the protégé, the benefits include:

- career advancement;

- personal support;

- encouragement;

- learning and development;

- increased confidence;

- assistance;

- acceptance; and

- feedback.

For the mentor, the advantages are:

- personal fulfilment;

- assistance on projects;

- increased self-confidence;

- networking; and

- revitalised interest in work.

However, Hansford, Ehrich and Tennent (2003) report that the mentor appears to receive substantially fewer benefits than the protégé. The organisation also benefits as *staff* are developed, turnover is reduced, there is increased commitment to the organisation and organisational communication is improved. However, the authors also warn that there is a dark side to mentoring. The protégé can have negative experiences because of unrealistic expectations, can be forced to neglect core aspects of his or her own job, and can experience role conflict between his or her boss and mentor. The mentors often experience a lack of time and have very few of the supposed benefits accrue.

Mentoring can develop any one of the elements within the categories of the HLO, or develop all the elements of the categories. Overall, though, mentoring is ideal for developing combinations of HLO categories and ensuring that this development is transferred into the workplace. It must be emphasised, though, that such development is a long-term investment. Organisations need to think carefully before entering mentoring programs and ensure that appropriate resources are assigned. For further reading on mentoring see Ho Law and Hussain (2007) and Scandura and Pellegrini (2007).

E-learning

Information and computer technology (ICT) has opened the door for a vibrant potential alternative to face-to-face (F2F) learning. F2F learning has some downsides, including pre-defined and immoveable offerings based on time and geography. For potential learners who are temporally and geographically challenged – for example, live in isolated areas or whose careers are based on shift work – F2F learning is an unviable proposition. However, the fundamental force limiting the use of ICTs has been recognised by key writers and researchers for decades (see, for example, Knowles 1970, Revans 1980 and Rogers 1983) – learning for humans is a social process and a social event. The view of the critical importance of social interactions in adult learning has been supported by recent research (Brown & Adler 2008). Learning through ICTs appears to contravene this basic need.

Defining e-learning

While ICTs have the potential to expand the possibilities of meeting the growing learning needs of adults (Isenberg 2007), there is some confusion over definition of the term. E-learning can cover a variety of facilities, including:

- *Having access to the internet.* There is a wide variety of search engines available that allow the curious adult access to a plethora of information. However, while some people are more likely to use the internet as a first port of call for information, this does not mean that they are skilled in dealing with and critically analysing information (Helsper & Eynon 2009). The learning process will still rely on an ability to search efficiently, high levels of motivation (see Chapter 9), and having the learning maturity to manage one's own learning.

- *The administration of learning.* Enrolments, the publication and presentation of learning course or workshop programs, the publication and presentation of course materials, record keeping, integrating successful completion of formal learning experiences into other HRM processes – are not only made easier by ICT but are reliant on it.

- *Computer Assisted Learning* (CAL), which may be based on a website or use CD-ROMS, is often used in conjunction with F2F learning in a classroom. The purpose of CAL is to enhance the learning experience; it can present at least seven types of learning activities – namely:

  - data reduction, where the computer can perform repetitive calculations, thus expediting other learning activities;

  - drill, a series of questions, answer, check answer, diagnose difficulties and prescription of next question;

  - tutorial, a more complex version of the drill, where learners can answer more multifaceted questions;

  - using newer technologies, such as iPads and apps, to bring the workplace into the classroom, for example with demonstrations. These applications emphasise the principle of learning from meaningful material (see Chapter 3);

  - simulations, where the learners learn and practise a complex combination of skills and knowledge (pilot training simulators and business games are common simulations);

  - problem solving (similar to simulations), where the learners develop strategies to solve a presented problem and receive scores on the effectiveness of their strategies; and

  - inquiry – which is a development of the problem-solving option and develops professionals' diagnostic skills.

- *Online e-learning* uses a computer-managed learning program (CML) to holistically manage each learner's activities in a way that optimises learning. The main processes of an online program are presenting a learning experience, testing the learner's knowledge, diagnosing the level of the learner's knowledge, selecting the appropriate next level for the learner, and maintaining a detailed record of each learner's progress.

Unfortunately, it is sometimes assumed that online e-learning equates with self-directed learning – an assumption that falls far short of the reality. Frequently, what is presented as online e-learning is merely the administration of learning – a process that is designed to minimise expenditure of the organisation, limit the amount of oversight that is needed, and dump the responsibility to make the learning system work entirely on the shoulders of the learner. While such a process could, in a moment of generosity, be called self-paced learning, it is certainly not self-directed learning. Rather, it is a glorified copying service, which saves the organisation the cost and trouble of mailing out a hard copy of the learning material.

Challenges to designing online e-learning

Holey and Oliver (2010) contend that, while the economies of scale may have encouraged organisations and educational institutions to adopt e-learning, the benefits to learners are questionable. Indeed, one manager is reported as suggesting that, if discussion time is cut out, this can strip down a one-day face-to-face event to a one-to-two hour e-learning session (Millen 2010). This is one manager who obviously has not heard of the importance of communicative learning! Writers such as Fiol (2003), Isenberg (2007) and Radwin and Leeds (2009) suggest that e-learning has several limitations.

- *Lack of focus on interpretation and meaning.* This results in incompatible 'information islands' because the same information may hold many different meanings.

- *Loss of complexity.* Tacit knowledge is simplified and made explicit so that it can be more easily disseminated through the online e-learning episode. The simplification that allows easy transmission also results in the loss of essential knowledge ingredients.

- *Formality.* This makes it difficult to change knowledge or discard knowledge. Outdated information can be as bad as, or worse than, no information.

- *Limited room for the informal,* the tacit, and the socially embedded. These learning approaches are where experience-based know-how lies and continuous updates occur. Unfortunately,, formalising knowledge-work through e-learning is likely to limit its usefulness and its flexibility. Further, such limits on flexibility are likely to negate the beginnings of new creations and new knowledge.

- *The focus of technologies* designed to support knowledge work. Such technologies tend to focus on individuals as decision makers in isolation, or the group as a homogeneous decision-making unit. Thus, such designs do not address the social quality of knowledge which supplies the rich give-and-take of diverse participants. Each member of the learning community has only partial knowledge, and learning will only occur when the incomplete parts come together through social interaction.

- *Learner isolation.* Learners can feel they are being marginalised with regard to having access to the HR developer and experience social isolation and disconnection from fellow learners.

There are four even greater pragmatic barriers to e-learning. The first two come from what some writers call the digital divide (Isenberg 2007). First, some learners do not have access to the level of computer technology that is required for e-learning – either having no technology at all, or simple dial-up rather than broadband. Even if the learner has the technology, the cost of downloading and using some of the more modern ICT process tools can quickly outstrip the contracted download maximums the learners have with their internet provider.

Second, some learners do not have the computer skills to use the technology even if it is available. Prensky (2001) first coined the term 'digital natives/digital immigrants'. Digital natives were seen as those who are:

- used to receiving information very fast;

- prefer random access (such as hypertext);

- like to parallel and multitask; and

- prefer graphics over text.

Prensky (2001) incorrectly assumed that this divide was based on age – the Generation X and Y and the Millenniums were the digital natives, and the Baby Boomers were the digital immigrants. Subsequent research (see Bennett, Maton & Kervin 2008; Helsper & Eynon 2009) has shown that age is not the defining criteria. Rather, *immersion in a digital environment* (the breadth of activities that people carry out on line) tends to be the most important criteria in predicting whether a person is a digital native. A digital native is therefore just as likely to be a Baby Boomer as a Gen Y.

Third (and this underlines the basic foundational problems with the current levels of e-learning technology), the successful use of the information presented by the e-learning technology will depend heavily on the learning maturity of the learner (see Chapter 8). Those who have a high learner maturity are more likely to benefit from e-learning, while those who are low on the scale will become very frustrated by the limitations of the present e-learning technology and, more than likely, will drop out of the learning experience.

The fourth barrier is linked to the more unstructured learning strategies needed for the deeper levels of the Hierarchy of Learning Outcomes (see Chapter 8). These unstructured learning strategies need a facilitator who manages the learning process – see the discussions on the role of the HR developer and change interventions earlier in this chapter. Accordingly, many of the so-called 'discussion sites' in e-learning web pages often degenerate into a meaningless whirl of personal agendas of some participants. For a classroom learning intervention, staying with managing process and avoiding content (see discussion on change interventions earlier in this chapter) is relatively easy for the skilled facilitator. However, the asynchronous nature of e-learning in its present form makes managing the learning process of a discussion site virtually impossible.

Potential benefits of online e-learning

In spite of the problems, however, online e-learning offers exciting potential for facilitating adult learning. For a start, it overcomes the problems of being time- or geographically challenged. Rudman (2010) defines e-learning (what we are referring to in this text as online e-learning) as the use of information technology to enable efficient, flexible, personalised, effective and engaging learning. As learning technology becomes more seamlessly integrated with other workplace technologies, online e-learning will become an increasingly attractive option in HRD (Australian National Training

Authority, 2003). Indeed, as Howarth (2010) points out, the emergence of Web 2.0 internet-based social networking tools, such as the LinkedIn professional network and Facebook, as well as blogs, wikis, Twitter and other online forums, are indicative of future developments. However, rather than the either/or arguments that are currently being championed, the immediate future of online e-learning in HRD is more likely to be an integration with F2F learning to create an even more dynamic learning environment both in the classroom and in the workplace.

Rudman and other authors (e.g. Noe 2009) suggest the benefits of e-learning include the following:

- it is self-paced so learners have control over when and where they receive training;

- it enables flexibility in timing and location;

- learners can access learning on an as-needs basis;

- after the initial investment, the costs of training are lower;

- learners can choose the type of media (print, simulations, graphics, video, sound) they prefer;

- administration (including enrolment, testing, and record keeping), can be handled electronically; and

- evaluation of learning can be incorporated and linked to other HR processes, such as performance appraisal and remuneration.

The future for e-learning is very positive. As technology progresses, so will the opportunities to use e-learning to support adult learning. In Australia, for example, the University of Southern Queensland uses a program called Terra Incognita which allows small groups to 'break off' from the central virtual classroom for discussions (Brown & Adler 2008). This facility has great potential for including the critical element of social learning, discussed earlier as a barrier to e-learning. The Web 2.0 tools and Twitter are likely to provide more options for optimising social learning (Dunlap & Lowenthal 2009).

Meeting the challenge

Online e-learning sites should not be merely slightly upgraded versions of hard-copy materials. Noe (2009) makes several broad suggestions to help make an online e-learning site a more dynamic learning experience. These include:

- repurposing the site from a face-to-face program design by including video, sound, text, and graphics to hold the learner's attention;

- ensuring that the site has meaningful material, relevant examples, and the application of the content to work problems and issues;

- basing the design on accepted adult learning principles (see Chapters 3, 10, and 11);

- developing learners in the skills needed to access and use the online site;

- allowing the learners the opportunity to collaborate by using chat rooms and discussion forums;

- using hyperlinks so the learners can access other relevant or interesting websites; and

- involving the ICT department in the design of the online site.

Recent research (Sun, Tsai, Finger, Chen & Yeh 2008 and Park & Wentling 2007) has shown several key variables to have a critical relationship with online e-learning. These include perceived ease of use of the technology, learner computer anxiety, instructor attitude towards e-learning learning program quality, and flexibility in assessment. From this research, we can make several conclusions about the design of online e-learning:

- Learners need development in the technology to be used. Research has found that computer anxiety and computer confidence are significantly correlated with the breadth, frequency, and overall amount of transfer of knowledge to the workplace. The researchers go on to recommend a pre-training intervention to enhance the learners' computer attitudes – particularly computer confidence and self-efficacy. Clearly, assuming that the learners are digital natives can be a terminal presumption.

- Good IT programmers must either be involved in the learning design or a good CML program needs to be selected in the first place. A user-friendly e-learning system is paramount. Confusion about the location of documents on the website will hinder the users' learning and further affect their performance. Unfortunately, a number of organisations expect the HR developer to create vibrant learning experiences within the constraints of limited or even defective CML programs.

- Learners will be anxious about using the technology. When the learner needs assistance, opportunities must be made available to provide ongoing support during the period of the online e-learning.

- These days, most adult learners are time poor as the result of competing life roles – family life, work life, social life and, if studying, their role as a learner. If the learning system cannot be used efficiently and effectively, the learners will become frustrated and lose interest. For example, if they have to spend too much time trying to locate information, or if the programmed knowledge is not presented logically (see 'Some basics for design' in Chapter 9), the learners' interest will wane rapidly.

- Sun *et al.* (2008) recommend that instructors should be selected not only on their topic content expertise and F2F facilitation skills but also on their willingness to facilitate learning through the online process.

Of critical importance, however, are the design of the learning program and the associated assessment. The design must be based on the principles discussed in Chapters 8 and 9, and the assessment must be flexible and relevant (see Chapter 12). Many online e-learning programs are based, at best, on structured learning strategies when the desired learning outcomes are at a deeper level of the HLO (see Chapter 8).

There are still several challenges for the design and implementation of online learning. Firstly, the current state of the art of digital technology does not mirror the unstructured learning strategies as they are used in F2F learning. Attempts have been made to emulate the discussion learning strategy, but with limited success. Most of the digital technology only offers asynchronous interactions (Jeffs, Richardson & Price 2009) – at the best slightly behind real time – allowing only simple, linear discussions that frustrate the learner as the discussion does not engage the externalisation and internalisation processes of knowledge generation. While some newer technology is becoming available to address the asynchronous issues, the cost of downloading the data in the conversations can be prohibitive to some learners and the non-verbal dimensions, such as eye-contact and facial expressions, are typically missing (Tisdell *et al.* 2004).

Secondly, critical barriers which slow the uptake of e-learning within organisations will need to be overcome. These include:

- entry costs of learning systems;

- content and access for all staff;

- the need for significant behavioural change in the workplace to realise the return on the investment;

- immaturity amongst training providers; and

- the technical complexity of e-learning solutions (Australian National Training Authority 2003).

Online e-learning is largely predicated on explicit knowledge. The likelihood of the learner turning explicit knowledge into tact knowledge (i.e. internalisation – see Chapter 3) depends compellingly on the learner's motivation and maturity as a learner (see Chapter 8). If the learner is stimulated by an interest level of motivation and is at the learner orientation stage 3 or 4 (see Chapter 8), then the learner is more likely to engage in internalisation.

As Nonaka and von Krogh (2009) point out, there are two types of knowledge movement. The first occurs when the individual alternates between his or her own explicit and tacit knowledge. The second is where knowledge is created as part of social learning. Online e-learning currently struggles to deliver social learning.

There are technological solutions mirroring some of the unstructured learning strategies used in F2F learning – for example, virtual environments and interactive avatars (see, for example, Falloon 2010). However, the design and development needed relies heavily on software design expertise, which is very expensive. In addition, few software design experts also have the necessary capabilities in designing learning for adults. This means an additional expense, as a learning designer needs to join the team. This team then needs to be developed as an effective production unit (expecting two strangers from different professions to gel immediately is a common mistake) and thus the expenses of the design mount. Considering e-learning is often driven by a CEO who wants to cut costs (Kidman 2003), such high expenses are not likely to be approved.

Organisational structure and culture are critical to the success of this type of learning (Forsyth, Pizzica, Laxton & Mahony 2010). Establishing a supportive organisational structure for online e-learning and developing an appropriate culture will take a lot of effort and investment which, unfortunately, some organisations will attempt to avoid.

In response to these challenges, the most common option chosen by an organisation is to use blended learning (Australian National Training Authority 2003).

Blended learning

Blended learning is a phrase that has entered the literature over the past few years. It combines online e-learning with traditional face-to-face education or training (Russell 2004). Blended learning is an attempt to meet the challenges facing the design of online e-learning discussed previously in this chapter. Ideally, blended learning should combine the best of online e-learning and F2F learning.

Given the challenges to online e-learning design discussed in the previous section, several conclusions can be drawn concerning an appropriate design for blended learning.

- Online learning is ideal for presenting programmed knowledge (see the HLO in Chapter 8). Learning strategies based on the skill and the theory sessions are quite easily designed for online e-learning. Information can be presented as part learning. For example, in the skill session, the show and show-and-tell steps can be presented very creatively using a video. The check-of-understanding can be conducted by using the 'question and answer' facility that many computer-managed learning (CML) packages offer. The supervised practice is a slightly greater challenge, but it can be accommodated by using local content experts to supervise the practice or by having the learners submit videos of their practice. The theory session, likewise, can be presented either with written materials or video for the explanation session, and with a variety of activities (for example, the question-and-answer facility, or showing an example of an event from a real workplace situation and asking for a response).

- The upper levels of the task and relationships categories can also be covered by online e-learning, although this will depend on the sophistication of the CML being used, and whether the learners have the computer facilities to receive this type of data.

- The deeper levels of the learning outcomes described in the HLO are best developed as F2F learning experiences.

- Accordingly, most blended learning designs have the learners cover programmed knowledge and the upper levels of the task and relationships categories by online e-learning. When the assessment indicates that they are proficient at this level, they are then brought into a F2F situation. Firstly, by this stage they have the basic building block knowledge (see Chapter 9) to cope with the more unstructured learning strategies. Secondly, appropriate learning strategies can be used in the F2F situation to develop the deeper level outcomes.

Some specific advice for successful blended learning (see, for example, Mitchell & Honore 2007) includes:

- Take care with balance in terms of blended learning – a ratio of 1:5 of online e-learning to F2F learning is about right.

- With F2F learning, a 'drip feed' approach is better than cramming a lot of learning into just a few days. Use spaced learning and active learning. First develop the learners and then allow them to develop the knowledge and skill on-the-job before bringing them in for another F2F session.

- Online e-learning should not be positioned or perceived as a cost-cutting activity.

- Acknowledge the cost of designing both online e-learning and F2F learning. In reality, both will eventually cost about the same.

- Initial impressions last for a long time. Some designers believe that it is better to commence the learning episode with an on-campus workshop (see, for example, Cooner 2010 and Tisdell *et al.* 2004).

- It takes time for people to become comfortable with online e-learning. Give them time to settle down; ensure that the initial tasks are simple enough to be met with success.

- Make sure that the learners do not experience any technical difficulties with the CML program (Sun *et al.* 2008). This means that the CML program should be well designed and tested, the learners provided with a developmental learning experience to ensure high levels of competence with the CML program, and there is a support service where they can gain advice (preferably 24/7).

A closer look 11.3

An example of blended learning

St George Bank's manager of design and technology, Bob Spence, says the bank's media choices were determined by the instructional design process.

'We defined the learning objectives, and then developed test items for these objectives. We then decided the best way to teach the material and chose appropriate media,' explained Spence.

St George, which won the 2003 Australian HR Awards e-learning category, rolled out e-learning in October 2001 (using its system called 'e-luminate') starting with its orientation program. It followed this with a management development program, and now hosts 120 online modules. New customer service officers are trained using three different media: e-luminate, a purpose-built simulated branch, and on-the-job supervision.

Spence says, 'e-learning is good for recall, remembering and stating facts, and works best for a lot of our compliance requirements, such as LEO, OHS, emergency evacuation procedures, and complying with the *Financial Services Reform Act (FSRA)*. We use our simulated branch as a classroom, applying the knowledge learned through e-luminate, and practising with security systems, cash systems, and so on. We then use on-the-job supervision to test performance.'

Management development programs lend themselves perfectly to a blended approach. St George uses e-luminate to teach the principles of management through self-paced learning, ensuring participants arrive in the classroom with the same level of knowledge. It has classroom sessions to discuss case studies and observe group dynamics, and then follows this with practical projects to be carried out in the workplace.

Spence says that the business case for blended learning is compelling. If you count the costs of accommodation, transport, and marking tests in a traditional face-to-face approach, blended learning is not only cost effective, but also very efficient, automating a lot of the administration. Almost all of St George's 8000 employees are enrolled in e-luminate; with a compliance deadline looming, they are currently completing from 800 to 2000 courses per day. To remain compliant with the FSRA alone, staff must complete an average of 11 courses per person per year.

'The biggest challenge we had designing e-luminate was to ensure we had adequate bandwidth and didn't clog the system. I've been surprised how well staff have accepted it. There were a few technical issues initially, but we got it pretty well right the first time,' says Spence.

Source: Russell 2004, pp. 14-15.

The implementing stage

It is worth re-emphasising that the HR developer may be the supervisor in the workplace, a trainer or facilitator in a staff role (for example, in a learning department in an organisation), or an external consultant. Whatever the primary role of the HR developer, the person facilitating the learning needs to be skilled in the learning strategies discussed in Chapters 10 and 11.

The structured–unstructured continuum discussed in the last two chapters moves from the highly content-oriented at the structured end to a focus on the management of the process of learning at the other. Each of the learning strategies is appropriate for a particular situation. The situations were discussed in Chapters 8 and 9; they were based on the combination of a number of variables:

- the hierarchy of learning outcomes (HLO);
- the learners;
- the strategic orientation of the organisation;
- the organisational culture;
- the key stakeholders; and
- the resources available.

It was suggested in Chapters 8 and 9 that particular learning strategies are more suitable to particular levels of the HLO.

The use of appropriate learning strategies ensures that effective learning occurs and that resources are not wasted on learning that goes nowhere. Just as important, however, is having HR developers who are adept and competent in using the various strategies. Without the facilitative endeavours of experienced HR developers any learning strategy is a ghost of its effective self. As a final comment, 'A closer look 11.4' highlights some energising principles to invigorate the learning experience for adult learners.

A closer look 11.4

Energising principles

Huey Long (2002, pp. 112-13) identifies ten critical principles that should be used in the design and implementation stages to energise teaching and learning.

- The context is activity oriented.

- The context provides the opportunity for learners to exercise control.

- Learners perceive the goals of the learning context to be useful and relevant.

- The context presents content *and* goals at the appropriate challenging level.

- Feedback is facilitated.

- The environment is nonthreatening.

- Humour and other anxiety-releasing activities are frequent.

- Prior abilities and knowledge can be applied.

- Students have choices among the senses and styles for expression, and appropriate objects are available.

- When they need it, students are helped to address attitudes, and state conditions that serve as distractions.

When designing a learning experience, the HR developer would do well to use these ten principles as a final checklist. After conducting a learning session, the HR developer could use the ten principles to review and reflect on her or his performance.

References

Argyris, C 1999, *On Organizational Learning*, 2nd edn, Cambridge, Mass: Blackwell.

Australian National Training Authority 2003, *Your future, your choice: Flexible learning futures*.

Bennett, S, Maton, K & Kervin, L 2008, The 'digital natives' debate: A critical review of the evidence. *British Journal of Educational Technology*, 39(5), pp. 775-791.

Boud, D 1985, 'Problem-based learning in perspective', in D Boyd (ed.), *Problem-based Learning in Education for the Professionals*. Sydney, NSW: HERDSA.

Brookfield, S 1995, *Becoming a Critically Reflective Teacher*, San Francisco: Jossey-Bass.

Brown, J S & Adler, R P 2008, 'Minds of fire: Open education, the long tail and learning 2.0', *Educause Review*, January/February, pp. 17-32.

Casey, D 1991, 'The role of the set adviser', in M Pedler (ed.), *Action Learning in Practice,* 2nd edn, Aldershot, England: Gower.

Chambers, D 2007, *How to succeed with problem-based learning,* Curriculum Corporation, Carlton, South VIC.

Cooner, T S 2010, Creating opportunities for students in large cohorts to reflect in and on practice: Lessons learnt from a formative evaluation of students' experiences of a technology-enhanced blended learning design. *British Journal of Educational Technology,* 41(2), pp. 271-286.

Dick, R 1992, 'Democracy for learners', in B Smith (ed.), *Management Development in Australia,* Sydney: Harcourt Brace Jovanovich.

Dunlap, J C & Lowenthal, P R 2009, 'Horton hears a tweet', *Educause Quarterly,* 32(4).

Falloon, G 2010, 'Using avatars and virtual environments in learning: What do they have to offer?', *British Journal of Educational Technology,* 41(1), pp. 108-122.

Fiol, C M 2003, 'Organizing for a knowledge-based competitiveness: About pipelines and rivers', in S E Jackson, Hitt, M A, & A S DeNisi, (eds.), *Managing Knowledge for Sustained Competitive Advantage: Designing Strategies for Effective Human Resource Management,* pp. 64-93, San Francisco: Jossey-Bass.

French, W L, Bell, C H & Zawacki, R A 2005, *Organizational Development and Transformation: Managing Effective Change,* Burr Ridge, Illinois: Irwin.

Forsyth, H, Pizzica, J, Laxton, R & Mahony, M J 2010, 'Distance education in an era of eLearning: Challenges and opportunities for a campus-focused institution', *Higher Education Research & Development,* 29(1), pp. 15-28.

Gettler, L 2002, 'Seeking advice – fewer models and newer roles', *Management Today,* September, p. 12.

Gonczi, A (ed.). 1992, *Developing a Competent Workforce. Adult Learning Strategies for Vocational Educators and Trainers,* Adelaide, SA: National Centre for Vocational Education.

Hallinger, P & Bridges, E M 2007, *A problem-based approach for management education: Preparing managers for action,* Springer, London.

Hansford, B, Tennent, L & Ehrich, L C 2002, 'Business Mentoring: Help or Hindrance', *Mentoring and Tutoring,* 10(2), pp. 101-15.

Hansford, B, Ehrich, L & Tennent, L 2003, 'Does mentoring deserve another look?', in R Wiesner & B Millert (eds.), *Human Resource Management: Challenges and Future Directions.* Brisbane: John Wiley & Sons Australia.

Helsper, E J, & Eynon, R 2009, Digital natives: Where is the evidence?, *British Educational Research Journal,* pp. 1-18.

Ho Law, S H & Hussain, Z 2007, *The psychology of coaching, mentoring and learning,* John Wiley & Sons, Chichester, UK.

Holey, D & Oliver, M 2010, 'Student engagement and blended learning: Portraits at risk', *Computers & Education,* 54(3), pp. 693-700.

Howarth, B 2010, 'Send in the cloud', *HR Monthly,* August, pp. 20-24.

Isenberg, S 2007, *Applying andragogical principles to Internet learning,* Cambria Press, New York.

Jeffs, A, Richardson, J & Price, L 2009, 'Students' and tutor perceptions of effective tutoring in distance education', *Distance Education,* 30(3), pp. 419-442.

Jeston, J & Nelis, J 2008, *Business process management: Practical guidelines for successful implementations*, Elsevier, Butterworth-Heinemann, Boston.

Kemmis, S 2007, 'Action research', in M Hammersler (ed.), *Educational research and evidence-based practice*, Sage, Los Angeles.

Kidman, A 2003, 'The integration challenge', *Human Resources*, 42, October, pp. 20-1.

Killen, R 2003, *Effective Teaching Strategies: Lessons from Research and Practice*, 3rd edn, Tuggerah, NSW: Social Science Press.

Knowles, M S 1970, *The modern practice of adult education: Andragogy versus pedagogy*, Association Press, New York.

Knowles, M S 1980a, 'How do you get people to be self-directed learners?', *Training and Development Journal*, May, pp. 96-9.

Knowles, M S 1980b, 'The magic of contract learning', *Training and Development Journal*, June, pp. 76-8.

Knowles, M S 1983a, 'Developing the Training Professional', *Training and Development in Australia*, March, pp. 3-7.

Knowles, M S 1983b, 'Developing the Training Professional: Part 2', *Training and Development in Australia*, June, pp. 3-9.

Knowles, M S 1984, *Andragogy in Action*, San Francisco: Jossey-Bass.

Knowles, M S 1998, *The Adult Learner: A Neglected Species*, 5th edn, Houston, Texas: Gulf.

Knowles, M S, Holton III, E F & Swanson, R A 2005, *The adult learner: The definitive classic in adult education and human resource development*, 6th edn, Elsevier, Boston.

Landsberg, M 2003, *The Tao of Coaching*, Profile Books: London.

Long, H B 2000, *Teaching for Learning*, Malabar, Florida: Krieger.

McLennan, N 1995, *Coaching and Mentoring*, Hampshire: Gower.

Marquardt, M J, Skipton, H, Freeman, A M & Hill, C C 2009, *Action learning for developing leaders and organisations: Principles, practices and cases*, American Psychological Society, Washington, DC.

McGill, I & Brockbank, A 2004, *The action learning handbook: Powerful techniques for education, professional development and training*, Routledge, London.

Mezirow, J 2009, 'Transformative learning theory', in Mezirow, J & Taylor E W (eds.) *Transformational learning in practice: Insights from community, workplace and higher education*, Jossey-Bass, San Francisco.

Millen, V 2010, 'Hitching a lift on the information superhighway', HR Monthly, August, pp. 32-35.

Mitchell, A & Honore, S 2007, 'Criteria for successful blended learning', Industrial and Commercial Training', 39(3), pp. 143-149.

Mumford, A 2004, *Management Development: Strategies for Action*, 4th edn, CIPD enterprises, London.

Noe, R A 2009, *Employee Training and Development*, 5th edn, McGraw-Hill, Boston.

Nonaka, I & von Krogh, G 2009, 'Tacit knowledge and knowledge conversion: Controversy and advancement in organizational knowledge creation', *Organization Science*, 20(3), pp. 635-652.

Odiorne, G S 1985, 'Mentoring – An American management innovation', *Personnel Administrator,* May, pp. 63-70.

Oncken, W 1997, 'A coaching key for any century', *Executive Excellence,* 14(4), pp. 12-14.

Park, J & Wentling, T 2007, 'Factors associated with transfer of training in workplace e-learning', *Journal of Workplace Learning,* 19(5), pp. 311-329.

Paton, R & McCalman, J 2008, *Change management: A guide to effective implementation,* Sage, Los Angeles.

Prensky, M 2001, Digital natives, digital immigrants, *On the Horizon,* 9(5), pp. 1-6.

Radwin, A & Leeds, E M 2009, 'The impact of face to face orientations on Online retention: A pilot study', *Online Journal of Distance Education Administration,* 10(4), pp. 38-42.

Ramaswami, A & Dreher, G F 2007, 'The benefits associated with workplace mentoring relationships', in T D Allen & L T Eby (eds.), *The Blackwell handbook of mentoring: A multiple perspectives approach,* Blackwell Publications, Maine, Mass.

Revans, R W 1980, *Action Learning,* London: Blond and Briggs.

Revans, R W 1982, *The Origins and Growth of Action Learning,* Sweden: Studentlitteratur.

Revans, R W 1997, 'Action learning: Its origins and nature', in M Pedler (ed.), *Action Learning in Practice,* Gower, Aldershot, England.

Revans, R W 1998, *ABC of Action Learning,* Lemos & Crane: London.

Rogers, C R 1983, *Freedom to Learn in the 80s,* Columbus, Ohio: Charles E. Merrill.

Rudman, R 2010, *Human Resource Management in New Zealand,* 5th edn, Pearson Education New Zealand, Auckland.

Russell, T 2004, 'Blended learning: Does it stack up?', *Human Resources,* 25 February, pp. 14-15.

Scandura, T A & Pellegrini, E K 2007, 'Workplace mentoring: Theoretical approaches and methodological approaches', in T D Allen & L T Eby (Eds.), *The Blackwell handbook of mentoring: A multiple perspectives approach,* Blackwell Publications, Maine, Mass.

Schein, E H 1998, *Process Consultation: Its Role in Organizational Development,* Reading, Mass: Addison-Wesley.

Smith, B J 1992, 'Mentoring, coaching and counselling', in B J Smith, (ed.), *Management Development in Australia,* Sydney, NSW: Harcourt Brace Jovanovich.

Somekh, B 2006, *Action research: A methodology for change and development,* Open University Press, Maidenhead, UK.

Stephenson, P & Galloway, V 2004, 'Problem- based learning'. In G. Foley (ed.) *Dimensions of Adult Learning: Adult Education and Training in a Global Era.* Crows Nest, NSW: Allen and Unwin.

Sun, P, Tsai, R J, Finger, G, Chen, Y & Yeh, D 2008, 'What drives a successful e-Learning? An empirical investigation of the critical factors influencing learner satisfaction', *Computers & Education,* 50, pp. 1183-1202.

Tisdell, E J, Strohschen, GLE, Carver, M L, Corrigan, P, Nash, J, Nelson, M, Royer, M, Storm-Mackey, R & O'Connor, M 2004, 'Cohort learning online in graduate higher education: Constructing knowledge in cyber community', *Educational Technology & Society,* 7(1), p. 115-127.

Vilkinas, T & Cartan, G 1992, 'Problem-based learning', in B J Smith (ed.), *Management Development in Australia.* Sydney, NSW: Harcourt Brace Jovanovich.

Woods, D 1985, 'Problem-based learning and problem solving', in D Boyd (ed.), *Problem-based Learning in Education for the Professionals.* Sydney, NSW: HERDS.

Yeo, R K 2010, 'Leading through problems: Recognizing the potential of getting their hands dirty', *Industrial and Commercial Training,* 42(3), pp. 128-134.

Zey, M 1988, 'A mentor for all reasons', *Personnel Journal,* January, pp. 46-51.

Chapter 12

Evaluation

LEARNING OBJECTIVES

After studying this chapter you should be able to:

1. Describe the three misconceptions that surround evaluation.

2. Explain the concept of constructive alignment

3. Describe the various types of assessment for learning.

4. Discuss scoring, formative assessment and summative assessment.

5. List and describe the eight levels of evaluation.

6. Discuss the scientific models of evaluation and cost–benefit analysis.

7. List the steps on an evaluation plan and the components of an evaluation report.

Misconceptions about evaluation

Evaluation – the fourth and final stage of HRD – is by far the most controversial. To the challenges and opportunities concerning evaluation in HRD there seem to be more questions than answers (Wang & Spitzer 2005). While it is professionally and theoretically desirable, there are doubts about its accuracy and usefulness. Neither does its cost win it very many friends in higher management. These concerns, however, are based on a misperception of evaluation's role in HRD.

Evaluation is a control system and, as with any control system, the likely pay-off has to be balanced against the cost. There are two types of costs associated with a control system. The first and most obvious is the cost of undertaking the evaluation itself – for example, the salary of the HR developer, the cost of materials, and the down time of staff involved in the evaluation. These expenditures are also immediate – the organisation has to undertake the expenditure at the time of evaluation.

The second cost is the risk of not conducting an evaluation – not knowing if the learning episode achieved what it was supposed to; not knowing if the organisation has benefited from the investment; not knowing if any mistakes were made, and worse, not knowing how to avoid these mistakes in the future.

The costs of such risks, however, are unlikely to surface until a time in the future; at the current time, they may seem questionable or even ephemeral. When balancing the advantages and disadvantages, it is easy to understand why some managers decide to avoid the evaluation stage – especially given the legitimate system's proclivity for pursuing efficiency (see Chapter 1). The reality, however, is that such risks will eventually translate into facts, and the dues will then have to be paid. It is far better to overcome small deficiencies in the present than let them escalate and become a major headaches.

It is true that the techniques used in evaluation are not an exact science. The results do not always translate into specific measures for future action. However, such deficiencies are true of any decision support system. The medical doctor interprets an X-ray to make a best-guess decision. The techniques of evaluation operate in the same kind of way. They provide indicators that give the professional HR developer the facts on which to make an informed decision. The more difficult the measurement of an attribute, the more the evaluation has to rely on the professional judgement of the HR developer.

The third misconception that undermines evaluation is not so obvious. Because the legitimate system deals with that part of the external environment that is closer to certainty, any serious misjudgement or lack of action is likely to show up reasonably quickly – that is, within a year or two. Because the signs are relatively noticeable, the evaluation techniques used in the legitimate system are likely to sense any aberrations.

The shadow system, however, operates in situations far from certainty; it not only deals with change but encourages change. Furthermore, the shadow system contemplates the distant future of the organisation. Therefore, evaluation of learning in the shadow system will be difficult, if not impossible. Some indicators of learning can be observed in the shadow system, but the first notice that the organisation is likely to have that its shadow system has not been performing, or has been starved of resources, is that the organisation does not have the new knowledge needed to meet the unknown challenges.

Accordingly, most of the evaluation techniques discussed in this chapter apply to the legitimate system. However, some effort to evaluate development in the shadow system has to be made. To the extent that the evaluation techniques discussed in this chapter can be adapted or used as surrogate measures in the shadow system, every effort should be made to evaluate the learning processes and outcomes in the shadow system.

So, despite the fact that evaluation techniques may not always provide exact answers and that these techniques are more applicable to the legitimate system, the evaluation stage cannot be ignored. There are at least four reasons for conducting evaluations of the HRD effort.

First, as Goldstein (2001) comments, all HRD interventions will be evaluated, either formally or informally. Therefore, the concern has to be with the quality of evaluation rather than with the question of whether to evaluate.

Second, legal imperatives have raised the awareness of organisations about evaluation. Some state and federal legislation require evidence that certain HR development activities (e.g. health and safety) have taken place. In Australia, the 2010 *Essential Standards and Conditions* for registered training organisations (RTOs) in vocational education and training (VET) demands that evaluation takes place. See:

www.licensinglinenews.com/Newsletter/Updated-AQTF/Updated-AQTF-Essential-Conditions-and-Standards-for-Registration-now-available.aspx

There are similar requirements for Industry Training Organisations (ITOs) in New Zealand. See:

www.nzqa.govt.nz/for-business/ito.do

In addition, some industrial relations decisions have shown that organisations have to demonstrate not only that HR development has taken place but that the development was successful (see Delahaye & Smith 1987).

Third, as Delahaye and Smith (1998) point out, evaluation is essential to the survival of the HRD function so that the contributions of that function can be demonstrated. So evaluation is, in fact, a vital part of the HRD endeavour.

Finally, the evaluator must have an acute sense of the likely costs and benefits of the different evaluation approaches. Above all, though, it should be clear who, and what purposes, one is serving (Easterby-Smith 1998). Fortunately, there is evidence that the application of evaluation is becoming more widespread (Tome 2009).

As Long (2002) points out, evaluation has at least two purposes. The first is to determine performance levels – of the individual, of the work group, and the organisation. The second is to provide another opportunity for learning to occur. To achieve these two purposes, the role of the evaluation stage is four-fold:

1. to measure what change has occurred;

2. to improve the other three stages – i.e. investigation, design and implementation – of the HRD system;

3. to see whether the change is attributable to the learning episode; and

4. to see whether the change was worthwhile.

The evaluation techniques that can be used to fulfil these roles will be discussed under five headings:

- assessment of learning;
- Kirkpatrick's four levels;
- presage elements;
- the scientific approach; and
- cost–benefit analysis.

Assessment of learning

The words 'assessment' and 'evaluation' are often used interchangeably in the literature. Brady and Kennedy (2007) suggest that assessment should be viewed as the gathering, interpreting and describing of information about learner achievement. Evaluation involves making judgements of worth. It is based on the information provided by the assessment process and information gathered via other processes, such as organisational control systems.

Assessment is inextricably entwined with learning strategies and the learning objectives, a process this textbook has referred to as 'constructive alignment'. Constructive alignment occurs where the behaviours described in the intended outcomes are mirrored in both the teaching/learning activities the learners undertake and in the assessment tasks (Biggs & Tang, 2007). Constructive alignment is a very important concept in the design of learning, as it integrates the three elements that impact on the experiences of the learner and emphasises that one element cannot be considered without the other.

Figure 12.1 Constructive alignment

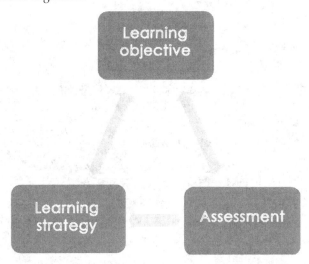

Source: Based on the work of Biggs & Tang 2007.

The assessment of learning addresses the big question, 'Just what changes have occurred in the learner's mind as a result of the learning episode?' This question presents the challenge of deciding how the change can be measured. After all, the change has occurred within the learner's mind and we cannot directly observe what has happened. So, most assessment procedures ask the learner to perform a behaviour and it is this behaviour that is then measured.

This conversion of a learning into a behaviour that can be observed has several potential weaknesses:

- The behaviour is only a *sample* of the total learning that has occurred. This limitation is best seen in a university or college examination where the learners have to answer a specific number of questions. The questions usually do not cover all the knowledge covered in the course. The learners tend not to write down all their knowledge of the question, because few people can recall everything on a given topic at one time.

- The behaviour represents only *explicit knowledge,* and explicit knowledge is often a very simplistic representation of tacit knowledge (see Chapter 3). So, tacit knowledge may not be reflected, or certainly not fully represented, in any behaviours, and yet tacit knowledge is an important reservoir of wisdom.

- The word *measurement* is often used in assessment and evaluation. It is important to recognise that measurement can only happen at the explicit knowledge level – and often not even there. For example, an assessor can measure whether a wall has been constructed vertically. However, when tacit knowledge is being assessed, the assessor can only use *indicators*. For example, an experienced HR developer can assess a theory session by counting the percentage of open questions used correctly, counting the number of times the overhead projector has been used correctly, and by timing the duration of the activity steps. These are only indicators of how well the theory session has been conducted. The experienced HR developer will use these indicators in conjunction with his or her tacit knowledge to judge the full worth of the theory session presentation. In assessment and evaluation, the HR developer should not confuse indicators for measures.

- The internalising process of knowledge generation for the individual may take place over a lengthy period of time, perhaps several years. So *timing* is very important in evaluation.

- The cue to convert the learning into a behaviour, usually some type of test, has to tap into the *appropriate knowledge* and not involve irrelevant knowledge. This is called *validity.* Validity is an important component of a test because the test must measure what it is supposed to measure. For example, if the test is a written examination, the examination is a test of literacy as well as the content knowledge of the topic – an illiterate person may have the topic knowledge but would not be able to write about it.

- The cue to convert the learning into a behaviour (i.e. the test) has to tap into the *same potential knowledge* each time it is used and for each learner on whom it is used. This is called *reliability.* The test must measure the same way each time it is used.

In summary, then, a cue that converts learning into a behaviour must be both valid and reliable. It must also be recognised that the converted behaviour is only a possible sample of the learning that has occurred, and usually only represents explicit knowledge. Finally, the cue must be administered at the appropriate time – for the learner, this appropriate time occurs at the end of the internalising process.

Unfortunately, the appropriate time for the learner may not be the appropriate time for the organisation: this presents yet another quandary for the HR developer in the evaluation process.

Types of assessment

The further down the hierarchy of learning outcomes (HLO), the more difficult impartial measurement becomes. For example, measuring the successful performance of a procedural skill (in the programmed knowledge category) is much easier than measuring the gain in mental agility from the meta-abilities category. Accordingly, the six types of assessment:

- skills testing;
- objective written;
- subjective written;
- performance tests;
- learning diaries; and
- portfolio assessment

are discussed in that order, from easiest to most difficult.

Skill tests

Skill testing is used for procedural skills. It is the most direct form of testing and follows exactly the learning objective. If the learning objective is 'To repair a basic fault in the slide mechanism of a Type 0411 photocopy machine in three minutes' then the test is simply that: repair the slide mechanism in three minutes. This behaviour can be observed directly and the slide mechanism must be repaired and working within the three-minute time frame for the learner to pass the test. The skill test demonstrates the learner's competence at procedural training in the programmed knowledge category of the HLO.

Objective written tests

Delahaye and Smith (1998) differentiate between objective and subjective written tests. The scoring of objective written tests requires no interpretation by the examiner. There are four types of written objective tests:

1. *Multiple choice tests,* that pose a question, usually referred to as a stem, and then provide alternative answers from which the learner can make a selection, as shown in the example below.

   'An open question allows the interviewee to:

a.   Choose from a limited number of options from which the answer comes.

b.   Choose from a wide number of options from which the answer comes.

c.   Discuss some new area.

d.   Ask the interviewer for some additional information.'

When designing multiple choice questions, the answer options should be kept as short as possible. As much information as possible should be included in the stem, and all alternatives should appear to be equally likely to the uninformed reader. It is better to avoid negative constructions (e.g. using the word 'not') in the answer alternatives as this tends to confuse the reader; the aim is to test content knowledge, not mental agility or linguistic skills.

2.   *True–false tests*, that provide a statement to which the reader has to respond 'true' or 'false', for example:

'The funnel sequence of questions starts with an open question. *T/F*'

There is a 50 percent probability that the reader can guess the answer, so true–false tests have limited use. When using a true–false test, ensure that the statement is unequivocally true or false, avoiding the use of qualifiers such as 'never' or 'always'. Qualifiers tend to make the statement both true and false, no matter what the content of the statement.

3.   *Matching tests that* examine relationships between pieces of information. In matching tests a series of stimuli is listed in the left hand column and a series of responses is listed in the right hand column. For example:

Canberra	USA
Paris	United Kingdom
Tokyo	France
London	India
Washington DC	Japan
	Australia

The items in each list should be homogeneous and the lists should be of unequal length so that the last connection is not self-evident.

4.   *Completion tests*, which are constructed by leaving a key word or phrase out of a statement. For example:

' [...] questions allow the interviewee to answer from a wide variety of options.'

The statement in completion tests has to be designed carefully so that the key word or phrase is the only logical option.

Objective written tests tend to test recognition rather than recall. Each of the objective written tests provides enough clues for a knowledgeable respondent to recognise the possible answer. In addition, objective tests examine only very specific pieces of information. The objective written test assesses the explicit knowledge of the learner at the programmed knowledge level of the HLO.

The advantage of objective tests is that they can be scored reliably because the answer is always the same. They are ideal for checking factual, professional, or technical information in the programmed knowledge category of the HLO. A good discussion of objective written tests is included in Thorndike (2007).

Subjective written tests

Subjective written tests are usually referred to as 'essay tests'. The cue to an essay test is a reasonably detailed question that examines a complex topic that contains several interrelated concepts. The learner then has to write an essay to answer the question. These essays may be several pages long or just one paragraph, the latter being referred to as a 'short essay'. Unlike objective tests, the questions in essay tests have few direct clues for the reader about the content being examined and therefore test recall of information. An example is:

'What is the difference between reliability and validity?'

Delahaye and Smith (1998) suggest that, when constructing an essay test, the designer should list the main issues and interrelationships first and then formulate the question so that the issues and relationships will be covered by the informed reader.

Essay tests are called 'subjective' because the scoring depends on the opinion of an expert. In an attempt to provide some reliability and validity to the scoring process, the examiner is often given a list of issues or concepts that the learner would be expected to discuss. However, given the variety of individual approaches each learner may take, the examiner is still required to make complex judgements on the worth of the learners' offerings. These judgments are, of course, based on the examiner's tacit knowledge. It should be acknowledged that subjective tests are also assessing the learner's literacy ability, and this very fact may contaminate the outcome or even deny the use of the assessment method.

Essay tests are ideal for probing the detailed complexity level of professional or technical information of the HLO. Essay tests can also be used to explore the learners' knowledge of the linear and diagnostic analysis, the goal identification and administrative proficiency elements of the task category of the HLO, as cue questions can include words that encourage analysis, synthesis, or evaluation.

Performance tests

Performance tests are used where assessment of a complex process is needed. This complex process simulates an actual situation in the workplace and usually represents a major responsibility in the workplace. The complex process is a combination of programmed knowledge and outcomes in the task and relationship categories of the HLO. A good example of such a complex process would be an interview. So, if the learning objective is 'To conduct a 20-minute research interview', the learner would have to demonstrate a complex combination of programmed knowledge (e.g. of the professional or technical information being investigated and also of interviewing techniques), task outcomes of diagnostic and complex analysis, interpersonal elements of interacting at an objective and perhaps an emotional level, and intrapersonal elements of self-confidence and inner strength. Several other elements of the HLO could also be involved, depending on the type of interview.

In evaluating such complex processes, the examiner may assess the process itself (as in observing an interview) or the product of the process (as in a piece of artwork). If assessing the process itself, the examiner may observe the event live, or may view a video recording. Observing a video recording has the advantage of the replay and the slow motion facilities.

Scoring performance tests is a multifarious task and is heavily dependent on the professional ability of the examiner as, again, the judgment is based on the examiner's tacit knowledge. In fact, nothing can replace this professional competence. Often, a pre-designed observation form is used to provide assistance. An example of a pre-designed observation form is shown in Figure 12.2.

Thorndike (2007) suggests four steps in designing an observation form.

1. *Describe the process or end product that is to be assessed.* For most processes, this step merely involves displaying the learning objective to be achieved; for a product, a definition may be needed.

2. *List the important behaviours and characteristics.* Any behaviours or characteristics that anyone could achieve or that cannot be assessed should be omitted. In Figure 12.2, there is no mention of 'standing in front of the class' (everyone could do this action) or 'comfortably analyses all situations' (cannot be assessed as it is too general). Rather, behaviours and characteristics that are critical to successful performance should be listed.

3. *Include common errors.* It is also important to note the presence of specific behaviours that are considered inappropriate.

4. *Put the list into an appropriate format.* The list of appropriate and inappropriate behaviours and characteristics should be organised into a sequence that is most useful to the observer and can be used easily in the 'heat of the moment' of the observation process.

Figure 12.2 Example of a pre-designed observation

SKILL SESSION FEEBACK SHEET				
Name		Date		
Session title				
Directions: Listen carefully to the session, and place a check mark in the column to indicate your option.				
Introduction: Did he/she		**No**	**Partly**	**Yes**
1. Clearly and precisely state the session objective(s)?	1			

2. Include time/quality standards in objective(s)?	2			
3. Utilise past experiences to introduce the session?	3			
4. Check current knowledge?	4			
5. Motivate the group?	5			
Show (demonstrate): Did he/she				
1. Do the job in a professional manner?	1			
2. Observe the time factors – good methods – safety – housekeeping?	2			
Show and tell: Did he/she				
1. Tell – Show – Illustrate one stage at a time?	1			
2. Stress key points – pause between stages?	2			
3. Ensure that all trainees could clearly see?	3			
4. Follow the breakdown – no backtracking, etc?	4			
5. Observe correct methods – good housekeeping – safety?	5			
6. Make adequate provision for trainees to ask questions?	6			
Check of understanding: Did he/she				
1. Ask trainees to name stage and key points?	1			
2. Perform the task to trainees' instructions?	2			
3. Ensure that all trainees knew how to do the job?	3			
Practice: Did he/she				
1. Have everything ready and properly arranged?	1			
2. Correct errors as they occurred by *constructive* criticism?	2			
3. Ensure correct methods – good housekeeping –safety factors?	3			
4. Structure adequate trainee practice (50% +)?	4			
Conclusion: Did he/she				
1. Briefly review critical stages and key points	1			
2. Ensure that trainees were aware of the standards expected?	2			

3. Ask for new ways or difficult parts?	3			
Job breakdown:				
1. Did he/she provide each trainee with a job breakdown?	1			
2. Did the breakdown have sufficient steps?	2			
3. Did the explanatory points cover 'how', 'why', 'when', and 'where'?	3			
4. Was safety emphasised?	4			

Source: Delahaye & Smith 1998, p. 52.

As a further assistance in the scoring process, rating scales and rubrics are sometimes added to the observation forms. The example in Figure 12.2 merely notes the presence or absence of the behaviour or characteristic. Rather than these columns, a five-point scale, for example, could be added. A rubric identifies the qualities expected for each behaviour or characteristic and also provides a hierarchy of potential responses. So, for questioning techniques, the following simple rubric may be given:

3 points:	Uses more than six open questions with 'stem plus query' structure.
	At least two demonstrations of a funnel sequence.
	Combines paraphrasing and open questions at least twice.
2 points:	Uses more than six open questions with 'stem plus query' structure.
	Combines paraphrasing and open questions at least twice.
1 point:	Uses more than six open questions with 'stem plus query' structure.

For a more detailed discussion of rubrics see Thorndike (2007). Performance tests are used to assess the more complex outcomes in the task and relationship categories of the HLO. They can also be used for the critical thinking category.

Learning diaries

Learning diaries are journals written by the learner to record events and the thoughts and reflections of the learner. In a learning diary, the learner:

- describes the learning events that have occurred (this record is made fairly soon after the event has transpired, preferably before going to sleep that night);
- discloses the feelings and inner thoughts that the events engendered;
- reflects on the personal effect and personal meaning of the events; and
- becomes involved in critical reflection (see Chapter 3) to challenge and change hegemonic assumptions.

Learning diaries encourage the development of high levels of analysis and critical reflection. They frequently highlight small, important incidents which would otherwise have been overlooked (Biggs & Tang 2007; Bennett & Kingham 1993). Smith (1992) suggests that there are three types of diaries:

1. the analytic diary;

2. the organised diary; and

3. the free flow diary.

In the analytic diary, four headings are used. The first, 'a brief description of the experience', records data gathered from as many different observers as possible (e.g. the learner, the facilitator, peers, and other actors in the event). The data will include both subjective (impressionistic) information and objective information. The second heading, 'detailed observations', classifies this data into four categories – what the learner observed about the experience, what the learner observed about his/her own feelings and behaviour, what others observed about the experience, and what others observed about the learner. The third heading, 'synthesise', allows the learner to analyse and reflect on the outcomes compared to the expectations, the worth and use of formal theories, and the worth and use of personal frames of reference. The fourth heading, 'future behaviour', concentrates on plans for the future – what changes can be made and how these changes will be instigated. The parallels of this structure with the Honey and Mumford learning cycle (see Chapter 10) are most marked.

The organised diary is usually in prose format. It is characterised by careful construction, clear expression, attempted objectivity, and a preoccupation with cognitive logic. The organised diary is based on the assumption that people tend to be naturally logical and are more likely to see strengths and flaws in their thought processes when they write their thoughts down on paper. The discipline of writing allows the learner to review the material gathered, identify key concepts, and link concepts.

The free-flow diary is a 'cathartic experience' allowing the learner to express thoughts and feelings creatively. The emphasis of this type of diary is on raw perceptions, and emotions and reactions with little attempt on external objectivity. These diaries usually include a number of astute observations as the learner 'gets in touch' with himself or herself. There are three advantages to the free-flowing learning diary. First, it allows the learner to clarify the reality of feelings. Second, this recognition of feelings, expressed appropriately, decreases the chance that they will interfere with learning (see Chapter 3 for the role of feelings in changing hegemonic assumptions). Third, the record preserves significant aspects of the original raw data. The free-flow diary is often employed as a precursor to using the organised or analytic learning diaries.

Learning diaries are powerful tools in the knowledge-generating process of externalisation. As Biggs and Tang (2007) comment, reflective learning diaries are especially useful for assessing outcomes relating to the application of content, professional judgment, reflections on past decisions, and problem solving with a view of improving them. There are, however, some criticisms of this assessment approach.

Firstly, they are susceptible to being based on faked data, and secondly (particularly with the free-flow diary), there are serious questions about validity and reliability. Thirdly, justifying decisions made for summative assessment is difficult. Finally, assessing diaries can be delicate, as they often contain personal content (Biggs & Tang 2007). Learning diaries, however, assess both the lower levels of the task and relationships categories and the problem solving and creativity elements of the critical thinking category of the HLO; correctly used, they are invaluable as a means of progressing learning.

Analytical critiques

An analytical critique examines an issue or a situation for both its strengths and weaknesses; it is based on complex professional knowledge. The issue or situation will be scrutinised and analysed from all perspectives. Usually, the report produces workable and justified recommendations. Accordingly, the critique is likely to be based on complex theoretical concepts which are used, in many ways, as an auditing standard. The analytic critique demonstrates ability at the critical thinking category of the HLO; the learner demonstrates complex problem solving, creativity, evaluation, didactic thinking, and logical reflection.

Portfolio assessment

Portfolio assessment is used extensively in the arts but can be useful in HRD. Portfolios are based on a collection of the learner's work that provides evidence of achieving specific learning outcomes. They often consist of a number of the other types of assessments described above. For example, if the program was designed to develop HR developers, the learners would have copies of their session plans, videos of sessions they have conducted, copies of the observation sheets completed by their trainees, and a report from their assessor and even notes and preliminary models, all gathered into a portfolio.

A portfolio, however, is more than a collection of the learner's achievements. A covering report, justifying and integrating the evidence is also needed. The assessor would be looking for:

- the extent to which the evidence is applicable to specific learning outcomes (this criterion indicates the extent to which the learner understands the learning outcome and is able to judge evidence – as Biggs and Tang (2007) comment, the learner needs to be wisely selective in placing in their portfolios what they think best addresses the learning outcomes and why);

- the learner being able to apply the theoretical concepts covered in the program to the evidence;

- the learner's grasp of the interrelationships between the pieces of evidence;

- the learner's grasp of the interrelationships between the theoretical concepts covered in the program;

- the learner's ability to self-assess, seeing not only the positive applications in the evidence but also the areas for future improvement; and

- the learner providing a plan for future development clearly enunciating what should be improved, in what order, and how the improvement will occur.

Portfolio assessment, however, is different from other forms of assessment on three counts. First, it takes a long-term view to evaluating the learner's performance – sometimes up to 12 months. Second, it focuses on quality of work more than on a raw score. Third, and perhaps most importantly, the learner has to reflect on his or her own work and thoughtfully evaluate their own history as learners. Learners are expected not only to identify strengths and weaknesses, but changes that have occurred over time, what they are satisfied with and why, and any negative personal reactions to their own work. Simple portfolios can be used to assess the lower levels of the task and relationship categories; more complex portfolios can be used to examine the learner's abilities at the critical thinking and meta-abilities categories of the HLO.

Overall, some advantages of portfolios include that the learners:

- are respected as independent, self-directed learners;

- take responsibility for making decisions on the evidence;

- are encouraged to reflect on what they have learned; and

- demonstrate reflective and thinking skills (Marsh, 2004).

Portfolio assessment is susceptible to the same criticisms as the learning diaries, but is a dynamic tool for developing and assessing the self-perpetuating learning element of the meta-abilities category of the HLO. (For further information on portfolio assessment see Belgrade, Burke & Fogarty 2005).

Assessment and the HLO

These assessment types can be mapped against the HLO (from Chapter 8) to establish the basic representation of constructive alignment – that is, the contention that there is a relationship between the learning outcomes, the learning strategies of choice, and the assessment types of choice (see Figure 12.1).

The caution given in Chapter 8 on the use of the HLO should be repeated here. Any model is a rudimentary representation of reality and the model on constructive alignment should not be followed slavishly. However, the constructive alignment model in Figure 12.3 does provide a logical starting point for making decisions on appropriate assessment types. The initial decision may be adjusted for other variables – for example:

- there can be a range of complexity within each of the assessment types (e.g. the subjective written test may require the learner only to reiterate the material presented or there may be a requirement for the learner to demonstrate some application of the concepts explained);

- while each of these assessment types has been described individually, for more accurate assessment the HR developer will tend to use a number of them in combination;

- a growing trend in education to use authentic assessment (Brady & Kennedy 2007) [Authentic assessment is a reaction to the reliance on traditional assessment in the classroom. Authenticity arises from assessing what is important, rather than assessing what is most convenient (Marsh 2004).

Accordingly, authentic assessment emphasises appraisal in the workplace and has been driven by the competency movement (see Chapter 5).];

- the characteristics of the learner (for example, level of motivation or current level of knowledge) – see Chapter 8;

- any issues raised in the HRDNI.

Figure 12.3 Constructive alignment based on the hierarchy of learning outcomes

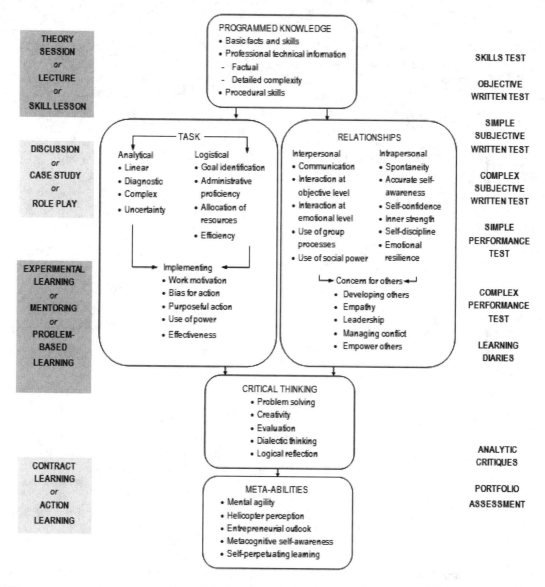

The caution given in Chapter 8 on the use of the HLO should be repeated here. Any model is a rudimentary representation of reality and the model on constructive alignment should not be followed slavishly. However, the constructive alignment model in

Figure 12.3 does provide a logical starting point for making decisions on appropriate assessment types. The initial decision may be adjusted for other variables – for example:

- there can be a range of complexity within each of the assessment types (e.g. the subjective written test may require the learner only to reiterate the material presented or there may be a requirement for the learner to demonstrate some application of the concepts explained);

- while each of these assessment types has been described individually, for more accurate assessment the HR developer will tend to use a number of them in combination;

- a growing trend in education to use authentic assessment (Brady & Kennedy 2007) [Authentic assessment is a reaction to the reliance on traditional assessment in the classroom. Authenticity arises from assessing what is important, rather than assessing what is most convenient (Marsh 2004). Accordingly, authentic assessment emphasises appraisal in the workplace and has been driven by the competency movement (see Chapter 5).];

- the characteristics of the learner (for example, level of motivation or current level of knowledge) – see Chapter 8;

- any issues raised in the HRDNI.

Self-assessment

As suggested at the beginning of this chapter, assessment and learning are inextricably intertwined and this complex relationship becomes even more so if we heed the advice of Rogers (1983) that the best and richest form of assessment is self-assessment.

This advice suggests that, as HR developers, we should develop the learners to such an extent that they value their own self-assessment above all else. It could even be argued that such development is evidence of the learner finally becoming an independent learner (see also learner maturity in Chapter 8).

The HR developer's dilemma

As with much of HRD, assessment imposes on the HR developer a number of conflicting choices. Skills tests reflect a simple situation; it is a simple matter for the HR developer to show reliability and validity based on the desired learning objectives. Observed behaviours, however, are blurred shadows of the quality that is being assessed.

When using portfolio assessment, the HR developer has to rely on the honesty of the learner. When the development of the learner is the main objective of the assessment it is a major strength.

After all, in this situation, any dishonesty will only damage the learner. When the assessment is for other purposes, however (e.g. monetary gain for the learner, as in salary increment or the award of a qualification), the use of the more complex assessment types such as the learning diaries or portfolio assessment becomes more problematical.

A third dilemma is the amount of information that should be disclosed to the learner prior to the assessment. Improving the clarity of assessment requirements can improve the learning experience (Misko & Priest 2009), but providing too much information may negate the purpose of the assessment because only the recent memory of the learner is tested rather than the true level of learning. So, once again, the HR developer is placed in a situation of making professional judgements.

The meaning of scores

When a test has been examined and the result given in a quantitative score, the result is called a *raw score*. Now, this seems quite straightforward – after all, a score is a score. Well, not necessarily so. Suppose a learner has received 11 out of a possible 20. Is this a pass? If several hundred people have taken the test and the lowest anyone else received was 18, one would have to wonder about the learner who received 11 out of 20. Or perhaps the test was for a rigger on tying knots. How would you feel halfway up a 200 metre cliff knowing that the person who tied the knots on your safety belt had achieved only 11 out of 20 on the knot-tying test? In that situation, most people would opt for a test with a pass mark of 20 out of 20!

Raw scores can be interpreted in a number of ways. One way is called *criterion-referenced scoring*. Criterion-referenced scores reflect the level of mastery of a certain content or domain of knowledge. A criterion-referenced score is the way people usually interpret a raw score. A 'criterion' is given to define a correct score (e.g. an open question has a structure of stem-plus-query). Marks are given for each correct answer and none for incorrect answers. The result is a raw score out of a total score (e.g. 11 out of 20) and this ratio – usually given as a percentage – reflects the learner's supposed level of knowledge. Usually, 50 percent is accepted as a pass mark.

Another way to interpret a raw score is called *norm-referenced scoring*. The raw score is compared to the average of a nominated group. The group may be the current class that the learner is attending, everyone in the organisation who has taken the test, or a nation-wide group. Usually, the comparison point is the average of the nominal group. This comparison point is called the standardised score. In norm-referenced scoring, the raw score is compared to the standardised score and if it is above, the learner has passed.

A raw score can also be considered as a formative assessment or summative assessment. *Formative assessment* is used where the HR developer is interested in identifying the learner's strengths or weaknesses. The raw score is used in this instance as feedback. First, the learner can gauge his or her progress. Second, the HR developer can adjust the learning experience. *Summative assessment* provides concluding evidence of the level of achievement of the learner; this is the usual accepted purpose of the raw score.

Overlap of the four HRD stages

Previously in this book, the point was made that dividing the HR process into four stages – investigation, design, implementation and evaluation – may present an overly simplistic view. The four stages are, in fact, highly interactive. One such interaction occurs between the implementation stage and the assessment of learning in the evaluation stage.

In the implementation stage, the assessment of learning provides dynamic feedback. The feedback on the learning is often immediate. Indeed, good learning design provides a sequence of a learning experience followed by assessment (i.e. formative assessment) so that the learner can gradually improve over the period of the learning episode. Most assessment of learning provides irrefutable evidence that a learner finds difficult to ignore. Positive evidence gives satisfaction and support. Negative evidence provides the opportunity for the learner to challenge frames of reference. Negative evidence also allows the HR developer to adjust the learning process.

McAllister (1997) believes that better learning and deeper commitment is enhanced when the HR developer and the learner begin to reframe assessment as an essential part of everyday learning. She presents real concerns that blanket application of assessment rules remove creativity for the HR developer–learner relationship, promote uniformity and blind adherence to rules, and reduce knowledge to the technical level – all in the quest for efficiency.

In the evaluation stage, on the other hand, assessment of learning provides some initial evidence of the success or otherwise of the learning experience. Recognising the two roles of assessment – developmental at the implementing stage and judgemental at the evaluation stage – is critical to the HR developer. These dual but conflicting roles are an important consideration when designing learning episodes and when planning the evaluation stage.

The importance of assessment

The six types of assessment – skill, objective written, subjective written, performance, learning diaries, and profile assessment – have been discussed in a hierarchy that corresponds roughly with the HLO to show the most suitable use of each type of assessment. Further, at the easiest end of the continuum (skills tests), the judgement of the assessor can be more objective, while at the opposite end, the assessor has to rely on professional, albeit subjective, judgement.

Assessment of learning is important for two reasons. First, the measurement provides an indication of how well the learner understands the concepts. This is particularly valuable for the legitimate system that needs to ensure that acceptable levels of procedural knowledge are maintained for the continued viability of the organisation.

The second important reason for assessment is that it provides feedback. This feedback allows both the learner and the HR developer to make adjustments to the learning process by identifying strengths and weaknesses.

Kirkpatrick's four levels

The most commonly used model of evaluation for HRD in organisations is Kirkpatrick's (Kirkpatrick 1959a, 1959b, 1960a, 1960b, and Kirkpatrick & Kirkpatrick 2005) four levels:

- reaction;
- learning;
- behaviour; and
- results.

These four levels are arranged in ascending order of value of information. There is also an assumption that each level affects the following level.

Reaction

This level simply measures the reactions of the learners to the learning episode – their liking for and feelings for the program. The assumption underlying this level of evaluation is that if the learners did not enjoy the learning experience, the dislike will affect the amount they will learn. The *reaction level* is usually measured with a questionnaire, sometimes derisively called 'happy sheets', which cover such areas as the content, the HR developer, the learning strategies used, and the physical location in which the learning took place.

Kirkpatrick and Kirkpatrick (2005) and Wexley and Latham (2002) believe that measuring the reaction level is important for three reasons. First, positive reactions encourage organisational support. Second, reaction is a measure of customer satisfaction and the customers will most probably not be motivated to learn if they are not satisfied (see the two-factor theory in Chapter 8). Third, the feedback from the reaction questionnaires can be used by HR developers to improve future programs. Kirkpatrick and Kirkpatrick (2005) provide a detailed discussion on designing reaction feedback sheets.

A useful option is to add to the reaction feedback sheet a list of the program learning objectives with two feedback scales (similar to the feedback sheet suggested in Chapter 6 on performance appraisal). The first can be a Likert scale (for example a 1 to 5 scale on a continuum from not achieved at all to fully achieved) and a few lines under each to provide qualitative information to the question 'Why not a 5?'

Learning

Evaluating learning has been discussed under the previous section, 'Assessment of learning', and is aimed at identifying the knowledge gained by the learners. As Kirkpatrick and Kirkpatrick (2005) point out, one or more of the following occurs:

- attitudes are changed;
- knowledge is increased; and
- skill is improved.

One or more of these changes must take place if a change in behaviour is to occur.

The assessment of learning should be linked directly to the learning objectives of the learning episode. The assumption is that successful learning is needed before the increased knowledge can be transferred to the job.

Behaviour

The behaviour level of evaluation examines the change in the behaviour of the learner on the job. The behavioural level is concerned with *actual ability* rather than *potential ability* as measured by the amount of learning. As Delahaye and Smith (1998) comment, this is the payoff for the organisation in investing in the learning episode. The assumption is that the behavioural change will have an impact on the organisation, improving its viability. It should also be noted that the competency movement has contributed significantly to the recognition that learning must be transferred back to the job. The underlying theme of competencies is that they should be assessed several times under workplace conditions.

The issue that then arises is deciding how the behaviour level can be assessed. The simplest answer, but one that is often ignored by organisations, is to repeat the investigation methods used in the HRDNI. For three reasons in particular, the performance appraisal system should play a big role in the behavioural level of evaluation:

- the performance appraisal process can readily identify changes that matter the most – those at the workface;

- a performance appraisal can evaluate changes in the more complex categories of the HLO, particularly at the task, relationship, and critical thinking levels (a performance appraisal is possibly the only approach to assessing the meta-abilities category).

- by focusing on the benefits of the learning episode, the performance appraisal process (particularly the interview) can extend the learning of the participant.

In addition, an experienced and astute appraiser can use the knowledge-generation processes of internalisation, externalisation, and socialisation to reinforce and extend the learning. The other methods used in the HRDNI – organisational records, questionnaires, interviews, focus groups – also have the potential to identify improvements simply by comparing the facts and data when used in the HRDNI with that in the evaluation.

Brinkerhoff (2009) suggests that the behaviour level of evaluation produces a number of benefits.

- It gives positive and negative feedback, allowing the HR developer to *revise the learning program,* as knowing what went right is just as important as knowing what did not work. Further, while the learning program may have successfully improved performance in the desired area, it may now become obvious that the staff are having difficulty with the subsequent process. For example, the technicians now may be able to repair the equipment but are having difficulties with diagnosing repair needs. This would indicate that the original HRDNI did not analyse the situation deeply enough and another round of the four HRD stages is required. This example highlights the fact that the behaviour-level evaluation not only evaluates the learning program but also evaluates the assumptions and methods used in the original HRDNI.

- It allows interventions to be planned to support *increased transfer of learning.* While learners may graduate successfully from a learning program, the most that can usually be said at this point is that they have achieved some accepted minimal standard. The very fact that the on-the-job behaviour is being screened tends to concentrate the focus of the supervisor and the returning learner on the learned behaviour often resulting in opportunities that ensure the new skills are practised and used.

- It identifies *unintended consequences.* For example, new trainers are usually told that their introductions to sessions should include a motivational component.

Unless specifically warned, new trainers may use negative motivational statements like 'If you do not learn this you will not have much chance of being promoted' and 'Customers can become very violent if you do not fill out this form correctly'. If not warned, their use of negative messages can become an habitual part of their repertoire, giving their sessions a decidedly gloomy atmosphere – a consequence that was not intended in their original development.

- It allows plans for the next level, *results,* to be formulated and for information from the behaviour level to be integrated. For example, the logic of the increase-in-value-to-the organisation argument will often require a demonstration of changes in the on-the-job performance.

However, the type of work culture that the participants will face when they return from the training program is also important (Kirkpatrick & Kirkpatrick 2005). So, the fact that there has been no change in the on-the-job behaviour of a participant may not indicate that the training program was a failure. The rewards to the participant (both extrinsic and intrinsic) may not exist in a non-supportive work culture. As Kirkpatrick and Kirkpatrick (2005) point out, for this very reason, it is important that the previous levels of evaluation – reaction and learning – are always conducted and recorded by the HR developer. The culture of the workplace will be examined further in Chapter 14.

Results

This level measures the impact of the learning episode on the organisation as a whole. The organisation may be looking for indicators such as improved profits, a decrease in accidents, an improvement in morale, or a decrease in turnover. In addition, results that are less tangible, such as increased motivation, should also be assessed as positive because changes in the less tangible outcomes should eventually have an effect on the more tangible measures (Kirkpatrick & Kirkpatrick 2005). However, it is important that the real impacts of the learning events are evaluated (calculating the differences the investment in learning made) rather than just counting the occurrences of outcomes (Tome 2009). This level, however, is the most complex to evaluate. So, what can the HR developer do? Again, repeating the measures used in the HRDNI can identify the benefits at the organisational level, although organisational records tend to be the predominant approach used. More recently, organisations are making use of survey questionnaires to take pre- and post-measures of staff attitudes. Another approach to managing the complexities of evaluating at the results level is the Successful Case Method (Brinkerhoff 2003). The rationale for the approach is based on the question 'If the learning program was successful, what is the best that it has achieved?' The overall steps in the Success Case Method (SCM) are:

1. focusing and planning a success case study;

2. creating an 'impact model' that defines what success should look like;

3. designing and implementing a survey to search for best and worst cases;

4. interviewing and documenting the success cases; and

5. communicating findings, conclusions, and recommendations.

However, the biggest challenge for the results level is that there is invariably a long time delay between when the learning program was conducted and when results begin to appear in the organisational control systems. Some managers are not patient enough to wait this long.

A closer look 12.1

Possible results measures

Behavioural measures	Computational formula
Absenteeism rate (monthly)	$\dfrac{\Sigma \text{ Absence days}}{\text{Average workforce size x working days}}$
Tardiness rate (monthly)	$\dfrac{\Sigma \text{ Tardiness incidents}}{\text{Average workforce size x working days}}$
Turnover rate (monthly)	$\dfrac{\Sigma \text{ Turnover incidents}}{\text{Average workforce size}}$
Internal stability rate (monthly)	$\dfrac{\Sigma \text{ Internal movement incidents}}{\text{Average workforce size}}$
Strike rate (yearly)	$\dfrac{\Sigma \text{ Striking workers x strike days}}{\text{Average workforce size x working days}}$
Accident rate (yearly)	$\dfrac{\Sigma \text{ of accidents, illnesses}}{\text{Total year'y hours worked}} \times 200{,}000$
Grievance rate (yearly)	Plant: $\dfrac{\Sigma \text{ Grievance incidents}}{\text{Average workforce size}}$ Individual: $\dfrac{\Sigma \text{ Aggrieved individuals}}{\text{Total yearly hours worked}}$

Productivity

Total	$\dfrac{\text{Output of goods or services (units or \$)}}{\text{Direct and/or indirect labour (hours or \$)}}$
Below standard	Actual versus engineered standard
Below budget	Actual versus budgeted standard
Variance	Actual versus budgeted variance
Per employee	$\dfrac{\text{Output}}{\text{Average workforce size}}$

Quality

Total	Scrap + customer returns + rework – recoveries ($, units, or hours)

Below standard	Actual versus engineered standard
Below budget	Actual versus budgeted standard
Variance	Actual versus budgeted variance
Per employee	$\dfrac{\text{Total}}{\text{Average}}$ workforce size
Downtime	Labour (\$) + repair costs or dollar value of replaced equipment (\$)
Inventory, supply, and material usage	Variance (actual versus standard utilisation) (\$)

Comments on Kirkpatrick's model

Kirkpatrick's model is a simple and seemingly robust paradigm that recognises the impact of a learning episode should extend beyond the individual learner. It has provided an easily remembered checklist that has broadened people's perception of the role of evaluation. In addition, each of the levels provides a unique examination of the worth of a HRD intervention.

There are criticisms of the model. Alliger and Janak (1989) have been the most cogent of the critics. They argue that the levels are not co-dependent – for example, successful learning might occur even if the participants do not like the location or the HR developer. Delahaye and Smith (1998) point out that the model concentrates on outcomes and process only, paying little attention to inputs.

In addition, if the four levels are considered a continuum from reaction to results, an interesting relationship exists with three issues (Delahaye & Smith 1998). Gathering data at the reaction level requires much less effort than gathering data at the results level. However, counteracting this, the data becomes more useful the further towards the results end of the continuum the evaluation progresses. Further to complicate the relationship, the more the evaluation moves towards the results end, the more the data can become contaminated. Data gathered at the reaction level is easy to collect and tends to reflect the true representation of the learning episode because the information is specifically about the learning episode. However, other than providing feedback on how to improve the specific learning episode if it is repeated, the information is of limited use to the organisation as a whole. At the other end of the continuum, proving that the learning episode has had an impact on the results of the organisation (e.g. increased profits, lower accident rate) is valuable information. Unfortunately, gathering such data is often complex, and showing causality – that the learning episode was solely responsible for the organisational changes – is very difficult.

Recent research has found that the lowest level (that is, the reaction level) is the most used of the four levels by organisation (Patel 2010) – indicating that there are still many challenges facing organisations in mastering the more complex levels of evaluation.

The presage factors

The evaluation processes discussed so far have concentrated solely on the outcomes of the learning episode – how much learning occurred; what changes to behaviour on the job eventuated; and whether the investment in the learning episode had any impact on the continued viability of the organisation. This post-facto orientation has been criticised for not being dynamic and pro-active. There is a belief that certain presage factors should be evaluated. Presage factors are those factors or events which can be examined to predict a particular outcome. Further, examining presage factors can keep the program moving in the intended direction, as changes can be made during the planning and implementation stages. One writer, Brinkerhoff (2009), has proposed a six-stage model that extends evaluation so that it includes a formative, improvements-oriented focus. The six stages are:

- Stage I: *evaluate needs and goals* – which we have referred to as the HRDNI. It is interesting that Brinkerhoff regards the needs investigation as part of the evaluation process. This stance underlines the interactive and overlapping nature of the HRD process.

- Stage II: *evaluate HRD design* – which focuses on evaluating the design of the program *before* it is implemented to ensure maximum payoff.

- Stage III: *evaluate implementation* – which examines and provides feedback on the program as it is being implemented. This allows adjustments to be made as the program is being conducted.

- Stage IV: *evaluate learning* – which is similar to Kirkpatrick's learning level.

- Stage V: *evaluate usage and endurance of learning* – which is similar to Kirkpatrick's behaviour level.

- Stage VI: *evaluate payoff* – which is similar to Kirkpatrick's results level.

So, Brinkerhoff adds three presage factors to the evaluation model proposed by Kirkpatrick – evaluating needs and goals, evaluating the design, and evaluating the program as it is being implemented. From the educational field, Kyriacou and Newson (1982) add another presage variable – the HR developer who conducts the learning program.

Evaluating needs and goals

While Brinkerhoff saw this first stage as ensuring that the HRD intervention was indeed a good idea, the original needs investigation provides the evaluation stage with some significant directional insights. In short, the investigation tools of the needs investigation stage should also be used in the evaluation stage. So, if the original HRDNI used information from the performance appraisal system, from interviews and organisational records, then the evaluation should re-check this information to see if an improvement has occurred.

Evaluating the program design

Brinkerhoff (2009) sees that, where stage I (the investigation) is concerned with whether HRD is a good idea in the first place, stage II focuses on the quality of the HR plan. A stage II evaluation should be conducted when the program design is unique or experimental, the costs are high, the HRD needs are crucial, or life or death issues or the participant groups are volatile, influential or demanding.

An initial, yet simple, approach to evaluating the design of the learning program is to use the Hierarchy of Learning Outcomes (see Figure 8.2). This comparison will provide a quick analysis of the appropriateness of the proposed learning strategies.

Conducting a more complex stage II evaluation will involve having the design of the program reviewed by a variety of stakeholders – potential learners, the supervisors of potential learners, the customers of potential learners, managers, the CEO, and other HR developers who are experts in both the content and the learning strategies (compare this to the platform model of design in Chapter 9). These reviewers should be asked to examine the theoretical adequacy of the design, the compatibility with the environment and culture, its practicality and cost effectiveness, its potential to satisfy the defined needs, the appropriate use of adult learning theories and techniques, any legal or ethical considerations, and the overall clarity of communication of the plans themselves. Another option at this stage II evaluation is to conduct a 'pilot study'. Conduct the program with a small sample of potential learners with the prime objective being the evaluation of the program rather than the development of the learners. However, for reasons of organisational politics, this option is not always viable.

The benefits of conducting a stage II evaluation include the following:

- The design can be improved prior to implementation.

- Opinions and advice from those who will be most affected by the program can be solicited. This increases the commitment of the key stakeholders (e.g. the learners, managers, and upper management).

- The transfer of training (see Chapter 3) is facilitated as the learners and immediate supervisors are better informed about the purposes of the program and are more likely to look for opportunities to use the learning after the program.

- The stage II evaluation process is likely to reveal and shape the expectations of both parties – the HR developers and the learners and supervisors. In this way, unreasonable expectations can be resolved before the event, new ideas and interpretations can be tried out, and the continuing dialogue between the HR development section and its clients will increase.

Evaluating during implementation

The primary purpose of the stage III evaluation is to monitor the implementation of the program and to provide the data that will help 'shepherd' the learning event to a successful conclusion (Brinkerhoff 2009). Brinkerhoff's stage III performs at least one sterling service – it highlights one of the covert activities of the conducting HR developer.

This covert activity is to continually monitor what is really happening as the program is progressing and compare this reality with the program plan.

- Did the learning strategy have the expected effect?

- Were there any unintended consequences?

- Are the learners alert?

- Is a dominant learner contaminating the experiences of the other learners?

A variety of questions should be flowing through the mind of the HR developer. Being a classic control system, the stage III also incorporates an action step. If a discrepancy is identified, the HR developer has two courses of action. Either the discrepancy can be altered (e.g. clearer instructions are given to the role players in a role play) or the outcomes can be accepted but a re-design of the program is undertaken. For example, if the role play has not gone as expected, the HR developer may decide to debrief what has happened and glean any possible lessons that can be learned, and then conduct a second role play that achieves the learning objectives missed by the first role play. So, the stage III evaluation should be a natural activity of the conducting HR developer.

However, the organisation may wish to invest more in this stage by using another HR developer to conduct the evaluation. This option, though, is usually undertaken only as a developmental activity for the conducting HR developer rather than an evaluation *per se*. Brinkerhoff (2009) highlights some critical points that may be worthy of particular attention during a stage III evaluation:

- functionally critical areas, where, if a breakdown occurs, major damage or bottlenecks to a program will be caused (e.g. if the learners do not understand the programmed knowledge presented in a theory session and this means that the learners would not be able to do the following skill session);

- areas of theoretical shakiness or concern, where a new idea is being tried out for the first time – this new idea may be new programmed knowledge or the trial of a new learning strategy;

- where experience has shown that problems may arise (e.g. where groups have had difficulty in confronting a long-held organisational cultural issue);

- where there is some specific research and development interest that the HR development section or upper management may wish to investigate (e.g. if there are any gender or sociocultural differences in learners who prefer unstructured learning strategies); and

- where there is a need for special records (e.g. for government regulations on equity or health and safety).

The conducting HR developer

Being responsible for the management and implementation of the designed program, the conducting HR developer is obviously a key variable in the success of the program. Usually, evaluation emphasises that HR developers – whether they be trainers, facilitators or teachers – be assessed by the participants at the end of the program. More often than not, this data is collected by using questionnaires – reaction sheets, structured questionnaires, and unstructured questionnaires. There has been quite a deal of literature on this issue over the years and a most detailed and concentrated analysis is offered in a special edition of the *Journal of Educational Psychology* (Perry 1990).

These measures are, again, post facto. They are only really useful for predicting whether the particular HR developer is likely to be suitable for the next similar program. This dilemma reflects the perennial problem of selecting staff. The selection decision can be made only on the past performance of the selectee. So, when evaluation is pro-active and concentrates on the presage variable of the conducting HR developer, the decision makers have to operate on the information about the past performance of that HR developer.

If the HR developer has conducted programs similar to the planned program, and the developer has been assessed, then the information used in the subsequent decision is more valid. If the HR developer has not conducted a similar program, then the decision makers have to use less valid information – that is, use information from a somewhat similar program and extrapolate the likely behaviours of the HR developer in the planned program from that less valid information.

An overview of the evaluation levels

These recommendations on evaluation of Kirkpatrick and Kirkpatrick (2005) and Brinkerhoff (2009) can be compiled to provide a comprehensive overview of the evaluation levels that can be examined – see Table 12.1.

Organisations face various situations when faced with evaluation, so some of the levels may become more important than others, depending on the circumstances. For example, some RTOs or ITOs use external consultants to deliver programs that the RTO or ITO has designed. In this situation, the RTO or ITO will need to use levels 3, 4, 5 and 6, and after the program has been completed, Levels 7 and 8. This allows the RTO (in Australia) or the ITO (in New Zealand) to demonstrate to the relevant authorities at auditing time that the 2010 Conditions and Standards have been met (see http://www.licensinglinenews.com/Newsletter/Updated-AQTF/Updated-AQTF-Essential-Conditions-and-Standards-for-Registration-now-available.aspx).

Table 12.1 Conducting evaluation at the eight levels

Level Number	Evaluation level	When to use it	How to do it
No.1	Evaluating needs and goals	If you are the designer and someone else has conducted the HRDNI	Review the accuracy /transparency of the qualitative research and the validity/reliability of the quantitative research
No.2	Evaluating the program design	If an external consultant is recommending a specific program they have designed or if you are the conducting HR developer using a program designed by someone else.	Use the HLO and the Constructive Alignment Model to make an initial examination of the design. Then make a second review with the learner and organisational needs in mind. Then a third review, using other

Level Number	Evaluation level	When to use it	How to do it
			considerations (number of learners to attend, resources available etc.)
No. 3	The conducting HR developer	Ideally, this should be undertaken prior to the program being implemented to ensure that the conducting HR developer does have the required content knowledge and the facilitating skills.	The HR developer needs to have the ability to facilitate the learning strategies that will be used in the program and also the appropriate micro-skills (see Chapters 10 and 11). Preferably the decision maker should have seen the HR developer conducting similar sessions but, if not, then a typical selection process should be undertaken.
No. 4	Evaluation during implementation	Firstly, the conducting HR developer should do this constantly throughout the program. Secondly, a representative of the client organisation may wish to ensure that the program is likely to be successful.	Self-evaluation by the conducting HR developer Observation by the organisational representative
No. 5	The reaction level	A well designed feedback sheet that is valid and reliable and will encourage honesty (see Kirkpatrick & Kirkpatrick 2005)	At the end of each session and/or at the end of the program. It is also useful to conduct an unstructured discussion (see Chapter 10) so the learners can provide greater detail than the written feedback on their reaction sheet.
No.6	The learning	During the program, at the end of the program and as an assignment to complete when back on the job.	Make sure there are frequent activities in each session (see the theory session in Chapter 10, for example) that can be used as both formative and summative assessment and also a text at the end of the program for summative assessment.
No.7	On-the-job behaviour	When the learners have returned to the job.	Should be conducted by the supervisor (for example, at least a performance appraisal – see Chapter 6). If the HR developer is not the supervisor then this information should be fed back to the Learning and Development

Level Number	Evaluation level	When to use it	How to do it
			Department.
No.8	Organisational results	Several times over the next 2 years.	Monitor the strategic control systems of the organisation.

To be or not to be

Brinkerhoff and other writers who have championed the evaluation of the presage variables have raised an interesting issue. In a perfect world, reviewing the design, carefully selecting the HR developer, and conducting an on-going evaluation while the program is in progress has the potential to ensure a close-to-perfect learning experience. As Brinkerhoff (2009) comments, HRD is like any other human activity – it is fraught with error, it is based on incomplete knowledge and understanding, it is difficult to control, and it is as likely to run off course as it is to succeed. Hence, the steering control of evaluating presage variables has definite attractions.

However, widening evaluation to include the presage variables increases the cost of evaluation. Organisations have to decide which cost they are willing to bear – the cost of increased evaluation or the cost of risk.

Timeout

Let us take time out to get our bearings. At the beginning of this chapter, it was suggested that the evaluation stage had four roles:

1. to identify what change has occurred;

2. to improve the other three stages – investigation, design and implementation – of the HRD system;

3. to see whether the change is attributable to the learning episode; and

4. to see whether the amount of change was worthwhile.

Basing an evaluation plan on Kirkpatrick's model – reaction, learning, behaviour and results – and also including an assessment of the presage factors (i.e. using Brinkerhoff's model) would provide answers to the first two of the four roles. Some information on the last two may have been gathered but usually further data has to be gathered to substantiate these two claims. That the change was attributable to the learning episode may be shown by using the scientific model, and a cost–benefit analysis exercise has to be undertaken to see if the change was worthwhile.

The scientific models

The scientific models of evaluation are based on the experimental methods used in research laboratories and are aimed at demonstrating causality. These scientific models are used in the evaluation of HRD programs to verify whether any change has occurred either in the individual or the organisation or both, as a result of the learning program. As such, the scientific models can provide some very useful and important insights and confirmatory evidence.

The five models:

- post-test;
- pre-test–post-test;
- time series;
- control group; and
- Solomon four

are discussed in order from the simple and less costly to the complex and more costly.

Post-test

The simplest scientific model, the post-test method of evaluation, can be represented as:

learning experience/evaluation

The learners experience a learning episode and an evaluation is then conducted. This evaluation may be conducted immediately after the learning episode or up to several months later. The post-test method proves whether the learners achieved a certain level of performance. However, there is no indication whether a change actually occurred as the levels of performance may have been achieved without the learning experience.

Pre-test–post-test

In the pre-test–post-test method the same evaluation is taken before and after the learning episode, as follows:

evaluation/learning experience/evaluation

The evaluation is referred to as a 'test' for two reasons. First, the term is a residue from the physical sciences of laboratory experimentation where tests were performed on the subject, item, or element being researched. Second, in the HRD sense, the learners are often given an examination or test to evaluate their performance or knowledge. The pre-test–post-test evaluation does show whether a change has occurred. However, we cannot say with certainty whether the change has occurred because of the learning experience or if some other fortuitous event intervened.

Time series evaluation

One such fortuitous event may be an unknown bias in the tests themselves or perhaps the whole group of learners made lucky guesses in the post-test. The time series method uses a number of pre-tests and a number of post-tests, as follows:

pre-test/pre-test/pre-test//learning experience//post-test/post-test/post-test

The time series evaluation, while showing conclusively that a change has occurred, still does not prove that the change occurred because of the learning experience.

Control group

In the idealised version of the control group method, potential learners are assigned randomly to an experimental group and a control group. In less idealised versions, the members of each group may be matched on certain characteristics (e.g. gender, level of responsibility in the organisation, profession, or salary scale). Another less idealised option is the 'group of convenience' – whatever groups are conveniently available are used. In the less idealised versions, the opportunity for a rogue variable to cause systematic bias becomes increasingly likely.

However they are selected, both groups are submitted to a pre-test and a post-test – but only the experimental group undertakes the learning episode (or, in scientific terms, is given a 'treatment').

Experimental group – pre-test/learning experience/post-test

Control group – pre-test/usual duties/post-test

The control group method provides improved confidence that the change occurred because of the learning experience and not because of extraneous factors. However, it is possible for other contaminating factors to bias the result. For example, the members of the control group were resentful because they did not receive the training (and therefore achieved a lower score) or perhaps the experimental group believed that they were an elite band because they were selected and therefore tried harder on the post-test. It is also theoretically possible that the experimental group learned from the pre-test and the control group did not.

The Solomon four

The Solomon four, the deluxe model of scientific evaluation, involves an experimental group and three control groups, as follows:

Experimental group – pre-test/learning experience/post-test

Control group A – pre-test/usual duties/post-test

Control group B – no pre-test/learning experience/post-test

Control group C – no pre-test/usual duties/post-test

The Solomon four design counters most of the possible arguments over causality; a successful demonstration of results provides high levels of confidence that the learning experience was successful. The Solomon four design presents the HR developer with practical problems, three of the more important being as follows:

- It is a very expensive design with high levels of expenditure in terms of money and time.

- The logistics can be quite formidable. Negotiating with managers for the release of the high number of people (three control groups and one group of learners) can be difficult, and organising the pre-testing and post-testing can take quite some effort.

- There are ethical considerations if one group receives developmental opportunities and the other three do not. The industrial relations implications also have to be considered.

A complex decision

The aim of the scientific models is to prove causality – that the learning experience was responsible for the changes at:

- the learning level; and/or

- the behaviour level; and/or

- the results level of evaluation.

While the simplest approach – the post-test – is less costly and easier logistically, it only goes marginally towards proving causality. At the other end of the continuum, the Solomon four design provides close to conclusive proof, but the costs escalate considerably.

Accordingly, the HR developer needs sound justification for using the more costly methods. There may be legal reasons for proving causality – for example, in a safety course, not only was the training provided but it did, without question, change the behaviour and attitudes of the participants. Also, some HR departments need to show causality if they are to maintain their status, and therefore an appropriate budget, in the organisation.

Being able to use the scientific models depends heavily on the ability to measure change in individuals and organisations. As discussed in Chapter 3, measuring improvements in tacit knowledge or changes in personal frames of reference can be very difficult, if not impossible. In addition, these evaluation measurements usually have to occur at a time that is decreed by the organisation. Whether these changes have in fact occurred by this decreed time depends on a variety of variables (e.g. the individual ability of the learners, opportunities arising in the workplace for the learners to use the new skills or knowledge). These issues were discussed when we examined the assessment of learning, and are a perennial concern in evaluation. Indeed, we will encounter them again in the next segment on cost–benefit analysis.

Cost-benefit analysis

The logic behind cost–benefit analysis is quite simple:

- identify the costs, in dollar terms, for the learning experience;

- identify the benefits accruing from the learning experience in dollar terms;

- the ratio between costs and benefits should be in favour of the benefits.

The costs of mounting a learning experience can cover a multitude of items – the salary or wages of the learners, the salary or wages of the HR developers, the rental of the classrooms, the depreciation on the training equipment, copying costs, cost of stationery, payment to guest speakers, travel costs, hiring (e.g. of videos), advertising costs – to name a few. Some benefits can also be reduced to a monetary value – for example, the reduction in accident numbers can be converted into time not lost on the job. Other benefits can be estimated with a 'shadow value'. For example, one way of calculating the value of the development an individual receives over the years is to assess the value of the promotions the individual achieves. However, at this point we quickly run into the two basic problems facing cost–benefit analysis.

The first problem encountered is converting benefits into monetary values. Most benefits from a learning experience, particularly with the more complex outcomes from the HLO (the task, relationship, critical thinking, and meta-abilities), are difficult to measure, let alone convert to a monetary equivalent. Think of the most common sequence – a change in a learner (e.g. increased emotional resilience) that produces a benefit in the workplace that can be measured and then converted to a monetary value. This is quite a tall order. Then add to this the perennial problem of when the benefit surfaces, which may be some considerable time after the learning experience.

The second problem with cost–benefit is deciding on the cut-off point, where the costs and the benefits stop. For example, when a learner attends a learning event, the cost of the learner's salary is usually included. However, what about the costs back at the workplace? The learner's duties still have to be performed. Often, the person one level below the learner is temporarily promoted to do the learner's job at an increased pay rate. Should this increased pay rate be included? What about the duties of the person who has been temporarily promoted? If someone else is promoted temporarily to perform these duties, is their increased pay rate to be included? What about the extra work that these temporary promotions have caused in the pay office? And so we could go on. A similar situation exists with benefits. For example, the learner's interpersonal skills have improved because of a designed learning experience and the learner performs customer relations better because of this new-found skill. What about the effects on the learner's peers? Perhaps their work becomes easier and more productive. Perhaps modelling occurs and the peers' customer relations improve also. Again, you get the idea. At some stage a decision has to be made on the cut-off points for both the costs and the benefits. Defining acceptable cut-off points may be a matter of:

- *logic* – for example, the time spent by the manager and the learner during the appraisal interview (the results of which are used in the HRDNI) is not considered part of the costs of the learning experience;

- *organisational culture* – for example, the organisation may have decided some decades ago that only the learner's salary will be included as the temporary promotion costs are the responsibility of the learner's workplace; or

- *organisational politics* – for example, the manager of the HR department holds early discussions with the chief executive officer to decide on what will and will not be included in the costs and benefits.

Why bother?

With these real and well-documented difficulties, one has to wonder why a HR developer should bother with a cost–benefit analysis. As Delahaye and Smith (1998) comment, the answer is simple – survival! Particularly in the legitimate system, success is measured in monetary terms. A cost centre such as a HR department has to show that it is providing demonstrable assistance in ensuring the organisation is viable – in other words, showing that the learning episode has contributed to the 'bottom line' is generally regarded by management as an imperative (Owen with Rogers 1999).

Another reason for conducting cost–benefit analyses is to select the learning programs that have the most impact. Few HRD departments are over-resourced, so the HRD manager needs some data on which to make decisions for selecting the programs that will have the most impact. So, despite the difficulties, the HR developers need to do everything in their power to ensure that defensible decisions are made on defining the appropriate costs and benefits involved in any planned learning event.

In addition, a professional cost–benefit analysis report acknowledges the problems with cut-off decisions and converting benefits to monetary values. The cut-off decisions should always be acknowledged in the report. Where it is not possible to convert benefits to a monetary value, the benefits should be fully described and such qualitative descriptions given full recognition in the final cost–benefit comparison.

The evaluation plan

Earlier in this chapter we discussed the overlap that occurs between the assessment of learning and the implementation stage. Another overlap occurs between the evaluation stage and the design stage. Planning the evaluation starts during the design stage. As well as ensuring that appropriate evaluation occurs at appropriate times during and after the implementation, producing an evaluation plan during the design stage allows the two roles of the assessment of learning – developmental and judgemental – to be coordinated. This ensures that one role does not interfere with the other.

Planning for the evaluation of a learning episode should include the following:

- Develop the assessment of learning for developmental purposes first.

- Incorporate appropriate developmental assessments into the evaluation plan and add further assessment of learning processes as required for the evaluation at the learning (or Level 6 in Table 12.1) level.

- Decide what presage variables will be evaluated and when. If the design is to be reviewed, arrange for this to occur. If the conducting HR developer and the location are to be evaluated, plan for the process (e.g. include items on the reaction sheets) and the personnel (e.g. for another HR developer to review the conducting HR developer).

- Review the investigating instruments (e.g. questionnaires, performance appraisals) used in the HRDNI and decide which will be used in the evaluation. Also ensure that the results of these investigating instruments are recorded for later comparisons in the evaluation report.

- Design daily and course or workshop reaction sheets.

- If the scientific models are to be used, plan the pre-test and post-test instruments. Decide when these tests will be implemented and plan logistics.

- Identify the methods that will be used to examine the behaviour (or Level 7 of Table 12.1) and results (or Level 8 of Table 12.1) levels of evaluation. Plan the measuring processes to be used and plan the logistics.

- If a cost–benefit analysis is to be implemented, arrange for the details of the costs to be collected. Identify all possible benefits and arrange for the collection of objective (e.g. monetary value) and subjective (e.g. managers' opinions) data to be collected. Ensure exact definitions of cut-off points are promulgated.

- Prepare a budget for the evaluation plan (include financial, staff and time requirements, and submit it for approval.

- Send the evaluation plan to staff who are affected (e.g. the conducting HR developer) or who will be involved (e.g. evaluators).

The evaluation report

As the saying goes, the job is not complete until the paperwork is done. There is little sense in conducting an evaluation unless the results are communicated. An evaluation report should at least include the following points:

- an *executive summary*, of about one page, that provides a précis of the report emphasising the objectives of the report, the approach taken, and the main findings;

- a *findings/recommendations section*, briefly describing the findings of the evaluation and the main recommendations and supporting recommendations,

- a *table of contents* listing the main topic headings and the associated page number;

- the *main body*, including:

    - the reasons for the evaluation, leading to the objectives of the investigation,

    - a list of the personnel involved in the evaluation,

    - a discussion of the various types of evaluations undertaken and how the data were collected and analysed,

    - a discussion of the findings, an examination of the options and a presentation of the conclusions, and

    - a list and a discussion of the recommendations (the recommendations should flow logically from the findings and conclusions); and

- *appendices*, some of which will include supporting data from the evaluation and others which will provide a detailed discussion or examination of important issues. This allows a précis of this detailed data to be included in the main body.

The evaluation report can have three significant roles in an organisation. The first is a communicative role. The evaluation report is usually distributed to the key stakeholders of the learning experience, and particularly to those who occupy the influencing and decision-making buying roles (see Chapter 9). Some parts of the report may be contentious and therefore abbreviated versions may be sent to other people.

Secondly, of course, the report has a role in decision-making:

- Was the learning design useful?

- Should it be used again?

- What further learning is required?

Notice here the overlap between evaluation and the HRDNI.

Thirdly, the report becomes an historical record that can be used to prove that certain events did take place (for example, if there is a safety enquiry) or to analyse later for any organisational trends.

Whose responsibility?

In 'A closer look 4.2' the question was asked, 'Whose responsibility is the development of staff in an organisation?' At the operational level, the responsibility is that of the line managers and supervisors. It is well to be reminded of this basic fact at the evaluation stage.

The line manager and supervisor should be fully involved in the evaluation of learning, whether the learning has occurred off-site or onsite. Further, as is the case in the HRDNI, the line manager or supervisor is the only person who can undertake some of the evaluation processes – the performance appraisal comes to mind again.

However, the line manager or supervisor may delegate the authority for a HR developer to do some types of evaluation, because the HR developer often has a unique combination of knowledge and skills – that is, the skills and knowledge on evaluation discussed in this chapter – to carry out evaluation projects.

At the strategic level, though, the organisation will also be involved in evaluation. This responsibility is often delegated to the Learning and Development Department in large organisations. The Learning and Development Department also needs to ensure that the operational and strategic strata of evaluation are coordinated. For further discussion on this issue see Browning and Delahaye 2010.

The need for dialectic thinking

At the beginning of this chapter, we discussed the misunderstandings that have plagued the evaluation stage over the years. In many ways, these misperceptions can be explained by a concept discussed in Chapter 3 – dialectic thinking. It is believed that dialectic thinking may separate adults from youths. Dialectic thinking consists of the ability to view artefacts (objects, operations or concepts) as having more than one characteristic. Further, these characteristics of an artefact may be conflicting. So, for example, electricity has positive benefits (keeps us warm in cold weather) but can also have negative consequences (it can kill us).

Evaluation must be approached with the wider viewpoints provided by dialectic thinking. Evaluation has a number of opposing characteristics and we have discussed two of these:

- Evaluation can be both developmental and judgemental.
- The more objective the measure used, the less rich the insights.

On the other hand, the more subjective measurements may provide richer, more contextual and realistic data, but the process of subjective analysis lacks validity and reliability.

Evaluation also shares a conflicting characteristic with the implementation stage. Chapters 10 and 11 were divided into structured and unstructured learning strategies based on two philosophies of learning. One, the traditional school, held that knowledge was finite, could be passed on by experts, and should be delivered in a controlled environment. The artistic school held that learning should be holistic and at the behest of the learner. As indicated in Chapter 10, both of these philosophies are correct, depending on the situation. Chapters 8 and 9 suggested that the situation could be gauged, to a certain extent, by such variables as the HLO, the learner, the strategic orientation of the organisation and the resources available. The evaluation at the learning (or stage IV) level should therefore consider the conflicting assumptions of structured and unstructured learning.

Evaluation also brings to the surface one of the oldest arguments in education. Bantoch (1992) believes the distinction between liberal and vocational education goes back to ancient Greece where liberal education was for living, and what we call today vocational education, was for earning a living. This belief has survived for centuries, where the slaves and craftsmen received an education that was trade-focused and gave society the products and services it needed. The upper classes became involved only in learning that trained the mind and cultivated the intellect (Sanderson 1993). Thus liberal education had a continuing popularity among the self-styled elite because of its original association with high culture and dignity. However, Thorndike (1931) deflated this balloon of pomposity by finding that studies in Latin and Greek did not necessarily generalise to other types of knowledge and abilities.

Writers such as Barcan (1992) and Wiggins (1989), however, report that the more modern interpretation of liberal education focuses on the identification of general but controlling principles rather than techniques, and emphasises the world of values rather than uniform behaviour. Liberal education develops the ability to accept other people with more knowledge and listen to them, perceive which questions are the most important to ask, challenge values and hidden agenda, and imagine that a new and strange idea is worth attending to. It has also championed learning for its own sake and placed a high value on academic freedom (Davies 1995). This stance brought stringent criticism in the 1990s where the emphasis was on economic rationalism. Vocational education is more specialised, technical, and productivity oriented. It is much easier to prove causality with vocational education; the results of such learning tend to surface more quickly and readily. With the competency movement (see Chapter 5) and economic rationalism, vocational education has received a resurgence of support from governments and other sources in the last few years.

However, as emphasised in Chapter 1, indulgence in unitary thought – for example, that vocational education is more valuable and critical to organisational viability – is a luxury that cannot be afforded in these complex times. Dialectic thinking must be substituted. Key stakeholders in organisations (be they CEOs, managers or HR developers) must recognise that evaluation supports and serves a variety of roles. Evaluation has to be objective and subjective and judgemental and developmental. All the four HRD stages – investigation, design, implementation and evaluation – have to consider structured and unstructured learning as equally valuable, and be based on the values of both liberal and vocational education.

Balancing these conflicting roles is the new challenge for organisations which have to accept that knowledge is a valuable but delicate resource that needs careful management. This is the topic of the next, and last two chapters in this book.

References

Alliger, G M & Janak, E A 1989, 'Kirkpatrick's levels of training criteria: Thirty years later', *Personnel Psychology,* 42, pp. 331-342.

Bantock, C 1992, 'Finn and vocational education', *Education Monitor,* 3(1), pp. 10-12.

Barcan, A 1992, 'Is there room for liberal education?', *Education Monitor,* 3(2), pp. 2-3.

Belgrade, S, Burke, K., & Fogarty, R 2008, *The Portfolio Connection: Student work linked to standards,* 2nd edn, Pearson Education Australia, Frenchs Forest, NSW.

Bennett, J & Kingham, M 1993, 'Learning diaries', in J Reed & S Proctor (eds.), *Nurse Education: A Reflective Approach,* London: Edward Arnold.

Biggs, J & Tang, C 2007, *Teaching for quality learning at university,* 3rd edn, Open University Press, Maindenhead, UK.

Brady, L & Kennedy, K 2007, *Curriculum Construction,* 3rd edn, Pearson Education Australia, Frenchs Forest, NSW.

Brinkerhoff, R O 2003, *The success case method,* Berrett-Koehler Publishers, San Francisco.

Brinkerhoff, R 0 2009, *Achieving results from training,* Pfeiffer & Co.

Browning, V & Delahaye, B L 2010, 'Enhancing workplace learning through collaborative HRD', in M Clarke (ed.), *Cases and readings in HRM and sustainability,* Tilde University Press, Melbourne, Vic.

Davies, P 1995, 'Time to tear down the universities?', *The Australian,* 12 April, p. 27. Delahaye, B L & Smith, B J 1987, 'Warning – Now you have to prove you have trained them'. *Human Resource Management Australia, 25(1),* March, pp. 5-8.

Delahaye, B L & Smith, B J 1987, 'Warning – now you have to prove you have trained them', *Human Resource Management Australia,* 25(1), p. 5-8.

Delahaye, B L & Smith. B J 1998, *How to be an Effective Trainer.* New York: Wiley

Easterby-Smith, M 1998, 'Training evaluation and follow-up', in J Prokopenko (ed.), *Management Development: A Guide for the Professional,* Geneva: ILO.

Goldstein, I L 2001, *Training in Organisations,* 4th edn, Pacific Grove, Cal.: Brooks/Cole.

Hall, W C 1995, *Key Aspects of Competency-based Assessment.* Adelaide, SA: National Centre for Vocational Education Research

Kirkpatrick, D L 1959a, 'Techniques for evaluating training programs: Part 1 Reaction', *Journal of ASTD,* 13(11), pp. 3-9.

Kirkpatrick, D L 1959b, 'Techniques for evaluating training programs: Part 2 – Learning', *Journal of ASTD,* 13(12), pp. 21-26.

Kirkpatrick, D L 1960a, 'Techniques for evaluating training programs: Part 3 Behaviour', *Journal of ASTD,* 14(1), pp. 13-18.

Kirkpatrick, D L 1960b, 'Techniques for evaluating training programs: Part 4 Results', *Journal of ASTD,* 14(2), pp. 28-32.

Kirkpatrick, D L & Kirkpatrick, J D 2005, *Evaluating Training Programs: The Four Levels,* 3rd edn, Berrett-Koehler, San Francisco..

Kyriacou, C & Newson, G 1982, 'Teacher effectiveness: A consideration of research problems', *Educational Review,* 34(1), pp. 3-12.

Long, H B 2002, *Teaching for Learning,* Malabar, Florida: Krieger.

McAllister, M 1997, 'Enriching Values: An Educational Criticism Approach to the Role of Assessment in Teaching Mental Health', unpublished doctoral thesis, Queensland University of Technology, Brisbane.

Owen, J M with Rogers, P J 1999, *Programs Evaluation. Forms and Approaches,* 2nd edn, St. Leonards, NSW: Allen & Unwin.

Marsh, C J 2004, *Key concepts for understanding curriculum,* 3rd edn, Routledge Falmer, London

Misko, J & Priest, S 2009, *Students' suggestions for improving their vocational education and training experience,* NCVER, Adelaide, SA.

Patel, L 2010, 'Overcoming barriers and valuing evaluation', *T+D,* February, pp. 62-63.

Perry, R P 1990, 'Special section: Instruction in higher education', *Journal of Educational Psychology,* 82(2), June, pp. 183-274.

Rogers, C R 1983, *Freedom to Learn in the 80s,* Charles E Merrill, Columbus, Ohio.

Sanderson, M 1993, 'Vocational and liberal education: A historian's view', *European Journal of Education,* 28(2), pp. 189-196.

Smith, B J 1992, 'Learning Diaries', in B J Smith (ed.), *Management Development in Australia.* Sydney: HBJ.

Stacey, R D 1996, *Strategic Management and Organisational Dynamics,* 2nd edn, London: Pitman.

Thorndike, E L 1931, *Human Learning,* New York: Appleton-Century-Crofts.

Thorndike, R M 2007, *Measurement and Evaluation in Psychology and Education,* 7th edn, Prentice Hall, Upper Saddle River, New Jersey.

Tome, E 2009, 'The evaluation of HRD: A critical study with applications', *Journal of European Industrial Training,* 33(6), pp. 513-538.

Wang, G G & Spitzer, D R 2005, 'Human resource development measurement and evaluation: Looking back and moving forward', *Advances in Developing Human Resource,* 7(1), pp.5-15.

Wexley, K N & Latham, G P 2002, *Developing and Training Human Resources in Organizations,* 3rd edn, New York: Harper Collins.

Wiggins, G 1989, 'The futility of trying to teach everything of importance', *Educational Leadership,* 47(3), pp. 44-48.

Chapter 13

Workplace learning

LEARNING OBJECTIVES

After studying this chapter you should be able to:

1. List the advantages of off-site learning and workplace learning.

2. Explain the nine elements of managing workplace learning.

3. Explain the seven phases of individual adult learning.

Moving into the shadow system

So far in the book, we have concentrated more on the processes used in the legitimate system. Accordingly, we have explored practices that tend to emphasise negative feedback loops and single loop learning.

We are now going to move towards the shadow system of the organisation, although workplace learning is, perhaps, more accurately depicted as being part of both the legitimate and the shadow system, as shown in the shaded area of Figure 13.1.

The workplace as a site for learning

Many scholars (see, for example, Billett 2002; Choy & Delahaye 2008; Stavenga de Jong, Wierstra & Hermanussen 2006; Hager 2004) believe that the workplace provides the most authentic learning environment for a competent workforce. Learning that is based in the workplace is founded on the theory of constructivism (Vygotsky 1978) where learners make meanings by contextualising the content within the socio-cultural environment and functions of the workplace (Choy & Delahaye 2010).

As a learning site, the workplace presents a number of advantages – the learning is focused on specific tasks, the principles of meaningful material and transfer of learning (see Chapter 3) are automatically integrated within the learning experience and feedback is immediately available.

Figure 13.1 The two basic systems

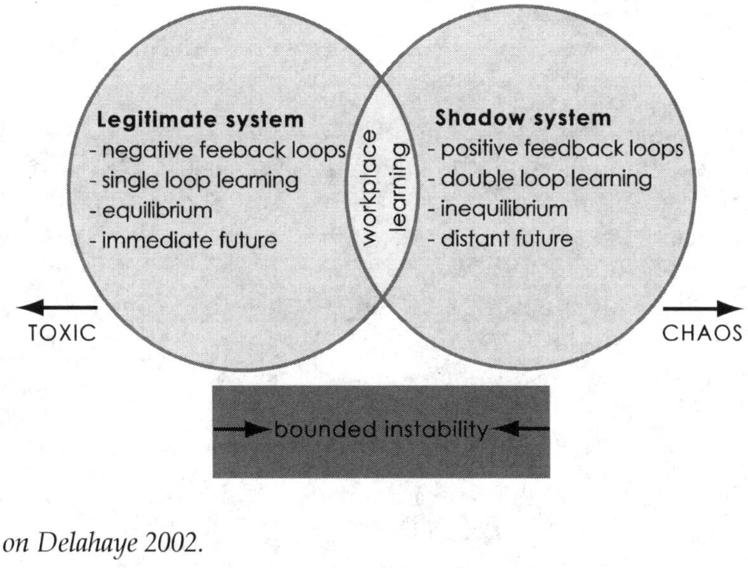

Source: Based on Delahaye 2002.

In workplace learning, the supervisor undertakes the full role of the HR developer. As Watson and Maxwell (2007) found, supervisors play a key role in the implementation of HRD. Basically, when the need for learning arises, the supervisor will make the decision on whether the learning should take place at the *work site* or *off-site*, when the supervisor will authorise some other HR developer to conduct the development (for example, in a training room or at a university).

Table 13.1 Advantages of off-site and workplace training

Advantages of off-site learning	Advantages of workplace learning
The time of the learners is not contested	Learning opportunities occur as immediate and problem based
Learning can be efficiently programmed	The learning is contextualised
Costs can be decreased	The learners are readily motivated because of the immediate application of the knowledge
The learning can be made specific and appropriate	Learners can have continual guidance on-the-job.
The knowledge is readily accessible to the learners	New learning can be integrated readily into the individual's existing knowledge base
The learning can be readily assessed	
Learners can interact with experts from a variety of fields	

Beckett (2001) believes that at the core of all workplace educative activities, and not beneath or beside them, is some element of skill acquisition. *Formal learning* (or off-site) programs are usually the most effective and efficient process for learning basic skills. Workplace learning allows further development and reflection within a rich and relevant context. Supervisors need to examine the needs of the learners and, in collaboration with the learner, decide which option – formal learning or workplace learning – or combination of options is best suited for the learner, the learning objectives and the organisation.

Further, supervisors have the responsibility for the total learning of their staff and this responsibility cannot be delegated (Browning & Delahaye 2010). Sending staff to an in-house training course or to an educational institution for a qualification does not herald the end of the supervisor's responsibilities. The HR developer conducting the training course, or the academic directing the award program, is only relieving the supervisor of the time and effort of conducting the learning experience. The supervisor must ensure that learning outcomes from off-site learning locations are translated into work-site productivity. Supervisors, then, must use both off-site learning and workplace learning to full effect and ensure that each staff member has a continuing and total learning experience.

Workplace learning is not an alternative form of developing staff. It is the principal developmental process for staff with formal (off-site) learning being an important adjunct and companion. After a formal or off-site learning experience, the learner must apply that learning back on the job. Further, the outcomes from a formal or off-site learning experience are often at only the coping level – the learner must develop deeper competence by application and practice of the skills and knowledge imparted during the formal learning experience.

Case study example

See the PLP case study on page 13 of the workbook that accompanies this text for off-site and on-site learning.

Challenges to workplace learning

While workplace learning is a critical part of the continuing development of staff, most organisations tend to ignore the concept altogether. This lack of awareness occurs despite clear research evidence that a well-trained, multi-skilled workforce is essential to economic survival and that investment in human resources has a positive relationship with share market performance and profits (Stone 2010).

Learning in the workplace faces a number of challenges including:

- learning must compete for time and recognition with the normal workday activities;

- there may be a lack of expertise in the workplace;

- individuals may be unwilling to participate in learning (see Chapter 10 for a discussion on the characteristics of adult learners);

- the catalyst for learning at the workface often depends on the sporadic or serendipitous occurrence of a problem or opportunity;

- the sporadic occurrence of a problem or opportunity must be accompanied by a motivation on the part of the learner to overcome the problem or take advantage of the opportunity;

- an instructor or guide or mentor needs to be available,

- even when available, experts may be reluctant to undertake the role of instructor or guide or mentor;

- the instructor or guide or mentor needs to have at least some of the skills and knowledge of a HR developer; and

- the instructor or guide or mentor needs to be given sufficient resources, including time, to undertake the role of instructor or guide or mentor.

Supervisors, with the active support of their organisations, must look for ways to overcome these challenges.

The supervisor as the HR developer

Workplace learning is a multi-faceted process, with the supervisor being the initiator and the linchpin throughout. This leads to a critical insight – *all supervisors must be highly accomplished HR developers*. This critical conclusion is the absolute antithesis of current practice in most organisations, where people are promoted on their knowledge and ability in a trade or profession. They are usually given little in the way of management development, let alone in facilitating workplace learning.

So, ideally, all supervisors should be able to facilitate learning in the workplace. This means that they would have the tacit knowledge and the complex skills discussed previously in this book, in particular:

- have the managerial competence to oversee the surveillance stage of the HRDNI and conduct the investigation stages when necessary;

- formulate learning objectives correctly;

- design learning episodes appropriately and be able to evaluate a learning design presented by an outside party (see Evaluation Level 2 in Figure 13.1);

- Conduct learning episodes [certainly, the supervisor should be able to competently conduct the more structured learning strategies (see Chapter 10) for the programmed knowledge and the upper parts of the task and relationships categories of the HLO (see Figure 8.2) and be adept at the associated micro skills; for the deeper, more complex outcomes and the associated learning strategies in the HLO, the supervisor may have the knowledge or skills to facilitate the learning episode or may prefer to bring in an outside consultant with these skills and knowledge];

- conduct evaluations of learning.

Needless to say, the time that the supervisor needs to undertake this role of HR developer in the workplace should be represented in the supervisor's workload – yet another managerial practice that is more honoured by its absence that its presence.

Learning spaces

As well as having the appropriate levels of skills and knowledge to facilitate the learning, the supervisor will need to plan for and organise the resources needed. The most critical resource needed for workplace learning is *learning spaces*. Learning spaces, or workplace affordances as Billett (2002) calls them, are the physical sites and the time that has been dedicated to allowing the staff member to learn.

The physical site will be a location together with the supporting learning technology and learning resources that have been specifically reserved for the learning episode. This site may be a space separate from the learner's usual workplace that also has the technology, such as: a computer; a particular type of machine which will allow the learner to practice new skills; and sufficient materials that the learner can use as part of experiential learning or practice.

So, for example, if the learner is to learn how to use a new milling machine, a milling machine in a safe location and sufficient raw materials will need to be set aside to give the learner time to practice and try out different techniques.

The learner will also need to be given an appropriate amount of time to learn the new skills or knowledge. If the physical site is the same as the learner's workplace, sufficient time for learning will still have to be allocated, with the added stipulation that the learning period should be interruption free.

Managing workplace learning

Managing workplace learning requires a consistent effort from the supervisor and is, therefore, a major part of any supervisor's duties. Writers such as Browning and Delahaye (2010) and Coetzer (2006) believe that the supervisor is responsible for:

- continually monitoring their staff as well as the internal and external environment of their organisation, to ensure that the staff have the needed knowledge and to identify what additional knowledge they need;

- providing their staff with a range of learning opportunities – such as observing new ways of working and providing challenging workplace activities;

- creating an organisational climate that supports and encourages learning;

- removing barriers to learning;

- providing appropriate learning support processes, such as coaches and mentors; and

- encouraging employees to engage in learning behaviours which include actively seeking out feedback on performance, and asking for assistance.

At first glance, these responsibilities may appear to be complex and demanding. However, taken stage by stage, the process of managing workplace learning can be examined under a number of key headings, as shown in Figure 13.2.

Case study example

See the PLP case study on page 15 of the workbook that accompanies this text for an example of using the managing workplace learning model.

Performance appraisal

Learning in the workplace begins with performance appraisal. As discussed in Chapter 6, the performance appraisal interview, especially the developmental type, allows the supervisor and staff member to begin a meaningful communication process. As such, they are involved in communicative learning and, as a matter of course, must engage in both the externalisation and internalisation knowledge generation processes (see Chapter 3). Therefore, as part of workplace learning, the performance appraisal:

- commences the learning episode;
- is a learning experience as and of itself; and
- results in an action plan for further targeted learning.

Figure 13.2 Managing workplace learning

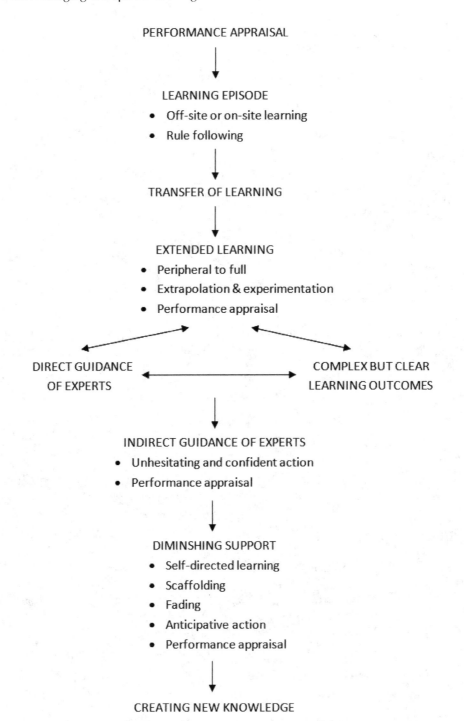

It is well to recognise, however, that the performance appraisal could have been initiated by a wider HRDNI. For example, the strategic plan may have specifed that the organisation will move into a new market. The senior managers, through their strategic and tactical planning process, would have identified what new skills and knowledge staff would need and would also have provided the resources for the development of the staff. On receiving this advice, the supervisor would undertake performance appraisals of all staff who would be affected and thereby create learning action plans. As another example, the supervisor may have noticed that one of the control systems has indicated a decrease in quality and this would have initiated performance appraisals with identified staff with, again, the creation of learning action plans.

The result of these actions plans are, of course, learning episodes for specific staff.

The learning episode

The learning action plan from the performance appraisal may have identified one learning episode or a series of related learning episodes. Either way, the supervisor will have to decide whether the learning should occur off-site or on-site. If off-site, the supervisor should:

- check that the learning objectives of the off-site learning program are appropriate to the work area; and

- evaluate the learning design (see Evaluation Level 2 in Figure 12.1).

If the learning is to occur on-site, the supervisor will need to design the learning, organise all the resources, arrange the learning spaces, and conduct the learning.

The learning may be conducted by the supervisor or by an expert in the content who is also a work colleague. Of course, the content experts would also need the appropriate learning facilitation skills.

The learning outcome is usually to a level that Beckett (2001) calls *rule following*. Rule following is a basic level of learning where the learner follows a specified sequence of steps – for example, in doing a skill or undertaking some type of problem solving. This rule-following sequence is valid under 'normal' circumstances.

So, for example, if the learning episode was to achieve the learning objective of 'complete a sale transaction where all information is available', the learner would be able to complete that simple type of sale transaction but would not be able to complete the transaction if some complexity was present – for example, if there was no tag attached showing the selling price of that item. Similarly, the learner would not know how to interact with an irate customer who is disputing the sale price of the item.

This initial learning episode, then, is often aimed at providing the learner with the absolute basic skills and knowledge so that the learner can complete the routine tasks in the workplace. The more the learning objectives for the learning episode become complex, the longer the learning episode will take, with a concomitant increase in training costs. Accordingly, most organisations opt for the achievement of the *rule following* level only.

Transfer of learning

One of the problems with off-site learning, and to a lesser extent on-site learning, is encapsulation. Encapsulation occurs when the learners achieve the desired learning objectives or learning outcomes in the off-site training room but do not take the learning back to the workplace. The learning is encapsulated in the learning situation and stays there. As Tennant (1999) comments, historically in education there has been a greater value placed on de-contextualised knowledge with a concomitant schism between 'knowing' and 'doing'. Knowing was seen as the mandate of the privileged and doing the role of the labouring class. However, recent research irrefutably demonstrates that deep learning depends on the combination of both knowing and doing. Therefore, the designer must constantly focus on the need to ensure that the planned learning will be transferred back to the workplace situation.

As discussed under 'the program and session plans' in Chapter 9, the HR developer can encourage transfer of learning during the off-site program itself by using the principles of learning of meaningful material and transfer of learning. In addition, at the design and implementation stage of the off-site learning program, the HR developer may be able to incorporate activities in the learning program – for example, have the learners commence projects during the learning program which have to be completed on-the-job, or arrange some follow-up training once the learner the returns to the workplace.

However, the most enduring effect on transfer of learning occurs after the learning episode when the learner returns to the workplace. Thus, transfer of learning is heavily dependent on the supervisors in their role of workplace HR developer to ensure that the skills and knowledge from the formal learning episode are used at the worksite as part of the normal, everyday activities.

To achieve this learning transfer, the learner needs what Tennant (1999) calls a positive transfer climate. In a positive transfer climate, the learner:

- is provided with opportunities to reinforce and further develop the 'routinised problem-solving' knowledge and skills covered in the learning program;

- is given both informational and motivational feedback; and

- operates in a supportive atmosphere. This support comes from both the supervisor and the learner's peers.

In this transfer of learning stage, the knowledge generation process of combination is emphasised, although internalisation tends to occur to an extent as well, depending mainly on the motivation levels of the learner (see Chapter 8).

Extended learning

The extended learning phase is the responsibility of the learner and the immediate supervisor; it takes the learner from the rule-following level to the *extrapolation and experimentation* level (Beckett 2001). With extrapolation, learners expand their skills and knowledge gained in the learning episode by finding out how to change and add to the basic rules they have been following. In other words, they are moving from operating under conditions of certainty to conditions that are less certain and more complex. In our example of the sales transaction, they would now learn how to cope with an irate customer and what to do when a price tag is not attached to the item being purchased.

In extended learning, then, the learner moves from peripheral to full engagement with the tasks to be undertaken in the workplace.

Figure 13.3 Progressive development

Low complexity	High complexity
Low accountability	High accountability
Stand-alone task	Interdependent task
Single input source	Multiple input sources
Limitation of risks	Full exposure to risks

Source: Based on Billett 2001.

At the commencement of the ordered pathway, the learner would be engaged in peripheral participation. The task would be of low complexity, usually based on a single decision path. The accountability would be low, in that any errors would be of low cost, or easily restored, or repaired. The tasks or tasks being performed would be stand-alone, in that the learner would not have to be concerned about the output or results; the manager or supervisor or guide retains this responsibility. The prompts or the information for the task or tasks would come from a single source, such as one conventional customer request. Finally, the learner would be protected from any undue risks. This protection may come from a barrier (e.g. by having some of the initial work completed), or by the security of close supervision. In this way the learner is protected from unusual events requiring other decision-making skills and knowledge.

Case study example

See the PLP case study on page 15 of the workbook that accompanies this text for the use of peripheral to full engagement.

The learner would then move gradually towards full participation via more integrated and complex tasks. Initially, the learner is given tasks that require a more complex combination of skills and knowledge, and would be expected to cope with information coming from more than one source. Then the learner could be exposed gradually to the results of the outputs of the efforts so that he or she realises how a less-than-desirable product or service affects the next user, or even the customer. Finally, the learner is expected to be accountable for the product or service, be able to recognise when the customer is happy with the product or service, or be able to improve the product or service to the standard required by the customer.

In providing support to the learner during this movement from peripheral to full participation, the supervisor should ensure that the appropriate learning strategies are used. It could be expected that the most useful of the strategies for the progressive development of the learner would include the skill session, the discussion (see Chapter 10), and mentoring (Chapter 11).

At some stage in the extended learning phase, often when the learner has accomplished a number of separate tasks under complex conditions, it is time for the learner to bring all the tasks together in a complete whole that represents a full job or a significant part of a job. Accordingly, the next two phases – complex but clear learning objectives and direct guidance of experts – are combined with extended learning, and the learners will continue to move through the three phases as they gain complete mastery of their jobs.

Complex but clear learning outcomes

Chapter 5 emphasised the need for clear learning objectives for a learning experience. Such learning objectives provide a clear purpose for the design of the learning experience and also give learners a specific goal that helped them shape and modify their behaviours. Learning objectives are very useful for routine tasks – tasks that form the basis of any job. The outcome of routine tasks can usually be phrased in the terminal-behaviour-standards-conditions phraseology of learning objectives and this is what occurred in the learning episode and, to a lesser extent, in extended learning.

However, by its very definition, the expansion towards full participation predicates a movement away from routine tasks to non-routine tasks. Non-routine tasks are usually more complex and incorporate more responsibility. Further, the results of non-routine tasks are usually more inclusively defined by learning outcomes rather than learning objectives (see Chapter 5). Further, the learner will gradually combine the routine tasks and the more complex tasks into a whole.

Accordingly, more sophisticated techniques are needed to communicate the full complexity of such learning outcomes. The learner needs to have a clear understanding of the required learning outcomes and this clarity is best communicated by:

- observing experts;
- visiting customers; and
- discussing standards.

Observing experts allows the learner to gauge the nuances that are often present in undertaking the task, to judge the standard of the final product, and to generate new knowledge using socialisation (see Chapter 3).

Visiting the customers who use the learner's output as part of their input to complete their own tasks allows the learner to witness the results of the actions. Billett (1993) gives the example of warehouse workers accompanying truck drivers to supermarkets to witness the delivery of the goods they had packed on pallets and noting the rigours on the packed pallets of both the road journey and the unloading procedures.

Discussions on what standards customers expect and/or possible problems that may occur and/or the effect of new material or technology or competition allow the learner to conceptualise the required learning outcomes.

Direct guidance of experts

The direct guidance of experts and other experienced workers is central to the quality of workplace learning because close guidance provides contributions that go far beyond learning through direct or indirect modelling (Billett 2001). Direct guidance is often undertaken by a mentor (see Chapter 11) although a person providing the direct guidance need not necessarily be a mentor in the full sense of the word. Specifically, Billett (2001) sees the role of the guide as:

- securing the learner's access to a sequence of activities at the time and place required by the learner;

- ensuring that the activities are suitable to the dictates of work practice;

- guarding against the development of bad habits or dangerous work practices;

- providing, when appropriate, for the learner's developmental progression, additional knowledge, or underlying theory that will enhance the learner's understanding of the work practice (see mentoring in Chapter 13); and

- demonstrating (see the skill session in Chapter 12), modelling, re-modelling (see modelling in Chapter 3) and providing feedback (see feedback as a principle of learning in Chapter 3) that enhances progressive development of vocational procedures that are difficult or need a highly refined level of competency.

Selecting the guide

While it would be easy for an organisation simply to appoint a guide for the learner, research indicates that the selection process may not be simple. Andrews and Delahaye (2000) found that individuals make complex decisions before accepting knowledge from another and make similar complex decisions before sharing knowledge. They call this process the psychosocial filter. When importing knowledge from another, an individual appears to make three judgements.

The first judgement appears to be a personal construct – whether the individual has the social confidence to approach another. To initiate contact, an individual needs to feel at ease in instigating a working relationship. If an individual feels personally comfortable in approaching another then the first hurdle in accepting knowledge from that person is cleared.

Then the individual will assess the approachability of the knowledge giver. In particular, the personal style and the status of the knowledge source are gauged as important by the individual when making this judgement as to whether to seek knowledge from the other person.

The individual will then move onto the third judgement – the credibility of the knowledge source. The knowledge source has to be seen as an 'expert' – competent and well-informed in the area of knowledge being sought.

Case study example

See the PLP case study on page 15 of the workbook that accompanies this text for the psychosocial filter.

Once the individual has worked through her or his psychosocial filter – that is, feels that he or she is socially confident in approaching the other person and that the other person is approachable and is indeed an expert – then that person is more likely to be accepted by the individual learner as a guide or mentor.

In summary, then, at this stage of workplace learning, the learner will be moving through the three steps of:

- extended learning;
- complex but clear learning outcomes; and
- direct guidance of experts

as an iterative process. When the learner has achieved a sufficient level of development to move onto the next phase, the supervisor should conduct a developmental performance appraisal.

Indirect guidance

At the indirect guidance stage, the learners have achieved a level of competence where they no longer need the direct support of an expert. They can become more independent learners. However, they will still need the influence and support from more indirect sources.

The indirect guidance provided by the workplace environment can impart a powerful influence on the learner. First, being surrounded by experienced co-workers and peers provides a continual reminder of what is acceptable good practice. Note, however, that this continual reminder can only occur if accepted good practice is part of the culture of the workplace. Bad practices can be acquired just as easily. So managers and supervisors must continually expect, monitor, and demand good practice. A second prospect for indirect guidance can occur when employees meet away from tasks, for example during tea or coffee breaks. Such breaks provide opportunities for learners to hear stories of disasters and successes, to have standards reinforced, to listen to reasons for certain procedures, to discuss problems, and to hear about useful contacts or sources of information.

Case study example

See the PLP case study on pages 11 and 15 of the workbook that accompanies this text for experienced co-workers providing indirect guidance.

At the indirect guidance phase, the learner is achieving a level of competence that Winch (1995) calls unhesitating and confident action.

At the end of this indirect guidance phase the supervisor should again conduct a developmental performance appraisal.

Diminishing support

As the learner becomes competent, it is important that the learner is encouraged to become independent. Collins *et al.* (1989) has suggested that such encouragement towards self-directed learning can be achieved by decreasing the support given to the learner by using scaffolding and fading.

Scaffolding implies a temporary and adjustable support that achieves two important outcomes:

- the support will give the learners the confidence to continue with the full task; and

- the support will encourage learners to take responsibility for their own learning – that is, to inspire them to become self-directed learners.

Such scaffolding may include providing the learner with a source of information such as a website or an instruction manual that the learner can refer to when a new circumstance arises. Alternatively, rather than referring a new situation to the guide, the learner may be asked first to define the new circumstance accurately and nominate a procedure that will solve the circumstance, and then go to the guide. The guide can then check the learner's reasoning, make any adjustments necessary to the learner's proposed procedure, and then allow the learner to continue with the solution. *Fading* refers to the process of the guide gradually removing parts of the scaffolding so that the learners gradually assume full responsibility for the full task and their own learning.

At the end of the diminishing support phase, the supervisor would conduct a developmental performance appraisal and may even consider widening to interaction to include career development (see Chapter 6).

Case study example

See the PLP case study on page 5 of the workbook that accompanies this text for scaffolding and fading.

Creating knowledge

At this stage of the staff members' development, they are primed to move onto creating new knowledge – identifying new and more efficient ways of doing tasks; looking for new knowledge on workplace tasks; and determine how changes in the external environment will affect the workplace and what should be done about it.

Creating knowledge is the responsibility of the shadow system. Therefore, the topic of creating knowledge and the role of the individual in the process will be discussed further in Chapter 14.

Some concluding comments

Learning activities in which individuals engage in the workplace influence what knowledge the individual constructs because such activities are framed by the workplace's norms and values (Billett 1999). The combination of engaging in work tasks of increasing complexity and accountability, the close guidance of other workers and experts, and the more indirect ongoing guidance provided by the setting appears to be the basis for robust knowledge in the workplace (Billett 1999). Further, this process allows the dynamic combination of both theory and practice (see Tennant 1999) and the development of knowledge and skills in the 'non-routinised problem solving' arena (see Billett 1999). Accordingly, the immediate supervisor should ensure that the learner is:

- provided with opportunities to become engaged in tasks that are progressively more complex and hold more accountability based on the knowledge and skills originally developed in the learning program;

- given feedback that is both informational and motivational;

- given opportunities to observe models of expert performance; and

- encouraged to develop expertise using the process of successive approximations.

During workplace learning, the learner should be encouraged to engage in externalisation. Socialisation is also a powerful influence as the learner associates with experts and models of excellence. Provided that sufficient time is allowed for reflection, internalisation is an automatic process.

It is very important to recognise, though, that the workplace curriculum must be based solidly on the concepts discussed in the previous chapters in this book. The theories of adult learning and the four stages of HRD are fundamental to any developmental process. Whether the workplace learning is managed by a worksite supervisor, the owner of a small business, or by a community educator in a learning partnership, the techniques and methods within the stages of needs analysis, design, implementation, and evaluation are the practical tools that encourage learning and ensure that learning is effective and efficient.

Individual change

As individuals learn and change, the transition may not always be as smooth as some supervisors expect. The individual change transition model proposed by French and Delahaye (1996) provides some understanding of the stages that individuals work through as they grow and change. As individuals transition through a change experience, they progress through four phases:

- security;

- anxiety;

- discovery; and

- integration.

Security

Security is a pre-change mode where the individual is surrounded by familiar habits, processes, and patterns that have been used to accomplish past success. Self-esteem stays the same or may even rise. It is from this safe, secure position that individuals face change. The catalyst for change may come from an internal source (such as a perceived need to change a behaviour or even a frame of reference) or an external source (e.g. the threat of becoming obsolete in a career).

The energy that propels the individual away from the apparent safety of the security phase is creativity. This creativity is harnessed by self-awareness, knowledge, vision, intuition, and environmental scanning. However, the proposed adoption of new ideas into new behaviour patterns leads to the second stage.

Anxiety

Anxiety is caused by the loss of old familiar patterns and behaviours – the process of decathexis (letting go of present attachments) and recathexis (embracing new attachments). Some individuals stay for long periods on the cusp of change between the two. Feelings range from mild confusion and self-doubt to anger, panic, numbness, and immobilisation.

These negative emotions may be so strong that an individual may choose to return to the perceived safety of the security phase – i.e. returning to the present attachments. The individual will stay in this security stage until some energy – either internally or externally sourced – forces the individual down the transition path again.

The energy that propels the individual through the anxiety phase is learning. The stages of needs analysis and design are of strong assistance during this stage. Defining achievable learning objectives or outcomes and designing learning experiences that are firmly based on the principles of learning ease the learner through the anxiety phase by providing a non-threatening path that leads to the next phase.

Discovery

During the phase of *discovery*, new information, skills, and behaviours are uncovered. This is the energetic phase of the change transition because it is about the exploration of new and exciting concepts previously unknown to the individual. It is important to recognise that the discovery stage may need a considerable time investment as reflecting on the past, identifying old behaviours that caused problems, and making new discoveries is time consuming. An interesting theme of the discovery stage is that 'learning how to learn' (see self-perpetuating learning in Chapter 8) accelerates the movement through the stages of security, anxiety, and discovery.

Interestingly, some people so enjoy the discovery phase that they stay in it. The energy that propels the individual out of the discovery phase is *decision-making*. Choices facing the individual include:

- ignoring the need to change;
- modifying goals;

- modifying strategies for achieving goals; and

- adopting some or all the requirements to make the successful transition.

Integration

During the final phase, *integration,* the new information, skills, and behaviours are assimilated into the current tasks and processes. This may be a straightforward process of refining or adding skills, or may be a deeper and more emotional activity of changing frames of reference (see Chapter 3). The individual may undertake trials and will need to undertake self-evaluation through reflection. Self-evaluation is a precursor to building commitment to the new attitude and behaviour. Commitment builds a new form of reality – the old behaviours have been abandoned and the new behaviours are now the new phase of security – until the next catalyst arrives to re-commence the change transition.

This model of individual change transition provides a prototype for a workplace educator or mentor to gauge the stages of development so that scaffolding and fading can be accomplished with care and respect.

A word of caution on workplace learning

As Livingstone (2001) points out, win–win is not the only outcome in workplace learning; disparities of power are at work and workplace democracy can be partial at best. Livingstone continues that learning organisations can mask the reassertion of employer rights with new forms of oppression and control in the workplace. Such a stance, though, merely exerts the rights of the legitimate system over the shadow system with an overemphasis on negative feedback loops and single-use learning. Referring to such a process as 'a learning organisation' is merely a sham and, as discussed in the next chapter, will only lead to a toxic organisation rather than a learning organisation.

For a sustainable organisation, workplace learning must have multiple outcomes – new professional and technical knowledge for the individual, new knowledge for the individual about social relations at work, and benefits for the organisation (Livingstone 2001).

Individual adult learning

Underpinning workplace learning is the way that individual adults go about learning. Based on their own life experiences, adults have established learning patterns that suit their own particular needs and personalities. Research (see for example, Barber 2003; Billett, Hernon-Tinning & Ehrich 2003; Delahaye & Ehrich 2008) has provided some insight into the ways individual adults learn new skills and knowledge and create their tacit knowledge. While a somewhat simplified version of complexities associated with individual learning, Figure 13.4 provides a 'map' that can help supervisors identify where they can best intervene to facilitate the learning of individuals.

For the supervisor, the words 'opt out' indicate an opportunity to intervene in the learning process, ensuring that the decision of the learner – to opt out or to continue – is based on valid information (see Model II theory-in-use in Chapter 3).

Figure 13.4 Individual adult learning

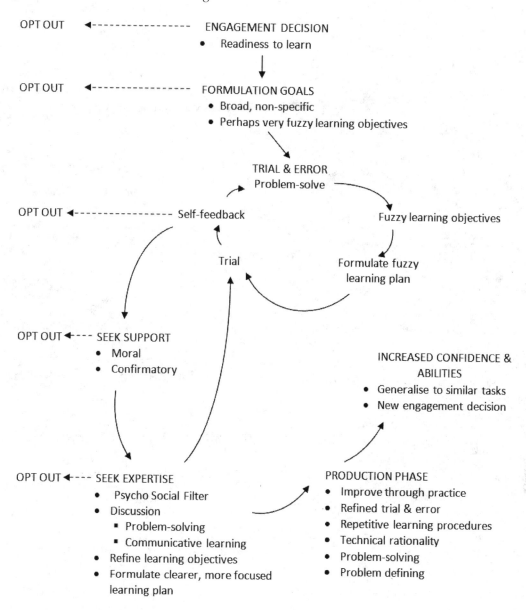

Engagement decision

Generally, a learning episode is initiated by the presentation of a problem or the realisation by an individual that they do not have the skills to start, or continue with, a task. This leads to the *engagement decision*. The decision to engage in a learning episode is largely based on one of the principles of learning, *readiness to learn* (see Chapter 3).

Billett *et al.* (2003) suggest that the individual's readiness to learn is predicated on four considerations.

First, there is a judgement on skills and knowledge that the individual already has. If the new knowledge and skills required are fairly closely aligned to current levels that the individual possesses, then the individual is more likely to progress with the learning (see *expectancy one* in the expectancy–valence motivation theory in Chapter 8).

Second, there is a judgement on the amount of technology and infrastructure support. If the computer programs currently in use, for example, do not need much alteration or if no new computer programs need to be purchased and subsequently learned, then the individual is more likely to progress with the learning.

Third, if the topic to be learned is within the individual's current interests, the individual is more likely to progress onto learning (see *utility, achievement and interest motivation* of Biggs' three levels of motivation in Chapter 8).

Fourth, if the individual's confidence is high, then the learning is more likely to progress.

Depending on the levels of motivation, the individual will either continue with or opt out of the learning. The supervisor may decide to intervene at this point.

Formulating goals

The next step in the learning process is formulating **goals** for going about the learning (Billett *et al.* 2003). These goals are based on a judgment of how far the learning has to go. For example, one individual may only wish to identify the reason for a work-based problem but decide not to progress with the acquisition of any further skills. In this case, if the problem arises again, the individual may just refer the matter to an expert to fix the problem.

Another individual may wish to have the skill and knowledge to fix the problem. Accordingly, that person will need to invest more money, time and energy in a more extended learning effort. Generally, the individual sets goals that are broad and non-specific at this stage; if learning objectives are identified, they tend to be very fuzzy.

If the supervisor decides to intervene at this point, a review of the *hierarchy of learning outcomes* in Chapter 8 will provide a way of categorising the variety of learning outcomes that can be chosen. The hierarchy will also present an understanding of the relationship between the complexity of the desired learning goal and the complexity of the learning strategy needed.

It is worth noting that the engagement decision and goal formulation is often carried out by the learner very quickly. The urge to move on to, or even begin with, the third step is often quite strong.

Case study example

See the PLP case study on page 15 of the workbook that accompanies this text for the learning process of a staff member.

Trial and error

One of the most common reactions of adult learners when faced with the challenge of learning a new skill is to jump in and 'have a go' (Delahaye & Ehrich 2008). Ge and Hardre (2010) call this the *discovery stage* where the learner explores new domain knowledge and discovers possible meanings. This hands-on approach is typified by the individual undertaking some initial approximations of the task. In undertaking these initial approximations, learners provide themselves with feedback (see the principle of learning *feedback* in Chapter 3) and, concomitantly, undertake a gap analysis (see *HRDNI defined* in Chapter 5), albeit subconsciously.

When broken down into smaller actions, the trial and error learning is often a series of iterative or cyclical steps, some taken quite consciously others more at the subconscious level. These steps are:

1. Problem solving, as the individual examines the challenge, identifies possible alternatives for action, and then settles on one.

2. A notion of a learning objective is formulated, although usually at the subconscious level – sometimes as a blurred visual image or as a vague impression of what the outcome may be.

3. A learning plan is then formulated, with resources being gathered and an idea of some steps in a possible solution. At this stage, the plan is incomplete; the first few steps in the sequence of sub-tasks may be fairly clear but the later sequence of steps quite hazy.

4. The trial is undertaken.

5. Self-feedback is given, usually accompanied with dissatisfaction, as the learner wrestles with the obscure learning objectives providing a less than edifying view of the gap between reality and the vague impression of what that reality should be.

6. Then the cycle begins again, with a clearer image of the learning objective and a more focused and purposeful learning plan.

The learner may continue with this iterative process, depending on the strength of motivation. The lower the level of motivation, the more likely the learner is to opt out – often just after the self-evaluation step. Again, the supervisor may choose to intervene at this point.

If the motivation is high, and the trial and error approach has not produced an acceptable resolution of the challenge, the learner will then go on to the next phase.

Seek support

The learner may seek some general support at this stage. The learners will look for two types of support. The first is moral support – the assurance that the learning goal is worthwhile. The second is confirmation not only that the learning goal is worthwhile, but the way they are going about learning is the most sensible approach.

Depending on the type and quality of the support, the learner may opt out of the learning or may continue. The supervisor can be an excellent source of support at this phase.

Seek expertise

Seeking expertise may coincide with seeking support; the same person can easily fulfill both roles. The individual may seek support and expertise from potentially uninformed sources – such as family members – or from people who do have the expert knowledge needed – such as co-workers, professional or technical experts (Billett *et al.* 2003). The choice of 'expert' depends on the individual's psychosocial filter – the social confidence of the learner and the perceived approachability and credibility of the 'expert' (see discussion earlier in this chapter). Interestingly, this process of seeking the knowledge of experts is encouraged by both Knowles (1998) in contract learning and Revans (1998) in action learning (see Chapter 11) so that individuals develop as self-directed learners. The learning processes used in this support and expertise step are frequently the discussion and the skill session (see Chapter 10).

As part of this interaction with the expert, the learner will refine the learning objective and formulate a clearer, more focused learning plan. Often, the expert will assist with the refinement of skills or expansion of knowledge. Accordingly, Ge and Hardre (2010) call this the *knowledge construction and integration stage* and this stage involves organising, restructuring and selecting information that is worth learning. Depending on the level of motivation, the learner will opt out or continue with the learning. The supervisor can be of great support to the learner at this stage – by being the expert, by recommending an expert, or helping the learner work through her or his frustrations (see Figure 3.3).

The learners may then return to the trial and error stage or, if feeling particularly confident in their competence, move into the production phase.

Production phase

In the production phase, learners carry out the skill or use the knowledge in the 'real' world. This real world may be their workplace or may be in an area of personal interest, such as a hobby. In this production phase, they will improve through practice as they refine and add to their explicit knowledge and develop their tacit knowledge. Ge and Hardre (2010) call this the *automation and tuning stage* as the learner becomes more proficient and efficient.

They will often use a variety of learning strategies, with a number of the approaches often being combined:

- The individual will often return to the third phase of *trial-and-error*. This would be combined with self-feedback (see the principle of learning *feedback* Chapter 3).

- Barber (2003) reported that the most frequently used learning process was *repetitive learning procedures* – the learners repeating the procedure until they become expert (see principles of *active learning* and *overlearning* in Chapter 3).

- Another learning approach used is *technical rationality* (Barber 2003). This approach depends on the technical knowledge of the individual and the willingness of the individual to indulge in reflection. The technical knowledge is based on the relevant trade and professional theories; the willingness to reflect allows the individual to use this theoretical knowledge to recognise why the problem existed in the first place and to create a plan of action to overcome the difficulty.

▪ Very much aligned with the other learning approaches is *problem solving* (Billett *et al.* 2003). When the trial in the trial-and-error failed, the learner would use a problem-solving process. This problem-solving process may vary from, 'Well, let's try this,' involving little thought, to a more disciplined method such as the scientific problem-solving model (see Chapter 3).

▪ A final learning approach is *problem defining* (Barber 2003). This is really the first step in the scientific problem-solving model (see Chapter 3), but it is interesting to see it identified as a separate learning approach. Coming, as it tends to do, near the end of the learning cycle is also interesting. In problem defining, the learners use the tacit knowledge (see Chapter 3) built up during the previous phases to take an educated guess at the cause of the problem. Barber (2003) gives the example of a car mechanic confronted with the problem of a car not starting. There can be many causes for a car not to start. Based on the limited information available, the mechanic will use a store of personal tacit knowledge to choose the most likely cause of the problem and, if this does not work, to choose the next most likely cause.

What is also very interesting about this sixth phase is that the learner will move, at various times, back to phases three, four and five – trial and error, seeking support and expertise, and then returning to the production phase.

Increased confidence and abilities

Increased confidence and abilities occur when the individual believes that the initial or revised goal has been achieved. The idea of a revised goal occurs because, as the individual progresses through the previous phases, the individual continually makes conscious and subconscious checks of the initial goal. As the iterative process of moving through each phase continues, new information is gathered and new knowledge accumulated, and the individual may alter the initial goal based on this new knowledge. At some stage, though, the learner decides that 'enough is enough' and less and less effort is invested in the particular learning episode. At this stage, Billett *et al.* (2003) found that the individual often reported a feeling of increased confidence and ability to tackle new learning challenges, thus leading to a new engagement decision.

Some final comments

The model of individual adult learning presented in Figure 13.3 is a reasonably accurate picture; it can be used as an initial indicator in how to facilitate learning of an individual in the workplace. However, one should always have great respect for individual differences and be prepared to deviate from the model when evidence suggests another approach is needed. For example, if the learner exhibits one of the avoidance behaviours of freeze, fight or flight (see Figure 3.3) then there is a distinct possibility that the learner's personal frame of reference is being challenged and that counselling could be the preferred option.

The challenge of workplace learning

There is no doubt that the workplace offers a most natural environment for learning. The andragogical assumptions of Knowles (see Chapter 3) automatically apply in the work setting because:

- the learning is relevant to real-life situations;

- incorporates the rich, work-based experiences of the learner; and

- involves the learner so that their sense of self-responsibility is engaged.

Further, the following list which, while based only on instrumental learning (see Chapter 3), provides basic evidence for the power of workplace learning (relevant principles of learning are included in brackets):

- the need for learning quickly becomes obvious (readiness to learn);

- active learning is fully utilised (active learning);

- if the learner is encouraged to move through the model in Figure 13.3, then the elements of learning are repeated (over learning);

- the learner has to watch what is being done, as well as listen (multiple-sense learning);

- the supervisor and/or the workplace expert provide continual updates on progress (feedback);

- the content to be learned is highly relevant (meaningful material); and

- the learning is immediately used in the workplace (transfer of learning).

If the supervisor ensures that the learning task is divided into small parts separated by practice, the learning principles of part learning and spaced learning are also incorporated.

There is no doubt, though, that workplace learning is the exception rather than the rule in most organisations. The need to produce, and produce efficiently, are often the most primary forces in most organisations and, accordingly, the legitimate system will deem any 'time wasting' activities as objectionable. Unfortunately, learning, training, and staff development are often viewed as time wasters.

In addition, very few supervisors are proficient in facilitating the learning of adults. As can be seen from our discussions here, facilitating adult learning needs elaborate skills supported by complex knowledge. Accruing these levels of skills and knowledge will take a long time because the spontaneous combination of skills and knowledge needs a highly developed level of tacit knowledge.

As the research by Armstrong and Mahmud (2008) found, tacit knowledge can only be created by in-depth experiential learning and extensive related experience. Workplace learning, though, is the crucible for maintaining and creating knowledge. If organisations want to remain viable, they will need to make the conscious decision to provide realistic support for workplace learning.

Finally, there are two key points about workplace learning that are worth repeating:

- supervisors are fully responsible for the learning of the staff under their control; and

- the most important factor in workplace learning is the individual adult learner.

References

Andrews, K M & Delahaye, B L 2000, 'Influences on knowledge processes in organizational learning: The psychosocial filter', *Journal of Management Studies,* 37(6), September, pp. 797-809.

Armstrong, S & Mahmud, A 2008, 'Experiential learning and the acquisition of managerial tacit knowledge', *Academy of Management Learning & Education,* 7(2), pp. 189-208.

Barber, J 2003, 'The informally trained mechanic: Skill acquisition in the workplace', *Journal of Vocational Education and Training,* 55(2), pp. 133-48.

Beckett, D 2001, 'Hot action at work: A different understanding of 'understanding'', in T Fenwick (ed.), *Sociocultural Perspectives on Learning through Work,* Jossey-Bass, San Francisco, pp. 73-84.

Billett, S 1993, 'Authenticity in workplace learning settings', *Australian and New Zealand Journal of Vocational Education Research,* 2(1), pp. 1-29.

Billett, S 1999, 'Guided learning at work', in D Boud & J Garrick (eds.), *Understanding Learning at Work,* Routledge, London.

Billett, S 2001, *Learning in the Workplace: Strategies for Effective Practice,* Crows Nest, NSW: Allen & Unwin.

Billett, S 2002, Workplace pedagogical practices: Co-participation and learning, *British Journal of Educational Studies,* 50:4, 457-481.

Billett, S, Hernon-Tinning, B & Ehrich, L 2003, 'Small business pedagogic practice', *Journal of Vocational Education and Training, 55(2),* pp. 149-67.

Browning, V & Delahaye, B L 2010, 'Enhancing workplace learning through collaborative HRD', in M Clarke (ed.), *Cases and readings in HRM and sustainability,* Tilde University Press, Melbourne, Vic.

Choy, S & Delahaye, B L 2008, 'Chapter 10: Leadership development: Implementation of an organization centred curriculum', in S Billett, C Harteis & A Etelapelto (eds.), *Emerging perspectives of learning at work,* Sense Publishing, Roterdam.

Choy, S & Delahaye, B 2010, 'Partnerships between universities and workplaces: Some challenges for work integrated learning', *Studies in Continuing Education,* 32(3).

Coetzer, A 2006, 'Managers as learning facilitators in small manufacturing firms', *Journal of Small Business and Enterprise Development,* 13(3), pp. 351-362.

Collins, A, Brown, J S & Newman, S E 1989, 'Cognitive apprenticeship: Teaching the crafts of reading, writing and mathematics', in L B Resnick (ed.), *Knowing, Learning and Instruction: Essays in Honour of Robert Glasser.* Hillsdale, New Jersey: Lawrence Eribaum and Associates.

Davidson, P & Griffin, R 2002, *Management – An Australian Perspective,* 2nd edn, Brisbane: John Wiley & Sons Australia.

Delahaye, B L & Ehrich, L C 2008, 'The complex preferences and strategies of older learners'. *Educational Gerontology*, 34(8), pp. 649-662.

French, E & Delahaye, B 1996, 'Individual change transition: Moving in circles can be good for you'. *Leadership and Organizational Development*, 17(7), 22-8.

Ge, X & Hardre, P L 2010, 'Self-processes and learning environment as influences in the development of expertise in instructional design', *Learning Environment Research*, 13, pp. 23-41.

Hager, P 2004, Conceptions of learning and understanding learning at work, *Studies in Continuing Education* 26, no. 1: 3-17.

Knowles, M S 1998, *The Adult Learner: A Neglected Species,* 5th edn, Gulf, Houston, Texas.

Livingstone, D W 2001, 'Expanding notions of work and learning: profiles of latent power', in T Fenwick (ed.), *Sociocultural Perspectives on Learning through Work,* pp. 31-40. San Francisco: Jossey-Bass.

Revans, R W 1998, *The ABC of Action LearningLemos & Craner,* London.

Schein, E H 1978, *Career Dynamics: Matching Individual and Organisational Needs,* Reading: Addison-Wesley.

Stavenga de Jong, J A, Wierstra, R F & Hermanussen, J, 2006, 'An exploration of the relationship between academic and experiential learning approaches in vocational learning', *British Journal of Educational Psychology*, 76(1), pp. 155-169.

Stone, R J 2010, *Human Resource Management*, 7th edn, John Wiley & Sons Australia, Brisbane.

Tennant, M 1999, 'Is learning transferable?', in D Boud & J Garrick (eds.), *Understanding Learning at Work,* Routledge, London.

Vygotsky, L 1978, *Mind in society: The development of high psychological processes.* Harvard University Press, Cambridge, MA.

Watson, S & Maxwell, G A 2007, 'HRD from a functionalist perspective: The views of line managers', *Advances in Developing Human Resources*, 9(1), pp. 31-41.

Winch, C 1995, 'Education needs training', *Oxford Review of Education,* 21, pp. 315-25.

Chapter 14

Creating and embedding new knowledge

LEARNING OBJECTIVES

After studying this chapter you should be able to:

1. Provide an overview of the shadow system.

2. List and describe the guiding principles of the shadow system.

3. Discuss the three roles of the shadow system.

4. Describe the extraordinary management processes.

5. Explain how new knowledge can be exported to the legitimate system.

From maintaining to creating

Thus far, we have assumed that the knowledge needed for organisations to operate successfully is available somewhere. We have also assumed that we only have to look hard enough to find the required knowledge. Such assumptions, of course, have at least two weaknesses. First, there is the belief that everything that is worth knowing is already known. Such a suggestion is nonsense, as a reading of any newspaper will show. New knowledge is being discovered and created all the time. Second, there is the assumption that the there is a finite reservoir of knowledge – all we have to do is find it and mine it. Again this assumption is untrue. As can be seen by the thousands of new inventions, new insights on political and social interactions and the occurrence of new happenstances such as the discovery of penicillin, knowledge can be created. Maintaining the current viable knowledge of the organisation is the responsibility of the legitimate system and is a vital pursuit – but not the full story.

We will now turn to the second major system predominantly responsible for creating and importing new knowledge into the organisation – the shadow system. Before proceeding, the warning raised in Chapter 1 needs to be repeated. This textbook is based on the model that, in any organism, there are two basic systems – the legitimate system and the shadow system. These two systems are not separate; they are not independent bodies. They are overlapping and dependent. The shadow system needs the legitimate system for its supply of energy to allow the shadow system to search for and to create new knowledge. The legitimate system needs the shadow system so that the organisation can face and meet the unknown and potentially fatal challenges of the future.

Indeed, we have seen this interdependency and overlap in the previous chapter when we looked at workplace learning. In many ways, workplace learning is a hybrid of the two systems – there is knowledge that is beyond dispute; this has been referred to as programmed knowledge in the hierarchy of learning outcomes in Chapters 8 and 12. Workplace learning uses programmed knowledge, but workplace learning is also about learning how to operate under conditions of uncertainty – for example, see the learning outcome called 'analysis under uncertainty' in the task category in the hierarchy of learning outcomes. Ultimately the worker needs to operate at this complex level.

For this chapter, though, we will move into what Stacey (2000) refers to as 'operating under conditions of far-from-certainty' and what Mintzberg calls 'emergent strategic planning' (Mintzberg 2009) – that is, the shadow system.

An overview of the shadow system

As Stacey (1996) points out, the problem with an omnipotent legitimate system is that it traps the organisation into an endless repetition of its past. Such omnipotence quashes creativity because negative feedback dampens any variation in behaviour, and single-loop learning continually reinforces current values and behaviour. Therefore, a key management task is one of enabling and managing the knowledge creation and deployment processes associated with innovation (Tranfield *et al.* 2006). Such innovation is dependent on the fact that the closer an organisation is pushed towards chaos, the more the organisation is likely to generate new and more complex forms of behaviour based on more robust and realistic values. Thus the only way that an organisation can avoid the trap of obsolescence is to allow the shadow system to search for the new ideas that will ensure the future viability of the organisation.

A closer look 14.1

The young guns

One common and easily managed knowledge-creating strategy for the shadow system is to bring together a group of young, first-line managers as a project team. Rather than implementing some specific project, these 'young guns' are charged with a general objective – to identify future organisational responses if some basic assumption on which the organisation operates is suddenly altered. For example, consider a manufacturing organisation that has had a competitive edge based on an exclusive agreement with a government department for the long-term supply of a particular product. The 'young guns' may be given an objective like 'Suppose the Department of Works and Machinery advised us that we would have to bid competitively for the supply of the particular product every three months; what changes would we have make to our organisation?'

The underlying objective of this strategy is twofold. First, the 'young guns' are being developed and the learning strategy (and incidentally the control strategy) is usually action learning. Second, the shadow system is given an opportunity to analyse and challenge the assumptions of the legitimate system and to ponder, analyse, and dissect a possible future scenario. The 'young guns' will be operating on two levels – their own development and identifying new knowledge for the organisation.

When operating on these two levels, they will be conducting several needs investigations (as the objective is multi-faceted) at once. As they investigate, they will be learning new information. At the same time they will have to consider how the organisation will be changed to accept the new scenario. While doing this they will have to evaluate each new idea and proposed strategy for change. As they could be operating on several new possibilities, some of which will need to be integrated and some of which will be 'standalone', each possibility could be at a different stage of investigation, design, implementation, and evaluation. To complicate the issue for them further, they will be operating at two levels (personal and organisational development) and in two different directions (the assumptions of the legitimate system that need to be challenged and the future external environment of the organisation).

Before they start, the 'young guns' will need to be competent at the various practices and have a thorough understanding of the principles of the stages of:

- investigation;
- design;
- implementation; and
- evaluation.

The essence of the shadow system is embodied in a conversation the author had with the CEO of a government department. I was making the point that, in the 1960s when NASA was initially charged with the responsibility of landing a human on the moon, there was no inkling of products like Teflon that would be discovered during the quest. The CEO said that the issue was much deeper than that. It was not simply that new products were discovered, but that these unforeseen products solved unforeseen problems that had arisen between the 1960s and the 1980s. This then is the role of the shadow system – not just to identify new products or new values for the organisation, but to arm the organisation with sufficient options that will help combat any unforeseen problems, or allow the organisation to take advantage of any new opportunities that may arise in the future.

Of course, based on the Newtonian paradigm of thinking, it is tempting to view the legitimate system and the shadow system merely as two separate sections of the organisation. Again, this perception is too simple. Indeed, sometimes staff do work separately in the shadow system, as suggested by 'A closer look 14.1' (see following). In this example, there are a group of 'young guns' who are working 100 percent of their time on a developmental project. The segment 'A closer look 14.2' provides some more techniques that have been used to operate in the shadow system. These examples described in 'A closer look 14.1' and the 'A closer look 14.2' segments are often raised when the discussion turns to the shadow system, most probably because they provide a readily identifiable picture of what is possible.

The examples in 'A closer look 14.1' and 'A closer look 14.2', though, are really special cases, albeit more visible. More commonly, staff move in and out of the shadow system several times a day. As Andrews (1999) comments, the generation of knowledge in an organisation is more about the everyday actions of many than the plans of a few. For example, the manager of the registry and records branch of an organisation may be driving to work one morning listening to the radio. The DJ on the radio makes some comment that triggers an idea in the mind of the manager. Thinking on this idea, the manager sees an improved way of managing the records of the organisation. Once at work, over a period of several months, the manager works steadily towards introducing the change. The manager does not spend this time working solely on the new idea. Rather, he invests a few minutes one day, an hour the next, and ten minutes the next. The majority of the manager's time is still spent in the legitimate system. However, the times the manager is thinking on the new idea, and working to introduce it, represents the time the manager is spending in the shadow system.

A closer look 14.2

Some techniques for the shadow system

Some typical examples of ventures that managers can use in the shadow system include:

- projects;
- matrix teams; and

- the meeting place.

Projects

Similar to the 'young guns' example, projects are often the venture of choice by managers – most probably because the investment can be justified to the legitimate system. There are a number of variations but typically each project has three objectives:

- there must be an improvement to a product or service;

- there must be a financial return on the project; and

- the project must be a learning experience for the staff involved.

Matrix teams

Matrix teams work well where the organisation is divided into product or service departments. For example, an organisation servicing rural industries may be divided into Intensive Crops, Organic Crops, Animal Husbandry and Native Fauna. These four departments represent one arm of the matrix. Members from each department are then asked to form teams – with each team having at least one representative from each department. These teams are often given creative names – for example, the Constructing Larger Emus team and the Environmentally Friendly Crops and Animals team – to emphasise the alternative thinking that is needed. The objectives of the teams are to:

- identify knowledge from the other departments that may be useful in the team member's department; and

- identify new products or services or different future organisational values and culture from combining the knowledge from each department.

The meeting place

Staff tend to meet naturally in places around the organisation. This may be at the store room while they are waiting for equipment and materials, at the records department while waiting for a file, or even outside the elevators. The legitimate system would regard these waiting periods as a waste of time. For the shadow system, however, these interludes are fertile periods where knowledge can be exchanged. For the shadow system, these sites are worthy of development so that the staff can exchange ideas and knowledge. The development may be simply the provision of some comfortable chairs or even a coffee station.

This view of staff moving in and out of the shadow system several times a day most probably represents the majority of the activity in the shadow system. If we use the metaphor of large and small business, it is reported that at least 60 percent and perhaps up to 90 percent of business in Australia and in New Zealand is conducted within the small business stream. Similarly, it is likely that at least 60 percent of the activity in the shadow system is conducted by the staff's frequent daily visits. The more overt examples given in 'A closer look 14.1' and 'A closer look 14.2' most probably represent only 30 percent to 40 percent of the activities in the shadow system. For the CEO, managing the special projects in the shadow system is relatively straightforward. However, supporting the frequent visits of staff to the shadow system requires discrimination and subtlety; discrimination (in that the intention of some staff may not be the welfare of the organisation) and subtlety (in that heavy handed support of the well intentioned can in fact kill off the creative endeavour).

As an overview, then, the organisation needs to develop its absorptive capacity – the ability to identify, assimilate and exploit knowledge from the environment (Schmidt 2010). The responsibility of the shadow system in increasing the organisation's absorptive capacity can best be described by the D-R-N model (Tranfield *et al.* 2006):

- a *discovery phase* which emphasises the need to scan and search both the internal and external environments;

- a *realisation phase* which examines how the organisation can successfully implement the innovation, growing it from an idea through various stages of development to final launch; and

- the *nurturing phase*, where the organisation involves maintaining and supporting the innovation through various improvements and learning how to manage the process better.

The shadow system follows the D-R-N phases by conforming to its guiding principles, undertaking three basic roles and by using extraordinary management.

The guiding principles of the shadow system

The shadow system is predicated on the search for *creativity*. Negative feedback loops kill off creativity, so the shadow system uses positive feedback loops and double-loop learning:

- *positive feedback loops* enhance different behaviour – in many ways it is like spreading fertilizer to encourage growth; and

- *double loop learning* encourages the questioning of underlying values.

The combined application of positive feedback loops and double-loop learning provide a very fertile ground for encouraging the growth of creativity.

Accordingly, the shadow system focuses on the individual and relationships. *Individuals* should be allowed to develop and create their own paths for work, and are left to their own devices – they thrive best on working things out for themselves (Huq, Raja & Rosenberg 2006). Further, extraordinary management emphasises *relationships*. As Read (2004) contends, the rational world of systems, processes and procedures can only be effective if built on a strong foundation of relationship capabilities. Indeed, the 'non-rational world' of feelings, emotions, values and beliefs are the heart of creating and sustaining workplaces where people flourish and business results are achieved.

It is important to recognise, though, that we are not referring the individual and relationships as separate entities. The shadow system is about *individuals in relationships*.

A focus solely on the individual would suggest that there is a state of anarchy in which everyone does whatever they please (Stacey 2000). However, when an individual operates within relationships, the others in the relationship exert a certain level of constraint. A further constraint is that the supervisor or manager has a greater capacity to instruct, persuade and influence, simply because of their positional power in the organisation.

So, as a contrast to the legitimate system where the negative feedback loops provide a direct control mechanism (ordinary management), the shadow system establishes boundaries of constraints beyond which the actors in the shadow system do not venture. This is a more indirect form of restraint and is referred to as *extraordinary management*. Extraordinary management, then, sees the energy of individuals within relationships as a power to be harnessed over and above the ordinary management approach of using position power to energise, coerce, and direct. In extraordinary management, the supervisor encourages double-loop learning as the catalyst for creativity and positive feedback loops to maintain the momentum of the creativity. If a certain type of creativity is not wanted, the momentum of that creativity is starved by denying it nutrition – that is, by withholding positive feedback loops.

The three roles of the shadow system

Extraordinary management is obviously a very subtle and very complex form of management. To understand the supervisors' role in extraordinary management, we will first examine the three roles of the shadow system.

The first role

The primary responsibility for the shadow system is to identify new knowledge for the organisation. This is the discovery stage of the D-R-N model; it uses three generic routines:

- search;
- capture; and
- articulate (Tranfield *et al*. 20006).

There are two basic sources for this new organisational knowledge. One option is to import the new knowledge from another system (e.g. from another organisation or from some new research finding by a university or professional body). In this case the knowledge may not be new to the world at large but is 'new' to the organisation. The second source of new knowledge for the organisation is to create the new knowledge.

While the literature in the area of managing the shadow system is in its infancy, there is considerable agreement that the shadow system cannot be managed by the mechanistic processes of ordinary management. Rather, the shadow system is managed by establishing a value system that *reveres and celebrates learning* – a key element of extraordinary management. Individual staff members need to know that they will be encouraged to create new knowledge and pursue such opportunities. The supervisory and management team need to know that they have to encourage such pursuits so the 'many' visit the shadow system for short periods every day.

An organisational culture that reveres and honours learning will exhibit three characteristics.

- It will accept failure as a natural process in learning. The actors in the shadow system need to know that failure is not a dire consequence but an opportunity to examine information as a feedback process and to reflect on different options. As Scott and Harker (2004) comment, where blame is not present, organisational learning is facilitated.

- It will promote a climate of trust and openness. Fiol (2003) and Roberts (2006) believe that, without trust in social relations, knowledge is withheld rather than disseminated and protected rather than enlarged upon.

- It will embrace positive feedback. Using positive feedback has an amplifying effect that amplifies small changes (Stacey 1996). For the legitimate system with its high needs for control, the idea of positive feedback generates high levels of anxiety. Indeed, there is some basis for this fear. Continuous positive feedback may push the organisation into anarchy. Without positive feedback however, creativity is lost; and creativity is the name of the game in the shadow system.

By exhibiting these characteristics, the shadow system is more likely either to import or create new knowledge.

The second role

As well as creating new knowledge, the shadow system is continually challenging the fundamental values of the legitimate system. These fundamental values are important because they allow the legitimate system to make decisions efficiently and, often, automatically.

However, these fundamental values of the legitimate system are only effective in the present time. There is no guarantee that they will continue to serve the organisation successfully in the future. The role of the shadow system, therefore, is to test and challenge these fundamental values continually. The theoretical basis of this challenging process is achieved by:

- using the Theory-in-use Model II (Argyris 2004) where any interaction is based on valid information, the participants have free and informed choice, and the participants keep testing the validity of the choices – especially as the choices are being implemented; and

- accepting that the shadow system is the realm of double-loop learning (Argyris 1992). The actors in the shadow system must always question the underlying values of current decisions, activities, and even the culture of the legitimate system.

The third role

The third role of the shadow system is to store potentially useful knowledge and information. This potentially useful knowledge consists of three types:

- basic information and raw data;

- unrelated knowledge; and

- knowledge of how to learn.

A reservoir of *basic information and raw data,* such as customer profiles and demographics, details on future technology, data on non-customers, and overseas trends should be readily available for analysis. Such information usually needs some considerable lead time to gather; having it readily available considerably cuts the time needed for analysis and creating solutions. This means that the organisation needs to invest in knowledge systems such as capture processes to ensnare information, data bases to store the information, and decision tools to analyse the information – systems Earl (1997) calls 'knowledge configurations'. The nature of this of basic information and data goes beyond what the legitimate system would consider necessary. This is another of the tensions between the two systems: the legitimate system sees the cost of gathering and storing such information as inefficient, whereas the shadow system sees such a reservoir as a priceless gold mine.

A cornucopia of *unrelated knowledge,* usually kept in the minds of the staff, may come from experience in previous jobs or organisations, from hobbies or other interests outside of the work situation, or even from past failures. A valuable source of such potential knowledge comes from the diversity of the staff – the more diverse, the more the potential for rich knowledge (see Chapter 4). Such a cornucopia of knowledge becomes an invaluable asset when the organisation is facing an unanticipated problem.

The most valuable asset in knowledge management may be *knowledge of how to learn.* As Bessant (2006) points out, the strength of continuous improvement as a learning capability is that it embeds a high frequency learning cycle across much of the organisation. This process of knowing how to learn has been discussed in Chapter 8 under the meta-abilities of mental agility, helicopter perception, and self-perpetuating learning. These meta-abilities present the organisation with an energy that will allow the organisation to survive the most catastrophic surprise.

Extraordinary management processes

Based on the discussion so far, we might expect the process of implementing extraordinary management to:

- be subtle and complex;

- be based on individuals in relationships; and

- use positive feedback loops and double-loop learning.

This is in contrast to the direct and mechanistic processes used in the legitimate system with ordinary management.

Extraordinary management, then, focuses on:

- identifying and encouraging self-organising groups;

- tapping into communities of practice;

- developing internal and external networks; and

- accessing learning partnerships.

While the following will discuss each of these elements in turn, it is important to recognise that they are highly interactive and interdependent.

Self-organising groups

Self-organising groups (SOGs) are the heart of the shadow system. However, SOGs are dissipative structures. The term 'dissipative structure' comes from the concept of synergetics in systems theory. Dissipative structures form during states of instability in the organisation; they generate new forms through a process of spontaneous self-organisation (Stacey 2000). A dissipative structure, though, requires some considerable effort to retain its structure and relatively little to change it. When challenged by the legitimate system (which requires no effort to retain its structure and a lot to change it) a dissipative structure is very vulnerable.

This self-organising capability does not rely on pre-ordained planning; neither does it respond to overt controls. There are often no centralised causes for these coherent collective actions. SOGs occur because of the inherent desire of individuals to come together and form relationships, particularly in times of tension. The interactions in these relationships closely mirror the knowledge-generation processes of combination, internalisation, externalisation, and socialisation (see Chapter 3), thus forming fertile grounds for creativity. The realisation that creative activity is linked to the self-organising process within social groups has now been incorporated into structures of many businesses and associations, including such giants as Microsoft and IBM (Davis and Sumara 2001). Interestingly, such self-organisation is more likely to occur in small businesses where the close ties and social contacts between staff present fertile grounds for SOGs.

A SOG occurs when two or more people come together over some mutual interest. In organisations, the most readily recognised SOGs are the 'whinge-and-bitch' groups. Managers need to recognise that 'whinge-and-bitch' groups are engaged in double-loop learning and are a rich source of energy. This energy is neither good nor bad. What differentiates a successful outcome from a calamity is how well the supervisor manages the energy of the group.

Of course not all SOGs in organisations are 'whinge-and-bitch' groups. Many, perhaps even the majority, are initiated by two or more members coming together over an exciting idea. Often this idea, because the members have only the organisation in common, is aimed at improving some aspect of the organisation. Frequently, an individual moves into a SOG when she or he is at the seeking-support and/or seeking-expertise stage of the individual adult learning model (see Figure 13.4).

As indicated earlier, the problem with SOGs is that they are 'dissipative structures' (Stacey 2000) – structures that are a new life form but are very vulnerable. The number of new ideas that founder on the reefs of lack of interest by upper management or are wrecked by the active displeasure of power centres in the legitimate system must be legion.

To ensure that the new ideas are eventually harvested, the organisation must ensure that SOGs are supported. The challenge for management, therefore, is to encourage SOGs to survive by providing energy – that is, by providing positive feedback loops. This energy can be in the form of money or time. Other forms of energy can be just as powerful – for example, the attention of upper management.

The creative learning processes of a SOG may be supported in a variety of ways:

- The provision of sufficient resources, such a time, money and the active interest of upper management.

- Ensuring that SOGs have ready access to knowledge systems, such as data banks and analytic tools, so they can quickly address problems and opportunities before the excitement of a new thought is swamped by everyday work demands.

- Ensuring that there is variety in the membership of the SOG. This variety may be based on knowledge of differing professions and trades. For example, a mix of marketers, fitters and turners, and administration staff would allow a wide investigation into client complaints. The variety in membership can also be based on the expertise of the members. Experts step back from their first overly simplistic interpretations of a problem or situation and question their own relevant knowledge (Ge & Hardre 2010). On the other hand, experienced workers can also learn through engagement with novices, as novices often bring with them a range of skills and knowledge that have been accumulated from elsewhere (Fuller *et al.* 2005). Finally, mature learners who can apply all the techniques of the four stages of HRD – needs investigation, design of learning experiences (usually their own), implementing these learning experiences and evaluating the outcomes – bring an overarching learning process to the SOG.

- The interactions within the SOG will be based on group dynamics. These processes need to be managed (see group dynamics in Chapter 8). Further, the SOG is likely to move through the *stages of group growth*. These stages (Tuckman 1965, Tuckman & Jensen 1977, Maples 1988) are:

  - *Forming* – where several individuals come together with such questions in mind as 'What is the purpose of this group?', 'How will I be treated?', 'What can I contribute?', 'Who is in charge?'

  - *Storming* – the stage where the group culture governing behaviour and values is gradually formed. This stage is marked by conflict in a variety of forms. Individuals try to impose their own values, agendas, and acceptable forms of behaviour on the group. There are usually power plays over leadership and authority roles and games are played (see transactional analysis in Chapter 10). Experiencing conflict is an essential part of group development. If issues of power, acceptable behaviour, and authority are not resolved at this stage, then the issues will come back to haunt the group at a later stage and will cause barriers to achieving the aims and goals of the group.

  - *Norming* – where the group becomes more cohesive. There is a sense of harmony and even euphoria. Members will want to protect the group from disintegration and any perceived threatening opinion or viewpoints form group members will be discouraged. The norming stage is a double-edged sword. On the one hand, the group gains a lot of energy and efficiencies from the cohesiveness. On the other hand, the group can easily become unaware of dangers to decision-making. In particular, the influence of 'group think' (Janis 1972) can cause the group to ignore evidence and sound advice because of the euphoric feeling that the group can never be wrong.

-   *Performing* – in this stage the group is fully functional and concentrates on the tasks to be achieved. The group is organised and can deal with complex challenges without descending into conflict. Efforts still need to be made to keep the group together and, therefore, the maintenance tasks (see Chapter 7) of the group are still important.

-   *Adjourning* – a temporary group like a SOG will disband at some point. This is called the adjourning stage. In the adjourning stage, the group needs to wrap up any outstanding tasks. The reactions of members often differ. Some find the end of the group a relief, eagerly anticipating returning to their usual work responsibilities, while others may still be experiencing the euphoria of being part of a group and excited with its accomplishments. Therefore, some form of recognition of the demise of the group should be undertaken.

It should be noted that the SOG will need time to progress through these stages and the supervisor must be willing to invest this time resource in the group.

Facilitating the knowledge development process in SOGs

For the development of more complex new knowledge, the organisation may need to appoint a facilitator (for example, the immediate supervisor or an in-house or external HR developer) to manage the group processes within the SOG. Many SOGs become so involved in the content of the problem or challenge they are investigating that they are unaware that certain process issues are inhibiting the efficient or effective achievement of successful outcomes (see Chapter 11, particularly the section on change interventions).

At the most obvious level, the process management may be based on one of the problem-solving models, such as scientific problem solving or system beta (see Chapter 3), or one of the unstructured learning strategies, such as contract learning or action learning (see Chapter 11). At a deeper level, the facilitator should ensure that each individual actor in the SOG moves through the knowledge generation steps of combination-internalisation-socialisation-externalisation.

At the deepest level of process management, a common overarching process management process for SOGs is based on Cavaliere's five-stage model (1992). Cavaliere based her model on the processes used by the Wright brothers as they developed the first successful flight in an aeroplane, back in the early 1900s.

Within each of these stages, there are four repetitive cognitive processes – goal setting, focusing, persevering and reformulation.

The five stages are:

1. *Inquiring,* where the members or actors in the SOG see a need to solve a particular problem.

2. *Modelling,* where the actors in the SOG cast around and observe similar phenomena (e.g. watching birds fly before designing an aeroplane). Similarities and differences are noted and a prototype model or solution is proposed. The observations of a similar phenomenon are used to build individual actors' tacit knowledge; then metaphors, analogies and models are gradually made conscious (that is, externalisation). A number of these will be discarded until a viable model is identified.

3. *Experimenting and practising,* where the actors build a model or representation of the solution and tests it against various standards of reality. This may mean trying out the prototype (e.g. testing a model of the aeroplane) or having the solution critiqued by experts. For the actors in the SOG, the proposed solution may be previewed by certain trusted members of the legitimate system.

4. *Theorising and perfecting,* where the model or solution is continually refined from a stage where it solves the problem in a barely acceptable manner to a stage where the model or solution gains high acceptance from the potential clients. The actors in the SOG will continually ask the question 'What possible objections could be made to this solution?' or the actor could use a decision-making model such as force field analysis (see Chapter 10).

5. *Actualising,* where the individuals (who have been both learners and actors in the SOG) receive recognition for the product of their creative efforts.

Thus, when working with the actors in the SOG, the facilitator is operating at three levels. At the first level, the facilitator is using the unstructured learning strategies – such as system beta or contract learning – to help the actors in the SOG explore the content of the problem or challenge.

At the second level, the facilitator is ensuring that each actor is moving through the knowledge-generation processes of combination-internalisation-socialisation-externalisation.

At a deeper third level, the facilitator can use the five-stage model of adult learning to help the actors understand the various stages of the knowledge development process that must be navigated. For example, most learners become quite excited when they identify what they see as a viable model or solution. The facilitator can used the five-stage model to point out that the job is only half done – the proposed model or solution needs further experimentation, justification by theorising, and perfecting. Similarly, during each of the five stages, the actors can become frustrated and even discouraged. The HR developer needs to point out that this is a natural cognitive process in the learning cycle and ensure that, at each stage, the actors move through the four repetitive cognitive processes of goal setting, focusing, persevering and reformulation.

At some point, either before or after the fifth stage – actualising – at least one of four outcomes will occur:

1. The SOG, being a dissipative system, dies before achieving much of note. Perhaps the idea did not live up to its original potential, or the SOG ran out of energy, or the legitimate system (for good or dubious reasons) terminated the SOG.

2. The original idea is expanded into a viable concept, but the concept is not yet useful to the organisation. In this case, the new knowledge will be stored in some knowledge configuration such as a data base (Earl, 1997).

3. The original idea becomes a viable product, knowledge base, or alternative for the organisation and can now be exported to the legitimate system. This option will be explored later in this chapter in the discussion of 'Bounded instability'.

4. The SOG evolves into a community of practice. This evolution is not dependent on whether the original intention of the SOG is successful or not, and may occur after outcomes 2 and 3 above. We will examine this outcome first.

Communities of practice

A community of practice (CoP) often develops out of a SOG, comprising of people who carry out similar tasks and who come together to discuss and investigate areas of mutual interest. CoPs are informally bound social collectives of experts either existing within or independent of organisational boundaries (Iverson & McPhee, 2002). So, as a SOG evolves into a community of practice, it may reside either within or outside the boundaries of the organisation. A number of existing professional bodies, for example the Australian Human Resources Institute and the Australian and New Zealand Academy of Management, are now very well respected *external CoPs* providing an invaluable service in the creation and proselytisation of knowledge, as well as being the stewards for the standards of behaviour for the profession.

Since being identified as a mechanism through which knowledge is held, transferred, and created, the idea of *internal CoPs* has become increasingly influential within management literature and practice (Roberts, 2006). This is understandable as, from a knowledge management perspective, the social connections and relationships within CoPs encourage greater knowledge sharing. In turn, this supports and promotes innovation (Lesser & Stock 2001).

Another advantage of internal CoPs is that they develop social capital as well as specialist content knowledge. Social capital is essential for the survival of any organisation, as it develops social factors (for example, social relationships, trust, and personal connections) which enable frequent interaction and communication between members to enhance the community aspect (Chua 2006). Accordingly, internal CoPs highlight the socially constructed nature of knowledge creation, transfer, and management systems within these communities (Mudambi & Swift 2009). Finally, internal CoPs can become one of the important reservoirs of content knowledge and knowledge of how to learn for the organisation.

Internal CoPs will need some of the same support mechanisms that are afforded to SOGs. Internal CoPs are, at least in the initial stages of their life cycle, dissipative systems. So, if an organisation believes that certain internal CoPs should continue, the organisation will need to provide positive feedback loops and encourage the CoPs to use double-loop learning.

Internal CoPs, though, are not always the benevolent and beneficial entities that some academic writers believe. Firstly, being organisms, they are subject to complexity theory. Therefore, while a CoP may commence as predominantly influenced by its relatively larger shadow system, the legitimate system of the CoP invariably develops. In other words, the CoP relies more and more on its own legitimate system to ensure the efficiency that is needed for the organism (the CoP) to survive. The rise of the legitimate system within the CoP means that negative feedback loops, single-loop learning and organisational defence mechanisms become more influential. At this stage, there is the ever present danger that the creativity of the CoP, the very reason for its existence, may be crushed or severely limited. As Ogilvie (2007) points out, CoPs have been known to restrict innovation by opposing the introduction of new techniques.

In addition, power dynamics arise in CoPs, becoming an issue for the organisation. Members who have full participation in the CoP will have a greater role and are therefore likely to wield more power in the negotiation of meaning (Roberts 2006). This politicised meaning of a concept, piece of knowledge, or value need not necessarily reflect the meaning preferred by the community in the organisation. This contest over meaning can lead to conflict within the CoP as well as the entire organisation.

However, there is no doubt that internal CoPs can become a wonderfully rich resource of knowledge. As Huq *et al.* (2006) found, research endorses the critical importance of a supportive climate through the development of a working environment that on a cognitive level supports and advocates the creation of these communities.

Networks

The power of networks can be seen in the powerful bonds of the *six degrees of separation* (Paulos 2001) – the assumption that everybody in the world is connected within six links of relationships. It can be shown that any person can be linked to any other person in the world within six steps. This has powerful consequences for the shadow system in locating new information and in communicating new information to the legitimate system in the organisation. In searching for new information, the actors in the shadow system must move beyond the first contact to discover the other contacts in the link of the six degrees of separation. In communicating the new information, the shadow system must recognise and encourage the ongoing effects of the six degrees of separation by harnessing the power of networking. As indicated by Tranfield *et al.* (2006), the discovery stage of the D-R-N model emphasises the need to scan and search both the internal and external networks of the organisation. One of the most effective and rewarding options comes from the extensive social networks of staff (Earl 1997).

External networks increase the potential for identifying knowledge that is new to the organisation or provide the catalyst for the creation of new knowledge. Two types of external networks are needed. Networks based on *weak ties* (sometimes referred to as loose links) occur when staff members come into contact with people they do not usually associate with (Regans & McEvily 2003). It has been shown that such weak ties are a dynamic catalyst for creating new knowledge (Granovetter 1973) – the impetus for most new knowledge comes not from familiar networks but from unusual sources.

A significant new insight into customer needs may come not from current customers but from that part of the population which has nothing to do with the organisation. For example, the CEO of a medical research company which depended on a continual production of patented medical drugs had a policy of sending his research scientists to at least one conference each year that had nothing to do with their area of expertise. A favourite ploy of the CEO was to send the scientists to a theological conference. In this way, the scientists were exposed to thinking that was completely different to their normal area of expertise.

The second type of external network should be based on *strong ties* (sometimes called tight links). Strong ties are signified by *relationship strength* (time spent developing the relationship, emotional intensity, mutual confiding, and degree of reciprocity) and *network density* (the extent to which network nodes are directly connected to each other) (Regans & Zuckerman 2001). This type of external network is most suitable for non-codified tacit knowledge – knowledge that is held by experts, is complex, and multifaceted. Such non-codified tacit knowledge is best exchanged by experts using thick communication channels (Sherwood & Covin 2008), such as when engaged in communicative learning (see Chapter 3). Such strong ties are more likely to occur through CoPs, professional conferences, and the social networks of the individual.

Internal networks perform three important roles for the shadow system. Firstly, internal networks can be useful in a similar manner to external networks – internal networks with weak ties can be a catalyst for a search for new knowledge; internal networks with strong ties can also be a source of thick communication to exchange non-codified tacit knowledge. Secondly, SOGs are often conceived during discussions in internal networks, whether they have weak or strong ties. Supervisors would do well to encourage such relationships based on internal networks. Thirdly, internal networks are also needed so that the new knowledge (either that imported through external networks or created by SOGs) can be exported to the legitimate system. This third role of internal networks, the exportation process, will be discussed later in this chapter under the discussion of 'Bounded instability'.

Case study example

See the PLP case study on page 5 of the workbook that accompanies this text for an example of building internal networks.

Learning partnerships

A special type of networking occurs when the organisation enters into learning partnerships. Learning partnerships are a relatively new phenomenon. Some 15 years ago, most organisations saw learning institutions such as universities and TAFEs as pools of potential employees. The development and education of their staff was seen as the responsibility of someone else, usually defined as 'the government'. However, especially in the last decade, organisations have become less satisfied with the mere transmission of information by learning institutions; rather there has developed a desire to ensure that the newly acquired knowledge is converted into significant organisational outcomes, as efficiently and effectively as possible (Delahaye & Choy 2008).

There are three types of learning partnerships. The first, *joint ventures,* creates a jointly owned organisation to achieve the goals of an alliance between at least two commercial/government organisations. The goal of these joint ventures is to create new knowledge in the form of products or processes that can be turned to a profitable outcome like broadening product lines or accessing new markets (Deeds 2003). In developing these new products or processes, new knowledge that the organisations in partnership can use is identified.

The second, *apprenticeship learning partnerships,* has its genesis in the changes that occurred in the vocational education and training (VET) area in the early 1990s. Under the new apprenticeship policies of the governments of Australia and New Zealand, the role of training apprenticeships was widened from the government-controlled TAFE colleges. This saw the rise of Registered Training Organisations (RTOs) in Australia and the Industry Training Organisations (ITOs) in New Zealand, with the aim of allowing a much wider choice of preferred educational entities. The new policy also expanded the concept of vocational education to include the addition of 'traineeships' to the existing apprenticeships. Further, there was an agreed 'common qualifications scheme' based on certificates and diplomas in VET that provided a nationally recognised set of qualifications.

The New Apprenticeship Scheme heralded the beginning of specifically intentional learning partnerships. Under the New Apprenticeship Scheme, the apprenticeship agreement is a three-way contract between the apprentice or trainee, the employing organisation, and the RTO/ITO. So the RTO/ITO became an active partner in the learning process – a partnership that was intended to benefit the learner, the organisation, and the RTO/ITO. The next significant step was the translocation of the New Apprenticeship Scheme into secondary schools. Students in their final years of high school were allowed to commence an apprenticeship. This change saw the students spend a couple of days at school, a day with a RTO/ITO, and a couple of days at paid work in an organisation.

So an additional type of apprenticeship learning partnership in which many organisations find themselves involved is with the local high school and a RTO/ITO. Such a partnership is far from an 'arm's length' affair. The organisation has a number of legal, ethical, and managerial issues to contend with. Their role in these learning partnerships places new demands on their HRM and HRD systems. Organisations now need to be very aware of their local environment. In particular, their recruitment and selection processes need to begin much earlier, focusing on potential employees in the high school system. Organisations also need to consider the employment contracts and ensure that, for apprentices and trainees, a learning contract (see contract learning in Chapter 11) is in place as part of an employment contract. This learning contract then becomes part of the HRD system in the organisation. In this manner, the organisation becomes a vital and involved part of the learning of the apprentice. Further, the organisation will find that the learning process of the new apprentice or trainee will, through workplace learning, engender new learning experiences and generate new knowledge creation opportunities for the organisation – see the comments on external networks above.

The third, *strategic learning partnerships*, occurs between an organisation and a tertiary educational institution such as a university. These partnerships exist in one or some combination of the four categories.

The first category focuses on *research*. By combining the strengths of each partner – the research capabilities and tacit knowledge of academic staff in the university with the practical applications and marketing capabilities of the organisation – the strategic learning partnership produces increased knowledge and a product or service, both of which have commercial value. So this type of learning partnership may be similar to a joint venture.

The second category in a strategic learning partnership focuses on *work integrated learning* (WIL) or work experience learning (WEL). Students from the university or college work in the organisation under close supervision. This allows the student to apply the theory learned at the university or college (a process called praxis) and to gain experience in working in an organisation. This work-experience learning is sometimes called a 'practicum'. The focus of WIL is on the development of the student, with the organisation providing an altruistic service for the benefit of the industry or profession – although some organisations use WIL as part of a selection process.

The third category within a strategic learning partnership is *customised work integrated learning* (CWIL). The focus of CWIL is also on the development of the student. The CWIL program, however, is an advance on the traditional university-centred approach in that the content of the official units are revised and amended so that there is a better alignment of the learning curriculum with real work tasks in the organisation or industry (Symes & McIntyre 2000).

The fourth category of strategic learning partnerships is called *work capacity integrated learning* (WCIL). WCIL differs from the other categories on three fronts. Firstly, the focus is on the learning of both the student and the organisation. Secondly, WCIL uses learning cohorts. Thirdly, the WCIL approach uses the authentic learning environment of the workplace which, according to Billett (2007), provides learning experiences that are not teachable in other environments. The process of using learning cohorts would include the following components:

- The two parties – the organisation and the university/college – must move away from the vendor model. The vendor model assumes that a product is provided for a set fee (Wright 2008), reinforcing the notion that the university must produce exact solutions to the problems identified (Choy & Delahaye 2009). Such values are detrimental to the effectiveness of learning cohorts.

- The two parties need to engage in a consultative knowledge relationship where the university is seen to be supplying multiple solutions, or where the university approaches the problem in a way that reveals that the corporation wasn't looking for the right solution in the first place. In examining a number of successful partnerships with universities, Wright (2008) identified three major factors in successful consultative knowledge relationships:

- the interaction became a lasting partnership that built new capabilities for the company;

- senior management was highly involved; and

- the organisations involved the universities in their strategy rather than merely in a technical task or isolated problem.

- The curriculum design for the learning cohort must be based on andragogical principles (Choy & Delahaye 2008) – see Chapter 3.

- There must be an on-going and open dialogue between the senior management of the organisation and the academics. This dialog will rely on at least three sub-issues (Choy & Delahaye 2009). First, there needs to be a thorough and communal understanding of the strategic plan and direction of the organisation. Of importance will be an acceptance of Mintzberg's (2009) notion of intended and emergent strategies – and the complexities and flexibilities surrounding such discussions. Second, the need for the organisation to plan and establish workplace affordances (see Chapter 13) – the physical spaces, resources, and time needed by the learners. Third, the need to decide how the WCIL project will become part of the performance appraisal process, so that the changes can be identified and categorised.

- The potential worker–learners are incorporated in the discussions as soon as the strategic and macro decisions have been made by the senior management and the academic facilitators (Delahaye & Choy 2008).

- A critical part of the sustainable learning partnership is the emphasis on the academics and worker–learners functioning together and using learning as a way to help organisations achieve strategic changes (Sims 2006). This collaboration may entail on-going changes to both the curriculum content and learning strategies where the worker–learners add to the agreed curriculum design while the facilitators guide them.

A recent development in strategic learning partnerships is a combination of the first category (research) and the fourth category (WCIL), where the strategic direction of the organisation demands that staff have a research orientation and research skills.

Delahaye, Choy and Saggers (2010) have reported on a process to develop a learning cohort in research, knowledge, and skills for an organisation. They suggest that the following parameters are important:

- The psychological contract of the expectations of all parties (the cohort member, the host organisation, and the university) must be fully explored prior to and in the early stages of the life of the learning cohort.

- An initial residential workshop must be held just prior to the beginning of the research program. This workshop provides some basic technical skills and knowledge, establishes the learning cohort as a supportive entity, and develops group relationships.

- The use of traditional course work subjects to provide research knowledge and skills. The knowledge and skills are at the programmed knowledge and the upper levels of the task and relationship categories, so are quite suited to structured learning strategies (see the hierarchy of learning outcomes in Chapter 8).

- The provision of follow-up workshops to allow the members of the learning cohort to interact, to develop their intra-dependencies further, to encourage the learning cohort to become a learning team, and to learn about research from each other as well as the academic facilitators. As these learning outcomes are at the deeper levels of the hierarchy of learning outcomes (see Chapter 8), unstructured learning strategies are used in these workshops.

- As researchers, the learning cohort must become independent learners who value self-assessment more than other-assessment (see the unstructured learning strategies of action learning, contract learning, and change interventions in Chapter 11).

Summary

The heart of the shadow system is the SOG. The supervisor or manager must nurture SOGs which show promise of identifying new knowledge by using positive feedback loop and encouraging double-loop learning. Further, SOGs will often benefit by having their group and learning processes managed by a facilitator. Extraordinary management, the process used to govern the shadow system, emphasises the role of relationships between individuals and encourages staff to become engaged in both external and internal networks. Learning partnerships are a special type of network where knowledge is reinforced and, in the case of WCIL, both then learner and the organisation are developed in strategically defined directions.

Exporting to the legitimate system

A key management task is one of enabling and managing the knowledge creation and deployment processes associated with innovation (Tranfield *et al.* 2006). In other words, success is not in identifying the new knowledge, but having that new knowledge embedded in the workplace so that the organisation becomes more efficient and/or takes advantage of the new product or service.

To achieve this success, the new knowledge must be exported to the legitimate system – and both systems have specific responsibilities to ensure that such success is achieved.

Defence mechanisms

The main barrier to the exportation of new knowledge is the defence mechanisms of the legitimate system – the organisational equivalent of individual hegemonic assumptions (see Chapter 3). The legitimate system is predicated on efficiency, and importing new knowledge is not an efficient process. Embedding new knowledge requires resources, time, and effort – energy that the legitimate system believes could be put to better use in production. These defence mechanisms will be raised automatically (again, very similar to an individual when his or her frames of reference are challenged) and tend to keep an organisation in single-loop learning so that the underlying governing variables are not examined.

Such defence mechanisms are based on theory-in-use Model I (Argyris 2004) and have a number of common elements:

- remain in unilateral control;

- maximise 'winning' and minimise 'losing';

- suppress negative feelings; and

- be as 'rational' as possible – by which people mean defining clear objectives and evaluating their behaviour in terms of whether or not they have achieved them.

A number of defence mechanisms used by managers in the legitimate system have been identified.

Case study example

See the PLP case study on page 24 of the workbook that accompanies this text for organisational defence mechanism.

Defensive routines

A defensive routine is used by individual managers. Argyris (2008) has identified the steps in a defensive routine as:

- send a mixed message – for example, *I like your recommendation and it is too complex to work;*

- pretend the message is not mixed – for example, *You can be proud of this contribution;*

- make the mixed message and the pretence beyond discussion – for example, *I am very pleased with this result and I am sure you are also;* and

- make the undiscussability itself beyond discussion – for example, *Now that everyone is happy with this conclusion, is there anything else we should discuss?*

The individual who has written the report tends to be too confused to think of an immediate response and is out of the manager's office before she or he can give a suitable response.

An appearance of positive action

The manager uses common business activities to give the appearance of taking positive action. Common examples include:

- sending the idea to a sub-committee (committees operate under negative feedback loops and negative feedback loops destroy creativity); or

- using an inappropriately designed training course (usually using highly structured learning strategies as instrumental learning to achieve complex learning outcomes.

It looks good in an annual report if 1 000 people have attended a one-hour lecture – *we have invested 1 000 hours in changing the culture of the organisation.*

Use up the energy

Give the initiator of the new idea lots of work to do on investigating the new idea. For example, recommend that the initiator interview more people, research customer records, or discuss the new idea with a number of organisational committees. The initiator of the new idea eventually runs out of energy and gives up.

Bowdlerization

The manager removes parts of the information or even censors information so that the full message is not understood by the recipients or the full meaning of the message is not communicated. This filtering process ensures that only information that supports current standards is communicated. The filtering may be from the manager to the staff or from the manager to upper management.

Purposes of defence mechanisms

Defensive mechanisms used by organisations are many and varied; they are often unique to a particular organisation. Defensive mechanisms are very powerful. They tend to be instigated automatically by the legitimate system. As far as the legitimate system is concerned, they serve several purposes:

- they assist the organisation to avoid double-loop learning;

- they protect key members of the organisation from embarrassment, threat, and surprises; they ensure that the organisation does not go in a direction that might cause discomfort to key members;

- they help to avoid the discomfort of change;

Defensive routines proliferate and grow in an underground manner. They are often used by the legitimate system to block proposals of the shadow system and frequently becomes part of the organisation's culture (see Chapter 15). The challenge for the shadow system is to overcome them.

The shadow system

Of course, as in any complex system, the paths that the new knowledge takes on its journey to the legitimate system can be many and varied. When the new knowledge is the result of a WCIL intervention that already has senior management approval and the knowledge is codified, it may move into the legitimate system quickly and relatively painlessly. This is because codified, explicit knowledge is easily transposed by using weak ties and thin communication channels (Sherwood & Covin 2008) – and because the new knowledge already has the imprimatur of senior management.

On the other hand, non-codified, tacit knowledge needs thick communication channels and strong ties (Sherwood & Covin 2008). Predominantly, new non-codified, tacit knowledge is created or imported by a SOG. The first challenge in exporting such knowledge to the legitimate system occurs if the SOG keeps expanding the new idea then, at some stage, the new idea becomes too far removed from the needs of the organisation. At some stage, someone in authority (often the supervisor) has to decide that the new knowledge is (a) useful to the organisation and (b) is ready to be exported to the legitimate system.

A second challenge in exporting the new knowledge may then occur. The members of the SOG invariably become very attached to the new knowledge. They are often intransigent in their belief that the new knowledge is so pure and so good that anyone who hears of it will be converted to the truth of it immediately. Of course, reality is often otherwise. The problem that the shadow system faces is that the legitimate system may see the new idea or knowledge as a threat – and automatically defend itself against the perceived menace using defence mechanisms.

The exportation of new knowledge to the legitimate system is frequently, therefore, a political process (Stacey 2000) – and some members of SOGs may be horrified to think that their 'pure' ideas will be sullied by such an underhanded process. The supervisor may find that a more constructive option is to hand the new knowledge to another party who is more adept at managing change.

The final task of the shadow system, then, is to prepare the new idea or knowledge so that the legitimate system will be more likely to accept it. This preparation is a *political activity*. Organisational politics can be functional or dysfunctional (Vredenburgh & Shea-VanFossen 2009). Organisational defence mechanisms can be dysfunctional, so political processes that are beneficial are needed. There are several options.

- Identifying a power centre in the legitimate system to become a sponsor or champion. This sponsor will need to have knowledge of organisational politics and credibility in the eyes of other power centres in the organisation.

- Preparing the path for the new idea or knowledge. This action may include discussing the new concept with members of various committees, identifying people in the legitimate system who will benefit from the new concept and providing them with special previews, and holding informal discussions at propitious opportunities or even holding trials. However, committees should be avoided in the early stages. Committees are governed by negative feedback loops and negative feedback loops kill creativity. Further, committees are often a disguise for defence mechanisms – devices used by the legitimate system to eradicate threats, real or perceived.

- Preparing the new concept as an acceptable package. Too many times, a new concept is presented in its raw state and the abrasive nature of the raw state tends to raise resistance. Further, a presentation of a new concept in its raw state smacks of indifference and carelessness. Rather, the champions of the new concept should think of the individuals who will make a decision on the appropriateness of the new offering. In one organisation, a SOG had designed a process that allowed new staff to identify problems and create possible outlandish solutions. The manager of the area was very wary of the new design until he was told that it was really a mentoring program. The manager said, 'Oh, a mentoring program. That's all right, then.' The new program had been linked to something familiar to the decision maker.

- Engaging in a *debate*. Note, debating is different from communicative learning (see Chapter 3). To be used as a political process for encouraging the legitimate system to accept the new idea, the debater would need to prepare well – in particular identifying all the objections of the legitimate system and planning counter-arguments.

- The Lisa virus. (This one came from one of my students, so I have named it in her honour.) Lisa was a trainer and, when she wanted to have a new idea implemented in the organisation, she would introduce the new idea as a session in each of her training programs. In this way she would 'infect' people who would return to their workplace and 'infect' their work colleagues.

Often, a combination of these approaches needs to be used. The supervisor should create a plan and organise appropriate resources to implement the plan.

The legitimate system

Rather than use defence mechanisms, the legitimate system can use a more positive approach to ensure that valuable new knowledge is embedded successfully into the everyday work life of the organisation. This *embedding process* uses four phases:

1. *The audit*. The legitimate system examines the proposal and makes decisions based on such criteria as alignment to the strategic plan, the extent to which the organisation has already been engaged in change (staff can become burnt-out by excessive change interventions), and whether sufficient resources are available. In making these decisions, the legitimate system needs to use theory-in-use Model II behaviour – use valid information, make free and informed choices, and test the validity of the choices (Argyris 2004).

2. *The plan*. If the new knowledge has significant strategic implications, then the planning for the new idea should proceed through the *strategic planning* process. However, if the new knowledge has more immediate operational implications then *standing plans* (policies, procedures, and rules) and *single-use plans* have to be considered. Training courses or workshops will have to be planned because any new idea includes new knowledge (i.e. the design stage of HRD). Appropriate *budgets* will have to accompany any single-use plans. In addition, developmental workshops may have to take into account the *unlearning* of staff (see Chapter 3), as old behaviours are often entrenched in their tacit knowledge.

3. *Implementation*. The plans have to be implemented – this means an investment of money and/or time.

4. *Extended learning.* Once the staff have been trained, they return to their operational area – but the management of knowledge does not stop here. The supervisor should encourage extended learning (see Chapter 13). Extended learning covers four steps. The learners should:

    a. be engaged immediately in the newly learned tasks;

    b. be developed by progressive approximations;

    c. be given feedback that is informational and motivational; and

    d. be exposed to models of expert performance.

Case study example

See the PLP case study on page 21. PLP uses the monthly management team's weekly meeting as an auditing process for new ideas.

The legitimate system, therefore, holds a responsibility to evaluate all new ideas to ensure that valuable resources are not wasted. The challenge to the legitimate system, though, is to accept ideas that may be a threat to its present culture – and this takes a highly mature body of managers. It is also interesting to note the path back towards the shadow system is encouraged by extended learning.

Limiting the defence mechanisms of the legitimate system and utilising the embedding process will achieve the most desirable outcome for the complex system of the organisation – *a state of bounded instability.* Bounded instability occurs when both the legitimate system and the shadow system have appropriate levels of power such that the organisation is neither dragged into a toxic state by the legitimate system's compulsion for efficiency nor thrown into a state of chaos by the shadow system's craving for creativity. When in a state of bounded instability, the organisation will continue to move forward and be suitably innovative to ensure that the organisation will survive both the near-to-certainty and far-from-certainty external environments.

Control – to be or not to be?

Managing the shadow system is not an easy process. The natural inclination, to increase control when faced with an unpredictable climate, is overwhelming but must be avoided. Direct control, with its emphasis on negative feedback, is the very antithesis of the management skills needed in the shadow system.

Of course, allowing open slather will also be an invitation to disaster. The manager, then, needs to use more indirect controls. For special cases and projects there are several options available:

- carefully selecting staff who will be given significant resources to operate in the shadow system; and

- providing 'sunset' clauses in any projects

to name just two. However, to manage the other, major part of the shadow system – the day-to-day forays of staff into creating new knowledge – is a much more subtle and difficult process. There are two 'controlling' processes operating in the shadow system. The first is the constraining effect of individuals operating in relationships, as discussed earlier in this chapter. The second is the 'invisible force' of organisational culture – building a climate that encourages and celebrates the individual victories that occur every day (see Chapter 15).

The nexus of work and learning

In contemporary society, an individual can rarely offer labour and time in exchange for payment. The individual's competitive advantage lies in a combination of a unique quality and quantity of knowledge. If this combination is of value to someone else, then the individual can exchange the knowledge for a reward. This reward is often monetary, as in the case of employment, although other rewards such as self-satisfaction can also be a potent inspiration.

Work and learning, however, have an uneasy relationship in today's society. Productivity is seen as paramount, and productivity is dependent on the quantity of work. Both the quantity and quality of work are dependent on learning, as the ability to work depends on the application of knowledge. But work and learning can rarely occur at precisely the same moment. Learning requires application, thought, reflection, and motivation. If time and energy are not invested in the design and process of learning, learning will be inefficient and ineffective. Inefficient and ineffective learning will eventually make an impact on the efficiency and effectiveness of work activities. Organisations must accept that the work site is the focus of both work and learning. Both activities are integral to each other, and both activities must be planned and given sufficient resources to prosper.

There should be a seamless interaction between workplace learning (Chapter 13) and the creation of new knowledge (this chapter). The interaction should be constant and cyclic – staff have to be developed in current valuable knowledge; as staff become more expert in and adept at applying current valuable knowledge, they should be encouraged to engage in double-loop learning so that new, efficient, and effective ways of doing are either imported from the external environment or are created by the staff members themselves. This new knowledge is then embedded in everyday work practices, either through the strategic planning process or operational planning; the staff members become expert and adept at this 'new' knowledge, so continuing the cycle.

Work and learning are not separate entities. They are inter-dependent, as work practices engender learning and learning engenders more efficient and effective ways of working. As Bessant (2006) points out, continuous improvement is an organisation-wide process of sustained and focused incremental innovation.

References

Andrews, K 1999, 'Knowing, learning and unlearning in a knowledge creating company: An inductive theory building case study', unpublished doctoral thesis, Centre for Professional Practice in Education and Training, Queensland University of Technology.

Argyris, C 1992, *On Organizational Learning*. Cambridge, Mass: Blackwell.

Argyris, C 2004, *Reasons and Rationalizations: The limits of organizational knowledge*, Oxford University Press, New York.

Argyris, C 2008, *Teaching smart people how to learn*, Harvard Business Press, New York.

Bessant, J 2006, 'Learning and continuous improvement', in J Tidd (ed.), *From knowledge management to strategic competence: Measuring technological, market and organisational innovation*, 2nd edn, Imperial College Press, London.

Billett, S 2007, 'Education: Supporting and guiding ongoing development', *Journal of Cooperative Education and Internship*, Vol. 41(2), pp. 37-44.

Cavaliere, L A 1992, 'The Wright Brothers' odyssey: Their flight of learning', in L A Cavaliere & A Sgrol (eds.), *Learning for personal development*, San Francisco, Jossey-Bass.

Choy, S & Delahaye, B L 2008, 'Chapter 10: Leadership development: Implementation of an organization centred curriculum' in S Billett, C Harteis & A Etelapelto (eds.), *Emerging perspectives of learning at work*, Sense Publishing, Roterdam.

Choy, S & Delahaye, B L 2009, 'A sustainable model for university-industry learning partnership : Issues for universities', in *Book of Abstracts for the ANZAM 2009 Conference*, 1-4 December 2009, Southbank, Melbourne.

Chua, A Y 2006, 'The rise and fall of a community of practice: a descriptive case study', *Knowledge & Process Management*, 13(2), pp. 120-128.

Davis, B & Sumara, D 2001, 'Learning communities: Understanding the workplace as a complex system', in T Fenwick (ed.), *Sociocultural Perspectives on Learning through Work*. pp. 85-95, San Francisco: Jossey-Bass.

Deeds, D L 2003, 'Alternative strategies for acquiring knowledge', in S E Jackson, M A Hitt & A S DeNisi (eds.), *Managing Knowledge for Sustained Competitive Advantage: Designing Strategies for Effective Human Resource Management*, San Francisco: Jossey-Bass.

Delahaye, B L & Choy, S 2008, *A learning partnership with a university: Some considerations for industry*, 22nd ANZAM conference, 3-6 December, Auckland, NZ.

Delahaye, B L, Choy, S & Saggers, B, 2010, *Developing managers as researchers using a learning cohort approach*, 24th ANZAM conference, 8-10 December, Adelaide.

Earl, M 1997, 'Knowledge as strategy: Reflections on Skandia International and Shorko Films', in L Prisak (ed.), *Knowledge in Organisations*. Boston: Butterworth-Heinemann.

Fiol, C M 2003, 'Organizing for a knowledge- based competitiveness: About pipelines and rivers', in S E Jackson, M A Hitt and A S DeNisi (eds.), *Managing Knowledge for Sustained Competitive Advantage: Designing Strategies for Effective Human Resource Management*, San Francisco: Jossey-Bass, pp. 64-93.

Fuller A, Hodkinson H, Hodkinson P & Unwin L 2005, 'Learning as peripheral participation in communities of practice: A reassessment of key concepts in workplace learning', *British Educational Research Journal*, 31(1), pp. 49-68.

Ge, X & Hardre, P L 2010, 'Self-processes and learning environment as influences in the development of expertise in instructional design', *Learning Environment Research*, 13, pp. 23-41.

Granovetter, M S 1973, 'The strength of weak ties', *American Journal of Sociology*, 78, pp. 1360-1380.

Huq, A, Raja, J Z & Rosenberg, D 2006, 'Linking organisational culture and communities of practice', in E Coakes & S Clark (eds.), *Encyclopaedia of communities of practice in information and knowledge management*, Idea Group Inc, New York.

Iverson, J O & McPhee, R D 2002, 'Knowldege management in communities of practice', *Management Communication Quarterly*, 16(2), pp. 258-261.

Janis, I L 1972, *Victims of Group Think,* Boston: Houghton.

Lesser, E L & Stock, J 2001, 'Communities of practice and organisational performance', *Systems Journal*, 40(4), pp. 831-841.

Maples, M F 1988, 'Group development: Extending Tuckman's theory'. *Journal for Specialists in Group Work,* Fall, pp. 17-23.

Mintzberg, H 2009, *Management*, Berrett-Koehler, New York.

Mudambi, R & Swift, T 2009, 'Professional guides, tension and knowledge management', *Research Policy*, 38(5), pp. 736-745.

Ogilvie, S 2007, 'Can we rehabilitate guilds? A sceptical re-appraisal', Faculty of Economics, University of Cambridge, UK.

Paulos, J A 2001, *Innumeracy: Mathematical Illiteracy and its Consequences*, 2nd edn, Hill and Wang, New York, Read, V2004, 'Foreword', in T Scott & P Harker, *The Myth of Nine to Five: Work, Workplaces and Workplace Relationships*, Thorogood, London.

Read, V 2004, 'Foreword', in T Scott & P Harker, *The Myth of Nine to Five: Work, Workplaces and Workplace Relationships,* Thorogood, London

Regans, R & McEvily, B 2003, 'Network structures and knowledge transfer: The effects of cohesion and range', *Administrative Sciences Quarterly*, 48, pp. 240-267.

Regans, R & Zuckerman, E W 2001, 'Networks, diversity and productivity: The social capital of corporate R&D teams', *Organizational Science*, 12, pp. 502-517.

Roberts, J 2006, 'Limits to communities of practice', *Journal of Management Studies*, 43(3), 623-639).

Schmidt, T 2010 'Absorptive capacity – One size fits all? 'A firm-level analysis of absorptive capacity for different kinds of knowledge', *Managerial and Decision Economics*, 31, pp. 1-18.

Scott, T & Harker, P 2004, *The Myth of Nine to Five: Work, Workplaces and Workplace Relationships,* Thorogood, London.

Sherwood, A L & Covin, J G 2008, 'Knowledge acquisition in university-industry alliances: An empirical investigation from a learning theory perspective', *Journal of Product Innovation Management*, 25(2), pp. 162-179.

Sims, R R, 2006, *Human resource development*, Information Age Publishing, Greenwich.

Stacey, R D 1996, *Strategic Management and Organisational Dynamics*, 2nd edn, London: Pitman.

Stacey, R D 2000, *Strategic Management and Organisational Dynamics*, 3rd edn, London: Pitman.

Symes, C & McIntyre, J 2000, 'Working knowledge: An introduction to the new business of learning', in C Symes & J McIntyre (eds.), *Working Knowledge: The new vocationalism and higher education*, SRHE and Open University Press, Maidenhead (pp.1-14).

Tranfield, Young, Partington, Bessant & Sapsed, J 2006, in J Tidd (ed.), *From knowledge management to strategic competence: Measuring technological, market and organisational innovation*, 2nd edn, Imperial College Press, London.

Tuckman, B W 1965, 'Developmental sequences in small groups', *Psychological Bulletin*, 63, June, pp. 384-99.

Tuckman, B W & Jensen, M C 1977, 'Stages of small-group development revisited', *Group and Organizational Studies*, 2, December, pp. 419-27.

Vredenburgh, D & Shea-VanFossen, R 2009, 'Human nature, organizational politics and human resource development', *Human Resource Development Review*, August, pp. 1-22.

Wright, R 2008, 'How to get the most from university relationships', *MITSloan Management Review*, 49(3), pp. 75-80.

Chapter 15

Organisational culture, leadership and knowledge management

LEARNING OBJECTIVES

After studying this chapter you should be able to:

1. Explain why knowledge is a unique asset.

2. Describe the basic assumptions of the legitimate system and the shadow system of an organisation.

3. Explain how the legitimate system manages the organisation's knowledge assets.

4. Explain how the shadow system manages the organisation's knowledge.

5. Describe the concept of bounded instability.

6. Describe organisational culture and explain its role in the management of knowledge

7. Discuss the role of leadership in the management of knowledge

8. Describe the role of the HR developer in an organisation.

Knowledge as an asset

As Scott and Harker (2004) comment, just like every other organisational issue, the organisation's capacity to learn is dependent on the learning capacity of the individuals who comprise it. There are two broad categories of learning of which organisations need to be aware. The first is the learning of the technical and professional knowledge that an organisation needs to create a market share and sell its product or service. This can be termed content knowledge. The second type of learning was discussed in Chapter 8 as self-perpetuating learning. Self-perpetuating learning is the individual's awareness of her or his personal processes of learning and how these processes affect his or her ability to learn.

Many organisations concentrate on the first category of learning – content knowledge. However, even more important to the survival of the organisation is each employee's ability to engage in self-perpetuating learning. This combination of self-perpetuating learning and content knowledge is the basis for that unique asset – organisational knowledge capital.

It was once held that the two most basic resources available to an organisation were money and time, and that one could be exchanged for the other. So, for example, if a project was falling behind schedule it was just a matter of buying more equipment or hiring more staff and thus catching up on time. This old dictum is no longer true.

Knowledge has now become an equally critical resource. Unfortunately, though, there is no simple exchange equation between money and time on the one hand, and knowledge on the other. Knowledge has to be created, learned, and maintained rather than simply purchased and maintained. Further, while a certain type of knowledge may be appropriate today, there is no guarantee of its relevance in the future. Some knowledge may even have to be unlearned. This means that, while creating and acquiring knowledge may indeed cost money and take time, simply investing money and time does not guarantee useful knowledge.

As discussed in Chapter 1, knowledge is a unique resource (Delahaye 2003, Sveiby 2007). With most resources that are available to an organisation, the more they are used the quicker they are depleted. This is true of raw materials or capital equipment. However, knowledge does not decrease with use; in fact, the more it is used the more it expands. Try to hold onto knowledge, and the world passes you by. Someone else (often several someone elses) will discover or create the same or more advanced knowledge. Conversely, spread your knowledge around and it comes back multiplied tenfold. As Gamble and Blackwell (2001) comment:

> Today the intention is to create enterprise integration through a knowledge-sharing culture, to recognize the value of something that is called intellectual capital and to understand that competition depends not on the differential possession of physical assets, or even of information, but on the ability to deploy and exploit knowledge. (Gamble & Blackwell 2001, p. 6)

Knowledge assets of organisations are now considered so important that Australia has established a national standard for knowledge management, the Australian Standard 5037-2005.

It is worth considering the difference between data, information, and knowledge. This delineation was discussed in Chapter 1, but it is worth reconsidering here. A number of publications provide definitions and differentiations (see, for example, Australian Standard 5037-2005, Fuller 2002; Gamble & Blackwell 2001 and Wilson 2005); these can be summarised as:

- *Data* – chunks of facts that reflect the state of the world, including symbolic representations. These chunks of facts, by and of themselves, do not usually have meaning. In combination, however, they may form the basis of information. So, for example, when looking at a speedometer, the figure '80' does not mean much nor does the figure '100' or '110'.

- *Information* – a combination of data such that the combination endows the data with meaning. So, for example, when the figure '80' on the speedometer is combined with the figure '100' on the speed limit signpost on the side of the road, the driver can make a meaning from the two figures – that is, the '80' is lower than the '100'. This information is needed before knowledge can be activated.

- *Encoded knowledge* – sometimes referred to as programmed knowledge or embedded knowledge. This type of knowledge is found in textbooks and in the manuals of procedures of organisations. When the driver links the '100' on the speed sign with the encoded knowledge contained in the traffic regulations, then the driver can make the decision that at the current speed of '80', he or she is driving under the speed limit. Interestingly, the driver may have the encoded knowledge from the traffic regulations stored as explicit knowledge (i.e. the driver can declare this knowledge – see Chapter 1).

- *Embedded knowledge* – knowledge that exists within systems and routines. These are the processes that the organisation uses to ensure smooth operations between the various internal and external systems and sub-systems.

- *Embodied knowledge* – a body of understanding and skills that is constructed by people. Incorporated in both the individual's tacit knowledge and their explicit knowledge, embodied knowledge represents the intuition, empathy, experience, emotions, and undocumented professional knowledge that allows individuals to make appropriate decisions – often instantaneously.

- *Encultured knowledge* – the shared understandings and cultural meanings that people have in organisations.

Knowledge, then, is a complex resource that needs careful management. Knowledge may be held in organisational systems, such as the computer systems and the manuals of procedures, but it also resides within the minds of individual staff members. Such repositories of knowledge are often termed 'knowledge reservoirs' or 'silos'. Knowledge, of itself, can be ephemeral; often the only physical evidence of its presence is the successful or unsuccessful use of the knowledge. Finally, it is often difficult to predict what future problems will occur, let alone what knowledge will be needed to overcome those problems. Organisations have to treat knowledge as the critical and valuable resource that it is – and this means *creating* and *maintaining* knowledge. AS5037-2005 suggests that knowledge management involves four processes that allow organisations to use and leverage knowledge. These processes are:

- presenting, distributing, and sharing knowledge;
- capturing and storing knowledge;
- revising and disposing of knowledge; and
- creating, discovering, and acquiring knowledge.

Case study example

See the PLP case study on pages 5 and 16 of the workbook that accompanies this text for knowledge silos.

Both the legitimate system and the shadow system have roles to play in each of these processes. The legitimate system is predominantly responsible for presenting, distributing and sharing knowledge; the shadow system is predominantly responsible for creating, discovering and acquiring knowledge.

A systems approach

As an overarching theme, this text has used a model based on complexity theory. Stacey (1996) suggests that any organism (including organisations) can be viewed as having two basic systems – the legitimate system and the shadow system.

The legitimate system uses negative feedback loops and single-loop learning to maintain the status quo. Negative feedback loops dampen any behaviour that is seen as aberrant by the legitimate system (Stacey 1996). Single-loop learning passes on current knowledge without challenging the veracity or usefulness of the knowledge (Argyris 2004). The role of the legitimate system is to ensure that the organisation survives the immediate future by the efficient use of the organisation's resources. The application of negative feedback loops and single-loop learning accomplishes this efficiency prerogative extremely well. The shadow system, on the other hand, provides the organisation with the energy, usually in the form of knowledge, that will ensure the organisation's long-term future. The shadow system is predicated on positive feedback loops and double-loop learning. Positive feedback loops enhance behaviour and increase energy (Stacey 1996, 2000). Double-loop learning occurs where an individual or a group challenges the underlying values of an idea, assumption, or concept (Argyris 2004).

Case study example

See the PLP case study on page 22 of the workbook that accompanies this text for an example of a postive feedback loop.

The role of the legitimate system is to pull the organisation towards a state of equilibrium. It is in that state of equilibrium that the organisation is at its most efficient. Unfortunately, if the organisation remains at the stage of total equilibrium for a period of time, the organisation will stagnate, become toxic, and slowly poison itself. The shadow system, however, pulls the organisation towards chaos. It is in the state of chaos that organisms are at their most creative, although at this time the organism is more likely to destroy itself. In the twenty-first century, then, managers have to manage the legitimate system and manage the shadow system so the organisation maintains a state of bounded instability. A state of bounded instability means that the organisation hovers between equilibrium and chaos, thus enhancing the strengths of both the legitimate system and the shadow system. The significant issue, of course, is how the manager can maintain this state of bounded instability. One of the most fundamental solutions to this conundrum is to concentrate on managing that most unique of organisational assets – its knowledge capital.

Figure 15.1 A model for managing knowledge

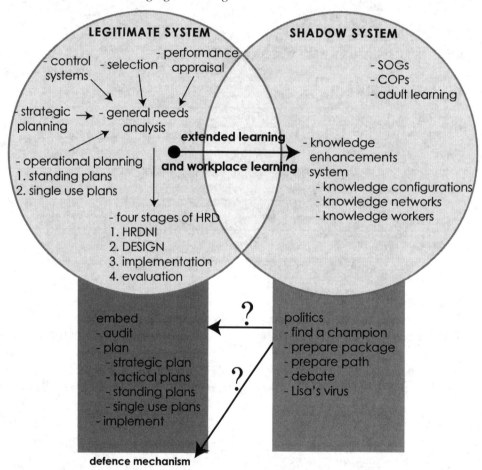

This chapter will examine the management of knowledge by discussing the roles of the legitimate system and the shadow system and the interaction between them. However, it is important to recognise that the two systems are strongly affected by two other forces – organisational culture and the leadership within the organisation. If the two systems undertake their roles appropriately and if the interactions between the two systems are managed correctly, the organisation can maintain a state of bounded instability by using its knowledge capital. Managing the two systems correctly, though, is heavily dependent on the existence of an appropriate organisational culture and a mature leadership style that can apply ordinary management and extraordinary management judiciously.

The legitimate system

In managing knowledge capital, the legitimate system's prime concern is maintaining the organisation's current valuable knowledge by ensuring that the accepted current core competencies – and only those competencies – are disseminated throughout the organisation. The second concern for the legitimate system is to identify new directions for the organisation. These new directions may be dependent on new knowledge.

Strategic planning

In traditional strategic planning, the legitimate system examines the direct (such as customers and competitors) and indirect factors (such as changes in technology and government laws) in the external environment, compares these with its own strengths and weaknesses (commonly called the SWOT analysis – strengths, weaknesses, opportunities and threats), and formulates strategies for future viability. This future viability may be seen as doing more of the same or as opening a new opportunity. Usually, organisations undertake a combination of the two. Mintzberg (2009) calls the result of this planning process the *intended strategic plan* as the SWOT analysis and resultant decisions are deliberate and logical.

Case study example

See the PLP case study on page 5 of the workbook that accompanies this text for an example of a strategic planning process.

Under the option of 'doing more of the same', the organisation uses the strategic planning process to check that the organisation's current valuable knowledge is indeed still valuable – that it is the type and quality of knowledge that will allow the organisation to service its market niche efficiently and effectively. If so, then the silos of knowledge, especially the standing plans (discussed later in this chapter), can remain unchanged. If the strengths/weaknesses analysis of the strategic planning process identifies gaps or defects in what was assumed as being current valuable knowledge, then the problem would need to be referred, through the general needs analysis, to the HRDNI process. For any gaps, new learning experiences (e.g. single-use plans in the form of training courses) would need to be designed and implemented and the results eventually evaluated. If there are any defects, then unlearning (see Chapter 3) would need to occur.

Under the option of 'opening a new opportunity', four important processes need to be initiated and conducted:

- Tactical plans would need to be generated from the intended strategic plan. There will be several tactical plans for each new strategic direction. It has to be said that tactical planning is one of the least well-handled processes in most organisations (most probably because of the legitimate system's search for 'efficiencies'). Each tactical plan would need to answer three questions and, far too often, upper management leave the answers to these questions to the operational staff. The questions are:

- What type of resources would be needed to achieve the tactical plan? The type of resources would be some combination of finance, time and knowledge.

- What amount of each resource would be needed? This may need some decisions on the most appropriate quantities. For example, if the objectives of the tactical plan need to be achieved in a hurry, then finance may be used to decrease the amount of time – perhaps by purchasing more equipment or hiring outside consultants rather than developing organisational staff in some type of skills.

- Where will these resources come from? Will the finance come from savings or from a loan? Should some operation in the organisation be closed down so that the staff released can be transferred to the new operation?

- A general needs analysis would need to be undertaken to identify the resources and to commence the planning process. The general needs analysis may indicate that equipment or property needs to be purchased or that staff will need to be developed in new knowledge and skills. Single-use plans (discussed later in this chapter) will be needed for each of these operational requirements. All single-use plans will need to be supported by a suitable budget.

- If new learning is needed, a HRDNI (see Chapter 5) must be carried out to determine what new knowledge is needed to take advantage of the opportunity. This would be followed by the other three steps of HRD – namely, design, implementation, and evaluation.

- Standing plans – policies, procedures, and rules – must be formulated to support the new knowledge.

It is surprising the number of CEOs who forget these four processes, assuming that osmosis or good luck will save the day once they have made the important decision on what new opportunity the organisation will exploit. Making the decision on adopting the strategic opportunity is the first ten percent of the task – the other 90 percent incorporates the processes of tactical planning, conducting a general needs analysis, generating single-use plans, and a HRDNI if needed – then designing, implementing, and evaluating the learning experiences and, finally, devising standing plans.

Operational planning

There are two types of operational plans – standing plans and single-use plans – each of which comes from the strategic plan and the associated tactical plans. *Single-use plans* describe how a specific objective will be achieved and what resources, including a budget, will be needed. If new learning is needed, the four stages of HRD come into effect and the designed learning program is, in itself, a single-use plan. *Standing plans*, with their policies, procedures and rules, form an important knowledge silo in an organisation as they identify and describe the core competencies of the organisation. As discussed in the previous section, standing plans come from the tactical plans. As such, standing plans can provide the content of procedural training courses that are based on instrumental learning. Frequently, the HRDNI will refer to the relevant standing plan to identify the content of the learning program. For further discussion on operational planning see Dickie and Dickie (2006) and Schermerhorn *et al.* (2011).

Case study example

See the PLP case study on pages 18 to 19 of the workbook that accompanies this text for an example of standing plans.

Organisation control systems

Control systems are essential for the efficient operation of the legitimate system; they ensure that the current valuable knowledge of the organisation is being used correctly. Most introductory management texts (e.g. Dickie & Dickie, 2006; Schermerhorn *et al.* 2011) suggest that control systems have four basic steps – a pre-determined standard, a measuring sensor, a comparative procedure, and a remedial action. These four steps represent a classic negative feedback loop where, once deviant behaviour is identified, action is taken to dampen the aberrant behaviour and bring it back to the pre-determined standard.

Case study example

See the PLP case study on page 21 of the workbook that accompanies this text for control systems.

For negative feedback loops and single-loop learning, the pre-determined standard is the crucial issue. The pre-determined standard represents the current valuable knowledge. This current valuable knowledge is found in a variety of sites, often referred to as knowledge silos. Knowledge silos include standing plans and single-use plans (see discussion above), job descriptions and specifications (see Chapter 6), and the skills, information, abilities, and attitudes of the organisational staff. Acceptable pre-determined standards should be sourced from any of these knowledge silos.

When the measuring sensor and the comparative procedure identify a behaviour or outcome that is aberrant, the remedial action becomes a *general needs analysis*. If the needs analysis indicates that a lack or inappropriate use of knowledge is the base cause then a HRDNI is undertaken (see Chapter 5). This HRDNI can then result in the design and implementation of a learning program, and this learning program may be conducted on-site (as workplace learning) or off-site.

Performance appraisal

Another human resource management process that acts in a similar manner – indeed some texts include it as a control system – is the performance appraisal system (see Chapter 6). The pre-determined standard for performance appraisal is based on the job description and the job specification. Whether undertaken for administrative or developmental reasons, staff performance is appraised and action plans should be developed to ensure that staff are developed in the identified shortfalls. These action plans should also become part of the surveillance stage of the organisation (see Chapter 5). Again, these action plans should feed into the HRDNI of the organisation.

Case study example

See the PLP case study on page 11 of the workbook that accompanies this text for the use of the performance appraisal process as a means of managing knowledge.

These two management processes – control systems and performance appraisals – uphold the veracity and primacy of the organisation's current core competencies. They are the major negative feedback loops used by the organisation. As the underlying values of these core competencies are not challenged, the two management processes become a major element of the single-loop learning assumption of the legitimate system.

Selection

Selection is another important HRM function that helps the legitimate system to manage the organisation's knowledge capital. At the minimum, the selection process ensures that only people who have skills, knowledge, and abilities that match the core competencies of the organisation are accepted – thus perpetuating single-loop learning. In a similar fashion to that performed for performance appraisal, the job description and specification provide the basis for the pre-determined standard, representing the organisation's view of the current valuable knowledge for the position being filled. If the person selected does not have all the required current valuable knowledge, then the selectee usually attends a learning experience – often a training course based on one or more of the categories discussed under the hierarchy of learning outcomes in Chapter 8.

However, the selection process not only helps the legitimate system maintain current valuable knowledge. New knowledge will also be imported into the organisation – although this new knowledge importation may be intended or unintended. If *intended*, selection will be the result of the strategic and tactical planning process which converts into a single-use plan to select staff with certain types of knowledge. In this case, the organisation will purposely select an individual because that individual possesses specific and new knowledge that the organisation needs. If this specific and new knowledge is an intended part of the selection process, the legitimate system usually supports the new member in disseminating the new knowledge by having that person involved in the four stages of HRD – that is, identifying the gaps in the knowledge of the present staff, designing and implementing learning experiences for those staff, and then evaluating the effect of those learning experiences.

New knowledge importation can also be *unintended*. Most new employees will have had unique experiences outside of the parent organisation; these experiences represent new knowledge for the parent organisation. However, if the new knowledge of the new employee is not an intended part of the selection process, then the new knowledge may be seen as aberrant behaviour and negative feedback loops will be instigated in the form of discipline or counselling.

Case study example

See the PLP case study on pages 4 and 9 of the workbook that accompanies this text for examples of using selection to import new knowledge.

The four stages of HRD

The four stages of HRD play a key function in the legitimate system's role in managing an organisation's knowledge capital. Indeed, the four stages are the very heart of the legitimate system's role in helping the organisation to manage its knowledge capital.

The four stages of HRD are usually described as HRDNI, design, implementation, and evaluation. These stages have been the central theme of this text:

- HRDNI – Chapters 5, 6 and 7;

- design – Chapters 8 and 9;

- implementation – Chapters 10 and 11; and

- evaluation – Chapter 12.

As has been discussed in this chapter, the management processes of control systems, performance appraisal, selection, operational planning, and strategic planning all flow into a general needs analysis. If the issue is deemed to be one of learning, the impetus flows into the HRDNI and then into the other three stages of design, implementation and evaluation.

In summary, then, when these six management processes, with the support of a culture that encourages extended learning, are used appropriately, the legitimate system is fulfilling its role in managing the organisation's knowledge capital and helping the organisation stay in the state of bounded instability.

Potential problems

The legitimate system uses at least six management processes to help the organisation manage its knowledge capital – strategic planning, operational planning, control systems, performance appraisal and selection. When well managed, the legitimate system plays a significant part in the management of the organisation's knowledge capital.

However, problems occur when the basic assumptions of the legitimate system – negative feedback loops and single-loop learning – are given unfettered power. Typically, with such unfettered power, these basic assumptions beguile the legitimate system into emphasising efficiencies. Combined with single-loop learning, this thirst for efficiency invariably means that some key activities in the six management processes – the four stages of HRD, strategic planning, operational planning, control systems, selection, and performance appraisal – are ignored.

The six processes are then used improperly. For example, in the search for efficiencies, the legitimate system will often forsake the evaluation stage of HRD. This means that the organisation does not know what learning experiences have worked, what have not worked, and what learning experiences have resulted in incorrect, inappropriate, and even dangerous or unsafe learning.

A closer look 15.1

The risk of killing knowledge

A business process re-engineering example based on losing sight of real knowledge might illustrate the point. At the height of the fashion for BPR in the early 1990s (Business Process Re-engineering) a major copier corporation took a close look at the activities of its field service engineers. It noticed that they spent a lot of time back at the depot, picking up work orders and parts or chatting in the coffee lounge. They decided to re-engineer the process. The coffee lounge was closed and a more efficient system for communicating orders and supplying parts was devised. A small department was set up to produce operating manuals for all the latest machines and every service van was fitted with a PC with a CD containing schematic graphics of the working parts of different machines. Engineers would be out on the road, facing customers more of the time, and their information support would be up to the minute. However, repair efficiency went down and servicing costs went up. Then one observant manager noticed that in many of the vans the latest manuals had not been removed from their plastic shrink-wrapping. It was apparent that the CDs had never seen the light of a laser. Further investigation revealed that the engineers were very uncomfortable with the new system. It did not tell them the tricks of the trade. Having to consult a manual made them feel foolish in front of customers, and the CDs were hard to use. Previously, when the engineers got together for a coffee, they were actually swapping ideas and tips about how best to tackle certain jobs. This information had high credibility because it came from other engineers who had actually done the job. So, back to square one. The coffee room was re-opened, a depot-based supply system was introduced, and the engineers were supplied with radio headsets that allowed them to talk to each other easily in the field and on the job: 'Hey Joe, how do you get the drum out of one of these ABC79Os?' 'No problem, I did one last week, you just …'. Efficiency and repair costs rapidly climbed back on track.

In this case, the BPR exercise had killed knowledge exchange at a time when the business need for knowledge was very strong. With a knowledge-based view rather than an ostensible cost-reduction focus, the initial management decision would have been different. This is where knowledge management has something in common with TQM. Too great a focus on process reengineering or on cost reduction can extinguish valuable intellectual capital and reduce profit rates. Reducing cost to a minimum can be more expensive than an investment in a knowledge-management program even though it might ostensibly increase short-run costs. Worse, a narrow focus on procedure or process might change the whole basis of customer value.

Source: Gamble & Blackwell 2001, p. 15.

Mistakes occur and are repeated unthinkingly (because of single-loop learning) – and the organisation is dragged by the legitimate system towards total equilibrium. Unfortunately, in today's fast changing environment, an organisation languishing in the vicinity of total equilibrium becomes toxic – a state readily recognised by the physical and psychological illnesses caused to staff members and by the existence of industrial problems. This toxic state can be described as follows.

> *Dysfunctional workplaces often have a feeling of tension, hostility, or sullen resentment. These are indicators that those who are employed here are not willingly engaged with the purpose of the enterprise. Work is being grudgingly performed because the needs of the human spirit are being ignored. Often these needs have been subordinated to the demands of individual ego, status, and power. The dichotomy of 'them' and 'us' is very evident. These are not effective workplaces.* (Scott & Harker 2004, p. 65)

To avoid this toxic state, the organisation needs to be continually drawn towards inequilibrium by an equally powerful shadow system. A powerful shadow system, though, depends on workplaces that support and celebrate learning.

Workplace learning

While the legitimate system undertakes formal learning using the four stages of HRD, the contemporary view is that the worksite is the crucible for learning in any organisation. Based on this view, the supervisor is the key actor in initiating and nurturing the learning of staff (Browning & Delahaye 2010). In managing the workplace curriculum, the supervisor follows a series of stages (see Figure 13.2) – namely:

- conducting a performance appraisal;
- organising the learning episode (either through a formal program, conducted by the in-house training department in the legitimate system or an outside consultant);

then through the three interconnected steps of:

- extended learning;
- complex learning; and
- outcomes-guided learning

before moving onto the indirect guidance of experts and diminishing support.

Workplace learning occupies a unique space in knowledge management as it spans both the legitimate system and the shadow system. A well-managed workplace learning curriculum then moves seamlessly into the creative process of the shadow system.

The shadow system

The shadow system is the location of the emergent strategic plans of the organisation. Emergent strategic plans are those that are generated in response to changes in the external environment and are dependent on the creativity and learning maturity of the staff at the work face (Mintzberg 2009). Accordingly, the shadow system is based on the assumptions of positive feedback loops and double-loop learning. As such, the shadow system needs to be governed by a different set of management processes than those used in the legitimate system.

The catch-cry in the shadow system is creativity. The role of the shadow system is to challenge the operating procedures and the culture of the organisation by importing and creating new knowledge. In this way, the organisation is drawn towards inequilibrium. The shadow system is neither part of the management hierarchy nor a separate entity. Lindberg (2001) describes the shadow system as operating behind the scenes: operating with hallway conversations, the grapevine, the rumour mill, and the informal procedures for getting things done. Usually staff spend most of their time in the legitimate system carrying out their duties. But every now and then they enter the shadow system, perhaps for only a few minutes a week, creating or testing or validating new ideas.

Before proceeding, one point needs to be repeated. The legitimate system and the shadow system are not separate entities. They are mutually dependent systems. The organisation will not survive without both systems. Indeed, the organisation will not survive for long if one system is too strong – that is, if the organisation does not operate in a state of bounded instability. Therefore, the two systems – legitimate and shadow – each need to have sufficient power and energy to keep the organisation in bounded instability. No more, no less.

Self-organising groups and communities of practice

The energy of the shadow system comes from self-organising groups (SOGs). A SOG occurs when two or more people come together over some mutual interest. In organisations, the most readily recognised SOGs are the 'whinge and bitch' groups. Managers need to recognise that 'whinge and bitch' groups are:

- engaging in double-loop learning; and
- a rich source of energy.

This energy is neither good nor bad. What differentiates a successful outcome from a calamity is how well the manager manages the energy of the group.

Case study example

See the PLP case study on pages 21 to 23 of the workbook that accompanies this text for examples of successful use of SOGs.

Not all SOGs, however, are 'whinge and bitch' groups. Many, perhaps even the majority, are initiated by two or more members coming together over an exciting idea. Often this idea, because the members only have the organisation in common, is aimed at improving some aspect of the organisation. From the point of view of the shadow system, such bodies are hotbeds of learning as members recount difficulties experienced and challenges overcome. Providing unobtrusive support for these groups can pay handsome dividends for the organisation.

The problem is that SOGs are 'dissipative structures' (Stacey 2000) – structures that are a new life-form but are very vulnerable. The number of new ideas that founder on the reefs of lack of interest by upper management or are wrecked by the active displeasure of power centres in the legitimate system are legion.

Some SOGs can last for long periods of time; the members can then be termed as a community of practice. A community of practice (COP) comprises of people who carry out similar tasks, coming together to discuss and investigate areas of mutual interest. CoPs that are important to the organisation may be internal or external. A community of practice differs from a SOG in that it will become a silo of knowledge of a particular profession, trade, or a specific topic. Further, the community of practice will also actively tend to search for new knowledge and share this knowledge readily with its members. Gamble and Blackwell (2001) suggest that a community of practice consists of three dimensions:

- the structural dimension – the informal networks that enable individuals to identify others with similar interests and who have potential resources;

- the relational dimension – addressing issues around trust, shared norms, values, obligations, and expectations; and

- the cognitive dimension – addressing the need for a common body of knowledge, a common context in which this body of knowledge can reside, and a common vocabulary.

The creative learning processes of a SOG or COP should be supported in several ways. Management needs to ensure that SOGs or COPs receive sufficient resources. Concomitantly, management must ensure that SOGs and COPs are protected from negative feedback loops. Negative feedback loops sound the death knell of creativity. Management must provide positive feedback loops in the form of money, time, and management interest and commitment. Support can be provided in a number of other ways, including:

- developing members of the SOC and COPs to the mature learner level so that they can apply all the techniques of the four stages of HRD – needs investigation, design of learning experiences (usually their own), implementing these learning experiences, and evaluating the outcomes;

- developing the SOG and COP through the stages of group growth – forming, storming, norming, performing, and adjourning;

- the learning process of the SOG or COP should be supported by a learning facilitator who uses Cavaliere's five-stage model, the small business learning model, and the unstructured learning strategies;

- encouraging members of the SOG or COP to develop extensive internal and external networks; and

- investing in knowledge systems. These systems include capture systems to ensnare information, data bases to store the information, and decision tools to analyse the information.

Networks

The shadow system needs both external networks and internal networks. External networks increase the potential of identifying knowledge that is new to the organisation. Some networks should be based on weak ties so that staff come into contact with people they do not always interact with. Weak ties provide insights into new ways-of-doing and alternative values and beliefs. Networks with strong ties occur where staff members already have strong relationships and network density with a system, such as a professional body or a group of friends with similar interests. Networks with strong ties tend to provide deep and non-codified tacit knowledge that is best communicated by thick communication channels. External networks often provide knowledge that, while known to other systems, is new to the organisation. External networks can also be a catalyst for creating new knowledge.

Internal networks are particularly important to the shadow system when exporting the new knowledge to the legitimate system as it is through these internal networks that the new knowledge can be conveyed into the everyday working life of the organisation or can provide the political path for the export of the new knowledge to the legitimate system. Internal networks can also be the genesis for the creation of new knowledge by being the midwife of an SOG.

Learning partnerships

There are three types of learning partnerships:

- joint ventures;
- apprenticeship learning partnerships; and
- strategic learning partnerships.

Strategic learning partnerships are central to the shadow system. For the shadow system, the Work Capacity Learning Partnership (WCIL) can have the strongest effect. In WCIL, both the learner and the organisation are the focus of the learning experience; the learning facilitates the achievement of the intended strategic plan of the organisation; the learning strategy is based on a learning cohort; and the workplace is used as the authentic learning environment. WICL provides a rich environment for creativity, double-loop learning and the creation of new knowledge. It has the advantage of simultaneously incorporating the new knowledge into the legitimate system, as the actors in the WCIL are also the workers who use the new knowledge in their everyday activities. Hence, the actors in WCIL are often called worker-learners (Choy & Delahaye 2008) – perhaps the ultimate aim for workplace learning.

Potential problems

However, if the shadow system is too strong, the organisation will be impelled beyond its appropriate niche and develop a total disregard for the needs of its customers. This is the state of chaos. It will also cause the death of the organisation, often in a spectacular fashion. Once again, we see the need for both systems – the legitimate and the shadow – to be given just enough power and energy to keep the organisation is a state of bounded instability.

Bounded instability

The most basic task of the legitimate system is to ensure the current viability of the organisation by emphasising efficiency. Change uses resources that could otherwise be utilised for normal production. The legitimate system needs to be assured that any change is likely to benefit the organisation. However, the legitimate system is notorious for its use of defence mechanisms – automatic processes that squash new ideas (see Chapter 14).

To overcome this automatic reaction, both the shadow system and the legitimate system need to take responsibility for embedding the new knowledge in the legitimate system to achieve a state of bounded instability. In bounded instability, both systems have sufficient and appropriate power to undertake their roles.

Case study example

See the PLP case study on pages 26 to 27 of the workbook that accompanies this text for a description of how an organisation achieves a state of bounded instability.

The responsibility of the shadow system

The problem with creativity is that it is a positive feedback loop. This energy encourages the actors in the shadow system to even greater efforts of creativity – which leads to the path of chaos.

Rather, when managing the shadow system, the manager needs to intervene at the appropriate moment. The appropriate moment occurs when the SOG has created something of value during a creative episode but is in danger of moving too far into chaos – good rule of thumb is at the end of step 4 (theorising and perfecting) in Cavaliere's model (see Chapter 14). This means that the fifth step (actualising) can be a signal that the shadow system needs to prepare the new idea for the acceptance of the legitimate system as well as celebrating the creative efforts of the SOG responsible for the new idea. This fifth step coincides with the fifth stage of group growth (adjourning) as discussed in Chapter 13.

Preparing the new idea for deployment by the legitimate system is a political process. There are at least four processes that the shadow system uses to prepare the new idea.

- identifying and using a sponsor or champion who has credibility in the legitimate system;

- preparing the product so that it is packaged in a way that the legitimate system is likely to accept it;

- preparing the path by marketing the new idea with key stakeholders in the legitimate system;

- Preparing for, and engaging in, debates to encourage the legitimate system to accept the new idea; and

- inserting the new idea in the approved training courses and workshops of the legitimate system – a process called the Lisa Virus (after Lisa, a student who first suggested the idea to me).

In summary, then, the shadow system has a responsibility to refine the new idea so that is acceptable to the legitimate system. This is a political process which is often alien to the actors in the shadow system. The SOG has to be developed in these political processes or another person may need to take responsibility.

The responsibility of the legitimate system

Rather than automatically reverting to such negative responses as defence mechanisms, the legitimate system should develop a logical and objective response to the new ideas suggested by the shadow system. This response is called the embedding process. It consists of four stages:

- *the audit* – the legitimate system examines the proposal and makes decisions based on the appropriate use of available energy;

- *plan the introduction* of the new idea either through the strategic/tacit planning process or through operational planning;

- *implement the plans*; and

- *extended learning.*

Case study example

See the PLP case study on page 20 of the workbook that accompanies this text for the embedding process.

A seamless transition

As has been emphasised, the two systems – the legitimate and the shadow - are linked and strongly interrelated. Indeed, when examining an organisation using this complexity theory approach, the relationship between the two systems is seamless, as one system gradually morphs into the other. So the model depicted in Figure 15.1 is a simplistic representation of reality and it will be up to you, the reader, to add the complexities of reality as you learn more about complexity theory and its use in analysing organisations and especially in managing the knowledge capital of the organisation.

The paradox

Good organisational governance, then, is based on a paradox – the need for conformity and creativity. Both are essential to the current and future viability of the organisation. To achieve the state of bounded instability, Scott and Harker (2004) make the following points:

- The accessibility of the leader seems to be important. Lack of accessibility causes at least two problems. First, the psychological separation between the leader and staff increases, exacerbating the 'them' and 'us' syndrome. Second, the leader must then rely on second-hand information concerning what is actually happening that is frequently filtered and contaminated. Rather, the manager should 'walk the talk'. The critical issue here is to engage the humanity of the people by knowing about them personally as well as their roles and tasks in the organisation.

- The manager must allow and encourage the employees to have a noteworthy and practical input into the issues of concern to the organisation by canvassing their opinions and knowledge *before* committing to organisational policy changes.

- Identify and negate the negative effects on communication of the trappings of status and power. These negative manifestations of status and power include a large office that is physically inaccessible to the workers, gatekeepers who exercise their power inappropriately, and dressing to emphasise the difference between the management and the worker.

- Establish informal spaces where all staff – workers, supervisors, managers and specialists – can meet. As well as informal spaces, informal times need to be incorporated into the culture of the organisation.

These four points indicate that both organisational culture and leadership are needed to turn the embedded knowledge into embodied and encultured knowledge (see the discussion in the first page of this chapter).

Organisational culture

The shadow system and the processes of auditing, planning the introduction, implementing the plan, and extending the learning are essential to ensuring that the new knowledge is embedded into the organisation. However, another critical element needs to be considered so that this knowledge is further entrenched – that is, becomes encultured knowledge. Organisational culture is a subtle yet pervasive force which guides the behaviour and often the decision-making in an organisation.

In most organisations, one of the key issues that must be addressed is the primacy of the legitimate system's culture. To achieve bounded instability, the organisation's culture must support *both* the legitimate and the shadow systems. To address this issue, we will examine:

- the concept of organisational culture;

- the current understanding of the literature which tends to suggest that organisational culture is uni-dimensional; and

- an option which suggests that organisational culture is multi-dimensional.

Definition

Organisational culture is a widely accepted phenomenon, although covering such a broad and variable concept there is some difficulty in identifying one particular definition (Kwan & Walker 2004). However, Schein (1985) has provided one of the most enduring definitions that has been supported by a number of other writers – for example, Goodman, Zammuto and Gifford (2001), Van Muijen, Koopman, Dondeyne and De Cock and De Witte (1992). The definitions of organisational culture have the following elements in common. They include patterns of basic assumptions:

- invented or discovered by the group;

- to cope with external adaptations and internal integration;

- that have worked well over a long period of time; and

- should be taught to new members – namely, the correct way to perceive, think, and feel in relation to those problems.

In other words, organisational culture reflects the underlying assumptions about the way work is performed in an organisation – what is acceptable and what is not; which behaviours and actions are encouraged and which are discouraged (Mullins 2007). It represents a collection of traditions, values, beliefs, policies, and attitudes that constitute a pervasive context for everything we do and think in an organisation (McLean & Marshall 1993). Organisational culture, then, performs a similar role for the organisation that frames of reference and tacit knowledge play for the individual.

Organisational culture is formed, usually over a period of time, by a number of influences. These include:

- the philosophy and values founding members;

- strategic orientation;

- primary function and technology;

- size; and

- the beliefs and values of the current senior management and other key staff (Mullins, 2007; Smith & Vecchio, 2007).

It binds employees together, drives the way things are done in an organisation, distinguishes one organisation from another, and affects the way an organisation operates (Zu, Robbins & Fredendall 2010).

Organisational culture is undoubtedly a complex concept but, as Smith (2008) points out, managing culture is more important than managing procedures and systems – even, perhaps than strategic planning (as I heard one senior manager say 'Organisational culture eats strategy for lunch'). Further, organisational culture may be the one long-term competitive advantage because it cannot be copied quickly (Boyd & Packer 2009). Undoubtedly, then, supervisors and managers must understand and be able to use organisational culture constructively.

Elements of organisational culture

The question can then be raised 'How can we identify the culture in an organisation?' As a starting point, Schein (2004) suggests there are three distinguishing levels:

Level 1: Artefacts and creations include the office layout, written and spoken language, and overt behaviour. This layer is usually the most easily identified. It includes dress codes, physical layout of the workplace, statements of philosophy and mission, and annual reports. This level is very similar to the observed behaviour in an individual. In a similar vein, while the artefact is easily identified, making accurate implications about the deep drivers of the organisational culture is much more difficult.

Level 2: Espoused values are the descriptions that members of the organisation use to describe the organisation. In many ways, this is an externalisation process (see Chapter 3) where the organisational members try to convert their tacit understanding of the organisational culture into explicit knowledge that can be shared. This explicit knowledge is then used to justify actions and behaviours. Espoused values cover the norms, ideologies, and charters that govern behaviour and that dictate appropriate and inappropriate behaviour. Kwan and Walker (2004) believe that the dimensions of the second level are easier to access than the third level, through interviews and questionnaires.

However, because the answers are subjective, they can only indicate what people say is their reason for their behaviour and what they ideally believe the reasons to be. Thus, the true underlying reasons for the behaviour may still remain hidden.

Level 3: Basic underlying values. When a solution (based on the organisation's beliefs and values) works repeatedly, the value becomes a basic assumption. Basic assumptions become unconsciously held learned responses, guiding behaviour and determining how group members perceive, think, and feel about things – similar to the way in which frames of reference act for an individual. Level 3 is the most abstract level and includes the shared, underlying, and predominantly unconscious assumptions that people use to make sense of the world. It is the least accessible level of culture. It influences a person's perceptions, thought processes, feelings, and behaviour. This is the deepest level of culture and therefore the driver of the behaviours and decisions of the group. Most people are unaware of many of these assumptions; therefore, as usual with externalisation, they have difficulty explaining why their group behaves in the ways it does.

From these three distinguishing levels, various writers (for example, Johnson, Scholes & Whittington 2005; Lewis 2001; Markoczy1994, Schein 2004) suggest a number of factors that can be seen as constituting organisational culture. The factors are often described as forming a web. They include:

- *routine behaviours* – how members behave towards each other and towards those outside the organisation, providing evidence of how things are done;

- *processes* – the methods the organisation uses to carry out its tasks, including the official communication channels, the socialisation procedures for new staff, and the rules on the conduct of meetings;

- *rituals* – the special events through which the organisation emphasises what is particularly important;

- *stories* – told by members; typically having to do with successes, failures, heroes, and mavericks (the stories flag important events or explain and justify why things are done the way they are);

- *symbols* – such as types of office furniture, logos, titles, language (particularly jargon) – all of which become a shorthand representation of the culture;

- *forms* – the official documents, speeches, newsletters, and memos;

- *power structures* – power centres and powerful individuals who may or may not be in senior management;

- *control systems* – the measurement and reward systems that emphasise and monitor what is important – they may be official or unofficial as in defense mechanisms; and

- *organisation structure* – which may reflect power structures and delineate what is seen as important activities in the organisation. Organisational structure should be read in conjunction with power structures.

When these elements are observed, some conclusions can be drawn about the organisational culture. Interestingly, many members of the organisation may have become so adept at interpreting these signals that they react unconsciously – again, underlining the similarity with individual frames of reference.

Accordingly, these elements facilitate the continuance of the social system and give a regulatory mechanism for attitudes and behaviours (Aamodt 2004).

Types of organisational culture

Over the years, a number of authors have presented models representing types of organisational culture. Deal and Kennedy (2000) categorised corporate cultures using two determining factors – namely:

- the degree of risk; and

- the speed of feedback.

A better known model (Cameron & Quinn 2006) presented an analysis of organisational culture based on two factors:

- process (from flexibility to control); and

- focus (from internal to external).

A combination of several of these models provides a model that encompasses most of the criteria used in a number of these more specific models.

The model in Figure 15.2 suggests four types of culture based on the criteria of internal environment (from mechanistic to organic – see the work of Burns & Stalker, 1961) and the external environment (from close-to-certainty to far-from-certainty – see complexity theory in Stacey, 2000). The four types are:

- teamwork;

- entrepreneurial;

- bureaucratic; and

- premeditative.

Figure 15.2 Organisational culture

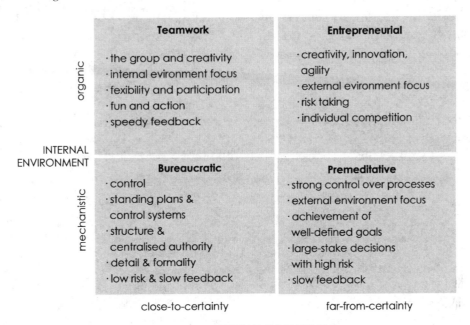

Teamwork

The focus here is on the group and creativity, using a formula of fun and action. The attention is on the internal environment. Flexibility and participation in decision-making is most highly valued, but there is an emphasis on minimising risk. Speed in feedback to staff is essential, not only to provide information but also to provide motivation to energise the fun–action dynamic. There is a strong push to ensure staff are empowered; the development of staff, using workplace learning in particular, is a key theme. Social events, especially celebrating achievements, are used to enhance morale with the aim of ensuring job satisfaction and involvement. Cohesion of activities is achieved by commitment to the group. The aim of this high energy teamwork is to produce volume, but this can be at the expense of quality.

Entrepreneurial

This form also depends on creativity as well as innovation and agility – but the energy is focused on the demands of the external environment rather than the needs of staff. Risk taking, individual freedom, and initiative are highly valued. Staff receive quick feedback, but only at the informational level. The behaviours encouraged are flexibility, resource acquisition, continual adaption to the external environment, and individual competition. Internal conflict and intense pressure is often the norm, and star performers are highly valued.

The aim of this high energy, frenetic pace is for the organisation to be at the leading edge but this can cause a non-cohesive and erratic culture, with a lack of trust and high staff turnover in.

Bureaucratic

The emphasis in this form is on the internal environment and control, particularly the control of the individual. The control is achieved by generating explicit standing plans (policies, procedures, and rules), associated control systems, regulation, and routine. The organisation has a clear structure, with power distributed accordingly and authority centralised. Staff find it difficult to measure what they do, and the emphasis is on low risks and slow feedback. The focus is on attention to trivial events, minor detail, formality, and technical perfection with no understanding of the reason for their efforts. The aim of this form is to maintain stability and predictability, the assumption being that the external environment operates under conditions of close-to-certainty.

Premeditative

This form focuses on the external environment, with a clear understanding of client needs, but insists on strong control over processes. Competition between individuals and between groups is encouraged, with the need for the achievement of well-defined goals being stressed. There is a sense of deliberateness throughout the organisation. It values clarity in tasks, task orientation, goal accomplishment, quality, and efficiency. There are large-stake decisions with high risk but slow feedback, so it may be years before it is known if the correct decision was taken. There is a hierarchical system of authority, with the decision-making from the top down. The long-term goals are market share, penetration through high-quality inventions and scientific breakthroughs, and a desire to be market leader. However, the culture moves very slowly and is vulnerable to short-term fluctuations.

However, the view that an organisation's culture may conform to one of these four types, even broadly, may not reflect the complex reality of organisational culture.

The multi-dimensional view

An organisation that is highly uni-cultural would not be the best for overall organisational effectiveness and, indeed, is likely to be somewhat dysfunctional, as such a uni-dimensional force would limit the roles and the behaviours of the staff (Belasen & Frank 2008; Zu, Robbins & Fredendall 2010). Cameron and Quinn (2006) suggest that, although there is usually one dominant culture, all organisations would be expected to have all four cultures to some degree.

However, an examination of the PLP case study at the end of this textbook provides some insight into the multi-dimensional view of organisational culture. At PLP there was a team culture. PLP's orientation booklet of emphasised the importance of people and a team culture. All staff interviewed mentioned the word 'team' several times and one editor commented, 'While each magazine is separate, as far as I am concerned the people from the design and production teams who are working on my magazine are also part of my team. We are always in each other's offices'.

This indication of interdependence is strong evidence that the groups at PLP were not simply work groups but true teams (for a discussion on teams, see Schermerhorn *et al.* 2011, pp. 425–427). There was also strong evidence that PLP was a fun place to work with staff, at interview, using words such as *relaxed, energetic, high achieving, friendly,* and *family atmosphere*. The orientation booklet frequently made references to fun, including the statement:

> *… all our offices are within a stone's throw of the beach and the ocean! Get out there at lunch or something! There are post-exercise hot showers in both the male and female toilets which staff are welcome to use, preferably one at a time.*

Note that the provision of hot showers is an artefact which helps tell the story about the organisational culture at PLP. This evidence supports the conclusion that PLP had a teamwork culture.

Case study example

See page 16 for a full description of PLP's teamwork culture.

However, there was evidence of another culture. The orientation booklet also emphasises the importance of deadlines and exceptional service to clients. At interview, most staff also spoke quite emphatically about meeting deadlines, being focused on the job, and maintaining a high quality of product. One staff member commented, 'We have to get the job done. If we need to work like Trojans, we do'. Another staff member commented, 'It all comes back to deadlines. If you don't meet them with good reason, you most likely haven't been pulling your weight'. A manager stated that he had no concerns if staff took a long lunch to have a surf 'as long as the deadlines are met'. This evidence supports the conclusion that PLP also has a *premeditative culture*, with a well-defined goal being stressed (the deadlines) and a clear understanding of client needs (high quality product, exceptional service to clients).

Case study example

See the PLP case study on page 17 of the workbook that accompanies this text for a full description of PLP's premeditative culture.

Interestingly, there was also evidence that the culture also linked these two organisational culture types. One staff member explained: 'You can go out surfing. But on the other hand, you don't take advantage. You would be letting everyone down'. The orientation booklet used phrases such as 'the workload of your colleagues' and 'a respect for your colleagues' needs'. So, as far as the staff were concerned, the deadlines had to be met otherwise they would be letting their team mates down.

So, how can we make sense of the organisational culture at PLP? It would seem that there are three parts to their organisational culture. Firstly, the teamwork culture supports the shadow system – have fun, be creative, positive feedback loops of enjoyment at work. Interestingly, this seems to be the most visible part of the organisational culture. Secondly, the premeditative culture supports the legitimate system. There is the unbreakable rule – meet the deadlines. While the 'fun' message may have been the most visible, the serious nature of 'deadlines' was a constant companion to all staff. Thirdly, the two apparently opposing culture types are linked by a third part – do not let your team mates down or increase their workload.

> ## Case study example
>
> See the PLP case study on page 27 of the workbook that accompanies this text for a multidimensional view of organisational culture.

Summary

As Hofsted (1981) pointed out, social systems can only exist because human behaviour is not random, but to some extent is predictable. The predictability is achieved, to a large extent, by the organisation's culture. Further, culture is viewed as one of the most stable and powerful forces working in organisations (Schein 1996). Therefore, organisational culture provides organisations with a level of predictability for a lengthy period. However, changing the culture of an organisation is not easy – it usually occurs only gradually (Mullins 2007).

It is important that the organisational culture supports the strategic planning process but it is also important to ensure that the culture supports the strategic changes that emerge from the shadow system. As can be seen from the PLP case study, an appropriate organisational culture that supports both the legitimate and shadow systems of the organisation will generate the apparently opposing goals of consistent strength and flexible creativity.

Leadership

We have seen that the role of the immediate supervisor or manager is central to the management of knowledge, organisational culture, and the learning of staff. As a final comment on managing the knowledge capital of the organisation, we must therefore examine the concept of leadership – a concept that is pivotal both to ordinary and extraordinary management.

Leadership has been the topic of a multitude of research projects and textbooks over the last 50 years, from the work in the 1950s which suggested that a leader had two roles – task orientation and relationship orientation – to the situational theories of the 1970s (for example, Blake & Mouton 1974; Hersey & Blanchard 1978) which suggested that the correct leadership style depended on the situation, for example the job maturity of the staff member. A thoughtful alternative was later provided by Bass (1985) who suggested that there were two leadership approaches – transactional and transformational.

Transactional leadership is based strongly on negative feedback loops and single-loop learning. The leader actively monitors deviations of subordinates from performance standards and encourages staff to maintain performance standards by developing staff expectations of rewards for accepted behaviour. Above all, mistakes must be avoided. As such, transformational leadership is likely to be most useful in situations where the group (leader and staff) is operating under near-to-certainty conditions and is faced with clear, familiar tasks – that is operating in the legitimate system of the organisation. In this situation, leaders can assert their authority and followers are more likely to comply.

Transformational leadership, on the other hand, appeals to the emotional, motivational and developmental needs of the leader's staff. Transformational leaders empower staff through emotional appeals; it may reframe stressful situations as opportunities while providing the necessary support throughout the performance process. Based on the work of Mezirow (2009) on changing emancipatory learning and Argyris (2004) on Theory-in-Use Model II, we can say that transformational leaders ensure that staff:

- have equal opportunities to participate;

- have free and informed choice;

- receive information that is valid;

- keep testing the validity of choices, especially when the choices are being implemented;

- are free from coercion and distorting self-deception; and

- are open to alternative points of view, caring about the way others think and feel.

In the literature of the 1990s, transactional leadership was inclined to be disparaged while transformational was lauded (for a discussion, see Lowe, Kroek & Sivasubramaniam 1996). To an extent, this may be correct. A study by Rank, Nelson, Allen and Xu (2009) found that transactional leadership negatively affected innovative behaviour while transactional leadership provided a positive force. In terms of our earlier discussion, negative feedback loops suppress creativity and positive feedback loops encourage creativity.

Complexity theory suggests that, in contemporary times, an *either/or stance* is seldom correct for managing organisations – rather we should look for a *both/and* position. Recent research has supported this statement. Morhart, Herzog and Tomczak (2009) found that a medium level of transactional leadership maximises the positive effects of transformational leadership as transactional behaviours are likely to be perceived by staff as helpful guidance, fair and constructive, and provide readily identifiable signs of appreciation. Transformational leadership supported by transactional leadership is the key to achieving bounded instability.

In the PLP case study we see how transactional leadership and transformational leadership combine to provide a dynamic knowledge-management process. Transactional leadership focuses on critical parts of the organisation. For example:

- one of the central control systems is the cash-flow budget with financial reports centred on each of the magazines with the financial director saying, 'Everything has a control, everything has to balance back' (see pages 19-20);

- task breakdowns are provided for every job, and policies are fully documented (see pages 18-19); and

- the CEO insists that a full proposal accompanies any new idea (see pages 20-21).

However, there is plenty of evidence of transformational leadership. For example:

- the emphasis on on-the-job training (see pages 13 and 14);

- the use of 360 degree performance appraisals (see page 25);

- the introduction of the two new magazines (see pages 21-22); and

- the emphasis on teamwork (see pages 7 and 16).

It should also be noted that these examples given for leadership are also appropriate for the organisational culture types – namely, teamwork culture and premeditative culture – used in PLP.

What the PLP case study also demonstrates is that an appropriate mix of leadership styles and organisational culture is essential. In PLP, this *judicious amalgamation of leadership and culture* has provided the ultimate support system for a knowledge-management process that emphasises both the maintenance of current valuable knowledge and a continuing search for new knowledge. In other words, the leadership styles and the organisational culture types combine seamlessly and are in mutual support and harmony.

The role of the HR developer

Over the last decade, the role of the HR developer has grown both in complexity and importance. The HR developer is the *steward of the knowledge resource* of the organisation. The HR developer accepts and operationalises this stewardship role directly or indirectly by:

- *creating new knowledge* by managing the knowledge-creating processes of externalisation, combination, internalisation and socialisation;

- *identifying and importing* relevant explicit knowledge from outside the organisation;

- *disseminating knowledge* throughout the organisation (This dissemination is most often achieved by the four stages of HRD – i.e. needs investigation, design, implementation, and evaluation that has been the main emphasis of this text. Assisting the shadow system to inculcate new knowledge into the legitimate system via the unstructured learning strategies, however, is a growing responsibility.);

- *maintaining* the knowledge resource through the four stages of HRD;

- recognising the difference between the two basic systems of the organisation – *the legitimate* and *shadow systems* – and assisting the managers to manage these two systems;

- providing *learning support to SOGs* by applying the skills and knowledge discussed in this textbook and by facilitating the learning processes of the groups by using such models as group growth and Cavaliere's five-stage learning model; and

- *developing and supporting supervisors* and managers as they manage the workplace curriculum.

The successful implementation of the HR developer's role is what helps the organisation to become that most robust and viable of entities, the learning organisation.

Career development for the HR developer

Several times throughout this text the point has been made that the responsibility for learning in the organisation rests with the supervisors and managers. Sometimes, however, supervisors and managers delegate this responsibility to an internal or external HR developer. An internal HR developer may operate under the name of trainer, learning consultant, workplace educator, or HR developer. The external HR developer is often called a consultant. Wherever the role exists – with a trainer, learning consultant, supervisor, or manager – consideration must be given to the career development of the HR developer or that portion of the supervisor's and manager's role that incorporates HR development.

As indicated throughout this text, the HR development role is complex and challenging. A HR developer is a researcher, a designer, a facilitator of adult learning, an evaluator of programs and projects, and the steward of the organisation's knowledge assets. The HR developer needs to be highly competent in all the skills and knowledge discussed in this text. It can be expected, then, that the developmental path of a HR developer will be complex and time consuming.

What is the best way to become a HR developer? There are, of course, many paths. The following path is an example of the most productive and efficient:

1. Start as a trainer or adult educator in the structured learning strategies (see Chapter 10). The structured models of the skill session and the theory session naturally integrate the principles of learning and the other adult learning theories (see Chapter 3). The novice HR developer can then concentrate on honing the basic micro-skills of questioning, responding, creating learning objectives, and using visual aids. Concurrently, the novice is learning the basics of evaluation as learning is tested in the practice stage of the skill session and the activity steps of the theory session.

2. One indication that these basic skills have been assimilated is when the novice begins to focus on the learners rather than focusing on personal security and anxieties. At this stage, the novice can then move onto the discussion. The discussion model (see Chapter 10) begins the HR developer's journey into concentrating less on the content being learned by the learners and more on the process of learning. The predominant processes used in the discussion to manage the learning processes are listening, questioning, probing, and summarising (see Chapter 7), and the use of visual aids (see Chapter 10).

3. From the discussion, the HR developer is ready for the case study (see Chapter 10). The case study focuses the learners' attention on a pre-set topic and the HR developer then surfaces the knowledge resident in the individual minds of the learners by again using questioning. At the same time, the HR developer is becoming accustomed to the sensation of transferring to the learners the responsibility of identifying the content to be learned.

4. The step up to the role play (see Chapter 10) brings the HR developer into contact with the learners' emotions. As indicated in Chapter 12, role plays are

designed to encourage learners to challenge their frames of reference. Such challenges invariably surface emotions and the HR developer must be able to use this additional energy as a learning resource.

5.   From the role play, the HR developer is ready to use the more complex unstructured learning strategies of problem-based learning, contract learning, action learning, and change interventions (see Chapter 12). In these learning strategies, the HR developer delegates fully to the learners the responsibility for the content to be learned. The HR developer concentrates on managing the learning processes discussed in Chapter 11.

6.   As the HR developer has been developing the skills and knowledge necessary to facilitate learning in the previous five points, he or she was also gaining knowledge and skills in evaluation. Specifically, the HR developer would have been observing the learning of the learners and making decisions based on these observations. These observations introduce the HR developer to the second stage of Kirkpatrick's evaluation model (see Chapter 12) – that is, learning. The HR developer needs to expand her or his focus gradually to the other stages of reaction, on-the-job behaviour, and organisational results. This focus on evaluation not only expands the HR developer's knowledge of the topic of evaluation but also provides feedback on the HR developer's efforts in facilitating learning, thus providing further opportunities for questioning one's own knowledge and skills in facilitation.

7.   Designing learning experiences can be the next stage in the development path. Often, this design stage can follow the HR developer's experience in facilitating learning (points 1 to 5 above). Designing lesson plans for skill and theory sessions is usually quickly followed by designing structured training courses or workshops based on the programming and task category of the hierarchy of learning outcomes (see Chapter 8). As the HR developer gains experience in the unstructured learning strategies, he or she is likely to become involved in designing learning experiences at the deeper levels of the HLO.

8.   Finally, the HR developer can become involved in HRDNI. The role is one of being a researcher; Chapters 5 to 7 discussed the basics of research. However, to be fully competent in research, the HR developer would need to undertake further study in research, a topic that has numerous textbooks and study programs.

These eight steps have provided a developmental path that is relevant for HRD activities in the legitimate system. Extensive experience in these activities will allow the HR developer to move into facilitating learning in that most dynamic, creative, and chaotic of learning cauldrons – the shadow system. Facilitating the learning in SOGs and developing supervisors to become competent in workplace learning is a challenging but gratifying experience.

For those of you who take the path of becoming an adult educator, a community educator, a trainer, an instructor, a workplace educator, a learning facilitator, or a HR developer – good luck and good life-long learning. I hope you enjoy the journey as much as I have.

References

Aamodt, M G 2004, *Applied industrial/organizational psychology*, 4th edn, New York: Thompson Learning.

Argyris, C 2004, *Reasons and Rationalizations: The limits of organizational knowledge*, Oxford University Press, New York.

Australian Standard 5037-2005 *Knowledge Management*. Sydney: Standards Australia International. <www.standards.com.au/ catalogue/script/search.asp>

Bass, B M 1985, *Leadership and performance beyond expectations*, The Free Press, New York.

Belasen, A & Frank, N 2008, 'Competing values leadership: Quadrant roles and personality traits', *Leadership & Organization Development Journal*, 29(2), pp. 127-143.

Blake, R R & Mouton, J S 1974, *The new managerial grid*, Gulf Publishing Company, Houston.

Browning, V & Delahaye, B L 2010, 'Enhancing workplace learning through collaborative HRD', in M Clarke (ed.), *Cases and readings in HRM and sustainability*, Tilde University Press, Melbourne, Vic.

Boyd, C & Packer, S 2009, 'All hands on deck', *HR Monthly*, August, pp. 18-20.

Burns, T & Stalker, G M 1961, *The management of innovation*, Tavistock, London.

Cameron, K S & Quinn, R E 2006, *Diagnosing and changing organizational culture*, Upper Saddle River, NJ: Prentice Hall.

Cavaliere, L A 1992, 'The Wright brother's odyssy: Their flight of learning', *Learning for Personal Development*, in L A Cavaliere and A Sgrol (eds.), San Francisco: Jossey-Bass.

Choy, S & Delahaye, B L 2008, 'Chapter 10: Leadership development: Implementation of an organization centred curriculum' in S Billett, C Harteis & A Etelapelto (eds.), *Emerging perspectives of learning at work*, Sense Publishing, Roterdam.

Deal, T E & Kennedy, A A 2000, *The new corporate cultures*, Perseus Books.

Delahaye, B L 2003). 'Human resource development and the management of knowledge capital', in R Wiesner & B Millett (eds.), *Human Resource Management.' Challenges and Future Directions*, Brisbane: John Wiley & Sons Australia.

Dickie, L & Dickie, C 2006, *Cornerstones of management*, Tilde University Press, Manly, NSW.

Fuller, S 2002, *Knowledge Management Foundations*, Boston: Butterworth-Heinemann.

Gamble, P R & Blackwell, J 2001, *Knowledge Management: A State of the Art Guide.* London: Kogan Page.

Goodman, E A, Zammuto, R F & Gifford, B D 2001, 'The competing values framework: Understanding the impact of organizational culture on the quality of work life', *Organization Development Journal*, 19(3), pp. 58-68.

Hersey, P Blanchard, K H 1978, 'So you want to to know your leadership style?', *Training and Development Journal*, February, pp. 1-15.

Hofstede, G 1981, 'Culture and organizations', *International Studies of Management & Organizations*, 10(4), pp. 15-42

Johnson, G, Scholes, K & Whittington, R 2005, *Exploring Corporate Strategy*, 7th edn, Prentice Hall.

Kwan, P & Walker, A 2004, 'Validating the competing values model as a representation of organizational culture through inter-institutional comparisons', *Organizational Analysis*, 12, pp. 21-89.

Lewis, D 2001, 'Organisational culture – theory, fad or managerial control?', in R Wiesner & B Millett (eds.), *Management and organisational behaviour*, John Wiley & Sons Australia, Brisbane.

Lindberg, C 2001, 'Listen to the shadow system', *Complexity Management.* <http://www.plexusinstitute.com!edgeware/archive/think/ mainprin8 .html>

Lowe, K B, Kroeck, K G & Sivasubramaniam, N 1996, 'Effectiveness correlates of transformational and transactional leadership: A meta-analysis review', *Leadership Quarterly*, 7, pp. 385-426.

Markoczy, L 1994, 'Modes of organizational learning: Institutional change and Hungarian joint ventures', *International Studies of Management and Organization*, 24(4), pp. 5-31.

McLean, A & Marshall, J 1993, *Intervening in culture,* Working paper, University of Bath.

Mezirow, J 2009, 'Transformative learning theory', in Mezirow, J & Taylor E W (eds.), *Transformational learning in practice: Insights from community, workplace and higher education.* Jossey-Bass, San Francisco..

Mintzberg, H 2009, *Management*, Berrett-Koehler, New York.

Morhart, F M Herzog, W & Tomczak , T 2009, 'Brand-specific leadership: Turning employees into brand champions', *Journal of Marketing*, 73, September, pp. 122-142.

Mullins, L J 2007, *Management and organisational behaviour,* 8th edn, Harlow: Pearson Education.

Rank, J Nelson, N E Allen, T D and Xu, X 2009, 'Leadership predictors of innovation and task performance: Subordinates' self-esteem and self=presentation as moderators', *Journal of Occupational and Organizational Psychology*, 82, p. 465-489.

Schein, E H 1985, *Organizational culture and leadership: A dynamic view*, San Francisco, CA: Jossey-Bass.

Schein, E H 1996, 'Culture: The missing concept in organization studies', *Administrative Science Quarterly*, 41(2), pp. 229-240.

Schein, E H 2004, *Organizational culture and leadership: A dynamic view*, 3rd edn, Jossey-Bass.

Schermerhorn, J R, Davidson, P, Poole, D, Simon, A, Woods, P & Chau, S L 2011, *Management*, 4th edn, John Wiley & Sons Australia, Brisbane.

Scott, T & Harker, P 2004, *The Myth of Nine to Five: Work, Workplaces and Workplace Relationships*, Thorogood, London.

Smith, A 2008, 'Human resource management in Australian registered training organisations', literature review and discussion starter, NCVER, Adelaide.

Smith, A 2008, *Human resource management in Australian registered training organisations: Literature review and discussion starter – Support document*, NCVER, Adelaide.

Smith, C G & Vecchio, R P 2007, 'Organisational culture and strategic leadership: Issues in the management of strategic change', in R P Vecchio (ed.), *Leadership: Understanding the dynamics of power and influence of organisations*, University of Notre Dame, Notre Dame, Ind.

Stacey, R D 1996, *Strategic Management and Organisational Dynamics*, 2nd edn, London: Pitman.

Stacey, R D 2000, *Strategic Management and Organisational Dynamics*, 3rd edn, London: Pitman.

Sveiby, K E 2007, 'Disabling the context for knowledge work: The role of managers' behaviours', *Management Decision*, 45:10, pp. 1636-1655.

Van Muijen, J J, Koopman, P L, Dondeyne, P, De Cock, G & De Witte, K 1992, 'Organizational culture: The development of an international instrument for comparing countries', in G Hunyady (ed.), *Proceedings of the 2nd European congress of psychology*, Budapest, Hungary, pp. 249-259.

Wilson, J P 2005, *Human resource development: Learning and training for individuals and organisations*, Kogan Page, London.

Zu, X, Robbins, T L & Fredendall, L D 2010, 'Mapping the critical links between organizational culture and TQM/Six Sigma practices', *International Journal of Production Economics*, 123, pp. 86-106.

Glossary

accuracy one of the twin pillars of scientific research, means that the research tools and analytic processes used are as precise and correct as possible

action learning an unstructured learning strategy that emphasises questioning and the need to implement what is learned

action plans the permanent record of the intended activities decided on in the developmental performance appraisal

action research the fundamental model used in managing the process in change interventions

active listening going beyond the technical skills of listening and responding to understand and feel what the learner is explaining

activity number 1 the activity used in the introduction to the interview to encourage the interviewee to talk

activity number 2 the first level in the rapport zone, where the interviewer uses interviewing skills to encourage the interviewee to provide information

adjourning the fifth and final stage of group growth when the group disbands

administrative performance appraisal one of the two types of performance appraisal; it concentrates on administrative decisions such as salary increments

adult learner after finishing high school; may be learning in the workplace, at a work-based learning course or at an educational institution such as a polytechnic, TAFE or university

analytic learning diary one type of learning diary, based on four headings – description of the experience, detailed observations, synthesis and future behaviour

analytical subgroup consists of four elements (linear analysis, diagnostic analysis, complex analysis and analysis under uncertainty) and is one of the three subgroups of the task category in the HLO

andragogy the art and science of teaching adults

anxiety the second stage in the individual change transition model, caused by the loss of familiar patterns and behaviours

apprenticeship learning partnership learning partnership of the apprentice or trainee, the host organisation, and the registered training organisation

approximation of the task the third step in the small business learning model

AS 5037-2005 the Australian standard for knowledge management

audit part of the embedding process that the legitimate system uses to import new knowledge from the shadow system

behaviour level the third level in Kirkpatrick's evaluation model, examines the change in behaviour on the job

behaviourally anchored rating scales a method of judging an individual's characteristics in the job specification

blended learning a combination of e-learning and face-to-face learning

boundaryless career where an individual moves between firms and projects because of changes in **a** person's interests, abilities and values as well as changes in the work environment. In a boundaryless career individuals need to continually upgrade skills and knowledge and expand personal networks. See protean career.

bounded instability a healthy state of tension within the organisation where the need for high productivity is balanced with a continual search for learning and change

Brinkerhoff's model a more extensive evaluation model than Kirkpatrick's, consists of six stages – I (needs and goals), II (design), III (implementation), IV (learning), V (usage and endurance of learning) and VI (payoff)

budget a plan documenting the expected income and expenditures of the designed learning experience

career counselling the first part of career development (see also career management) where the individual's needs are identified. Five steps – career anchors, personal environment, information on future careers, constructing action plans, and making change

career management the second part of career development (see career counselling), integrates the career needs of the individual with the strategic directions of the organisation

case study a learning experience where the learner reads a narration of a real-life event and answers set questions, and where the HR developer uses the discussion to encourage learning

causal assumptions the lowest level of an individual's frames of reference

Cavaliere's five stage model a process for facilitating SOGs

challenging the fundamental values of the legitimate system the second role of the shadow system

change interventions an unstructured learning strategy that uses group dynamics and action research to manage the learning process

collectivist cultures cultures that value obedience, duty, harmony, dependence and subordinate individual goals to group goals

combination combining another's explicit knowledge with one's own

communicative learning understanding the world of another person and establishing the validity for personal beliefs

communities of practice often develop out of SOGs, and comprises people who come together to discuss and investigate areas of mutual interest

competencies similar to learning objectives, but intended to cover skills, knowledge, abilities and attitudes to be assessed by observation several times in the work environment; used mainly for instrumental learning (see also learning objectives and learning outcomes)

complex but clear learning outcomes is the fifth element of the workplace learning model and combines with extended learning

complexity theory a combination of chaos theory and quantum mechanics

concern for others subgroup consists of four elements (developing others, empathy, leadership and managing conflict) and is the most complex of the relationships category of the HLO

constructive alignment occurs where the intended learning outcomes are mirrored by the learning strategies and learning assessment used

content analysis a way of analysing the qualitative data gathered during an interview or a focus group

contract learning an unstructured learning strategy that uses a learning contract to manage the learning process

control group the second most complex scientific model, uses a pre-test–post-test model with a control group as well as the group experiencing the learning

control systems systems that identify aberrant behaviour. Has four steps – a predetermined standard, a measuring sensor, a comparative procedure, and remedial action. One of the processes that the legitimate system uses to manage the organisation's knowledge assets

cost–benefit analysis an analysis that identifies the costs and the benefits of a learning episode and then expresses the results as a ratio

create new knowledge the first role of the shadow system

creating knowledge is the ninth and final element of the workplace learning model; the learner becomes a mature learner and can create knowledge

criterion-referenced scoring the marks achieved against predetermined criteria, usually presented as a percentage of the total possible score

critical reflection where an individual examines the very foundations and justifications for personal frames of reference

critical thinking consists of problem solving, creativity, evaluation, dialectic thinking and logical thinking and is at the third level of learning outcomes in the HLO

current knowledge the learner's present level of knowledge of a particular topic

cyclical model a model which suggests that the curriculum design process can start at any of the four steps of the rational model

data analysis the process of examining the gathered data to identify trends or conclusions

data gathering the collection of information that may define, explain or describe the opportunity or problem being investigated

defence mechanisms the automatic response of the legitimate system to a new idea coming from the shadow system

design stage the second of the HRD stages where aims, objectives and content are examined

developmental performance appraisal one of the two types of performance appraisal; it concentrates on the developmental needs of the individual

diminishing support is the eighth and second-last element of the workplace learning model. The guide gradually encourages the learner to become a self-directed learner by scaffolding and fading

direct guidance of experts central to the quality of workplace learning, this is the sixth element of the workplace learning model; the learner is given a mentor who can help plan the workplace learning and provide feedback to the learner

discovery the third stage of the individual change transition model, an energetic phase when new information, skills, and behaviours are uncovered

discussion a learning experience where the HR developer uses micro-skills to elicit the required information from the learners

disorienting dilemma a significant, undeniable, and usually traumatic fact or event that challenges a paradigmatic assumption

double-loop learning learning that challenges the underlying values of what is being taught

e-learning use of information and computer technology to deliver efficient, effective and engaging learning

emancipatory learning transforming frames of reference, especially hegemonic assumptions

embedding process the process used by the legitimate system to incorporate new knowledge into everyday work life; four steps include the audit, the plan, the implementation, and extended learning

encapsulation the phenomenon where learners leave the learning in the classroom

engagement decision the first of the six phases in the individual adult learning model; based on the readiness to learn, individuals decide whether to commence a learning episode

entrance investment time the time invested by the interviewer to bring the interviewee into the rapport zone

ethnocentricity the belief in the intrinsic superiority of one's own cultural norms

evaluation plan the plan, showing time lines and what evidence needs to be collected, allows the developmental and judgemental roles of evaluation to be coordinated

evaluation report records the decisions taken during the evaluation and presents the results and recommendations

evaluation stage the fourth HRD stage where the worth of the learning experience is assessed

exit investment time time invested by the interviewer to bring the interview to a close

expectancy–valence theory a motivational theory of four sequential steps

experiential learning a learning episode where the learner experiments with or experiences a specific situation and then reflects on it. Consists of several approaches including learning instruments, simulations, projects, and sensitivity groups

explicit knowledge knowledge that can be articulated

extended learning is the fourth element of the workplace learning model; the learner is moved from peripheral to full engagement to expand the learning gained in the learning episode **fading** together with scaffolding, a technique used in diminishing support, the guide gradually removes parts of the scaffolding

external networks such as professional bodies, a good source for new knowledge

externalisation allowing tacit knowledge to surface so that it can be articulated as explicit knowledge

extraordinary management new management theories, based on the concepts of chaos theory and dissipative structures, that are used to manage the shadow system; in particular, using positive feedback loops and double-loop learning

facilitator team the group of people who conduct and manage the focus group

facilitator the role the HR developer takes to manage the process of the unstructured learning strategies

focus group a means of gathering data from a group of people

formal learning learning that attracts a qualification; may occur off-site or be a combination of off-site and on-site learning

formative assessment assessing the strengths and weaknesses of a learner's knowledge and using this information as developmental feedback

forming the first stage of group growth where the individuals are concerned about the purpose of the group

formulating goals the second phase in the individual adult learning model; the individual decides on the goals of the learning episode

four stages of HRD HRDNI, design, implementation, and evaluation. The key processes that the legitimate system uses to manage the organisation's knowledge assets. Uses information from strategic planning, control systems, performance appraisal, and selection

frames of reference the deep-seated underlying values and belief systems that shape and dictate the everyday attitudes and behaviours of an individual

free flow diary one type of learning diary, is a 'cathartic experience', allowing the learner to creatively express thoughts and feelings

gender a word that denotes the different sex or sexual orientation of a person

gender models models in the literature that emphasise the emancipatory approach as the individual becomes free from hegemonic assumptions,

globalisation the involvement in the economic and industrial activities of another country; interacting on a global scale with people from a variety of cultures in the normal course of one's job

group composition the make-up of the membership of the group

group dynamics the forces that operate within a group

harassment a particular form of discrimination designed to humiliate, offend, intimidate or otherwise make a person feel unwelcome or inadequate

hierarchy of learning outcomes (HLO) a model that categorises learning outcomes into a hierarchy and links the categories to appropriate learning strategies

high-context cultures where 'how' a message is said (the context) is more important that 'what' is said (the content)

historical embeddedness historical moments experienced by an individual that affect the perception of that individual

holistic adult learning the total entity of a learning adult

HRDNI report the written document that describes the process used and the results of the investigation

human resource development needs investigation (HRDNI) the diagnostic process where data is gathered and then analysed to ensure the effective and efficient development of staff

impairment is the term used to cover the variety of disabilities – either mental or physical – and health issues that present a challenge to the individual learner

implementation stage the third HRD stage where formal or informal learning activities occur

implementing subgroup consists of five elements (work motivation, a bias for action, purposeful action, use of unilateral power, and effectiveness) and is the most complex of the subgroups of the task category of the HLO

import new knowledge the first role of the shadow system

increased confidence and abilities is the seventh and final phase in the individual adult learning model

indigenous Australians are the Australian Aboriginal and Torres Strait Island people

indirect guidance is the seventh element of the workplace learning model; the learner needs to be surrounded by experienced workers and by a positive learning culture

individual adult learning model is a seven-phase model that describes how an individual adult learns in the workplace; the phases include performance engagement decision, formulation of goals, trial and error, seek support, seek expertise, production phase, increased confidence and abilities

individual change transition model a four-step (security, anxiety, discovery and integration) model that can help the guide plan and judge the diminishing support element of the workplace curriculum model

individualist cultures a culture that values self-reliance, creativity, independence, solitude and equality

individuals in relationships the basis for extraordinary management

information the inert data that are contained in books and computer data banks

instrumental learning learning to control and manipulate the environment

integration the fourth and final stage of the individual change transition model; the new information, skills and behaviours are assimilated into the current tasks and processes

interaction model a model of curriculum design which suggests that the four steps of the rational model are interactive

internal networks assist the shadow system in exporting new knowledge to the legitimate system

internalisation converting explicit knowledge into tacit knowledge

interpersonal subgroup consists of five elements (communication, interaction at the objective level, interaction at the subjective level, using group processes, and using social power) and is one of the subgroups of the relationships category of the HLO

interpretation drawing conclusions about the complex behaviours, messages, forces and conditions of an event

interview a one-on-one interaction where one person is gathering information from another

interviewee the person being interviewed

interviewer the person conducting the interview

intimacy a deeper level in the rapport zone where the interviewee is willing to discuss emotions

intrapersonal subgroup consists of six elements (spontaneity, accurate self-awareness, self-confidence, inner strength, self-discipline, and emotional resilience) and is one of the subgroups of the relationships category of the HLO

investigation plan the action plan that describes how the investigation will be conducted

investigation stage a specific investigation of an opportunity or problem identified by the surveillance stage, consists of two phases data gathering and data analysis

job analysis the process of gathering and analysing data on a job, so that the two basic job documents, the job description and the job specification, can be formulated

job description one of the two basic job documents, lists the job title and other contextual information, the job duties and the performance indicators

job specification lists the characteristics (knowledge, skills and abilities) required by the job holder

joint venture a jointly owned organisation formed by at least two companies to learn about and create a specific product or process; the outcome is more specific than that of a strategic alliance

key stakeholders people with political knowledge who influence decisions within the organisation

Kirkpatrick's model the most common model used for evaluation, consists of four levels reaction, learning, behaviour and results

knowledge unique resource that does not adhere to the law of diminishing returns, grows from sharing and results from an individual accessing and enabling information

leadership a combination of transactional and transformational leadership that supports the management of knowledge and combines seamlessly with the organisational culture

learners the adult learners involved in the learning experience

learning diaries journals written by the learner to record events, thoughts and reflections, consisting of three types – analytic diary, organised diary and free flow diary

learning episode is the second element of the managing workplace learning model; the learning episode may occur in the work site or off-site

learning instrument an experiential learning approach where the learner completes an instrument, often a questionnaire, to uncover information about personal frames of reference

learning level the second level in Kirkpatrick's evaluation model, examines the amount of learning that occurred, using one of the testing processes – skill test, written objective test, subjective written test, performance test, learning diary, or portfolio assessment

learning objective a statement, usually written and consisting of a terminal behaviour, a performance standard, and conditions under which the assessment is to take place. Provides the direction for, and the final destination of, the learning experience

learning organisation organisation using both the legitimate system and the shadow system to ensure that knowledge is adequately maintained and created so that the organisation will continue to survive

learning orientation a model that categorises learners into four stages that reflect their predisposition for certain learning experiences

learning outcomes the expected outcome when the learning experience is based on communicative or emancipatory learning (see learning objectives and competencies)

learning partnerships a network of organisations or groups that come together to enhance mutual learning opportunities

learning set a group of learners involved in action learning

learning space is the resource that allows the learner to learn in the workplace, usually time and location

learning strategies the methods of instruction and/or facilitation used to provide adult learners with learning experiences

learning styles four preferences (diverger/reflector, assimilator/theorist, converger/pragmatist and accommodator/activist) for types of learning experiences

learning transfer having learning that occurred in an off-site learning experience being used in the workplace (see principles of learning in Chapter 3)

lecture a modified theory session which omits the activity step

legitimate system one of the two basic models of any system, including organisations. Uses negative feedback loops and single-loop learning to ensure that the organisation is operating efficiently (see also shadow system)

liberatory models are models in the literature that highlight the structures and systems that oppress women and other minority groups through power and control

logistical subgroup consists of four elements (goal identification, administrative proficiency, resources allocation, and efficiency) and is one of the subgroups of the task category of the HLO

logistics organising the resources needed to bring a focus group together

low-context cultures where 'what' is said (the content) is more important than 'how' the message is said (the context)

management of knowledge knowledge is considered to be a valuable asset and, as such, needs to be managed appropriately

management re-engineering the cost-saving approaches based on rational economics, designed to help the organisation to survive the rapidly changing environment

managing workplace learning model a nine-element model consisting of performance appraisal, learning episode, transfer of learning, extended learning, complex but clear learning outcomes, direct guidance of experts, indirect guidance of experts, diminishing support, and creating new knowledge; it governs how learning is best managed in the workplace

Maori the indigenous peoples of New Zealand

mentoring an unstructured learning strategy where a senior member of staff who is a superior performer acts as **a** model, coach, and adviser to the learner

meta-abilities category consists of the elements of mental agility, helicopter perception, and self-perpetuating learning, and is at the fourth, and most complex, level of learning outcomes in the HLO

micro-skills the skills of questioning, responding, using visual aids and constructing learning objectives used by the HR developer to enhance learning

motivation the internal force encouraging people to learn

movement from peripheral to full participation sequencing activities in the workplace so that the learner develops progressively; the first element in the workplace curriculum model

negative feedback loops feedback loops that dampen aberrant behaviour. Used by the legitimate system

networks two types, internal and external; assist with identifying new knowledge and transferring that knowledge to the legitimate system

Newtonian paradigm the assumption that all organisms can be analysed in a rational and linear manner

nonverbal behaviour the gestures and body language used by the interviewer and the interviewee during the interview

norming the third stage of group growth when the group becomes more cohesive

norm-referenced scoring the comparison of the raw score to the average of a nominated group

objective written test scoring requires no interpretation by the examiner; consists of four types – multiple choice, true-false, matching, completion

objectives model another name for the rational model

observation form aid used by the assessor in a performance test (see also rubric)

off-site learning learning that occurs in locations such as a training course or at an educational institution (see also formal learning)

older learners are generally regarded as those over the age of 45 years

ordinary management the conventional management theories that are based on the Newtonian paradigm

organisational culture the culture in an organisation that supports both the legitimate and the shadow system and combines seamlessly with leadership

organised diary type of learning diary, usually in prose format, with an emphasis on careful construction, clear expression, attempted objectivity, and cognitive logic

other sexual orientations include homosexuality, bisexuality and transsexuality

painting the path ensuring that the HRDNI report provides a sufficiently detailed description of the research process

paradigmatic assumptions highest level of an individual's frames of reference

paraphrasing repeating back to the interviewee, in a concise form, the essential elements of the interviewee's reply

pass time part of the introduction to the interview, used to decrease the stress levels **of** the interviewee

pattern of the interview the model of an ideal interview structure that enhances the interview results

performance appraisal a process that identifies the strengths and weaknesses in staff's knowledge. One of the processes that the legitimate system uses to manage the organisation's knowledge assets

performance indicators the observable and measurable outputs of the job

performance management the management of all systems that affect individual and organisational performance to ensure a strong strategic direction

performance test assessment of a complex test, usually based on both the procedural and task and relationships levels of the HLO

performing the fourth stage of group growth when the group becomes fully functional

platform model a model of curriculum design which reflects the more natural process of negotiation in human interactions

political knowledge is made up of political power and knowledge of the organisational procedures and processes

political processes or activities processes used by the shadow system to export new knowledge to the legitimate system

portfolio assessment collections of the learner's work across a significant time period

positive feedback loops forces that enhance small variations, used in extraordinary management and the shadow system

post-test the simplest of the scientific models, consists of conducting the learning episode and then conducting an evaluation

power distance the degree of deference that one individual gives another

presage factors the factors to be evaluated before the learning episode commences, are included in Brinkerhoff's model but not in Kirkpatrick's model

prescriptive assumptions the second highest level of an individual's frames of reference

pre-test–post-test the second simplest of the scientific models, consists of conducting an evaluation, conducting the learning episode, and then conducting the evaluation again

principles of learning ten principles on which instrumental learning is based

probing the combination of questioning and paraphrasing to explore the interviewee's ideas to a deeper level

problem-based learning an unstructured learning strategy which allows the learner to work on a professional problem to develop knowledge and skills

problem-solving interview where the appraiser and the appraisee have equal power and approach the appraisal process as a common problem-solving event

product marketing plan a plan to market and advertise the designed learning experience

production phase the sixth phase in the individual adult learning model; the individual uses a variety of learning approaches to improve knowledge and skill – these approaches include trial-and-error, repetitive learning procedures, technical rationality, problem solving, and problem defining

program plan a time plan of the designed learning experience

programmed knowledge category consists of the elements of basic facts and skills, professional/technical information, and procedural skills, and is the least complex of the learning outcomes in the HLO

project a defined activity from the workplace where the learner can experiment and reflect on the outcomes

protean career see boundaryless career

protégé the learner in the mentoring program

psychosocial filter is the process an individual uses to choose who would be best expert for a mentor; it comprises social confidence of the individual learning and the approachability and credibility of the expert

questioning a micro-skill where the HR developer queries the learner to externalise that learner's ideas and thoughts

questions queries asked by the interviewer to control the interview's direction

rapport zone the time in an interview when the interviewee experiences minimum stress and is more likely to voluntarily disclose information

rational discourse used in communicative learning, meaning to talk and listen respectfully to others, even when they hold differing views

rational model a model suggesting that curriculum design consists of four steps – objectives, instructional strategies, organising, and evaluation

raw score the overall quantitative score achieved in a test

reaction level the first level in Kirkpatrick's evaluation model, examines the reactions of the learners to the learning episode

referential adequacy ensuring that comments and descriptions are a sufficiently detailed and rich representation of the respondent's ideas

reflective discourse an assessment of beliefs or ideas to determine the truth or falsity, belief, or disbelief of the proposal

relationships category consists of the subgroups of interpersonal, intrapersonal, and concern for others, and is at the second level (the same level as the task category) of learning outcomes in the HLO

replicability one of the twin pillars of scientific research, means that the research should be able to be repeated with the same results

resource plan a plan that describes the resources needed to mount the designed learning experience – and when these resources will be needed

resources the assets available to the HR developer to conduct a learning experience; including time, physical resources, and other HR developers

responding a micro-skill where the HR developer uses paraphrasing, probing, and summarising to provide feedback and encouragement to the learner

results level the fourth level in Kirkpatrick's model, examines the impact of the learning episode on the organisational outcomes

ritual the polite greeting used to commence the interview

role play similar to a case study, where the narration is replaced by the learners enacting roles which are subsequently discussed

rubric an aid to the assessor in performance testing, identifies the expected qualities of each behaviour within a hierarchy of potential responses

sampling investigating a percentage of the whole population, and then drawing conclusions about the population from that sample

scaffolding together with fading, a technique used in diminishing support; the guide provides temporary and adjustable support for the learner so that the learner becomes a self-directed learner

scientific models aimed at proving causality, consist of five types – post-test, pre-test–post-test, time series evaluation, control group, and Solomon four

security the first stage of the change transition model; this is a pre-change mode where the individual is surrounded by familiar habits, processes and patterns

seek expertise, the fifth phase in the individual adult learning model where individuals, using their psychosocial filter, select an expert to provide help

seek support the fourth phase in the individual adult learning model; the individual looks for information from family, professional experts, and other small businesses

selection a process that identifies appropriate new staff. One of the processes that the legitimate system uses to manage the organisation's knowledge assets

self-evaluation where the learner evaluates his or her own learning, and values this above evaluation by others

self-organising groups (SOGs) dissipative structures that are the heart of the shadow system; they need to be supported by management and can become communities of practice

semi-structured learning strategy a learning strategy where the learner takes responsibility for deciding the learning objectives, the content to be covered, and the evidence to be presented to prove that learning objectives have been achieved

sensitivity groups where the HR developer uses group process to allow the learner to disclose deep personal issues and emotions

session plan a plan that describes the content to be covered in sequence and the associated overhead transparencies and board plans

set adviser the facilitator of action learning

shadow system one of the two basic systems of the organisation; responsible for creating new knowledge and for the distant future of the organisation; has four important roles – importation of new knowledge, challenging the fundamental values of the legitimate system, storing potentially useful knowledge and information, and exporting new knowledge to the legitimate system; uses self-organising groups (SOGs)

simulation an experiential learning approach which allows the learner to experience and reflect on a real work-based situation

single-loop learning learning that does not challenge the underlying values of what is being taught

single-use plans one-off plans to implement a new idea. A training course or a workshop is an example of a single-use plan

skill session a learning experience to teach a learner a procedural skill based on the steps of show, show-and-tell, check-of-understanding, and practice

skill test used to assess procedural skills

socialisation exchanging tacit knowledge with another

SOLER system a way of categorising and interpreting nonverbal behaviour

Solomon four the most complex of the scientific models, uses the pre-test–post-test on three control groups and the group undergoing the learning experience

stage models models of age categories in adults denoting transition periods and specific needs

stages of group growth forming, storming, norming, performing, and adjourning

standing plans policies, procedures and rules

store potentially useful knowledge the third role of the shadow system

storming the second stage of group growth when the group culture is gradually formed

strategic alliance a learning partnership based on a formal arrangement between independent forms; the outcome of the alliance is not specific, as in a joint venture

strategic human resource development planning the strategic plan for developing the staff in the organisation, derived from the corporate strategic plan

strategic orientation the market niche that the organisation is servicing

strategic planning a process that allows the organisation to confirm its current valuable knowledge and to identify new knowledge. One of the processes that the legitimate system uses to manage the organisation's knowledge assets

structured interview an interview where the interviewer relies on pre-planned questions that are asked in the same order

structured learning strategy a learning strategy where the HR developer takes responsibility for deciding the learning objectives, the content to be covered, and the evidence to be presented to prove that learning objectives have been achieved

subjective written tests sometimes called essay tests, this type depends on the opinion of the examiner

successive approximations process using a two-step process of identifying what the learner has done right and identifying one or two improvements only. This two-step process should be continued to guide the learner to full and complete accomplishment

summarising interviewer reviews the information provided by the interviewee

summative assessment the sum of all the tests of assessment on a learner, provides concluding evidence of the learner's achievement

supervisor the person who becomes the HR developer in workplace learning

supportive mechanisms the actions the facilitator takes to provide the learner with the confidence needed to undertake the unstructured learning strategies

surveillance stage the first stage of the HRDNI where the organisation constantly surveys its external and internal environment

tacit knowledge knowledge that is in the subconscious mind

tactical planning identifies the type and sources of resources that will be used to implement the strategic plans

task category consists of analytical, logistical, and implementing subgroups. At the second level of learning outcomes in the HLO, at the same level as the relationships category

tell-and-listen interview where the appraiser informs the appraisee of the decision but is also willing to listen to the responses from the appraisee

theory session a learning experience that imparts information, the body of which is divided into logical segments, each segment consisting of three components: the explanation step, the activity step, and the summary step

theory-in-use Model I a negative model used by managers to avoid making important decisions

theory-in-use Model II where an interaction is based on valid information and the participants have free and informed choice

three levels of motivation a model of utility, achievement, and interest motivation

time series evaluation in the middle of the simple/complex continuum of scientific models, this test consists of a series of pre-tests, followed by the learning episode, followed by a series of post-tests

traditional vertical career a career that moves upward in one organisation

transfer of learning is the third element of the workplace learning model; the supervisor must ensure that encapsulation is overcome and that the learning is transferred back to the worksite

trial and error, the third phase in the individual adult learning model; the individual will attempt to problem solve and then form fuzzy learning objectives and a fuzzy learning plan, have a go, and then engage in self-feedback

trustworthiness the quality of a qualitative researcher who reports with integrity and honesty

two-factor theory a motivational theory consisting of satisfiers and motivators

unlearning the process of discarding obsolete or ineffective knowledge

unstructured interview an interview where the interviewer relies on managing the process to control the direction of the interview

verification cross-checking research evidence and interpretations

visual aids resources such as the white board, overhead projector, and computer-assisted computer packages which the HR developer uses to maximise multiple-sense learning during presentations and learning sessions

workplace learning learning that occurs in the workplace

youth learners are generally regarded as those between the ages of 17 and 25 years of age.

Index

A

accuracy, 88, 137, 177, 178, 209, 330
  definition, 455
action learning, 164, 230, 253, 254, 262, 281,
  291, 297, 303, 304, 305, 307, 309, 313, 388,
  395, 404, 412, 450
  definition, 455
action learning project, 307
action plans, 147, 163, 172, 173, 375, 430
  definition, 455
action research, 307, 308, 309, 310
  definition, 455
active listening
  definition, 455
activity number 1, 183, 184, 185, 186, 195, 198
  definition, 455
activity number 2, 185, 186, 198
  definition, 455
adjourning, 404, 435, 437
  definition, 455
administrative performance appraisal
  definition, 455
administrative selection officer, 150, 152, 153,
  154, 155, 156, 157, 158
adult learner
  definition, 455
adult learning strategies, 228
analyser strategy, 250
analytic learning diary
  definition, 455
analytical subgroup, 218, 220, 226
  definition, 455
andragogy, 48, 49, 57, 234, 236, 237, 238, 274,
  292, 298, 300
  definition, 455
anxiety, 50, 92, 97, 319, 324, 382, 383, 400
  definition, 455
apprenticeship learning partnership, 409
  definition, 455
approximation of the task
  definition, 455
artefacts and creations, 440
AS 5037-2005
  definition, 455
assessment centres, 127
audit, 74, 110, 119, 306, 416
  definition, 455

B

behaviour level, 347, 348, 349, 352, 360
  definition, 456
behaviour modification, 50
behaviourally anchored rating scales
  definition, 456
blended learning, 321, 322, 323, 325
  definition, 456
boundaryless career, 166, 172
  definition, 456
bounded instability, 17, 22, 248, 417, 426, 431,
  434, 436, 437, 438, 439, 447
  definition, 456
Brinkerhoff's model, 357
  definition, 456
budget
  definition, 456

C

career anchors, 168, 169, 171, 456
  types of, 169
career counselling, 23, 168, 172
  definition, 456
  happenstance theory, 170
career management, 164, 165, 172
  definition, 456
case study
  definition, 456
causal assumptions, 64, 69, 76, 79, 80
  definition, 456
Cavaliere's five stage model
  definition, 456
challenging the fundamental values of the
  legitimate system
  definition, 456
change interventions, 251, 256, 291, 307, 309,
  310, 317, 404, 412, 416, 450
  definition, 456
classical conditioning, 49, 50
collectivist cultures, 100, 108, 111, 112
  definition, 456
combination
  definition, 456
combination (explicit to explicit), 53
communicative engagement, 146
communicative learning, 59, 60, 62, 63, 67, 69,
  98, 103, 109, 146, 209, 215, 219, 259, 260,
  269, 291, 305, 316, 373, 408, 416
  definition, 456
communities of practice, 401
  definition, 457
competencies
  definition, 457

competitive edge, 11, 55, 77, 120, 121, 123, 248, 395

complex but clear learning outcomes
definition, 457

complexity theory, 7, 13, 14, 21, 407, 425, 438, 442
definition, 457

concern for others subgroup, 224, 225, 302, 307, 310
definition, 457

constructive alignment, 212, 214, 329, 332, 342, 343
definition, 457

content analysis, 205, 206, 207, 208, 209
definition, 457

contract learning, 254, 262, 291, 297, 298–302, 313, 388, 404, 405, 409, 412, 450
advantage, 227
definition, 457
episodes, 300

control group
definition, 457

control systems, 73, 119, 125, 126, 133, 163, 311, 332, 350, 375, 429, 430, 431, 442, 444, 447, 459
definition, 457

conventional strategic management, 9

cost reduction, 7, 8, 432

cost–benefit analysis, 83, 332, 357, 360, 361, 362, 363
definition, 457

cost-saving syndrome, 6

create new knowledge, 11, 15, 394, 399, 400, 409
definition, 457

creating knowledge, 54, 381, 390
definition, 457

creativity, 15, 74

criterion-referenced scoring, 345
definition, 457

critical incident technique (CIT), 128, 154, 155

critical reflection, 63, 68, 69, 70, 71, 72, 75, 79, 227, 280, 282, 283, 284, 339, 340
definition, 457

critical thinking, 63, 71–74, 79, 280, 282, 284, 348
amalgam of, 75
definition, 457
problem solving element, 297

critical thinking category, 226, 229, 283, 284, 302, 310, 339, 341, 342
application, 226

cultural backgrounds, 87, 90, 101, 106, 108, 269

current knowledge, 7, 11, 15, 53, 72, 230, 237, 305, 338, 425
definition, 457

cyclical model, 255
definition, 457

D

data analysis
definition, 458

data gathering, 25, 119, 125, 149, 177, 179, 201, 208
definition, 458

debate, 59, 61, 74, 95, 98, 99, 101, 243, 324, 416

defence mechanisms, 17, 21, 136, 137, 251, 257, 407, 412, 413, 414, 415, 416, 417, 437, 438
definition, 458

defender strategy, 250

design stage, 20, 63, 83, 139, 362, 416, 450
definition, 458
learning outcomes, 215

developmental performance appraisal
definition, 458

diagnostic audit, 121

dialectic thinking, 74, 364, 366

diminishing returns, law of, 11, 462

diminishing support, 381, 433
definition, 458

direct guidance of experts, 378, 379, 380
definition, 458

discovery, 277, 382, 383, 387, 394, 398, 399, 407
definition, 458

discussion
definition, 458

disorienting dilemma, 68, 70, 71, 76
definition, 458

diversity training, 109

double-loop learning, 15, 17, 61, 279, 296, 398, 399, 400, 401, 402, 407, 412, 414, 418, 425, 434, 436
definition, 458

E

education, 32

e-learning, 260, 291, 314, 315, 316, 317, 318, 319, 320, 321, 322
definition, 458

e-learning episode, 316

emancipatory learning, 58, 63, 70, 71, 80, 83, 111, 131, 132, 151, 215, 221, 225, 260, 262, 291, 447
definition, 458

embedding process, 249, 416, 417, 438
definition, 458

empirical research, 55
encapsulation, 376
    definition, 458
engagement decision, 385, 386, 389
    definition, 458
entrance investment time, 182, 185
    definition, 458
entrepreneurial strategy, 250
equilibrium, 14, 16, 17, 425, 433
espoused values, 441
ethnocentricity, 88
    definition, 458
evaluation
    report, 362, 363
        definition, 459
    stage, 20, 63, 83, 137, 147, 269, 330, 331,
        345, 346, 352, 357, 362, 364, 431
        definition, 459
evaluation plan, 132, 260, 264, 357, 362–63
    definition, 459
exit investment time, 183, 187, 198
    definition, 459
expectancy–valence theory, 231
    definition, 459
experiential learning, 18, 112, 221, 223, 224,
    225, 226, 276, 280, 281, 287, 288, 291, 372,
    390
    definition, 459
explicit knowledge, 52, 53, 55, 58, 61, 71, 74,
    76, 80, 185, 207, 209, 215, 216, 257, 333,
    388, 424
    definition, 459
exploratory energy, 7, 8
extended learning, 376, 377, 378, 380, 386, 417,
    431, 433, 438
    definition, 459
external networks, 407, 408
    definition, 459
externalisation, 11, 53, 60, 61, 83, 128, 207, 221,
    225, 258, 273, 291, 320, 340, 373, 382, 402,
    404, 405, 448
    definition, 459
extraordinary management, 13, 15, 21, 22, 398,
    399, 401, 427, 446
    definition, 459

F

facilitator
    definition, 459
facilitator team, 201
    definition, 459
financial system, 124, 188
flatter structures, 5, 6
focus group, 83, 125, 134, 181, 198, 199, 200,
    201, 202, 203, 204, 205, 206

definition, 459
formal learning, 55, 95, 96, 315, 370, 376, 433
    definition, 459
formative assessment, 345, 346
    definition, 459
forming
    definition, 459
formulating goals, 386
    definition, 459
four stages of HRD, 21, 23, 83, 125, 126, 382,
    403, 428, 430, 431, 433, 435, 448, 459
four-phase paradigm of knowledge creation, 54
frames of reference, 58, 63, 221, 225, 228, 252,
    346, 360
    and critical thinking, 75
    as a learning hurdle, 93
    challenging using role plays, 450
    changing, 67, 70, 71, 384
    definition, 460
    insights about, 282
    problems in learning, 90
    role, 66
    worth and use, 340
free flow diary
    definition, 460
future careers, 168, 171, 456

G

gender
    definition, 460
gender models, 98, 99
    definition, 460
global financial crisis, 8, 91
globalisation, 110, 166
    definition, 460
graphic rating scales, 157
group composition, 199, 200, 201
    definition, 460
group dynamics, 202, 205, 277, 307, 308, 310,
    323, 403
    definition, 460

H

happenstance theory, 170
harassment, 9, 88, 89
    definition, 460
hegemonic assumptions, 66, 67, 90, 98, 224, 284,
    294, 339, 340, 412, 458, 460
hierarchy of learning outcomes (HLO), 215, 230,
    243, 256, 264, 279, 291, 297, 312, 314, 323,
    334, 342, 346, 361, 365, 372, 450
    definition, 460
    major categories, 215
    practical use, 228
high-context cultures, 100, 108

definition, 460
historical embeddedness
definition, 460
holistic adult learning
definition, 460
HR practitioners, 33
HRD needs assessment, 119
HRD strategic plan, 123, 124
HRDNI, 120
definition, 460
importance, 119
method, 133
need for, 139
purpose, 121
report, 215
HRDNI report, 132, 137, 138, 139, 205, 214,
219
definition, 460

I

impairment, 97
definition, 460
implementation stage, 20, 83, 113, 146, 269,
345, 362, 365, 376
definition, 460
implementing subgroup, 221, 225, 302, 307, 310
definition, 460
import new knowledge
definition, 460
increased confidence and abilities
definition, 460
indigenous Australians, 100, 101, 103, 104, 107,
297
definition, 460
indirect guidance, 380, 381, 433
definition, 461
individual adult learning model, 402
definition, 461
individual change transition model, 382
definition, 461
individualist cultures, 100
definition, 461
individuals in relationships, 398, 401
definition, 461
induction, 22
inequilibrium, 14, 15, 16, 17, 433, 434
information
definition, 461
instrumental learning, 55, 57, 58, 59, 63, 72, 77,
80, 83, 109, 111, 131, 132, 215, 218, 259,
260, 291, 390, 414, 429
definition, 461
integration, 98, 106, 111, 318, 382, 384, 388,
423, 440
definition, 461

interaction model, 255
definition, 461
internal environment, 124, 442, 443, 444, 469
internal networks, 408, 436
definition, 461
internalisation, 53, 54, 56, 59, 60, 61, 62, 72, 83,
146, 209, 219, 221, 225, 258, 274, 278, 291,
320, 373, 376, 382, 402, 404, 405, 448, 461
internalisation converting
definition, 461
interpersonal subgroup, 222, 223, 224
definition, 461
interpretation, 22, 60, 65, 100, 178, 239, 298,
309, 316, 334, 365
definition, 461
interview
definition, 461
interviewee
definition, 461
interviewer
definition, 461
intimacy, 183, 186, 189, 198, 201
definition, 461
intrapersonal subgroup, 223, 224
definition, 461
investigation plan, 132
definition, 461
investigation stage, 20, 63, 83, 125, 126, 132,
139, 352
definition, 462

J

job analysis, 127, 147, 148, 149, 151, 152, 153,
158, 164
definition, 462
job description, 149, 150, 151, 152, 157, 429,
430
definition, 462
job documents, 149, 462
job specification, 149, 152, 153, 154, 156, 157,
158, 159, 160, 161, 429
definition, 462
joint venture, 410
definition, 462

K

key stakeholders, 122, 138, 139, 248, 251, 252,
254, 256, 264, 284, 313, 323, 353, 363, 437
definition, 462
Kirkpatrick's four levels, 26, 332, 346
Kirkpatrick's model, 351, 357
definition, 462
knowledge
definition, 462
knowledge resources, 12, 91

L

leadership
  definition, 462
learners
  definition, 462
learning contract, 228, 298, 299, 300, 302, 409, 457
learning diaries, 53, 289, 334, 339, 340, 341, 342, 344, 346
  definition, 462
learning episode, 54, 56, 295, 347, 372, 375, 378, 385, 433, 462
  context, 101
  creative results, 109
  design, 56, 249
  evaluation, 330, 362
  formal and informal, 99
  impact, 351
  objectives, 300
  problem selection, 295
  reaction, 347
  type, 259
learning episode, 357
learning in the workplace, 38
learning instrument, 282
  definition, 462
learning level, 352, 360
  definition, 462
learning objective, 128, 205, 257, 278, 334, 336, 337, 375, 387, 388
  definition, 462
learning organisation, 10, 13, 16, 173, 384, 448
  definition, 462
learning orientation, 230, 234, 235, 236, 238, 239, 243, 244, 258, 292
  definition, 462
  stage 3, 237
learning outcomes, 128, 131, 132, 213, 217, 281, 343, 370, 378, 380, 414
  agreed, 239
  categorising, 215
  defining, 137
  definition, 463
  deriving, 214
  learning experience design, 138
  portfolio assessment, 341
learning partnerships, 21, 402, 408, 409, 410, 411, 436
  definition, 463
learning program, 108, 109, 113, 123, 128, 252, 253, 256, 257, 258, 263, 264, 269, 315, 319, 348, 349, 350, 352, 353, 357, 376, 382, 428, 429
learning set, 304, 305

definition, 463
learning space
  definition, 463
learning strategies, 49, 103, 164, 215, 216, 218, 219, 223, 225, 229, 230, 237, 238, 255, 260, 276, 313, 321, 323, 449, 450
  application, 269
  appropriate, 138, 213, 215, 229, 243, 250, 257, 378
  categories, 234
  definition, 463
  for surface learners, 95
  semi-structured, 276
  structured, 274
  unstructured, 291, 450
learning styles, 63, 64, 92, 230, 239, 240, 241, 242, 243, 244, 269, 282, 312
  definition, 463
learning transfer, 376, 463
lecture, 218, 219, 223, 224, 229, 230, 233, 234, 235, 239, 260, 276, 282, 301, 414
  definition, 463
legitimate system, 14, 15, 16, 17, 123, 248, 249, 259, 260, 361, 390, 394, 400, 407, 416, 425, 427, 429, 433, 436, 448
  and traditional management, 16
  assumptions, 395
  basic assumptions, 431
  defence mechanisms, 412, 417
  definition, 463
  exporting to, 412
  in tension, 17
  power centre, 415
  primacy, 439
  role, 425, 431
  task, 437
liberatory models, 98
  definition, 463
Likert scales, 157
logical reflection, 75
logistical subgroup, 220
  definition, 463
logistics, 199, 220, 275, 359, 362, 363
  definition, 463
low-context cultures, 100
  definition, 463

M

management by objectives, 5, 6, 150, 151
management of knowledge, 10, 20, 21, 23, 91, 417, 426, 446, 451
  definition, 463
management re-engineering, 20, 139
  definition, 463
managerial observation, 125

managing workplace learning model
definition, 462, 463
Maori, 104, 105, 106, 114
definition, 463
matrix teams, 397
mental models, 52, 78
mentoring, 58, 93, 164, 167, 221, 223, 224, 225,
226, 291, 311, 313, 314, 378, 379, 416
definition, 463
mentor–protégé, 312
meta-abilities category, 227, 259, 284, 302, 310,
313, 334, 342, 348
application, 228
definition, 464
micro-skills, 292, 293, 449
definition, 464
mind maps, 71
motivation, 49, 58, 168, 230–33, 282, 349, 387,
443
achievement, 233, 236
and stress, 82
career, 168
definition, 464
interest, 233
utility, 95
work, 221, 226, 282
movement from peripheral to full participation,
378
definition, 464

N

negative feedback loops, 14, 73, 369, 384, 399,
407, 414, 415, 425, 429, 430, 431, 435, 446,
447
definition, 464
networks, 21, 167, 168, 169, 401, 407, 408, 410,
412, 435, 436
definition, 464
Newtonian paradigm, 9, 10, 14, 396
definition, 464
nonverbal behaviour, 182, 194, 195, 199, 201,
205
definition, 464
norming, 404, 435
definition, 464
norm-referenced scoring, 345
definition, 464

O

objective written test, 336
definition, 464
objectives model
definition, 464
observation form, 337
definition, 464

observation method, 126
off-site learning, 370, 375, 376
advantages, 370
definition, 464
older learners, 92, 93, 392
definition, 464
operational management, 9
operational management functions, 9
optimal arousal conditions, 82
ordinary management, 13, 14, 16, 21, 22, 399,
401, 427
definition, 464
organisational culture, 22, 23, 89, 138, 248, 250,
251, 264, 323, 361, 400, 418, 426, 439, 440,
441, 442, 444, 445, 446, 448
definition, 464
organisational politics, 122, 136, 137, 353, 361,
415
organisational records, 125
organisational strategic plan, 123
organised diary, 340
definition, 464
other sexual orientations, 98, 99
definition, 464
outsourcing organisations, 7

P

painting the path, 179
definition, 464
paradigmatic assumptions, 64, 65, 66, 68, 69, 78,
79, 221, 224, 225, 228, 241, 252, 282, 296
definition, 464
paraphrasing, 53, 182, 185, 189, 190, 192, 195,
198, 271
definition, 465
pass time, 183, 184, 186, 187, 195, 198
definition, 465
pattern of the interview, 182, 187
definition, 465
performance appraisal, 23, 69, 126, 127
administrative, 147, 154
definition, 465
developmental, 147, 154, 163
importance, 143
interviews, 160
problem-solving interview, 161
system, 124, 143
tell-and-listen interview, 161
performance criteria, 129, 130, 131
performance indicators, 150, 151, 152, 153, 154,
155, 156, 159, 164
definition, 465
performance management, 124, 143, 144, 164,
173
definition, 465

performance management strategies, 6
performance test
    definition, 465
performing, 88, 97, 275, 291, 330, 435
    definition, 465
personal operating environment, 171
platform model, 256, 353
    definition, 465
political knowledge, 251
    definition, 465
political processes or activities
    definition, 465
portfolio assessment, 334, 342, 344
    definition, 465
positive feedback loops, 15, 16, 73, 398, 399,
    401, 403, 407, 425, 434, 435, 445, 447
    definition, 465
post-test, 358, 359, 360, 362
    definition, 465
power distance, 107, 230
    definition, 465
presage factors, 92, 352, 357
    definition, 465
prescriptive assumptions, 65, 67, 68, 69, 70, 224,
    296
    definition, 465
pre-test–post-test, 358
    definition, 465
principles for adult learning, 55
principles of learning, 55, 83, 192, 218, 257, 258,
    276, 376, 383, 385, 390, 449
    definition, 465
prior learning, 110, 131
probing, 53, 182, 185, 188, 190, 191, 195, 196,
    198, 201, 208, 271, 292, 336, 449
    definition, 465
problem-based learning, 221, 225, 226, 262, 291,
    294, 296, 297, 450
    advantage, 227
    definition, 466
problem-solving interview, 161
    definition, 466
procedural training, 55
product marketing plan, 262, 263, 264
    definition, 466
production phase, 388, 389
    definition, 466
professional tacit knowledge, 76
program plan, 354
    definition, 466
programmed knowledge category, 216, 218, 220,
    291, 302, 307, 334, 336
    definition, 466
project

definition, 466
projects, 283–84
prospector strategy, 250
protean career, 166, 167
    definition, 466
protégé, 58, 312, 313, 314, 466
psychosocial filter, 379, 380, 388
    definition, 466

Q

quality control system, 124
questioning, 53, 72, 182, 185, 187, 188, 194,
    198, 201, 270, 271, 273, 275, 277, 288, 292,
    307, 339, 398, 449, 450
    definition, 466
questions
    definition, 466

R

rapport zone, 182, 183, 185, 186, 195
    definition, 466
rational discourse, 60, 61, 63, 71, 72, 83, 294
    definition, 466
rational model, 255
    definition, 466
raw score, 342, 345
    definition, 466
reaction level, 347, 351
    definition, 466
real-life project, 304
recruitment, 22, 94, 101, 110, 409
reductionism, 13
re-engineering strategies, 5
referential adequacy, 179
    definition, 466
reflective discourse, 60, 69, 75, 312
    definition, 466
relationships category, 222, 224
    definition, 467
replicability, 137, 177, 209
    definition, 467
resource plan, 164, 260, 262, 264
    definition, 467
resources, 7, 252–54, 323, *See* knowledge
    resources
    allocating, 220, 279, 311
    definition, 467
    financial, 199
    learning, 372
    minimal, 7
    physical, 11, 252, 253, 254, 467
responding, 102, 270, 271, 273, 277, 286, 288,
    292, 293, 449
    definition, 467
results level, 349, 350, 351, 352, 360

definition, 467
ritual, 183, 184, 186, 187, 195, 198
 definition, 467
role play, 223, 224, 229, 251, 260, 276, 279,
 280, 281, 287, 291, 354, 449, 450
 definition, 467
rubric, 339
 definition, 467

S

sampling, 179, 180, 181, 200
 definition, 467
scaffolding, 96, 381, 384
 definition, 467
scientific models, 357, 360, 362
 definition, 467
security, 60, 91, 166, 167, 169, 172, 291, 322,
 377, 382, 383, 384, 449
 definition, 467
seek expertise
 definition, 467
seek support, 388
 definition, 467
selection, 22, 101, 110
 definition, 467
selection process, 172, 230, 295, 379, 409, 410,
 430
self-evaluation, 237, 293, 294, 384, 387
 definition, 467
self-organising groups (SOGs), 16, 21, 22, 401,
 402, 403, 404, 406, 408, 412, 415, 434, 435,
 448, 450
 definition, 467
semi-structured learning strategy
 definition, 468
sensitivity groups, 282, 285, 287, 307
 definition, 468
 well-managed, 287
session plan
 definition, 468
set adviser, 304, 305, 306
 definition, 468
shadow system, 14, 17, 123, 248, 256, 330, 394,
 395, 396, 394–99, 397, 398, 399, 425, 433,
 434, 436, 437, 438, 448
 aim, 15, 16
 and creativity, 15, 126
 and new management theory, 16
 creating knowledge, 381
 definition, 468
 evaluation, 331
 guiding principles, 398
 in tension, 17
 internal networks, 408
 management, 251, 417

moving into, 369
 responsibility, 398, 399
 roles, 15, 399, 400, 415
 strategic changes, 249
simulation, 283, 295, 307
 definition, 468
single-loop learning, 14, 17, 259, 279, 394, 407,
 413, 425, 429, 430, 431, 433, 446
 definition, 468
single-use plans, 416, 427, 428, 429
 definition, 468
skill session, 218, 219, 230, 235, 242, 274, 276,
 321, 378, 379, 388, 449
 definition, 468
skill test, 334
 definition, 468
socialisation, 51, 52, 54, 61, 64, 67, 68, 74, 83,
 182, 221, 225, 254, 291, 302, 378, 382, 402,
 404, 405, 441, 448
 definition, 468
SOLER system, 194, 195
 definition, 468
Solomon four, 358, 359, 360
 definition, 468
staff management practices, 89
stage models, 91
 definition, 468
stages of group growth, 21, 403, 435
 definition, 468
standing plans, 249, 416, 427, 428, 429, 444
 definition, 468
store potentially useful knowledge, 400
 definition, 468
storming, 435
 definition, 468
strategic alliance
 definition, 468
strategic business units, 5
strategic human resource development planning
 definition, 468
strategic human resource planning (SHRP), 22, 23
strategic orientation, 123, 134, 248, 264, 323,
 365, 440
 definition, 468
strategic planning, 8, 23, 121, 123, 138, 144, 248,
 249, 310, 394, 416, 418, 427, 431, 440, 446
 definition, 469
strategic planning process, 12, 123, 427
structured interview, 196, 197, 206
 definition, 469
structured learning strategy
 definition, 469
subjective written tests, 334
 definition, 469

successive approximations process, 81, 258
  definition, 469
summarising, 53, 193, 195, 271, 272, 277, 292, 449, 469
summative assessment, 341, 345
  definition, 469
supervisor, 21, 77, 81, 119, 123, 125, 154, 160, 181, 205, 252, 353, 364, 369, 371, 373, 375, 378, 381, 388, 399, 404, 433, 446, 449
  definition, 469
supportive mechanisms, 291, 292
  definition, 469
surveillance stage, 123, 125, 126, 137, 372, 430
  definition, 469
System Beta, 73, 74, 306

T

tacit knowledge, 6, 52, 58, 61, 74, 75, 78, 80, 207, 209, 215, 257, 316, 360, 384, 405, 408, 415, 424, 436
  definition, 469
  non-codified, 408
tactical planning, 375, 427, 428, 430
  definition, 469
TAFE. *See* Technical and Further Education (TAFE)
task category, 218, 220, 221, 222, 226, 229, 257, 279, 302, 307, 336, 394, 450
  definition, 469
Technical and Further Education (TAFE), 42
tell-and-listen interview
  definition, 469
theory session, 230
  assessment, 333
  choice of, 238
  definition, 469
  design, 321
  efficient transmission, 233
  initial elements, 219
  planning, 275
  stage 1 learners, 235
  structure strategies, 223
  use of, 218, 275
theory-in-use Model I, 413
  definition, 469
theory-in-use Model II, 416
  definition, 469
three levels of motivation, 232, 233, 386
  definition, 469
time delay in learning, 81, 83, 258
time series evaluation, 358
  definition, 470
traditional vertical career, 166, 167

definition, 470
training, 32
training needs analysis (TNA), 119
transfer of learning, 57, 138, 218, 258, 348, 369, 376, 390
  definition, 470
trial and error, 387, 388, 389
  definition, 470
trustworthiness
  definition, 470
two-factor theory, 231, 232, 233, 347
  definition, 470

U

unlearning, 75, 76, 77, 416, 427
  definition, 470
unstructured interview, 195, 196, 206
  definition, 470

V

verification, 119, 177
  definition, 470
VET. *See* Vocational Education and Training (VET)
visual aids, 56, 138, 199, 201, 205, 271, 272, 273, 275, 288, 449
  definition, 470
Vocational Education and Training (VET), 33
  future of VET, 42

W

wholly educational institution-based experiences, 39
wholly work-based experiences, 39
work-based experiences with direct guidance, 39
work-based experiences with educational intervention, 39
workplace learning, 372, 382
  advantages, 370
  and off-site learning, 370
  challenges, 371
  change intervention, 309
  definition, 470
  in knowledge management, 433
  learning spaces, 372
  management of, 21, 373
  outcomes, 384
  quality, 379

Y

youth learners, 94, 95, 96
  definition, 470